PHYSICAL EDUCATION HANDBOOK

Life is a series of games—games of finding answers, finding amusement, persuading people, winning friends, raising families, and performing rituals. Some persons relish the game of life and enjoy all the sub-games to the hilt. Others play them grimly, with their eyes fixed on the scoreboard, too much concerned with staying ahead to enjoy the game.

DON ROBINSON *(Phi Delta Kappan)*

PHYSICAL EDUCATION HANDBOOK

Seventh Edition

DON CASH SEATON
Former Chairman, Department of Health,
Physical Education, and Recreation,
University of Kentucky

NEIL SCHMOTTLACH
Professor of Physical Education,
Ball State University

IRENE A. CLAYTON
Former Director of Physical Education,
Bryn Mawr College

HOWARD C. LEIBEE
Former Professor of Physical Education,
The University of Michigan

LLOYD L. MESSERSMITH
Former Professor of Physical Education,
Southern Methodist University

PRENTICE-HALL, INC., Englewood Cliffs, New Jersey 07632

Library of Congress Cataloging in Publication Data

Main entry under title:

Physical education handbook.

    Includes bibliographies.
    1. Physical education and training—Study and teaching.
I. Seaton, Don Cash (date)
GV361.P49 1983   613.7'07   82-12215
ISBN 0-13-667535-2
ISBN 0-13-667527-1 (pbk.)

PHYSICAL EDUCATION HANDBOOK, Seventh Edition
Seaton/Schmottlach/Clayton/Leibee/Messersmith

© 1983, 1974, 1969, 1965, 1959, 1954, 1951
by Prentice-Hall, Inc., Englewood Cliffs, N.J. 07632

Editorial/production supervision and design: *Hilda Tauber*
Cover design: Debbie Watson. Drawing by *Rita Kaye Schwartz*
Art production: *Jenny Markus*
Manufacturing buyer: *Harry P. Baisley*

Printed in the United States of America

10 9 8 7 6 5 4 3

ISBN 0-13-667527-1 pbk

ISBN 0-13-667535-2

PRENTICE-HALL INTERNATIONAL, INC., *London*
PRENTICE-HALL OF AUSTRALIA PTY. LIMITED, *Sydney*
EDITORA PRENTICE-HALL DO BRASIL, LTDA., *Rio de Janeiro*
PRENTICE-HALL CANADA INC., *Toronto*
PRENTICE-HALL OF INDIA PRIVATE LIMITED, *New Delhi*
PRENTICE-HALL OF JAPAN, INC., *Tokyo*
PRENTICE-HALL OF SOUTHEAST ASIA PTE. LTD., *Singapore*
WHITEHALL BOOKS LIMITED, *Wellington, New Zealand*

In memory of
HOWARD C. LEIBEE
and
LLOYD L. MESSERSMITH

This edition is dedicated to
JANE, KRAIG, and GLENN
for their patience and understanding
and to the many others who would enjoy
a lifetime of active participation.

CONTENTS

PREFACE

The teacher or recreation leader is sometimes confronted by the necessity of teaching an activity with which he or she is not completely familiar or of giving enough guidance to "start the ball rolling." To master all activities in the present wide offerings in physical education would require too long a period of preparation; most student teachers tend toward specialization. Some activities, too, are more familiar to men than to women, and vice versa. Yet with the advent of Title IX and Mainstreaming, departmental organization of teaching personnel is such that both men and women are called upon to teach any or all activities. This is particularly true of individual and team sports such as golf, orienteering, cycling, flag football, and soccer.

With these facts in mind, the PHYSICAL EDUCATION HANDBOOK, 7th edition, has been written to serve as a teaching and reference tool for several types of people: physical educators, student teachers, recreational leaders, sports enthusiasts, physical education majors, and for all high school and college students who are interested in sports activities and physical fitness.

Previous users of the HANDBOOK will find that some activities have been dropped and new activities (Aquatic Games, Cycling, Cross-Country Skiing, Team Handball, Orienteering) have been added. In deciding which activities to include in this revision we relied on a survey of previous users who expressed their preferences and needs. The activities chapters have been thoroughly revised and updated. New illustrations, updated sport rules, emphasis on coeducational participation—these are some of the changes. The bibliographies have been expanded and refined with the addition of audio-visual materials.

In order to derive maximum utility from this HANDBOOK, it is essential to begin with a careful study of the two introductory chapters, which contain a wealth of pertinent information. Chapter 1,

Understanding Physical Education, covers four basic areas: the nature and purpose of physical education, the sociological aspects, the psychological aspects, and the mechanical (movement) aspects. Chapter 2, Physical Fitness Programs, explains the benefits of physical fitness and the proper ways to set up regular exercise programs. These two introductory chapters constitute the backbone and sinews of this manual; they provide both the meaningful principles needed for understanding and the practical suggestions needed in applying these principles to effective teaching and learning.

Format of the Activity Chapters

At the head of each activity chapter is a list of objectives highlighting its main concepts and features. These objectives are written in instructional terms to help the teacher in evaluating students. The activities chapters open with a discussion of the nature and purpose of the specific activity. Also included is information regarding rules, equipment, playing field dimensions, organizational setups, and so on. A section called *Suggested Learning Sequence* outlines the teaching progression—beginner to intermediate (and sometimes advanced)—that is normally used in most schools. Although this sequence is highly recommended, the order can be varied to meet program and teacher needs, so long as concepts are properly interrelated and not fragmented.

The *Skills and Techniques* sections are designed for the beginner-to-intermediate levels of skill development (more advanced skills are often covered in the selected references). Practical advice is given in the form of *Learning Cues* and *Practice Suggestions*, with specific aids to the teacher in formulating drills and planning lessons.

Other features include playing strategies, safety considerations, playing courtesies, and terminology associated with the specific activity. At the end of each chapter is a list of selected references, including books, periodicals, and audio-visual materials to supplement the material found in the chapter.

Use of Audio-Visual Aids

Many visual aids are available in the physical education field; the alert teacher will want to take advantage of these aids to increase teaching effectiveness. The Athletic Institute has pioneered in the production of film strips in a wide range of activities specifically designed to aid the physical education teacher. Other producers have both film strips and motion pictures available. The sources listed in Appendix D of this HANDBOOK should enable any teacher to select appropriate materials. Before using any visual aids, however, you are urged to read the guidelines given at the head of Appendix D. A wise use of audio-visual materials will enrich and improve most instructional programs.

Skills Tests

Skills tests in the various activities are not included, but resourceful teachers should be able to prepare their own tests or find such tests in the reading materials indicated. A bibliography of tests and measurement guides is included in Chapter 1 (see page 9).

Coeducational Teaching

With a few exceptions, all the activities described in this HANDBOOK can be used in a coeducational setting. Specific ways to modify activities and rules in order to play on a coeducational basis are outlined in Chapter 1 (see pages 6–7). Other suggestions are given in the activity chapters.

Planning the Lesson

The following suggestions are offered to assist the instructor, recreational leader, or student teacher in planning a lesson or a unit of instruction.

1. Determine your *goal.* What would you like the learner to have achieved at the conclusion of the lesson or unit of instruction?

2. Determine the *population* of your group. What are their ages, sex, characteristics (social, physical, emotional, mental)? What is their previous skill background in the activity or type of activity to be taught? What skills must they possess to begin the lesson?

3. Determine the *content* (skills, knowledge, strategy, etc.) based on the type of population represented.

4. Determine the lesson or unit *objectives* based on the lesson or unit content. Unit objectives will be broader whereas the lesson objective will be more specific.

5. Determine in what *sequence* the learning material may be presented most effectively. The Suggested Learning Sequence given in each activity chapter of the HANDBOOK is a good order to follow; or it can be altered to suit your needs and style of instruction.

6. Determine the instructional *equipment and supplies* (balls, bats, etc.) you will require.

7. Determine whether to supplement the lessons with *audio-visuals,* and select appropriate materials (see Appendix D).

8. Determine an *evaluation plan* for assessing: (a) performance skill achievement and (b) mastery of instructional material.

Use of the Appendices

In using this manual, we hope you will not overlook the valuable reference materials contained in the appendices. Appendix A lists sources of official rules, by type of activity. Appendix B gives the specifics on how to conduct tournaments. Appendix C shows diagrams of athletic fields and playing courts. Appendix D provides guidelines on the use of audio-visual materials and a list of sources of such materials. Appendix E will simplify making conversions of metric and English measurements.

Whether administering a program, planning a unit or lesson, directing a recreational activity, or for your own personal use, we hope this book will meet your needs and bring healthful enjoyment to all.

ACKNOWLEDGMENTS

We are indebted to the following professors and instructors who graciously contributed their knowledge and expertise to this revised edition:

DR. MARVIN GRAY, Ball State University
  Sociological Aspects of Physical Education

DR. ARNO WITTIG, Ball State University
  Psychological Aspects of Physical Education

DR. GALE GEHLSEN, Ball State University
  Mechanical Aspects of Physical Education

MICHAEL G. MARSHALL, Ball State University
  Physical Fitness Programs; Wrestling

CHARLES E. GUEMPLE, Ball State University
  Aquatic Games

DR. SUN JAE PARK, Ball State University
  Archery; Team Handball

WILLIAM L. RICHARDS, Ball State University
  Badminton

DEBBIE POWERS, Ball State University
  Basketball

WALTER R. HARVEY, Ball State University
  Cycling

DR. ADELAIDE M. COLE, Ball State University
  Dance (Folk, Square, Social)

SARAH MANGELSDORF, Ball State University
  Dance (Modern)

DR. CHARLES SIMONIAN, Ohio State University
  Fencing

DR. GERALD S. GEORGE, University of Southwestern Louisiana, Lafayette
  Gymnastics

TERRY HITCHCOCK, Muncie Northside High School, Muncie, Indiana
  Handball and Racquetball; Volleyball

JERRY RUSHTON, Ball State University
  Orienteering; Track and Field

JERRE MCMANAMA, Ball State University
  Soccer

DR. PETER W. EVERETT, Florida State University
  Softball

SCOTT B. PERELMAN, Vic Braden Tennis Academy
  Tennis

DAVID PEARSON, Ball State University
  Weight Training

We also thank the following people for their valuable assitance:

KAREN FITZPATRICK, Head Field Hockey Coach, Ball State University, for helping to revise the chapter on Field Hockey.

SAM ALFORD, Chairman Physical Education Department, Chrysler High School, New Castle, Indiana, for use of the weight room and for providing students for photographs.

The high school and college students who gave willingly of their time to pose for photographs.

BARBARA GOODEN, Business Department, Yorktown High School, Yorktown, Indiana, for the many hours spent typing and preparing the manuscript.

HILDA TAUBER, Development Editor, Prentice-Hall, Inc., whose creative genius, sharp eye, and questioning mind helped to organize the seventh edition of the HANDBOOK into a workable form.

PHYSICAL EDUCATION HANDBOOK

UNDERSTANDING PHYSICAL EDUCATION

Nature and Purpose
Sociological Aspects
Psychological Aspects
Mechanical Aspects

NATURE AND PURPOSE

The American Alliance for Health, Physical Education, Recreation, and Dance in a recent position paper, "Guidelines for Secondary School Physical Education," stated:

> In an increasingly complex society, probably the most pressing need of the students is to develop the skills and attitudes necessary for solving problems and coping with everyday stress.[1]

This statement applies not only to the secondary school student but to all individuals during their entire formative years, from pre-school to post-graduation. The stress and tension of modern living is on the rise everywhere. With lifestyles changing dramatically, futurists are forecasting radical changes in living patterns, especially an expanded leisure time. In order to survive in our society, people must learn to cope with changing conditions. But in a world largely controlled by technology, we have become less active, less adventuresome, and less willing to engage in risk-taking pursuits. Ironically, the more leisure time we gain from technological advances, the more we are reaching back into an earlier era to rediscover pastimes pioneered by our ancestors. To satisfy the needs for challenge, adventure, and self-actualization, many people are turning to vigorous exertion in various forms: orienteering, jogging, bicycling, swimming, tennis, racketball, cross-country skiing, and many others. Physical activity has become a medium by which the individual is better able to cope with the stressful conditions of modern life. The object of this section is to show that the best place, the most logical way to acquire the necessary coping skills is through a well-planned, coordinated program of physical education.

WHAT IS PHYSICAL EDUCATION?

The term *physical education* has been misinterpreted in several ways. To some it is associated with play—a concept denoting little or no purpose. To others it has become synonomous with the highly competitive endeavor we attribute to interscholastic and intercollegiate athletics. Still others see physical education as a regimented form of activity associated with military training. None of these interpretations is accurate. Physical education is *education* and is based on a common core of learning experiences planned on a sequential arrangement appropriate to the individual's stage of social, emotional, intellectual, and psychomotor development. Education is brought about as the individual interacts with the surrounding physical environment.

Physical education is that phase of education concerned with the teaching of skills, acquisition of knowledge, and development of attitudes through human movement. Most public schools, colleges, and universities recognize the importance of physical education by making it part of the required curriculum. This recognition is accorded to physical education by many nations throughout the world.

The school physical education program provides each person with several opportunities—from assessment of fitness levels and consequent activities that will strengthen personal weakness to development of lifetime skills and understanding enabling the student to lead a full and productive life while in school and afterward. In a broad view of

[1]AAHPERD, "Guidelines for Secondary School Physical Education" (Washington, D.C.: The Alliance, 1978).

FIGURE 1-1. Some skills provide a lifetime of pleasurable activity.

education, physical education's uniqueness lies in its contribution to physiological (fitness) and psychomotor (skills) development. It shares with other disciplines in contributing to the cognitive, social, and affective areas of development.

It is fitting therefore to say that the purposes of physical education are in accord with those of education in general as stated by the Educational Policies Commission:

1. To foster the development of individual capacities which will enable each human being to become the best person he/she is capable of becoming.
2. To serve society's needs.[2]

Physical education is a part of the total process of education that utilizes games, sports, aquatics, dance, and other vigorous activities to help the individual to achieve the goals of education.

SCHOOL PHYSICAL EDUCATION PROGRAMS

Well-defined programs of physical education endeavor to provide a systematic progression of movement experiences as the students pass through various developmental stages during their tenure in school. Recent federal legislation has dictated that these experiences must be equally available for both sexes (Title IX) for handicapped children (Public Law 94-142). We will discuss this legislation after we have examined the components of a well-

[2]Educational Policies Commission, "The Central Purpose of American Education" (Washington, D.C.: National Education Association, 1961), p. 1.

planned physical education program at the various levels.

Elementary School. Elementary school programs of physical education provide the basis for a wide range of learning experiences. Programs in the lower elementary grades are characterized by large muscle, vigorous activity featuring locomotor skills (walking, running, jumping, hopping, skipping, galloping, leaping) and nonlocomotor skills (bending, twisting, reaching, lifting, turning, lowering, raising). These skills incorporated in programs of dance, movement exploration, movement education, stunts and tumbling, rhythmics, fitness activities, and aquatics emphasize key elements such as self-expression, cooperation, coordination, body awareness in a variety of mediums, creativity, strength, endurance, flexibility, agility, balance, and spatial awareness. As children move into the upper elementary levels, the emphasis is on the development of fine manipulative skills. Children are taught the basic elements of a variety of physical activities such as softball, soccer, gymnastics, dance, fitness activities, swimming, and many more. The child's need to excel and compete are fostered through careful planning of movement experiences.

Middle School. Middle school programs are to some extent a continuation of the upper elementary school program. However, a greater degree of sophistication of skill development and a broader variety of activities is involved. Because this period is an age of rapid physical and social growth, challenging activities that provide an opportunity for the development of interpersonal relationships should be offered. Emphasis is on team sports for interpersonal and social growth; coeducational activities that avoid contact; gymnastics, track and field; continued emphasis on fitness activities, rhythms, aquatic activities, and the inclusion of lifetime or leisure time activities that will be used after schooling is completed. It is also a time when various disciplines (science, mathematics, social studies, physical education) in a school may plan joint cooperative ventures to enhance a particular learning experience. For example, the physical educator and science teacher may plan a camping trip in which camping, canoeing, and swimming skills will be used by the students while studying stream ecology, wildlife, and local fauna.

Senior High School. The senior high school physical education program has undergone several changes over the years. Many programs take place outside of the school—camping, cycling, orienteering, cross-country skiing, golf, hiking, and many others. Programs and activities are designed to answer the how and why of an activity. Attempts are made to design learning experiences that help the student to gain an understanding of mechanical principles and the effects of exercise on the body, to understand concepts that deal with the role of sport and physical activity in society, to make value judgments about their own well-being, to continue development of interpersonal skills through competitive activities, and to participate in a wide variety of lifetime skills (golf, tennis, camping, fitness skills, aquatic activities, etc.) that can be used upon completion of formal education. Physical education programs have turned from requiring specific activities to pupil interest-choice activity programs whereby the students are given the opportunity to determine and in some cases specialize in a given activity. Specialization gives the self-motivated student an opportunity to pursue an activity in greater depth. Along with skill development, counseling is done on how to make the correct choice to fit the individual's needs for self-fulfillment and self-actualization. More and more activities are being offered that contain an element of risk, compelling the individual to draw upon unknown potential. Situations that force the student to learn from a wide range of activities will enhance the development of coping skills.

College Program. College programs of physical education should be based upon a thorough analysis of the student's health, fitness status, and recreational needs. Many colleges and universities require students to enroll in some type of foundations course that exposes the students to the why, when, and how of physical education and then acquaints them with a wide variety of activities from which selection may be made according to individual need and interest. Several of the activities offered at the college level reflect the popular trend among the adult population in seeking new, challenging activities. Along with their carryover value, these activi-

ties provide a sharp test for discovering one's levels of potential, both physical and mental. Activities having this popular appeal include white water canoeing, back packing, cross-country and downhill skiing, cycling, orienteering, scuba diving, mountain climbing, jogging, yoga, karate, racketball and handball, weight training, aquatic activities, and conditioning. Because of recent federal legislative rulings, these activities are offered to both men and women. Other popular activities offered at several universities include archery, golf, tennis, bowling, angling, soccer, wrestling, volleyball, badminton, flag football, dance, basketball, and gymnastics.

FIGURE 1-2. Cross-country skiing provides a sharp test of endurance.

At all levels physical education programs are planned to meet and contribute to the overall aims of education. By the time students reach the later high school and college level, programs are designed in a systematic manner enabling students to develop a life plan for physical activity.

EXTRACURRICULAR PROGRAMS

Aside from the instructional program of physical education, there are other opportunities for students who are keenly interested in pursuing an activity on a more competitive level. These programs usually appear on a fuller scale beginning at the junior high level and extending through the college years.

Intramurals

Learning sports and gaining proficiency in competition is enhanced through participation in the intramural sports programs available to both sexes. In recent years these programs have played a vital role on most college and university campuses. Intramurals are a voluntary free-time program in sporting activities that provides an avenue for competition among various campus groups. On college campuses teams are recruited from fraternities, sororities, classes, housing units, and clubs. This program offers students who are not on varsity teams an opportunity to implement, in a competitive situation, the knowledge and skills they have acquired in the instructional phase of physical education. This experience enhances the values inherent in competitive sports, including the development of organic vigor, team play, sportsmanship, group loyalties, and the refinement of sport skills.

Extramurals

The growth of extramurals, sports clubs, and other similarly named college athletic organizations has been extensively promoted throughout the country. With the increasing demand for dollars, many colleges and universities are forced to offer these activities on a club basis. The purpose of the extramural program is to provide sports competition among colleges and universities for those students anxious to train and compete on a varsity-like level. Some of the current activities include volleyball, rugby, softball, lacrosse, weightlifting, sailing, and ice hockey.

Varsity Athletics

Varsity athletics have become an American tradition. The important role they play in our life along with recreational sports will be more extensively discussed in the next section. The varsity sports program found at all educational levels is a highly organized, competitive activity for the participant who has a high degree of psychomotor ability. Under Title IX, the program is available to all—men and women, boys and girls—who wish to participate at this level. The main educational values of athletics are their contribution to physical fitness; to acquisition of high levels of skill; to development of self-image, self-realization, individual worth, fair play, and cooperation.

HISTORICAL DEVELOPMENT OF PHYSICAL EDUCATION

It helps to examine the past in order to understand the present and plan for the future. Let us review briefly, then, the historical concepts of physical education.

First, it is well to point out that a highly systematized type of education is basically a product of the modern era. So also is the present system of physical education. *Second,* throughout human history, just as concepts and practices in education have changed, so have they changed in physical education. *Third,* although exercise is fundamentally a large part of physical education, a close examination of previous societies reveals that exercise alone is not a true representation of physical education. The natural urge for physical activity has always carried learning implications with it. *Fourth,* the dichotomy of mind and body has been replaced by a psychosomatic view in which the individual is seen as a total entity.

Early Beginnings

Various forms of physical activity and physical education have existed since primitive times. The earliest were of a survival nature: exercise was the result of completing daily tasks. In many primitive societies ritual dances were performed in all sorts of religious ceremonies. From the Greeks came the emphasis on the educational side of exercise and the idea of the "unified man," with harmony resulting from the blending of mind and body. A different view was held by the Spartans who saw the role of physical activity as one of preparation for military purposes—to build a strong, sturdy, well-conditioned body capable of withstanding the harsh rigors of military life. During the Middle Ages forms of physical activity fell into disfavor with the Church: salvation of the soul for the hereafter was more important than building strong bodies for life on earth.

Germany, Denmark, Sweden, and England were early pioneers in developing programs of physical education that were later to have a marked effect on programs in the United States. The German program was built around heavy gymnastic apparatus such as the high bar, parallel bars, rings, and horses. Sweden emphasized the medical side of gymnastics and subsequently developed a system of corrective exercises. Denmark developed a system of gymnastics particularly suited to the needs of its predominantly agricultural population. Examples of this type of activity may be found in conditioning or warming up exercises, sometimes called "grass drills," used for football and other vigorous sports.

England contributed numerous sports and the "sporting spirit" to America via the transplanted colonists.

Physical Education in the United States

Early Programs. Physical education as we know it today was not introduced into the schools of this country until about the time of the Civil War. The early settlers had little time for frivolity or entertainment. Play was for very young children. Recreation and sports were chiefly the property of the wealthy.

The first school programs of physical education were introduced by European immigrants who came to this country during the last century. These programs, reflecting the nationalistic ideals of their native homelands, were very formal in nature and restricted in content. Academic-minded educators reluctantly but gradually accepted these formal types of programs. The chief argument used in favor of physical exercise was that city boys no longer had chores or physical work to do. It was reasoned that physical education would counteract this deficiency. At about the same time, owing to an increase in leisure time, the working man had an opportunity for wider participation in sports and recreational activities.

Early efforts to introduce athletics into the school program were rejected by school directors. Students, however, persisted in promoting athletics under their own direction. As a result of increasing abuses associated with their promotion and also of changes in educational philosophy, educators, sensing the potential educational features of athletics, decided to take over control of school athletic programs. Some contended that athletics afforded students a way to relieve surplus energy or blow off steam, and to them athletics were a good means of keeping the boys busy and out of mischief. In most cases the administration and promotion of athletics and physical education were separately maintained. Thus there arose an artificial division of two naturally associated movements.

Impact of the Sciences. Since the turn of the present century, several factors have contributed toward bringing sports and physical education into an organic union. Most notable influences have perhaps been in the biological sciences and in the newer sciences of psychology and sociology, which in turn have considerably altered educational thought and practice.

Biology's chief contribution to education has been the principle of growth, which is closely akin to the idea of development so emphasized in education today. Other biological sciences, such as anatomy, physiology, chemistry, and nutrition, have provided vast quantities of knowledge that have broadened the scope of physical education.

Modern psychology has advanced the thesis that humans are an organic unity. All aspects of a person's makeup have a bearing on the final product. Education is no longer concerned merely with imparting knowledge to improve the intellect alone. Sport contributes to group adjustment by providing opportunities for developing sportsmanship and ethical behavior.

Psychology has also been responsible for advancing principles concerning the processes of learning and for improving techniques and methods of instruction. Mental hygiene, which is an offspring of psychology and psychiatry, has contributed new ideas on the emotional aspects of life.

All of the above ideas have played their part in shaping modern educational practices. A person must be well instructed in all of the above aspects or fall short of achieving a well-rounded and balanced personality that can be readily adapted to meet rapidly changing conditions of present-day society.

Present-day Programs. Today's physical education programs bear little resemblance to the earlier types of formal gymnastics. They now include popular team sports, body conditioning, recreational sports, and various forms of dance. Depending on locality and available facilities winter sports, horseback riding, and other specialized activities are also available.

Interscholastic and intercollegiate sports are closely associated with physical education, and in most cases are handled by the same personnel. Intramural sports provide a broad base for releasing the competitive urge of the student body. The required or service programs attempt to reach all students with a program that is basically instructional in content and purpose.

Physical education programs are becoming more flexible than ever before to take care of individual needs and interests. On the college and university level, more academic content is being included to give an appreciation of health, safety, and sports in one's personal life and in the American culture. The participants enjoy learning techniques and strategies, and about how the rules evolved. Whereas the previous emphasis in many of these activities was on exercise, today we also enable the students to acquire an interest, skill, and understanding that will remain with them for life.

LANDMARK DEVELOPMENTS

Two significant pieces of federal legislation have had a wide-ranging effect on physical education programs in recent years: Title IX outlawing sex discrimination, and Public Law 94-142 guaranteeing equal opportunity for handicapped children.

Title IX

Title IX of the Education Amendments of 1972 states:

> No person in the United States shall on the basis of sex be excluded from participation in, be denied the benefits of, or be subjected to discrimination under any education program or activity receiving federal financial assistance . . . .[3]

Under Title IX, females must receive equal opportunity to participate with males in athletics and physical education classes. This law has affected all phases of the physical education program, from planning to finances. The law mandates coeducational classes and provides for ability grouping within a class as long as it is not based on sex. Women and girls may not be excluded from participation in such sports as wrestling, boxing, basketball, and football. Title IX further provides for equal sharing of facilities, budgets, coaching, coach compensation, equipment, supplies, and many other items.

Coed Physical Education

Now that coeducational physical education has been mandated, it has necessitated a new way of thinking for teachers who plan and organize phys-

[3]U.S. Department of Health, Education, and Welfare. Office for Civil Rights (Washington, D.C.: Government Printing Office, 1975).

ical education programs. Almost all of the activities described in this *Handbook* can be used in a coeducational setting. In the activities chapters suggestions are made for modifying rules of play. In addition, the following specific ways to modify activities and rules will facilitate play on a coeducational basis.

Equipment

1. Use of junior-size balls, golf clubs, bats, etc.
2. Use of oversize balls—softball, beachball
3. Use of regulation-size heavy foam rubber balls having similar weight properties as their regulation-size counterparts
4. Larger target areas
5. Larger goals

Playing Area

1. Reduce dimensions of court or field
2. Enlarge boundary areas; use walls as an outside boundary
3. Design specific zones for males and females or restrictions on the numbers of opposite sex in a particular zone
4. Cut size of areas in half to allow for smaller teams yet more participation (for example: 7 on 7 soccer, 3 on 3 basketball, 2 on 2 volleyball, 6 on 6 field hockey)

Teams

1. Equalize competition by matching beginners against beginners, or heights and weights, or ability grouping, or experience grouping
2. Equalize numbers of boys and girls per team
3. Equalize playing time for each participant per game

FIGURE 1-3. Title IX legislation has brought about many changes in the school physical education program.

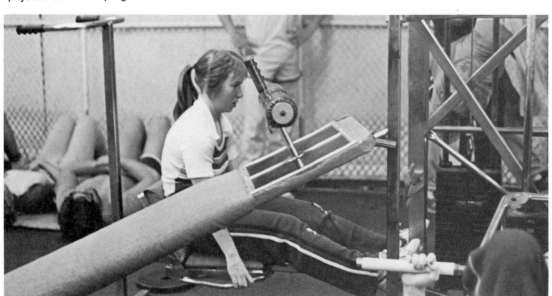

4. Male and female co-captains
5. Males substitute for males, females for females

Instructional Considerations

1. Develop individualized learning packages based on ability
2. Interest grouping—competitive and noncompetitive activities
3. Individual activities and team activities
4. Sport orientation or education approach for contact sports listed in the Title IX guidelines (boxing, wrestling, ice hockey, football, basketball, rugby)
5. Emphasis on individual and dual activities
6. Area emphasis on socialization activities—dance (folk, square, social), camping, outdoor skills, new games

Competition

1. Limited ball contacts by males before females touch the ball, and vice versa
2. Alternate the contacts or passes made
3. Assign a total number of contacts that must be made before shooting or kicking
4. Allow females only in scoring areas with a female goalie (examples: field hockey, soccer, team handball)
5. Only allow females to shoot
6. More points assigned to a score by a female than a male or if the ball changes hands a specified number of times
7. Shorten the distance of the shooting, throwing, swimming, or striking boundary
8. Alternate scoring opportunities for males and females
9. Shorten time periods
10. Modify some rules: no spiking, no fast breaks, 1 or 2 swings, no sliding, no tackling (soccer), females take direct or indirect kicks and penalty kicks
11. Place time limits on games
12. Award points based on team play and total player involvement

The Handicapped

In 1975 the federal government passed the Education for All Handicapped Children Act (Public Law 94-142). This law gives every handicapped child the opportunity to be integrated into the regular physical education program, whenever appropriate. Physical educators must now design programs that provide for the needs of the handicapped as well as the nonhandicapped child. This means that teachers have to understand the special requirements of handicapped students and be able to make program and activity adaptions that will allow for integration whenever possible. This concept, known as *mainstreaming,* will have a marked effect on the program

for students who are preparing for a professional career in physical education.

AAHPERD Publications. Included in the Selected References at the end of this section is a separate listing of AAHPERD publications that will be an invaluable aid to teachers and recreation directors in planning programs and activities for persons with all types of impairments, both physical and mental.

FUTURE TRENDS

A great deal of time and effort is now going into scientific laboratory research in physical education. This is particularly true in the fields of physiology, psychology, and kinesiology, as each area affects the teaching and learning of neuromuscular and sport skills. Testing is being used to a far greater extent because it enables individuals to monitor their progress and compare their rate of improvement with others. A number of sources on testing and measurement in physical education are listed in the Selected References at the end of this section.

Professional Needs

While still beyond the horizon, there are indications that future courses may be designed to tie in with professional needs. For example, the student of forestry or engineering would benefit from instruction in handling canoes, lifesaving, first aid, and survival in the open. The future newspaper or TV reporter would benefit from a knowledge of sports techniques. The artist or illustrator needs to know correct anatomical stances. The student of architecture can well utilize information on the construction of sports complexes, playgrounds, and recreational housing facilities. Likewise the student of municipal government should know about recreation commissions and about governmental taxes on sports. The music student would learn about musical accompaniment for various dance forms, the place of music in community recreation centers and camps, and the marching formations for school bands. The student of education would learn to teach and supervise the games played in the elementary grades and how to organize holiday or birthday parties for children and social gatherings for adults.

OBJECTIVES OF PHYSICAL EDUCATION

Students often question the necessity of fulfilling the physical education requirement. "What good will physical education do me?" "What am I supposed to get out of it?" "Why waste time playing silly games and learning pointless rules when I could be taking a subject that has more educational value?" "What's the use of working up a sweat—I'll get plenty of that in the Army!" When questions like these go unanswered, as they frequently do, a great deal of doubt is cast on the professed role of physical education—namely, to contribute to the development of the total person. Students who flounder about without understanding the purpose and value of their physical education program are being deprived of an important resource that can affect them now, in the immediate future, and for life.

The well-planned physical education program has the potential to contribute in a number of ways to all phases of individual development. In some areas physical education's contribution is unique; these objectives include the development of organic fitness and of neuromuscular skills. In other areas objectives are shared with other disciplines; these objectives include social development, emotional development, and cognitive development.

An outline of specific objectives is listed below. The objectives are classified here under three main categories: *cognitive* (dealing with knowledge and perception), *affective* (including social and emotional), and *psychomotor* (body movement and fitness). Some overlapping is inevitable (and maybe even desirable).

A. *Cognitive* (*Knowledge*) *Objectives.* These objectives deal with the individual's ability to perceive, comprehend, apply, analyze, synthesize, and evaluate. Common examples include:
   1. Learning the rules and techniques of a game.
   2. Acquiring knowledge of the strategy of a game.
   3. Developing an understanding of the present values of an activity or sport and of its carry-over values to later life.
   4. Analyzing facts and problems leading to an understanding of how the body moves.
   5. Understanding the "why" of an activity before performing it.
B. *Affective* (*Social and Emotional*) *Objectives.* These objectives deal with the individual's values, appreciations, attitudes, and interests. For example:
   1. Acquiring the attitudes and habits of loyalty, cooperation, initiative, self-control and courtesy.
   2. Demonstrating the concept of fair play as it relates to one's role in a sporting contest.
   3. Developing standards and ethics that must be observed to get along with other participants and team members.
   4. Appreciating physical skill development and its relationship to the use of leisure time.
   5. Appreciating the value of physical activity and its effect on the human body.
   6. Developing a healthy outlet for self-expression, creative energy, release of tension and emotional drives.

C. *Psychomotor Objectives* (*Organic Fitness and Neuromuscular Development*). These objectives deal specifically with the way the body functions, including the development of specific manipulative skills that affect the way we live, work, and play. For example, common objectives include:
   1. Developing specific skills (running, jumping, throwing, dodging, twisting, carrying, leaping, etc.) that allow the participant to play in a game or engage in a specific physical activity.
   2. Engaging in training and conditioning programs that develop the body to its fullest potential to meet the challenges of everyday living.
   3. Learning various ways to improve muscular strength, muscular endurance, cardiovascular endurance, flexibility, power, agility, speed, and eye-foot and eye-hand coordination.
   4. Acquiring skills for safety and survival, such as swimming, lifesaving, and boating skills.

SUMMARY

Physical education is more than exercise, more than a muscle builder or a circulation quickener. It is more than frivolous play or having fun. It is more than athletic competition. Physical education also has health knowledge to impart, group experiences to offer, the joy of effort and achievement to give. It has the responsibility to teach skills in lasting recreative interests and to develop an appreciation of sports whether as spectator, reader, or participant. Physical education is education. It must always be in step with the current practices and procedures in education. It must always contribute to the all-around development and education of students.

Physical education and physical activity play a vital role in guaranteeing our survival in future generations. Sound school programs of physical education are vital to developing positive attitudes toward physical activity. They should be planned in a systematic manner, based on carefully established aims, goals, and objectives, and should provide a variety of opportunities from which the individual can best meet his or her specific needs and interests. Programs of today and for tomorrow must draw upon the biological, physiological, psychological, pedagogical, sociological, and cultural parameters that are available to us now.

SELECTED REFERENCES

AAHPERD. *Physical Education for High School Students.* Washington, D.C.: The Alliance, 1970.

ANNARINO, ANTHONY A., CHARLES L. COWELL, and HELEN W.

HAZELTON. *Curriculum Theory and Design in Physical Education,* 2nd ed. St. Louis, Mo.: The C.V. Mosley Co., 1980.

BARROW, HAROLD M. *Man and His Movement: Principles of Physical Education.* Philadelphia, Pa.: Lea & Febiger, 1971.

BLOOM, BENJAMIN S., ed. *Taxonomy of Educational Objectives. Handbook I: The Cognitive Domain.* New York: David McKay Co., Inc., 1956.

BUCHER, CHARLES. *Foundations of Physical Education* (eighth ed.). St. Louis, Mo.: The C.V. Mosby Co., 1979.

DAVIS, ELWOOD C., and DONNA MAE MILLER. *The Philosophic Process in Physical Education,* 2nd ed. Philadelphia, Pa.: Lea & Febiger, 1967.

GERBER, ELLEN W. *Innovators and Institutions in Physical Education.* Philadelphia, Pa.: Lea & Febiger, 1971.

HACKENSMITH, C.W. *History of Physical Education.* New York: Harper & Row, 1966.

HARROW, ANITA J. *A Taxonomy of Psychomotor Domain.* New York: David McKay Co., Inc., 1972.

KRATHWOHL, D.R., et al. *Taxonomy of Educational Objectives. Handbook II: The Affective Domain.* New York: David McKay Co., Inc., 1964.

PARKS, JANET B. *Physical Education, the Profession.* St. Louis, Mo.: The C.V. Mosley Co., 1980.

STEIN, JULIAN. "Sense and Nonsense about Mainstreaming." *The Journal of Physical Education and Recreation,* January, 1976.

U.S. Department of Health, Education, and Welfare, Office for Civil Rights: Final Title IX Regulations Implementing Education Amendments of 1972—Prohibiting Sex Discrimination in Education. Washington, D.C., Government Printing Office, 1975.

ZEIGLER, EARLE F. *History of Physical Education and Sport.* Englewood Cliffs, N.J.: Prentice-Hall, Inc., 1979.

ZEIGLER, EARLE F. *Physical Education and Sport Philosophy.* Englewood Cliffs, N.J.: Prentice-Hall, Inc., 1977.

Books on Testing and Measurement

AAHPERD Skills Test Series: Archery, Basketball, Football, Softball, Volleyball, Tennis. Washington, D.C.: The Alliance, 1978.

BARROW, HAROLD M., and ROSEMARY MCGEE. *A Practical Approach to Measurement in Physical Education,* 2nd ed. Philadelphia, Pa.: Lea & Febiger, 1971.

CLARKE, H. HARRISON. *Application of Measurement to Health and Physical Education,* 5th ed. Englewood Cliffs, N.J.: Prentice-Hall, Inc., 1976.

COLLINS, D. RAY, and PATRICK B. HODGES. *A Comprehensive Guide to Sports Skills Tests and Measurement.* Springfield, Illinois: Charles C. Thomas Publisher, 1978.

JOHNSON, BARRY L., and JACK K. NELSON. *Practical Measurements for Evaluation in Physical Education,* 3rd ed. Minneapolis, Minnesota: Burgess Publishing Co., 1979.

Literature on Programs for the Handicapped

The following publications may be ordered from AAHPERD Publications (Dept. V), P.O. Box 870, Lanham, Maryland 20801.

Adapted Physical Education Guidelines: Theory and Practices for the 70s and 80s

Annotated Research Bibliography in Physical Education,

Recreation, and Psychomotor Function of Mentally Retarded Persons

Aquatic Recreation for the Blind

Choosing and Using Phonograph Records for Physical Education, Recreation and Related Activities

Dance for Physically Disabled Persons: A Manual for Teaching Ballroom, Square and Folk Dances to Users of Wheelchairs and Crutches

Guide to Information Systems in Physical Education and Recreation for Impaired, Disabled, and Handicapped Persons

Involving Impaired, Disabled and Handicapped Persons in Regular Camp Programs

Making Physical Education and Recreation Facilities Accessible to All

Materials on Creative Arts for Persons with Handicapping Conditions

Motor Fitness Testing Manual for the Moderately Mentally Retarded

Physical Activities for the Mentally Retarded (Ideas for Instruction)

Physical Education and Recreation for Impaired, Disabled, and Handicapped Individuals: Past, Present, Future

Practical Pointers: A new series of publications providing how-to-do-it information on: (1) using various activities to meet unique needs of handicapped indivduals, (2) adaptations, modifications, and creative approaches that have been successfully used in ongoing programs, and (3) ideas for finding innovative ways of meeting needs of participants in either special or regular programs and activities.

Audio-Visual Materials

The following films are available from AAHPERD, c/o NEA Sound Studios, 1201 16th St. N.W., Washington, D.C. 20036.

All the Self There Is (16 mm, 13½ min.). Interprets the "new physical education."

An Equal Chance through Title IX (16 mm, 22 min.).

A Very Special Dance (16 mm, 20 min.). Dance and mentally handicapped young adults.

Every Child a Winner (16 mm, 13½ min.). New physical education at the elementary school level.

SOCIOLOGICAL ASPECTS

In recent years there has been a growing awareness of the social implications of physical fitness and sports activities. A nation's attitudes toward recreational and leisure time pursuits reveals a great deal about its lifestyle and cultural patterns. The extent and kinds of participation in those activities reflect such factors as geography, historical tradition, religion, and economic status. In this section we will examine how some of those factors interrelate with leisure, recreation, and sport. We will conclude by speculating about future directions and trends. The bibliographical sources at the end of this section are strongly recommended for a fuller understanding of this subject.

CHANGING ATTITUDES ON WORK AND PLAY

Historically, participation in any form of recreation—play, games, sports—was frowned upon as sinful idleness that played into the hands of the devil. The Protestant work ethic, which many of our forefathers preached, held that hard work alone would inculcate the supreme ideals of thriftiness, morality, and purity. In many cases, particularly in Colonial New England, people who took part in sports and games, especially on the Sabbath, were subject to arrest. Only on rare occasions, after the work was done, would some forms of play take place. Even these were usually work-associated activities such as husking bees or barn raisings.

As time passed, leaders began to speak out on the benefits of recreation and sports. The medical and the physical education professions pointed out the advantages of regular exercise. Social scientists and psychologists cited the social and psychological benefits of recreational participation. And, contrary to the earlier belief, there was a gradual and growing acceptance of the notion that a meaningful leisure time activity could actually improve one's working efficiency.

Changing economic conditions and lifestyles further supported the concept that leisure time activity could be beneficial. With the shift from an agricultural toward an urban industrial society, manual outdoor farm work gave way to the factory assembly line and sedentary office jobs. As more and more machinery took over, jobs became routine, monotonous, with little chance for self-expression. The day of the village craftsman was past. In crowded cities fatigue, tension, and stress were undermining the health of many and becoming an important problem.

Today, more than ever people look to recreation for ways to relax, to restore themselves, to "recharge their batteries" both physically and mentally. The impetus to pursue an enriching leisure time activity is constantly accelerating. Furthermore as the use of computers is growing, the work day and the work week are shrinking. In some parts of the country the four-day forty-hour work week is becoming the norm. The mid-week half-day break and extended vacations are also more common. So every year more people are faced with more leisure time than ever. In the view of prominent economists and philosophers this represents a very serious social problem. When we add the fact that people are living longer, we see how vital it is to plan and prepare meaningful leisure-time activity while we are young, to fill the longer spare time hours and retirement years.

But in spite of those advances toward the ultimate goal of increased leisure time, it seems that we are busier and more rushed than ever before. We seem concerned constantly with how we will get everything done in a particular period of time. We seem to live in a stress society where our lifestyle is governed by the clock. In short, if we have all this leisure time, where is it?

THE NEED FOR RECREATION

During primitive times people were forced to engage in vigorous physical activity in order to survive. They hunted and fished for food and had to be strong and alert against danger and attack. Only on a limited basis did they sometimes amuse themselves with forms of play. In our contemporary society, those types of vigorous activities are no longer required for survival. Yet our body is basically the same as in earlier times; it still requires exercise in order to function at full capacity.

Today it is essential that we take part in a physical activity as a substitute for the vigorous pursuits in which our ancestors engaged. Fitness and health authorities are unanimous in emphasizing the advantages of recreation participation. While some forms of recreational activity provide more vigorous exercise than others, all pursuits involving body movement can be beneficial.

The benefits of a meaningful recreational activity go beyond the purely physical. Even if your work is enjoyable and satisfying you cannot perform at an efficient level indefinitely. Recreation offers a needed change from the work routine, an opportunity to relax, to be uplifted, to be "re-created" so as to return to work physically and mentally restored. Recreation contributes to the physical and mental stability that is greatly needed in our contemporary society.

Recreation Involvement: Spectator or Participator?

A potentially harmful trend in recreation and sport in our culture has been the growing tendency toward spectatorism. Sitting and watching others play tends to promote an inactive, unhealthy lifestyle. To blame, perhaps, is the impetus to build new stadiums and the heavy sponsorship of sporting events on television, particularly cable television. These shows are turning us into a nation of armchair players.

Fortunately, there are encouraging signs that the population is also moving in the direction of active participation. Each year more and more people are jogging, playing tennis, racquetball, and golf, skiing, camping, backpacking, and engaging in a host of other lifetime sport activities.

Both trends seem to be operating simultaneously—toward the spectator, inactive lifestyle on one hand and toward the participator, active lifestyle on the other. While something may be gained from watching someone else play or perform an activity (for instance, learning more about the game and appreciating the athletes' skills), it is generally agreed that active participation offers more total benefits.

Recreation Agencies

Because recreational activities are so varied, there is no one organizational setup in the United States covering all the types available. Agencies that promote recreational activities are operated by the local, state, or federal government. Numerous national parks and state forests are open to the public and offer camping, hunting, and fishing as well as many other activities. In addition, recreational programs are sponsored by many community groups, both public and private, including schools, hospitals, industrial plants, commercial establishments, churches, religious and fraternal organizations, and clubs.

EDUCATION AND LIFETIME SPORT

The historical tendency in American school sports has been to stress a few team activities, primarily football, basketball, and baseball. While team sports have many advantages and should be a part of physical education and interscholastic athletic programs, they fail to offer an opportunity to pursue a lifetime sport.

The term "lifetime sport" refers here to a recreational or sport activity in which one can participate long after graduation—indeed, for an entire lifetime. Examples of lifetime sports are golf, swimming, cycling, tennis, bowling, and the like. Generally, lifetime sports are characterized by requiring little equipment and only one or two participants in order to play.

Physical education programs in many schools, colleges, and universities offer lifetime sports that are of immediate value while at the same time contributing to lifelong well-being and enjoyment.

THE ECONOMICS OF RECREATION

As our society becomes more affluent and as leisure time increases, the amount of money spent on recreation-related activities is constantly soaring. According to one source, over $180 billion was spent in 1978 on recreational and leisure-time activities—

12 percent more than in 1977.[1] Even when the economy declines, Americans still find ways (perhaps through less expensive activities) to engage in some form of recreation. All in all, it is estimated that entertainment and leisure-time activities account for more than 10 percent of the United States gross national product, and that figure is likely to grow in the future.[2]

Government at all levels realizes a significant amount of revenue through recreation activities, in particular from federal and state sales taxes on equipment and supplies. Some types of activities, such as horse racing (for years, the nation's leading spectator sport), also provide substantial tax revenue. Another example is the sale of fishing and hunting licenses, which contributes millions of dollars annually to governments at all levels.

Nationwide the recreation industry provides employment for thousands of people in the manufacture and sale of sporting equipment and supplies. Furthermore, those employed in industry or in federal, state, and local recreation programs represent a substantial part of the work force.

The cost of taking part in recreational activities varies considerably, so that virtually everyone can find a meaningful leisure time pursuit that will fit his or her budget. Activities such as jogging, cycling, and bowling are relatively inexpensive. But for such sports as skiing, sailing, water skiing, and horseback riding, the expense involved is an important consideration.

COEDUCATIONAL SPORTS

Until recently American sport was marred by discriminatory practices. Through legal restrictions, policy, or outright male hostility, females were often barred or were given only limited opportunities for participation.

The myths that athletic competition would make a woman masculine, hurt her reproductive system, or build big muscles further discouraged participation. Research has shown that no scientific evidence supports the fallacies that girls or women undergo any form of harmful physiological change through athletic participation.

Title IX. Following testimony before Congressional committees which revealed discriminatory practices against girls and women in practically all athletic programs, the bill known as Title IX of the Education Amendments of 1972 was enacted into law (see p. 6). As a result of Title IX, recreational activities are now largely coeducational. There has been a tremendous upsurge in female participation in sports—a 500 percent increase by 1982.

[1]Lane Jennings, "Future Fun: Tomorrow's Sports and Games," *Futurist*, 13:417–420, December, 1979.
[2]*Ibid.*

OPPORTUNITIES FOR THE HANDICAPPED

We have pointed out the advantages to all people from participating in a lifetime sport. During the decade of the 1970s, there arose a public awareness of the need to improve education services for the handicapped. Perhaps most significant was the implementation of P.L. 94-142 (Education of All Handicapped Children Act of 1975) which provided for mainstreaming.

Mainstreaming established the opportunity for handicapped children to participate in regular public school classes. While the programs necessitated specially-trained teachers as well as modified facilities and equipment, the movement supported the trend that all people, regardless of their physical, mental, and emotional status, could benefit from physical activity.

Fortunately, this idea has caught on outside the formal school setting where numerous opportunities have been made available for our handicapped citizens, not the least of which is the Special Olympics.

BLACK AMERICANS IN SPORTS

The traditional view in America has been that sport was one of the few areas where there was no racial discrimination. Success in sports was generally agreed to be based solely on athletic performance and not on ethnic background or, for that matter, on socio-economic status. Indeed the relatively high percentage of blacks (about 11 percent) in relation to the total number of professional football, baseball, and basketball players in the United States was quite impressive. Furthermore, a high percentage of black Americans participated in high school and college athletic programs.

Despite these numbers, many people today maintain that black Americans' involvement in sport is still not wholly free from racial prejudice. They argue further that while equal opportunity may exist in the field of competition, the retired black athlete has a harder time when his career is over.

Among the leading black Americans who have spoken out against discrimination in sports are Dr. Harry Edwards, a sociologist at the University of California at Berkeley, Arthur Ashe, the professional tennis player, and Reverend Jesse Jackson, the civil rights activist. They point out that because of limited employment opportunities along with sport hero identification many black youngsters seek a career in sports. As a result, many young blacks spend a lot of time on playgrounds, neglecting their academic training and the learning of practical employment skills.

Furthermore, the belief persists among many blacks that a professional sports career can serve as a road out of the ghetto and to financial security. In fact, the odds of attaining success are so small that most blacks soon find themselves back where they started with no education or marketable skills. In short, the idea that sport serves as a "way out" is a myth; only a select few "make it." In his book *Sports in America,* James Michener states that in a typical year, an average of only 200,000 basketball-playing high school senior boys of all races graduate. Of that number only about six will eventually earn a starting spot on a pro team.[3] And those black athletes who do succeed often have a hard time finding jobs at the end of their relatively short professional careers.

Edwards, Ashe, and Jackson, along with many others, are speaking out to the black community and stressing the importance of staying in school and learning a marketable skill that will provide a secure lifelong income.

INTERNATIONAL SPORTS

As world travel becomes easier and faster, and international communication systems become more advanced, Americans are getting more firsthand information about sports in other countries. This trend is dispelling the belief that the United States is one of the few countries that emphasize sports. Americans tend to think that the World Series or the Super Bowl are major international athletic events. In fact these events pale in comparison with the global popularity of the World Cup matches sponsored by the International Federation of Soccer or the annual Tour de France sponsored by the International Cycling Union, and regarded by some authorities as the most grueling of all sporting events.

In Canada and the Scandinavian countries hockey, skiing, and ice skating are very popular. In the Latin American countries soccer and baseball capture a great deal of attention. Some of the Far Eastern countries, such as Thailand, India, and Malaysia, consider badminton a major sport. Volleyball is promoted widely in the U.S.S.R. and the Iron Curtain countries as well as in Japan and China. Baseball is the Japanese national sport. In China, table tennis and basketball are the most popular. In Mexico and Spain bullfighting and jai alai are national pastimes.

In many nations around the world, particularly in the Communist countries, sports are promoted for propaganda reasons and the government hunts for talented athletes who are trained to represent their nation in international sporting events. This practice is fostered in Russia and East Germany, where a great deal of emphasis is placed on the development

[3]James A. Michener, *Sports in America* (New York: Random House, 1976), p. 193.

of world-class athletes. The underlying philosophy is that a winning athlete represents a winning form of government. Or, as one Communist leader put it, "International sport is 'war without weapons'!"

The Olympic Games. Among the widely known international competitions are the Asian Games, the Pan American Games, the British Empire and Commonwealth Games, World Maccabee Games, and the World University Games. But the oldest and most popular are the Olympic Games. The ancient Olympics were first held in 776 B.C. at Olympia, Greece, and were conducted probably every four years until A.D. 394. At that time, the Roman Christian emperor, Theodosius, abolished the Games as sinful because they were traditionally held in honor of the Greek pagan gods.

The Modern Games were revived in 1896 by the Baron Pierre de Coubertin, who believed that they could serve as an instrument for peace and good will. It was his desire that the Modern Olympics be conducted in a spirit of fair play, free of political interference, and should honor the achievements of athletes from around the world.

In many respects de Coubertin's ideals have not been realized, for the Olympic Games have been embroiled in many problems. There have been numerous political disputes, some of which have resulted in boycotts and terrorist attacks. There have also been disagreements over the amateur status of some of the athletes. And, the Olympic Games have become so expensive to conduct that many countries can no longer afford to participate.

Some authorities believe that major changes are needed for the Olympics to survive. Perhaps the solution lies in opening Olympic competition to all—whether amateur or professional. It has been suggested that gold medals be awarded only when an athlete breaks a world record. This would reduce competition among athletes from different countries. Another proposal considered to ease the financial burden of the Games has been the location of a permanent Olympic facility, perhaps in Greece.

Whatever the future of the Olympic Games may be, they hold a potential promise to promote international good will and understanding.

LEISURE, RECREATION, AND SPORT IN THE FUTURE

As we approach the 21st century, it is clear that more and more people will face the problem of finding meaningful, enjoyable ways to fill their leisure time.

During the 1970s, the popularity of motorized sports reached an all-time high. Motorcycles, snowmobiles, and off-road recreation vehicles led the surge. However, soaring fuel costs have dampened some of that enthusiasm in the 1980s. Already we

are seeing a trend away from motorized sports toward hiking, backpacking, and, the fastest growing winter sport of all: cross-country skiing. Notwithstanding, the love of cars and motor vehicles remains very strong, and Americans will probably be reluctant to give up motorized sports entirely.

A recreational spin-off from our technological society has been the development of electronic games. Videogames first appeared in 1972 with simple move-the-dot-through-the-maze type challenges. From that beginning, and with the addition of microprocessor memory chips, highly sophisticated visual and sound effects are now produced. Currently there are games that feature spaceships with limited fuel supplies, machines that have three-dimensional movement capabilities, and "black hole" and gravity challenges.

These electronic games are only a beginning. With unbelievable reality and simulation accuracy, we will soon be "flying" space ships, "driving" race cars, "commanding" tanks on the battlefield, and "landing" a jet on the deck of an aircraft carrier. Other forms of effect will offer all the sensations of flying a stunt plane, riding a roller coaster, or taking a submarine ride. According to the promoters, the experience will be very realistic yet virtually eliminate the possibilities of injury, death, or potential lawsuit.

The drawback in these games is that they are a passive, non-vigorous form of diversion and we derive no benefits of physical exertion from playing them.

Further refinement of our satellite communications systems will develop the capacity for international sports audiences. Baseball and basketball are already played throughout much of the world and soccer is growing very rapidly in the United States. We can probably look for longer seasons as teams travel around the world to more desirable climates (or use the ever-increasing number of domed stadiums). Furthermore, we can also look for true world championships, since professional team sponsorships may well move away from the geographical concept and toward the multi-national corporation. How about the World Series being played between the IBM Yankees and the Tokyo Giants? Or the Super Bowl title being decided between the Mexico City Aztecs and the Royal Dutch Shell Rams?

But perhaps by the time we enter the 21st century, the World Series and the Super Bowl will no longer be popular. Soccer, however, is expected to grow in popularity since it is relatively inexpensive to sponsor and less injury prone than American football. Besides, unlike football, anyone, regardless of size, can play soccer.

No discussion of the future of sports would be complete without mentioning a factor that has had a major impact on its growth thus far. Television brought sports into our homes and, more recently, special electronic skills such as instant replay and slow-motion coverage have maintained viewing popularity. Some activities have modified their rules (tennis tie-breaks), or have gone to "sudden-deaths" and "shoot-outs" in order to maintain viewing appeal. Other sports by their very nature do not fare as well in the television medium. You cannot see the puck in televised hockey; and golf tournaments, open road races, and skiing competition are among those in which it is difficult for the television viewer to maintain a realistic perception of the activity. But it would appear that television sport-viewing will maintain its popularity—particularly on cable TV.

Some social scientists and psychologists are predicting an attitudinal change with regard to competition and the importance placed on winning. It has been suggested that the "number one" syndrome which permeates so much of our sport culture may be losing its appeal. Some believe that making winning the ultimate objective breeds deception, cheating, degradation, and fear. Furthermore, some researchers claim that even winners may wind up as losers, since the winners are often isolated and become the target for their opposition.

A more reasonable approach, according to some, would be to replace the highly competitive win-or-lose concept, which makes the losers miserable, with a cooperative, friendly, and trusting type of game environment in which everybody feels good. One such sport promoted by the California-based New Games Foundation is "earthball," in which two teams attempt to move an earth replica 16-foot weather balloon across a playing area. After each goal the team members switch sides to develop the concept "We all won!" instead of "They won!" Of course there are those who scoff at the idea of non-competitive games as being against human nature.

Further space exploration and new fuels may very well entail the expansion of sport into outer space—with novel, surprising possibilities. Imagine, for example, swimming within a space capsule in a gravity-free environment. Think of the stunts that could be accomplished off a diving board! You could actually swim *UP* to meet a group of friends. Imagine what feats of high jumping and pole vaulting one could accomplish in such an environment!

Back on terra firma the impetus will no doubt continue for increased participation in sports by women and handicapped persons. This development is the result not only of the equal access laws but also of changing attitudes.

SUMMARY

Our concepts and attitudes about recreation, sport, and leisure pursuits are shaped by many factors. At one time shunned in our society, leisure-time activities gradually began to gain acceptance. The benefits of recreational activity include physical and mental health restoration and the improved ability to work and function more efficiently.

The range of recreational activities is broad enough to enable everyone to select a leisure time pursuit that suits his or her preference and finances. Agencies of all types are to be found in almost every community, so it is easy to learn what recreational opportunities are available.

The long-range outlook forecasts a growing trend toward computer-type games and professional sport spectating. We must be on guard against the dangers of an inactive lifestyle in the 21st century.

SELECTED REFERENCES

BUCHER, CHARLES A. *Foundations of Physical Education,* 8th ed. St. Louis, Mo.: C.V. Mosby Co., 1979.

DE GRAZIA, SEBASTIAN. *Of Time, Work, and Leisure.* New York, 1962.

JENNINGS, LANE. "Future Fun, Tomorrow's Sports and Games," *Futurist,* 13:417–429, December, 1979.

KANDO, THOMAS M. *Leisure and Popular Culture in Transition.* St. Louis, Mo.: C.V. Mosby Co., 1975.

MICHENER, JAMES A. *Sports in America.* New York: Random House, 1976.

SEIDEL, BEVERLY L., and MATTHEW C. RESICK. *Physical Education: An Overview.* Reading, Mass.: Addison Wesley Publishing Co., 1978.

YIANNAKIS, ANDREW, THOMAS D. MCINTYRE, MERRILL J. MELNICK, and DALE P. HART. *Sport Sociology: Contemporary Themes.* Dubuque, Iowa: Kendall-Hunt Publishing Co., 1979.

PSYCHOLOGICAL ASPECTS

Psychology is the study of behavior. As such, it is concerned with all aspects of behavior. There are many areas of study in psychology but in this *Handbook,* we concentrate on principles that are most relevant for teachers and coaches, particularly those concerning learning and social interaction.

MOTIVATION

Whatever behavior is being studied, one important consideration is the motivation prompting it. *Motivation* is any condition that energizes, guides, and sustains responding. Motives may be unlearned, such as hunger or thirst, or learned, such as the desires for friends or for accomplishment.

Needs and Drives. Psychologists view *needs* as the physiological or psychological deficits a person experiences. *Drives* are the states resulting from needs. Motives often are viewed as the product of needs and drives.

Physiological needs include hunger or thirst, need for air, or need for relief from pain. Teachers and coaches may not be concerned with the first two, but the latter two provide good illustrations of problems that may prove important. For example, teaching swimming may be very difficult if the learner has a strong fear of suffocation and refuses to put his or her head in the water. And many runners experience painful "stitches" and simply stop practicing.

Psychological deficits may be more difficult to identify. Need for achievement may be important for the learner, for example, but if not expressed, the instructor may fail to realize the importance of the resultant drive. Lack of support for the learner's achievements may "turn off" the learner.

The same type of situation is possible for affiliation (friendship) drive. Research has shown that participation in sports for both physical education majors and non-majors often is prompted by a desire to be "part of the group." If the instructor fails to find ways to support this, an important motive may not be satisfied.

Level of Motivation.   Regardless of the type of motive being investigated, psychologists have tried to find ways to express the strength of the motive. Often this is accomplished by measuring *deprivation,* that is, how much time has passed since last satisfying the motive.

Psychologists also have studied the relationship of level of motivation to the resultant performance. The solid line in Figure 1-4 illustrates the typical results of such studies. Interestingly, as a task becomes more difficult, the level of motivation required to produce maximum performance diminishes. The broken line in Figure 1-4 shows this difference.

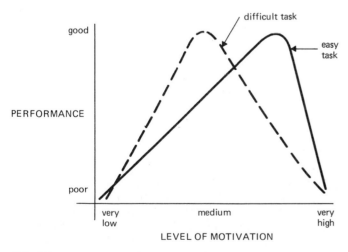

FIGURE 1-4.

Teachers and coaches are familiar with the results shown in these curves. The lazy, unmotivated student or athlete usually does not perform very well. The person who is interested and reasonably excited about the experience often does very well. But the responses of someone who is "super-motivated" often are quite poor. Teachers, coaches, and the public in general often talk about someone "choking." There are many examples of this last situation: the golfer who misses an 18-inch putt on the last hole and fails to win an important tournament, the student who "draws a blank" on a particularly difficult examination question, or the long-jump contestant who fouls on a crucial jump. All may experience motivation that is too high for them to perform well.

Functional Autonomy.   *Functional autonomy* refers to a situation where a response is first made to satisfy some external motivating condition, but after being repeated a number of times, comes to be motivating in and of itself. One example of functional autonomy found in physical education is that of jogging. Very few joggers start to jog because they really enjoy it. Rather, they are trying to get in shape, lose weight, quit smoking, or obey doctor's orders. Yet many joggers come to appreciate the jogging just for its own sake. Indeed, kept from exercising by bad weather, travel, job pressures, or other reasons, avid joggers often feel very deprived.

Conflict.   Another aspect of the study of motivation is that of *conflict,* a situation where two or more incompatible motives are operating at the same time. Psychologists have identified four basic forms of conflict. One is called *approach-approach conflict,* when the person must choose between two positively-valued or pleasant opportunities. For example, the person who has two "free" hours on a warm, sunny day and cannot choose between playing nine holes of golf or a couple of sets of tennis is experiencing an approach-approach conflict.

A second form of conflict is called *avoidance-avoidance conflict,* when the person must choose between two negatively valued or unpleasant circumstances. If the person with the two "free" hours feels obliged to either cut the lawn or clean the garage rather than pursue some recreation, an avoidance-avoidance conflict is experienced.

The third basic form of conflict is called *approach-avoidance conflict,* when one circumstance provokes both positive and negative values simultaneously. Many people experience such a conflict when trying to dive from a three-meter board for the first time. Accomplishing this would have much positive value, but the possibility of a mistake generates conflicting negative values.

Finally, the fourth basic form of conflict is a variation of the third. Called *multiple approach-avoidance conflict,* it occurs when the person is confronted with more than one possibility, each of which has both positive and negative values. Participating in an early-morning exercise program may create such a conflict. Actually starting to exercise has the positive value of getting in shape, but possible negative values such as experiencing some pain or having to change a sleeping schedule. Not starting has the positive values of maintaining a comfort level or not experiencing the pain, but the negative value of getting more and more out of shape.

Resolving any of these conflicts usually involves choosing a response that satisfies the strongest of the motives. Naturally, in the case of an avoidance-avoidance motive, the choice would be to satisfy the least unpleasant of the motives.

LEARNING-PERFORMANCE DISTINCTION

A second important consideration when studying behavior is the *learning-performance distinction. Learning* is defined as a relatively permanent change in behavior that occurs as a result of experience. This definition does not negate the importance of physical development. Physical growth often is a necessary condition for learning to take place, but physical growth alone is not sufficient. Experience must occur also.

Performance is the actual behavior shown by the person. It must be recognized that what is observed does not necessarily reveal what has been learned. For example, a tennis player may have learned how to hit a "cut shot," but not be confronted with a situation that requires such a response. The observable performance would not show the learning.

Process versus Product.   A variation of the concern with performance has been the choice of *process,* or how a response is made, versus *product,* or what result turns out. This debate often is expressed as "That's not the right way to do that" versus "But it works!"

Teachers and coaches constantly are confronted with this concern. It is awfully hard to tell a player with a .375 batting average that putting the "foot in the bucket" is poor form. The product is successful, even though the process is not ideal.

Effects of Practice.   Many students and athletes grow up believing that "practice makes perfect." This is an inaccurate statement unless the response being performed *is* perfect or is being modified constantly to approach perfection. Instructors should recognize that a more appropriate viewpoint is that "practice makes *permanent.*" The instructor's task is to try to help the student-athlete make permanent the very best response possible.

REINFORCEMENT

The condition that satisfies a motive is called a reinforcer. Although often thought of as reward, psychologists use the term *reinforcement* in a broader sense, defining it as any condition that increases or maintains the strength of a response.

Positive Reinforcement.   The conditions usually described as rewards are called *positive reinforcements,* events, *which when present,* increase or

maintain the strength of a response. These may include anything from a few words of praise to stickers pasted on a football helmet.

Negative Reinforcement.   Another form of reinforcement is called *negative reinforcement,* when the *removal or absence* of some stimulus increases or maintains the strength of a response. The unpleasant condition being removed is called an *aversive stimulus.*

Negative reinforcement is *not* punishment. *Punishment* occurs when a response *leads to* an aversive stimulus, while negative reinforcement occurs when the aversive stimulus does not occur or is stopped.

Teachers and coaches often use negative reinforcement. Particularly good responses are reinforced by the removal of some unpleasant condition, for example, cancelling the laps to be run at the end of class or practice. On the other hand, if the responses have been especially poor, adding laps to the end of practice represents punishment.

Extinction and Spontaneous Recovery.   When a response is no longer followed by a reinforcer, the response tends to become weaker. *Extinction* is both the process of no longer presenting the reinforcement and the result of this process, the weakening of the response strength. Eventually, the response strength may return to its pre-learning value.

Interestingly, sometimes there will be a reappearance of an extinguished response after a period of rest has followed the extinction procedure. This is called *spontaneous recovery* of the response and occurs when the stimulus conditions provoke the response, although there is no reinforcement present.

Both extinction and spontaneous recovery are familiar to instructors. For example, many young children learn to throw ineffectively, placing forward the foot on the same side of the body as the throwing hand. An instructor hoping to change this pattern may have to devote quite a bit of time to praising an appropriate response and extinguishing the less efficient pattern.

Despite this constant instruction, sometimes after the children have been away from class or competition for some time, there may be a reappearance of the inefficient form. Just why this spontaneous recovery of the response occurs is not understood. Regardless, instructors must realize that if it does, additional extinction of the inappropriate response will be necessary.

Partial Reinforcement Effect.   One condition that works against extinction is *partial reinforcement,* that is, when a response is followed by reinforcement only part of the time. The result of partial reinforcement is called the *partial reinforcement effect* (*PRE*). Responses learned under partial reinforcement are *more resistant* to extinction than responses learned under continuous reinforcement.

This works to the advantage of the coach or teacher if the response is a productive or efficient one. However, an inefficient response such as the throwing response mentioned above will work some of the time. In such cases, eliminating the response may be quite difficult.

This points to the need for effective instruction for motor responses very early in a child's life. When appropriate response patterns can be trained, they can become very resistant to extinction and should be maintained throughout life. On the other hand, lack of instruction or poor instruction may allow inefficient and inappropriate responses to be learned that will work against the pleasures and successes that could be experienced.

SHAPING

Shaping is defined as reinforcing closer and closer approximations of a desired behavior. It is one way of trying to satisfy the practice-makes-permanent concern expressed above. Shaping is one of the most common ways of establishing *instrumental conditioning*, when the probability of making a response is changed by manipulating the consequences of that response. Learning an instep kick in soccer can be accomplished by shaping. To begin, the player is encouraged whenever contact with the ball is made on the instep rather than the toe. Step-by-step, increasing proficiency is reinforced so that eventually the player can use either foot to make accurate, appropriate-speed kicks from a still or moving ball.

Modeling. *Modeling* occurs when a person observes the behavior of another, then performs some or all of that observed behavior. The instructor teaching the instep kick first demonstrates how it is done. The person learning then tries to imitate what has been seen. If combined with shaping, the instructor reinforces each imitation that gets closer to the ultimately-desired performance.

Another concern in modeling is *vicarious learning,* which occurs when the learner observes both the response being made and the consequences of that response. This is shown when the learner imitates the form of an expert archer when the resultant bullseye also is seen. On the other hand, observing an unsuccessful response may lead to learning to *avoid* making a response that does not work. For example, if a companion attempts to cast a fishing line while standing too close to a tree and snags the line, the observer can learn to avoid that response without actually having to perform the response.

Superstitious Responding. In some cases, a response is followed by a reinforcement that is *not* contingent upon the response being made, but the observer comes to believe there is a contingency.

FIGURE 1-5. Modeling is an important instructional principle.

The result, called *superstitious responding* because of this inaccurate belief, is repetition of the response pattern. Unfortunately, occasional response-reinforcement sequences, although not contingent relationships, are enough to sustain the superstition, illustrating the partial reinforcement effect.

While many superstitions may be harmless, such as putting a sock on the left foot before putting one on the right foot, the teacher or coach must guard against circumstances where the person believes the superstition so avidly that failure to satisfy the conditions produces an attitude of complete defeatism. The "now we can't win, because you didn't follow the superstition" attitude can be extremely destructive, while in reality, it is completely false.

GENERALIZATION AND DISCRIMINATION

Responses learned in one situation sometimes are made in other, similar circumstances. When this happens, *stimulus generalization*—responding not only to the original stimulus, but to other similar stimuli—has occurred. In other cases, when the response is made to the original stimulus, but not made to other stimuli that are judged dissimilar, *discrimination* or *differentiation* has occurred.

An important application of stimulus generalization can be found in teaching downhill skiing.

The learner can be taught that the same responses are appropriate for many similiar circumstances, such as differing snow conditions, or approaching turns or moguls. Discrimination also can be very important for the athlete. A fairly obvious example of this is when the quarterback readying to throw a pass must differentiate teammates from opponents.

ATTENTION

Almost any sport or activity environment has many aspects of stimulation. Response acquisition may depend upon the person's *attention* to the stimuli that are important for learning.

Teachers and coaches should realize there are three categories of attention. The first is involuntary and depends upon the properties of the stimuli. Almost anyone will react vigorously to a sudden, unexpected loud noise. If this occurs just as a player attempts to shoot a free throw, the distraction may be sufficient to upset the shooting pattern, something the fans for the opponent's team may hope will happen.

A second category is the voluntary attention produced as a conscious process of the person. The player concentrating on the free throw may consciously "block out" the noises made by the opponent's fans.

The third category, essentially involuntary but based upon learned experiences rather than the properties of the stimulus, is classified as *habitual attention.* Coaches often try to instill this into players, so they habitually attend to the cues that help make performance automatic. Examples include spotting the cues that allow the player to make appropriate defensive moves, or avoid a punch, or know when to release a pass.

PREPAREDNESS

Preparedness is a concept that suggests that heredity determines conditions that make learning possible. There are comparable suggestions that *unpreparedness* for learning responses or *contrapreparedness,* a predisposition not to learn a response, may exist also. Research has found that people often choose their competitive sports by the physical characteristics they have inherited. For example, people with the best vision and quickest reaction times become ice hockey goalies, while those with poorer vision and slow reaction times participate in synchronized swimming. It is important that teachers and coaches realize inherited characteristics may help determine the choices of activities or limitations of abilities for their students and players.

OTHER GENERAL FACTORS AFFECTING ACQUISITION

While many factors such as those mentioned above influence acquisition, there are a number of other variables that affect learning. This section presents some that seem most appropriate for physical education.

Overlearning. *Overlearning* is associated with the "practice makes permanent" concept. If some criterion is used to decide when learning has occurred, overlearning refers to the amount of time or number of trials spent practicing beyond that criterion level. Even if the shortstop and second baseman seemingly have mastered the double play pivot, repeated practice will ensure the learning.

Transfer of Training. When acquisition of a task is affected by some previous learning, *transfer of training* has taken place. Teachers should strive for *positive transfer,* that is, when learning one task facilitates the acquisition of another task. The throwing motion mentioned earlier provides a good example of positive transfer. The opposite hand-foot requirement can be transferred from throwing a ball to serving a volleyball, serving in tennis, or rolling a bowling ball. Some situations generate *negative transfer,* when already knowing one task interferes with, or makes harder, the acquisition of a second task. Something that seems as simple as learning the rules regarding out-of-bounds illustrates how negative transfer can occur. In baseball, tennis, soccer and a number of other sports, on the line is inbounds. The ball must be completely beyond the line to be out-of-bounds. But in football or basketball, on the line is out-of-bounds. Obviously, learning in one case may be detrimental to learning the same type of rule for some other sport. To further complicate the matter, some judgments involve *how much* over the line, as when a referee in wrestling must make a decision as to whether or not most of the body has crossed the boundary line.

It should be noted that there will be some instances where no transfer takes place, either positive or negative. This happens when one task has no bearing upon another.

Knowledge of Results. Also called feedback, *knowledge of results* is the information about success or failure a person receives after performing some response. In general, knowledge of results facilitates acquisition of a response, especially if it is provided immediately after the response is made rather than delayed.

Many motor tasks provide knowledge of results automatically. If a person tries a new type of turn while skiing and falls, there is immediate feedback about that response. Other circumstances require the feedback provided by a coach or instructor.

Comments about position on the playing area or time elapsed for running a particular distance are examples of feedback an outside observer can provide.

A popular way to provide feedback information in classrooms and athletic situations is the use of film or video tape. One advantage of this type of feedback is that it can be used repeatedly, allowing the learner to be certain to understand the point being made.

Distribution of Practice. A summary of research supports the finding that holding relatively short practice periods and distributing them over some period of time will produce best acquisition of a task. This often is called *distributed practice,* as opposed to *massed practice* where practice periods are bunched together.

Many teachers and coaches take advantage of this principle by scheduling a variety of tasks during any one session. The tasks may be repeated a number of times over several days, but are not practiced long enough in any one session to produce boredom or fatigue. Distributed practice also seems to allow for consolidation of learning to take place during the interim periods.

Active versus Passive Attitude. A principle that seems to apply to almost any acquisition situation in education and athletics is that an *active* approach to learning will produce better acquisition than will a *passive* attitude.

In addition, for some tasks acquisition improves if there is an initial *warm-up period* that provides adjustment and introduction to the task. Yet, in other circumstances repeated practice in an active manner may produce *fatigue* which in turn causes deterioration of performance. The teacher or coach must consider both possibilities when planning a class or practice period.

Physical versus Mental Practice. Generally, research has shown that acquisition of a motor task (often a sport behavior) is best when physical practice is used. However, it also has been found that mental practice, that is, simply thinking about what kinds of motor responses will be made and how they will be executed, is better for acquisition than no practice at all. Many psychologists recommend that mental practice be used when physical practice is impossible, for example, when traveling or when weather conditions make physical practice impossible.

Context of Learning. Evidence indicates that people often develop what is called *state-dependent learning,* where the response learned is attached to the physical context in which it is learned. This factor is one that is important for both acquisition and retention of the response. "Dress rehearsal" practices are conducted to try to satisfy this factor.

Practicing in game uniforms, on the actual playing field or court to be used, or in other circumstances that match the conditions that will be used when retention is actually demanded may help maximize performance.

RETENTION AND FORGETTING

Of major concern to instructors in all areas is whether responses that have been learned will be retained or forgotten. *Retention* is the storage of learning over some period of time, often called the *retention interval. Forgetting* refers to the loss of retention, or the inability to retrieve a response, from storage. It should be noted that we must always measure retention in some manner, not forgetting. Forgetting is only inferred from what appears to not be retained.

Storage. *Storage,* or the maintenance of a memory over the retention interval, is divided into three subcategories. *Sensory storage* refers to information that is held in an unprocessed sensory form for several seconds or *less.* It is proposed that if a sensory overload exists, the person may be unable to do more than receive the stimulation; it is not processed and therefore no learning occurs.

Short-term storage refers to the initial processing of information. Responses are held for several seconds up to thirty seconds and processing must continue or information will be lost or discarded. *Long-term storage* occurs when information in sensory or short-term storage is processed, encoded, rehearsed, or treated in some manner so that retention extends over some longer period of time. Long-term storage may last a lifetime.

Teachers and coaches need to recognize these different forms of storage and plan their training methods accordingly. A life-long activity such as bicycling provides good examples of all three forms of storage. Stimuli encountered while riding are held momentarily in sensory storage while initial evaluation decides whether to ignore or attend to them. These might include the visual scene, auditory stimuli such as a car's horn, kinesthetic stimuli such as position on the bicycle, and many other sensations.

Some stimuli may be incorporated into short-term storage. For example, the rider may be given directions and hold these in memory only long enough to execute them. Once completed, this information is discarded totally.

Finally, the act of riding the bicycle itself is good evidence for life-long, long-term storage of a series of responses. It has often been said that once one learns to ride a bicycle, the responses are never forgotten. There is much evidence to indicate this is correct.

Athletics provide comparable examples—in football there are many sensory stimuli that must be evaluated, short-term storage of the play that has been called which when used is then temporarily discarded, and long-term storage of all the plays and formations to be used over the course of a game or a season.

Failure to Retrieve.   One explanation of why responses seem to be forgotten is called *failure to retrieve.* This implies that the information is held in storage, but for some reason the person is unable to call upon the information and produce it. Often this is attributed to inappropriate retrieval cues.

The dance teacher who asked her young students to "start with the pattern you learned last Friday" may find the students unable to make the correct responses if they practiced two different dances at that last session. They have not forgotten the dances, but are confused by the instructions given and retrieval failure occurs.

Interference.   Another explanation for the seeming failure to retain is *interference,* which suggests that retention of one response conflicts or interferes with the retention of some other response. This may be previous learning interfering with the retention of something learned later (often called *proactive interference*) or later learning interfering with the retention of something learned before (called *retroactive interference*). In either case, more than one stored response is elicited by the retrieval cue and if the inappropriate one is given, forgetting will seem to have occurred.

Even something that seems as simple as warm-up drills can be used to illustrate interference. If the teacher or coach calls a particular pattern and one or more of the participants recalls the wrong sequence, collisions or bumping can result. This is sometimes painful and often embarrassing.

Motivated Forgetting.   One additional explanation for forgetting is to claim that it is motivated. Sometimes called *repression,* the concept is that the person forgets the response because making the response may be threatening, anxiety-provoking or embarrassing.

Instructors may observe this phenomenon with especially good performers. In circumstances where making the response might make a companion look very inferior, the knowledgeable person seems to forget. This forgetting is attributed to the motive conditions, such as friendship, that are operating at the time and supposedly lets the performer avoid the anxiety or pain that would be associated with creating problems for a companion.

PROBLEM SOLVING IN PHYSICAL EDUCATION

The Problem Solving Sequence.   *Problem solving,* that is, establishing a goal and then seeking ways to achieve that goal, is typified by a fairly common sequence of events. The five steps are (1) recognizing there is a problem, (2) defining the problem accurately, (3) producing hypotheses about the problem's solution, (4) testing the hypotheses, and (5) selecting the best solution.

Just recognizing that a problem exists may be a major step in initiating problem solving because lack of understanding stops the sequence before it gets started. For example, not realizing that the rules of a game are misunderstood means the problem is not recognized. If recognition occurs, defining the problem accurately requires identifying the most relevant concepts. When rules are misunderstood, discovering which are not grasped is essential if they are to be learned properly.

Once the areas to be worked on have been identified, hypotheses about how to resolve the problem can be generated. Sometimes it is best to generate as many possible solutions as possible before testing any or making judgments about any of the approaches. This helps to guarantee that the best possible solution will be found. For example, the teacher or coach may suggest holding rules classes, giving a rule book to each student or player, showing films depicting the rules, or taking the participants to a contest where the rules are enforced properly. Each of these possible solutions might be suggested before any evaluation was made.

Testing means that each hypothesis is either confirmed or disconfirmed. If disconfirmed, it is discarded as unworkable. If confirmed, the solution should be compared to any others that also are confirmed to determine which is most acceptable. Taking the students to a contest might be an acceptable hypothesis, but prohibitively expensive when compared to renting a film. The latter solution would be more likely to be adopted.

Variables Affecting Problem Solving.   The reader is invited to review the earlier sections of this chapter and try to develop applications of the principles presented to a problem solving situation. To illustrate the complexity of problem solving and how many variables may be important, consider the coach or teacher trying to teach novice swimmers to make a flip-turn. The heightened motivation level generated by submersion and disorientation may reduce performance effectiveness considerably. Repeated practice almost certainly will be needed and may use modeling as one solution and the principles of shaping as well. Knowledge of results will show how a well-executed flip-turn reduces the turn-around time required at the end of the pool. Finally, interference may exist in the form of other rolling-motion activities the swimmers have learned previously. What may seem to be a fairly simple goal to achieve may actually be rather complicated and require thorough study before a practice plan is initiated.

SOCIAL CONCERNS IN PHYSICAL EDUCATION

Many recreational pursuits, games, and organized sports require the participation of more than one person at the same time. How the people interact and what effects the interactions have upon the behavior of any one of the people is part of social psychology, the study of the behavior of an individual within a group setting.

Competition and Cooperation. *Competition* is the attempt to do better than someone else. Competition often requires a positive attitude, whether the someone else involved is another person or the previous accomplishments of the person competing. Research indicates that a successful competitor strives for and expects accomplishments that an unsuccessful competitor does not. Additionally, studies have shown that anxiety about competition varies as a function of many variables including perceived threat, level of motivation, or sex role endorsement. Coaches may need to evaluate competition anxiety before establishing contest strategies.

Cooperation refers to working with or helping someone else in hopes of achieving some mutual goal. Both competition and cooperation often are fostered by sport or game situations. In many cases this refers to cooperation with teammates, but cooperation with officials, opponents, and even spectators may be a part of the sport or game situation.

One problem coaches or teachers often face is the competition *versus* cooperation dilemma. The person who has a high level of competitive motivation may find it difficult to cooperate with others, even though cooperation would facilitate pursuit of the goal desired. An example of this occurs when a player wishes to be a starter and must compete against teammates for the starting positions available, yet is required to cooperate by the very nature of the game. Convincing players that both competition and cooperation are possible simultaneously in such situations is difficult.

Conflict in Social Situations. Comparable to the conflict situations described above, social situations can produce approach-approach, avoidance-avoidance, and approach-avoidance circumstances. Choosing the sport in which to participate or the physical education class to take might serve as an example of one or more of these conflicts. If the player has a choice between field hockey and cross-country, the problem may be that friends are playing both (approach-approach), that both are disliked but soccer is not offered (avoidance-avoidance), or that friends are playing the one that is liked least, while the better-liked sport or class has only strangers (multiple approach-avoidance). Because social motives such as friendship can be extremely powerful, teachers and coaches are cautioned to evaluate such possibilities when working with their participants.

Social Expectations. Social expectations may influence a person's behavior especially when the behavior appears to occur in order to satisfy some previously expressed expectation. Instructors have to be particularly careful to avoid repetitive demeaning remarks when dealing with behaviors that are easily changed. Comments such as "You will never get it right" become the expectation and yield inadequate performances. Teachers and coaches must also guard against peer group ridicule which can produce the same kind of effect. Correspondingly, establishing positive expectations often will generate performance improvement. The "You're getting better. I know you'll get it soon" attitude can be expected to help produce improved responding.

Social Facilitation and Social Interference. The phenomena of *social facilitation* and *social interference* refer to the effects the presence of others may have upon performance. Social facilitation means the presence of others tends to make performance better than when others are not present. Social interference refers to situations where the presence of others tends to make performance poorer than when others are not present. The most obvious example of these phenomena comes when performance is required in front of a class or when a crowd is present for an athletic contest.

In general, studies have shown that social facilitation is most likely to occur when the response to be performed is one that has been well learned. Social interference occurs more frequently with relatively new responses. Again, teachers or coaches who understand these results can try to establish conditions that create facilitation or avoid interference. The implied reinforcement of social facilitation or punishment of social interference can be expected to affect later performances.

SUMMARY

This brief look at psychological principles is sufficient to indicate the need for coaches and teachers to be aware of the many variables that may affect performance. The references listed below will help the reader explore in more detail those areas that are of particular interest.

SELECTED REFERENCES

Journals

Probably the most appropriate journal would be the *Journal of Sports Psychology* published by Human Kinetics Publishers, Inc., Box 5076, Champaign, IL 61820. This journal publishes a wide variety of papers in the area of sports psychology and, in addition, includes a digest of related works found in other publications, book reviews, and commentaries.

Other journals likely to include some work related to sports psychology are *Journal of Motor Behavior, Perceptual and Motor Skills, Journal of Applied Psychology, The Physician and Sports Medicine, Research Quarterly,* and *International Journal of Sports Psychology.*

Books

The ongoing series *Psychology of Motor Behavior and Sport* selects papers from the annual conventions of the North American Society for Psychology of Sport and Physical Activity. Seven volumes exist at present. A wide range of papers is found in each.

Psychology in Sports: Methods and Applications. Edited by Richard M. Suinn. Burgess Publishing Co., 1980. Divided into three parts, this book presents sections on concepts in sport psychology, the personal view (experiences) and applications.

Social Science of Play, Games, and Sport: Learning Experiences by Glyn C. Roberts, Maria T. Allison, Susan L. Greendorfer, Kevin S. Spink, and Linda S. Koehler, Human Kinetics Publishers, 1979. Includes 20 practical learning experiences on research methods, sociology of sport experiences, and psychology of sport experiences.

The Inner Athlete: Mind Plus Muscle for Winning by Robert M. Nideffer. Thomas Y. Crowell Company, 1978. An overview of applications of sports psychology principles to actual practice in sport.

Sports Psychology: An Analysis of Athlete Behavior. Edited by William F. Straub. Mouvement Publications, 1978. Eleven general areas are presented, showing how psychological principles can be applied in sports settings.

Sport Competition Anxiety Test by Rainer Martens. Human Kinetics Publishers, 1977. Illustrates the use of a research technique in numerous sports settings.

MECHANICAL ASPECTS

This section examines certain movements found in everyday and sport activities such as standing, sitting, walking, lifting, carrying, pulling, pushing, running, jumping, throwing, and catching. Discussion will focus on the physical principles related to basic movement skills. For additional information, the reader should explore the selected references in the interrelated fields of anatomy, kinesiology, and biomechanics that are listed in the bibliography.

BODY BALANCE

Basic to all activity, both ordinary and sports related, is an understanding of how the body maintains a balanced position. The degree of stability, or balance, a body possesses is dependent upon several factors, including: (a) the area of the base of support, (b) the height of the center of gravity, and (c) the proximity of the center of gravity within the supporting base.

A balanced position is defined as a position wherein the center of gravity is placed over the support base. The center of gravity is the point around which the body balances in all directions. The base of support includes not only the feet in contact with the ground but also the area between the feet. If the center of gravity is placed outside the supporting base, balance is destroyed and downward motion results. Balance can be regained by reestablishing the support under the center of gravity. Locomotion therefore is accomplished by a continuous process of placing the center of gravity outside the base, thus losing balance, and then regaining balance by placing the foot under the center of gravity.

The area of the base of support is an important stability factor. As the area of the base increases, balance increases. When standing in a side stride position one has a greater degree of balance than in the feet together position. A side stride position increases balance in a lateral direction; a forward stride position increases balance in an anterior-posterior direction.

The degree of balance is also influenced by the height of the center of gravity. A low center of gravity increases balance and a high center of gravity decreases balance. In athletic situations an increase in balance is often accomplished by bending the knees to lower the height of the center of gravity.

If the center of gravity falls over the middle of the supporting base, equal balance on all sides of the body is established. However, if the center of gravity is placed over the back edge of the base, the degree of balance increases toward the front of the body and decreases toward the back edge of the supporting base. In other words, as the horizontal distance from the center of gravity to the front edge of the support increases, balance increases. As the horizontal distance from the center of gravity to the edge of the base decreases, balance decreases. To stop quickly and maintain balance the center of gravity should be moved to the back edge of the supporting base. To move quickly in the forward direction the center of gravity should be placed to the front edge of the base. This allows the balance to be destroyed very quickly because the center of gravity only has to be moved a short distance to be outside the supporting base.

BODY STRUCTURE

In addition to balance, the structure of the body has an influence on efficient movement.

The body is not one solid mass, but is composed of a series of segments. Each segment is connected to the next segment by joints, which are held together by muscles and ligaments. If the body segments are stacked so that the line of gravity passes

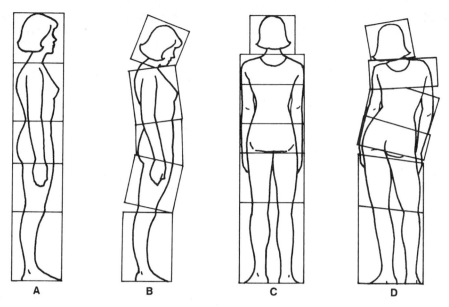

FIGURE 1-6. In (A) and (C) each segment is balanced above the segment below. In (B) and (D) the alignment is unbalanced.

directly through the center of each segment less stress will be placed upon the muscles and ligaments. There is little stress on the muscles and ligaments because the segments are perfectly balanced one over the other. Therefore, a good standing position is one in which each body segment is centered over the segment immediately below it (see Figure 1-6).

STANDING

Standing posture varies among individuals, and is affected by such factors as health (including mental attitude), body build, and occupation. Although there is no single description of good standing posture, proper body alignment is an essential element.

In the standing position with perfect alignment, a straight line should pass through the ear lobe, center of shoulder joint, slightly behind the hip joint, slightly in front of the center of the knee joint and in front of the ankle joint. The total picture of the best standing posture shows shallow curves of the upper and lower back, a slight tilt forward-upward of the pelvis to help decrease the curve of the lower back, the head back and the chin comfortably down, the abdominal wall flattened, the chest lifted, and the shoulders relaxed and back. This posture is not only mechanically sound but also attractive in appearance.

In good standing position the feet are usually placed parallel, four to six inches apart. Although some authorities consider a toeing-out position to be normal, those who advocate the parallel position appear to have sounder reasons. In this latter position, the base is firm in both forward-backward and lateral directions, as compared with the weaker triangular foot position (smaller base) resulting from the toeing-out position. The parallel foot position also places less strain on the leg muscles, and the body weight can be transferred along the entire longitudinal arch of the foot.

SITTING

On the average, individuals spend over 60 percent of their waking hours in a sitting position. As in the standing position, body alignment and balance are the two essential considerations in sitting and in the act of getting into and out of a chair.

In preparing to sit down, stand near and in front of the chair, with the calf of one leg next to the chair. This is necessary so that in the act of sitting, the trunk and upper body will move in an almost erect position, with the leg muscles controlling the action. As the body is lowered the trunk should bend slightly forward from the hip joint. This will keep the center of gravity over the supporting base. The body weight should first be placed on the front edge of the chair, thus establishing a new base of support, and then pushed back in the seat (chair).

When sitting on a straight chair, full use should be made of the chair seat and the chair lower back for support. Sit with the buttocks well back into the seat, with the body against the back of the chair. The upper torso should rest slightly against the upper back of the chair. Good body segment alignment, as in standing, is the major criteria for sitting.

To get up from the chair, reverse the order for sitting down. Place one leg in front of the other, slide forward, bend the trunk forward from the hips. When the center of gravity is over the feet, lift the body upward.

LIFTING AND CARRYING

The principles of balance and body alignment also apply in lifting and carrying. Keeping an aligned position will avoid strain and stress on muscles and joints.

When lifting an object from below, stand close to it, place one foot slightly in front of the other, keeping the back straight, the ankles, knees, and hips flexed. In this position the entire body remains over the center of the supporting base. To straighten up, the strong leg muscles (not the weak back muscles) are used to lift the body and object to the erect position.

During lifting, the weight of the object alters the location of the body's center of gravity. The object is momentarily a part of the body, and tends to move the body center of gravity in the direction of the object. Therefore, a wider supporting base is required.

A weight carried on one side of the body should be carried close to the body, with only a slight shift of the center of gravity. If the weight must be carried away from the body, raising the arm on the opposite side will move the center of gravity back toward the middle of the base. A weight carried in front of the body necessitates a backward shift of the center of gravity. The shift should be only enough to keep the center of gravity over the base. The most economical way to carry a load is that observed in more primitive people. Carried on top of the head the load is directly in line with the body.

PUSHING AND PULLING

Many pushing and pulling tasks are not strenuous but several involve the application of considerable force and make economy of effort and avoidance of strain prime considerations. The more nearly the body segments are aligned to apply the force of either pushing or pulling, and the better the base over which the body moves, the easier the task. The height and weight of the object to be pushed or pulled determine the amount the body's center of gravity must be lowered. To push a heavy object, the hands should be placed in line with the object's center of gravity. The body should be in line with the arms. If the object tends to tip, the position of the hands must be lowered.

In pulling, the body should be inclined in the direction of motion. In this position the body exerts its force most economically by using the strong leg muscles. The force should be applied as nearly as possible in the direction of the desired movement. Whenever the force is applied at an angle to the line of movement, only the component of the force in the direction of movement is effective in accomplishing the desired result.

FORCE AND FRICTION

All locomotor tasks (running, jumping, skipping, etc.) propel the body by applying a force against the ground. The force that actually moves the body is a reaction force (ground reaction force) which is reacting to the muscular force applied to the ground in accordance with Newton's Third Law: for every action there is an equal and opposite reaction. The greater the force pushing against the ground, the greater will be the reaction force pushing the body forward.

Friction, a force which opposes motion, tends to influence the ground reaction force. In order to move the body forward there must be sufficient friction between the foot and the ground to invoke the ground reaction force. Everyone knows that it is easier to walk or run on a hard solid surface than on a slippery surface or on a surface which gives. In the latter situation, the foot slides backward against the surface or the surface moves, thereby reducing the ground reaction force. That is why rubber-soled shoes or cleats are used in athletics—to provide adequate friction, thereby assuring the best possible ground reaction force.

Newton's Second Law states that acceleration is directly proportional to force. It is apparent that the greater the force exerted against the ground, the greater the reaction force and the faster the body moves.

The direction in which the force is applied is another factor that contributes to speed and efficiency of locomotion. In almost all locomotor tasks (except for some forms of jumping and hopping), the muscular force is applied to the ground in a backward-downward direction; the reaction force is then in a forward and upward direction. The upward (vertical) component is effective in lifting and supporting the body against the pull of gravity; the forward (horizontal) force component results in the forward movement of the body. If the body can apply only a limited amount of force and if the force is exerted in two directions, then it is better to divide the force unequally, putting more force in the desired direction. In running and walking, where the vertical force is greater than the horizontal, the body appears to bounce upward with each step. A greater horizontal force provides more speed in the horizontal direction, giving the motion an appearance of smoothness. An increase in the forward lean allows the body to pull more backward than upward, thus increasing the horizontal force component.

FIGURE 1-7. **A:** Backward component of pushing force. **B:** Downward component of pushing force. **C:** Forward component of reaction force. **D:** Upward component of reaction force.

In some locomotor activities (walking, skipping, galloping, and sliding) the forward foot strikes the ground well ahead of the body's center of gravity. This action exerts a backward and upward reaction force against the body. The backward component of this force provides a resisting action to the body's forward momentum and makes it possible to stop the forward progress. This retarding force component remains in action to a lessening degree until the foot is directly under the center of gravity. From this point until the foot leaves the ground, the propelling forward-upward reaction force is invoked.

The ideal foot placement is one in which the toes are pointed straight ahead. This provides the best possible position to apply force in a direction opposite to the desired movement. A toeing-in or a toeing-out position not only places undue stress on the ankle and knee joints but also is less efficient because the force is applied at an angle to the foot.

WALKING

Walking is the process of locomotion in which the body weight is transferred from one forward swinging leg and foot to the other. It differs from other locomotor tasks in that at no time is there lack of contact with the floor. The outstanding characteristic of the walk is the period of double support. For clarity the walk will be described in terms of leg action and arm swing.

Leg Action. From the double support position with one leg in front of the other, the back leg moves backward until it breaks contact with the ground. Then the knee and the hip begin to bend, starting the forward swing of the leg. The leg is describing somewhat of an arc. When the approximate mid-

point of the arc is reached, there is more flexion of the knee and hip to permit clearance from the ground. The leg is then extended and the heel contacts the floor. As the heel of the swinging leg touches the floor, the leg extends; the body then shifts forward and the cycle is repeated.

Arm Swing. In walking, the arms hang relaxed at the sides and swing forward and backward in opposition to the leg movement. This oppositive action occurs in all movements and is controlled at the reflex level of the nervous system. It is possible to interfere with this reflex through conscious control of movement. However, it is not desirable to do so, since this oppositive action of the arms and shoulder girdle counterbalance the rotation of the hips and the resultant forces are applied straight ahead.

In efficient walking, the heel should first contact the ground (toes pointed straight ahead), the body weight should be transferred to the outer border of the foot and then the ball, followed by a push off from the toes. Foot placement is considered best when the inner border of each foot falls closely (within 1 to 2 inches) along an imaginary line. Care should be taken not to cross this line in a weaving motion.

In summary, a natural walk is one in which the arms and legs swing easily, although the length of the stride and the frequency of steps taken will vary with the individual. The essential factors causing this variation are the individual's height, particularly the leg length, and speed of walking. An increase in walking speed is accomplished by either an increase in the stride length (distance covered per stride) or an increase in the frequency of steps, or both. In most people the stride length is increased until a given acceleration, at which time stride length is decreased and the stride frequency increases.

There should be little up and down bouncing movement of the body caused by the vertical force component. Increased walking speed is also accompanied by an increased body inclination. Horizontal movement is facilitated by this position because (a) the body is more in line with the driving leg, (b) the center of gravity is shifted forward to the front edge of the supporting base and gravity is used to assist in overcoming the body's inertia, and (c) the stride length is increased from the center of gravity to the release.

RUNNING

Running, like walking, is a locomotor task in which the body weight is transferred from one forward swinging foot to the other. Running differs from walking, however, in that there is a short period of non-support (no contact with the ground), whereas in walking there is always contact with the ground. Running is generally divided into three phases: (a) recovery phase, (b) support phase, and (c) driving phase.

The recovery phase starts the instant the rear or driving leg leaves the ground and ends when the same leg has moved forward and again contacts the ground beneath the individual's center of gravity. As the foot leaves the ground (the beginning of the recovery phase) the hip begins its forward movement and the lower leg folds up toward the upper leg. As the speed of running increases there is a greater tendency for the heel to kick up toward the buttock. This kick-up is not a fault, as it was once thought. The kick-up shortens the lever of the leg, and permits the swinging leg a smaller moment of inertia. The advantage of the small moment of inertia is that it can be moved very quickly without a great deal of muscular force.

As the leg continues forward in the recovery phase, the height to which the knee is lifted depends upon the running speed. The lift is highest in sprinting and lowest in jogging. The forward swinging leg reaches its highest point as the rear leg completes its full extension. After reaching the limit of its forward swing the recovery leg (front leg) reverses its direction and moves the foot first forward and then downward. The recovery phase is completed as the foot strikes the ground. Several factors must be considered in the foot striking. First the foot should be placed under the center of gravity and moving backward at moment of contact. This positioning of the foot enables upward and forward ground reaction forces to be invoked. Overstriding is characterized by the foot contacting the ground in front of the center of gravity and by the forward movement of the foot at contact. The foot should be moving backward at the time of contact in order to invoke the forward ground reaction force. The contact of the foot in front of the center of gravity tends to create a backward driving force or blocking action which will determine the running momentum.

The support phase of running begins with the landing of the forward foot and ends when the center of gravity passes in front of the supporting foot. As the foot contacts the ground, the knee bends to absorb the shock of landing, which is the first function of the support phase. The second function of the support phase is to arrest the body against the force of gravity. The final function of this phase is to move the body to a position for an effective driving phase.

The driving phase begins as the supporting phase ends—as the foot leaves the ground. In this phase the body is propelled forward by exerting muscular leg force against the ground and behind the center of gravity. As the body progresses forward the heel is lifted, the knee extends, and finally the ankle and toe extend well behind the body. It has been shown that failure to obtain complete extension of the driving leg is a very common characteristic of the poor runner.

Arms. In running, the upper body (shoulders and arms) moves in opposition to the leg action in order to balance the rotation effect of the leg swing on the trunk. The upper arms move relatively straight backward and forward. However, the lower arms move in a slight cross body direction in front but do not cross an imaginary vertical plane bisecting the body into right and left halves.

In sprinting, the elbows tend to be bent at an angle of approximately 90 degrees. This angle increases as the hand swings in front of the body and decreases as the hand passes the hip to the rear. The smaller moment of inertia (small lever arm) allows the arms to be moved very rapidly. The amount of bend in the arms decreases as the running speed decreases. The distance that the arms are carried away from the side of the body (lateral distance) seems to be dependent on the width of the hips. The heavier the hips in relation to the arms the farther from the body the arms must be carried. The hands are usually carried in a relaxed, cupped position.

Body Lean. When the rate of acceleration of a runner is the greatest, the forward lean of the trunk is the greatest. Thus a sprinter has a tremendous lean at the start of a race. From the instant the sprinter starts to reach top speed, the rate of acceleration is gradually diminished and the forward lean becomes less and less. The body lean at a uniform rate of speed is nearly erect. This slight lean is necessary in order to maintain balance, i.e., keep the body from rotation or falling forward.

Stride Length—Stride Frequency. The speed at which a runner moves is dependent upon two factors: (a) the stride length and (b) the stride frequency. The stride length is the distance the body is moved in one stride. The frequency is the number of strides taken per unit of time. If a runner has a stride length of 2 meters per stride and a frequency of 3 strides per second the running speed (distance per time) equals 6 meters per second. Any increase or decrease of these two elements will cause a corresponding change in the running speed.

JUMPING, HOPPING, LEAPING

The jump, hop, and leap are all forms of locomotion which involve projecting the body into the air. The hop is defined as any movement involving a takeoff and landing on the same foot. In the leap there is a takeoff from one foot and a landing on the other foot. For the jump the takeoff is from one foot or both feet and the landing is on both feet simultaneously. Many sports skills involve a form of jumping, hopping, and/or leaping.

The essential factors to be considered in jumping, hopping, and leaping are: (a) initial force, (b) angle of takeoff, and (c) gravity.

In preparing to jump, hop, or leap, the legs bend in preparation for the strong, explosive leg action. The depth of the bend of the legs (or crouch) is dependent upon the strength of the leg muscles and the nature of the sport skill. A deep crouch requires a great deal of leg strength and a long period of time to lift the body. Therefore, in most situations the crouch should never form a 90-degree angle at the knee. The angles between 65 and 90 degrees tend to produce the best jumps.

The initial force is produced by the explosive leg action pushing down against the ground. In accordance with Newton's Third Law, an equal and opposite ground reaction force is produced, which pushes the body into the air. An arm swing in an upward direction produces an increase in the ground reaction forces and a transfer of momentum.

If the purpose of the jump, hop, or leap is to move the body upward as far as possible (i.e., a vertical jump), all force should be applied straight down against the ground with the center of gravity directly over the feet. This will produce a ground reaction force with only a vertical component and all energies used to lift the body vertically. If, however, the purpose of the task is to propel the body forward and upward, the force should be applied against the ground at an angle. The forward lean of the body and the arm swing forward contribute to this angle of projection. When the takeoff force is applied at a 45-degree angle, half of the ground reaction force is used to move the body upward and half is used to move the body forward. A higher angle of pushoff, for example 70 degrees, provides a greater vertical force than horizontal; a lower angle, for example 30 degrees, provides greater horizontal motion and less vertical motion. Thus the angle of takeoff is dependent upon the goal of the skill.

Once the body is projected into the air, gravity will slow its vertical velocity and bring the body back to earth. The height that a body will achieve is dependent only on the magnitude of the ground reaction force and the angle of application. An angle of projectile of 90 degrees will provide the greatest amount of time in the air, because all available force is in a direction to resist gravity. Any other angle divides the ground reaction force vertically and horizontally, producing less time in the air.

In landing from a jump, hop, or leap the force must be absorbed in order to avoid injury. A force can be absorbed by its gradual slowing over the greatest possible time and distance (i.e., giving with the force). Therefore, all joints of the legs must "give" in sequence as contact with the ground is made, in order to absorb the force.

CATCHING

Catching is a skill that requires the body to stop the momentum of a moving object. The mechanical principles are (a) absorb the force over the greatest possible distance, i.e., "give" and (b) absorb the force over the greatest possible surface area.

The absorption of the force over the greatest possible distance involves exerting a force on the object in the opposite direction of the moving object. This can be accomplished by first, moving in line with the oncoming object; second, reaching out as far as possible to meet the object; and third, contacting and slowly allowing the object to move toward the body. A step taken in the direction of the oncoming object not only increases balance but also, for an increase in the distance and time, permits the object's velocity to be reduced.

For balls that are to be caught above the waist, the thumbs of both hands should be placed together and the fingers pointed upward. For objects to be caught below waist level, the little fingers should be placed close together and the fingers pointed downward. These positions are important in order to avoid injury and to present the largest possible surface area. In baseball, the padded glove increases the area over which the force is received.

THROWING

Throwing an object involves the transfer of momentum from the body to the object. An object held in the hand acquires the speed and direction of the hand and when released continues to move at this velocity and in the same direction until acted upon by other forces, such as gravity and air resistance. Of primary concern are the methods for developing speed and controlling the direction of the hand.

The faster the hand is moving when a ball is released, the greater the speed of the throw. The speed of hand movement can be increased by increasing the period of time the ball is moving in the direction of the throw. In other words, increasing the length of the backswing. To increase the backswing: (a) turn the side opposite the throwing arm toward the direction of the throw, (b) rotate the body away from the direction of the throw, and (c) place the feet in a stride position with the foot opposite the throwing arm forward.

The total effective force is the sum of the force produced by all the muscle groups contributing to the action. The contributing body parts brought into action in timed sequence provide more speed. The sequence is: step, rotate, throw. The step should be taken in the direction of the throw. The rotation refers to the rotation of the trunk, and the throw refers to the forward arm swing. Any movement of the body in the direction of the throw adds to the velocity of the throw. A run up or hop preceding the throw gives the body added momentum which is transferred to the thrown object. Follow through, a gradual reduction of the body's momentum, is essential to avoid injury and to insure maximum transfer of momentum to the object.

In addition to the speed of release such factors as angle of release, air resistance, gravity, height of release, and spin will affect the distance an object can be thrown. When throwing for distance, the ball must be released at an angle no greater than 45 degrees. Top spin on a ball will cause a ball to have a shorter period of flight. The greater the distance above the ground the ball is released the lower the projectile angle should be. The angle of release should also be decreased when throwing against high air resistance.

SELECTED REFERENCES

BARHAM, JERRY N. *Mechanical Kinesiology.* St. Louis, Mo.: C.V. Mosby Company, 1978.

BROER, MARION R., and RONALD F. ZERNICKE. *Efficiency of Human Movement.* Philadelphia, Pa.: W.B. Saunders Company, 1979.

BUNN, J.W. *Scientific Principles of Coaching,* 2nd ed. Englewood Cliffs, N.J.: Prentice-Hall, Inc., 1973.

COOPER, JOHN M., and RUTH B. GLASSOW. *Kinesiology,* 4th ed. St. Louis, Mo.: C.V. Mosby Company, 1976.

DYSON, GEOFFREY H. *The Mechanics of Athletics,* 4th ed. London: University of London Press Ltd., 1967.

HAY, JAMES G. *The Biomechanics of Sports Techniques,* 2nd ed. Englewood Cliffs, N.J.: Prentice-Hall Inc., 1978.

KELLY, DAVID L. *Kinesiology: Fundamentals of Motor Description.* Englewood Cliffs, N.J.: Prentice-Hall Inc., 1971.

LOGAN, GENE, and W. MCKINNEY. *Anatomic Kinesiology.* Dubuque, Iowa: Wm. C. Brown Company, 1970.

MILLER, DORIS, and R. NELSON. *Biomechanics of Sports.* Philadelphia, Pa.: Lea & Febiger, 1973.

MORTON, DUDLEY J., and DUDLEY D. FULLER. *Human Locomotion and Body Form.* Baltimore, Md.: The Williams and Wilkins Company, 1952.

NORTHRIP, JOHN W. *Biomechanic Analysis of Sport,* 2nd ed. Dubuque, Iowa: Wm. C. Brown Company, 1974.

O'CONNEL, ALICE L., and ELIZABETH B. GARDNER. *Understanding the Scientific Bases of Human Movement.* Baltimore, Md.: The Williams and Wilkins Company, 1972.

PLAGENHOEF, STANLEY. *Patterns of Human Motion.* Englewood Cliffs, N.J.: Prentice-Hall Inc., 1971.

RASCH, P., and R. BURKE. *Kinesiology and Applied Anatomy.* Philadelphia, Pa.: Lea & Febiger, 1975.

WELLS, KATHERINE F., and KATHRYN LUTTGENS. *Kinesiology: The Scientific Basis of Human Motion,* 6th ed. Philadelphia, Pa.: W.B. Saunders Company, 1976.

PHYSICAL FITNESS PROGRAMS

THIS CHAPTER DISCUSSES:

♦ The physiological benefits of physical fitness.
♦ The physiological and sociological values of regular exercise.
♦ Modes of fitness appraisal, with corresponding development schemes.
♦ The relation between exercise and weight control.
♦ Supplemental training activities: weight, interval, circuit (parcours), and continuous.
♦ Exercise for the handicapped.

UNDERSTANDING PHYSICAL FITNESS

We live in a labor-saving, highly mechanized society which is eliminating more and more physical exertion from our everyday lives. But the effects of a sedentary lifestyle can be seen in the people around us. Overweight, diminished muscle tone, sluggishness, lack of breath when performing even simple tasks—these are some of the common signs that something is wrong with the way we live. At the same time the pressures of everyday life continue to mount as we grapple with a corresponding rise in our fears and anxieties to meet pressing problems and deadlines. These stresses also affect our health and help to cultivate our unfitness.

It is unfortunate, despite advances in modern medicine, that we have matured in a society that does not require us to exercise vigorously, does not expect us to exercise, and to a certain extent does not positively reinforce us for exercising. This paradoxical consequence has produced an overfed, overweight, sedentary individual expected to meet the stresses of our highly complex and competitive society.

The human body is similar to a machine. If mistreated and not properly maintained, the machine will malfunction and cease to run efficiently. Our bodies are similar in that improper maintenance fosters deterioration of the numerous physiological systems within the body. This in turn may make the individual more susceptible to numerous diseased states thereby leading to increased medical costs, decreased productivity, disabling physical impairments, and, if very severe, higher mortality rates.

An estimated 40 billion dollars is lost annually, in earnings and medical care, from cardiovascular

and related diseases alone.[1] Although exercise is not a panacea, it may be the cheapest preventive medicine in the world.

Exercise is an essential element in the achievement and maintenance of physical fitness. The consensus of scientific opinion today is that exercise is essential. Experts further agree that to be effective, exercise must be regular, vigorous, of sustained duration, and suited to the individual.

Dr. Bud Getchell, a renowned physical fitness expert, defines physical fitness as "the capability of the heart, blood vessels, lungs, and muscles to function at optimal efficiency."[2]

The basic components of physical fitness include:

1. *Muscular strength*—the ability of a muscle to contract maximally against a resistance.
2. *Muscular endurance*—the ability of a muscle to contract repeatedly over a long period of time.
3. *Flexibility*—the ability to move a muscle or joint through a full range of motion.
4. *Cardiorespiratory endurance*—the ability of the cardiovascular and respiratory systems to transport oxygen and function efficiently during exercise over a long period of time.

BENEFITS OF PHYSICAL FITNESS

A regular, vigorous exercise program results in numerous training effects that enable the body's

[1]J.W. Farquhar, *The American Way of Life Need Not Be Hazardous to Your Health* (New York: W.W. Norton and Company, 1978).

[2]Bud Getchell, *Physical Fitness: A Way of Life,* 2nd ed. (New York: John Wiley and Sons, 1979), p. 9.

TABLE 2-1. Physiological Effects of Training

At Rest	Increase	Decrease	No Change
Cardiac hypertrophy	X		
Heart rate		X	
Stroke volume	X		
Blood volume	X		
Blood pressure		X	
Pulmonary ventilation	X		
Ventilatory efficiency	X		
Lung volume	X		
During Submaximal Exercise			
Lactic acid accumulation		X	
Heart rate		X	
Stroke volume	X		
Cardiac output			X
Vo$_2$			X
Pulmonary ventilation	X		
Ventilatory efficiency	X		
Lung volume	X		
During Maximal Exercise			
Lactic acid accumulation	X		
Heart rate			X
Stroke volume	X		
Cardiac output	X		
Vo$_2$	X		
Pulmonary ventilation	X		
Ventilatory efficiency	X		
Lung volume	X		
Other Changes			
Body fat		X	
Serum cholesterol		X	
Serum triglycerides		X	
Serum high density lipo-proteins	X		
Serum low density lipo-proteins		X	
Stores of ATP	X		

physiological systems to function more efficiently. As the individual becomes better adapted to meet everyday demands and stresses there is a corresponding improvement in general health. Table 2-1 indicates the physiological effects on the body as the result of training.

Cardiorespiratory System

The beneficial training effects of exercise on the cardiorespiratory system are very evident. The heart, which in essence is a muscular pump, becomes stronger and more efficient. Cardiac output, or the total amount of blood pumped from the heart per minute, is a product of stroke volume and heart rate. Through a regular exercise program the cardiac output increases due to an increased stroke volume or, in essence, an increased efficiency of the heart to pump more blood per heart beat. Consequently the heart does not need to beat as many times per minute to supply the same amount of blood, thereby conserving valuable energy. Due to this training effect the heart of the trained individual actually saves many valuable heart beats per minute at rest and during exercise.

With a regular exercise regimen the individual is able, due to the training effects derived from exercise, to breathe in larger quantities of air and fill the lungs more efficiently. In addition, the trained individual has a higher concentration of hemoglobin (a carrier of oxygen) available within the bloodstream. Since a trained heart is more efficient it is able to increase cardiac output to the lungs. With an increase in the concentration of hemoglobin, a greater number of oxygen molecules are transported from the lungs via the bloodstream to the cells of the body.

The trained individual is also able to extract a greater percentage of the oxygen at the cellular level. Furthermore, a greater percentage of waste products produced by the exercising muscles is extracted for disposal, thereby slowing the onset of fatigue. Since the trained individual has a greater capacity to utilize larger quantities of "fuel" and to extract waste products, the ability to endure long-term exercise bouts is enhanced. The term used to denote the maximal capacity of the individual to consume and extract oxygen is "aerobic capacity." The trained individual has a greater aerobic capacity than the untrained person. Though this capacity varies with the individual because of hereditary factors and other personal limitations, a 20 to 30 percent increase is possible with adherence to a vigorous exercise program.[3]

Research has also demonstrated the effects of regular exercise on blood serum levels of two fatty substances, cholesterol and triglycerides. These substances make up the fatty atherosclerotic deposits lining the blood vessels which have been linked to the development of heart disease. Excessively high levels of these two substances within the blood serum are considered dangerous. With regular exercise the concentration levels of these substances, especially the triglycerides, are lowered.

In addition, research has shown a strong correlation between the types of proteins which serve as carriers of cholesterol and the incidence of heart disease. Two types of carriers, low density lipoproteins (LDL) and high density lipoproteins (HDL) have been found to play important roles in the occurrence of heart disease. LDLs transport cholesterol from the liver to the various tissues for use and

[3]Getchell, *Physical Fitness*, p. 28.

have been linked to the formation of the fatty plaques deposited on the inner linings of blood vessels. HDLs transport excess cholesterol from the tissues back to the liver and have been found to prevent the fatty plaques from being deposited on the vessel linings. Research has demonstrated that physically fit individuals tend to have greater amounts of HDL and lower amounts of LDL in the bloodstream. Thus exercise may serve a role in the prevention of heart disease.

Hypertension, or high blood pressure, has also been linked as a risk factor in the development of heart disease. Though still under dispute, several studies have demonstrated a reduction in blood pressure in borderline hypertensive patients engaged in a regular exercise program. So in some cases exercise may be effective in the treatment of hypertension without the use of medicines.

Longevity

Although there is as yet no conclusive proof that adherence to a vigorous exercise program will prolong life, much of the evidence we have does support that conclusion.

What is more important is that exercise will add to the *quality* of life, thereby enabling the individual to participate in meaningful activities with greater enjoyment and less fatigue. In fact, a healthy, fulfilling life often leads to a long life.

PSYCHOLOGICAL AND SOCIOLOGICAL VALUES

Regular exercise affects not only the body but the mental and emotional states as well. Exercise can serve as an outlet for pent-up emotions through socially accepted channels. Stress, anxiety, and depression may be relieved by exercise, without the ills and side effects of mood-altering drugs. Physically fit individuals speak of their enhanced mental acuity, mental energy, concentration, and feelings of well-being. These feelings have been documented in several studies. In addition, physically fit individuals have an enhanced self-image, a definite sign of excellent mental health.

The late President Kennedy, an exponent of the strenuous life, summed it up in this way:

> . . . Physical fitness is not only one of the most important keys to a healthy body, it is the basis of dynamic and creative intellectual activity. The relationship of the body and the activities of the mind is subtle and complex. Much is not yet understood, but we do know what the Greeks knew: that intelligence and skill can only function at the peak of their capacity when the body is healthy and strong; that hardy spirits and tough minds usually inhabit sound bodies.
>
> In this sense, physical fitness is the basis of all the activities of our society. And if the body grows

soft and inactive, if we fail to encourage physical development and prowess, we will undermine our capacity for thought, for work, and for the use of those skills vital to an expanding and complex America. Thus, the physical fitness of our citizens is a vital prerequisite to America's realization of its full potential as a nation, and to the opportunity of each individual citizen to make full and fruitful use of his capabilities.

FITNESS APPRAISAL

Before a proper exercise program can be set up for an individual, there must be an appraisal of his or her physical fitness. Such an appraisal also provides motivation, a key ingredient in any exercise program, in that goals may be established and improvements confirmed.

A battery of tests has been adopted from the American Alliance for Health, Physical Education, Recreation, and Dance to evaluate the major areas of fitness of boys and girls in grades 5 to 12. The tests included in this battery are:

1. Pull-up (Boys)
2. Flexed Arm Hang (Girls)
3. Situp
4. Shuttle Run
5. Standing Long Jump
6. 50-Yard Dash
7. 600-Yard Run

These tests are designed to measure individual strengths and weaknesses by comparing their performances against established norms. Further information may be obtained from the AAHPERD.[4]

For individuals over age 12, the following tests developed by Dr. Bud Getchell may be used.[5]

Females—1½ Mile Run

Fitness Category	1.5 Mile Time
Super	Faster than 11:30
Excellent	11:30 to 12:59
Good	13:00 to 14:29
Fair	14:30 to 15:59
Poor	16:00 or slower

Males—2 Mile Run

Fitness Category	2.0 Mile Time
Super	Faster than 12:00
Excellent	12:00 to 13:59
Good	14:00 to 15:59
Fair	16:00 to 17:59
Poor	18:00 or slower

[4]American Alliance for Health, Physical Education, Recreation, and Dance. *Youth Fitness Test Manual* (Washington, D.C.: The Alliance, 1976).

[5]Bud Getchell, *Physical Fitness: A Way of Life*, 2nd ed. (New York: John Wiley and Sons, 1979), pp. 68–69.

Determination of Body Fat

Body fat can be measured most accurately by such methods as hydrostatic (i.e., underwater) weighing and by taking skinfold measurements at various body sites. But these methods require special equipment and are therefore expensive and impractical in most instances. Two simple alternative methods may be employed to determine if excess body fat is present. The first method involves self-inspection, while standing naked in front of a mirror, to see whether there are any excessive fat deposits in any part of the body. The second method, which is more precise, involves pinching a skinfold at a site on the body, usually near the waist. If the individual is able to pinch one inch or more of fat, he or she is probably overweight. If less than a half-inch of skinfold is pinched, then body fat is relatively normal or at an acceptable level. Though less precise than scientific measurement, these two methods provide adequate estimations of body fat.

EXERCISE PRESCRIPTION

Prescription of exercise should follow basic guidelines established by the American College of Sports Medicine, which are applicable to all individuals regardless of age or functional capacity.[6] Four factors are involved: intensity, frequency, duration, and type of activity.

Intensity.   Intensity refers to the degree of exertion which the individual demonstrates during an exercise bout. Research has shown that an individual should exercise at a level corresponding to 70 to 80 percent of maximal capacity in order to derive the maximal benefits of exercise. This can be monitored by knowing the heart rate per minute during exercise. By simple computation a training heart rate (THR) can be established corresponding to an average level of 75 percent between maximal and resting heart rates. At this heart rate level the individual will increase functional capacity without overtaxing the body, thereby reducing the risk of injury. To compute the training heart rate the individual must estimate the maximal heart rate and also establish a resting heart rate. A good approximation of maximal heart rate can be established by subtracting one's age from 220 (i.e., 220 − age = maximal heart rate). The resting heart rate can be determined by taking a pulse count for one minute. These values are put into the following formula to establish a training heart rate:

$$(\text{Maximal h.r.} - \text{Resting h.r.}) \times .75 + \text{Resting h.r.} = \text{THR}$$

[6] American College of Sports Medicine, *Guidelines for Graded Exercise Testing and Exercise Prescription* (Philadelphia, Pa.: Lea & Febiger, 1975).

In order to monitor the exercise heart rate the individual can take a pulse at the radial artery on the wrist, the carotid artery on the neck, or at the chest just to the left of the sternum using the index and middle fingers. The individual should stop occasionally and immediately take a pulse count for 10 seconds before the heart has a chance to recover. Then by multiplying the value by 6, a one-minute value can be obtained. Staying within a "ball park" range of the training heart rate will insure that the individual is working at the correct level. Exercising at a rate far below the THR suggests that the individual is not exercising hard enough to elicit maximal benefits. Furthermore, if the recorded heart rate far exceeds the THR, then the individual is exercising too hard and risks injury.

Frequency.   Frequency refers to the number of days per week that the individual should exercise in order to derive the maximal benefits of the exercise program. The recommended frequency is 3 to 4 days per week. Exercising less than three days per week will not maintain a fitness level adequately. More than four days per week should not be initially prescribed as it may overtax the body, which may lead to injury. For the trained individual, more than four days of exercise may be prescribed according to personal needs and desires.

Duration.   Duration refers to the amount of time spent exercising per training bout. The individual should strive to reach 30 minutes of continuous exercise. This amount has been demonstrated to cause a sufficient stimulus to the various physiological systems of the body to elicit a training effect and maintain a desired fitness level. It must be noted, however, that the individual just beginning an exercise program should not strive for the 30-minute time period initially. A gradual increase in duration from an initial 10 to 15 minutes should be prescribed to allow the body to adjust to the stress of exercise. After reaching the 30-minute continuous time period, the individual may increase the duration according to personal preference.

Type of Activity.   The type of activity should be continuous, aerobic (using oxygen), and rhythmical in nature. Activities such as walking, running, swimming, cycling, and cross-country skiing fit this requirement. These activities adequately stimulate the cardiorespiratory system, producing an increase in functional capacity. They also involve the entire body, thereby promoting total body fitness. Activities such as bowling, golf, softball, and others, though excellent recreational activities, do not provide an adequate stimulus to the cardiorespiratory system. Table 2-2 rates various activities according to their relative development of three specific fitness components: endurance, strength, and flexibility.

TABLE 2-2. Rating of Activities

Activity	Endurance	Strength	Flexibility	kcal/min. 123 lb.	kcal/min. 150 lb.
Aquatic Games	H	H	M	7.2	8.7
Archery	L	M	L	3.6	4.4
Badminton	M	M	M	5.4	6.6
Basketball	M	M	M	7.7	9.4
Bicycling	H	H	M	5.6	6.8
Bowling	L	M	H	3.7	4.0
Canoeing	M	H	M	2.5	3.0
Fencing	M	M	H	7.2	8.0
Field Hockey	H	M	M	7.5	9.1
Golf	L	L	M	4.8	5.8
Handball	H	M	H	7.8	9.5
Hiking	H	M	M	5.5	6.3
Orienteering	H	H	H	10.8	13.1
Racquetball	H	M	H	7.8	9.5
Running (9 min./mile)	H	M	M	10.8	13.1
Skiing—Cross Country	H	H	H	13.7	15.1
Skiing—Downhill	H	H	H	8.7	10.0
Soccer	H	M	H	7.8	9.5
Softball	L	M	M	3.6	4.7
Swimming	H	H	H	7.2	8.7
Table Tennis	L	L	M	3.8	4.6
Team Handball	M	M	M	7.5	8.7
Tennis	H	M	H	6.1	7.4
Touch/Flag Football	M	H	M	5.4	6.0
Volleyball	M	M	H	2.8	3.4
Wrestling	H	H	H	—	14.2

Key: L = Low. M = Medium. H = High. Letter pertains to degree of development of the specific fitness component. The last two columns indicate the number of calories (in thousands) burned by an individual weighing 123 or 150 pounds, in performing each activity.

Individualized Prescription

The exercise program may be modified according to the individual's personal needs or limitations. Adjustments may be made within all four areas of prescription (i.e., intensity, frequency, duration, type of activity) to meet the basic requirements for development of fitness. For example, if an individual is unable to maintain an intensity level of 75 percent, due to a personal limitation, the individual may increase the duration of the activity in order to fulfill the basic fitness requirements.

If the capacity exists, the individual may also step up the frequency of the exercise program. Participating more days per week will enhance the development of fitness, but one must be careful not to overdo it to avoid risk of injury.

For an individual who cannot pursue a walking or running program due to a physical impairment a cycling, swimming, or other suitable program may be prescribed.

Many different factors such as age, fitness level, medical restrictions, availability of facilities, work or school schedules, influence the development of an exercise program. A further important consideration is the individual's personal schedule. To be effective the exercise must become an integral part of one's lifestyle—as much a habit as eating or sleeping.

Warm-up and Cool-down

Before starting the exercise bout it is necessary to prepare the body for the workout. The warm-up may consist of easy walking followed by stretching exercises to gradually increase the blood circulation in the muscles. The warm-up also makes the body more flexible, and prepares the joints and muscles for the added stress of exercise. In addition to preparing the body for exercise, warm-up activities serve as a preventive measure against injury and undue muscle soreness.

FIGURE 2-1. Trunk rotator.

FIGURE 2-2. Legover.

FIGURE 2-3. Low-back stretcher.

FIGURE 2-4. Hamstring stretch. Extend arms slowly to the floor and hold for a few seconds—do not bounce.

FIGURE 2-5. Quadricep stretch.

FIGURE 2-6. Achilles stretch.

FIGURE 2-7. Bent-knee situps. Note arms folded across chest.

The cool-down is instituted after the exercise bout to assist the body in recovery. Easy walking and stretching activities aid in ridding the body of waste products produced in the exercising muscles, and thus prevent muscle soreness. Furthermore, cool-down activities help to restore flexibility, some of which is lost due to the fact that exercise tends to shorten the muscles, thereby reducing flexibility.

The following stretching exercises are recommended for use in both the warm-up and cool-down activities:

1. Arm circles
2. Side stretches
3. Trunk rotator
4. Legovers
5. Low-back stretches
6. Hamstring stretches
7. Quadricep stretches
8. Achilles stretches
9. Bent-knee situps

Fatigue, Clothing, and Related Concerns

At the start of any exercise program the participant should be told to expect some muscle soreness, but that it will disappear once the body adapts to the stress of new exercise. Moreover it is important never to plunge into a conditioning program, because the risk of injury is always greater at the outset.

Following the exercise session the participant should feel slightly tired but not exhausted. If the individual still feels very tired an hour or more after the exercising session, the workout is too demanding. As a rule of thumb, the participant should be able to converse with another person while exercising. If so out of breath that conversation is impossible, the participant is exercising too hard. Exercise should be an enjoyable activity, not a torment. In the words of Bill Bowerman, former head track and cross-country coach at the University of Oregon, "Train, don't strain."[7]

In maintaining an individualized program the workout may take place at any time of the day that is convenient. There is no reason to suspend the workout during extremely hot and humid weather or very cold weather provided that the individual dresses properly and observes any necessary precautions.

[7]W.J. Bowerman, *Jogging* (New York: Grosset and Dunlop, 1967).

TABLE 2-3. Two-week Walking/Jogging Program

WALKING PROGRAM

	Mon.	Tues.	Thur.	Fri.
First Week	Walk 20 min.	Walk 20 min.	Walk 24 min.	Walk 24 min.
Second Week	Walk 28 min.	Walk 28 min.	Walk 32 min.	Walk 32 min.

JOG-WALK PROGRAM

	Mon. and Tues.	Thur. and Fri.
First Week	Walk 20 min.	Walk 17 min.
	Jog/walk ½, ½, ½, ½	Jog/walk ½, ½, ½, ½, ½, ½
	Walk 10 min.	Walk 10 min.
Second Week	Walk 15 min.	Walk 12 min.
	Jog/walk ½, ½, ½, ½, ½, ½, ½, ½, ½	Jog/walk ½, ½, ½, ½, ½, ½
	Walk 10 min.	Walk 10 min.

*Note: ½ = 110 yds. or 30 to 45 sec. Individual should alternate on the Jog/Walk routine—i.e., Jog ½, Walk ½, Jog ½, etc.

JOGGING PROGRAM

	Mon.	Tues.	Thur.	Fri.
First Week	Jog 2 miles	Jog 4 miles	Jog 3 miles	Jog 5 miles
Second Week	Jog 3 miles	Jog 4 miles	Jog 2 miles	Jog 5 miles

Table 2-3 represents a sample two-week workout for an individual on a walking, jog-walk, or jogging program. All walking should be done at a brisk pace in order to elicit the necessary training response. Remember that all workouts should progress slowly to avoid injury.

Clothing. Basically, clothing should be light and loose-fitting to provide adequate ventilation. During hot, humid weather it is best to wear as little as possible to facilitate heat loss from the body. During cold weather multiple layers of light clothing are adequate for warmth during workouts. Excess layers can be shed if one becomes too warm, without losing important body heat. In extremely cold weather protection for the extremities is a must and hence a warm knit cap or head covering and mittens or gloves should be worn.

Footwear. The type of footwear is another important consideration. Shoes should provide adequate support and cushioning to protect the feet. Shoes should be flexible in the forefoot region and provide good lateral stability within the heel area. The fit should be snug, not tight, with enough room for the toes. Buying a pair of quality name-brand shoes from a reputable dealer is the best investment an individual can make before beginning a fitness program. It is well to avoid the so-called bargain brands because they do not give adequate protection and support.

EXERCISE AND WEIGHT CONTROL

A by-product of sedentary living is the problem of obesity. Millions of dieters embrace the slogan "thin is in," yet a recent survey estimated that between 80 and 90 percent of all adults in the United States were at least 5 percent over their ideal weight.[8]

The solution to weight control is quite simple and easy to understand. To maintain constant weight, energy intake (in the form of foods) must equal energy output. If the intake exceeds the output, the unused energy is stored in the body as fat. The only way to lose weight is by getting the body to "burn up" or use up its excess fat. This is accomplished by either decreasing food intake or by increasing physical activity. What could be simpler? Yet, unfortunately, for many people weight control remains an insoluble problem.

Research has shown that the real problem in weight control is not overeating but rather inactivity. It has also been shown that exercise is a positive aid in weight control maintenance. With the proper exercise regimen and a sound diet plan, weight control is possible. Dr. John W. Farquhar states:

> Weight losses from other shortcuts such as jaw wiring, diet pills, or fasting are usually temporary because, again, they do not change the underlying habits that cause the weight problem. The mere act of "going on a diet" implies that one will eventually "go off." . . . Unless you build new habits and become comfortable with them as you shed your pounds, you will regain the pounds eventually. You have to be able to live with the new program and enjoy it.[9]

[8]J.W. Farquhar, *The American Way of Life Need Not Be Hazardous to Your Health* (New York: W.W. Norton and Company, 1978), p. 143.
[9]*Ibid.*, p. 142.

FIGURE 2-8. Jogging is an excellent way to burn calories and develop cardiovascular endurance.

In several studies it has been demonstrated that the distance covered during the exercising bout is more important than the intensity at which it is accomplished. The average adult uses up approximately 100 calories per mile, with slight variations for different body sizes. With so little time available for most of us in our modern society, the time we can spare for daily exercise is at a premium. Here the physically fit individual is at an advantage in that he can cover twice the distance in a given time than a less trained person can. In other words, the trained individual is able to expend twice the number of calories per exercise session as the untrained person.

When you first glance at the numbers, exercise may not appear to be such an excellent way to control weight. In order to shed one pound of body fat, for example, 3,500 calories must be expended. Furthermore, the trained individual who is able to run three miles in 30 minutes (i.e., 10 minutes per mile pace) will use up only about 300 calories (100 calories per mile). But as further investigation has shown, the individual who exercises four times per week over the same distance will expend roughly 1,200 calories. At this rate of caloric output, with dietary food intake remaining constant, 15 pounds of fat would be shed in a year.[10] In addition, if the individual could reduce the food intake by 400 calories per day and could expend 300 calories per exercise session, the total caloric expenditure would equal 4,000 calories per week. At this rate the individual would be able to shed approximately one pound of fat per week.[11] An additional bonus that

exercise provides is the toning of flabby muscles; this contributes to a more attractive shape.

Sweating and Other Weight Loss Myths

Contrary to popular belief, sweating during exercise does not help use up excess body fat. This misconception has encouraged the use of rubberized sweat suits, which may be potentially hazardous to the body. Rubberized suits do promote excessive sweating, and weight loss is observed. But this is temporary weight loss caused by the loss of body fluids and has nothing to do with actual loss of fat. If carried to excess, dehydration of the body can occur with harmful effects for the individual. Once fluids are again consumed, the weight loss observed will quickly return.

Another disadvantage of rubberized suits is that they do not allow the heat which is produced during exercise to escape from the body. Excess body heat is normally removed through the evaporation of sweat. The cooling effect of evaporation helps bring the body temperature back to normal. When a rubberized suit is worn, sweat cannot evaporate so excess body heat is trapped, thereby increasing body temperature above the normal range. This in turn puts added stress upon other heat regulating mechanisms of the body. Blood is shunted to the exercising muscles in an attempt to regulate body temperature. This decreases the blood volume, causing the heart to work abnormally hard to compensate for this loss. This may lead to heat stroke, a life-threatening situation which, if not treated immediately, may lead to circulatory collapse. It must be stressed that sweating during exercise is a normal and healthy function. The sweating mechanism monitors excess body heat and, through dissipation of sweat from the body, regulates and maintains proper temperature. An individual who tampers with this precise regulating mechanism is courting a dangerous risk.

Proper weight management requires self-motivation and a sound exercise program in addition to a proper diet plan. Promises of quick weight loss devised by manufacturers of various gadgets and exotic diets prescribed to assist in such endeavors are not an effective means of weight control. Claims regarding spot reducing of various areas of the body have also been disproven by scientific research. Furthermore, exercise and a sound diet plan will aid in weight maintenance with weight loss occurring throughout the entire body. There is no easy method by which to maintain a trim, aesthetically pleasing figure. It takes effort to get into shape and then to maintain a desired fitness level.

SUPPLEMENTARY TRAINING CONCEPTS

For the individual who wishes to go beyond the level of general physical fitness, there are a number

[10]Bud Getchell, *Physical Fitness: A Way of Life,* 2nd ed. (New York: John Wiley and Sons, 1979), p. 244.

[11]*Ibid.,* p. 245.

of supplemental activities. These include weight training, interval training, circuit (parcours) training, and continuous training.

Weight Training

Muscular strength and endurance are important components of a physical fitness program. In order to produce an increase within these components the muscles involved must be overloaded with a resistance. This basic principle applies to all individuals regardless of age or functional capacity. Furthermore, weight training should involve all parts of the body to facilitate improvements in total body fitness. It must be noted, however, that a weight training program does not greatly benefit the cardiorespiratory fitness of an individual and consequently it should not be the sole fitness activity.

For years the myth has been perpetuated that weight training produces abnormally large, bulging muscles in women, making them look unfeminine. Numerous studies have demonstrated that women may increase their muscle strength substantially without an accompanying increase in bulk. The capacity to increase muscle bulk is genetically determined by the amount of the male hormone, testosterone, present within the body. The level varies among individuals. On the whole, females have very small amounts of testosterone present and are therefore very unlikely to develop massive muscles.

Two forms of weight training are available: *strength* (or *power*) *weight training,* which uses heavy weights and few repetitions (i.e., the number of times a weight is lifted or the muscle is contracted), and *endurance weight training,* which uses light to moderate weights with many repetitions. These specific activities produce strength/power gains and endurance gains respectively. In both types, weight training workouts should be performed three days per week, alternating a day of rest with each workout day to facilitate adequate recovery from the previous session.

Three methods of weight training have been developed to enable the individual to pursue these improvements:

1. **Isometric**—contraction of a muscle without permitting the muscle to change in length by pushing or pulling against an immovable object.
2. **Isotonic**—contraction of a muscle against a constant resistance through a full range of motion allowing for shortening of the muscle.
3. **Isokinetic**—contraction of a muscle against a variable resistance at a constant speed and through a full range of motion allowing for shortening of the muscle.

All three methods provide significant strength gains, but they have certain advantages and disadvantages

TABLE 2-4. Interval Training Program

			MEN	
First Week	Day 1	Set 1	4 × 220 at 0:38	(1:54)*
		Set 2	8 × 110 at 0:18	(0:54)
	Day 2	Set 1	2 × 440 at 1:20	(2:40)
		Set 2	8 × 110 at 0:18	(0:54)
	Day 3	Set 1	1 × 880 at 3:00	(3:00)
		Set 2	2 × 440 at 1:20	(2:40)
Second Week	Day 1	Set 1	2 × 660 at 2:15	(4:20)
		Set 2	2 × 440 at 1:20	(2:40)
	Day 2	Set 1	2 × 880 at 3:00	(3:00)
		Set 2	2 × 440 at 1:20	(2:40)
	Day 3	Set 1	1 × 880 at 3:00	(3:00)
		Set 2	2 × 660 at 2:15	(4:20)
			WOMEN	
First Week	Day 1	Set 1	4 × 220 at 0:45	(2:15)
		Set 2	8 × 110 at 0:25	(1:15)
	Day 2	Set 1	2 × 440 at 1:30	(4:30)
		Set 2	8 × 110 at 0:25	(1:15)
	Day 3	Set 1	1 × 880 at 4:00	(4:00)
		Set 2	2 × 440 at 1:30	(4:30)
Second Week	Day 1	Set 1	2 × 660 at 2:45	(5:30)
		Set 2	2 × 440 at 1:30	(4:30)
	Day 2	Set 1	2 × 880 at 4:00	(4:00)
		Set 2	2 × 440 at 1:30	(4:30)
	Day 3	Set 1	1 × 880 at 4:00	(4:00)
		Set 2	2 × 660 at 2:45	(5:30)

*Explanation
4 = number of repetitions
220 = training distance, in yards
0:38 = interval of training time in minutes:seconds
(1:54) = interval of recovery period in minutes:seconds

in the matter of equipment, availability of facilities, and personal preferences.

Before beginning a weight training program it is important to learn how to use the equipment for proper performance with safety. Briefly, weight equipment should be properly maintained, spotters should be available for assistance, and proper lifting form should be utilized to obtain maximum benefits in addition to maximum safety. For further information consult the Weight Training chapter in this *Handbook.*

Interval Training

Interval training refers to exercise performed at very high intensity for short duration, with a brief rest period between each repeated interval. This type of training will reap excellent fitness benefits but is more taxing upon the body than other activities. Because of the extremely high intensity level of the workout, the exercising muscles have to work anaerobically, that is, without oxygen. This causes large quantities of lactic acid, a metabolic waste product, to accumulate in the exercising muscles, inducing the early onset of fatigue. Adjustment of the body to this increased stress results in an adaptation of the body to work at a higher intensity level without the rapid onset of fatigue, thereby promoting an advanced fitness level.

Interval training should be based on the overload principle. Thus each week of training should be progressively more difficult than the previous week's workout. This may be accomplished by (1) increasing the intensity of the repetitions; (2) shortening the recovery period; (3) performing more sets per bout; or (4) a combination of any of the first three methods. Initially, the individual should start slowly to allow the body a period of adjustment to the stress of interval training. Table 2-4 provides a sample two-week interval training program with workouts indicated in a prescription form. In addition, interval workouts should be executed three days per week. Continuous running may be utilized on days between the interval workouts to supplement the training regimen.

Circuit Training (Parcours)

In circuit training, exercises are performed at a series of workout stations arranged within a specific area. The object is to develop total body fitness. The exercises prescribed involve all major muscle groups of the body put on an overload in order to produce significant fitness gains. These activities are performed at very high intensity levels and promote muscular strength and endurance, cardiorespiratory endurance, and flexibility. Each station should emphasize different fitness activities for developing different areas of the body. A typical circuit might include the following activities:

Station	Activity
1	Run 110 yards
2	Bench stepping
3	Push-ups
4	Situps
5	Squats with weights
6	Shuttle run
7	Pull-ups
8	Jumping on and off a bench
9	Rope skipping
10	Curls with weights
11	Burpees
12	Run 110 yards

Parcours. A new concept of circuit training developed in Europe has been adopted recently in

FIGURE 2-9. A parcours fitness circuit in a community park.

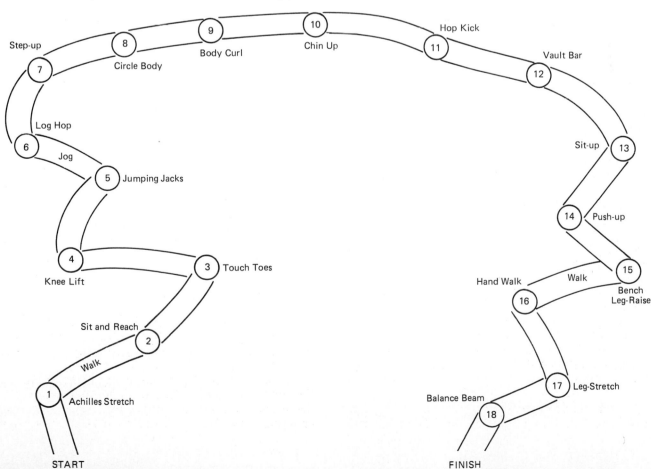

the United States and Canada. Called *parcours* (or *parcourse*), it consists of a series of stations set up over a 1 to 2½ mile path, to provide a recreational exercise circuit for individuals of all ages and abilities. Figure 2-9 illustrates a typical parcours circuit suitable for a community park. Various fitness levels are designated which stress muscular strength and endurance, cardiorespiratory endurance, and flexibility activities. Participants are taught at the beginning of the circuit how to monitor their pulse rate and are reminded to check their pulse at various stations along the route. In addition to park sites, the circuit is often set up along existing bike or hiking paths. Most exercises may be performed during any season of the year and therefore the system encourages year-round participation. Additional information may be obtained from the reference readings.

Continuous Training

For the individual who has achieved the ability to run, cycle, or swim for 30 continuous minutes and wishes to pursue a higher fitness level, continuous training may provide the answer. Termed "LSD (long, slow distance) training," it refers to the ability of the individual to continue in exercise at or around a training heart rate level for longer than 30-minute periods. Besides promoting muscular and cardiorespiratory endurance, continuous training aids in caloric expenditure, a key to proper weight maintenance.

EXERCISE FOR THE HANDICAPPED

Regardless of functional capacity or age, all individuals require regular, vigorous physical exercise. This principle also applies to handicapped individuals of all ages. Under Public Law 94-142, all handicapped school-age children are guaranteed equal opportunities for educational services, including physical education. Furthermore activities such as the Special Olympics and wheelchair marathons have demonstrated the remarkable feats that handicapped individuals can achieve. Experts state that there is little negative relationship between the handicapping condition and athletic prowess in a majority of cases.[12] Also psychological benefits are gained from regular physical activity, promoting self-confidence, self-discipline and enhanced self-image.

Physiological alterations derived from a vigorous training program can be demonstrated in all individuals, with a corresponding improvement in general health. Whether or not there is physical or mental impairment, every person has unique abilities and limitations. It is important to individualize

[12]*Special Olympics Instructional Manual: From Beginners to Champions,* ed. Julian Stein, (Washington, D.C.: AAHPERD, 1972).

the exercise program in harmony with the participant's special needs. By slight modifications in exercise prescription a program may be adapted to provide the stimulus necessary to elicit a training response. When dealing with impairments, however, one must use good judgment in establishing the rate of progression in training intensities, duration, and frequency. It is furthermore important to examine which practical modes of exercise are conducive to optimal fitness achievement with the least physical discomfort or risk of injury.

With recent advances in the fields of adapted physical education and corrective rehabilitation education, numerous programs have been devised to meet the needs of the handicapped. New developments should be followed closely.

TERMINOLOGY

Aerobic capacity A measure of cardiorespiratory endurance. Refers to the maximal amount of oxygen consumed per minute.

Atherosclerosis A thickening and loss of elasticity in the linings of the arteries due in part to the buildup of fatty deposits on the inner walls.

ATP (Adenosine triphosphate) A high energy substance found in all cells of the body.

Blood pressure The pressure exerted against the walls of the blood vessels by the blood that makes blood flow through the circulatory systems.

Calorie A unit of measure for the rate of heat or energy production in the body.

Cardiac output A product of stroke volume and heart rate. Refers to the total amount of blood pumped from the heart per minute.

Cardiorespiratory endurance The ability of the heart and lungs to work at optimal efficiency during continuous exercise.

Cardiorespiratory system System involving the heart, blood vessels, and lungs.

Cholesterol A fat-like substance found in the body and thought to be a factor in atherosclerosis. High levels of cholesterol in the bloodstream have been linked with an increased risk of heart disease.

Circuit training A routine of selected exercises or activities performed in sequence at individual stations at a predetermined pace.

Duration The length of time spent exercising per conditioning bout; 30 minutes is recommended for fitness maintenance.

Flexibility The ability to move a joint and its corresponding muscle groups through a full range of motion.

Frequency The number of days per week that an individual exercises. Three to four days is the recommended frequency.

Functional capacity The ability of an individual to perform various activities or skills.

Heart rate The number of times per minute the heart beats.

Hemoglobin An iron-containing protein which serves as a carrier for oxygen throughout the circulatory system.

Hypertension Abnormally high blood pressure—usually at or above 140 for the systolic pressure and at or above 90 for the diastolic.

Intensity The degree of exertion put forth by the body during exercise. May be determined by taking a pulse count immediately after an exercise bout.

Lipoprotein A type of protein which serves as a carrier for cholesterol and triglycerides within the bloodstream.

Lung volume Amount of air the lungs will hold.

Maximal heart rate The highest heart rate that an individual can attain. May be estimated by subtracting one's age from 220.

Muscular endurance The ability of a muscle to exert a force repeatedly or hold a static contraction for a long period of time.

Muscular strength The ability of a muscle to produce a maximal force against a resistance.

Parcours A type of circuit training offering recreational exercise for all ages.

Pulmonary ventilation Amount of air breathed per minute.

Training effect Bodily changes that occur with adherence to a regular, vigorous exercise program.

Training Heart Rate (THR) The exercise heart rate per minute at which the individual reaps cardiorespiratory benefits.

Triglycerides Fatty particles found in the body. A high level within the bloodstream has been linked as a possible risk factor in the development of heart disease.

VO$_2$ (Oxygen uptake) The amount of energy the body uses.

Warm-up Flexibility exercises performed prior to the workout to prepare the body for the stress of exercise.

SELECTED REFERENCES

American Alliance for Health, Physical Education, Recreation, and Dance. *Adapted Physical Education Guidelines: Theory and Practice for the Seventies and Eighties.* Washington, D.C., 1976.

American Alliance for Health, Physical Education, Recreation, and Dance. *Youth Fitness Test Manual.* Washington, D.C., 1976.

American College of Sports Medicine. *Guidelines for Graded Exercise Testing and Exercise Prescription.* Philadelphia, Pa.: Lea & Febiger, 1975.

American College of Sports Medicine. *Physiological Aspects of Sports and Physical Fitness.* Chicago, Ill.: The Athletic Institute, 1968.

ASTRAND, PER O. *Textbook of Work Physiology,* 2nd ed. New York: McGraw-Hill, 1977.

BOWERMAN, W.J. *Jogging.* New York: Grosset and Dunlap, 1967.

CALHOUN, M.F. *The Parcourse Guide to Fitness.* San Francisco: Parcourse Books, 1979.

COOPER, K. *The Aerobics Way.* New York: Evans Publishing Company, 1978.

CURETON, T. *Physical Fitness and Dynamic Health,* 2nd ed. New York: Dial Press, Inc., 1973.

FARQUHAR, J.W. *The American Way of Life Need Not Be Hazardous to Your Health.* New York: W.W. Norton and Company, 1978.

FIXX, J.F. *The Complete Book of Running.* New York: Random House, 1977.

FIXX, J.F. *Second Book of Running.* New York: Random House, 1980.

GETCHELL, BUD. *Physical Fitness: A Way of Life,* 2nd ed. New York: John Wiley and Sons, 1979.

GLASSER, W. *Positive Addiction.* New York: Harper and Row, 1976.

KOSTRUBALA, T. *The Joy of Running.* New York: Pocket Books, 1977.

KUNTZLEMAN, C.T. *Rating the Exercises.* New York: William Morrow and Company, Inc., 1978.

O'SHEA, J.P. *Scientific Principles and Methods of Strength Fitness.* Reading, Mass.: Addison-Wesley, 1976.

POLLOCK, M. *Health and Fitness Through Physical Activity.* New York: John Wiley and Sons, 1978.

ROSS, J. *Understanding the Heart and Its Diseases.* New York: McGraw-Hill, 1976.

WILMORE, J. *Athletic Training and Physical Fitness.* Boston, Mass.: Allyn and Bacon, Inc., 1976.

Audio-Visual Aids and Filmstrips

Coping with Life on the Run. (Motion Picture) Locust, N.J.: Sports Productions, 1977, 1 reel, 27 min. Summary: Discusses the physical and mental benefits of jogging.

Keeping Fit: The Physiology of Exercise. (Slide Carousel) Sunburst Communications, 1976. Distributed by Center for Humanities, White Plains, N.Y. 142 slides, 2 cassettes, 27 min.

Run Dick, Run Jane. (Motion Picture) Brigham Young University, 1971, 16 mm color, 20 min. Narrated by Dr. Ken Cooper. Summary: Importance of regular exercise and its effect on physical and mental health.

SHEEHAN, GEORGE. *Exercise as a Lifestyle.* (Phonotape) Guest presentation at Ball State University, Muncie, Ind., April 27, 1977. 1 cassette, 45 min.

Walk, Jog, Run. (Sound Recording KEA 1143), Kimbo Educational Activities, 1977. Created by Health and Physical Education Department, Educational Research Council of America. Summary: Interval training for cardiovascular fitness.

What Makes Millie Run. (Motion Picture) Provo, Utah: Brigham Young University, Media Marketing, 1977. 1 reel, 16 mm, 45 min. Summary: Reasons and ways for women to become physically fit.

AQUATIC GAMES

THIS CHAPTER WILL ENABLE YOU TO:

♦ Move about in all directions in water three or more feet deep, using various modes of propulsion.
♦ Have water splashed in your face, and place your face and head in and under the water without panicking.
♦ Breathe normally in the water while keeping your eyes open.
♦ Respond to directions given as you are performing in the water.
♦ Participate in and contribute to team efforts in games and contests.

NATURE AND PURPOSE

Aquatic games are organized games, contests, and relays played in a pool. They are designed to start on a simple level and progress to a more advanced level as a natural outgrowth. The ability to swim is helpful but is not a prerequisite. Participants often learn how to swim as a natural outcome of aquatic games. One area of aquatics that is improved for all levels is water adjustment, that is, the ability to put one's face in the water without holding the nose or rubbing the eyes, and to breathe at a normal rate of 15 to 20 times per minute.

In addition to water adjustment, the purpose of the games is to improve aquatic skills and team techniques, and to improve cardiovascular and cardiorespiratory functions. Men and women can participate in all forms of aquatic games on an equal basis; although males are generally stronger, females are generally more bouyant. Aquatic games are most helpful for those unable to jog or restricted by other physical handicaps, because natural bouyancy takes the strain off the ankles and hips. Flexibility, agility, balance, and strength can be improved with regular participation in water activities.

EQUIPMENT

Most of the equipment needed is generally found in and around aquatic facilities. Special equipment is minimal and inexpensive. The pool may vary in size from a backyard pool (20' by 30') to a full-size Olympic pool (56' by 162.5'). What is extremely important is the water's depth, because that will determine what age group can play. In most competitive pools ten or more years old, the shallow end will be approximately 3 feet 6 inches deep; in pools built since the mid-seventies, the shallow end will be 4 or more feet deep.

SUGGESTED LEARNING SEQUENCE

Most games and contests begin with participants either in the water, at the wall, or on the deck at the water's edge. All participants should be taught correct methods for entering the water such as by using available steps, sliding in from the pool's edge, and jumping or diving into shallow water. Climbing out of the water may be accomplished by an arm extension press on the edge of the pool as in a push-up.

Each skill to be taught should follow a learning sequence that names the activity, explains the skill, demonstrates the skill, and allows a trial run. Listed below is a program of games for beginner, intermediate, and advanced levels. All the games will be described later.

A. Class organization
  1. Safety considerations around the pool
  2. Safety and rules during play
B. Skills and Techniques
C. Aquatic Games
  1. *Beginning Level*
    a. Follow the Leader
    b. Treasure Hunt
    c. Fabyan's Water Music
    d. Beater Wades Round
    e. Water Tag
    f. Water Volleyball
    g. Musical Rings
    h. Kingfish
    i. Water Chain Tag
    j. Catfish and Minnow
    k. Water Line Dodge Ball
    l. Bull in the Ring
  2. *Intermediate Level*
    a. Artillery Battle
    b. Rub-A-Dub-Tub
    c. Guess Who

d. Ball Tag
e. The Lifter
f. Water Balloon Ball
g. Corks
h. Float Tag
3. *Advanced Level*
a. Underwater Football
b. Jump or Dive
c. Water Baseball

Practice Suggestions

The best way to learn to perform the skills is to practice them regularly and often.

Begin each class session by having all students get in the water and warm up on their own for about 5 to 10 minutes by running in place, leg lifts, arm circles, or jumping jacks. If and when necessary, give directions to those individuals or groups needing help. Call the class together. Explain, demonstrate, and then perform in unison some of the skills to be used in the games you are going to play. Make positive suggestions so as to ensure success for all participants.

SAFETY MEASURES

Pools are generally safe if the proper precautions are taken. But because of potential dangers in and around water, safety practices are of the utmost importance. To maintain a safe atmosphere, watch out for the following:

1. Over-aggressive participants, who may get too rough.
2. Under-aggressive participants, who may get frightened or intimidated by rough participants.
3. Overfatigue—signs are heavy breathing, flushed skin on shoulders and back of neck, and clinging to edge of pool.
4. Abrupt change in depth of pool from shallow to deep.
5. Obstacles possibly protruding into moving lanes.
6. Areas under diving boards, starting blocks, and ladders.
7. Water depth over swimmer's head.
8. Poorly lit deep water.
9. Sharp edges on underwater light covers, water inlet fittings, and drain covers; sharp or missing tiles.
10. Overflow troughs which impede players from entering and leaving water.
11. Equipment which may have or may develop sharp edges while in use.
12. Objects large enough to hide or obstruct players from one another or from the instructor's view.
13. Water temperature so cold (70° or less) that respiratory problems may arise.
14. Water so highly chlorinated as to present a hazard to eyes or skin.
15. Items on or near edge of pool that might be pulled or pushed into the water.

SKILLS AND TECHNIQUES

This chapter is by no means intended as a complete instructional manual of swimming techniques. The following list represents a series of skills the participant will use in the various aquatic games that are described. For the physical education teacher or leader it is recommended that the participant practice the skills first before playing the game. These techniques may be practiced in total or they may be practiced as they apply to skill requirements of a specific game. Many of the skills can be practiced in formation, facing the instructor, and can serve as an exercise program or warm-up before playing the game. In addition, several of the techniques, when done to command and in a series, can become an excellent method for developing physical fitness.

1. Move freely in water of varying depths.
2. Jump or dive from the edge of pool into water from 3 to 12 feet deep.
3. Run forward, backward, or sideward from point to point.
4. Move from point to point by hopping, skipping forward or backward, or by side straddle hop.
5. Use less than the four extremities to propel self and/or an object through or on the water's surface, as in a rooster hop or a candle carry.
6. Propel an object under, on, or above the water's surface to a teammate.
7. Propel an object to hit a target, as in the game of "splashketball."
8. Recover an object from the bottom of the pool in water from 3 to 12 feet deep.
9. Propel an object along the bottom of the pool at all depths (3 to 14 feet), using one or more extremities.
10. Maintain self plus an object of varying size and weight in water over one's head.
11. Maintain self plus a constant weight; receive an object as in a pass, propel the object to a teammate or prevent an opponent from receiving the object over a period of time.

General Playing Procedures

1. Teams should be chosen by the instructor and, when possible, team rosters should be announced early, with names listed alphabetically.
2. The stronger members of each team should be used in lead-off and anchor positions in relay races, ballgames, etc.
3. Lanes should be switched after each game, so that

no team gets a constant advantage because of water depth, lighting, or obstacles present.

4. Unless otherwise indicated, games should begin and end in the water; a maximum depth of five feet is recommended.

5. When games begin from any point on the deck or when determination of the winning team is difficult, the game should not end until all members of all teams are seated on the deck in original starting lineup.

General Rules

The following rules apply to all the games. Any special rules or exceptions are given under the particular game.

1. No one may be pushed into water from pool edge.
2. No ducking is ever permitted. This applies to opponents and to own team members.
3. Splashing of water is inevitable but is not to be part of the game.
4. No throwing of any object not specifically required and supplied for the game.
5. Participants may not leave the water or pool decks without instructor's authorization.
6. No one allowed on the diving board during games and relays.
7. No switching lights on and off.
8. No pulling on anyone's swim suit to gain an advantage or as an annoyance.

GAMES

For ease of reference, the games described below have been numbered, and the level is indicated in parentheses: Beginning (B), Intermediate (I), Advanced (A). Many skills serve as lead-up activities to the more advanced games.

Beginning Level Games

1(B). Follow the Leader
Purpose: Water adjustment and skills of diving and jumping in.
Participants: Any number.
Equipment needed: None.
Time limit: Class period.
Water depth: From 2 to 5 feet.
Procedure: One person with a high level of aquatic skills leads the class in performing various moves in the water. Moving through water by running, jumping, stroking, and kicking.

2(B). Treasure Hunt
Purpose: Water adjustment and ability to retrieve objects from the bottom of a pool.
Participants: Two teams, any number of players.
Equipment needed: 5 to 10 pennies per player to

be dropped in the water at random in the pool.
Time limit: Game ends when all pennies are found.
Water depth: From 2 to 12 feet.
Procedure: At a given signal, both teams try to find the "treasure." The team that retrieves the most pennies from the bottom of the pool and gives them to the teacher is the winner.
Rules: No stealing of pennies from other players' hands.

3(B). Fabyan's Water Music
Purpose: Water adjustment and various movements done to music. This game offers excellent opportunities for reviewing skills and getting acquainted in swimnastics classes, recreational and handicapped groups, parents-day shows, and a host of other places. With a little ingenuity and creativeness the instructor can expand the possibilities for water adjustment.
Participants: Any number.
Equipment needed: Cassette or record player and suitable folk dance or square dance records. Steps or dance calls are usually given in the album (or you can consult the chapter on Dance in this *Handbook*).
Water depth: Any depth.
Procedure: Each student is to respond to the directions given by the instruction on the record or the instructor on the deck in time with the music.

4(B). Beater Wades Round
Purpose: Water adjustment and water mobility are natural outcomes.
Participants: 12 to 20 players.
Equipment needed: None.
Time limit: None.
Water depth: 3 to 5 feet.
Procedure: One player is chosen to be "It." All other players join hands in a circle. The person who is "It" wades around the outside of the circle and tags one of the players in the circle. The tagged player must wade around the outside of the circle in the opposite direction from that in which It is wading. Both try to reach the vacant space. The unsuccessful one is It for the next round.
Rules: "It" must wade around the outside of the circle. "It" and the tagged player must wade in opposite directions.

5(B). Water Tag (Water Tap)
Purpose: Water adjustment and awareness; agility to avoid being tagged.
Participants: Any number.
Equipment needed: None.   *Time limit:* None.
Water depth: Shallow for beginners, deep when participants are ready for deep water.
Procedure: One player is chosen to be "It."

FIGURE 3-1. Players join hands in a circle.

Other players try to avoid being tagged (touched anywhere).

Rules: The person who is "It" may not tag the person who was "It" the previous round.

6(B). Water Volleyball
Purpose: Water adjustment and lead up to volleyball.

Participants: Two teams, 6 members each (may vary).

Equipment needed: One rubber volleyball. Volleyball net or rope suspended 3 to 15 feet above water.

Time limit: 10 minutes, or 15 points.

Water depth: 3 to 4 feet.

Procedure: Players try to hit ball over net (or a goal line); score of 15 points wins.

Rules: A player may not hit the ball twice in a row. A maximum of 3 hits may be used to hit the ball across the net. Basic rules of regular volleyball apply, but less strictly (illegal hits, etc.). Boundaries are the shallow end, both sides, and deep water.

Variations: Use a beach ball; lower or raise the net.

7(B). Musical Rings
Purpose: Water adjustment and kinetic awareness.

Participants: 2 teams, any number of players.

Equipment needed: Diving rings for all except

FIGURE 3-2. Line volleyball—no net, ball must be kept airborne.

one of the total number of participants; music.

Time limit: None.

Water depth: Shallow water—chest deep.

Procedure: When music stops, everyone stands on a ring. The person not standing on a ring drops out of the next round. After each round, remove one more ring until you are down to two players and one ring. Music should be played until all students are moving, then stopped abruptly.

Rules: No pushing or pulling.

8(B). Kingfish

Purpose: Water adjustment and safe transition from deck edge to water and from water to deck edge.

Participants: 10 to 16 players.

Equipment needed: None.   *Time limit:* None.

Water depth: Chest-deep water.

Procedure: Players sit in a row on edge of the pool with chin on hands, elbows on knees. At a signal, all dive or jump in, swim or wade across the area, and climb out and assume same pose. The last one out is eliminated. The one who remains the longest is "kingfish."

Rules: No pushing or horseplay while getting into or out of the water and crossing the pool.

9(B). Water Chain Tag

Purpose: Water adjustment and teamwork toward a common goal.

Participants: 15 to 20 players. One player chosen to be "It."

Equipment needed: None.   *Time limit:* None.

Water depth: Shallow area.

Procedure: The player who is "It" tags another player. While holding hands the two of them tag a third player. Every player is to be caught by being tagged by player at the end of the line. Only those players at the end of the line are allowed to tag another player. Last one tagged is "It" for the next game.

Rules: No breaking of hands to tag. No one allowed out of the water.

10(B). Catfish and Minnow (Cat and Mouse)

Purpose: Water adjustment plus the ability to put the head and body under water and between obstacles in an attempt to escape.

FIGURE 3-3. Relay finish—single line, seated, arms folded, legs crossed.

FIGURE 3-4. A shallow water game of tag with "It" in the middle.

FIGURE 3-5. Cat and Mouse—two circles, one "mouse" and one "cat."

Participants: 8 to 14 players.
Equipment needed: None.
Time limit: None.
Water depth: Shallow.
Procedure: One player is chosen to be the minnow and another the catfish. The other players join hands in a circle and by raising or lowering their arms, try to protect the minnow from capture by the catfish. The minnow is "caught" when touched on top of the head by the catfish. Then two others are chosen to be catfish and minnow.
Rules: No releasing of hands and no holding of the minnow or catfish.
Variations: Switch positions of minnow and catfish. Use two or more concentric circles.

11(B). Water Line Dodge Ball
Purpose: Water adjustment and agility to avoid being hit. The ability to hit a moving target is an outgrowth.
Participants: Three teams of 4 to 8 players each.
Equipment needed: A water ball, slightly deflated (a ball bladder will do nicely).
Time limit: A limit of two or three minutes is usually set for the team in the middle.
Water depth: Shallow.
Procedure: Divide the group into three teams. Teams one and two line up at each side of the swimming area while team three stands between them. The object is to hit the team in the middle with the thrown ball. The team receiving the least

FIGURE 3-6. Numbers line keep away—ball carried across own goal line.

number of hits, while in the middle, wins. The time limit applies for team change.

Rules: No glasses or goggles may be worn. To count as a hit, the ball must be thrown by player's nondominant hand (i.e., a righthander must throw lefthanded, and vice versa).

12(B). Bull in the Ring

Purpose: Water adjustment and ability to control feet and hands while being pushed and pulled.

Equipment needed: None.   *Time limit:* None.

Water depth: Shallow.

Procedure: Players join hands in a ring with the "Bull" in the center. Bull tries to get out of the ring in any way he can while the others try to prevent his escape. If Bull breaks through, the two players between whom he escaped give chase. The player who catches the Bull by encircling Bull's waist becomes the next Bull.

Rules: No tripping, kicking, or holding of the Bull. No hitting, pinching, or butting by the Bull.

Intermediate Level Games

13(I). Artillery Battle

Purpose: Water adjustment; the ability to move about in deep water and to hit a moving target.

Participants: Two teams of 12 to 30 players.

Equipment needed: 2 water balls, underinflated, or football bladders.

Water depth: Deep.

Procedure: Two teams line up facing each other. Each team is given a ball, and the players try to hit as many opponents with it as possible. When a player is hit by an opponent's ball, that player must drop out. When only one player is left, that team wins.

Rules: Boundaries are the edge of the pool in deep water. To count as a hit the ball must be thrown by the player's nondominant hand. When a player is eliminated, that player sits on the edge of the pool.

14(I). Rub-A-Dub-Tub

Purpose: Above water adjustment and balance while using a paddle.

Participants: At least 4 on each team with half of each team on opposite sides of the pool.

Equipment needed: One inner tube and canoe paddle for each team.   *Time limit:* None.

Water depth: 3 to 4 feet minimum, preferably 5 feet or over.

Procedure: Relay race to beat the other team(s) to the finish line. By turns, each player is seated in the inner tube and must paddle across to the other side of the pool. Another paddler makes the return trip.

Rules: Player must remain seated in the inner tube. No tipping of "canoes" allowed.

15(I). Guess Who

Purpose: Water adjustment; ability to open eyes under water to locate an object.

Participants: Any number.

Equipment needed: One water balloon for each class member.   *Time limit:* None.

Water depth: Shallow or deep water.

Procedure: Offensive (balloon carriers) must attempt to swim across to other side of pool, under or above the water, without breaking the balloon. Defensive players try to locate and break the balloons before they can reach the other side. Participants "huddle" before each play to choose offensive and defensive sides.

Rules: No rough-housing; no ducking the balloon carrier.

16(I). Ball Tag

Purpose: Water adjustments plus the ability to hit a moving target or to escape being hit by moving through the water.

Participants: 10 to 20 players.

Equipment needed: Water ball (soft).

Time limit: None.

Water depth: Entire pool.

Procedure: "It" tosses the ball and tries to tag (hit) somebody with it. The one who is tagged becomes "It" and must hit a different player.

Rules: No tag backs (i.e., hitting the player who just hit you). No one allowed to leave the water.

17(I). The Lifter

Purpose: Deep water adjustment and the ability to move on bottom of pool in deep water.

Participants: 5 or more players per team.

Equipment needed: 2 diving bricks.

Time limit: None.

Water depth: 10 feet or more.

Procedure: A player carries a brick under water over to his teammate who is on opposite side of the pool; the teammate then carries it back in a shuttle relay race. First team which carries the brick over and back once per team member is finished and seated is the winner.

Rules: If a player comes up for air he must go under at the same spot and finish carrying the brick. The teammate who is waiting to carry it back must be under water when the brick is transferred.

18(I). Water Balloon Ball

Purpose: Deep water adjustment and ability to keep ball airborne as a team member.

Participants: Two equal teams, any number of players.

Equipment needed: A large balloon or large water ball.

Time limit: None.
Water depth: Shallow to deep water.
Procedure: Each team selects a goalkeeper to be stationed with back to edge of pool. The goalkeeper is responsible for preventing the ball from passing the goal line, i.e., edge of the pool to be defended. All other players line up in the center of the playing area, facing each other. A balloon or ball is tossed up by the instructor and the players attempt to advance the ball by batting it in the air with the open hand. If the ball touches the water, it is given to the team which did not touch it last. A team advancing the ball over their opponent's goal scores a point. First ten points win.
Rules: No carrying the ball.

19(I). Corks

Purpose: Deep water adjustment and teamwork.
Participants: Two teams, any number of players.
Equipment needed: 25 or more corks or Ping Pong balls. Baskets or boxes for goals.
Time limit: None.
Water depth: Any depth.
Procedure: Two equal teams line up on opposite sides of the swimming pool in front of their respective goals (use a basket or box). The corks (or Ping Pong balls) are thrown into the center between the two teams and at the signal, each team member attempts to pick up a cork and place it in the team's goal. Each cork is taken to the goal separately; players go in turn. The team with the greater number of corks in its basket wins.
Rules: No ducking, holding, or kicking. Splashing is allowed.

20(I). Float Tag

Purpose: Deep water adjustment and ability to take feet off the bottom of pool and float.
Participants: Two equal teams.
Equipment needed: None. *Time limit:* None.
Water depth: 5 feet or over.
Procedure: Several members of the class are appointed "It." To avoid being caught, one must be doing a back or face float. A player may be tagged only while not floating. The last three to be tagged are "It" for the next game.
Rules: A tag is a touch on the shoulder. Sculling is allowed.

Advanced Level Games

21(A). Underwater Football

Purpose: Underwater adjustment and prolonged breath holding.
Participants: Two equal teams.
Equipment needed: One diving brick.

Time limit: Two 10-minute halves.
Water depth: 10 feet or more.
Procedure: Brick is dropped in middle of the deep end by teacher. Object is to push or swim the brick to the opposite wall, keeping the brick on the bottom at all times. A goal is scored when brick touches opponent's wall. After each goal, brick is re-dropped in the middle. Two-minute rest at halftime.
Rules: Person carrying the brick must stay near the bottom. No one may be held under water.

22(A). Jump or Dive

Purpose: Water adjustment and ability to respond to verbal commands quickly and correctly.
Participants: Any number.
Equipment needed: Diving board or diving area.
Time limit: None.
Water depth: Deep end.
Procedure: One player at a time makes a walking approach to the diving end of the board. As he reaches the end of the board, the commander calls out either "jump" or "dive." The player must correctly do what the commander calls out.
Rules: The commander must be fair (equal) to *all* the players; he can say "J-J-Dive" but discretion must be used as to what is fair. The player tries to do what the commander says as his feet retouch the board on the hurdle and must perform what is called out.

23(A). Water Baseball

Purpose: Water adjustment and hand-eye coordination. An excellent game for skills or getting acquainted. Suitable for any age group.
Participants: 2 teams with 9 players per team (number of players may vary with class size and ability); at least 1 umpire.
Equipment needed: 1 large wiffel bat and wiffel ball; 4 nonfloating bases, designated as 1st, 2nd, 3rd, and Home.
Time limit: 9 innings (or a number agreed upon by both teams).
Water depth: Any depth in keeping with swimming ability and height of players.
Procedure: Played like baseball, the object being to score the most runs by the end of the game.
Rules: 1. Three outs per team per inning. 2. It is an out if: (a) a ball is caught in the air; (b) a swimmer is touched with the ball while not on base; (c) first base is tagged before the swimmer reaches it; (d) a batted ball hits the batter. 3. No rough play or dunking allowed. 4. Three strikes or misses of the ball by the batter is an out; two strikes and a foul, in that order, is an out.
Variation: If inner tubes are available, batters and/or fielders or the entire team may sit in the inner tubes and paddle around bases.

ARCHERY

THIS CHAPTER WILL ENABLE YOU TO:

♦ Identify and demonstrate the ten basic steps of shooting in target archery.
♦ Identify and demonstrate terms related to the bow and arrow.
♦ Understand the basic terminology associated with target archery.
♦ Identify and describe the rules associated with target archery.
♦ Identify and observe the necessary safety precautions.

NATURE AND PURPOSE

For the past several years, interest in archery has grown tremendously throughout the world. Many schools and colleges include archery in their physical education programs. Consequently, archery has become a modern sport form. In the 1972 Olympic Games held at Munich, archery appeared as an Olympic event for the first time. Several archers from the United States have captured not only Olympic medals but also medals from other international competitions.

Archery is an easy to learn activity, and it is possible for both sexes of all ages to develop proficiency in archery skills in a relatively short period of time. As an individual sport it is relatively inexpensive and can be practiced year-round. The benefits of archery are both physical and emotional.

EQUIPMENT

Archery equipment as a whole is known as "tackle." The minimum essential tackle for the beginning archer includes: (1) a bow of correct length and weight, (2) one dozen matched arrows, (3) a finger tab or glove, and (4) an arm guard. The selection of a proper bow and matched arrows are the two most important steps for successful archery practice.

Bows

Bows are constructed of many materials including wood, fiberglass, or laminated wood core and fiberglass. To overcome the disadvantages of the wooden or fiberglass bow, a laminated (composite) bow was designed. This bow is smooth-shooting and is not subject to changes due to weather.

Bow weight refers to the weight in pounds required to bring a bow to full draw. The most important factor in determining bow weight is the individual archer's muscular strength. For the beginner, it is best to start with a bow that is easier to draw and handle rather than using "overbow." The bow weight may be gradually increased as the archer improves shooting technique and develops muscular strength. Table 4-1 shows the recommended bow weights according to the standards established by the Archery Manufacturers Organization.

TABLE 4-1. Recommended Bow Weights

	Under 20 lbs	20 lbs	25 lbs	30 lbs	35 lbs	40 lbs	Over 40 lbs
Children 6–12	X	X					
Teen (girl)		X	X				
Teen (boy)		X	X	X			
Women		X	X	X			
Men					X	X	X	
Hunting							X

Arrows

Arrows are made of wood, fiberglass, or aluminum. The least expensive, wooden arrows, are used by most beginning archers. Glass and aluminum arrows are used by more advanced archers. Each type of arrow has its own advantages and disadvantages, but it is very important that one select arrows closely matched in weight, length, and stiffness (spine).

A beginner should start to shoot with arrows that are two inches longer than the needed proper length in case of an overdraw. To determine the proper length, one should place the nock of the arrow on the center of one's chest and extend arms full length forward, palms facing, so that the point of the arrow extends past the fingertips. When purchasing a bow and arrows, one should seek advice from an expert to determine the proper bow and arrows that fit best.

Arm Guards

Arm guards have two main functions: (1) the most important is to protect the bow arm from the slap of the bow string; (2) the other is to keep a long sleeve close to the arm so it will not interfere with the bow string. The arm guard is worn on the inside of the forearm below the elbow, near the wrist of the bow arm. The arm guard is usually made of leather with elastic straps to hold the guard on the forearm.

Finger Tabs or Gloves

Friction between the fingers and the bow string can produce not only soreness to the fingers, but it can also have effects on proper shooting. Tabs or gloves will protect the fingers and aid in developing a smooth and consistent release. Many beginners have difficulty in using finger tabs or gloves, but with a little patience and practice one can overcome this difficulty.

Target

A target consists of a target face, a mat, and a stand. Ready-made targets can be purchased from a sporting goods dealer. Schools and colleges usually use a 48-inch target face. Target mats are easily made from tightly compressed hay. The mat should measure at least 50 × 50 inches.

RULES OF TARGET ARCHERY

1. Any bow except a crossbow may be used for competition.
2. Arrows should have a distinctive crest in order to distinguish each archer's arrow.
3. After the signal to shoot, arrows should be nocked.
4. Arrows that fall from the bow and cannot be reached with the bow from the shooting line, are considered to be shot.
5. Only six arrows may be shot at the designated target; if more than six are shot, only the lowest six scores are counted, and any arrow(s) shot at any other target shall not be scored.
6. An archer should shoot from the longest distance first, the second longest distance next, and so forth.
7. Scores are recorded from the highest score to the lowest score.

8. Arrows should be retrieved only after the signal is given.

SCORING

The scoring values of target archery are 9 points for gold; 7 for red; 5 for blue; 3 for black; and 1 for white rings. An arrow that goes completely through the target or that bounces off the target counts 7 points regardless of the part of the target it passes or hits. An arrow that lands on the line between two rings counts as hitting the higher scoring ring.

All target archery rounds (competitions) are shot at a regulation 48-inch target face unless otherwise specified. The common target archery competitions are the American Round, Columbia Round, Hereford Round, York Round, Women's and Men's Metropolitan Rounds, and Scholastics Round. Each competition round differs in the number of arrows and the distance from which the arrows are shot.

For physical education classes, a modified institutional round should be implemented to enable a round to be completed within a given time period. For example, the Ball State Round consists of 12 ends: 4 ends each shooting from 20 yards, 25 yards, and 30 yards, and requiring approximately sixty minutes to complete. Each end consists of shooting 5 arrows. The scoring values of the Ball State Round are 5 points for gold; 4 points for red; 3 for blue; 2 for black; and 1 for white. This gives a maximum total of 300 points (5 arrows × 5 points × 12 ends = 300 points). If a class period is only forty-five minutes, a round should consist of 8 ends: 4 ends from 25 yards and 4 ends from 30 yards.

SAFETY

Bows and arrows are weapons capable of inflicting serious injury, and should be handled with care. Here are some specific precautions to follow. Remember that the continued enjoyment of archery depends upon everyone observing these safety rules.

1. Always check the bow and string to see if it is properly placed at both ends of the string notch before starting to shoot.
2. Shoot only at the target.
3. Don't draw the bow when anyone is between you and the target area.
4. Never allow anyone to retrieve arrows until all arrows have been shot.
5. Never shoot into the air or in any direction where it might destroy property or endanger life.
6. Always be sure that the area in back of the target is clear or has an adequate back stop.
7. Do not overdraw the bow.
8. Be sure arrows are of the correct length and stiffness for the bow.

9. Do not release a fully drawn bow without an arrow.
10. Obey all commands given for shooting and retrieving arrows.
11. Always wear an arm guard and finger tab to prevent injury.
12. Do not wear bulky clothing or dangling jewelry when shooting.
13. No fooling around or horseplay on the shooting line.
14. Never run with arrows in your hand; when carrying arrows, keep the pile ends toward the ground.
15. When you have finished shooting, stand behind the other archers until the end has been completed.

SUGGESTED LEARNING SEQUENCE

Open space with good lighting and a proper backdrop, well-organized lessons, and an emphasis on safety are all important aspects of creating a successful atmosphere for archery. Safety should be stressed from the very beginning. Instructions should include the care of the equipment (bow, bowstring, and arrows) and the ten essential steps for shooting described in this chapter. A good learning sequence is the following.

A. Introduction
B. Nature of the Activity
  1. Archery as a sport and family recreation
  2. Discussion of equipment
  3. Safety
C. Skills and Techniques—Ten Basic Steps of Shooting
  Static Stage: Practice without arrows
  1. Proper stance
  2. Nocking the arrow
  3. Setting the hook
  4. Holding the bow
  5. Raising the head
  6. Raising the unit
  Dynamic Stage: Practice with arrows
  7. Drawing and anchoring
  8. Aiming and holding
  9. Releasing
  10. Follow-through
  Steps 7 and 8 should be practiced several times before moving into steps 9 and 10.
  The first shooting practice should start from 15 yards, then 20 yards, 30 yards, and so on.
D. Rules and Scoring—Once some proficiency in shooting technique has been achieved, participants can be taught the rules governing target archery and the scoring method.

SKILLS AND TECHNIQUES

Stringing the Bow

Push-Pull Method

1. Take the bow handle in your left hand with the back of the bow toward you.
2. Holding the left arm in front of the body and angling the bow's upper limb toward the right, place the lower nock against the instep of the left foot, but not touching the ground.
3. Place the right hand on the upper limb just below the upper loop of the bowstring; then keeping both arms straight, pull with the left hand and push with the heel of the right hand, and slide the string into the upper nock with fingers. While stringing, keep your face away from the bow.

Step-through Method

1. Hold the bow in your right hand and the string with the other hand.
2. Place the back of the lower limb of the bow across the ankle of your left foot.
3. Step through the bow with your right leg.
4. Place the bow handle high on your right thigh.
5. Press the upper limb of the bow forward with the open right hand and slide the string into the nock with the left hand. Always check both notches for proper string insertion and alignment after each stringing.

Shooting: The Ten Basic Steps

Archers should always follow the ten basic steps of the shooting sequence in their proper order. Consistency is very important for becoming a good archer. Repetition of these ten steps will help you develop rhythm in shooting and help you become a satisfied archer. The steps described below are for the right-handed person; adjustments are required for left-handers.

Step 1—Establishing a Proper Stance
The stance is the foundation of good archery form. The square and open stances are the most commonly used. For both stances, the archer should spread both feet apart (approximately shoulder width) to achieve a comfortable feeling. The archer's weight should be equally distributed upon both feet, and the knees should be locked to maintain balance. Once you decide on a stance—either the square or open stance—you should take the same stance each time you shoot.

1. *Square Stance.* The square stance is recommended for beginning archers. In this stance, the archer's feet straddle the shooting line with both feet parallel to each other, and toes line up with the center of the target. The body should be

FIGURE 4-1. Square stance.

upright with head turned toward the target (see Figure 4-1).

2. *Open (Oblique) Stance.* To assume the open stance, the archer draws the foot closer to the target back about 4 to 6 inches from the square stance. At the same time, hips and shoulders must also turn so that the body is at about a 45-degree angle to the target (see Figure 4-2). The open stance is recommended for advanced archers.

FIGURE 4-2. Open stance.

Step 2—Nocking the Arrow
Nocking the arrow means placing the arrow on the bowstring in preparation for drawing.

Learning Cues

1. Hold the bow with the left hand and the palm of the bow hand facing the ground.
2. The right hand holding the shaft of the arrow, with index finger pointing upward, slip the nock

onto the string at a 90-degree angle with the string. Make a small mark with ink on the string to ensure that the nocking is always done in the same place. If a bow with the nocking point is already fixed on the string, the arrow is usually nicked below the nocking point. After nocking, the archer makes sure there is no gap between the string and the throat of the nock.

Step 3—Setting the Hook
After nocking the arrow, the archer must establish a proper hook. The hook is set using three fingers (index, middle, and fourth fingers) of the archer's right hand. Hook first three fingers around the string at the first knuckles of these fingers. Hold the arrow lightly between index and middle fingers but do not squeeze the arrow (Figure 4-3). Thumb

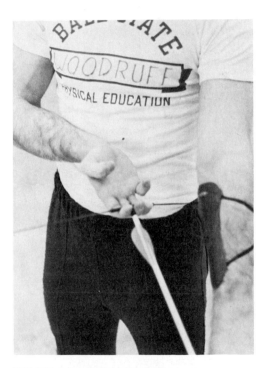

FIGURE 4-3. Setting the hook.

and little finger of the right hand should be touching each other over the palm. After shooting for a while the thumb and little finger should be relaxed. It is important to keep the back of the right hand straight.

Step 4—Establishing a Bow Hold
As in all other aspects of archery, consistency is also required in establishing a proper bow hold. First, extend your left arm at the shoulder height toward the target with left hand in a "handshake" position, then place the pivot point of the bow handle (midsection of the bow) in the "V" formed by the thumb and index finger. Now the handle of the bow should rest against the base of the thumb, and

FIGURE 4-4. The bow hold.

other fingers should be placed lightly around the handle. This keeps the bow from falling at release of the arrow. Make sure that you do not grip the bow. Before releasing the arrow, the elbow of the bow arm must be turned down to avoid slapping by the bowstring (Figure 4-4).

Step 5—Raising the Head

Before raising the unit (bow and arrow), the archer's head should be in a natural position turned to look directly at the center of the target without any tilt (Figure 4-5).

FIGURE 4-5. Note head position.

Step 6—Raising the Unit

At this point, the archer has prepared mechanically for shooting by establishing a proper stance, nocking an arrow, setting the hook, establishing the grip, and raising the head. Now the archer is ready to do the dynamic parts of shooting. The archer raises the entire unit (bow with a nocked arrow) to shoulder height. The bow is now in an upright position facing the target, bow arm is extended toward target, and the drawing arm is forming an extension of the arrow. The elbow of the drawing arm is better slightly higher than lower in relation to the arrow (Figure 4-6).

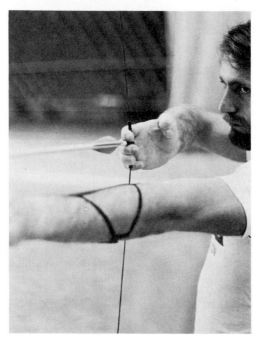

FIGURE 4-6. Eyes on target, drawing arm slightly higher than arrow.

Step 7—Drawing and Anchoring

Drawing is the act of pulling the bowstring into the shooting position, and anchoring is the point where the drawing hand is placed. The drawing and the anchoring should be done with one smooth deliberate motion.

Learning Cues—Drawing

1. Before drawing, keep in mind that the three fingers of the drawing hand are just hooked onto the string at the first knuckles.
2. The drawing hand should be relaxed with special attention given to relaxing the back of the hand.
3. The elbow of the drawing arm should be slightly elevated.
4. Now the archer draws the bow by letting the shoulder and back muscles do the pulling with one smooth and deliberate motion.
5. At the full draw, the string should make contact with the center of the nose, lips, and chin.

FIGURE 4-7. Anchoring.

Learning Cues—Anchoring

1. Anchoring must be done at the same point for each draw. This lets the arrow be drawn exactly the same distance and place each time.
2. The index finger of the drawing hand should be under the tip of the jawbone with the thumb relaxed against the neck (low anchor point).
3. While drawing, the archer should take a deep breath, exhale about half of the air and hold the rest until the arrow has been released (Figure 4-7).

Step 8—Aiming and Holding
Three methods of aiming in archery are by using a bow sight attached to the bow, by "point of aim," and by "instinctive shooting."

1. Shooting with a bow sight is the most accurate aiming technique. The archer should line up the string and bow sight with the center of the target. If the arrow hits high, move the sight up and if low move the sight down. The sight can also be adjusted left or right.
2. Point-of-aim shooting is aiming at some spot with the point of the arrow. The spot may be in front of, on, or above the target. The selection of the aiming spot depends upon the height of the archer, length of the arrow, and bow weight. When shots are low, move the spot up; when shots are high, move the spot down. String alignment is also important and should be done directly in front of the right eye and lined up vertical with the bow.
3. Instinctive shooting is shooting without a sight or point-of-aim marker. The archer's eyes are focused on the center of target and the bow arm will adjust itself toward target. Accuracy of this technique depends upon the archer's shooting form, eyesight, depth perception, and kinesthetic awareness.

Concentration may be the single most important part of aiming. You should hold your breath and relax a few seconds until the arrow is released. You should also be aware that the sight will oscillate while you are aiming, but make sure it oscillates within the target center.

Step 9—Release
Releasing the arrow should be done with unconscious effort. The archer simply relaxes the entire drawing hand and lets the string roll off the fingers by itself. No other parts of the body except the drawing hand should be moved. During the release, the archer must continue aiming and maintain the contraction of the upper back muscles. Furthermore, the archer should not let the drawing hand move forward nor come off the anchor position to release the string.

Step 10—Follow-Through
Follow through is the act of maintaining the body position and mental condition assumed at release until the arrow hits the target. The bow arm is pushed slightly forward and the drawing hand rubs the chin as it moves back behind the archer's neck. During the act of release and follow-through, the archer must continue aiming at the target center rather than following the flight of the arrow and keeping the tension of the upper back muscles (Figure 4-8).

FIGURE 4-8. Release and follow-through.

Retrieving Arrows

To retrieve an arrow from the target, place the palm of your left hand against the target face with the arrow resting between the index and the middle finger, and push the target face lightly. With your right hand, grasp the arrow by the shaft close to the target and, twisting it slightly counterclockwise, pull the arrow directly backward. If the arrow goes through the target but the fletchings (feathers) remain inside the mat, go to the back of the target and pull the arrow carefully forward without any twisting motion.

HINTS FOR IMPROVING TECHNIQUE

Upon release, movements of certain parts of the body will cause faulty arrow flights. Be aware of these movements so that you can avoid them.

1. *High arrow flights are usually caused by:*

   a. Peeking (looking up to watch the arrow in flight)
   b. Heeling the bow (putting pressure on the low part of the bow handle with the low portion of the bow hand)
   c. Body leaning backward
   d. Overdraw (pulling arrows beyond normal anchor point)

2. *Low arrow flights are usually caused by:*

   a. Creeping (letting the drawing hand move forward before arrow is released)
   b. Overhold (maintaining the hold position too long)
   c. String hitting the arm guard upon release
   d. Hunching the shoulder of the bow arm

3. *Arrow flights to the left are usually caused by:*

   a. Cupping the drawing hand instead of having the back of the drawing hand relaxed and straight
   b. Bringing the string away from the face (anchor point) to release the arrow
   c. Improper alignment of the bow, body, or string

4. *Arrows falling off the arrow rest of the bow are caused by:*

   a. Pinching of the arrow nock with the fingers of the drawing hand. To remedy this, the archer should separate the index and middle fingers to insure a light touch with the nock, hook the string with the first knuckles of drawing fingers, and utilize back muscles to draw
   b. Tight finger tab
   c. Cupping of the drawing hand

TERMINOLOGY

Addressing the target Standing ready to shoot with a proper shooting stance.
Anchor point Specific location on the archer's face to which the index finger comes while holding and aiming.
Archery golf An adaptation of the game of golf to the sport of archery. Players shoot for the holes, and score according to the number of shots required to hit the target.
Arm guard A piece of leather or plastic that is worn on the inside of the forearm to protect the arm from the bowstring.
Arrow plate A protective piece of hard material set into the bow where the arrow crosses it.
Arrow rest A small projection at the top of the bow handle where the arrow rests.
Back The side of the bow away from the shooter.
Bow arm The arm that holds the bow; this would be the left arm for a right-handed person.
Bow sight A device attached to the bow through which the archer sights when aiming.

Bow weight Designates the amount of effort (in pounds) needed to pull a bowstring a specific distance (usually 28 inches).

Cant The act of holding the bow tilted or slightly turned while shooting.

Cast The distance a bow can shoot an arrow.

Clout shooting A type of shooting that uses a target 48 ft in diameter, laid on the ground at a distance of 180 yards for men and 140 or 120 yards for women. Usually 36 arrows (6 ends with 6 arrows) are shot per round.

Cock feather Now called the "index feather." The feather that is set at a right angle to the arrow nock; differently colored than other two feathers.

Creeping Letting the drawing hand move forward at the release.

Crest The archer's identifying marks shown just below the fletchings on the arrow.

Draw The act of pulling the bow string back into the anchor position.

End A specified number of arrows shot at one time or from one position before retrieval of arrows.

Face The part of the bow facing the shooter.

Finger tab A leather flap worn on the drawing hand to protect the fingers and provide a smooth release of the bow string.

Fletchings The feathers of the arrow, which give guidance to its flight.

Flight shooting Shooting an arrow the farthest possible distance.

Handle The grip at the midsection of the bow.

Hen feathers The two feathers that are not set at right angles to the arrow nock. See *Cock feather*.

Hold Steadily holding the arrow at full draw before release.

Instinctive shooting Aiming and shooting instinctively, rather than using a bow sight or point-of-aim method.

Limbs Upper and lower parts of the bow; divided by the handle.

Nock The groove in the end of the arrow in which the string is placed.

Nocking point The point on the string at which the arrow is placed.

Notch The grooves of the upper and lower tips of the limbs into which the bow string is fitted.

Overbow Using too strong a bow that is too powerful to pull a bowstring to proper distance.

Overdraw Drawing the bow so that the pile of the arrow is inside the bow.

Petticoat That part of the target face outside the white ring.

Pile (point) The pointed metal tip of the arrow.

Pinch To squeeze the nock of the arrow.

Plucking Jerking the drawing hand laterally away from the face on the release, which will cause arrow flights to the left.

Point-blank range The only distance from the target at which the point of aim is right on the bull's-eye.

Point-of-aim A method of aiming in which the pile of the arrow is aligned with the target.

Quiver A receptacle for carrying or holding arrows.

Recurve bow A bow that is curved on the ends.

Reflexed bow A bow whose limbs spring toward the back when it is unstrung.

Release The act of letting the bowstring slip off the fingertips.

Round The term used to indicate shooting a designated number of arrows at a designated distance or distances.

Roving Archery game played outdoors in which natural targets (stumps, trees, bushes, etc.) are selected for competition.

Serving The thread wrapped around the bowstring at the nocking point.

Shaft The long, body part of the arrow.

Spine The characteristic rigidity and flexibility of an arrow.

Tackle Archery equipment referred to as a whole.

Target face The painted front of a target, usually replaceable.

Trajectory The path of the arrow in flight.

Vane Plastic feather of an arrow.

SELECTED REFERENCES

American Alliance for Health, Physical Education, Recreation, and Dance. *Archery: A Planning Guide for Group and Individual Instruction.* Reston, Va.: AAHPERD, 1972.

The Athletic Institute. *How to Improve Your Archery.* Chicago: The Athletic Institute,

BARRETT, JEAN A. *Archery.* Pacific Pallisades, Calif.: Goodyear Publishing Co., 1973.

BURKE, EDMUND H. *Field and Target Archery.* Greenwich, Conn.: Fawcett Publications, Inc., 1961.

HERRIGEL, EUGEN. *Zen in the Art of Archery.* New York: McGraw-Hill, Inc., 1964.

KLANN, MARGARET L. *Target Archery.* Reading, Mass.: Addison-Wesley Publishing Co., 1970.

McKINNEY, WAYNE C. *Archery.* Dubuque, Iowa: Wm. C. Brown Co. Publishers, 1966.

NIEMEYER, ROY K. *Beginning Archery.* Belmont, Calif.: Wadsworth Publishing Co., Inc., 1967.

Audio-Visual Materials

Available at school libraries and community libraries. For more information, contact the following organizations:

Athletic Institute, 705 Merchandise Mart, Chicago, Ill. 60654. Super-8 loop films and 16 mm films.

Ben Pearson Archery, Consumer Division Brunswick Corp., P.O. Box 270, Dept. S., Tulsa, Okla. 74101. 35 mm slides and other equipment.

Archery Organizations

American Archery Council, 618 Chalmers, Flint, Mich. 48503.

Archery Manufacturers Organization, 618 Chalmers, Flint, Mich. 48503.

National Archery Association, Box 48, Ronks, Pa. 17572.

Professional Archers Association, 1500 N. Chatsworth St., St. Paul, Minn. 55117.

5 BADMINTON

THIS CHAPTER WILL ENABLE YOU TO:

♦ Understand the fundamental techniques involved in the various strokes in the game of badminton, and be able to execute these shots.
♦ Demonstrate proper footwork and positioning in both singles and doubles.
♦ Display an understanding of basic strategy in both singles and doubles.
♦ Identify and understand rules for the singles and doubles games.
♦ Understand the basic terminology used in the game.

NATURE AND PURPOSE

Badminton is a relatively new addition to the family of sports in America. Despite the late date of its recognition as a valuable leisure-time activity, its popularity has recently grown. This growth is due in part to the game's adaptability. It can be played fast or slow, hard or easy, in or out of doors; by men, women, and children, young or old.

At a beginning level it is usually possible to keep the shuttle in play, which makes the game enjoyable and rewarding for the participants. In advanced play it is a very fast, competitive game that calls for a high level of skill, overall athletic ability, and physical conditioning. Singles, doubles, or mixed doubles may be played; thus badminton is an excellent coeducational activity.

Although courts can be set up outdoors, almost all competitive badminton is played indoors where the wind will not affect the shuttle.

EQUIPMENT

The choice of equipment is important in badminton. High-quality rackets and shuttlecocks can have a favorable bearing on performance. When purchasing rackets and birds, buy the best you can afford.

Racket

Badminton rackets are quite light and can be made of either metal or laminated wood. Metal or composition rackets are quite popular now because of their extreme lightness which allows quick and rapid movement. Most people feel this allows them to react more quickly and to hit the shuttle with greater velocity.

Choosing a racket is a matter of personal preference. You should use what feels comfortable, not what looks good. Tournament players may spend four or five times as much for a racket as do recreational players.

Strings can be either gut or nylon. Gut is used by most tournament players because it is said to be more resilient than nylon. However, gut strings are far more expensive and usually will not last as long as nylon. It is safe to say that nylon is more practical for all but the tournament player.

Shuttlecock

A shuttlecock (also called bird or shuttle) weighs approximately one-sixth of an ounce and is made of either goose feathers or nylon. The feather shuttle is better but also more expensive and will usually not last as long as nylon.

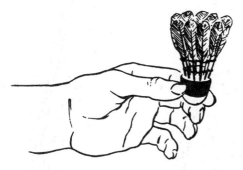

FIGURE 5-1. Holding the bird for delivery.

Major tournaments use feather shuttles while nylon is generally used for most recreational and class play. Shuttles are not very durable (especially the feathered ones) and often will not last through even one match.

BADMINTON COURT

The official badminton court is shown in Figure 5-2. The playing court for doubles is the entire court, while for singles it is the same length, but three feet narrower. The service court for doubles is shorter and wider than that for singles, which necessitates a different service concept. The net is 5 feet 1 inch at the net poles and 5 feet at the center. The lines of the court must be 1½ inches wide and may be either painted or taped on the court surface. Games can be played outdoors but are usually played indoors so the wind will not affect the shuttle. The ceiling of an indoor court should be at least 20 feet high and preferably 25 feet. Most major tournaments will have ceilings at least 30 feet high.

RULES OF BADMINTON

1. Toss for serve. Before a match begins opponents shall toss (usually spin the racket), with the side winning having the option of:
   a. Serving or receiving or
   b. Choosing ends.
   The side losing the toss may have the choice of any alternative remaining.
2. Fifteen points constitute the usual game except for women's singles, in which 11 points are played. Occasionally men's singles may be 21 points instead of 15. When the score is tied at 13-all (in a 15-point game), the side reaching 13 first chooses to finish the game at 15 or to set the game at 5 points. When tied at 14-all the choice is to play 1 or 3 points. Similarly, in 11-point games, the score may be set at 3 when the score is 9-all and at 2 when 10-all. In a 21-point game the same method of scoring is used substituting 19 and 20 for 13 and 14.
3. The service must be delivered to the diagonal service court. A bird that lands on a line is considered good. In singles the bird must land in the long, narrow court and in doubles in the short, wide court. After the serve in doubles the deep back line is the boundary. Thus the short back line is used only on the doubles serve.
4. Only one service (trial) per player is allowed per inning, unless the bird is missed entirely in which case another attempt is allowed. The service alternates courts, starting in the right-hand court for doubles at all times. In singles, the service starts in the right-hand court at the beginning of the game, but thereafter service is made from the right-hand court when the score is even (for that side) and from the left-hand court when the score is odd (for that side). Only one hand is allowed the side beginning the serve in doubles the first inning, and two hands are allowed each inning thereafter. However, a member of the team can be in either court when the score is even (or odd),

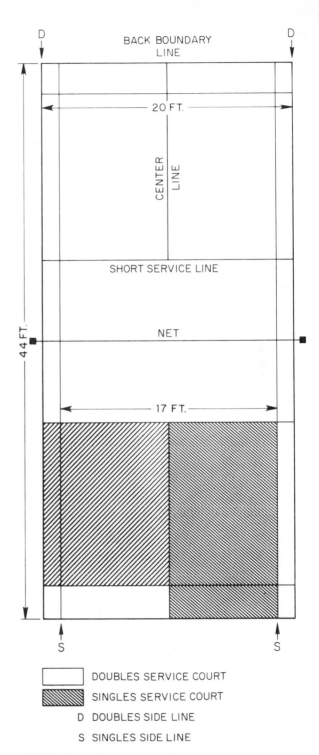

FIGURE 5-2. Badminton playing courts.

but all members must be in their proper court, i.e., the same sides they were in when they made their first point. An easy way to remember: When their score is even, partners should be in the courts (sides) in which they started the game.
5. Opponents play the best of three games, unless otherwise agreed. Players will switch ends of the court at the beginning of the second and third

games. In the third game (if there is one) the players will switch ends when the leading score reaches:

8 in a game of 15
6 in a game of 11
11 in a game of 21

6. It is a fault (loss of service or hand for the serving side and loss of point for receiving side) when:
   a. Service is illegal, i.e., the bird is struck when above the waist, or the head of the racket is higher than the hand when hit.
   b. Service or played shot lands outside the specified court, passes through or under the net, or hits a player or obstruction outside the court.
   c. If server or receiver steps out of the proper court before delivery of serve or feints in any way before the service. Only the person served to may return the bird.
   d. A player reaches over the net to hit a bird. (The follow-through, however, may break the plane of the net.)
   e. A player touches the net with the racket or any part of the body.
   f. A player hits the bird twice or momentarily holds or throws it with the racket.
   g. A player fails to return the bird to the opponent's proper court. (The player cannot hit, catch, or be struck by a doubtful bird and call "out".)
   h. The server steps forward when serving.
   i. On a doubles serve, the server's partner unsights the server. (Hand out or side out.)
   j. A player obstructs or hinders an opponent.

SUGGESTED LEARNING SEQUENCE

It is important to develop an overall understanding of the game before one works on specific skills. But some activity should take place early in the learning sequence. The following outline includes everything that needs to be covered, but the exact teaching sequence will vary according to circumstances.

A. Nature of the Game
   1. The playing court
   2. The singles and doubles games
B. Grips
   1. Forehand
   2. Backhand
C. Rules
D. The Strokes (Skills and Techniques)
   1. Deep singles serve (forehand underhand clear)
   2. Overhand clear (forehand and backhand)
   3. Overhand smash (forehand and backhand)
   4. Block (off of smash)
   5. Drops
      a. Overhead
      b. Underhand
      c. Hairpin
   6. Short doubles serve
   7. Drive serve
   8. Backhand low serve
   9. Round-the-head clear
   10. Round-the-head smash
   11. Round-the-head drop
   12. Footwork and movement
E. The Singles Game
   1. Strategy and positioning
F. The Doubles Game (Regular and Mixed)
   1. Strategy
   2. Formations (Positioning)
      a. Side-by-side
      b. Up and back
      c. Combination

SKILLS AND TECHNIQUES

Many different skills and techniques must be utilized effectively to be a good, fundamentally sound badminton player. In this section we will describe each stroke or skill, and give learning cues and practice suggestions for each.

The Grips

Forehand. To acquire the proper grip for a forehand stroke, hold the racket by the shaft in the left hand with the face of the racket perpendicular to the floor, and shake hands with the handle with the right hand. Grasp the handle lightly with the little finger on the leather base and the forefinger slightly separated from the others. Care must be taken not to grasp the handle too far up from the end, or the wrist action will be prevented by the

FIGURE 5-3. The forehand grip. Note that the palm of the hand is basically parallel to the face of the racket.

protruding end. The thumb should be on the left side of the handle with the "V" formed by the thumb and forefinger being on top of the handle, resting above the third finger. Basically, the grip should permit the palm of the hand to be parallel to the face of the racket. There will be slight variations among individuals and it is difficult to say exactly where each part of the hand should be. Many players like to touch the thumb and the third finger.

Backhand. This same grip may be used for backhand shots, but most of the better players today use what is known as the "thumb-up" grip. To assume this grip, turn the top edge of the racket frame over slightly to the right and place the thumb along and parallel to the wide side of the handle. The power of the thumb is thus added to that of the body, arm, and wrist on the wrist snap during the forward swing of the racket. This grip permits a longer reach, more power, and, in strokes where the bird must fly long distances, greater accuracy. Another advantage is that a quicker recovery can be made because not as much body movement is required as when the same grip is used for forehand and backhand strokes. Beginners have a tendency to grip the racket too tightly.

Footwork

Movement and footwork seem to go hand in hand. Some people are innately quicker than others, but any well-conditioned person should be able to cover the badminton court adequately.

1. *Ready position.* Good movement begins with a good ready position. The feet should be shoulder width apart, the knees slightly bent with the weight on the balls of the feet.
2. *The first step.* Getting to the shuttle on time requires a good first step. When moving forward and to the right or left, the first step should be a cross-over step in the direction of the intended point of contact. The opposite foot will be dropped back a short distance so as to push off efficiently and generate quick movement. When moving left to the front, drop the left foot back, push off, and take the first stride as a cross-over step with the right foot.
   When moving back and to the right, drop the left foot slightly forward so as to push off and establish movement with the right foot to the intended point of contact. These same principles hold true when moving to the left back court (using opposite movement of back-right).
3. *Turn sideways in preparation.* It is important to turn the body sideways to the net when hitting the shuttle. This will allow the full rotation of the upper body and hips in generating power.
4. *Return to center.* After each shot is hit, the player should return quickly to the center of court and prepare for the next return.
5. *Use short steps.* Generally, short steps help you to stay balanced and to transfer the weight into the shot.

The Strokes

There are five basic groups of shots: serves, clears, smashes, drops, and drives. All except the drives will be described below.

I. Serves

There are two basic badminton serves: the singles serve, which is hit high and deep, and the doubles serve, which is hit short and low. To a large degree, rules dictate this difference. The back court boundary is deeper in singles thus allowing more court to hit into. The high serve is not effective in doubles because the shuttle cannot be hit deeply enough due to the shorter boundary. The concept in the doubles serve is to force your opponent to hit up on the shuttle by keeping it short and low. On the singles serve, one hopes that a good high, deep serve will force the opponent to hit the shuttle shallow in the court so as to allow the server to be on the offensive. Some variance in these serves is advisable because if the same serve is hit every time, the receiver will know exactly what to expect.

Rules also dictate technique to a certain extent. As previously pointed out in this chapter, the shuttle must be hit below the waist level and the racket head must be below wrist level. For these reasons, the underhand motion is used.

A. The Singles Serve. When positioning oneself for the singles serve, the key is to be centrally located on the court. Therefore one should stand about halfway between the net and the back line and near the center service line. Remember that the server must be positioned in the proper service court.

The body should be sideways to the receiver's service court, with the feet about shoulder width apart. Using the forehand grip, the server assumes the service position with both hands chest to shoulder high (Figure 5-4). The wrist of the hitting arm should be cocked up as much as possible. The weight is on the back foot and the knees are slightly bent. It is important to be as relaxed as possible. When ready, drop the shuttle. A good drop should be at about a 45-degree angle to the net, i.e., not directly to the side and not directly at the net, but approximately halfway between. As soon as the shuttle is dropped, the hitting arm is brought down and forward, keeping the wrist cocked (Figure 5-5). At the last instant the wrist snaps and the forearm rotates upward and forward at point of contact (Figure 5-6). It is primarily this snap and rotation that allows the racket head to accelerate and gener-

FIGURE 5-4. The singles serve position.

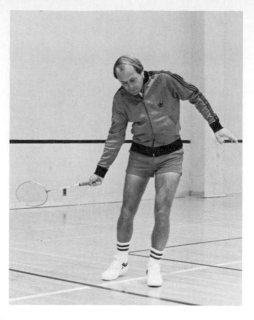

FIGURE 5-5. For the singles serve, after the shuttle is dropped, bring the racket downward and forward, keeping the wrist cocked.

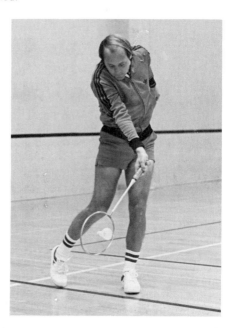

FIGURE 5-6. Notice the weight transfer and point of contact for the singles serve.

FIGURE 5-7. The follow-through position after a vigorous wrist snap and rotation of the forearm and body.

ate the power to send the shuttle high and deep. The hips and shoulders rotate to the net and the racket will finish across the body (Figure 5-7).

Through the stroke, the weight has shifted from the back to the front foot to help generate power. The lifting with the knees as the body extends upward through the stroke also helps to get the body weight into the shot.

The singles serve can be described as a basic underhand motion with a vigorous wrist snap and forearm rotation.

Learning Cues

1. Stand sideways to receiver's service court with feet shoulder width apart and weight primarily on the back foot.
2. Make sure the hitting wrist is cocked up as much as possible.
3. Drop the shuttle far enough away from the body to force the hitting arm to reach slightly for it.
4. Drop the shuttle before starting the swing.
5. Be as relaxed as possible and try to generate maximum racket head acceleration by snapping the wrist and rotating the forearm at point of contact.
6. The racket face will be open (tilted back) at point of contact to allow the upward trajectory. Too much height without depth indicates too much of

an open face. A low trajectory indicates that the racket face was too flat.

7. Follow through with your whole body. Transfer the weight to the front foot and lift up with the knees at point of contact.
8. Rotate the shoulders and hips at point of contact to help generate power and allow the racket to finish across the left shoulder.
9. Concentrate on watching the shuttle.

Practice Suggestions

Get as many shuttles as possible and hit the deep singles serve. This is one skill that can be worked on successfully without a partner.

The two keys to look for are height and depth. Hit the shuttle high enough to get it over the out-reached arm and racket of an average-size individual and hit it deeply enough to land near the back line. Few people can consistently achieve both of these goals when starting. Work to get the shuttle to the doubles service line first and then try to keep moving it deeper. Remember: a short or low serve will usually put you on the defensive.

If you have difficulty in achieving the desired trajectory, review the learning cues and look for the problem. More often than not the primary problem is related to lack of wrist snap and forearm rotation.

B. The Doubles Serve (Short and Low). Positioning for the doubles serve is approximately one or two feet behind the short or front service line and near the center service line. This is assuming server and partner are playing the up and back style of doubles. If playing side-by-side, then the server would move deeper and more to the center of the service court.

The stance is basically the same as for singles, except that the hands will be held somewhat lower and the wrist of the hitting arm not cocked as much. The reason for this is that the motion is much shorter. The idea is to hit the shuttle so it will stay low and drop just behind the front service line. Because little power is needed to achieve this, the wrist remains in the cocked position throughout the stroke. The racket face is only slightly open and there is very little follow-through. Minimum hip or shoulder rotation is utilized. The shuttle should reach its maximum height at the net and immediately start to drop.

Learning Cues

1. Hold the shuttle chest high and lower the hitting hand to waist high.
2. Keep the wrist cocked (do not snap it).
3. Point of contact should be just below the waist. (This is slightly higher than the singles serve.)
4. Primary movement is from the shoulders.
5. Think of guiding the shuttle, not hitting it.
6. Keep the shuttle as low and short as possible.

Practice Suggestions

With as many shuttles as possible, hit the doubles serve trying to keep the shuttle crossing the net by no more than one foot (preferably much less), and landing no further than six inches behind the short service line. Problems usually arise as a result of too much motion or making contact with the shuttle too low.

NOTE: The doubles serve may effectively be hit with either the forehand or backhand.

FIGURE 5-8. The doubles service position. Note that the wrist of the hitting arm is not cocked as it was for the singles serve.

FIGURE 5-9. Because the shuttle is hit short and low, the racket face is quite flat at the point of contact.

FIGURE 5-10. Note the short follow-through for the doubles serve.

II. Clears

There are two types of clears: overhand and underhand. These can be hit with either the forehand or backhand. The forehand is usually hit whenever possible because it is easier to generate power.

A. Forehand Underhand Clear. This is the same motion as the deep singles serve. This particular shot is hit out of necessity when the shuttle drops too low to use the overhead motion. Note: For Practice Suggestions, see Singles Serve.

B. Forehand Overhead Clear. The forehand overhead motion is similar to the basic throwing motion. In clearing the shuttle with this motion, it is important to get the racket back (with the arm bent) in the back-scratching position while moving to that location of the court where contact will be made (see Figure 5-11). The body should be sideways to the net and the shuttle overhead. It is difficult to clear a shuttle that is too far in front of the body.

The arm straightens from the elbow as the hitting hand reaches upward (Figure 5-12). The wrist remains cocked back as the arm straightens out. At point of contact the wrist snaps and the forearm rotates causing the racket head to accelerate and move very quickly (Figure 5-13). (This is the same general concept as discussed for the singles serve.) The shoulders and hips rotate to help bring the racket through (similar to the throwing motion). Follow through slightly across the body with the racket head pointing down (Figure 5-14).

To achieve the proper upward flight, the racket face must be facing slightly up at point of contact.

Learning Cues

1. Good preparation is a must. The racket should be taken back to the back-scratching position as one moves into position.
2. When the racket is taken back, it is important that the wrist be cocked up.
3. Turn sideways to the net.
4. Hit the shuttle, extending as high as possible with the racket face pointing slightly up.
5. Transfer weight forward, snap the wrist, and rotate the forearm at point of contact.

FIGURE 5-11. Preparing to hit the forehand overhead clear. Note position of the racket and the body.

FIGURE 5-12. It is important to contact the shuttle with an extended arm.

FIGURE 5-13. The quick wrist snap and forearm rotation cause the racket head to accelerate.

FIGURE 5-14. For the forehand overhand clear, note the position of the shoulders and racket on the follow-through.

FIGURE 5-15. To practice the clear: place bird, cork up, on racket, toss it high into the air, then hit it as it comes down.

6. Rotate the shoulders and hips as one would when throwing a ball.
7. Hit the shuttle hard. Pretend to be throwing the racket as far as possible.
8. Hit the shuttle high and deep.

Practice Suggestions

Standing near the back line of your court, place a shuttle (feathers down) on the forehand side of the racket. Push the shuttle up as high as possible, get the racket back, and clear the shuttle using the forehand overhead motion. As with the underhand clear, try to keep the shuttle higher than an opponent's outreached arm and racket, and try to place it near the back line.

With a partner, work on clearing the singles serve.

Lack of success is usually due to poor preparation, i.e., not turning sideways and letting the shuttle drop too low.

C. Backhand Underhand Clear. As with all backhand strokes, it is imperative to switch to the backhand grip previously described. From the ready position the body turns sideways to the net (right shoulder pointing to the net) as the racket is taken back. The racket head will point down as a result of having the wrist cocked down. The arm will bend as the racket is drawn back around the body. As the shuttle drops, the whole body lifts up as contact is made. The wrist snap, forearm rotation, and upper body rotation all help to generate power. The follow-through will be across the right side of the body with the palm of the hand facing up. This is a result of the forearm rotation and wrist snap. Point of contact should be further towards the net than on the forehand because the shuttle is struck with the front arm on the backhand and thus it is easier to reach in front. A great loss of power will result if the shuttle is back even with the body.

Learning Cues

1. Switch to the backhand grip while turning sideways.
2. Cock the wrist down, bend the arm and reach behind the back when preparing.

FIGURE 5-16. The ready position for the backhand underhand clear.

FIGURE 5-17. The backswing and body turn for the backhand underhand clear.

FIGURE 5-18. Point of contact on the backhand underhand clear. The body weight has transferred forward as the entire body lifts up into the stroke.

FIGURE 5-19. Note the forearm and shoulder rotation for the backhand underhand clear.

FIGURE 5-20. The end of the follow-through.

3. Extend the arm outward at point of contact and try to generate as much power as possible by snapping the wrist and rolling the forearm.
4. The shoulder rotation is critical. It will be impossible to generate any power without extensive use of the shoulders.
5. Reach in front of the body (towards the net) to make contact.

NOTE: See learning cues for all clears as there are similarities among them.

Practice Suggestions

Standing near the back line, lay the shuttle (feathers down) on the backhand side of the racket. Push the shuttle up, let it drop, and hit it with the backhand underhand motion, looking for the same results as with other clears previously discussed.

D. Backhand Overhead Clear. The concept of this shot is the same as that of the forehand overhead clear. As previously indicated, the success is usually not as great because, as a motion, it is not as natural. Again, whenever possible hit the forehand.

The preparation is the same as the underhand clear except that the racket and arm will be higher. As the arm extends upward to the point of contact, the same sources of power are utilized.

A final note concerning clears: As a general rule it is advantageous to clear often to your opponents' deep backhand corner of the court. This is an extremely difficult shot to return, especially at the beginning to intermediate level.

III. Smashes

The smash is the basic offensive shot in badminton. In order to smash the shuttle it obviously has to be above net level. For this reason the overhead motion is used on either the forehand or backhand side. As with clearing, it is usually easier to smash with the forehand.

Whether hitting the forehand or backhand, the motion is exactly the same as it is for the clears. The shuttle must be hit further in front in order to get the downward flight. By the same token the racket face must be angling down as compared to up for the clear (Figures 5-21 and 5-22).

The object of the smash is to hit down on the shuttle. In order to achieve this the shuttle has to be kept in front of the body. It is possible to clear a shuttle that is behind the body but it is impossible to smash. Therefore positioning and timing are crucial factors when smashing.

It is also necessary to extend upward at point of contact. The higher you reach the greater the angle becomes down to the court. This is also advantageous when clearing because complete extension will increase the motion.

Learning Cues

As far as preparation and motion are concerned the same learning cues apply to both the overhead clears and the smashes. These additional key points apply to smashes:

1. Get into position so contact can be made in front

FIGURE 5-21. For the clear, the racket face is pointing slightly up and point of contact can be slightly behind the body.

FIGURE 5-22. For the smash, racket face angle is down and point of contact is in front of the body. Note the difference with position for the clear.

of the body with the racket face angling down toward the court.
2. It is far easier to smash from the forecourt than backcourt because of the angle the shuttle must travel. Also the shuttle slows down rapidly and therefore may be easily returned when struck from deep in the court.
3. Sharp downward angle is just as important as sheer speed. The smash is a power stroke.

Practice Suggestions

Standing in midcourt, push the shuttle up as previously described. Working separately on the forehand and backhand, smash the shuttle down across the net trying to achieve both power and a sharp downward trajectory.

IV. Drop Shots and Blocks

In a drop shot the shuttle is hit in such a way that it softly drops over the net and lands shallow in the opponent's forecourt. A drop shot can be (and should be) hit using any of the previously described stroking motions—forehand or backhand, underhand or overhead. Other drop shots include blocks and net drops.

A. Overhead or Underhand Drops. To hit the drop off of an overhead or underhand motion it is important to execute the motion as if clearing, smashing, or driving the shuttle. Just as contact is made the racket head will slow instead of accelerating. If executed properly the shuttle will drop as it

reaches the net. The object is to make your opponent think you are going to clear or smash, and then let up and hit the drop shot. This shot depends to a great extent on finesse and deception. Because the timing is so difficult, most individuals must spend countless hours perfecting this shot.

Learning Cues

1. Preparation has to be the same as if one were going to clear or smash. Anything different will tip off the opponent that dropping is intended.
2. On the overhead motion the racket face should be flat or pointing slightly down.
3. On the underhand motion the racket face will be open similar to the position when clearing.
4. The racket head should move slowly at point of contact.
5. The shuttle should drop immediately after crossing the net.

Practice Suggestions

Use the same practice suggestions as for the clears and smashes. The object now, of course, is to keep the shuttle low and shallow. If the shuttle is hit too high, the opponent will have added time to react.

B. Net Drops. The net drop is hit from near the net when the shuttle is near or below net level. Usually it is in answer to a drop shot from one's opponent. Because of the closeness to the net, the shuttle must be hit almost directly up. A very short motion is used and it can be hit off of either the

FIGURE 5-23. Forehand net drop. The shuttle should be hit as close to net level as possible.

FIGURE 5-24. Backhand net drop. Because the shuttle has dropped below net level, it has to be hit almost directly up.

forehand or backhand (Figures 5-23 and 5-24). As with all drops the idea is to keep the shuttle low (as near net level as possible) and shallow in the court. This often is described as a "touch" shot.

Learning Cues

1. Contact the shuttle as near net level as possible. (Don't let it drop.)
2. Using a short stroke, guide the shuttle over the net.
3. Keep the shuttle low.

4. The racket face should be completely open (pointing up) at point of contact.

Practice Suggestions

Standing near the net, push the shuttle up in the air. Let it drop, then using the described technique, try to drop the shuttle over the net. Contact the shuttle at various heights using both the forehand and backhand. Keep the shuttle as low and shallow as possible.

C. Blocks. The block is hit in response to a

FIGURE 5-25. The forehand block—a reflex shot.

FIGURE 5-26. The backhand block. Place the racket in front of the shuttle as if trying to let it hit the racket.

smash or a drive. Many times it is a reflex movement. When the shuttle has been hit hard, one may only have time to block.

When blocking, one should try to get the racket in front of the shuttle as if trying to catch it on the strings. Similar to other drops, the object is to drop the shuttle over the net shallow in the opponent's court. This shot can be hit off of the forehand or backhand (Figures 5-25 and 5-26). Point of contact will be dictated by the line of flight of the shuttle, but usually it will be low.

Learning Cues

1. Do not try to take the racket back as there will not be sufficient time.
2. React as quickly as possible trying to get the racket head out in front of the shuttle.
3. Try to keep the shuttle low. Aim for just over the top of the net.
4. If the shuttle is smashed at the body, block it with the backhand.
5. Both forehand and backhand blocks will be hit with the forehand grip, because there won't be enough time to change grips.

Practice Suggestions

It is impossible to practice blocks without a partner. With a partner clear the shuttle and alternate smashing and blocking off of the smash.

PLAYING STRATEGY

Although there is no set sequence of shots that one can use to win a rally, there are definite situations that call for a specific shot, or demand that a specific shot not be used. Basically, shots made from below the net are *defensive* and those made from above the net are *offensive*. Also, there are certain principles concerning the use of the body that make for a more enjoyable game. The following suggestions will be helpful.

Singles

1. Serve long the majority of the time unless opponent is playing back for just such a shot, then serve short to take advantage of the poor position. Serve short often enough to prevent the opponent from consistently taking up a position near the back of the receiving court. A long serve puts the server and the receiver on an equal basis. It is difficult to make an accurate drop shot from the back court; it takes too much accuracy and power on the part of the waiting player to smash repeatedly from the back court; and it takes too much power to clear from the back court time after time. Thus, a receiver can rarely have an advantage on a well-executed long serve.
2. To receive in the right-hand court, stand on the

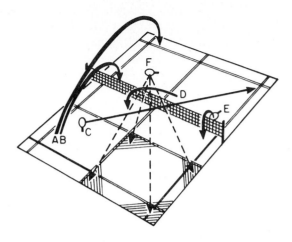

FIGURE 5-27. Lines of flight and placement of basic strokes: (A) high clear; (B) drop shot; (C) smash; (D) cross-court net flight; (E) hairpin net shot; (F) serves—shaded areas indicate desired areas for placement of service.

left side about midway back from the front service line, so that most serves can be received by the forehand. Likewise, when receiving in the left court, stand to the left, so that most serves can be received by the forehand.
3. Return a high serve with a drop or clear. Do not smash a high serve unless it is of insufficient length, or unless your opponent has a very weak smash defense and you have accurate smashing ability; even then, use it sparingly. Drop shots to your opponent's forehand and clears to the backhand are usually the most difficult to handle. Variation is essential in returns to prevent successful anticipation of your shot by your opponent.
4. The safest reply to a short low serve is a clear, although a net drop can be made if the bird is hit before it falls too low below the level of the net.
5. Do not return a net drop with another net drop unless you are sure of winning the rally, as the bird will probably be flicked quickly over your head to the back court without any possible chance to recover it.
6. After every shot, return to your base of operations located on the center line and from two to four feet behind the short service line. Do not make any shot that will not give you time to get back to this base; otherwise you will be out of position and unable to play the return shot properly, if at all.
7. Try not to be moving at the time your opponent makes the shot, or the bird will probably be played to the spot you vacated. On the other hand, if your opponent is moving to cover an open spot on the court when you make your shot, play the bird to the position being left. The most difficult maneuver on the court is that which requires a quick change of direction in your movement, for retracing your steps de-

mands the utmost agility and speed.

8. Other than shots played directly at your opponent, play the bird to a point within a foot of the restraining lines whether on the serve or during a rally.

9. When smashing, use cross-court shots or smash at your opponent's right hip or shoulder.

10. Return a smash with a drop shot to the point on the court farthest from the point at which the smash was made.

11. Build your game on a basis of alternately dropping and clearing, then use smashes and drives as openings occur. Run your opponent from front to rear and from side to side on alternate shots, unless the provisions of paragraph 7 apply.

12. Do not drive cross-court unless the shot is a sure winner. The safest drives are those made straight down the sidelines, passing your opponent.

13. Do not use net shots unless your opponent is clearly out of position and will be unable to reach the shuttle for a reply.

14. Take advantage of any weakness your opponent may have. Before playing to a weakness, disguise your intention by first playing to the other side of your opponent's body or to the farthest part of the court from the point of weakness.

15. Do not try fancy shots unless they are the only ones possible under the circumstances, and do not try deception through wrist action until you have thoroughly mastered the basic strokes.

16. At the beginning of a game or match, play your shots near the center of the court and then spread gradually to the boundary lines.

17. Watch the bird closely. Most players have a tendency to take their eyes off the shuttle just before or at the time it is hit. This action will result in a miss, a throw, or in a "bad" shot.

Doubles

Before considering the principles of doubles play, it is necessary to understand the various formations used. This is important as it is the first decision that must be made by a doubles team in any game. In fact, the choice of formation and agreement on how the court is to be covered must be made even before the first service is made. Without this agreement, partners will be running into each other in some cases, and at other times the bird will hit the floor with neither partner having made an attempt to return it. There are any number of formations, only three of which will be discussed here: the side-by-side, the front and back, and a combination of the two.

Side-by-side Formation. In this formation, each partner is responsible for his or her half of the playing court. The base of operations for each player

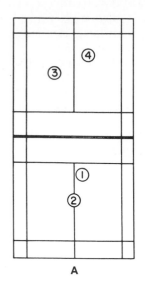
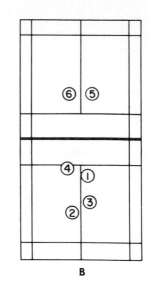

FIGURE 5-28. Recommended serving and receiving positions in doubles. **A**—In men's or women's doubles: (1) server; (2) server's partner; (3) receiver; (4) receiver's partner. **B**—In mixed doubles using forward and back system: (1) server's position if a woman; (2) her partner's position (man); (3) server's position if a man; (4) his partner's position (woman); (5 or 6) woman's position when her partner is receiving.

is midway between the center line and the side boundary line of the player's half court, and approximately 4 feet behind the service line. The main disadvantage of this formation is that it is more difficult to cover 22 feet from net to rear boundary line than it is to cover 20 feet from side to side. This fact is easily understood when it is realized that standing still, a player can reach out 7 feet. By reaching 7 feet to each side, the court can be covered laterally by moving only 3 or 4 feet to the right or left from the center of the court. On the other hand, it is necessary to move 3 feet forward and 12 feet backward from the base of operations in covering the 22 feet from net to rear boundary. Only one reach of 7 feet can be used due to the fact that you cannot reach backward very far to make a shot.

Another disadvantage of this formation is that it is almost impossible to determine who is going to hit those shots played down the center line, despite the accepted rule that the player to the left should take these shots because they are on the forehand side.

Still another drawback of this formation is that few players of average ability can move from the net to the rear court and still smash—often meaning a possible loss of attack.

Front and Back Formation. In this formation, one member of the team plays the front portion of the court, with a base of operation on the center line and just in back of the short service line; the partner plays the rear portion of the court from a base on the center line and just in front of the doubles rear service line. The front player is responsible for all drop shots and any other shots that can be intercepted and returned with an equal or better shot than the partner; the back player takes all shots that the net player cannot comfortably return while standing on the short service line. This system is usually used for mixed doubles with the woman playing near the net while the man covers the back court.

Although the front and back formation facilitates greater attacking power, it definitely has certain disadvantages. One of the most important is that it affords poor defense against smashes and drives down the sidelines. This formation also puts a premium on a very low, accurate short serve, because any bird over a few inches above the net will be pushed back straight at the server, or quickly put out of reach of both players.

Combination Formation. The combination system, sometimes called the "in and out" system, combines the best of the other two systems, using the side-by-side position for defense, and the front and back formation for attack. The basic principles to be followed in the combination system are as follows:

1. When the receivers start in the front and back formation, the server's initial formation is determined by the server's ability to make a good short serve. If the server is an accomplished server, the team should start in front and back formation; otherwise they should use the safer side-by-side formation.
2. On a long, high serve, the serving team should play side-by-side and the receiver, going back for the serve, should play the back court, while the receiver's partner should move forward to play the front court as the receiver goes back.
3. On any high shot that gives the opponents the advantage and opportunity to smash, the team making the stroke should take up the defensive side-by-side formation. The player making the shot should cover the half of the court from which the shot was made.
4. The first opportunity should be taken to revert to the front and back formation, going clockwise or counterclockwise in the direction taken in playing the shot. Any shot returned, other than the clear, affords this opportunity. Which partner covers what part of the court on the return is determined by who plays the return shot from what spot on the court. If the return stroke is made near the net and on the right side of the court, the partner playing the right half of the court would naturally make the shot. Since that individual must move forward to make the shot, he or she would then play the front position, while the partner would fade back and play the back court. If the right half-court guardian drifts back to play a return from the back court, he or

she should remain in the back position, and the partner should move up and play the front court.

Doubles Tactics. Regardless of the system of teamwork selected, the following tactics and strategies will make for better play:

1. Always play for your partner. Make shots that will be returned so as to leave an opening for your partner's best shot, which could possibly finish the rally. Never play a shot that leaves your partner open to blistering smashes, or to returns that will take a great deal of scrambling to retrieve.
2. Always make an attacking shot unless any other return would leave you, your partner, or both out of position for the return. This implies that all shots should be hit down, thus preventing your opponents from doing the same. Your partner should move forward on all smashes (and drops from the back court) to protect against returned drop shots and cross-court drives.
3. Make most serves short and low, preferably to the off-hand corners. Use a high service only when your opponent is consistently rushing the serve, and then play the bird so it is just out of reach, giving little time to run back and get under it. When a lob serve is used, the best spot is to the receiver's backhand. The drive serve should be used sparingly and then to the corner formed by the center line and rear doubles service line.
4. Rush short serves by standing close to the service line with the left foot forward. As soon as the bird is served, step forward with the right foot, turn the racket so the face is parallel with the net, and push the right arm forward, hitting the bird while it is still above the level of the net. Hit it down. Little backswing is needed.
5. Usually smash a long serve, but occasionally play a drop shot for variation.
6. Do not play too close to the net, but rather take up a position around the short service line when playing net.
7. If the servers are playing a front and back formation, the best return of a low service is a half-court shot down the side boundary line. A drive clear to the backhand corner of the court is probably the best return against a team using the side-by-side system.
8. Avoid quick, flat shots and sharply angled shots unless opponents cannot intercept the bird and return it before you can recover.
9. Have the left-court player in the side-by-side system play the shots down the center of the court (assuming that person is right-handed).
10. Make placements to the least obvious spots.
11. Keep your racket up in front of your body, and your weight on the balls of your feet.

PLAYING COURTESIES

Like tennis, badminton emphasizes sportsmanship and playing courtesies. Use good judgment at all times with regard to your own behavior as well as your attitude toward your opponent. Be cordial and respectful. As in any sport, be a good loser as well as a gracious winner. Try to maintain a positive rather than negative attitude. This will make the game more enjoyable for all participants. Some courtesies specific to badminton are:

1. If in doubt about the bird's landing, always call it in favor of the opponent.
2. If there is any question of your fouling at the net, be sure to call it on yourself.
3. If there is any question about your throwing a bird, be quick to call it a throw.
4. Do not question the call of your opponent.
5. Do not smash at your opponent if the point could be easily won by placing the shuttle elsewhere. Although it is often good strategy to hit at your opponent, this should be avoided on a "set-up."
6. Never under any circumstances should the racket be thrown in anger. This is not only poor sportsmanship but dangerous, because the racket could hit and injure someone.

TERMINOLOGY

Alley The 1½ foot wide extension on both sides of the court used in doubles play.

Backhand Any stroke made on the side of the body opposite the racket side.

Bird Another name for the shuttlecock.

Block A stroke whereby the racket is placed in front of the shuttle almost as if trying to catch it. Very little motion is used.

Carry An illegal shot where the shuttle does not rebound immediately off the racket at point of contact.

Clear A high shot (or lob) which falls close to the back line.

Cross-court A shot in which the bird crosses the net in a diagonal direction.

Double hit An illegal shot wherein the shuttle is hit twice in succession on the same stroke.

Drive A hard-driven stroke which just clears the net and does not rise high enough for an opponent to smash.

Drive serve The flight of a serve similar to a drive. Used mostly in doubles from the right court to a right-handed player.

Drop A shot which barely clears the net and immediately drops sharply.

Fault Any infraction of the rules, either on the serve or after the shuttle has been put in play, the penalty for which is loss of serve or point.

Foot fault Illegal position or movement of the feet by either the server or receiver.

Forehand Any stroke made on the racket side of the body.

Game point The point which, if won, allows the server to win the game.

Hairpin net shot A shot hit near the net after the shuttle has dropped quite low. The shuttle will rise almost straight up, barely clearing the net, and drop sharply.

Handout Term used in doubles to show that one player has lost service.

Inning The time during which a player or team holds service.

Let The stopping of play due to some type of outside interference. The point is replayed.

Love The term used to indicate zero in scoring.

Match point The point which, if won by the server, makes that person the winner of the match.

Overhead A motion used to strike the shuttle when it is above the head.

Rally An exchange of shots either in practice or during a match.

Receiver The player to whom the shuttle is served.

Round-the-head stroke An overhead stroke used to hit the shuttle on the off-hand side of the body.

Server The player who puts the bird into play.

Setting Choosing how many more points to play when certain tie scores are reached.

Short serve A serve that scarcely clears the net and lands barely inside the opponents' front service line. This serve is used primarily in doubles.

Shuttlecock (or **Shuttle**) The feathered, plastic, or nylon "bird" which is batted back and forth in badminton.

Side-out When the individual (in singles) or team (in doubles) loses serve and becomes the receiver.

Smash The hard overhead stroke hit downward with great velocity and angle. It is the principle attacking stroke in badminton.

Throw An illegal shot in which the shuttle is carried or thrown by the racket.

Underhand A stroke that is hit upward when the shuttle has fallen below shoulder level.

Unsight Illegal position taken by the server's partner so the receiver cannot see the shuttle as it is hit.

SELECTED REFERENCES

American Alliance for Health, Physical Education, Recreation, and Dance; National Association for Girls and Womens Sports. *Badminton—Squash—Racquetball Guide.* Washington, D.C.: AAHPERD, 1980.

ANNARINO, ANTHONY. *Individualized Instructional Program in Badminton.* Englewood Cliffs, N.J.: Prentice-Hall, Inc., 1973.

ARMBRUSTER, DAVID A., FRANK F. MUSKER, and DALE MOOD. *Sports and Recreational Activities for Men and Women* (7th ed.). St. Louis: C.V. Mosby Co., 1979.

Badminton U.S.A. (monthly magazine), 333 Saratoga Rd., Buffalo, N.Y. 14226.

DAVIDSON, KENNETH R., and L.R. GUSTAVSON. *Winning Badminton* (rev. ed.). New York: Ronald Press Company, 1964.

DAVIS, PAT. *Badminton Complete.* New York: A.S. Barnes and Co., Inc., 1967.

JOHNSON, M.L. *Badminton.* Philadelphia, Pa.: W.B. Saunders Co., 1974.

PELTON, BARRY C. *Badminton.* Englewood Cliffs, N.J.: Prentice-Hall, Inc., 1971.

POOLE, JAMES. *Badminton* (2nd ed.). Pacific Palisades, Calif.: Goodyear Publishing Co., 1969.

ROGERS, WYNN. *Advanced Badminton.* Dubuque, Iowa: Wm. C. Brown Co., 1970.

VARNER, MARGARET. *Badminton* (2nd ed.). Dubuque, Iowa: Wm. C. Brown Co., Publishers, 1971.

Audio-Visual Materials

All American Productions, P.O. Box 801, Riverside, Calif. 92502. *Badminton* (16 mm film).

Ideal Pictures, 417 N. State St., Chicago, Ill. 60610. *Badminton.*

Athletic Institute, 805 Merchandise Mart, Chicago, Ill. 60654. *Beginning Badminton Series.*

BASKETBALL

THIS CHAPTER WILL ENABLE YOU TO:

♦ Know the playing court, equipment, and rules of basketball.
♦ Practice and develop skill in the fundamentals of passing, dribbling, shooting, rebounding, individual offense, and individual defense.
♦ Identify the objectives and strategies of team offense and team defense.
♦ Identify and describe coeducational modifications pertinent to the game of basketball.

NATURE AND PURPOSE

Basketball is an extremely popular game, played in all parts of the world and at every conceivable level. In America, the extremes are very evident—from rickety backboards attached to outdoor garages to multi-million dollar arenas that hold thousands of spectators. Basketball can be played at a highly organized level or very spontaneously at a neighborhood playground. Children can play on school teams beginning with elementary school, continuing through college. Highly skilled men and women can earn basketball scholarships to play for colleges and universities. There are amateur tournaments and professional leagues for both men and women. The United States has a men's and women's Olympic Basketball Team. Recreationally, basketball is played in the YMCA, YWCA, Boys Club, church leagues, and community centers. It is a vital part of school intramural programs, oftentimes being played coeducationally. Basketball presents the opportunity to teach skills, coordination, agility, speed, and body control. Participation in the game can contribute toward maintenance of total fitness of the individual. For these reasons, basketball is an attractive physical education class activity.

This sport, which originated in America, has very broad applications: large groups can participate at relatively low cost; the game can serve for competitive as well as recreational purposes; and it has the necessary appeal to make it a popular spectator sport.

FACILITIES AND EQUIPMENT

The Court. The playing area of basketball is called the court. The dimensions of the rectangular court measure a maximum of 94 feet long and 50 feet wide, or a minimum of 74 feet long and 42 feet wide.

The baskets are suspended 10 feet above the floor at the endline of each court. The backboards, to which the baskets are attached, are either fan-shaped or rectangular, and are made of glass or wood. The court has three restraining circles and two free-throw areas (Figure 6-1). The court can be modified (made smaller) and the baskets lowered to accommodate younger participants. Basketball can be played on half of a court if large numbers of participants want to play in an intramural, class, or recreational situation.

The Ball. The official ball is round with a circumference of 29½ to 30¼ inches. In competition, a ball of high-grade leather is used. Less expensive balls are made of rubber or synthetic materials. Smaller balls are available for younger participants.

THE GAME

Each team is composed of five players. Two or sometimes three officials regulate the game. The purpose of the game is to score a larger total number of points than the opponent. The score is compiled by shooting the ball through the basket either from the field (called a field goal) or from the free-throw line (called a free-throw or a foul shot). The ball is passed, thrown, bounced, batted, or rolled from one player to another. A player in possession of the ball must maintain contact with the floor with one foot (called the pivot foot), unless the player is shooting, passing, or dribbling. Dribbling consists of a series of one-hand taps, causing the ball to bounce on the floor. Physical contact with an opponent can result in a foul if the contact impedes the desired movement of the player.

The game is divided into 20-minute halves for college and university teams, and 8-minute quarters for high school teams. Teams composed of players younger than high school age should have 6-minute quarters. The length of the game in a recreational, class, or intramural situation can be adjusted by shortening the quarters or halves, or by having "running time," wherein the clock does not stop on the dead balls.

There are slight variations of rules between high school and collegiate play, as well as between the men's and women's collegiate game. Nevertheless, there are basic rules of basketball governing play at any level.

BASIC RULES

Players

1. Even though only five players play at a time, any number of substitutions can be made at any time during the game. Substitutes must report to the scorer and wait to be beckoned onto the court by an official.
2. One of the five players is the captain and may address the official on matters of interpretation or information. Any player may request a timeout.

Scoring and Timing

1. Field goal = 2 points
   Free-throw = 1 point
   The ball must enter the basket from above.
2. Timeouts are restricted to a total of five. One additional timeout may be granted each team for each extra period of the game. A timeout lasts one minute and can only be requested during a dead ball or anytime by the team in possession of the ball.
3. If the score is tied at the end of regulation time, play continues an extra period. As many extra periods are played as are necessary to break the tie.

4. Time stops each time an official blows the whistle indicating a dead ball (violation, foul, jump ball, out of bounds).

Play

1. Putting the ball into play at the start of the game and at the start of each succeeding quarter or half or extra period is by a jump ball in the center circle between two opponents. After each goal, the ball is put into play by the team that did not score from the out-of-bounds area at the end of the court at which the basket has been scored.
2. A player is out of bounds when touching the floor on or outside the boundary line.
3. The ball is out of bounds when it touches a player who is out of bounds or any other person, the floor, or any object on or outside a boundary, or the supports or back of the backboard.
4. The ball is caused to go out of bounds by the last player touching it before it goes out. The ball would be awarded out of bounds for a throw-in by the opposing team. The ball is awarded out of bounds after a violation, successful free-throw or field goal, or a common foul until the bonus rule goes into effect.
5. While the ball is alive, an offensive player cannot remain for more than three seconds in that part of the free-throw lane between the endline, the free-throw line, and the free-throw lane lines.
6. If two opponents are both firmly holding the ball, or an offensive ball handler is closely guarded by the defense for five seconds, a jump ball is called.
7. Violations include causing the ball to go out of bounds, double dribbling, running with the ball, kicking the ball (positive act), striking the ball with the fist, interfering with the basket, illegal throw-in (taking more than five seconds or stepping on the line), and the three-second lane rule.
8. Fouls are classified as: (a) *personal*—involving

FIGURE 6-1. The basketball court.

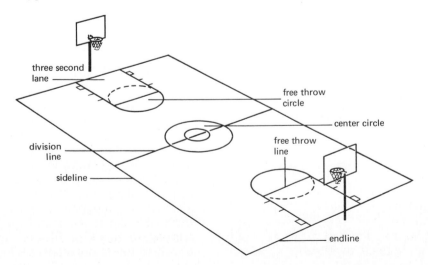

pushing, charging, tripping, holding, body contact; or (b) *technical*—involving delay of game, unsportsmanlike conduct, illegal entry, excessive timeouts. For personal fouls, the offender is charged with one foul; a fifth personal foul results in disqualification. The offended player is awarded:

a. one free-throw if the foul occurred during a field goal attempt and the basket was made.
b. two free-throws if the foul occurred during a field goal attempt and the basket was missed.
c. no free-throw, but the ball is awarded to the offended player's team out of bounds if it was before the fifth common team foul of the half (in a game played in quarters) or before the seventh common team foul of the half (in a game played in halves).
d. one free-throw plus a bonus free-throw if the first one is made, when the fifth common foul or seventh common foul (see above) has occurred. This is called the bonus rule.

For technical fouls, the offended team is awarded a free-throw as well as the ball out of bounds.

MODIFICATIONS FOR COEDUCATIONAL PLAY

1. Teams can consist of 2 males and 3 females or 3 males and 2 females. Only a male can substitute for a male; only a female can substitute for a female.
2. Adjust the point value of field goals and free throws as follows:

    field goal by a male = 2 pts.
    field goal by a female = 4 pts.
    free-throw by a male = 1 pt.
    free-throw by a female = 2 pts.

3. Males are assigned to guard males; females are assigned to guard females. *At no time* can a male guard a female.
4. Do not allow males in the area of the free-throw lane from the free-throw line to the baseline *at any time* on either end of the court. Suggested penalties for violation of #3 or #4:

    Offensive violation: out of bounds for opponent
    Defensive violation: award a field goal (2 pts.) to the offense

SUGGESTED LEARNING SEQUENCE— BEGINNERS

1. Conditioning
2. Basic game concepts
3. Basic rules
4. Fundamental skills:
    a. pivoting
    b. catching and holding the ball
    c. passing—chest, bounce, overhead
    d. dribbling—high, low
    e. shooting—set, layup
    f. rebounding—jumping
5. Individual Offense:
    a. cutting—V-cut, front
    b. driving
6. Individual Defense:
    a. basic stance and movement
    b. guarding a player with the ball
    c. guarding a player without the ball
7. Team Play:
    a. *Offense*—basic concepts on how to attack a player-to-player defense
    b. *Defense*—player-to-player
    c. *Other*—jump ball alignment, free-throw alignment

SUGGESTED LEARNING SEQUENCE— INTERMEDIATES

1. Conditioning
2. Additional rules
3. Review beginners unit
4. Intermediate skills:
    a. passing—one-hand bounce, baseball
    b. dribbling—cross-over
    c. shooting—free throw, jump shot, layup from various angles
    d. rebounding—blocking out, outlet
5. Individual Offense:
    a. cutting—backdoor (reverse)
    b. fakes and feints
6. Individual Defense:
    a. defense against a player one pass away and two passes away
    b. denial defense
    c. defense against a ball handler
7. Team Play:
    a. *Offense*—basic concepts on how to attack a zone defense
    b. *Defense*—combatting picks and screens zones
    c. *Other*—fast break in-bounds plays

SKILLS AND TECHNIQUES

Pivoting. Pivoting is the only legal maneuvering a player standing and holding the ball is allowed. One foot (the pivot foot) must be kept at its point of contact with the floor, while the other foot can step in any direction. A good technique for the beginner is to imagine that a spike has been driven through the pivot foot into the floor; this would afford faking movements with the opposite foot, but the spike can be removed only through dribbling, passing, or shooting. Illegally moving the pivot foot or taking too many steps while stopping constitutes "traveling." The result is a loss of possession of the ball for that team.

Passing

Good passing is necessary in order to maintain possession of the ball and be able to move into scoring position. The key to an effective offense is accuracy in passing. Passing is the quickest way to move the ball, thus allowing the offense to catch the defense off balance or out of position.

Chest Pass. This pass is probably the most commonly used pass. The ball is held in both hands, the fingers spread on the sides of the ball with the thumbs behind the ball. The ball is held about chest high with the elbows held comfortably at the sides of the body. The ball is released by extending the arms fully, snapping the wrists, and stepping in the direction of the pass. The palms should be facing downward or slightly outward with the elbow chest high on the follow-through. The chest pass should be received chest high.

Bounce Pass. This pass is a short distance pass used to avoid a deflection or interception when a player is being closely guarded. It is executed in the same manner as the chest pass except the ball is bounced into the hands of the receiver. The ball should bounce at approximately two-thirds of the distance between the passer and receiver, and should rebound waist high. This pass can also be released with one hand by stepping out to either side of a close defender and bouncing the ball around him. It is also possible to make this pass directly off of the dribble.

Overhead Pass. This pass is used to pass over a defensive player, usually to a post player or a cutter. The ball is held overhead with both hands, thumbs under the ball and fingers spread on the sides of the ball. The passer steps forward toward the intended receiver and transfers the body weight to the front foot. The arms, which are slightly bent, are brought forward sharply, with a snap of the wrists releasing the ball. This pass is best utilized by a player who is taller than the defending opponent.

One-Hand Overhead Pass (Baseball Pass). This pass is used most frequently to cover long distances, especially in initiating the fastbreak. When this pass is thrown with the right hand, the ball is brought back to the right ear, close to the head, with the fingers well spread in back of the ball. The left hand can steady the ball when it is in this position, ready to be thrown. The weight of the body is shifted to the right rear foot as the ball is brought back. The weight shifts forward to the left foot as the right arm is brought forward to release the ball. The ball is released about one foot in front of the body with the wrist snapping forward and downward.

Learning Cues

1. Passes should be crisp.
2. Always fake before each pass.
3. Take a step in the direction of the pass.
4. Weight should be balanced when passing.
5. Do not "telegraph" the pass; be deceptive with your eyes.
6. Aim to hit your receiver between the waist and shoulders.

FIGURE 6-2. The overhead pass.

7. Put as little spin as possible on the pass.
8. Pass to the side of your teammate away from the defender.
9. Always lead a running teammate.
10. Learn to catch and pass in one motion.

Catching and Holding the Ball

Possession of the ball is so important that receiving and holding the ball are as essential as passing. A player should attempt to catch every pass regardless of how it is thrown. To help eliminate deflections, a player should cut toward each pass to meet it. The hands should be held out in front of the body to provide a target and to maintain balance when moving in any direction to meet the ball. It is also possible to hold one hand up in the air (the hand furthest from your defender) to provide a high target for a pass. The ball should be caught with the pads of the fingers and brought toward the body to protect it before dribbling, passing, or shooting. If a player must stand for a few moments in possession of the ball, it is best to step back slightly with your free foot, away from your defender, pulling the ball back with you. This places your body between the ball and the defender for added protection.

Learning Cues

1. Provide the passer with a target by holding a hand up or both hands forward.
2. Move to meet passes thrown to you.
3. Hands should be comfortably spread and relaxed when catching.
4. Keep elbows flexed, not stiff.
5. Watch the ball all of the way into your hands.
6. Hold the ball close to the body for protection.

Practice Suggestions for Passing and Catching

1. Stand approximately 8 feet from a wall. Execute different passes against the wall, concentrating on form and accuracy.
2. With a partner, stand in positions as either two guards, or as a guard and a forward. Pass back and forth, faking before each pass and practicing deception. Add two defenders. Add a cut to the basket after each pass to receive a return pass. (The cut could also be toward the passer in order to receive an underhand pass.)
3. To practice the baseball pass, stand 30 feet from a partner. Pass back and forth. To practice this pass on the move, both players position themselves near the backboard. One player rebounds the ball off the board, dribbles toward the sideline, and releases a baseball pass to the other player cutting downcourt. Add defenders.
4. Three-player weave: Three players start on the endline approximately 15 feet apart. The player in the middle has a ball. He passes to a wing and subsequently cuts behind him. This receiver, in turn, passes to the third player and cuts behind him. The three players continue passing and moving downcourt. Vary the passes. Add one, two, or three defenders.

KEY TO MANEUVERS

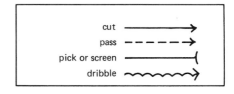

FIGURE 6-3. Preparing to catch a pass against a defender.

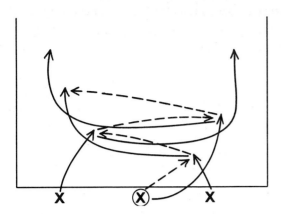

FIGURE 6-4. Three-player weave.

5. Variation: Five-player weave.

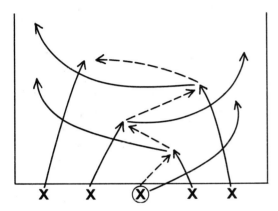

FIGURE 6-5. Five-player weave.

6. Four corner passing: With players in a box formation, one player makes a long pass to the first player in the next line. She follows her pass and receives a shorter pass back. She hands off to the same player and goes to the end of that line. Continue with a long pass to the next corner. *Variation:* Add another ball. Start them in opposite corners.

FIGURE 6-6. Four-corner passing.

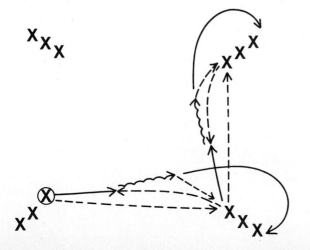

7. Shotgun passing: One player stands apart from a half-circle of teammates who are arranged so that two players are just in the peripheral vision of the single player. Using two balls, the half-circle players and the single player pass very quickly back and forth.

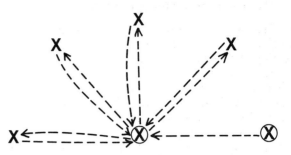

FIGURE 6-7. Shotgun passing.

8. Reaction pass drill: One partner has a ball, while the other player stands approximately 15 feet away with his back turned to the ball. The player with the ball calls out the other player's first name, followed by a pass to the player. Upon hearing his name, the player quickly turns and attempts to catch the ball and gain control of it. The pass should vary, making the receiver jump, reach, stoop, etc. to secure every pass.

9. Monkey in the middle: Players form a circle with one player ("monkey") in the middle. Using one ball and any type of pass, a player in the circle attempts to get the ball to any other player in the circle, other than the two players immediately adjacent to her. The "monkey" attempts to touch, deflect, or intercept the pass, at which time she changes place with the passer.

10. Shuttle pass drill: Form two lines in a shuttle formation. The first player in one of the lines has a ball. The first person in the opposite line defends as the player attempts to pass across to the other line. Continue passing between the two lines with the passer each time becoming the next defender.

Dribbling

Dribbling is slower than passing as a means of moving the ball. Therefore it should not be overused. The dribble should be used only to: (1) penetrate or drive for the basket; (2) create a better passing lane; (3) get out of a crowd; and (4) bring the ball down the court. A good rule to remember is never to dribble the ball when a pass can be completed successfully.

With the hand cupped, the pads of the fingers control the direction of the ball, while the wrist and finger flexion provide the force. The ball should be pushed downward and slightly forward, with the body in a crouched position. The opposite arm and forward foot should provide protection between the ball and the opponent. There are basically two types of dribbles that are identifiable by observing the rebounding height of the ball and the proximity of the defender. These are the high-speed dribble and the low-control dribble.

High-Speed Dribble. The high-speed dribble is used when a player is unguarded and moving quickly—leading a fastbreak, driving to the basket, bringing the ball down the court without opposition. The body is erect with only a slight forward crouch. The ball rebounds between the waist and chest. The dribbling arm pushes the ball forward and slightly to the side of the body. A full running stride is used, limited only by the dribbler's ability to control the ball.

Low-Control Dribble. This dribble is used when a player is closely guarded or in a congested area. Both the body and the ball should be kept low. The ball should rebound knee high and close to the dribbling side of the body. The more frequent contact with the ball allows for control and change of direction when under pressure.

FIGURE 6-8. Low-control dribble. (From David H. Strack, *Basketball.* Prentice-Hall, Inc., Englewood Cliffs, N.J., 1968.)

Crossover Dribble. In order to change directions, the crossover dribble can be used. It is effective only if the defender is guarding loosely. The dribbler simply pushes the ball to the floor so that it rebounds across in front of the body to the opposite hand. This must be done very quickly and with only one bounce in order to avoid an interception. The shoulder opposite the dribbling hand should always

be lowered to protect the ball. The dribbler can now continue dribbling in the opposite direction.

Learning Cues

1. Keep your eyes and head up.
2. Be able to dribble with either hand.
3. Protect the ball with your body and opposite arm.
4. Control the dribble with your fingers and wrist; not the palm.
5. Keep your knees bent for balance.
6. Dribble with the right hand when dribbling to the right, and dribble with the left hand when dribbling to the left, *especially* when being guarded.

Practice Suggestions for Dribbling and Ball Handling

(Work to keep your head up during all dribbling and ball handling drills.)

1. Rotate the ball around the body, starting with the head. Go all the way down around the legs, and back up.
2. Rotate the ball around each ankle—right and left. Rotate the ball in a figure 8 around the ankles in a continuous motion.
3. Dribble the ball around the legs in a figure 8. Keep the ball low.
4. Straddle flip: With the legs shoulder width apart, hold the ball low in front with both hands. Flip it up slightly between your legs, bringing your hands around behind the legs to catch the ball before it hits the ground. Flip it up again and bring the hands back to the front. Repeat as quickly as you can. *Variation:* Start with the hands alternately on the ball—one in front and one in back. Flip the ball up, alternating the hands quickly.
5. Dribble the ball around your body while on one knee, both knees, sitting, lying.
6. Standing 2 feet from a wall, tap a ball with the right or left hand high against the wall. *Variation:* Tap two balls simultaneously.
7. Circle keepaway: Within the boundaries of a restraining circle, try to dribble and maintain possession of a ball while another player attempts to steal it. *Variation:* Both players have a ball, trying to dribble *and* steal the other player's ball.
8. On a half court, try to dribble and maintain possession of a ball while two or three players try to pursue and steal the ball.
9. Dribble tag: On a half court, with all players dribbling a ball, play "tag." *Variations:* (a) More than one player is "it." (b) Restrict all players to use their nondominant hand.
10. Column dribbling drills (players at the endline in three columns): Dribble the full length of the court:
    a. In a zigzag pattern, executing a crossover dribble or a reverse dribble at each corner.

b. Doing a crossover, reverse, or stop on the coach's signal.
c. Going around obstacles.
d. Against defenders trying to steal the ball.

Shooting

The primary objective of the game of basketball is to score goals. Therefore all players should be able to shoot. Being able to shoot a variety of shots from varying distances increases the effectiveness of any player.

Point of Aim. There are two targets that can be used in aiming at a basket—the rim, or a spot on the backboard for a bank shot. The easiest point of aim for a beginner is the rim of the basket, due to its permanent position from anywhere on the floor. The player should concentrate on dropping the ball just beyond the front of the rim. The bank shot is typically used when a player is positioned at a 24–45-degree angle from the basket. A spot on the backboard is sighted with the purpose of allowing the ball to hit this spot and rebound into the basket. Selecting the correct spot and judging the force to put on the ball makes this a skill for experienced players. A square box is painted on most backboards to aid in spot selection. In aiming, the brain sights the target, computes the distance, and determines the correct trajectory to put on the ball. It is important for the eyes to be focused on the target before each shot, during the release, and after the follow-through. It is obvious why shooting demands so much practice.

One-Handed Set Shot. This shot is used for most long shots. The feet should be positioned in a forward-backward stride position with the foot under the shooting hand slightly forward. The ankles, knees, and hips should be slightly flexed. Weight is easily balanced over the feet, and the shoulders are square to the basket. The ball is held below the chin (sighting the basket over the ball), or above the forehead (sighting the basket below the ball). It might be noted that the higher the ball is held, the less chance the defense has of blocking the shot. The ball should be held with the fingers, never in the palms of the hands. The shooting hand is behind and slightly under the ball with the fingers spread and wrist cocked (hyper-extended). The non-shooting or guide hand is placed on the side and slightly under the ball with fingers spread. In executing the shot, the legs extend upward while the shooting arm extends toward the basket. The wrist flexes forward, while the guide hand comes off of the ball. The wrist flexion releases the ball, with the fingertips coming off last, creating a slight backspin on the ball. A proper follow-through should have the guide hand held high, with the palm of the shooting hand facing the floor. The one-handed set shot is also used by most players when shooting free-throws.

FIGURE 6-9. One-handed set shot.

Jump Shot. The jump shot is a very effective offensive weapon, due to its high point of release. The initial body position and the placement of the hands on the ball are the same as in the one-handed set shot. The shooter jumps into the air by pushing off with both legs. The ball is brought high above the forehead. At the apex of the jump, the body should be in a near-stationary, balanced position. Keeping the eyes focused on the basket, the shooting

FIGURE 6-10. Jump shot. (From Strack, *Basketball.*)

2. Eyes should be focused on the target before, during, and after the shot.
3. Fingertips should control every shot.
4. Use the backboard to bank a shot from an angle.
5. Maintain body balance; try not to lean or fall.
6. The shooting hand should follow through toward the basket.
7. Backspin on the ball is desirable.
8. Generally, a higher arc on the ball results in greater accuracy.

Practice Suggestions for Shooting

1. Add shooting to various passing and dribbling drills.
2. Column shooting drills (two lines of players facing the basket):
   a. one line shoots lay-ups; the other line rebounds. Vary the angles for the lay-ups. Add defensive pressure from the rebounding line.
   b. same as above, only use jump shots or set shots.
3. Around the world shooting: One player shoots, moving to a new spot after each shot, while another player rebounds and quickly passes to the shooter. *Variations:* (a) The passer-rebounder applies defensive pressure on each shot. (b) Have two rebounders and two balls, so the shooter must move and shoot quicker.
4. Shuffle and shoot: Using two balls, a player shuffles between two spots, picking up the ball at each spot and shooting. Two rebounders work at rebounding the balls and replacing them at each spot.

arm is uncocked and releases the ball with the same action as the one-handed set shot. The player should land in a balanced position. Since the force for the jump shot is supplied primarily by the arms and wrist, the range of this shot is limited, as compared to the set shot which incorporates leg power as well as arm strength.

Lay-Up. This shot is one of the highest percentage shots in the game, due to its closeness of range. It is used when a player has received a pass close to the basket, or has driven past the defense near the goal. It is best executed on a diagonal in relation to the basket, using the backboard to bank the ball in. At the last dribble the ball is firmly grasped with the fingers of both hands, and carried above the head. When shooting with the right hand, the take-off should occur with the left foot, while the right knee thrusts upward to achieve maximum height. At the same moment, the ball is set in the shooting hand and the left hand falls away. The shooting arm and fingers extend upward to "lay" the ball against the backboard. A proficient basketball player will develop the ability to shoot a lay-up with either hand being the dominant hand—the left hand when on the left side of the basket, the right hand when on the right side.

Learning Cues

1. Knees should bend to help generate power and provide balance.

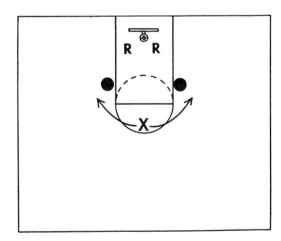

FIGURE 6-11. Shuffle and shoot.

5. One-on-one: A player passes the ball to a player being guarded. The receiver practices various shots against the defender. *Variations:* (a) The receiver "posts up" to practice hook shots and moves with her back to the basket. (b) The receiver is allowed to use the passer again if she gets stuck.
6. Rebound-pass-shoot drill: X shoots from one of

the spots, after receiving a pass from the passer. The rebounder rebounds and passes the ball to the passer. In the meantime, the shooter has moved to the next spot, ready to receive the pass there. Use two balls as the action is continuous.

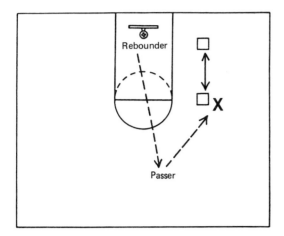

FIGURE 6-12. Rebound-pass-shoot.

7. Follow the leader: Each player has a ball. One leader is designated. He shoots from various spots, while every player follows him.
8. Competitive shooting: Two teams compete against each other from various shooting spots. *Variations:* (a) Timed shooting. (b) Designated number of completed shots. (c) Least number of misses. (d) First team to finish.

Rebounding

Rebounding is gaining possession of the ball after an unsuccessful shooting attempt. Since approximately 60 percent of field goal attempts are missed, rebounding skill is essential to any team. Rebounding is categorized as being either defensive (at your opponent's basket), or offensive (at your own team's basket). The keys to effective rebounding are positioning, aggressiveness, and timing of the jump.

Positioning for the rebound is called "blocking out" or "boxing out." The defensive player has a distinct advantage here, already being closer to the basket. With anticipation and a quick move, however, the offensive player can gain the inside position. Blocking out is done by pivoting to face the basket, putting the opponent behind you. It is important here to spread the feet far apart, bend the legs, lower the hips, and hold the elbows out away from the body. This helps to create a stable position, not allowing an opponent to get around. Since both the offensive player and the defensive player want the inside position, a player must be very aggressive in order to maintain this desired position. This means the player that is blocking out must slide and maintain physical contact with his opponent until the rebound is secured.

FIGURE 6-13. Blocking out.

Once the inside position is attained, the player must observe the ball, and anticipate how and where it will rebound off of the rim or backboard. The player should jump high and grasp the ball firmly with both hands. On the downward move, after getting the ball, spread the legs and hold the ball high and away from the opponents. If it is a

FIGURE 6-14. Rebounding. (From Strack, *Basketball.*)

defensive rebound, outlet the ball away from the basket to a teammate near the sideline, or dribble the ball out away from the basket. An offensive rebound should be tipped back up to the basket, shot after a fake, or passed to a teammate in better shooting position.

Learning Cues

1. Work hard to attain or maintain the inside position, closest to the basket.
2. Do not get crowded too far under the basket.
3. Be aggressive.
4. Jumping:
   a. initiate the jump with the arms
   b. explode off of the floor by bending the legs
   c. reach high with both arms extended
   d. time the jump in order to grasp the ball as high as possible, attempting to keep the ball on line with the forehead
5. Go for the ball; do not let it come to you.
6. Keep a firm hold on the ball, jerking it down and away from any nearby opponents.
7. Land with feet comfortably spread and elbows out.

Practice Suggestions for Rebounding

1. Standing 20 to 25 feet from a partner, have her toss a ball high into the air toward you. Jump high and grasp the ball firmly with both hands, bringing it down aggressively.
2. Standing in front of the backboard, toss the ball high against the board. Jump and grasp the rebound, concentrating on good rebounding form. *Variations:* (a) Execute an outlet pass after rebounding (defensive rebound). (b) Shoot or tip the ball into the basket (offensive rebound).
3. Second effort drill: Stand in front of the backboard with a partner holding a ball behind you. On your partner's command, jump high into the air as if rebounding. After you have jumped, the partner tosses the ball against the board, forcing you to spring back up immediately to rebound.
4. Circle block-out: Place a ball in the center of a restraining circle. Align three pairs of players around the outside of the circle—facing each other (one inside player with her back to the ball). On the whistle, the player on the inside turns and blocks out the other player, trying to keep her from touching the ball for approxi-

FIGURE 6-15. Circle blockout.

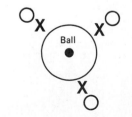

mately 5 seconds. *Variation:* Place a ball on the floor near each pair. Have each player block out her opponent from their ball for 30 seconds.
5. Three-on-three Block-out: With 3 offensive players and 3 defensive players positioned around the basket, the coach shoots the ball. Both teams attempt to secure the rebound. The offensive player should shoot the ball again or tip it in, while the defensive player should outlet the ball.

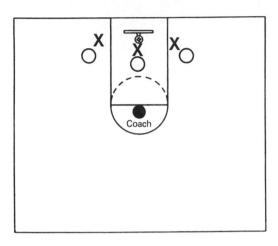

FIGURE 6-16. Three-on-three blockout.

Individual Offense

To be a good basketball player, you must always be a threat to the opponents when your team has possession of the ball. This means being able to score when the ball is in your hands, as well as being able to move effectively on the floor without the ball in order to free yourself or a teammate.

Driving. Driving is a means of getting past opponents by faking them off balance, accelerating, and dribbling hard past them. It is important to dribble with the hand farthest from the defender when driving. Fakes can be executed with the head, ball, or free foot. By holding the ball close to your body, away from the defender, a series of "jab" steps or "rocker" steps can lure the opponent off balance so that you may drive. It is essential that a player not dribble immediately after receiving a pass. This would eliminate the fake and drive—a prime individual offensive weapon.

Cutting. Cutting is sharp, angular movement involving starting, stopping, and changes of direction. This enables a player without the ball to get free from defenders. All cuts should be preceded by a fake in the opposite direction. Cuts can be in front of the defender (front cut) or behind a defender (reverse or backdoor cut). A V-cut is a sharp, angular cut (in the shape of a V) used to clear an area for a pass.

All offensive movement should be purposeful—not aimless, wasted motion. An offensive player with the ball is constantly looking for open shots,

FIGURE 6-17. Jab step.

passes, or drives. An offensive player without the ball is cutting and moving to get free, or to set a screen for a teammate. Of course, offensive team patterns or plays are a means of regulating and structuring every player's movement on the floor.

Individual Defense

Defense involves preventing a team from scoring, or, at least, limiting the maneuvering ability of the offensive team. Defense is as important as offense, but is considered less glamorous than scoring baskets. It requires hard work, concentration, and determination. Body balance is the key to good defense. The feet must be ready to move, preventing

leaning and reaching with the upper body. It is a general rule (with only a few exceptions) that a defensive player should try to stay positioned between the offensive opponent and the basket. Foot movement is accomplished by sliding, keeping the feet as close to the floor as possible to enable quick shifts in direction.

There are two general situations to consider in individual defense: guarding a player with the ball (a ball handler), and guarding a player without the ball.

Against a Player with the Ball. Note the fundamental defensive stance (Figure 6-18) of the player: weight low and evenly distributed on the balls of the feet, head up, knees flexed, arms flexed,

FIGURE 6-18. Defensive stance.

FIGURE 6-19. Defense against a player without the ball.

hands relatively close to the body, palms up. The eyes should be focused on the opponent's hips rather than on the eyes or the ball. This prevents being faked out of position. Rather than reaching with the hands, a player should constantly be sliding the feet to maintain good body position. The arms should extend upward or outward from the body only to deflect a pass or a shot. The distance between the defensive player and the ball handler depends on the quickness and shooting range of the offensive player. Once a player stops dribbling, a very close defensive position should be established, with arms extended to prevent passes or a shot.

Against a Player without the Ball. It makes sense that a player without the ball is not a scoring threat. Thus, in playing defense, you must work hard to prevent your opponent from *receiving* the ball. This is accomplished by keeping the player and ball in view at all times. Also, one arm should constantly be extended between the ball and your defender to "deny" the pass. If your opponent is not close enough to the ball to receive a pass, you may have to open up your body position, using your peripheral vision to keep the ball and your opponent in view. Again, like defending a ball handler, you want to dictate your opponent's moves.

Practice Suggestions for Individual Offense and Defense

(Either the *offensive* or *defensive* portion can be emphasized.)

1. Cutting: B attempts to free himself for a pass from A by executing V-cuts, front cuts, or reverse cuts (backdoors). X tries to deny the pass.

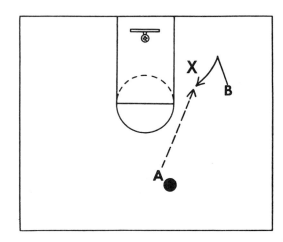

FIGURE 6-20. Cutting.

2. Individual Offense: After receiving a pass from A, B must do three offensive maneuvers enroute to

FIGURE 6-21. Individual offense.

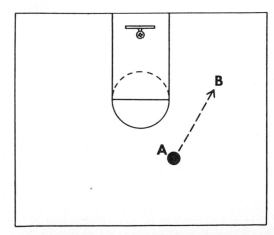

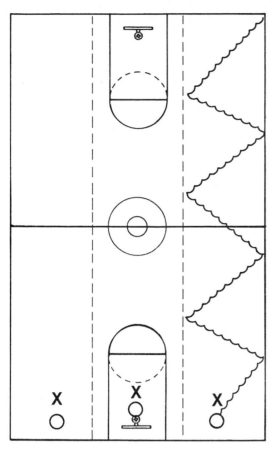

FIGURE 6-22. Zigzag.

the basket for a shot. (Example: jab step, reverse dribble, head fake.) May add a defender.

3. Zigzag: Divide the court into thirds. Staying in their third of the court, the offensive player dribbles in a zigzag pattern down the floor. The defensive player stays with her, practicing good defensive form and positioning. *Variation:* The dribbler stops her dribble enroute, making the defensive player move closer, straighten, and extend her arms.

4. Denial Defense: Both defensive players (X) work hard to deny any pass to the player they are

FIGURE 6-23. Denial defense.

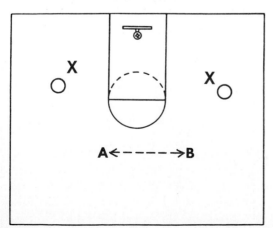

guarding. A and B pass the ball back and forth trying to get it to the Os.

5. Denial in a Box: Within a 10 to 15 foot square, X must work hard to deny B from receiving a pass from A.

FIGURE 6-24.   Denial in a box.

TEAM PRINCIPLES

Team Offense

Offensive tactics in basketball vary according to the defensive tactics employed by the opposing team. Thus the offensive patterns will vary in order that the most efficient attack may be developed against the particular defense. Generally speaking, there are two types of offense: (1) that which is employed against the player-to-player defense, and (2) that which is employed against the zone defense.

Offense Against a Player-to-Player Defense. The offense used against the player-to-player defense is a combination of passing and player movement. Even though the offense consists of five players, it is most common for only two or three players to work together for a shot while the others employ decoying or rebounding roles. Against a player-to-player defense, it only takes one defensive player to falter to enable an open shot for the opposing offensive player. Working together to accomplish this, it is possible to do a give-and-go and a variety of screens and picks. These maneuvers employ only two or three players and confuse the defense, putting them out of good defensive position. Of course, individual offensive moves such as cutting and driving may be incorporated also.

FIGURE 6-25.   Give-and-go.

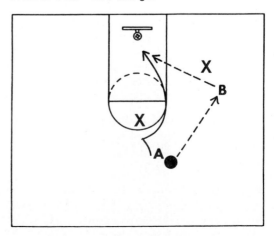

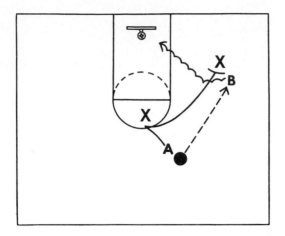

FIGURE 6-26. Pick.

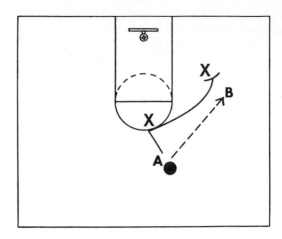

FIGURE 6-27. Screen.

These maneuvers can be incorporated into set plays, or used spontaneously in a freelance situation. Thus, 5-player plays are actually a combination of 2- and 3-player maneuvers.

Offense Against a Zone Defense. The offense used against the zone defense is primarily one of moving the ball with short, quick passes to force the defensive players out of their assigned positions in order that a good shot may be taken. The offensive players move to positions that will force the defense to alter their zone and thus weaken its strength. Even if an offensive player gets past a defender, in a zone defense there is another defender waiting to cover. Therefore, the following principles should guide the offense in defeating the zone defense:

1. Quick passing
2. Outside shooting
3. Penetrate the zone with a dribble or a pass, then quickly pass out to a free teammate

4. Cut through the zone, splitting two defenders
5. Overload one side of the zone with offensive players
6. Dribble very sparingly
7. Screen a shifting defensive player

Team Defense

The Zone Defense. This style of defense calls for the placement of the defensive players in designated areas in and around the defensive basket in order to give a maximum protection against good shots. The alignments are numbered. The alignment selected must take into consideration the size, speed, and abilities of the players, as well as the area of the court desired to be covered. The most common zone defenses are the 1-3-1, the 1-2-2, the 3-2, the 2-1-2, and the 2-3. The zone is a type of defense where each player is assigned a certain area on the court to cover, and guards only that offensive player

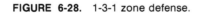

FIGURE 6-28. 1-3-1 zone defense.

who comes into that area. The defense shifts in relation to the ball, rather than in relation to the position of the offensive players. The zone defense is valuable in securing rebounds, in cutting off inside shooting, against taller opponents, and in protecting players who are tired, weak defensively, or in foul trouble.

The Player-to-Player Defense. The principle behind the player-to-player defense is the assignment of each player to guard one offensive player, and thus the area element that is prominent in the zone defense is eliminated. Instead of shifting as a unit in relation to the position of the ball, each player must follow one player all over the defensive court. This defense takes extraordinary skill, stamina, and teamwork, since any free offensive player is a scoring threat. Since the offensive team will be working screens, picks, and cuts to free a teammate, the defense must communicate and have tactics to avoid such maneuvers. One such tactic involves immediate on-the-floor switching of defensive assignments if an offensive player has gotten free. Another tactic involves defensive players allowing room for each other to slide through picks and screens, enabling them to stay with their assigned players.

The Pressing Defense. In recent years, pressing defenses have taken on great significance at all levels of basketball competition. The main objectives of pressing defenses are to harass opponents into ball-handling errors, to force opponents into changing their game strategy, and to force the offensive team to use up valuable time in bringing the ball down the court. The press can be administered full-court, ¾ court, or ½ court, and can incorporate zone or player-to-player principles.

TERMINOLOGY

Backcourt players (Guards) Players who set up a team's offensive pattern; usually the smaller players on the team or the best ball handlers.

Backdoor An offensive maneuver whereby a player cuts toward the baseline to the basket, behind the defenders, and receives a pass for a field goal attempt.

Baseline The endline.

Blocking out (Boxing out) A term used to designate a defensive player's position under the backboard which prevents an offensive player from achieving good rebounding position.

Charging Personal contact against the body of an opponent by a player with the ball.

Corner players (Forwards) Tall players who are responsible for the rebounding and shooting phases of the team's operation. They make up the sides of the offensive set-up.

Cut A quick offensive move by a player trying to get free for a pass.

Denial defense Aggressive individual defense where the defensive player works hard to keep the offensive player from receiving a pass.

Double foul When two opponents commit personal fouls against each other at the same time.

Dribble Ball movement by a player in control who throws or taps the ball in the air or onto the floor and then touches it. The dribble ends when the dribbler touches the ball with both hands simultaneously, permits it to come to rest while in contact with it, or loses control.

Drive An aggressive move toward the basket by a player with the ball.

Fake (Feint) Using a deceptive move with the ball to pull the defensive player out of position.

Fastbreak Moving the ball quickly downcourt in order to score before the defense can set up.

Field goal A basket scored from the field. Worth two points.

Freelance No structure or set plays in the offense.

Free throw The privilege given a player to score one or two points by unhindered throws for a goal from within the free throw circle and behind the free throw line.

Give-and-go A maneuver in which the offensive player makes a short pass to a teammate, and then cuts in toward the basket for a return pass.

Held ball Occurs when two opponents have one or both hands firmly on the ball, and neither can gain possession without undue roughness.

Inside player (Center, Post, Pivot) Most often the tallest player on the team. This player is situated near the basket, around the three-second lane area, and is responsible for rebounding and close-range shooting.

Jump ball A method of putting the ball into play by tossing it up between two opponents in one of the three circles.

Outlet pass A term used to designate a direct pass from a rebounder to a teammate, with the main objective being the start of a fast break.

Personal foul A player foul which involves contact with an opponent while the ball is alive or after the ball is in possession of a player for a throw-in.

Pick A special type of screen where a player stands so the defensive player slides to make contact, freeing an offensive teammate for a shot or drive.

Pivot Takes place when a player who is holding the ball steps once or more than once in any direction with the same foot; the other foot, called the pivot foot, being kept at its point of contact with the floor. Also, another term for the inside player.

Posting up A player cutting to the three-second lane area, pausing, and anticipating a pass.

Rebound A term usually applied when the ball bounces off the backboard or basket.

Restraining circles Three circles of six-foot radius, one located in the center of the court and one located at each of the free throw lines.

Running time Not letting the clock stop for fouls or violations. Usually used in a recreational situation.

Screen An offensive maneuver where a player is positioned between the defender and a teammate in order to free the teammate for an uncontested shot.

Switching A reversal of defensive guarding assignments.

Team's back court That part of the court containing the opponent's basket.

Team's front court That part of the court containing a team's own basket.

Technical foul A noncontact foul by a player, team, or coach for unsportsmanlike behavior or failure to abide by rules regarding submission of lineups, uniform numbering, and substitution procedures.

Telegraphing a pass Indicating where you are going to pass by looking or signaling.

Throw-in A method of putting the ball in play from out of bounds.

Traveling When a player in possession of the ball within bounds progresses illegally in any direction.

Violation An infraction of the rules resulting in a throw-in from out of bounds for the opponents.

SELECTED REFERENCES

BARNES, MILDRED J. *Women's Basketball,* 2nd ed. Boston: Allyn and Bacon, Inc., 1980.

BROWN, LYLE. *Offensive and Defensive Drills for Winning Basketball.* Englewood Cliffs, N.J.: Prentice-Hall, Inc., 1965.

Coaching Clinic's Complete Guide to Offensive Basketball. Editors of *The Coaching Clinic.* Englewood Cliffs, N.J.: Prentice-Hall, Inc., 1979.

COUSY, BOB, and FRANK POWER JR. *Basketball: Concepts and Techniques.* Boston: Allyn and Bacon, Inc., 1970.

EBERT, FRANCES A., and BILLYE ANN CHEATUM. *Basketball—Five Player.* Philadelphia, Pa.: W. B. Saunders Company, 1972.

HOLZMAN, RED, and LEONARD LEWIN. *Holzman's Basketball: Winning and Strategy and Tactics.* New York: Macmillan Publishing Company, 1973.

JEREMIAH, MARYALYCE. *Coaching Basketball: Ten Winning Concepts.* New York: John Wiley and Sons, 1979.

MEYER, RAY. *Basketball as Coached by Ray Meyer.* Englewood Cliffs, N.J.: Prentice-Hall, Inc., 1967.

NEWSOM, HERBERT. *Basketball for the High School Coach and the Physical Education Teacher.* Dubuque, Iowa: Wm. C. Brown Company, Publishers, 1966.

WOODEN, JOHN R. *Practical Modern Basketball.* New York: The Ronald Press Company, 1966.

WOODEN, JOHN R., and BILL SHARMAN. *The Wooden-Sharman Method.* New York: Macmillan Publishing Company, 1975.

Magazines

Athletic Journal, 1719 Howard Street, Evanston, Illinois 60202

Coaching Women's Athletics, Coaching: Magazines, P.O. Box 867, Wallingford, Connecticut 06492

Scholastic Coach, 902 Sylvan Avenue, P.O. Box 2001, Englewood Cliffs, New Jersey 07632

Film and Cassette Sources

Medalist Sports Education—Library, P.O. Box 95694, Chicago, Illinois 60694

Sports Films and Talent, Inc., 7431 Bush Lake Road, Minneapolis, Minnesota 55435

Sports Techniques Instructional Films, Athletic Institute, 705 Merchandise Mart, Chicago, Illinois 60654

BOWLING

THIS CHAPTER WILL ENABLE YOU TO:

♦ Select a proper fitting bowling ball and a pair of bowling shoes.
♦ Bowl a game according to the official rules of the American Bowling Congress.
♦ Practice and use the four-step approach and delivery, the straight ball, and the hook ball.
♦ Score a complete game using the appropriate symbols to indicate the line score.
♦ Improve your strategy by converting spares.
♦ Understand the terminology, observe safety rules, and utilize proper etiquette associated with the sport.

NATURE AND PURPOSE

Bowling appeals to people of all ages and is easily adapted for special populations. Because a relatively small expenditure of energy is required in bowling it is not an activity that lends itself to the development of physical fitness. However, participants may play the game for years after more strenuous activities have been abandoned. Bowling is an activity that any person who has a degree of motor fitness can enjoy as a lifetime sport.

The typical bowling center of today has become an almost 24-hour enterprise. It caters to housewives leagues in the morning, to junior leagues in the afternoon, to leagues (separate or mixed) for men and women in the evening, and to late night-early morning bowlers who work the second shift. Most establishments are clean and well kept, thus providing suitable entertainment places for the whole family.

The modern game of tenpins is played on indoor wooden lanes, 60 feet long from the foul line to the center of the number one pin, and 41 or not more than 42 inches wide (see Figure 7-1). The tenpins are set up (or "spotted") in a diamond formation on pin spots 12 inches apart, center to center (Figure 7-2). A regulation tenpin is 15 inches high, with a diameter of 2¼ inches at the base. Pins are constructed of clear, hard maple and are usually coated with a plastic outer covering. They must conform to American Bowling Congress specifications. The object of the game is to roll the ball down the lane and knock down all the pins located in the diamond formation.

The lane is bordered on either side by gutters, which prevent an errant ball from moving into another adjacent lane. It is constructed of two types of wood: maple, a hardwood to take the constant punishment of the ball, and pine, a soft wood that aids in gripping the ball. As you will notice (Figure 7-2), a lane has several markings some of which appear to be off the lane (the approach area). All of the marks serve as points of reference for the bowler. The initial sets of dots, found in the approach area, serve as a point of reference for the bowler's stance and approach. The set of points in arrow formation beyond the foul line serve as a point of reference for aiming the ball.

EQUIPMENT AND FACILITIES

Bowling is one of the few sports that a participant can enjoy without having to buy expensive equipment. For the recreational or occasional bowler, bowling centers provide "house balls," and for a small fee shoes may be rented. However, if you are planning to become a regular bowler, it is best to own your own equipment. Studies that have been conducted indicate that men and women who own their own equipment have higher bowling averages. Therefore, if you want to improve as a bowler, it is best to own your own equipment. Basically, all the bowler needs is a ball, a carrying bag, and a good pair of bowling shoes.

For a school physical education class, it would be expensive and impractical to have bowling lanes in the gymnasium. Several companies manufacture bowling sets consisting of plastic bowling pins, a plastic sheet on which to place the pins for proper distance and placement, and a hollow rubber bowling ball containing several holes so the learner can properly fit the ball to the hand. Markings and distances can be measured and painted on the floor with a water-based paint for easy removal. Many techniques can be learned in the gymnasium before proceeding to the bowling center.

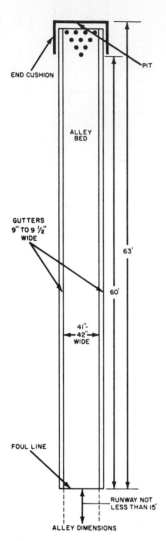

FIGURE 7-1. Lane dimensions.

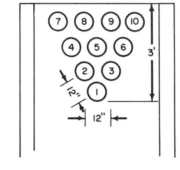

FIGURE 7-2. Position and number of pins.

are drilled with three holes, one for the thumb and two for the third and fourth fingers. If you buy your own ball, the ball is fitted to your hand span. This ensures a proper fit that will allow you to handle the ball fairly easily. The holes should be large enough for the fingers to slip in and out easily. The thumb hole should be comfortably loose. The bowler should be able to turn the ball around the thumb without binding, grabbing, or excessive rubbing of the skin.

FIGURE 7-3. Position of fingers in three-hole ball.

To determine the proper fit, the bowler must decide the type of grip that will be used. There are three grips: the conventional, the semi-fingertip, and the full fingertip. Advanced bowlers use the latter two grips; beginners should use the conventional grip since it is the easiest to control. To determine proper hand span for the conventional grip, place the thumb completely in the thumb hole, keeping the fingers relaxed and spread over the finger holes. The crease of the second joint of the two middle fingers should extend ¼ inch beyond the inside edge of the finger holes (Figure 7-3). The finger holes are cut at a certain pitch or angle to aid the bowler in grasping the ball.

In practice bowling sets used in most schools, the hollow rubber ball generally comes with several finger holes in order to accommodate the various hand spans.

Bowling Shoes

Another important item in the bowler's list of equipment is proper footwear. At first glance, both shoes of a pair of bowling shoes look the same. Closer inspection of the soles of the shoe will reveal a difference. For the right-handed bowler the left shoe should have a leather sole to facilitate sliding at the release point, and a rubber heel; the right shoe

Bowling Ball

Choosing a Ball. Bowling balls are made of hard rubber or plastic and come in a variety of colors. The hard rubber ball is black and is the type of ball found in most bowling centers. Although all bowling balls are the same size, 27 inches in diameter, the weight varies from 8 to 16 pounds. When selecting a ball, the beginner should choose the weight that feels most comfortable. Young junior bowlers use a light ball, women generally use a ball that weighs 10 to 13 pounds, and men usually use a ball weighing 14 to 16 pounds. The primary considerations in making your decision should be comfort and how well you can control the ball. If you consistently use a house ball, find a ball that best fits you. House balls are marked with an identification number and the weight; try to use the same ball each time you bowl.

Fitting the Ball. It is also important to select a ball equipped with holes that fit your fingers. Balls

should have a rubber sole with a leather tip, and a rubber heel. For the left-handed bowler the order is reversed. Most bowling centers have rental shoes for both right-handed and left-handed bowlers.

For the physical education class, it is important for the student to wear smooth-soled shoes that would enable sliding during the approach and release. Crepe soles or heavy-treaded rubber soles such as used in jogging shoes would be inappropriate.

Ball Bag

The serious bowler and the bowler who owns equipment should have a bag in which to store and carry the ball. With the versatility of materials today, any amount of money can be spent on a bag. The plastic or vinyl and canvas bags are the least expensive. Many discount department stores have bags on sale regularly.

BASIC RULES

In league or tournament play, two contiguous lanes are used, and the bowling of ten complete frames on these lanes constitutes an official game. Members of contesting teams successively and in regular order bowl one frame on one lane and the next frame on the other lane, so alternating frames until the game is completed. Each player bowls two balls in each frame. If a strike is made on the first ball, the second ball is not rolled (except that in the tenth frame if a strike or spare is made, the player immediately rolls on the same lane the additional balls or ball to which the strike or spare entitles him).

In case of a tie game, each team bowls an extra complete frame on the same lane in which the tenth frame was bowled. The extra frame is bowled and scored in exactly the same manner as the tenth frame. If a tie still exists at the completion of the first extra frame, the teams must change lanes for the additional frames that may be required to determine the winner.

It is a foul if a bowler permits any part of his foot, hand, or arm, while in contact with the lanes or runways, to rest upon or extend beyond the foul line at any time after the ball leaves the bowler's hands and passes beyond the foul line. No count is made on a foul ball, and any pins knocked down are immediately respotted. A foul ball counts as a ball bowled by the player. If a player commits a foul which is apparent to both captains or one or more members of each of the opposing teams competing in a league or tournament on the same pair of lanes where the foul is committed, and the foul is not seen by the foul judge or umpire, or recorded by an automatic foul detecting device, a foul shall nevertheless be declared and so recorded.

Pinfall—Legal

Every ball delivered by the player shall count, unless declared a dead ball. Pins must then be respotted after the cause for declaring such dead ball has been removed.

1. Pins knocked down by another pin or pins rebounding in play from the side partition or rear cushion are counted as pins down.
2. If, when rolling at a full setup or in order to make a spare, it is discovered immediately after the ball has been delivered that one or more pins are improperly set, although not missing, the ball and resulting pinfall shall be counted. It is each player's responsibility to detect any misplacement of pins and have the setup corrected before he bowls.
3. Pins knocked down by a fair ball, and which remain lying on the lane or in the gutters, or which lean so as to touch kickbacks or side partitions, are termed dead wood and counted as pins down, and must be removed before the next ball is bowled.

Pinfall—Illegal

When any of the following incidents occur, the ball counts as a ball rolled, but pins knocked down shall not count.

1. When pins are knocked down or displaced by a ball which leaves the lanes before reaching the pins.
2. When a ball rebounds from the rear cushion.
3. When pins come in contact with the body, arms, or legs of a pinsetter and rebound.
4. A standing pin which falls upon removing dead wood or which is knocked down by a pin setter or mechanical pinsetting equipment shall not count and must be replaced on the pin spot where it originally stood before delivery of the ball.
5. Pins which are bowled off the lane, rebound, and remain standing on the lane must be counted as pins standing.
6. If in delivering the ball a foul is committed, any pins knocked down by such delivery shall not be counted.

Bowling on Wrong Lane

When only one player or the leadoff players of both teams bowl on the wrong lane and the error is discovered before another player has bowled, a dead ball shall be declared and the player, or players, required to bowl on the correct lane. When more than one player on the same team has rolled on the wrong lane, the game shall be completed without adjustment, and the next game shall be started on the correctly scheduled lane.

Scoring

All players should learn how to score. It adds considerably to the enjoyment of the game if the player can keep an accurate record of the score as the game progresses. There are ten numbered boxes on the score sheet to correspond to the ten frames in a game. At the top of each frame box are two small squares in which to write the number of pins toppled with the first ball and the second ball. Some simple scoring rules must be remembered in order to score a game accurately.

1. The score that is entered from box to box is cumulative, i.e., it represents the total number of pins toppled up to that point.
2. If a bowler does not get a strike or spare in any frame, scoring is just a matter of adding on the number of pins knocked down in each frame.
3. If all pins are knocked down with the first ball, it is called a *strike* and a cross (×) is marked in the small square in the upper right-hand corner of the frame box. The strike will count 10 pins plus the number of pins knocked down on the next two successive balls. A score will not be entered in the frame box until those two balls have been rolled.
4. If all pins are knocked down with two balls, it is called a *spare* and is indicated by a diagonal mark (/). The spare will count 10 pins plus the number of pins knocked down on the next ball rolled. A score will not be entered in the frame box until the next ball has been rolled.
5. If you spare or strike in the tenth frame, then you roll one more ball if a spare, or two more balls if a strike, and add that to your total score.

In order to illustrate scoring we will score a hypothetical game. But first let's review the symbols used and the scoring procedure.

(X)   Indicates a *strike:* 10 plus the score of the next two balls.

(/)   Indicates a *spare:* 10 plus the score of the next ball rolled.

(O)   Indicates a *split:* score will depend on number of remaining pins knocked down by next ball rolled.

(Ø)   Indicates a *converted split:* 10 plus the score of the next ball rolled.

(-)   Indicates a *miss* or *error:* no score.

(F)   Indicates a *foul:* no score.

(G)   Indicates a *gutter ball.*

The score sheet of a completed game is shown and analyzed in Figure 7-4.

Frame	1st Ball	2nd Ball	Total Score
1.	7 pins Enter score in first square	2 pins	9 pins
2.	5 pins	3 pins	17—cumulative score of first two frames: 9 + 8 = 17
3.	Strike. Enter (X) in first square		46—2 strikes (20) + 9 pins (see frame five) + 17 = 46
4.	Strike (X)		65—Strike (10) + 9 + 46 = 65
5.	9 pins—add to the two consecutive strikes	Miss (−) no pins	74 (65 + 9)
6.	8 pins	Spare. Enter (/) in second square	89—Spare (10) + 5 pins + 74 = 89
7.	5 pins—add to spare from frame six	4 pins	89 + 9 pins = 98
8.	9 pins	(−) no pins	98 + 9 = 107
9.	7 pins—a split	(O) no pins, missed converting the split	107 + 7 = 114
10.	Strike (X)—Player rolls two more balls, which are also strikes		114 + 3 strikes (30) = 144

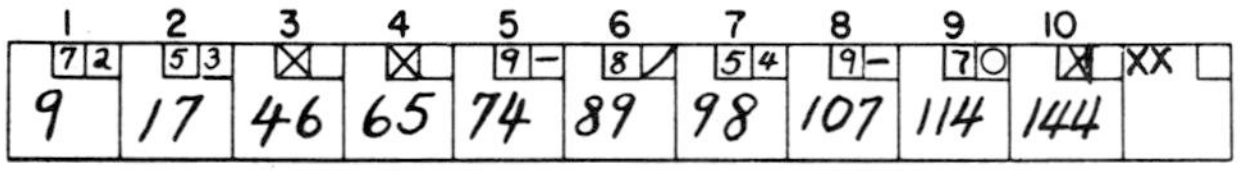

FIGURE 7-4.   Score sheet of a completed game.

SUGGESTED LEARNING SEQUENCE

A. Nature of the game
  1. Equipment
  2. Fitting a bowling ball
  3. Safety; Lane courtesy
B. Techniques. Rules should be introduced early in the learning progression to coincide with specific techniques.
  1. Stance
  2. Approach
  3. Straight ball
  4. Hook ball
C. Scoring. May be introduced as the situation warrants and is most appropriate.

D. Strategy
   1. Pin bowling and Spot bowling
   2. Making spares

SKILLS AND TECHNIQUES

Bowling is a relatively easy game to learn, but like all sporting activities it is important to learn the techniques involved in order to develop consistency. For the physical education teacher, much of the technique involving the grip, stance, approach, and release can be taught in the gymnasium. The two basic skills to be learned are the swing coordinated with a specific number of steps.

The Stance

There is no definite or prescribed stance assumed by all bowlers preparatory for the start of the approach. However, there are some important points to remember.

1. Hold the ball with both hands in front of the body. For a man this may be waist high, for a woman a little higher in order to attain a longer swing for increased speed.
2. The feet are spread slightly apart, weight evenly distributed, perhaps one foot slightly ahead of the other.
3. Most of the weight of the ball should be supported by the nonthrowing hand at this point.
4. The ball is gripped with the thumb in a 12 o'clock position for a straight ball or the 10 o'clock position for a hook ball.

Whether the bowler stands erect or crouched, it is necessary to have good balance and to feel comfortable with the ball in hand.

The Approach

Bowlers vary in the number of steps taken in the approach. The number of steps range from three to five, but most experts recommend the four-step approach. The beginning bowler should experiment with the delivery and determine which works best. The following discussion will center around the four-step approach for the right-handed bowler. The left-handed bowler will reverse the starting procedure.

In proper execution of the approach, the bowler will take a series of steps in a smooth, rhythmical manner, and will end with a slide and follow-through as the ball is released. Women bowlers begin on the 12-foot line with feet straddling the second dot from the right for right-handers or the second dot from the left for left-handers. The eyes should be fixed on the second arrow from the right

(right-hander) or left (left-hander) located on the lane. Men will begin the approach approximately 18 inches further back from the 12-foot line. As the steps are taken and the delivery is executed, it is important for the bowler to walk in a straight line. Let the dots near the foul line be your guide.

Learning Cues

Step 1. The push away. Step with the right foot and at the same time push the ball out to an arm's length in front of the body. Do not overextend the push away or loss of balance and direction may result.

Step 2. The ball moves to the bottom of the arc on the downswing as the left foot completes the second step.

Step 3. The ball reaches the top of the backswing (shoulder high), as the right foot completes the third step. The ball must swing in a straight line, shoulders square to the foul line.

Step 4. As the last step is taken the ball swings forward, the wrist is firm, and the ball is released toward the target. The nonthrowing hand will help serve as a means of balance. The left toe will be pointing at the target.

If the timing is correct the ball is released out in front of the body and laid rather than dropped on the lane. The bowling ball when properly delivered has a double motion. When first released it slides and revolves, sliding in the direction toward the pins. After sliding a distance, once it reaches the nonoiled surface, friction increases and the ball begins to revolve, causing it to hook, roll straight, or back up, depending on the type of ball that is thrown.

Practice Suggestions

1. Allow students to move to the ball rack and demonstrate proper technique for picking up the ball.
2. Pick up the ball and assume a good, well-balanced stance with ball held comfortably and in proper position.
3. From a designated line on the floor or on the approach try a four-step approach without the ball. To determine the length of your approach, move to a position short of the foul line and take four steps toward the beginning position. Try to coordinate steps, arm swing, follow through without the ball. Check the line from step one to step four.
4. Bellisimo recommends a one-step delivery with a ball.[1] Place students in a position to take the last step. Allow them to first take a practice swing with a ball then allow students to take the last

[1]Lou Bellisimo and J. Bennett, *The Bowler's Manual,* 4th ed. (Englewood Cliffs, N.J.: Prentice-Hall, Inc., 1982), p. 10.

A

B

C

D

FIGURE 7-5. The four-step approach.

step and delivery. Concentrate on a straight pendulum swing and a good follow-through with the hand finishing high.

5. Allow bowlers to try a four-step approach and delivery using the ball.

The Straight Ball

Beginning bowlers should concentrate first on perfecting a straight ball before attempting to roll a hook. It is also recommended that the woman bowler who lacks ball speed continue the use of a straight ball.

Learning Cues

1. The thumb should be held in a 12 o'clock position with the fingers underneath the ball.
2. The hand position should be maintained throughout the swing, with no arm rotation during release of the ball.
3. The wrist remains firm, the palm faces the pins as the ball is delivered; maintain a straight follow-through.
4. The ball should be started from the right side of the lane and directed toward the 1-3 pocket.

The Hook Ball

Most good bowlers use a hook ball; beginning bowlers will want to learn this delivery as soon as possible. To obtain maximum pin action, the ball should strike the pins at an angle, but the angle of the straight ball is limited by the width of the alley. The straight ball revolves forward, but the hook ball revolves at an angle, thus giving it greater pin splash or action by imparting a revolving action to the pins. This delivery is sometimes called the "handshake" delivery because the position of the hand is similar to that used in an ordinary handshake.

Learning Cues

1. The wrist is firm, the thumb is in a 10:30 o'clock position. This position must be maintained throughout the swing.
2. As the ball is released, the thumb comes out first, the fingers lift and impart a rotational effect to the ball.
3. Release the ball with the V formed by the thumb and forefinger pointing toward the target.
4. The hand should be carried upward and forward toward the pins in the follow-through. Do not side-wheel, twist the arm, or intentionally spin the ball.

There are two other types of deliveries, the curve ball and the backup ball. However, because of the difficulty of controlling them, they are not recommended for the beginning bowler.

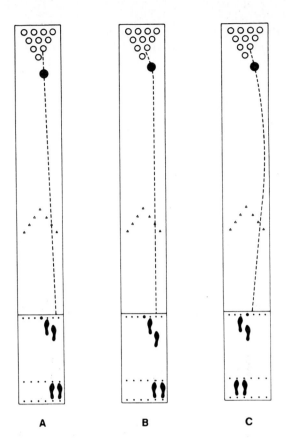

FIGURE 7-6. Path of (A) straight ball, (B) hook ball, (C) curve ball.

Practice Suggestions

1. For the physical education class, use partners. Roll a straight ball or a hook to each other. Concentrate on proper wrist and hand position as well as swing consistency.
2. At the lanes, practice the swing first, holding the ball in the correct position. Some experts recommend rolling the ball back and forth between partners to practice the proper release technique.
3. The bowler will continue to roll the ball over the second arrow from the right (right-hander). However, experiment with your starting position by moving over one or two boards toward the left to find the most consistent path for your hook.

PLAYING STRATEGY

Spot Bowling and Pin Bowling

An individual sport, bowling has no complicated playing strategies similar to those found in many team sports. You should plan your game so as to knock down the greatest number of pins possible. This is accomplished by individual control and accuracy, rather than cooperation with teammates in the execution of plays.

Playing strategy should include, first, a mastery of a definite approach and delivery style. The good bowler will settle upon a definite pattern as early as possible, making every effort to throw each ball with the same motion. Most bowlers are classified as "spot" or "pin" bowlers. The spot bowler selects a spot on the alley a few feet from the foul line and attempts to roll the first ball in each frame over that spot. The pin bowler looks at the pins while approaching and making the delivery. Whether you prefer throwing a hook or a straight ball, you should follow your selected style on all balls and concentrate on developing accuracy with a smooth and rhythmical delivery.

Spares

To bowl a good score, the bowler must pick up spares consistently. Accuracy is essential for good spare bowling. Unlike rolling a strike ball, the spare may force the bowler to vary the starting position and the spot over which the ball may be rolled. For the right-handed bowler, pins left on the right side of the lane such as the 1, 3, 6, 10 or 3, 5, 6, 9, 10, the starting position should be on the left side of the lane. For pins on the left side, the ball will be delivered from the right side of the lane. Pins that are left one directly behind another should be hit head-on, otherwise the bowler runs the risk of having the ball glance off the front pin thereby missing the rear pin. Conversion of spares will make a marked difference in your scores; practice and experience are two important factors in increasing the score.

SAFETY

Bowling is a relatively safe activity. Accidents are few, and good common sense will prevent them from occurring. The following are a few guidelines for safe bowling.

1. With a large class, plan formations well in advance so there is plenty of space between each participant during the approach, backswing, forward swing, and follow-through.
2. Be aware of people around you; swing the ball only on the designated alley.
3. Check to make sure the approaches are free of oily or rough substances that may interfere with the approach.
4. Use a towel to wipe the ball or dry your hands before each roll. A ball can become oily from the lanes and the oil may get on your hands.
5. When picking up the ball from the rack, always keep your palms parallel to the sides of the bowling rack (Figure 7-7).
6. Be aware of your fellow competitors; make sure

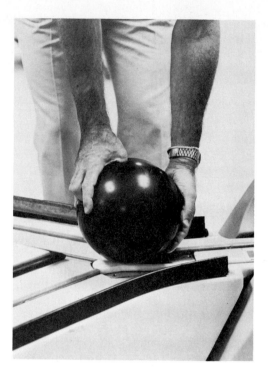

FIGURE 7-7. Proper method of picking up a ball from the rack.

the approach area is cleared before rolling the ball.
7. If students are used to set the pins, make sure the pinsetter is clear of the alley before rolling the ball.

LANE ETIQUETTE

As in other sporting activities, certain playing courtesies should be extended to your bowling competitors and teammates.

1. Do not talk to or otherwise disturb a bowler who is on the approach and ready to bowl.
2. Do not walk in front of a bowler to secure your ball from the rack when the bowler is ready to bowl. Wait for your ball to return.
3. When bowlers on adjacent lanes are both ready to bowl, the one on the right (as you face the pins) should always be permitted to bowl first.
4. Do not use a ball that is the personal property of an individual unless you have the owner's permission to do so.
5. Be at your post, ready to bowl when your turn comes.
6. After delivering the ball and noting the result, turn and walk back immediately to the rear of the runway, being careful to stay in your approach lane.
7. Do not argue with the foul line judge over deci-

sions even though you think an unjust call has been made against you.

8. Be punctual when scheduled to bowl. Nothing upsets a team more than having to wait for a late member.
9. Control your temper. Public exhibition of anger disturbs fellow bowlers and detracts from your efficiency.

TERMINOLOGY

Anchor   The person who shoots last on a team.

Baby split   The 1-7 or 3-10 railroads.

Backup   A reverse hook. A backup rotates toward the right for a right-handed bowler.

Bed posts   The 7-10 railroad.

Blow   An error; missing a spare that is not a split.

Box   The same as a frame.

Brooklyn   A crossover ball, one that strikes in the 1-2 pocket.

Bucket   The 2-4-5-8 or 3-5-6-9 leaves.

Cherry   Chopping off the front pin on a spare.

Crossover   Same as a Brooklyn.

Double   Two strikes in succession.

Double pinochle   The 7-6 and 4-10 split.

Dutch 200 or Dutchman   A score of 200 made by alternating strikes and spares for entire game.

Error   Same as a "blow." Failure to make a spare that is not a split.

Foul   To touch or go beyond the foul line in delivering the ball.

Frame   The box in which scores are entered. There are ten frames to each game.

Gutter ball   A ball that drops into either gutter.

Handicap   A bonus score or score adjustment awarded to an individual or team based on averages.

Head pin   The number one pin.

High hit   Hitting the head pin full in the face or head-on.

Hook   A ball that breaks to the left for a right-handed bowler. For a left-hander a hook ball breaks to the right.

Jersey side   Same as a Brooklyn.

Kegler   Synonym for bowler, derived from the German *Kegel* (game of ninepins).

Lane   A bowling alley.

Leave   Pin or pins left standing after a throw.

Light hit   Hitting the head pin lightly to the right or left side.

Line   A complete game as recorded on the score sheet.

Mark   Obtaining a strike or spare.

Open frame   A frame in which no mark is made; at least one pin remains standing after rolling both balls in a frame.

Pocket   Space between the head pin and pins on either side.

Railroad   Another term for a split. There are several kinds.

Sleeper   A pin hidden from view.

Spare   All pins knocked down on two balls.

Split   A leave, after the first ball has been thrown, in which the number one pin plus a second pin are down, and seven pins remain standing. Indicated by 0 on score sheet.

Spot   A place on the alley at which a bowler aims.

Strike   All pins knocked down on the first ball.

Striking out   Obtaining three strikes in the last frame.

Tap   When a pin is left standing on an apparently perfect hit.

Turkey   Three strikes in a row.

SELECTED REFERENCES

American Bowling Congress. *ABC Bowling Guide* (current ed.). Milwaukee: American Bowling Congress, 1572 East Capitol Drive.

BARSANTI, RENA. *Bowling.* Boston: Allyn and Bacon, Inc., Co., 1974.

BELLISIMO, LOU, and J. BENNETT. *The Bowler's Manual,* 4th ed. Englewood Cliffs, N.J.: Prentice-Hall, 1982.

BELLISIMO, LOU, and LARRY L. NEAL. *Bowling.* Englewood Cliffs, N.J.: Prentice-Hall, 1971.

COSTELLO, PATTY, and ALFRED GLOSSBRENNER. *Bowling.* New York: Mason/Charter, 1977.

American Association for Health, Physical Education, Recreation, and Dance: Division for Girls' and Women's Sports. *Official Bowling, Fencing and Golf Guide* (current ed.). Washington, D.C.: AAHPERD.

MACKEY, RICHARD T. *Bowling,* 2nd ed. Palo Alto, Calif.: Mayfield Publishing Co., 1974.

MARTIN, JOAN L. *Bowling,* 3rd ed. Dubuque, Iowa: Wm. C. Brown Company, Publishers, 1975.

SCHUNK, CAROL. *Bowling,* 2nd ed. Philadelphia, Pa.: W.B. Saunders Co., 1976.

SHOWERS, NORMAN E. *Bowling.* Santa Monica, Calif.: Goodyear Publishing Co., 1980.

CROSS-COUNTRY SKIING

THIS CHAPTER WILL ENABLE YOU TO:

♦ Select equipment best suited to your needs.
♦ Consider the advantages and disadvantages of waxless skis and waxable skis, and know how to wax them.
♦ Understand and apply the concept of "layering" in clothing.
♦ Perform the techniques of getting up from a fall, poling, turning, and striding while moving on flat, downhill, and uphill terrains.
♦ Know what safety precautions to observe when cross-country skiing.

NATURE AND PURPOSE

The great increase in popularity enjoyed by cross-country skiing can be attributed to many factors. *First* is the relative ease with which Nordic skiing can be learned. To move from one point to another the skier only has to initiate a walking action, thus it is a very natural activity. Unlike Alpine skiing, the touring skier has no lines to wait in, no crowds to endure, no long rides to the ski area, and no tow tickets to purchase. *Second,* the individual can engage in ski touring almost any place where there is no traffic: a country road, over fields, through woods, on hills, or on prepared tracks—these are all appropriate places to cross-country ski. *Third,* there are no limits as to age or sex; touring provides a good, clean form of recreation for all. It is not uncommon to find family groups—children, parents, and grandparents—gathering on a crisp, winter weekend day to ski tour in local and state parks, woods, or other scenic areas. In addition, many touring centers or local clubs in the United States now sponsor Citizens Races of varying distances, much like the marathons engaged in by many joggers. The purpose of the Citizens Races is not only competition but the opportunity to participate with hundreds of other people and to test yourself.[1] *Fourth,* ski touring is an excellent physical conditioner, especially when performed in a smooth, rhythmic manner over a prolonged period of time. Research studies indicate that the cross-country skier expends a great deal of energy in this physically demanding sport. *Finally,* ski touring equipment is reasonably priced at the beginner level. Many stores offer ski packages that include

[1]Further information about the Citizens Race can be obtained by writing to the Citizen and Club-Cross Country Racing Committee, United States Ski Association, 1726 Champa Street, Denver, Colorado 80202.

bindings, boots, poles, and skis for under $100. For the person who wishes to try out the activity, several outdoor stores or state parks will rent the necessary equipment for less than $10 a day.

School Programs. Several high school and college physical education programs include cross-country skiing as part of the regular curriculum. Many stores and state parks will rent equipment to schools for a reasonable price and in some instances will provide basic instruction. Many of the beginning techniques can be learned in two or three sessions, so the student can soon participate on flat and slightly rolling terrain. Obviously the more rugged terrain and steeper hills and valleys require more advanced techniques that take longer to develop. Although advanced techniques are beyond the scope of this chapter, information may be found among the Selected References.

Handicapped Programs. Cross-country skiing is an activity that also appeals to the blind and the partially sighted, the deaf, and the one-legged skier. Instruction programs for the handicapped enable special populations to enjoy this wonderful form of exercise and recreation. Several organizations that can supply additional information are listed under the Selected References.

EQUIPMENT

Ten years ago, the individual interested in ski touring would have found a limited selection of equipment from which to choose. Today, however, almost every Alpine ski manufacturer has also added a line of ski touring equipment. For the beginning skier, the selection process can indeed be mystifying and frustrating; therefore it is best to consult an expert before buying any equipment. The most important consideration for the beginner is that the equipment will function properly and will serve the skier through and after the initial stages of learning and participation.

Skis

When selecting cross-country skis, it is important to understand that they are categorized according to their use. *Racing skis,* which are narrow (35 to 45 mm) and very light, are designed specifically for competitive skiing. *Mid-touring skis* are heavier and slightly wider (40 to 50 mm). Beginners and recreational skiers frequently use the mid-touring ski, and it would be appropriate for the novice to use. The *touring ski* is still wider (45 to 60 mm) and heavier than the racing or mid-touring ski. Many beginners learn on this type of ski because it is heavier, provides greater stability, and can withstand greater abuse. Many learn-to-ski programs rent this type of ski to the person who is just learning to ski. The touring ski is also used by the expert for deep powder skiing, because the extra width helps keep the ski above the surface rather than sinking into the snow.

Skis come in assorted lengths and should be selected according to your body build and sex. The following is a general guide to use in selecting proper ski length. While standing on the floor, raise your arm straight up. For a woman or girl the tip of the ski should come to the wrist; for a man or boy the tip should come to mid-palm of the hand (Figure

FIGURE 8-1. Determining proper ski length. Tip comes to mid-palm for men and to the wrist for women.

8-1). If you are a heavy person, consider a stiffer ski; if you are light, consider a more flexible ski.

One very important factor is whether to choose the waxable or waxless type of ski. Cross-country skis are designed to grip the snow's surface in order to obtain a good forward motion. The gripping action can result from the use of various waxes, or, in the case of waxless skis, from either a strip of mohair or a specially designed surface in the form of fishscales or a step pattern (Figure 8-2). Although cross-country skis are generally made of a combination of wood and synthetic materials, most bottom surfaces are synthetic rather than wood, making them more impervious to moisture.

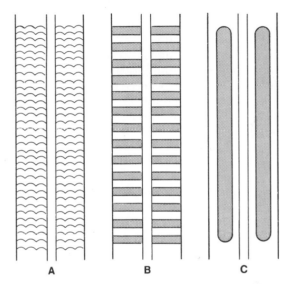

FIGURE 8-2. Types of bottom surfaces found on "waxless" cross-country skis: (A) fishscale pattern, (B) step pattern, (C) mohair strips.

The waxless ski is easy to maintain and for that reason would perhaps better serve for the occasional skier. There are, however, some disadvantages to this type of surface. The waxless bottom is not as adaptable to changing snow conditions as waxable skis. Application of different waxes in the kick zone is generally not possible, thus prohibiting maximum gripping performance. Additionally, the waxless ski sacrifices high level performance and speed. However, a majority of beginners and recreational skiers find the waxless type ski to be very satisfactory for their purposes. Ski surfaces with the mohair strips have a further disadvantage of sometimes becoming too moist and causing snow to cling to the ski bottom, thus greatly reducing skier performance.

Waxable skis are used by the ski purist and by the skier who wants the fun of waxing skis. The obvious advantage is that different waxes can be applied for different snow conditions, thus insuring a good kick and glide. Waxing skis takes time and requires some basic knowledge of snow conditions. It is also an additional expense and bother that some skiers would rather do without.

Bindings

Bindings enable the boot to be attached to the ski. There are several types: some have cables that go around the bottom of the boot; others have cables that clamp the top of the boot to the ski. For the beginner and recreational skier the traditional three pin binding is most commonly used (Figure 8-3). It consists of three pins which are projected or inserted into the sole at the toe end of the boot; a metal bar or clamp called a bale is then pushed down and held by a projection on the binding. The bale can generally be released by applying pressure to the projection on the bar or clamp. Most toe bindings are made of metal, although some manufacturers have developed a plastic binding. All bindings are "norm fit," that is, they will fit any size boot. The norm for bindings is 75 mm (width of the boot toe). However, newer developments are producing a "norm fit" of 50 mm for the recreational skier. Bindings can be purchased separately, but it is best that they be mounted by an expert.

FIGURE 8-3. A three-pin binding. The bale and binding shown are made of plastic.

Boots

A proper-fitting boot is perhaps the key to successful cross-country skiing. Boots should be selected on the basis of comfort to the skier. The boot should be flexible enough across the crease so that it does not cut off circulation to the toes or cut across the toes. The skier should try the boot on, wearing the socks used for skiing. The heel of the boot

FIGURE 8-4. A low-cut, light touring boot.

should be snug, there should not be much side-to-side flexibility, and there should be plenty of room in the toes. Generally, a space about the width of a finger at the end of the big toe indicates proper length.

A light touring boot is best for the beginner and recreational skier (Figure 8-4). This boot is usually made of leather and comes in either a low cut or a high cut (gives more warmth), and has a molded sole with three holes drilled in the sole at the toe for the binding. The holes should be set in a reinforced plastic or metal plate. Boots usually range in price from $20 and up. Before the first use it is important to apply a waterproofing conditioner and let the boots dry well. If properly taken care of, boots will last for several years.

Poles

Poles are used to aid in propelling the skier forward or as a means of balance and support. The pole consists of a grip, a strap, a basket, and a metal point that is bent to facilitate extraction from the snow. The poles can be made of a carbon fiber material, fiberglass, aluminum, or bamboo (Tonkin poles). Since poles tend to take a lot of abuse, the bamboo pole is the least durable. Most skiers prefer the fiber material pole which can be found in most stores.

The three key factors to look for when selecting a pair of poles are the length, the type of strap, and the size of the basket. To check for proper length, the pole, as you stand on a floor, should fit snugly under the armpit (Figure 8-5). Too long or too short a ski pole will hinder the skier's movement. The strap should be adjustable in order to allow the skier to make adjustments to the size of the gloves or mittens worn on the hand. Baskets, which are generally made of plastic, should be of medium size. Large baskets are used for deep powder snow, whereas smaller baskets are used by the competitive racer. Poles usually begin at $10.

FIGURE 8-5. Judging the right height of the ski pole.

Clothing

In addition to comfortable boots, what clothing to wear and how much are very important considerations. Remember that cross-country skiing involves total body movement and a great expenditure of energy. As a result, tremendous amounts of heat can be generated, and therefore overdressing will result in overheating. The best way to dress, as recommended by many experts, is on the "layering" principle, i.e., by wearing layers of loose-fitting clothing. Layering enables the skier to add or subtract articles of clothing according to the prevailing weather conditions. The following are important points to remember in selecting suitable ski wear.

1. Cotton should be worn next to the skin (underwear, inner socks) because it helps to absorb moisture and perspiration.
2. Avoid fabrics that do not breathe because they tend to hold in heat and moisture. Fabrics that are water repellent are preferable to fabrics that are waterproof.
3. Outer garments should be of a nonabsorbent material. Occasionally a skier falls and then snow clings to the material and may wet the inside layers.
4. Since much heat is lost through the head, wear a warm woolen knit hat or head covering big enough to be pulled down over the ears.

5. Loose-fitting pants or knickers are recommended to allow freedom of movement. A wool sweater or turtleneck shirt plus a nylon shell will keep the skier warm and dry under most conditions.
6. Wear a light inner pair of cotton socks and a pair of woolen knee length socks on top to keep the feet and legs warm and dry.
7. Wear mittens with a down fill or a light wool lining and a leather outer shell. Leather gloves with a warm lining are preferred by many because they give better control in handling the poles.

Other accessories include gaiters, an outer covering that keeps the lower legs dry (Figure 8-6); a fanny pack or knapsack to carry emergency materials, a repair kit, waxes, or extra clothes; and insulated vests. The cost of these items varies with the type and the quality. The important thing to remember, no matter what you spend, is that the layering of loose-fitting garments permits the cross-country skier to adapt to all types of weather conditions.

FIGURE 8-6. A pair of gaiters helps keep boots and ankles dry.

SUGGESTED LEARNING SEQUENCE

Cross-country skiing can take place during various weather conditions and on different types of terrain (uphill, downhill, the flat). The sequence suggested here begins on the flat, preferably with prepared tracks, and then procedes to the uphill and downhill. The skills and techniques described are for the beginner to beginner-intermediate level of recreational cross-country skiing.

A. Nature and Purpose
   1. Ski touring as a recreational sport
   2. Selecting equipment
   3. How to dress—what to wear
   4. Safety—introduced at appropriate times, when most meaningful

B. Conditioning—should begin prior to instruction on the slopes and should continue during the ski season
C. Waxing Techniques
D. Skills and Techniques
   1. On the Flat
      a. Getting up from a fall
      b. Diagonal stride
      c. Diagonal stride/Single poling
      d. Double poling
      e. Double poling/Stride
      f. Kick turn
   2. Uphill
      a. Diagonal stride
      b. Side step
      c. Traversing
      d. Herringbone
   3. Downhill
      a. Straight running
      b. Snow plow turn
      c. Step turn
      d. Traversing

SKILLS AND TECHNIQUES

The skills and techniques discussed in this section are for the beginner and beginner-intermediate recreational cross-country skier. There are several pre-techniques that can be practiced prior to beginning on the snow. These can be done on a carpeted area. If waxable skis are used they should be free of wax.

Practice Suggestions—Carpeted Area

1. Familiarize yourself with how the binding on the ski works. Put on the boots and insert the toe in the binding so that the three pins are inserted into the three holes at the bottom of the toe.
2. With both skis on, side step; move the tails of the skis keeping the tips fairly stationary, move around in a circle.
3. Slide the skis forward, approximating a walking action. Get the feel of the opposite arm and leg moving forward as the skis slide forward.
4. Learn to grasp the pole properly (Figure 8-7). Insert the hand through the strap, with thumb up, grasp the strap and pole grip. The skier should feel pressure at the bottom of the V of the thumb and index finger if gripping properly. As the arm pushes backward during the poling phase, the hand will release the pole; however pressure of the strap should always be felt at the junction of thumb and index finger.
5. Lift one ski then the other to note the action of the ski to boot and to develop a sense of balance. Because the heel is free from the binding, often the tail will fall causing the beginner to catch the snow and fall during side stepping or a kick turn.

Skiing on the Flat

It is best to start learning to cross-country ski on the flat. A facility that has pre-made tracks aids the beginner by placing the skis in the proper track while skiing. (When skiing alone in the wilderness

FIGURE 8-7. Grasping the pole.

FIGURE 8-8. The diagonal stride.

you are not very likely to find any pre-laid tracks.) If no tracks are available, any flat ground with a shallow covering of powder snow will also serve the purpose.

Getting Up from a Fall

All skiers at one time or another find themselves on the ground either as a result of a fall or as a deliberate means of slowing down. If on a hill or flat, the following method will enable you to resume a standing position (Figure 8-13).

Learning Cues

1. Holding a pole in each hand, assume a position perpendicular to your skis. If you are on a hillside, the skis must also be perpendicular to the slope with the skis on the downhill side. Now tuck the knees up under the body.
2. Roll to a kneeling position on the skis, poles planted and held to either side for stability.
3. Slide one ski forward so one knee is at a 90-degree angle, then merely stand up.

Diagonal Stride—Single Poling

The diagonal stride is to cross-country skiing as walking is to moving forward. The diagonal stride is a smooth, vigorous, rhythmical walking action that must be mastered by all beginners. (Figure 8-8). Opposite arm and leg action are used just as when walking in a vigorous fashion, while the other arm and leg serve as a counterbalance to maintain proper body position. The stride involves a kick (push off) of the ski and forward slide followed by the repeat action of the other ski as it is brought forward. A planting and downward and backward push of the ski pole aids the glide forward. This skill is used on flats and going up slight inclines. An accentuated motion can be used for moving up steeper inclines.

Learning Cues

1. The head is looking up and forward; body leans forward slightly, knees are comfortably flexed, weight is forward over the center of the skis on the balls of the feet.
2. The right arm reaches forward as left leg slides

forward. Place left pole opposite the left foot, push downward and backward with pole and push off with right foot. As glide slows, repeat action on opposite side.

3. From the pole plant the arm will extend behind as the push is completed, knees remaining flexed through the action. The pole is released from the snow and the arm is swung forward as the pole is regripped.

Double Poling/Kick

Double poling is a variation used as a change of pace from the single poling done with the diagonal stride. It is a powerful action that may be used when the skiing surface is crusty or a bit icy. Both arms are brought forward, the poles are planted opposite the toes, and a vigorous downward and backward push of the arms combined with a bending and compression of the upper body forward at the waist is initiated (Figure 8-9). The arms travel past the hips and the hands are released from the poles. A kick or stride may be added to this movement by simultaneously sliding the right or left ski forward as the arms swing forward. The opposite leg initiates the kick; near the end of the push the poles are

planted and arms and upper body execute the double poling technique (Figure 8-10).

Learning Cues

1. Weight should be evenly distributed on both skis, knees flexed, weight on balls of the feet.
2. As the arms are brought forward and poles are planted, the arms will be slightly flexed at the elbow.
3. The upper back is compressed forward at the waist as the arms continue to push downward and backward through extension.

Kick Turn

The kick turn is a technique used to change the skier to an opposite direction while standing on the flat or hillside. Although it may appear difficult, it is quite easy for the beginning skier to master.

Learning Cues

1. While standing with the skis together, plant poles (used as balance) behind the body.
2. Turn body to the right, pick up the right ski and turn so it faces opposite direction of the left ski.
3. With weight on the right ski, pick up the left ski, swing it around so that it is parallel to the right ski.

Practice Suggestions—On the Flat

1. Without poles, begin by walking with the skis, to develop a sense of balance and rhythm. Emphasis should be on sliding the skis forward.
2. Without poles, kick (push off) on one ski and return to starting position then push off with the opposite ski. Combine a kick (push) followed immediately by the same action of the opposite ski. Add a vigorous pumping action with arms to approximate action used during single poling.
3. Combine poling with the diagonal stride. Emphasis should be on the forward plant opposite the foot with one pole while the other arm is fully extended behind and then the consequent downward push and extension of arm. The same drill may be used to practice double poling.

FIGURE 8-9. Double poling. Note compression of the back and extension of the arms upon completion.

FIGURE 8-10. The double pole and kick.

4. To practice double poling with a stride, begin by striding with only the left or right leg until you feel comfortable coordinating the kick, pole plant and push; then add alternating strides.
5. Practice kick turn on flat without poles, then try using poles. Next proceed to the hillside and practice there.

Moving Uphill

Obviously not all cross-country skiing is done on a flat surface. The skier must learn to negotiate slopes as well. The easiest method for going uphill is using the diagonal stride described above. Where the slope is fairly steep, the action resembles a running motion with little or no glide during the concluding phases of the stride. The kick and stride will be shorter. It is important to remember to keep the weight well forward and knees flexed as you are moving uphill.

Side Stepping

When the beginning skier encounters a slope too steep to execute by means of the diagonal stride, the side stepping skill may be used for moving uphill.

Learning Cues

1. Assume a position crosswise to the hill.
2. With the edges pressing into the side of the hill,

step off with the downhill ski, step up with the uphill ski.
3. Use the downhill pole to help push off with the downhill ski, keeping weight into the hill.

Traverse

Traversing is another means to travel uphill. Traversing is merely a diagonal stride combined with a slight uphill movement. The skier strides toward a point, then executing either a kick turn or turn using a herringbone side stepping action, changes direction going uphill across the face of the slope. The skier actually will move back and forth across the face of the hill while moving uphill toward the top.

Learning Cues

1. Setting the skis crosswise to the hill, move forward using a diagonal stride. The movement is slightly uphill.
2. Weight should be forward keeping the edges of the skis set into the hill. The steeper the hill the greater amount of edge setting will be necessary.

The Herringbone

Although the herringbone is the most tiring way to climb a hill, it must be used when climbing up a steeper slope. The technique can best be described

FIGURE 8-11. The herringbone, a method of climbing uphill.

as a series of V's made by an alternating series of steps in which the ski tips are spread apart and the tails are kept fairly close together. In a V position, the poles are planted behind the skis; the edge of the skis are set with weight on the inside edge. As the right foot picks up the ski the right pole is planted and used to maintain balance and push off; the process is then repeated on the other side.

Learning Cues

1. With weight forward and knees flexed, spread tips of skis apart and keep heels together.
2. Set the weight on the inside edges by shifting weight to inside of each foot.
3. Plant pole behind skis; step up, plant the other pole, and step up.

Practice Suggestions

For the beginning skier, these uphill techniques can be practiced first on the flat, then on a gradual incline before attempting a steeper hill.

1. On a moderate incline, practice setting an edge as might be used in side stepping. Emphasis should be on rolling the ankle so weight is on the inside of the downhill ski and on the outside of the uphill ski. Practice climbing 10 to 12 steps.
2. The same exercise may be used for the herringbone as previously described. However, note the weight is set on the inside of each ski as the step is made.

Moving Downhill

Once the skier reaches the top of a hill it is usually necessary to go down. On slight inclines the skier may go straight down, but on steeper hills it becomes necessary to slow down and even to turn in some manner to avoid running into an obstacle. At times the best way to slow down is simply by sitting down. Before you use this method, however, make sure you know how to assume a standing position once again.

In moving downhill, it is important to remember a few key points. First, the weight must be centered or slightly forward over the skis; if not, loss of balance and a fall might result. Secondly, the hands must be held in front of the body so that the weight is placed properly over the skis. If the hands are allowed to fall behind and to the back of the body they cause the weight to shift backward thus resulting in a loss of balance and control. Finally, the skier should prevent the poles from dragging behind or becoming snagged in the snow, on a bush, or on any obstacle, because this would also result in a loss of balance and possible fall.

Straight Running

As the name implies, in straight running the skier goes straight down a hill. For the beginning skier, this technique is used on hills with a gradual incline. Remembering the points previously discussed, the following points are important.

Learning Cues

1. Body weight is over the center of the skis; the skis are shoulder width apart.
2. The knees must be flexed, the upper body is bent at the waist, hands held in front, head up and looking ahead, poles tucked under the arms, parallel to the skis.

Snow Plow—Snow Plow Turn

An easy method to learn for slowing down is the snow plow. To slow down, the skis are pushed apart at the tails and weight is transferred to the inside edges; the tips remain 6 to 8 inches apart forming a V. To turn in this position, the weight is merely transferred to the inside of one ski.

Learning Cues

1. The knees are flexed more than normal as the body is lowered. The ski tails are spread apart while the tips remain close together.
2. Body weight is slightly forward; pressure is placed on the inside edges of the ski by moving knees inward and slightly rolling the ankles.
3. To turn in this position merely transfer more weight to the inside of one ski and you will turn in the opposite direction. Pressure to the inside of the left ski will result in a right turn, and vice versa.

Step Turn

A step turn is frequently used to change direction, to go around a corner, or to avoid an object on the ground (Figure 8-12). The turn is executed from a glide, while running straight downhill or while on the flat. The skis should be flat preparatory to initiating the turn. The steps themselves are a series

of short steps, tips leading to the side, rather than wide steps. If going downhill, the stepping action is quicker than on a slight incline.

Learning Cues

1. Turn the head and drop the shoulder slightly in the direction of the turn.
2. While lifting the tip of the inside ski, shift the weight from the outside ski stepping on to the inside ski in the direction of the turn.
3. For tighter turns, quicken the steps.
4. Keep the hands in front of the body throughout the movement.

Practice Suggestions—Downhill Techniques

Begin developing the downhill techniques on a gradual slope before moving on to a slope that is steeper.

1. On a long gradual hill begin by first straight running. Execute a snow plow with tails apart, then allow skis to return to a straight run position, then repeat snow plow. Practice using this combination several times.
2. For snow plow turns, place stakes on a long gradual hill several feet apart and practice turning around one to one side and then another to the other side. Practice until you feel comfortable turning in both directions.
3. For the step turn, use stakes to design a course that forces you to step in different directions while moving on the flat and downhill.
4. Practice getting up from a fall while on the flat and while on a hillside. Emphasis should be on assuming a good base of support (crouch position) and use of poles.

FIGURE 8-12. The step turn. Note the head and shoulder drop in the direction of the turn.

FIGURE 8-13. Getting up from a fall.

Waxing

The art of waxing becomes more important as the skier's approach becomes more serious. Waxing is optional on the waxless ski but it is essential on the waxable ski. For the waxless ski (fishscale pattern, step pattern or mohair strip bottom) you may apply a base wax to the whole surface and a glide wax on the tips and tails of the skis. The base wax is applied with a hot iron and then ironed on evenly on the surface. Care must be taken to move the iron quickly over the surface so as not to burn the base. The glide wax may be rubbed on by hand then smoothed down with a cork. Most recreational skiers will never need to wax their waxless bottomed skis.

For waxable skis a two-wax system is recommended, one wax for snow conditions below freezing and the other wax for above freezing temperatures. The wax is applied to the kicker zone of the ski so that the ski will grip when pressure is applied to that area but will release and glide smoothly when the pressure (kick) is completed. Manufacturers have color-coded the waxes to give the best results at varying snow temperatures. Usually the green to blue colored waxes, which are harder waxes, are used for lower temperatures while the red and violet colored waxes, which are softer, are used for higher temperatures.

For the beginning skier using waxable skis, it is recommended that the base wax be applied at the ski shop at the time of purchase. For subsequent care, a ski wax kit can be purchased containing all the equipment needed to wax the skis. Such a kit should contain two to three kicker waxes and two to three glide waxes, a scraper to remove old wax, and a cork to smooth the surface. Further information on how to iron on a wax will be found in the list of Selected References.

SAFETY CONSIDERATIONS

1. If skiing alone, let someone know where you are going to be.
2. Dress appropriately for the prevailing weather conditions. Remember that as the temperature falls, wet clothes are very uncomfortable.
3. Carry extra clothing when planning a long day of skiing.
4. Check equipment before you start out to make sure it is in proper working condition.

5. Be aware that the wind-chill factor can make it feel much colder than the actual temperature, therefore increasing the danger of frostbite.
6. Wear a good pair of sunglasses on bright, sunny days to cut the glare and prevent possible snow blindness.
7. Wear a hat or carry one along. One-third of the body's heat loss is lost through the head.
8. Cover and protect the extremities against frostbite: ears, nose, fingers, and toes are especially vulnerable.
9. If touring for a long day, carry an emergency kit that contains ski wax, extra clothing, a wax candle, matches or lighter to start a fire, high energy food bars, and duct tape for temporary repair of broken ski tips.
10. Ski under control at all times; if you find yourself going too fast, sit down.
11. Ski on terrain appropriate to your level of skill.
12. Ski in areas free of traffic, including cars and snowmobiles.
13. Prepare yourself in advance before engaging in a vigorous touring program or racing program. Good physical condition is an important prerequisite, so start getting ready several weeks before the snow falls.
14. When in a crowd, be careful with your ski poles; the pointed tips can cause injury.

OTHER CONSIDERATIONS

1. Use good judgment when skiing with other people.
2. If skiing on a course that has pre-made tracks, let faster skiers have the right of way.
3. If skiing in rural areas, request permission of the property owner before crossing someone's land.

TERMINOLOGY

Alpine skiing Downhill and slalom skiing as opposed to cross-country or Nordic skiing.
Bale A metal device that presses the sole of the boot over three pins, thus securing the boot to the ski.
Basket Circular portion, usually made of plastic, near the bottom end of the ski pole that prevents the pole from sinking too deeply into the snow.
Binding Metal or plastic device for fastening the boot to the ski.
Camber The curved portion built into all skis that touches the snow when force is applied and lifts off when weight is lifted. The ski appears bowed as it lies flat on the ground.
Diagonal stride A skiers gliding action that resembles walking as it is executed.
Fishscale A type of surface resembling fishscales found on the bottom of waxless skis.

Gaiter A water repellent covering that fits over the boot, ankle, and lower leg. It is designed to keep snow out of the boot.
Groove Indentation that runs the length of the bottom of the ski allowing the ski to run straight.
Herringbone A technique used to climb uphill that leaves a V pattern on the snow.
Kick The force (push) that is applied during the stride, allowing the skier to glide on the snow.
Kick turn A technique used to change direction 180° while standing still on the flat or hillside.
Klister A type of sticky wax used on the bottom surface of a ski. Klister is the Norwegian name for paste.
Layering Wearing loose layers of clothes over undergarments so that the skier may easily add on for extra warmth or remove excess if too warm.
Mohair strips Strips of a fuzzy material found on the bottom of a type of waxless ski, to allow the ski to grip during the kick stage and flatten during the glide.
Nordic skiing Cross-country skiing and ski jumping.
Pin binding A type of toe binding that has three pins that are projected into the sole of the boot, securing the boot to the ski.
Pole plant Action in which the poles are put into the snow at a particular place and during a particular time.
Setting an edge A technique used to prevent a skier from slipping by angling the edge of the ski into the hillside.
Side step A technique used to climb a hill on skis. The skis are parallel to each other as the skier steps up along the length of the ski.
Snow plow A technique used to slow the skier down while going downhill by spreading the tails and keeping the ski tips close together.
Step A type of ski bottom design found on waxless skis resembling a series of steps.
Tail The back or end portion of a ski.
Tip The front end or leading point of a ski.
Track The trail that is left by skis as the skier moves through snow. These may be machine made.
Traverse Movement back and forth across the face of a hill; the technique may be done uphill or downhill.
Wax A petroleum-based product applied to the bottom of a cross-country ski that enables the ski to grip and also to slide.

SELECTED REFERENCES

BALDWIN, NED. *Skiing Cross Country.* Toronto: McGraw-Hill Ryerson Limited, 1977.
BRODY, MICHAEL. *Cross-Country Ski Gear.* Seattle: The Mountaineers, 1979.
BRUNNER, HANS, and ALOIS KAHN. *Cross-Country Skiing.* Translated and adapted by Wolfgang Ruick. Toronto: McGraw-Hill Ryerson Limited, 1972.
CALDWELL, JOHN. *The New Cross-Country Ski Book,* 4th ed. Brattleboro, Vermont: The Stephen Greene Press, 1976.
———. *Cross-Country Skiing Today.* Brattleboro, Vermont: The Stephen Greene Press, 1977.

FOSS, MERLE, and JAMES G. GARRICK. *Ski Conditioning.* New York: John Wiley & Sons, 1978.

GILLETTE, NED. *Cross-Country Skiing with John Dostal.* Seattle: The Mountaineers, 1979.

HELLER, MARK, ed. *The Skier's Encyclopedia.* New York: Paddington Press Ltd., 1979.

JENSEN, CLAYNE R. *Winter Touring: Cross-Country Skiing and Snow-Shoeing.* Minneapolis, Minnesota: Burgess Publishing Company, 1977.

LEDEREC, WILLIAM J., and JOE PETE WILSON. *Complete Cross-Country Skiing and Ski Touring,* 2nd ed. New York: W.W. Norton and Company, Inc., 1975.

SCHARFF, ROBERT, ed. *Ski Magazine's Encyclopedia of Skiing.* New York: Harper & Row, Publishers, 1974.

THORNTON, PAT. *Contemporary Cross-Country Skiing.* Chicago: Contemporary Books, Inc., 1978.

Periodicals

Cross Country Skier (5 times yearly) P.O. Box 1203, Brattleboro, Vermont 05301.

Audio-Visual Materials

Available from The Travelers Film Library, One Tower Square, Hartford, Connecticut 06115. *I Hope I Get a Purple Ribbon* (1977). Featuring Bill Koch—silver medalist, 1976 Olympic Games. 16 mm sound film. 15 min.
———. *It's as Easy as Walking* (1975). 16 mm sound film. 10 min.

Available from Modern Talking Picture Services, 5000 Park St., North, St. Petersburg, Florida 33709. *Skiing Is Believing.* 16 mm sound film. 24 min.

Organizations for the Handicapped

National Handicapped Sports and Recreation Association, Penn Mutual Building, 4105 E. Florida Ave., Denver, Colorado 80222.

National Blind Organization of Leisure Development (BOLD), 533 East Main St., Aspen, Colorado 81611.

Ski For Light, Inc., c/o Sons of Norway, 1455 West Lake Street, Minneapolis, Minnesota 55408.

U.S. Deaf Skiers Association; Simon Carmel, Adviser; 10500 Rockville Pike, #405, Rockville, Maryland 20852.

9 CYCLING

THIS CHAPTER WILL ENABLE YOU TO:

♦ Discuss the advantages and disadvantages of single-, three-, five-, and ten-speed bicycles.
♦ Select and fit a bicycle to individual needs and body. Select equipment for everyday use, touring, racing, and repair.
♦ Describe the gearing theory and apply it to everyday cycling.
♦ Demonstrate proper procedures for preventive maintenance and for routine adjustments.
♦ Demonstrate techniques for safe and efficient cycling in city and country, including ankling, balancing, body positioning, cadence, emergency stops, maneuvering, pacing, braking, mounting and dismounting, short radius turning, and straight roadside riding.
♦ Demonstrate proper hand signals, be familiar with bicycle safety rules of the road, and properly operate a bicycle.

NATURE AND PURPOSE

The popularity and growth of bicycling as a recreational activity enjoyed by the entire family has been phenomenal. In 1980 the estimated number of bicycles in use in America was 95 million. In recent years the bicycle has come to be regarded by many Americans not only as a vehicle for pleasure and sport but also as a means of transportation—a role it has long played for millions of people throughout the world. While it is not likely to replace the automobile in this country, the bicycle is relatively inexpensive, durable, cheap to operate and maintain, and does not use up natural resources nor emit pollutants into the atmosphere. In energy-conscious communities such as Davis, California, bicycles outnumber other forms of transportation. To most Americans, however, cycling is primarily a good outdoors sport that provides physical exercise often combined with vacation touring. This chapter will introduce you to the fundamentals of this enjoyable activity. Racing enthusiasts will find sources on competitive cycling among the Selected References.

RULES OF THE ROAD

In most states a bicycle driver is subject to the same laws that govern the operation of motor vehicles on the roadways. The following rules generally apply to bicycle drivers:

1. Observe and obey all traffic regulations, one-way and stop signs, stop or go and yield signals, and all applicable markings.
2. Obtain a copy of and observe all local, city or county, and state ordinances pertaining to bicycle use and operation in your area.
3. Keep to the right side of the road or street, drive with the traffic in a straight line, and ride single file.
4. Do not carry other riders.
5. Never hitch a ride on other vehicles.
6. Do not carry sacks or packages that obstruct vision or otherwise interfere with the proper control of the bicycle.
7. Always use proper hand signals to indicate turning or stopping.
8. Have the proper lights and reflectors for night cycling.
9. Be on the alert for car doors opening, for cars pulling out into traffic in front of you, for drain grates, stones, glass or other obstacles on the roadway, and for pedestrians.
10. Keep your brakes in good operating condition, and maintain your bike in excellent mechanical condition.

The bicyclist should become familiar with the guide, regulatory, service, and warning signs that are used to facilitate traffic movement. Additionally, the cyclist should review the meaning of roadway markings such as standard yellow center lines, the meaning of traffic signals, and the meaning of the colors and shapes of signs. Several of the important types of signs are illustrated in Figure 9-3.

Other signs and their meaning may be found in a driver's manual in the state where you reside. Refer to it for other rules specific to your state regarding cycling.

If dogs are encountered, the cyclist should tell the dog to "GO HOME," or stop the bicycle and place it between the dog and cyclist while passing through the area. Commercial repellents are available which are effective and harmless to dogs. Do not kick at the dog or swing at it with a tire pump. These methods are usually not effective and may cause a severe accident to the cyclist.

FIGURE 9-1. Touring is fun and provides an excellent way to exercise.

FIGURE 9-2. This cyclist enjoys pleasure riding. Note the safety helmet worn.

FIGURE 9-3. Road signs.

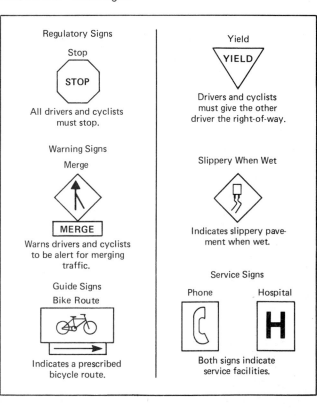

Regulatory Signs

Stop

STOP

All drivers and cyclists must stop.

Warning Signs

Merge

MERGE

Warns drivers and cyclists to be alert for merging traffic.

Guide Signs

Bike Route

Indicates a prescribed bicycle route.

Yield

YIELD

Drivers and cyclists must give the other driver the right-of-way.

Slippery When Wet

Indicates slippery pavement when wet.

Service Signs

Phone   Hospital

H

Both signs indicate service facilities.

The bicyclist should recognize hazards such as poor road conditions (sand, potholes, glass, oil spots, ice-covered, etc.), and, when possible, avoid them. Potholes may be "jumped" by lifting the front wheel to the far side of the hole by unweighting, i.e., pulling strongly upward on the handlebars and putting most of your weight on the pedals.

Brightly colored clothing should be worn during daylight hours so that motorists may see the cyclist easier. Also, reflective or white clothing should be worn at night, and the bicycle should have the proper lights and reflectors.

Hand Signals

All cyclists should become acquainted with the proper hand signals with regard to turning or stopping.

Left Turn. The rider should look behind and signal before turning left. Abduct the left arm so that it is horizontally extended to the left before moving in that direction, and then turn toward the left only when it is safe.

Right Turn. The right turn signal is also indicated by the left arm. The elbow should be flexed 90 degrees and the shoulder joint abducted the same amount. Turn to the right after checking for cross traffic, obeying signals, and when safe.

Stop. Signal a stop with the left arm. The upper arm is moved away from the body at a 45-degree angle, the lower arm hangs straight down, and the palm of the hand faces toward the rear.

BICYCLES AND EQUIPMENT

Bicycles come in various models, styles, and colors, and with different components. They are priced from under $100 to over $1,000. Bicycles may be classified as utility, touring, recreational, racing, or other bicycles. The beginning cyclist should select a bicycle according to the kind of use it is to serve, whether for recreation, road or track racing, touring, commuting to work, or whatever. The beginning cyclist should visit a local professional bicycle dealer for help in selecting an appropriate bicycle to meet his or her needs.

The middleweight, a single-speed bicycle, is recommended for the beginner since the bicycle is durable and is generally equipped with coaster (foot) brakes. The lightweight, a three-speed recreational or a five- or ten- or fifteen-speed touring bicycle, is recommended for the cyclist who needs or wants to drive more effectively and efficiently by using the various gear ratios provided by the multi-geared bicycles.

The three-speed recreational bicycle weighs about 38 pounds, comes in different frame and wheel sizes, has either caliper hand brakes or an optional coaster rear brake, and may have either flat or dropped handlebars. The gear mechanism is enclosed in the rear hub and allows for a normal speed, a low gear for pedaling against resistance, and a high gear for pedaling with the wind, downhill, or on level roadways.

The touring bicycle weighs anywhere from about 15 to 25 pounds, generally has caliper brakes, "turned-down" handlebars, and pedals with toe clips and straps. The *derailleur* moves the chain from one of several (usually five) freewheel sprockets to another in the rear and (if so equipped) from one chain wheel to another in the front.

Basic Parts of a Bicycle

The touring bicycle illustrated in Figure 9-4 will serve to identify the basic parts of a bicycle:

1. *Frame,* usually made of alloy steels or carbon steel.
2. *Front fork,* usually made of tubing.
3. *Crank* (or *hanger*) *sets,* which are either a one-piece or a three-piece forged unit.
4. *Handlebars*—standard or dropped.
5. *Saddle* (seat)—standard, racing, or touring type.
6. *Wheels,* consisting of hubs, rims, spokes, tires, and nipples (which hold the spokes to the rim). Standard, racing, or touring type.
7. *Brakes*—coaster type (foot-operated) generally used in the rear; rim type with either a center-pull or caliper (hand) type.
8. *Tires*—lightweight touring type or racing (tubular).
9. *Pedals*—three types: the classic rubber tread, the thin cage, or the metal platform. Toe clips may be used with the latter two types.

Fitting the Bicycle

It is recommended that the prospective bicyclist go to a professional bicycle shop to select a bicycle. The bicycle shop as opposed to a department store will generally have a greater selection of bicycles and component parts. The shop bicycles are assembled, adjusted, and maintained by qualified mechanics who are usually factory trained. Department store bicycles are roughly assembled by a stockperson. Have the bicycle shop's mechanic make whatever adjustments to the bicycle are necessary so that it fits your personal body build.

When fitting the bicycle, of utmost importance are the height of the saddle and the position of the handlebars. It is important to follow these steps: keeping the feet flat on the ground, fit the frame first, fit the saddle height second, and then adjust the handlebars. When fitting the frame, make sure that the bicycle top tube can be comfortably straddled while keeping both feet flat on the ground. For

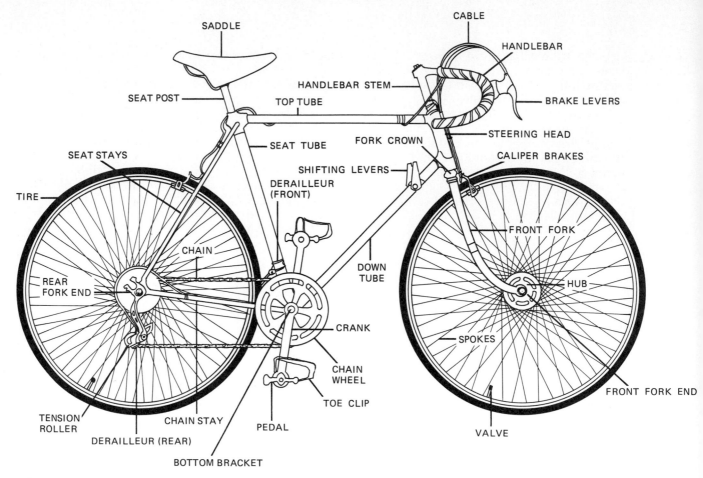

FIGURE 9-4. Parts of a bicycle.

proper saddle height, sit on the seat in the normal riding position, place the heel of one foot on the pedal while in its lowest position, adjust the saddle so that the leg is straight; your knee will now be slightly flexed when the ball of the foot is on the pedal in the pedal's lowest position. In fitting the handlebars, check the handlebars so the top bar is level with or lower than the nose of the saddle. In addition, be sure to check the tire pressure and check for proper operation of the brakes.

Checking Tires and Brakes

When checking tire pressure, inflate the tires to the recommended pressures that are stamped on the sides of the tire. The tires should bulge only slightly when you are riding, and should be checked frequently with a tire pressure gauge. Tire pressure gauges can be purchased for an inexpensive amount of money.

The brakes should stop the bicycle firmly and quickly. With caliper brake systems, check to ensure that the brake shoe contacts the rim properly. The brake cable should not be frayed or loose and should be lubricated with a water-displacement

product that attracts little dirt. These checks should be done on a monthly basis for the normal cyclist, but more frequently if the bicycle is used on a daily basis.

Accessory Equipment

In addition to the standard equipment, most states require that bicycles must have a braking system that will stop the driver within a certain distance (15 feet) from a certain speed (10 mph) on dry pavement. Bicycles operated at night must have a headlamp that is visible from a distance of at least 500 feet to the front. New bicycles must have front, rear, pedal, and side reflectors.

Other equipment that is recommended includes protective headgear, gloves, lock and chain, tool bag with tools, water bottles, and cycling shoes.

When the bicycle is purchased it may be a good idea to buy a basic tool kit at this time. A compact case with several tools is available for under fifteen dollars. The minimum basic tool kit one needs is dependent upon the type of bicycle; however, the minimum would include an adjustable wrench and a screwdriver.

SUGGESTED LEARNING SEQUENCE

A basic learning progression for the beginning level is listed below.

A. Cycling Needs
1. Bike selection and fitting
2. Saddle selection and adjustment
3. Basic tool and repair kits
B. Safety Considerations—specific points are covered on appropriate occasions.
1. Bike safety inspection
2. Safety equipment and clothing
3. Safe, efficient, and effective cycling
C. Skills and Techniques
1. Mounting and dismounting, body positioning, and pedaling skills
Ride: a short and slow check-out trek
2. Tire, wheel, and quick-release maintenance
3. Traffic hazards, laws, and skills
Ride: a short city ride
4. Brake maintenance and adjustment
5. Preventing accidents
Ride: a medium-length city ride
6. Steering skills
7. Identifying appropriate riding locations
Ride: a long city ride
8. Derailleur maintenance and adjustment
9. Preventive maintenance and adjustment procedures
Ride: a short country ride
10. Emergency situations
11. Wheel maintenance and adjustment
Ride: a hill climb and time trial
12. Bearing maintenance and adjustment
13. Vehicular and motorist hazards
Ride: a medium length country ride
14. Crank sets and pedals—maintenance and adjustment
15. Movement in traffic
Ride: a long country ride
16. Inclement weather riding
17. Night riding
Ride: a hill climb and time trial
18. Power train maintenance and adjustment
19. Practice reacting to road hazards
20. Physical fitness
21. Clubs, organizations, racing, touring, bikeways, etc.
Ride: extended country ride
Ride: bikeway
Ride: overnight trip

SKILLS AND TECHNIQUES

For the beginning cyclist there are several fundamental concepts to remember and a few skills (mounting, dismounting, changing gears and ankling) to learn in order to enjoy the pleasure of recreational cycling. The skills will be described later; the list below identifies and briefly explains some important concepts to remember as you enjoy cycling.

1. *Balancing.* Balance is generally easier to control on a faster moving bicycle although the bicycle is in a dynamic state of imbalance. The cyclist makes corrections as the state of imbalance is felt or sensed. To help maintain balance, the cyclist should look ahead and not look at the bicycle or feet.
2. *Body Positioning.* The body should be centered on the bicycle, the hands should be relatively close to the brakes (hand brakes), the vertebral column should be flexed, the head should be held upright, and the balls of the feet should be on the pedals.
3. *Cadence.* The efficient cyclist should maintain between 65 to 85 strokes per minute; however, this number fluctuates considerably depending on the technique used and the condition of both the bicycle and the rider.
4. *Emergency Stops.* The cyclist should evenly apply the brakes, keep the body low, and shift the weight backwards.
5. *Maneuvering.* Most maneuvering is done by leaning in the desired direction. For quick turns, pull on the handlebar end opposite to the desired direction of turning. For rough road surfaces, keep the body upright while leaning the bicycle. Finally, keep the bicycle upright and lean the body when maneuvering on slick surfaces.
6. *Pacing.* The cyclist should pace himself by shifting gears in order to maintain a nearly constant revolution per minute sequence. One becomes less fatigued if the rpm's are kept constant as opposed to pushing very hard just to be able to move the pedals.
7. *Braking.* Under normal braking conditions, the rear brake should be applied first and then the front brake. Equally increasing tension should then bring the bicycle to the desired slower speed or stop.

Mounting and Dismounting

The first basic skills to practice are mounting and dismounting, straight line and curve riding, starting and stopping, and turning. When mounting, the cyclist should straddle the frame, place one foot on the pedal, raise the pedal to a high position, and then push off and sit down on the saddle. When dismounting, the cyclist should coast with one pedal low, bring the other foot over the frame and downward as you leave the saddle, and then apply the brakes and touch the ground. Apply brakes evenly, being sure to understand which lever controls the

FIGURE 9-5. Mounting the bicycle. The mount starts with the foot on the pedal at the 11 o'clock position and the other foot adjacent to the bicycle on the ground.

FIGURE 9-6. Dismounting—note the position of the foot on the pedal and the leg swinging over the frame.

rear and which the front brakes. When straight line riding, remain relaxed and maintain a steady pedal pressure; when making a turn, slow down somewhat but continue to pedal as the bicycle turns.

Practice Suggestions

Practice straight line riding by pushing (scooter fashion) along a long part of the roadway. Next practice riding straight/forward along a 2-foot wide boundary, trying to keep from weaving.

FIGURE 9-7. The derailleur system.

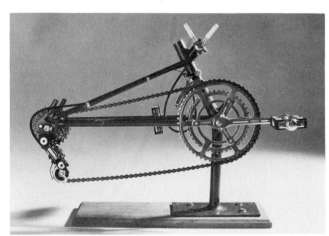

Using the Gears

When you know how to mount and dismount, how to straight line ride, start and stop, and how to make turns, you are ready to use the gears. Notice how one gently discovers the right gear by moving the levers back and forth. Always try to maintain about 65 revolutions per minute while pedaling. It is suggested that the cyclist check out a book and look up a gear ratio and cadence chart in order to calculate speed.

FIGURE 9-8. By adjusting the limit screw which controls the distance that the rear derailleur can move the chain, the rider can set the low and high gears.

To find your gear ratio, count the number of teeth on the chain wheel and each of the freewheel sprockets of your bicycle, measure the diameter (in inches) of your rear tire, and use the following formula:

$$\text{GEAR RATIO} = \frac{\text{Number of teeth on chain wheel}}{\text{Number of teeth on sprocket}} \times \begin{array}{c} \text{Diameter} \\ \text{of rear} \\ \text{wheel} \\ \text{(in inches)} \end{array}$$

Practice Suggestions

1. Exchange bicycles with friends who have different types of bicycles (classic, roadster, tourist, commuting, or racing) to learn the gearing techniques for both internal hub and external gearing systems.
2. *Gear selection.* Take a five-mile time trial and record your time and gear selection. After a few weeks repeat the ride and see how your time and gear selection compare with the first trial. These rides should be completed over the same route with all variables being controlled as much as possible in order to make a valid comparison. The terrain, weather conditions, time of day, attire worn should be as nearly the same on both rides. The gear selection may vary as will the time to complete the ride due to better physical conditioning or more efficient technique.
3. *Balance.* Pedal 50 feet very slowly within a two-foot wide boundary taking as much time as you can with feet remaining on the pedals and moving only in a forward direction.
4. *Speed and Coordination.* Begin 30 feet before the starting line and pedal at top speed through a course that is 8 feet wide but gradually narrows to 2 feet during the 50-foot run.

5. *Steering.* Place pylons 10 feet apart on each side of a 50-foot line. Cycle on opposite sides of the pylons with both front and rear wheels without knocking them over as you traverse the distance; i.e., simply weave in and out of the line of pylons.
6. *Pedaling and Braking.* Pedal at averge speed toward a goal and stop the bicycle without skidding 10 feet short of a marked line.
7. *Evasion.* Pedal at a fast speed toward a barricade and react to instructor's command of "left" or "right," which is given at a preselected point. The cyclist must maneuver the bicycle in the correct direction without hitting the barricade or going outside boundaries.
8. *Signaling and Turning.* The cyclist should look back over the left shoulder to check traffic without wobbling; demonstrate proper signals for turns in both directions or stopping; then execute the maneuver.
9. *Left and Right Spiral.* The bicyclist follows a spiral to the center without touching any lines on the 2-foot-wide course, which tests left and right turning skill and balance.

Bicycle Repairs

It is advisable for the beginning cyclist to get some practice in repairing a flat before being stuck miles from home or from a shop. Several of the listed bike books provide a complete section on tire repairs and should be consulted. Other skills that should be practiced by the novice cyclist include emergency stop braking whereby the cyclist transfers his weight to the rear of the bike, avoiding obstacles by maneuvering around obstacles in the riding line, the technique of ankling, and proper gearing.

FIGURE 9-9. Adjusting the center pull brakes so that the brake shoe properly contacts the rim.

FIGURE 9-10. Check the air pressure in the tire frequently.

A   B   C   D

FIGURE 9-11. Ankling positions. (A) At the top of the stroke the toes are higher than the heel. (B) The toes move to a lower position as the downstroke continues. (C) At the bottom of the stroke the toes are lower than the heel. (D) The toes move to a higher position as the upstroke continues.

Ankling

Pedaling correctly, or ankling, should be done with the ball of the foot on the pedal in the following manner: As the pedal approaches the 12 o'clock position, the heel should be dropped slightly as it is pushed; at the 3 o'clock position, the heel is slightly higher as the foot continues pressing the pedal backward through the 6 o'clock position where the heel is upward at about a 45-degree angle relative to the toe, and the heel remains slightly higher than the toe until the pedal reaches the top. It is important to keep a steady foot pressure throughout each pedal revolution. Toe clips with straps help considerably in ankling.

After several city and country rides, the beginning cyclist may want to be challenged by hill climbing or time trialing. These are excellent activities, and should be augmented with extended trips. If the novice cyclist has a desire to completely overhaul the bicycle, in addition to the recommended periodic maintenance, please consult the local bicycle mechanic and/or the Selected References.

TERMINOLOGY

Ankling   Technique of pedaling in which the foot follows through 180 degrees or more.

Bikeway   Paths or roads designated as bicycle routes.

Cadence   Pedaling at a more or less constant pace; should be around 65 to 85 pedal revolutions per minute for beginners, around 95–100 for tourists, and upwards from 120 for racers.

Caliper brakes   Hand brakes.

Chain wheel   Large wheel with gear teeth on the right crank.

Coaster brakes   Foot-activated internal hub rear brakes.

Derailleur   A mechanism to move the chain from one gear to another.

Down tube   Part of frame extending from the steering head to the bottom bracket.

Gear ratio formula   Number of teeth on front sprocket/ Number of teeth on back sprocket × wheel diameter.

Head tube   Large-diameter tube holding front fork assembly.

Saddle   Seat of a bicycle.

Seat tube   Part of frame extending from the bottom bracket to the seat.

Top tube   Horizontal part of frame extending from the head tube to the seat tube.

Variable gear hub   Rear hub with internal gears.

Wheel   Includes the hub, rim, spokes, and tire.

SELECTED REFERENCES

Books

All About Bicycling. Chicago: Rand McNally & Co., 1974.

BALLANTINE, RICHARD. *Richard's Bicycle Book.* New York: Ballantine Books, 1978.

Bike World Editors. *Bike Book Quarterly Series.* Mountain View, Calif.: World Publications, 1974.

DELONG, A. FRED. *DeLong's Guide to Bicycles and Bicycling.* Radnor, Pa.: Chilton Book Co., 1978.

FARIA, IRVIN E., and PETER R. CAVANAGH. *The Physiology and Biomechanics of Cycling.* New York: John Wiley and Sons, 1978.

FICHTER, GEORGE, and KEITH KINGBAY. *Bicycling.* Gold Leisure Library. New York: Golder Press, 1974.

SCHULTZ, BARBARA A., and MARK P. SCHULTZ. *Bicycles and Bicycling: A Guide to Information Sources.* Detroit, Michigan: Gale Research Company, 1979.

SLOANE, EUGENE A. *The New Complete Book of Bicycling.* New York: Simon & Schuster, 1974.

TOBEY, PETER W., ed. *Two Wheel Travel: Bicycle Camping and Touring.* New Canaan, Conn.: Tobey Publishing Co., 1972.

Periodicals

Bicycling. Emmaus, Pa.: Monthly Bicycling Magazine, monthly, general, beginning.

Bike World. Mountain View, Calif.: World Publications, monthly, general & technical, beginning through advanced.

Competitive Cycling. Carson City, Nevada: Jim McFadden, monthly, racing.

League of American Wheelmen Bulletin. Palatine, Illinois: League of American Wheelmen, periodically, general, beginning to advanced.

Audio-Visual Materials

Huffman Manufacturing Co., P.O. Box 1204, Dayton, Ohio 45401. *Bicycle Built for You.*

Valdhere Films, 3060 Valleywood Drive, Dayton, Ohio 45429. *Bicycle Driver Education—We Must Do More.* 1975. Available for purchase 16 mm, sound-color, 20 min., safety, all ages.

Association-Sterling Films, 600 Grand Avenue, Ridgefield, New Jersey 07657. *Magic of the Bicycle.* 1965. 16 mm, sound-color, 28 min., all ages.

Raleigh Industries of America, 1170 Commonwealth Avenue, Boston, Massachusetts 02134. *Pedal Power.* 1973.

Sales Promotion Department, Schwinn Bicycle Company, 1856 North Kostner, Chicago, Illinois 60639.

Ramsgate Films, 704 Santa Monica Blvd., Santa Monica, California 90401. *Bicycling on the Safe Side.* 16 mm, sound, color, 15 min., safe driving techniques.

Association Sterling Films, 600 Grand Ave., Ridgefield, New Jersey 07657. *Bikeways for Better Living.* 16 mm, sound, color, 24 min., bikeways.

Canadian Cycling Association, 333 River Road, Vanier City, Ontario, Canada KIL 8B9. *Tour of the Scioto River Valley.* 16 mm, sound-color, 20 min., young adult-adult.

Organizations and Clubs

Amateur Bicycle League of America, Box 669, Wall Street Station, New York, New York 10005

American Youth Hostels, National Campus, Delaplane, Virginia 22025. (Consult your local directory to see if there is a chapter in your area.)

Bicycle Federation, 1101 Fifteenth Street, N.W., Washington, D.C. 20005

Bicycle Manufacturers Association of America, 1101 Fifteenth Street, N.W., Suite 304, Washington, D.C. 20005

Bikecentennial, P.O. Box 8308, Missoula, Montana 59807

International Bicycle Touring Society, 2115 Pasco Dorado, La Jolla, California 92037

League of American Wheelmen, Inc., National Headquarters, 19 South Bothwell Street, Palatine, Illinois 60067

National Bicycling Foundation, P.O. Box 1368, Homestead, Florida, 33030

Youth Activities Department, National Safety Council, 444 North Michigan Avenue, Chicago, Illinois 60611

DANCE

Square Dance
Folk Dance
Social Dance
Modern Dance

MOVEMENTS COMMON TO ALL DANCES

All forms of dance involve movement. Although dance movement may at times be confined only to the body (axial movement), more commonly it requires the use of various forms of locomotion in which the body weight is transferred to the feet or from one foot to the other. All forms of locomotion can be reduced to five fundamental steps: walk, run, leap, jump, and hop. Any other type of locomotor activity is a combination of these basic steps. Closely related to the five fundamental steps are the skip, slide, and gallop, and often reference is made to the eight fundamental means of locomotion.

Walk. The weight is transferred from one foot to the other, alternately, one foot always being in contact with the ground. The usual foot action is a transfer of weight from the heel to the ball of one foot, during which time the other leg is pushing off, then swinging through to assume its position in the sequence of action.

Run. The speed of the walk is increased and there is a brief period when neither foot is in contact with the ground.

Leap. By means of a strong push-off from *one* foot, the body is lifted off the ground momentarily; the body weight then returns on the *opposite* foot. The leap differs from the run in that more energy is needed, and there is a longer period between transfer of weight due to a longer period of suspension in the air. The leap may be done either for height or for distance.

Jump. The body springs into the air by one of the following means:

1. A single-foot take-off, landing on both feet.
2. A two-foot take-off, landing on one foot.
3. A two-foot take-off, landing on two feet.

A jump may be made for either height or distance.

Hop. By means of a strong push-off from one foot, the body is lifted off the ground momentarily; the weight then returns to the *same* foot.

Graphic Representation. The walk, leap, jump, and hop are all done to an even beat, sometimes designated as long, and represented graphically as _____ _____ _____ , etc. The run, usually twice as fast, is short and represented as __. In relation to the long beat, it is shown == == , etc. Should the pattern become uneven (long-short), each of the three remaining related forms of locomotion would fit into the rhythm: skip, slide, gallop. The graphic representation would be _____ __, which total time is equivalent to one beat, thus ===.

Skip. A combination of a step and a hop, done to an uneven beat in which the step is given the long time-value and the hop the short value:

=== === ===.

Note: Were each part given equal time value, a step-hop would result instead of a skip.

== == == == == ==
step hop step hop step hop

In performing the skip, there is a feeling of elevation resulting from the natural tendency to swing the free leg forward and upward.

Slide. The weight is transferred from one foot to the other by means of a step on one foot followed by a quick drawing up of the other foot with an immediate transfer of weight to it, a sideward movement.

Gallop. A leap step combination in which the foot executing the step is brought up to but not beyond the foot that has completed the leap. The leap, a forward movement, is done with slight height; distance is not a factor.

SQUARE DANCE

Although square dance still retains the starting formation of four couples facing the center of a square with one couple on each side of the square, there have been radical changes in the calls, style, and music of contemporary square dance. Square dance calling requires a great amount of practice, understanding, voice control, and ability to handle large groups. Anyone who attempts calling must have a distinct and pleasing voice, a sense of timing so that the calls will immediately precede the figure and produce continuity in the dance, and a thorough knowledge of the dance figures. Excellent recordings of square dance music with calls are available.

SUGGESTED LEARNING SEQUENCE

Honor	Couple Promenade
Shuffle	Grand Right and Left
Forward and Back	Star Left, Right
Do-sa-do	Pass Thru
Seesaw	Ladies Chain
Allemande Left (Right)	Right and Left Thru
Swing	Square Positions
Promenade Single File	Half Promenade

These steps are described below in alphabetical order.

SQUARE DANCE TERMS AND FIGURES

Allemande Left. Gentleman gives his left forearm to the lady on his left. With left forearms joined, they walk around one another (exchange places) and then both return to place. This figure is sometimes followed by an allemande right, in which the gentleman executes the same figure but with his partner. More frequently, the allemande left is followed by a grand right and left (described below).

Circle Left (or Right). Three or more dancers circle to the left or to the right, as directed. Hands are joined with elbow comfortably bent so that the hands are above the elbow, man's palm up, lady's palm down.

Corner. The person to the man's left or the lady's right.

Courtesy Turn. The man takes the lady's left hand in his left, places his right hand in the small of the lady's back. Turning counterclockwise, the man backs up and the lady walks forward one half turn.

Do-sa-do. (French *dos-à-dos* meaning back to back.) Two dancers face each other and advance passing right shoulders. Each person slides behind the other person and moves backward to place.

Forward and Back. Persons or couples designated move forward 3 rapid steps and stop; then 3 steps backward and stop.

Grand Right and Left. In a square or circle formation partners face and take right hands. Men going counterclockwise and the ladies clockwise,

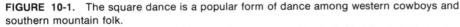

FIGURE 10-1. The square dance is a popular form of dance among western cowboys and southern mountain folk.

each partner moves ahead giving the left hand to the next and pull by, right to the next and pull by, left to the next and pull by, and stop. In square formation, partners will be facing and ready for the next call.

Honor.   The men bow while the ladies curtsey to their partners (or to the "corner" person, depending on the call).

Ladies Chain.

A. *Two Ladies Chain.* With couples facing, men stand still as the ladies go forward, take right hands, pull by, give the left hand to the opposite man who completes a courtesy turn.
B. *Four Ladies Chain or Ladies Grand Chain.* In square formation, all four ladies star right and move clockwise to their opposite man who gives them a courtesy turn.

Partner.   The lady on the man's right; the man on the lady's left. Sometimes partners are changed temporarily before returning to the original partner.

Pass Thru.   Two facing couples move forward and pass right shoulders with the one in front and remain facing in the same direction until the next call.

Promenade:

A. *Couple Promenade.* This is the most commonly used promenade in square dance. Standing side by side, couples join left hands, then join right hands on top of the left hands. The couple moves forward in a counterclockwise direction.
B. *Half Promenade.* Two couples indicated by the call use a couple promenade position to move counterclockwise and exchange positions in the square.
C. *Promenade Single File.* Dancers face counterclockwise and move one behind the other.

Right and Left Thru.   With couples facing, each person gives a right hand to the opposite and pulls by. The left hand is given to the partner and each couple does a courtesy turn.

Seesaw.   Two dancers face and pass left shoulders. Each slides to the left, back to back, and backs up to original position.

Separate.   Each dancer, or dancers, turns his back on his partner and they move in opposite directions. This movement is followed by a directional call.

Shuffle.   Comfortable short steps in which the feet slide smoothly along the floor. The boisterous skip or hop of early square dance is now regarded as unacceptable style.

Square Positions.   A square is an arrangement of four couples who stand facing the center in a square formation. The couples are numbered con-

secutively to the right, beginning with couple number 1, whose backs are closest to the music or caller. Couples 1 and 3 are the "head couples"; couples 2 and 4 are the "side couples."

Star Left (or Right).   When couples or designated dancers star, those involved form a palm star (hands about eye level, palms touching) with the specified hand, elbows bent, and walk forward. Dancers return to their original positions.

Swing.   This is a modified social dance position in partners. The gentleman's left arm is extended to the side, his right arm around the lady's waist. The lady puts her right hand in the gentleman's left, her left hand on the gentleman's shoulder. They stand to the side so that right hips and right feet are in line with one another and almost touching. Using the right foot somewhat as a pivot, they push with the left foot so that partners circle about in place, in a clockwise direction. As the swing is performed, partners lean away from one another, which results in a vigorous turn.

Practice Suggestions

1. The most common mistake made by the inexperienced square dance teacher is selecting a specific square dance and then directing the dancers to walk through the basic movements and figure of this dance. These movements require a great deal of time, are done without music and resemble uninteresting drills more than dance. Basic calls should be taught in a single circle. This method enables the teacher to see quickly all dancers, to use music immediately, and to eliminate the necessity for a specific number of students for squares. Dance to music can begin, for example, with:

2. When the movements can be done effectively, teach a Do-sa-do, Seesaw, Swing, and Couple Promenade. All calls may be combined then in varied sequence or in the following manner:

> Honor your partner
> Honor your corner
> Join hands, circle left, circle right
> Walk into the middle
> Come right back
>
> Face your corner, do a Do-sa-do
> Seesaw your partner
> Join hands, circle right
> Circle left
> Face the center, go forward and back
> Allemande left your corner
> Allemande right your partner
> Swing your corner
> Swing your partner and promenade

Go single file
Face the center
(Repeat)

3. A Grand Right and Left may be taught by designating a certain number of hands until a new partner is reached. For example, a right hand to the partner would be "one" and a left the next would be "two." Any number may be chosen, but seven hands enables the dancers to learn the principle involved and eliminates the confusion of counting a large number of hands. Once the Grand Right and Left is mastered, an Allemande Left with the corner may precede this figure. These movements are ready to be combined with those already learned.

4. The group of dancers may move smoothly from the single circle formation to a double circle with partners facing. One may direct calls already acquired to make dancers comfortable in this new formation, for instance:

> Honor your partner
> Do-sa-do your opposite
> Swing your partner
> Circle left, Circle right
> Allemande right your partner
> Allemande left your opposite
> Do-sa-do your partner
> Seesaw your opposite
> Swing your partner

5. In the double circle formation, Star Left and Right and Pass Thru may be taught rapidly. This permits dancers to work with different couples while being at ease with the basic calls. Two Ladies Chain and Right and Left Thru may be added to the figures. All basic calls except the Grand Right and Left and the promenades may be combined to music.

The teacher will be able to teach the square formation using previously taught calls and may add more advanced figures as selected dances require. Happy Dancing!

Square Dances for Beginners

Oh, Johnny

Winchester Cathedral

Little Red Wagon

Little Ole Winemaker

Gentle on My Mind

Ragtime Banjo Ball

If You Knew Susie

Marina

Just Because

Big Daddy

FOLK DANCE

They are of all ages, from all societal levels, and have vastly different backgrounds, yet individuals gather to participate in the shared activity of folk dance. Since the early 1940s in the United States, there has been increased interest and participation in international folk dance. This activity has become a common element in education, recreation groups, dance clubs, and senior citizen programs.

The growth of folk dance has been fostered through national organizations, state federations, and ethnic group leadership. Participation ranges from informal recreation gatherings to regular club meetings; from holiday celebrations to international festivals; and from weekend workshops to highly specialized exhibitions.

Folk dance has many values. It can contribute physically through the development of fitness, balance, and poise. Socially, it may help people to relate to each other, is a social group experience, and may foster understanding between different cultures. For the beginner and the experienced dancer and from youth to old age, folk dancing is a pleasurable, varied, vigorous, and social pursuit. It is a healthful experience to be enjoyed as a lifetime activity.

SUGGESTED LEARNING SEQUENCE

The following progression is recommended for beginners. Each step will be fully described below.

Two-Step

Schottische

Polka

Mazurka

Waltz

BASIC FOLK DANCE STEPS

Two-Step.   Three steps are taken in the rhythm *quick, quick, slow,* using four counts. Thus, step left (count one), closing step right to left (count two), step left (count three), and hold (count four). The pattern may be repeated starting right.

Schottische.   This four-count pattern is most frequently done by taking three small running steps following by a hop, each using one count. It is an easy, smooth pattern.

FIGURE 10-2. Folk dancers enjoy the exhilaration of rhythmic group activity.

Polka. Two long-short intervals based upon two counts make up the timing for one polka step. Depending on which part of this step one selects as a starting point, it becomes either a hop-step-close-step or a step-close-step-hop. To suggest one of the most satisfactory methods of learning it, let us use the second analysis. Students who have experienced difficulty in executing the step in sequence have picked it up readily by using a gallop as a basis. A gallop four times with the left foot leading, then a change to four gallops with the right foot leading, will establish a pattern that can then be reduced to two gallops with one foot followed by two gallops with the other foot. When this pattern is fixed, the tempo can be increased, and a hop substituted for the second close in the two-slide sequence. Thus, we have gallop gallop, and the polka step results.

Mazurka. This step required three even long counts to be performed once. One example is a high brush step right to the side on count one, a closing step on the left to the right on count two, and a hop left on count three. At the time of the hop the right leg is swung out, then the right knee is bent so that the foot comes close to the left knee. The foot is then lowered to the left ankle in readiness for the next mazurka step. This is a strong, vigorous step, done continuously to the same side unless a variation is introduced.

Waltz. A three-count pattern consisting of *step, step, close,* in which it must be remembered that the weight is transferred from one foot to the other. Thus, step left (count one), step right (count two), closing step left to right (count three). The pattern is then repeated starting with a step right.

Practice Suggestions

1. The primary concern of the teacher should be the selection of dances which are suited to the level of ability of the dancers. While there are many values of folk dancing, it should also be a joyous activity. There is no better way to discourage students and to create dislike for the activity than to attempt to teach beginners a long, complicated dance.
2. Before teaching a new dance, the teacher should review the basic step or steps that are involved. Basic steps may be practiced in a single or double circle, moving counterclockwise, which is the most common line of direction in folk dance.
3. The teacher should be thoroughly familiar with the dance and the music before attempting to present the material. A short background introduction to the dance may be given, but students should get into the activity as soon as possible. The teacher should then demonstrate the complete dance to music.
4. In the starting formation, the teacher can break down the parts of the dance into small units while verbalizing with one descriptive word for each action. If necessary, this may be done somewhat slower, speeding up until the skill approximates the rhythm of the dance. In beginning any dance part, the teacher might give a two word signal such as "Ready, and . . ." to alert dancers and allow for reaction time. When combining parts, the teacher may cue the dancers as to what will be next. Upon completion of the dance, corrections in skill or techniques may be given to the entire group. When the dance is repeated, any errors may be corrected individually.

Folk Dances for Beginners

Dance	Basic Step
Alunelul	Walk
Black Forest Mazurka	Mazurka
Doudlebska Polka	Polka
Hora	Walk
Jugo	Schottische
Kalvelis	Polka
Korobushka	Schottische
Laz Bar	Two-Step
Little Man in a Fix	Waltz
Miserlou	Two-Step
Polka zu Dreien	Polka
Salty Dog Rag	Schottische

SOCIAL DANCE

Social or ballroom dancing really began in the United States at the time of World War I with the introduction of many new forms of couple dances. The Charleston was followed by a series of "jitterbug" dances and the Latin-American rhythms which were performed to big swing bands. Rock and Roll music influenced an individual type of dance which led to performances of disco. Novelty and fad dances seem to fill a need at a particular time and may reflect changing trends in music. They may stimulate interest and participation, but they seldom last long enough to merit a place in the repertory of traditional social dances.

BASIC CONSIDERATIONS

Dance Positions

Closed. Partners facing, standing toe to toe, looking over opposite's right shoulder, man facing line of direction. Man's left hand holds lady's right hand about shoulder height, arms are relaxed and slightly bent at elbows. Man's right hand, fingers closed, placed on partner's back below her left shoulder blade or slightly above her waist. Lady's left hand placed on man's right shoulder, forearm relaxed on man's right upper arm (Figure 10-3).

Semi-Open. From closed position partners turn slightly away from one another looking in line of direction—man's right and lady's left sides are near each other.

Open. From semi-open position, turn apart so that both are facing in line of direction.

Reverse Open. Partners turn so that both are facing in reverse line of direction—man's left and lady's right sides are near each other. Man's right arm and lady's left arm may hang down at side (Figure 10-4).

Line of Direction

In general, couples move about the floor in a counterclockwise circle known as the line of direction (LOD). Couples may, however, move forward, backward, or sideward within this pattern; and, there are many new dance steps in which the couples dance in much the same spot.

Style and Etiquette

Every type of dance is performed with a certain style. The particular dance form, its tempo, and rhythm determine the style with which a particular dance is executed.

A man asks a woman to dance in a simple and direct way. "May I have the next dance?" or "Will you dance with me?" are the two customary approaches. It is polite to escort the woman to and from the floor and to thank her for the dance. Usually a man may cut in on a couple at a private party, but at a public dance, cutting in is not condoned. Dancers should always be courteous and well-mannered on the dance floor.

How to Lead and Follow

The man must indicate his steps and leads sufficiently in advance so that the woman can follow with confidence. He does this primarily with his upper torso, shoulders, and right arm and hand. The right hand becomes the steering rudder.

FIGURE 10-3. The closed position.

FIGURE 10-4. Reverse open position.

The woman's principal method of following is to remain relaxed so that her partner may guide her easily.

SUGGESTED LEARNING SEQUENCE

There is no set sequence for learning basic social dance patterns. The teacher might consider the interests and ages of the students, variety in rhythm, available music, and then select the order of dances that best fits the students. The following dances are described below in detail: Foxtrot, Waltz, Tango, Rhumba, Cha Cha Cha, Jitterbug.

KEY TO ABBREVIATIONS

Fwd—Forward
Back—Backward
R—Right
L—Left
S—Slow
Q—Quick
Close—Bring one foot to the other and
       take weight on it.

All steps indicated as slow use two beats of the music, and all steps indicated as quick use one beat of the music. Unless otherwise indicated, the steps described are for the man's (or lead) part; the lady's is opposite. For example, man's "forward left" would mean lady's "backward right."

Foxtrot 4/4 Time

Magic Step. Basic Rhythmic Pattern: *S S Q Q*

1. Closed Position
    Fwd left—*S*
    Fwd right—*S*
    Side left—*Q*
    Close right to left—*Q*

LEAD CUE: *Lift right arm, lean forward.*

2. Semi-open Position
    Side left—*S*
    Cross right over left—*S*
    Side left—*Q* (return to closed position)
    Closed right to left—*Q*

LEAD CUES:
    Pressure with heel of right hand.
    Pressure with finger tips of right hand.

3. Turn—Under
    Man's part same as semi-open position
    Lady's part:
    Side R; start to turn under R arm—*S*
    Complete turn under R arm onto L foot—*S*
    Side R—*Q* (return to closed position)
    Close L to R—*Q*
    Lady's right and man's left hands are released during turn.

Box Step. Basic Rhythmic Pattern: *S Q Q*

    Fwd L—*S*
    Side R—*Q*
    Close L to R—*Q*
    Back R—*S*
    Side L—*Q*
    Close R to L—*Q*

Waltz 3/4 Time

Basic Rhythmic Pattern: *Q Q Q*

1. Box step
    Same as Foxtrot except each step is *Q*

2. Crossover
    Do one-half Box
    Cross R over L (semi-open position)
    Side L (return to closed position)
    Close R

LEAD CUES:
    Pressure with heel of right hand.
    Pressure with finger tips.

Tango 4/4 or 2/4 Time

Basic Rhythmic Pattern: *S S Q Q S*

1. Basic step (closed position)
    Fwd L—*S*
    Fwd R—*S*
    Fwd L—*Q*
    Side R—*Q*
    Draw L to R, weight remaining on R—*S*

2. Semi-open Position
    Side L—*S*
    Cross R over L—*S*
    Fwd L—*Q*
    Side R—*Q*
    Draw L to R—*S*

LEAD CUES:
    Pressure with heel of right hand.
    Pressure with finger tips.

Rhumba 4/4 Time

Basic Rhythmic Pattern: *Q Q S*

1. Box (closed position)
    Side L—*Q*
    Close R—*Q*
    Fwd L—*S*
    Side R—*Q*
    Close L—*Q*
    Back R—*S*

2. Cuban Walk
    Walking forward or backward in the *Q Q S* rhythm.

Cha Cha Cha 4/4 Time

Basic Rhythmic Pattern: *S S Q Q S*

1. Basic Step (closed position)
   Dancing toward each other with hands held:
   Fwd L—*S*, Back R—*S*
   Back L—*Q*, Back R—*Q*
   Back L—*S*, Back R—*S*
   Fwd L—*S*, Fwd R—*Q*
   Fwd L—*Q*, Fwd R—*S*

2. Cross Step
   Cross L—*S* (reverse open position) Man's L and Lady's R hands joined
   In place R—*S*
   Side L—*Q*, Close R—*Q*, Side L—*S*
   Cross R—*S* (open position) Man's R and Lady's L hands joined
   In place L—*S*
   Side R—*Q*, Close L—*Q*, Side R—*S*

Jitterbug 4/4 Time

Basic Rhythmic Pattern: *S S Q Q*

1. Basic Step (closed position)
   Touch L, then take weight on L—*S*
   Place R, then take weight on R—*S*
   Back L—*Q* (semi-open position)
   Fwd R—*Q* (return to closed position)

2. Basic Turn Man's Part same as Basic Step
   Lady's Part:
   Start to turn to R under R arm on R foot—*S*
   Complete turn under R arm on L foot—*S*
   Back R—facing partner—*Q*
   Fwd L—*Q*
   Start to turn to L under R arm on R foot—*S*
   Complete turn under R arm on L foot—*S*
   Back R—facing partner—*Q*
   Fwd L—*Q*

LEAD CUES:
   Pressure with heel of right hand.
   Pressure with finger tips.

Once the basic step patterns are learned the teacher may introduce variations or the students may be encouraged to create their own modifications.

Practice Suggestions

Since leading and following are basic elements for partner dances, the teacher should introduce them by using a simple dance walk. Today's young persons are not accustomed to dancing in contact with a partner, traveling on a dance floor, or following a definite basic step. The teacher, therefore, should try to begin in a fundamental manner.

Using a free formation, the basic step of any social dance should be learned without a partner. The teacher, prior to presenting the foot pattern,

might have students clap hands to the music which will be used for the dance, because being able to recognize the underlying rhythm is essential. The basic step pattern should be performed next with partners, all couples moving in line of direction. While the individuals keep dancing, the teacher may give verbal cues in relation to position, rhythm, or step pattern. If necessary, individual assistance may be continued through additional demonstration or dancing with the student. Students may receive extra ideas or be encouraged to create variations with partners learning together.

In the teaching of social dance, it is important to provide a relaxed learning atmosphere; to suggest and implement partner changes; to build confidence through words of encouragement; and to give opportunities for everyone to practice good social etiquette.

MODERN DANCE

Unlike the types of dance discussed earlier in this chapter, modern dance is considered an art form on a par with painting, sculpture, music, and ballet. It began as an experimental movement away from the restrictions of classical ballet, and today it encompasses a broad spectrum of techniques and thematic concepts. Many colleges and universities now offer undergraduate majors in modern dance, and some offer advanced degrees. For many students who are not looking to a professional career, this dance form offers an opportunity to develop a strong, supple, well-coordinated body, and to use the whole body as an instrument of expression. In this section the beginner will obtain some basic understanding of the elements of modern dance, and practical suggestions for techniques, improvisation, and choreography.

PRINCIPLES OF MOVEMENT

Movement Determined by the Body Structure

Students of dance must train their instruments—their bodies—to be as fully responsive as possible to the demands of beautiful, skilled movements. Flexibility, coordination, strength, control, and balance are among the basic tools one should acquire in technique classes. These abilities also enable the dancer to perform special skills such as complex turns, spirals, and falls. The beginning dancer should be guided in the correct alignment of the body to enable freedom and clarity of movement. Each bony portion of the body should be lined up directly over or under another. The head is held

FIGURE 10-5. A roll from a standing position.

level and tall above relaxed (not collapsed) shoulders, under which is a very high (not forward) chest, narrow waist, and pulled-up abdomen. The hips are lined up directly under the chest, not pushed forward or back. The legs are pulled up straight, not locked or hyperextended. The body weight is held up from the center of each relaxed foot. The posterior and anterior torso should be high and strong enough to allow the extremities to remain relaxed and free to move. Nothing should be "gripping." Poor posture or alignment not only hampers technical facility, but can ultimately lead to sprains and dislocations or can aggravate other injuries.

The beginner should be encouraged to use the body as freely and fully as possible. This develops an appreciation of movement and a realization of actually dancing. Later, as the body becomes more finely "tuned," the dancer is trained to control specific parts of the body for subtler, more economical expression. The modern dancer has many ways to portray the emotional and psychological content of a performance, and searches for ways to move to modern, dissonant, and rhythmically complex music and sounds. An acute kinesthetic sense must develop in the dancer so that the sensation of movement, the visual shape, becomes the guidepost. Depth, quality, and dynamics of the sensation are conveyed by the dancer to the observer, creating an enriching experience shared by both. Beside such training, the dancer should clearly comprehend the limited number of ways a human being can move. These may be categorized as axial movements and locomotor movements.

Axial movements occur in space but do not transport the body from place to place. They include:

1. Flexion—bending
2. Extension—raising or stretching
3. Rotation—twisting
4. Adduction—moving a body segment toward the central axis of the body
5. Abduction—moving a body segment away from the central axis of the body
6. Circumduction—circling the entire torso or any body part
7. A combination of the above

Locomotor movements involve moving from one place to another in space. They include the walk-step, run, leap, hop, jump, and combinations such as the skip-step and hop; gallop-step and leap; slide-step and leap moving sideways.

Movement Determined by the Environment and the Demands of Dance

There are a number of elements of movement that can be analyzed. We move within a specific rhythmic structure, and with a variety of muscular forces, all having relationship to physical forces such as gravity, acceleration, and momentum. We move in space making designs, and through space by means of locomotor patterns.

Rhythm. The rhythmic structure organizes the movement into repeatable units of time. Rhythm is composed essentially of both force and time factors. Dynamics is a frequently preferred term for describing the relationship between force and time. Rhythmic factors include:

1. Tempo—variation from fast to slow.
2. Underlying beat—the steady pulse inherent in a particular movement phrase. Three ways to arrive at a basic beat are through:
   a. Metric or movement counts determined by the accompaniment.
   b. Breath rhythm determined by the intervals of inhalation-exhalation and carried like a pulse through the body.
   c. Emotional rhythm determined by the inner motivation of the dancer and the expressive content of the work.
3. Phrase—sequence of long and short beats with a feeling of unity; an idea suggested but not complete in itself, though having its own beginning and dynamic line followed by a pause before a new phrase begins.
4. Accent—emphasis given in movement, sound, force, space, tempo in the beat. Silence, or arrested movement, can be as much an accent as a loud sound or abrupt movement.
5. Syncopation—an unexpected or displaced accent in the general pattern. This engenders surprise

and excitement as heard in jazz or felt in clapping two beats while walking three in the same given time.

— — — walk
—— —— clap
———————— time length

Force. Force conveys the quality, texture, or kinesthetic and emotional energy underlying a dance. Energy or force is that factor which enables one to feel the qualitative differences. Muscles and joints are capable of moving with varying degrees and combinations of forces; each is as different as the texture of velvet is from silk or tweed. These forces may be expressed as:

1. Sustained—an evenly timed, controlled flow of energy. The muscles resist gravity in varying degrees from very, very strong to light and airy. There is an equalization of muscle tension, as in movements requiring careful balance or slow motion.
2. Swing—an alternate swaying, suspended, to-and-fro use of energy. There is a passive acceleration as the dancer gives in to gravity and a more active retardation as the dancer completes the arc of the swing. The swing has a characteristic beat of three for each phase.
3. Ballistic—a piston-like thrusting use of energy. The dancer attacks out against gravity and recovers with an equal action before momentum is overcome. There is a gradual dying down of the movement between the two attacks. Such movements usually have an underlying beat of two and need far more energy than does the relaxed swing. A series of vigorous leaps or fast, stiff-kneed, high marching steps require ballistic force.
4. Percussive—a sharp, explosive use of energy. The muscles fixate against gravity as the movement comes to an abrupt halt, rather than "following through." The halt usually occurs in one beat, though the preceding and following movements may be in any other quality and time. Percussive moments are the strongest peaks of a movement. Much of the excitement felt in watching primitive and jazz dance is due to a continual use of percussive energy.
5. Vibratory—a continuous back-and-forth use of energy. Short, percussive movements done very

rapidly produce this effect but are difficult to prolong because of the high tension and control required to keep them even.

6. Collapsing—a letting go of muscular energy. The dancer's body or a part of it gives in to the force of gravity. To recover from the fall requires any other use of energy called for to convey the idea in mind. A true collapse occurs in one time interval, a long or short beat.

Space. The special element limits and defines the movement through the factors of:

1. Direction
   a. Line of motion—forward, backward, sideward, diagonal, turning, circular.
   b. Focus—use of eyes or a body part, such as a leg, to emphasize a point of attention.
2. Range
   a. Distance covered—by locomotion.
   b. Degree and number of joint actions—in axial movement, from narrow to broad. For example, a greeting by a slight nod or a deep, sweeping bow.
3. Levels—low through high.
4. Body facing—front, side, diagonal, back, up, down—all in relation to the location of the *front* of the given work space.

SUGGESTED LEARNING SEQUENCE

Dance classes are conducted in various manners but they all consist of the same basic elements. There is a time for warm-up, locomotor and axial combinations, creative endeavors, and concluding activities. The student learns how the elements of rhythm, force, and space can be used in dance during these class experiments.

Warm-up. The warm-up often consists of stretches starting with the large muscle groups and then progressing to the small muscle groups. Stretching helps the dancer gain flexibility, control, and balance in movement, and also places emphasis on the correct body alignment necessary to execute the movement. It is important to execute the warm-up exercises in a dance-like manner so that the students realize the relationship between the warm-up and actual dancing. Stretches vary in intensity and acceleration but have a common factor of being in motion, always attempting to increase the range of motion.

Locomotor Movement. Locomotor movements enable the student to discover space. The use of change in direction, level, and focus for basic movements creates an awareness of the emotional expressions possible and of the dimensions of movements to fill the shape of the space. Locomotor and axial movements are combined to develop the balance and control stressed in the warm-up. These movement phrases aid in exploring movement combinations which can create possible sections of dance compositions.

The beginning dance student finds satisfaction in completing movement sequences using familiar and unfamiliar material. Combining walks, runs, falls, rolls, and pauses allows the student to experiment with the changes in force and rhythm, and to become comfortable with the floor through contact with all parts of the body and not just the feet. This often allays the fear of injury many beginners have when working on a bare floor and also broadens their experience in movement. The beginner must be guided in creative activities through a series of movement problems ranging from the simple to the complex.

Improvisation. Improvisation can be an exciting experience for the dance student. It is essential to create a comfortable atmosphere of freedom for exploration to take place. The dancer should be familiar with all areas of the space and be aware of the other persons in the space. Improvisation may take place employing a large group of dancers or an individual. One example of developing a series of movement explorations is by working with a circle and the parts of a circle. Circular floor patterns, large and small, may be shown by using basic locomotor movements such as walks, runs, or leaps. The full circle pattern then can be changed to half-circles with full circles, sometimes developing into spirals. This same series may be executed by isolating different parts of the body to include swinging motions, figure eights, and turns.

Improvisation may be an end in itself or a tool for developing choreography. It is important during improvisation that the student learn to make decisions in movement sequences, to recreate patterns explored, and to develop new techniques and styles on the body instrument.

Conclusion. The concluding activity of a class session varies with the material presented. It may include stretches to relax and cool down the body or a presentation of movement sequences developed during the time period. Students become aware of the dramatic implications of movement through observation. Discussions concerning the sequences and causes of the effectiveness increase awareness

and appreciation in the student for other dances and dancers.

Warm-up and Stretch Techniques

Listed below are some specific ideas for class use.

A. Bend Series

1. Stand in easy wide stride.
2. Bend forward from the hips, lengthen the spine parallel to the floor.
3. Lateral flexion to the right, extend left arm reaching to the right over the head.
4. Repeat lateral flexion to the left.
5. Bend backwards by bending the knees and lead with the head, arching the upper torso toward the backward direction.

Variations

1. Stretch in all directions for 8 counts and then in diminishing counts of 4-2-1.
2. Bounce in all directions in diminishing counts of 8-4-2-1.
3. Same series sitting with straight legs in wide stride.
4. Same series sitting with soles of the feet together.

B. Leg Swing Series

1. Stand straight with right leg extended to the back.
2. Swing the right leg forward and backward from the hip with a relaxed knee for 7 counts and step on count 8.
3. Repeat with left leg.
4. Swing the right leg across the body and then out to the right side for 7 counts; step on count 8.
5. Repeat with left leg.
6. Swing the right leg in a circle moving from side right to the left and returning to the right; and step on the right foot.
7. Repeat with the left leg and continue alternating legs through 8 counts.
8. The arms move in opposition to the motion of the legs, forward, backward, sideward, and circling.

C. Foot Series

1. Stand with feet in parallel position a few inches apart.
2. Extend right leg until only the ball of the foot and toes touch the floor.
3. Push the toes into a point.
4. Pull back onto the ball of the foot.
5. Plié both legs placing the heels of the feet on the floor (feet will be in fourth ballet position, parallel).
6. Relevé on both legs (extend both legs and rise onto the balls of the feet).
7. Plié again.
8. Point the right foot.

9. Pull the right foot back into parallel position.
10. Repeat on the left foot and execute as many repetitions as desired.

NOTE: Cue words for this series are: *"ball of the foot, point, ball of the foot, plié, relevé, plié, point, pull back."*

These are examples of parts of a warm-up which need to be combined with other techniques to prepare the body for vigorous activity. It is essential to sufficiently warm-up the feet and legs if leaps, jumps, and hops are to be stressed during the class session. A warm-up does not necessarily consist of only axial movements. Locomotor combinations of the walk using pliés and relevés, lunges and leg swings also may be used. Variations on stretches may be executed by working with a partner and using specific parts of the body, such as the ribs, hips, shoulders, or knees as the impulse for the stretch. The partner acts as an opposing force and also serves as protection against injury in case the dancer who is stretching begins to topple over.

Locomotor Movements

A. Slide Series

1. Slide to the right and then the left in diminishing counts of 8-4-2-1.
2. Three slides, then half-turn on the fourth slide.
3. Three slides then a full turn jump on the fourth slide.

B. Triplet Series

A triplet is three forward steps with an accent on the first step.

1. Triplets moving forward.
2. Two triplets forward and a turning triplet.
3. Two triplets, a turning triplet, a reach in relevé to the free side and a side fall in the opposite direction.

C. Hop Series

1. Three runs forward then hop.
2. Three runs then turn the hop.
3. Two steps and a hop.
4. Step, hop, step, leap.

Locomotor movements should include the use of the arms in a variety of ways to complement and contrast the basic movements. Arms may move in opposition to each other, in parallel positions, in a static pose, or only one arm moving at a time. The beginning student often has difficulty coordinating the arms with other dance movements; therefore, simplicity in arm positions is essential until some mastery of the movement has been accomplished. The challenge of different arm, leg, and torso move-

ments and their combinations stimulates the dance student to strive for achievement and more complexity of movement.

Creative Activities—Improvisation

A. Individual dancers create a floor pattern to fit a designated space.
B. Individual dancers explore with movement the elements of weight and weightlessness.
C. Create a movement sequence.

The dancers execute the sequence using various images to change the quality and emotional expression of the sequence, for example, being by a lake, moving through a haunted house, or moving in a comic style.

Ideas for creative activities evolve from numerous sources. The beginning dancer may wish to work with a basic movement such as the swing and discover how the parts of the body swing, then combine these swings with changes in focus and level, then the changes in rhythm and then how the movement develops as a locomotor or axial action.

The images and impulse for the movement may be abstract or literal in nature. A prop such as a rope, a cape, or a box may be used to stimulate activity. Exploring movement using various points of attachment with another person or persons can be interesting and create awareness of dancing with other dancers.

The problems presented to stimulate creativity must be clearly designed and have specific goals, especially for the beginner. Improvisation and exploration of movement should develop an expansion of emotional expression as well as technical accomplishment.

FIGURE 10-6. Dancers exploring compositional designs.

ELEMENTS OF CHOREOGRAPHY

As in music, painting, and the other arts, dance must have both subject and structure—content and form. The subject may be something as concrete as a story or character study (representative, denotative) or as abstract as an emotional or mood idea (manifestative, connotative). Movement itself is often used as an initial stimulus to begin a dance; the gestures, principles of movement, and kinesthetic experience of the dancer will suggest further material. For example, the performer may move forward three beats with the arms rised, then discover a natural swaying of the arms could be used to good advantage by making them move in small arcs. This may suggest a leg gesture of a similar style the next time a forward movement is used; this could be executed in five beats, then with stronger tension and a different focus. Eventually, a whole phrase or dance assumes shape.

Modern dancers have been experimenting with many abstract ideas as subject matter. Among these, a student may find interest in explorations of physical principles, such as the movement and structure of the atom, and the effects of centrifugal force on the body. Atonal and twelve-tone music, as well as sounds from nature, cities, and electronic machines, are other fields of interest. The use of objects such as elastic ropes or large discs, innovations in costume design and material such as stretchable tent-shapes, and stage sets such as slanting boards and mesh-wired enclosures—all open many possibilities for original and meaningful dances. There is virtually little in life that could not be the source of creative work. A student may find that nature ideas—the wind, seas, birds, fire, the seasons—suggest qualities and themes that can become a full-length work. Themes based on work, play, routine—sowing and harvesting, a basketball game, geometric shapes—are all fruitful sources for beginning choreographers.

After the subject has been chosen, the dancer must begin to find the movements expressive as a theme or basic material from which many of the later combinations will come. Improvisation is one of the most valuable tools for discovering movement. The student simply moves spontaneously with or without music, then employs dramatic actions or dances freely with other persons. Gradually, the movements will be molded into a concrete, rhythmic, spatial form. New ideas will arise from work on the dance itself. One should take care to be specific about what one is trying to say. It is important to develop good work habits, including the ability to make decisions, to change something, and to stay with the problem at hand until it is resolved. Sometimes it is helpful to ask someone to observe parts of a dance to determine whether that one is feeling or attempting to say is really conveyed in the movement.

Another way to begin a dance is within an already set form. Literary forms such as poetry, plays, and short stories may be used. Musical forms lend themselves well to dance; for example: ABA, rondo, ABC, theme and variations. Different instruments in a quartet may be copied in movement—the oboe, drum, violin, and flute, for example. Early musical dance forms such as the pavane, gigue, or gavotte, can bring excellent results.

Whether or not a dancer works within a set framework, the overall design is still the prime concern. Some of the following aesthetic principles must be observed not only in a finished dance but in any art work.

1. *Balance:* Alternations of length, energy, symmetrical and asymmetrical designs, and so on.
2. *Repetition:* Needed for familiarity of the themes; for making one "whole" of a piece, for emphasis.
3. *Contrast:* In force, time, space; needed for interest, heightened drama.
4. *Unity:* Again, to make a dance a satisfying whole structure.
5. *Sequence:* Phrases and sections need to follow each other for coherence.
6. *Transition:* The way in which movements and phrases change from one to another. Transitional movements must not be important within themselves, but should be smooth and part of the dance proper.
7. *Variety:* For interest, by manipulating any principle or dramatic idea.
8. *Climax:* A structural high point in a dance; pre-

FIGURE 10-7. Dancers exploring group design.

sent in a classical approach to composition, needed for developing the conclusion of the dance.

In today's dance theater, the more experimental avant-garde choreographers often depart from many of these principles. The novice, however, will produce more fruitful results when given disciplines to follow.

To compose a dance, the beginning student may find it best to use one or only a few dancers and stay within the limits of an idea small in scope and length. It is wise to select an idea about which the student has some knowledge or experience. Choreographing for a large number can become as complex as writing for a symphony orchestra. As in any art, simplicity and honesty in staying with one idea, no matter how limited it may seem at first, are necessities in learning the discipline demanded by dance. Too many philosophical ideas incorporated into a dance tend to weaken the real value of the piece. The value lies in the movements, not in words. The medium of the dance is movement; its province is one in which moods, feelings, and meaningful activities in space and time can put into visual forms what words cannot express. Every human being who can move can find personal and shared values in the dance.

SELECTED REFERENCES

ANDREWS, EMILY, et al. *Physical Education for Girls and Women,* 2nd ed. Englewood Cliffs, N.J.: Prentice-Hall, Inc., 1963.

COHEN, SELMA JEANNE. *The Modern Dance.* Middletown, Conn.: Wesleyan University Press, 1966.

DeHAAN FREED, MARGARET. *A Time to Teach, A Time to Dance.* Sacramento, Calif.: Jalmar Press, Inc., 1976.

DeMILLE, AGNES. *To a Young Dancer.* Boston: Little, Brown and Company, 1960–62.

ELLIS, HAVELOCK. *The Dance of Life.* New York: Modern Library, Inc., 1923.

HAYES, ELIZABETH R. *Introduction to the Teaching of Dance.* New York: The Ronald Press Company, 1964.

HAYS, JOAN F. *Modern Dance: A Biomechanical Approach to Teaching.* St. Louis, Mo.: The C.V. Mosby Company, 1981.

HORST, LOUIS, and CAROLL RUSSELL. *Modern Dance Forms in Relation to the Other Modern Arts.* Brooklyn, N.Y.: Dance Horizons.

LOCKHART, AILEENE, and ESTHER PEASE. *Modern Dance,* 5th ed. Dubuque, Iowa: Wm. C. Brown Company, 1977.

PEASE, ESTHER. *Modern Dance.* Dubuque, Iowa: Wm. C. Brown Company, 1966.

PENROD, JAMES, and JANICE GUDDE PLASTINO. *The Dancer Prepares.* Palo Alto, Calif.: National Press Books, 1970.

SHERBON, ELIZABETH. *On the Count of One,* 2nd ed. Palo Alto, Calif.: Mayfield Publishing Company, 1975.

FENCING

THIS CHAPTER WILL ENABLE YOU TO:

♦ Identify the types of equipment used in foil fencing, and name the parts of the French foil.
♦ Perform some of the basic skills of foil fencing while participating in a bout, including the grip, salute, on-guard, advance, retreat, lunge, defense, parries, engagements, and attacks.
♦ Identify and apply some of the basic strategies used during a foil fencing bout.
♦ Identify and apply the rules of foil fencing as participant in a bout or as a spectator.
♦ Officiate as a judge at a bout and apply the rules.
♦ Know and use the proper safety precautions.
♦ Define and use the terminology generally associated with foil fencing.

NATURE AND PURPOSE

Modern fencing is a combat sport practiced by men and women of all ages from 8 to 80 and at every level from novice to Olympic. A fencing bout retains many of the characteristics of a real fight but without the attendant dangers usually associated with the use of swords. Foils of course are not sharp, and the fencer scores a point by touching an opponent anywhere on the torso.

To touch the opponent without being touched is the name of the game. In days long past, a duelist certainly knew when he had been touched by a sharp sword. In modern foil competition, the weapons are wired so that when a touch lands, a scoring box shows a light and a buzzer sounds. Such equipment is now required at most competitions, but in the typical physical education class it is impractical and expensive to use the electrical foil. In such classes, student judges stand alongside the fencers and watch for touches.

For most people, fencing is a new athletic experience and even the early lessons are fun. At first, the emphasis is on footwork, body position, and maintaining correct distance. As these are mastered, concentration shifts to the proper use of the foil. By the end of a course, a student can expect to do some actual fencing and to know some of the rules and terms of the sport. Bouting experience with a wide variety of opponents is an important part of any fencer's development; therefore after the basic skills are learned, the student should seek opportunities to test these skills against other fencers.

EQUIPMENT

Fencing Weapons

The three types of competitive weapons used are the épée, the sabre, and the foil (Figure 11-1).

The épée, a direct decendant of the rapier, has a large bell guard. Touches may be made only with the tip of the épée, and the entire body is valid target. The sabre (or saber) is principally a slashing weapon, although the tip may also be used; the target area includes all body parts above the hips. The foil is a light thrusting weapon, and the target area is the torso. This chapter will deal with the French foil, because most teachers favor its use by beginners. Figure 11-2 shows the parts of the French foil.

The usual class equipment consists of a mask, a foil, and a half-jacket. The mask comes in three sizes: small, medium, and large. The jacket sizes are small, medium, large, and extra-large, and are either right- or left-handed depending on the sleeve placement.

Foil grips are right- or left-handed, and the teacher might mark them as such to expedite issue. The foil tip should be covered with adhesive tape or a rubber tip, and a slight downward bend should have been worked into the first one-third of the blade.

The glove worn by a fencer is usually leather with a padded gauntlet. The gauntlet should be long enough to cover the end of the jacket sleeve so the point of an opponent's foil will not slide inside the sleeve. The beginner may wear any type of glove during the initial stage of learning in order to get used to the "feel" of a glove on the hand.

RULES

All fencing rules are identical for both men and women. However, men do not normally compete against women.

Touches and Target. In foil fencing the target is the body exclusive of the head and appendages. It begins at the top of the jacket collar and extends in front down to the groin and in back to the top of the hips. The sleeve seams mark the side limits.

A valid touch is one made with the foil point on valid target area. Contact made with the side of the blade never counts and is simply referred to as a slap. If the point slides along the target without momentarily fixing, it does not count. Touches made with the point on invalid target areas (mask, legs, arms) do not count but do cause the bout to be stopped.

Playing Area. For class purposes, any large room will serve very well for instruction and bouting. When judged bouts are held, boundaries can be quickly marked with masking tape. Precise measurement is seldom needed and a rectangular strip 46 feet by 6 feet should be laid out. Two on-guard lines need to be marked 6 feet in both directions from the center, and warning lines are placed 3 feet from each end. A diagram of a regulation strip is shown in Figure 11-3.

At the start of a bout and also after each scored point, the fencers begin at the on-guard lines and must remain on the strip during the bout. Stepping off the side with both feet is a violation. The director stops the bout and positions the fencer on the strip one meter further back from where he or she went off. Whenever the rear foot of a retreating fencer reaches a warning line, the director calls a halt and informs the fencer about being on the meter line. This warns the fencer that continued retreat beyond the end line with both feet will result in a point being awarded.

Officiating. In nonelectric fencing, a foil jury is made up of a director and four side judges. Two judges stand beside each fencer and watch for touches made against the opposing fencer. The director maintains a central position in order to observe the entire jury as well as the competitors (Figure 11-4). The judges and the director must move around as the fencers move, so as to maintain their relative positions.

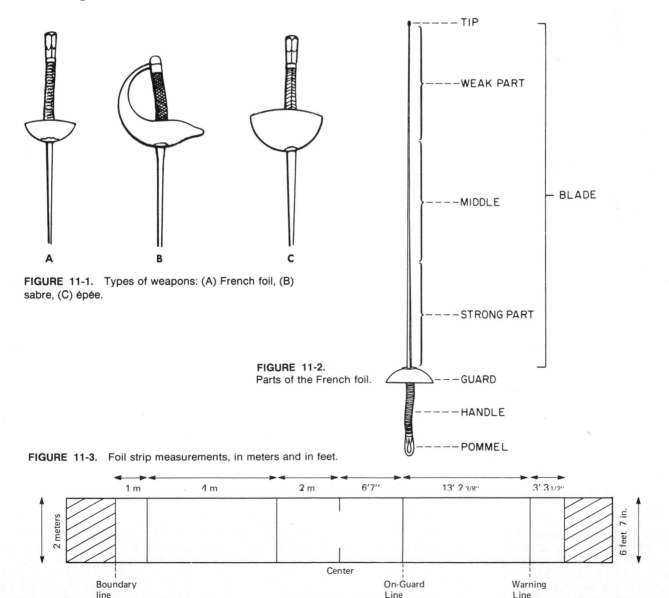

FIGURE 11-1. Types of weapons: (A) French foil, (B) sabre, (C) épée.

FIGURE 11-2.
Parts of the French foil.

FIGURE 11-3. Foil strip measurements, in meters and in feet.

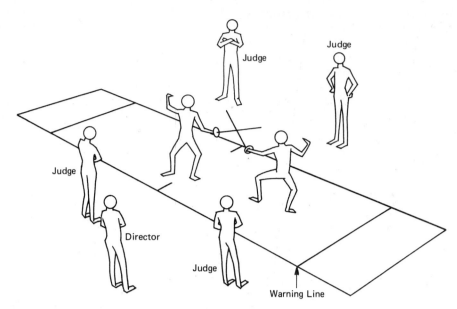

FIGURE 11-4. Positions of jury for non-electric foil. (Adapted from Charles Simonian, *Basic Foil Fencing.* Kendall/Hunt Publishing Company, 1979.)

The director is in total control of the bout and gives the orders to fence or to halt. The judge's primary responsibility is to observe when a touch is made on either valid or invalid target, and to signal by raising an arm to indicate that a touch landed. While the director also watches for touches, it is the sole responsibility of the director to determine which fencer had the right of way in any situation where both fencers received touches at about the same time.

When a judge raises a hand, the director immediately calls a halt and proceeds to analyze the action just completed. As each step is described, the director polls the two judges from whose side the action was initiated. The analysis and voting continue until a decision has been reached to award or not award a point.

Votes. The judge will vote *no* if the attack missed or was parried.

The vote is *yes* if the attacking point clearly fixed on valid target.

The vote is *abstain* if the judge could not see the action clearly or is unsure of a touch.

The vote is *yes, but invalid* if the point was seen to fix on invalid target.

The vote of each judge is worth one point, while that of the director is one and one-half points. Thus, if two judges have agreed on the vote, they could override a contrary vote of the director by 2 to 1½. If the director and one judge have the same opinion about the touch, they prevail over the other judge by 2½ to 1. An abstention carries no point value in the voting. If the two judges have contradictory opinions while the director abstains, there is a one to one tie that results in a *doubtful touch* decision, and no point is awarded.

If the jury decides that a particular action landed on invalid target, no further voting is needed and fencing is resumed. In other words, any touch on invalid area stops the action and nullifies any other touches that might have landed during that phrase. There is no penalty for invalid (off-target) hits.

Scoring. Each time the director awards a point, that point is recorded next to the name of the fencer who was hit. Therefore, the fencer with the lower score at any time is leading in the bout. When one fencer has been hit five times, the bout ends. The bout may also end if time expires, and the winner will be the fencer who led at that moment. When time runs out, enough points are added to the scores of each fencer to bring the loser's score up to five points.

Time limits are seldom used in informal or intramural meets. Where time limits are in effect, the competitors will need to be aware of the time that is allowed. Normally, a one-minute warning is given as the limit is approaching.

Types of Competitions

Most amateur meets are run on either a pool or a direct elimination system. In a pool, each fencer meets every other fencer in the pool in a specified order, with the winner having the best won-lost record. In the direct elimination format, the fencer advances with a win or is out of the competition with a loss.

Men's intercollegiate meets consist of a total of 27 bouts, nine in each of the three weapons. Each team has three men per weapon who fence against the three men from the opposing team.

Women's intercollegiate teams usually have four women in foil who meet each of the opponent's four entries. Thus sixteen bouts are fought, and the team having the majority of wins is the winner. In the event of a tie in bouts won, there is a count of the number of touches scored by and against each team.

SAFETY CONSIDERATIONS

Fencing ranks among the safest of all sports, but common sense must be exercised at all times. The following safety measures should be adhered to while participating in this sport.

1. Any time that partners face one another, a mask must be worn.
2. The tip of the foil must be covered with adhesive tape or a rubber tip.
3. Be aware of a broken blade. Blades may break upon the slightest touch, and the jagged end could cause injury.
4. Masks which show rust or weak places and jackets which are torn should be discarded.
5. A fencing half-jacket or full jacket should be worn in class; sweatshirts offer no protection against a broken blade.

SUGGESTED LEARNING SEQUENCE

The skills should be learned in the order outlined below. A beginner can fence effectively if the skills through the *one-two* are learned. The counter-parries, the double, the beat, and the low line offense and defense can be added when more time is available.

A. Nature and Purpose of Foil Fencing
  1. Equipment requirements
  2. Safety considerations
B. Rules—A discussion of rules and officiating practice can begin when most appropriate and applicable to a situation. This discussion should be ongoing throughout the learning sequence.
C. Terminology—A discussion of terminology, like rules, is most meaningful in the learning experience when dealing with that particular reference to a term at a given time. The learning of the language of foil fencing should occur throughout each segment.
D. Skills and Techniques
  1. Gripping the foil
  2. Salute
  3. On-Guard
  4. Advance
  5. Retreat
  6. Lunge
  7. Defense
  8. Right of Way
  9. Guard Positions and Engagements
  10. Advance Lunge
  11. Disengagement Attack
  12. Compound Parries
  13. One-Two
  14. Counter Parries
  15. Double
  16. Low Line Parries
  17. Beat Attack
E. Strategies—Beginning strategies should be discussed once the fencer begins engaging in elementary bouts and at times most meaningful to the learner.

FOIL SKILLS AND TECHNIQUES

While it is much more fun to fence than to practice, you must realize that fencing too often and too soon will lead to bad habits. Fencing requires self-control and correct execution of skills, and there is no shortcut to success. Therefore, it is important to spend a large portion of class time doing drills to perfect the lunge, the footwork, and the blade skills. Some fencing must be done in order to relate the drills to the reality of the bout.

Gripping the Foil

Most beginners learn to fence with the French foil. As shown in Figure 11-5, the thumb and forefinger oppose one another on the broad surfaces of the handle, while the remaining three fingers rest lightly along the side. There is slight curvature to the rectangular handle, and the curves should be directed toward the palm and toward the thumb. The following instructions are directed to the right-handed student.

Learning Cues

1. Curve of the handle to the thumb side.
2. Index finger and thumb on handle near pad of bell guard.
3. The three remaining fingers rest lightly on the handle.
4. The forearm should be at approximately a 45-degree angle from the elbow joint.

FIGURE 11-5. Gripping the French foil (right-handed).

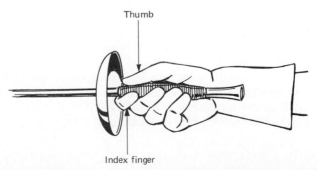

Salute

It is customary to salute your opponent or partner before a bout or a practice session. Stand erect with the heels together, the right foot pointing straight ahead and the rear foot placed at a right angle to the lead foot. From this position, bring the foil bell up to eye level and then smartly straighten the elbow to swing the foil downward.

On-Guard

Flex your sword arm enough to bring the foil point up to face level while maintaining a fairly straight line between the blade and your forearm. Bend the left arm and raise your elbow to about shoulder height; the forearm should be vertical and the wrist flexed and relaxed. While holding the arms in this position, take a short step forward, and bend both knees to a slight squat as in Figure 11-6.

FIGURE 11-6. The on-guard stance.

Learning Cues

1. Feet must be in line, weight evenly distributed on both legs; feet are 14 to 18 inches apart.
2. Flex the sword arm enough to bring the foil up to the face level while maintaining a fairly straight line between the blade and forearm.
3. Bend the left arm and raise the elbow to about shoulder height; the forearm should be vertical and the wrist flexed and relaxed.
4. While holding the arms in this position, take a short step forward and bend both knees to a slight squat.

Practice Suggestions

1. Place students on a line, check grip, have them go through a routine of the salute and then assume on-guard positions.
2. An effective drill for advance and retreat involves a leading partner who advances or retreats one or more steps at a time while the follower reacts and moves accordingly. Footwork should be varied so that the steps are sometimes slow and sometimes fast. Step lengths should range from quite short to fairly long.

This on-guard stance is designed to permit movement in either forward and rearward directions and to allow the effective launching of an attack. Your body weight should be evenly distributed onto both legs, and your feet should be spaced somewhere between fourteen and eighteen inches apart. The heels are in line and the feet are held at a right angle.

Advance

Whenever the opponent is too far away, one or more steps forward need to be taken. This is done by moving first the right foot a few inches forward and then the left foot an equal distance. Neither foot should slide on the floor.

Retreat

If the opponent is too close, the fencer will need to take one or more steps backward. The left foot will move first followed by the right foot.

Footwork must be responsive to the opponent's movements. The ability to change direction quickly in order to maintain a desired distance is very important.

Lunge

When two fencers maintain the correct distance, neither can hit the other by merely reaching out with the arm and foil. It will be necessary to take a long stretching step with the right foot in order to be able to touch the target with the foil tip. This is known as the *lunge* (Figure 11-7). Start by extending your sword arm toward the opponent. Your right

FIGURE 11-7. The lunge. (Courtesy of The Athletic Institute.)

hand will be shoulder high and the tip of the foil will be aimed at your opponent's chest. Next, lift the right foot, toes first, while simultaneously straightening your left knee and swinging your left arm to the rear in a large arc. The lunge ends with the right foot landing well out ahead, while the left foot remains where it was in the on-guard stance.

If the lunge results in a touch, it makes no real difference how the fencer recovers. But if the attack fails, it is most important that the fencer be able to recover quickly to a defensive position. This is done by bending at the left knee while pushing hard with the right foot. As the legs complete the recovery, the arms return to their proper positions in the on-guard stance.

The lunge is one of the most important movements in fencing and must be practiced diligently. The first lunges made by a beginner should be of medium length, because the muscles might be injured if long lunges are attempted before the student has the necessary flexibility. The need to fully extend the sword arm just before lifting the front foot must be stressed. A bout director must decide who the attacker is at any given time and does this by observing which fencer extended first to present a definite threat to the opponent. When two touches land at approximately the same time, the fencer who first extended will receive the priority in the decision.

Learning Cues

1. The sword arm is first extended toward the opponent.

2. The right foot, toes first, are lifted while simultaneously straightening the left knee and swinging the left arm to the rear in a large arc.
3. The right foot lands well out while the left foot remains anchored as in an on-guard position.
4. To recover, the left knee is bent while pushing off with the right foot.

Practice Suggestions

NOTE: Because of the sudden lunging movement forward it is important to do a series of stretching exercises with particular attention given to the major muscle groups of the leg and back.

1. Begin with students in a line in an on-guard position. Practice taking short to medium steps, then gradually lengthening the forward step.
2. With a partner, practice lunge at a partner then recover to guard.
3. With a partner, practice an advance-lunge-recover-and-retreat sequence.

Defense

When being attacked, a fencer generally has two broad options. One is to retreat and cause the attack to fall short, and the other is to deflect the attacking blade. If the attacking blade is to the left of your own, move your foil sharply to the left just enough to contact and deflect the blade away from your target. This is known as the *parry four*, the most common and strongest of the eight simple parries (Figure 11-8). Deflection of the attacker's blade to the

FIGURE 11-8. The simple parry four. (Photos by Ted Rice.)

FIGURE 11-9. The simple parry six.

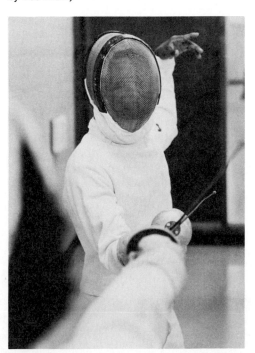

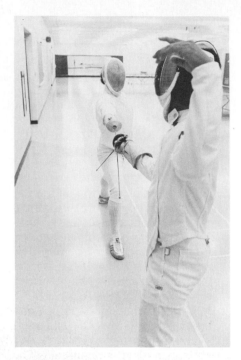

FIGURE 11-10. The simple parry seven being made by the near fencer. (Photos by Ted Rice.)

FIGURE 11-11. The simple parry eight being made by the far fencer.

right is made with the *parry six* (Figure 11-9). In both of these parries, the hand and blade should move horizontally right or left; the tip and the hand do not change level, and the elbow remains bent.

Following a successful parry, the defender now has the opportunity to make a counterattack through the use of a *riposte.* This may be a simple reaching out to touch the opponent, but if the attacker is quick enough to recover after having been parried, the defender may have to lunge to score with the riposte.

Right of Way

Any time that there is a single touch landing, the director has no problem in awarding the touch. However, if both fencers hit at the same time, the director must decide which, if either, had the *right of way.* An attack is correctly made and has the right of way when the swordarm is fully extended as the lunge begins. The opponent must take defensive action by retreating or parrying. If the parry is successful, the right of way now passes to the defender who may riposte, and the former attacker is obliged to take some defensive action. Thus the right of way can change back and forth several times in any given flurry of action.

Suggestions for Practice Bouts

Students could have some early bout experience as soon as the skills and rules described above have been learned. In a practice bout without judges, two fencers get on guard a few feet apart and begin to fence. After a bit of maneuvering, perhaps one will chance a lunge. The opponent might step back,

parry, or be hit. If the parry is made, the defender may fail to riposte immediately, thereby losing right of way, and either fencer may initiate the next attack. However, if the riposte is attempted, the new defender may recover, parry, or be hit. If both fencers attack correctly at the same moment and both touch, neither hit is counted. It is very helpful for the students to acknowledge being touched, but this is not required by the rules.

Guard Positions and Engagements

When in the on-guard stance, the swordarm can be held pretty much anywhere—to the right, to the left, low or high. It is best normally to hold the foil in the *sixth guard position,* which is identical to the sixth parry position in Figure 11-9. From this guard, the fencer may use the strong parry four. If the fencer chooses to stand on-guard while maintaining contact with the blade of the opponent, the blades are said to be *engaged.* Engagement numbers derive from the numbers of the comparable parries. For example, if your opponent's blade is to the left of your own, the contact is termed a *fourth engagement.*

Advance Lunge

Since defenders often retreat to avoid being touched by a lunging fencer, the attacker may put together an advance and a lunge in order to reach the target. There should be no pause between the advance and the lunge, and the right of way should be obtained by extending the swordarm during the advance. The beginner should be careful to make the advance only long enough to make up for the distance that the defender will retreat.

Disengagement Attacks

When a fencer's direct attacks are being repeatedly parried, it will soon occur to the attacker that the parry must somehow be avoided. One method for doing this is by means of a two-part action called the *disengagement*. The first move is the extension of the swordarm to give the impression that a direct attack is being started. If this feint convinces the defender of the need to parry, the attacker then deceives the parry by lowering the point and then raising it again as the parry goes past. This disengagement is of course followed by a lunge to complete the attack.

Properly executed, the disengagement avoids any blade contact by the defender. The swordarm remains extended throughout. As the attacker, you have to convince the defender that your initial extension is a real attack that must be parried. However, when you are the defender, you must not parry a mere feint. Until you learn to distinguish between a feint and a real threat, you should retreat as your first response to an attack.

Learning Cues

1. Extend arm to give illusion of an attack.
2. As a parry is made, lower the blade and then return it to a raised position.
3. Follow up with a lunge to complete the attack.

Practice Suggestion

For developing disengagement skills as well as defending skills, there is a very effective drill in which the defender may not retreat but may parry four or six. The attacker is permitted the options of direct lunge or disengagement lunge. In this drill, a well-made disengagement should touch, because the defender will be convinced that the feint is really an attack to be parried. On the other hand, a poorly made feint should get no response from the defender and the disengagement will be easily parried. To avoid guessing by the defender, it is important for the attacker to make a number of direct attacks in a row, all of which will be parried.

Compound Parries

As an attacker's disengagement is being attempted, the defender may parry a second or even a third time in an effort to contact and deflect the blade. Combinations of parries are termed *compound parries,* and these are reflexive responses by a defender who realizes that his initial parry failed to make contact.

One-Two

A pair of parries can be deceived by an attacker who makes two disengagement movements. The first disengagement serves as a feint to draw a defender's second parry which is then deceived by the second disengagement. As with most attacks, the swordarm should remain extended throughout so as to maintain the right of way.

Counter Parries

Defensive variety is necessary against more skilled opponents. Constant use of simple parries will be answered by disengagements and one-twos. Against a direct lunge, a defender in the sixth guard position may make a clockwise rotation of his or her foil in order to contact and carry the attacking blade to a sixth parry. From a fourth guard position, the rotation is counter-clockwise and terminates in a parry four.

Double

Against an opponent who utilizes counter parries, the attacker must deceive such parries by first making a feint of a direct thrust to draw the counter parry. As the parry is being made, the attacker's foil must circle in the same direction as that of the counter parry. By the use of the double, blade contact is avoided and the accompanying lunge should deliver the touch to the target.

Low Line Parries

When an attack is aimed at the lower target, the normal parries four and six cannot be used. Instead, the defender should lower the point and move the swordhand in the direction of the attacking blade in order to deflect it. The *parry seven* is used against attacks to the lower left side (Figure 11-10), while the *parry eight* is used when the threat is to the lower right target area (Figure 11-11). As with the high parries, the hand should move horizontally and remain higher than elbow level.

Low line parries may be deceived by feinting to a low target and then disengaging to a high target. Similarly, an attack may begin with a high feint and terminate with a disengagement to the low target.

Practice Suggestions

1. With a partner, practice counter parrying of attacks. (In this instance, the drill requires one fencer to attack in a predetermined manner in order that the one practicing the parry can have an opportunity to experiment with and learn the actual execution of the parry.)
2. Practice low line parries with a partner.
3. With a partner, practice the riposte from the parry. The partner should attack while the defender practices execution of riposte.

4. Practice riposte from disengagement.

NOTE: Once single skills have been well learned, drills that encourge a combination of the elements of the lunge, attack, parry, riposte, disengagement, advanced lunge, beat, advance, and retreat should be practiced.

Beat Attack

When an opponent is standing on-guard with an extended arm and a threatening point directed at your chest, a beat action can be used to remove this right of way. The *beat* is a sharp blow given to the defending blade to momentarily knock it aside and create an opening for an attack. Be careful not to wind up and thereby telegraph your intention to beat.

STRATEGIES

1. Your first concern should be to make it difficult for your opponent to hit you. The maintenance of good and consistent distance is important, so never let your opponent get closer than full lunge distance unless it is part of your game plan.
2. A retreat is the simplest and most effective defense against any attack; use it more often than you use your parries.
3. Offensively, you must analyze what your opponent is doing to stop your attacks. You cannot devise a good attack plan if you have not been able to recognize the defense being used against you.
4. Generally speaking, use the simplest attack that has a chance of scoring. Get more complex only if the opponent forces you to.
5. Attack with confidence as though you expect to hit. Too often the beginner is unsure and attacks timidly.
6. When you parry, the right of way is yours only if you riposte immediately. Be unpredictable in your defense—sometimes parry, sometimes retreat.
7. Remember that every fencer is different, and you must adjust your game accordingly. Unorthodox fencers and left-handers can be problems, and experience with a variety of opponents is necessary for anyone who wishes to become a good fencer.
8. Use each practice bout as an opportunity to improve your observational and fencing techniques. Don't try to win at the cost of damaging your hard-earned fundamental skills. In practice bouts it is better to lose while perfecting a particular skill or strategy than to win by resorting to sloppy tactics. Above all, enjoy each bout, and be sure to shake hands afterwards.

TERMINOLOGY

Advance A step taken toward an opponent while remaining on-guard.

Advance lunge An attack that combines an advance and a lunge.

Attack The initial forward movement of the weapon with an extended arm to threaten the opponent's valid target.

Beat attack A sharp blow given to the opponent's blade to create an opening for an attack.

Bout A competition between two fencers.

Corps-à-corps Physical contact between two fencers at close quarters.

Counter parry A circular parry that deflects an attacking blade into a line opposite to that of a simple parry.

Cutover A disengagement attack in which the blade is lifted over the defender's foil. Also called a coupé.

Deceive To offensively avoid contact by a defender's blade.

Director The official in charge of a jury. In Europe the director is called the president.

Disengagement An attack in which the blade passes under the defender's foil.

Double An attack comprised of a feint followed by a complete circle around the defender's counter parry.

Double touch A situation in which both fencers had equal right of way and both landed touches. No point is awarded.

Doubtful touch This is the decision whenever the polling of the jury does not produce a majority opinion. No point is awarded.

Engagement A held contact of blades when neither fencer is attacking.

Épée One of the three competitive weapons. Only the electrical version is used in meets. The bell is large and the entire body is valid target. There is no right of way.

Feint Any movement of the blade or body that will obtain a parry or other reaction from an opponent.

F.I.E. Fédération Internationale d'Escrime—the world governing body for amateur fencing.

Flèche (pronounced *flesh*) An attack in which the rear foot crosses in front of the leading foot. It is often followed by a short run because of the momentum developed. Potentially dangerous, this attack is not recommended for beginners.

Infighting Close combat that is permitted so long as there is no body contact or other violations such as use of the left hand or turning the back.

Invitation Any deliberate exposure of target that is intended to draw an opponent's attack.

Judge An official who stands beside one fencer to watch for touches made upon the other fencer.

Jury Made up of the director and the four judges.

Line A target area; may be referred to as high or low, inside or outside. It is also the term used to define a defender's position when the arm is fully extended and the point is threatening, that is, in line.

Low line   That part of the target that is below the defender's hand level in the on-guard stance.

Lunge   A means of delivering a touch by moving the leading foot substantially forward while the rear foot remains stationary.

Maître d'armes   French term for fencing master. A coach who has undergone a period of formal training and has passed an accrediting examination.

Match   A contest between two teams in any weapon. A series of bouts between the fencers of two different teams.

Meet   A full tournament between teams or individuals. A series of matches, bouts, or pools of bouts.

N.F.C.A.A.   National Fencing Coaches Association of America.

On-guard   The position assumed by a fencer when ready to fence.

One-two   An attack made up of two disengagements.

Parry   A deflection of an attacking blade. It is *simple* if it moves directly to the blade and *counter* if it describes a circle.

Phrase   Any unbroken series of offensive and defensive exchanges.

Pool   A group of fencers who will meet one another in round-robin competition.

Redoublement   A new action made after the original attack is parried but no riposte is forthcoming.

Remise   An immediate continuation of an attack that has been parried. A touch by remise can be allowed only if the riposte misses or is delayed.

Retreat   A step taken backward away from an opponent.

Right of way   A fundamental rule in foil and sabre that determines which fencer had priority in a phrase.

Riposte   The return action that follows a successful parry.

Sabre (saber)   One of the three competitive weapons. The cutting edge is used more often than the point, and the target area is all parts of the body above the hip level, including the head and arms.

Salle d'armes   French term for fencing school or club.

Salute   A universal gesture used before practice or a bout. A simple version is the raising of the weapon to a vertical position, bell at face level.

Strip   The fencing area. It may be of any material and is marked with the boundary and warning lines. In electric foil and épée fencing, a copper strip is used in order to ground out touches made on the floor.

U.S.F.A.   United States Fencing Association, the governing body which organizes U.S. fencing competitions and develops rules.

SELECTED REFERENCES

ALAUX, MICHEL. *Modern Fencing.* New York: Charles Scribner's Sons, 1975.

SELBERG, CHARLES A. *Foil.* Reading, Mass.: Addison-Wesley Publishing Company, 1976.

SIMONIAN, CHARLES. *Basic Foil Fencing.* Dubuque, Iowa: Kendall/Hunt Publishing Company, 1979.

U.S.F.A. Rules Book. 1982 edition available through the U.S.F.A. Secretary, 601 Curtis St., Albany, CA 94706.

FIELD HOCKEY

THIS CHAPTER WILL ENABLE YOU TO:

♦ Identify the field markings.
♦ Describe the basic rules of the game.
♦ Analyze and demonstrate the techniques of holding the stick, dribbling, the drive, fielding, various passes, the tackle, the dodge, the penalty corner, the free hit, defense hit, and push in.
♦ Identify and describe the common goalkeeping techniques.
♦ Describe basic offensive and defensive tactics.
♦ Understand and use the basic terminology.

NATURE AND PURPOSE

Field hockey has changed significantly in recent years. Although the traditional 5-3-2 system is still used, more teams are moving to a style of play characteristic of the game of soccer. A spectator should expect to see a variety of systems being employed by a team based on the talents of the individual players.

The game is played by two teams of 11 players usually designated as forwards, midfielders (links), defensive backs, and a goalie. The forwards are offensive players and therefore they must be quick, good stick handlers, possess good dribbling skills, and must shoot well. The midfielders serve as links, transforming the game from defense to offense. The midfielders must be in good physical condition to play both offense and defense; they must be good playmakers to set up the forwards and sure tacklers to stop the offensive thrust of the opponent. The backs or defenders must be aggressive and well conditioned in addition to being good tacklers. They must have good enough stick skills to make long clears when necessary. The sweeper, the last link outside the goalie, directs play, shores up the defense, and must possess patience and good fielding skills. The sweeper must have a "nose" for the ball. Obviously, the goalie is the last link in the defensive chain. The goalie must have "catlike" reflexes and be aggressive. Although some players are by nature offensive or defensive, many coaches now emphasize total team offense and defense.

Each player carries a hockey stick (described later), with the exception of the goalkeeper, who is permitted certain kicking privileges. The only way players can move the ball is by the use of the stick.

Goals count one point and can be scored only if an attacker's stick touches the ball inside the strik-

ing circle. The official game is played in two periods of 35 minutes each, unless otherwise agreed, and with no more than 5 minutes between halves, at which time the teams shall change ends. The game is started by the center forwards taking a bully on the center line. After each goal, the center bully is repeated.

Although field hockey has been a predominantly girls and women's sport, it is also played by men in the United States. In other parts of the world it is recognized as an Olympic sport for men. Because of the vigorous nature of the game, and the skill, coordination and conditioning needed, field hockey would be an acceptable activity for both boys and girls and men and women in a school or college physical education program. Whether played by all boys or all girls or on a coeducational basis, it is important to emphasize the rules of play, particularly those governing the field hockey stick. On a coeducational basis there should be emphasis on the wearing of shinguards and other protective gear.

For coeducational play, any or all of the following rule modifications may be made.

1. Use of a softer rubber ball rather than official field hockey ball.
2. Forwards restricted to girls rather than boys or shots on goal by girls only.
3. Placing girls at every other position to encourage passes to boys and/or to girls.
4. Reducing the size of the field and the number of players (6 on 6) so the emphasis is on skill rather than on speed or strength.
5. All penalty shots taken by girls, the short or long corner pass made by the boys.
6. Eliminate the drive and allow only a push.
7. Eliminate the scoop or flick when shooting at goal.

PLAYING FIELD

The field is about the size of a football field, 100 yards long and 60 yards wide, with a goal at each end (Figure 12-1). Goal posts are 4 yards apart and 7 feet high, joined by a cross bar. The posts and cross bars are square and painted white. The goal is usually enclosed with a net or screen, supported by two additional posts approximately 6 feet behind the goal. A straight line is drawn 16 yards in front of the goal and 4 yards long. This line is continued to the goal line by quarter-circle arcs of 16-yard radius with the goal posts as centers, thus forming the striking circle. Lines are 3 inches wide.

EQUIPMENT

The Ball

The official ball is hard and slightly larger than a baseball. It is made of cork and string, covered with leather, and painted white. For class purposes, however, a seamless polyurethane ball would be more practical.

The Stick

The field hockey stick ranges from 32 to 36 inches in length and weighs from 18 to 21 ounces.

FIGURE 12-1. The hockey field.

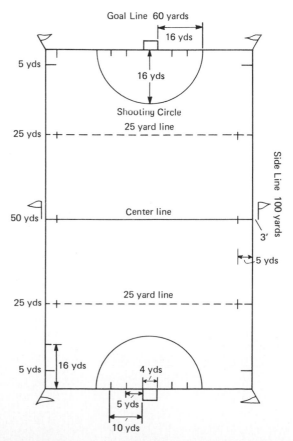

The thin portion above the heel has a polyfiber wrapping around the wood to give greater strength to this critical part. The blade is made of mulberry wood and is somewhat shorter today than it used to be. The left side of the blade is flat and is used for hitting the ball. The right side of the blade is rounded and may not be used for hitting the ball at any time.

When selecting a stick, it is important that the handle be comfortable, thin, and strong. The grain of the wood in the blade should follow around the curve to the toe of the stick to prevent splintering. The stick should be light enough to facilitate techniques and ease of control. The proper length for the stick is determined by the distance of the player's hands from the ground, and has nothing to do with the player's height or length of the legs. To determine the suitable stick length, the individual should stand erect, grasp the stick as for a drive, and swing it in front of the body. The stick should "feel" comfortable and should not hit the ground behind the ball at contact. For physical education classes there are junior sticks available for less than $10 which would serve the purpose.

Shin Guards and Pads

Light shin guards are wise protection and will not interfere with a player's ability to run. They will protect the ankle bones as well as the shins. Goalkeeper's pads should cover the leg from the thigh down. If the pads do not extend over the instep, kickers should be worn.

BASIC RULES

The following are the basic rules that apply to the game of field hockey. For coeducational play it may be necessary to modify some rules and perhaps add other rules to ensure safe play.

Fouls

1. When Playing the Ball, a Player Shall Not
   a. Raise any part of the stick above the shoulder at either the beginning or end of a stroke.

FIGURE 12-2. The hockey stick, right and left view.

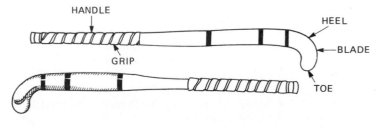

b. Hit the ball dangerously; i.e., into a player at close range, a hard ball that rises, or a ball hit on the fly.

c. Undercut—a drive type of stroke with the blade of the stick laid back and the ball raised dangerously.

d. Use the rounded side of the stick.

e. Stop the ball with any part of the body except the hand. When using the hand the ball must fall perpendicularly and not rebound in any direction. The foot may not be used to stop the ball. *Exception:* Provided the player is within the striking circle, the goalkeeper is permitted to kick the ball or allow the ball to rebound from the hand (the player may not bat it). The goalie shall not be penalized if the ball is deflected off the body, providing the player is within the striking circle.

f. Hit the ball between the player's own feet.

g. Back up the stick with the foot.

h. Take part in the game without having the stick in the hand.

2. With Regard to an Opponent, a Player Shall Not

a. Push, charge, shove, trip, strike at, or in any way personally handle the opponent.

b. Strike, hook, hold, lift, or in any way interfere with an opponent's stick.

c. Place the body between the opponent and the ball.

d. Allow the feet, shoulder, or any part of the body to interfere with an opponent playing the ball.

e. Run in front of an opponent so as to break the strike.

3. Offside

When the ball is last touched by one of the player's own team, a player may not be ahead of that teammate unless there are at least three defenders between the player and the goal the player is attacking, or the player is in his/her own half of the field. This does not prevent a player running forward to meet a pass after the ball has been hit.

Penalties for Fouls

1. Outside the Circle
A free hit is awarded to the team not committing the foul.

2. Inside the Circle

a. By the attack—a free hit by the defense anywhere in the circle or any spot within 16 yards of the inner edge of the defending team's goal on a line drawn through the place where the foul occurred and parallel to the sideline.

b. By the defense
1. A short, or penalty, corner is awarded to the attacking team.

2. A penalty stroke if the foul had stopped a sure goal.

Out-of-Bounds Play

In all cases, the line is considered "in the field of play," whether it be the circle, goal, or sideline.

The umpire *must* decide which team touched the ball last, since there is no provision in the rules for co-responsibility (off two sticks).

1. Over the Sideline
A push-in by a member of the team opposite that of the player who last touched the ball before it crossed the sideline.

2. Over the End Line, Not Between the Goal Posts
a. Off the attack—a defense hit.
b. Off the defense—
1. When the ball is *unintentionally* hit over the goal line—a long corner.
2. When the ball is *intentionally* hit over the goal line—a short or penalty corner.

3. Over the End Line Between the Goal Posts
a. A legal goal, when the ball was touched by the stick of an attack inside the striking circle. Play resumed by a center bully on the center line. The goal counts even if the ball was last touched by the stick or person of the defense.
b. When the ball was not touched by a stick of the attack inside the circle and:
1. was touched by a stick of the defense—a long corner.
2. was not touched by a stick of the defense inside the circle—a defense hit.

SUGGESTED LEARNING SEQUENCE

There are a number of ways to list the sequence of skill development for field hockey. In the one proposed, dodging is introduced early in order to teach students to move *around* rather than *into* a player. The drive and fielding will be taught at the same time; passes are taught in conjunction with types of passes (drive, flick, scoop) to make it more meaningful. As with several team sports, it's best to introduce a technique along with a rule that may apply to it, a definition of it and some strategy involved. Therefore, this sequence cuts across many elements, skills, rules and strategy, at any one time.

A. Nature and Purpose
B. Conditioning Aspects—plan drills and exercises that might be related to movements found in field hockey. Emphasis of all areas of fitness particularly on upper body strength, agility, speed, and flexibility.
1. Circuit training with sticks
2. Some long distance running

C. Basic Game Concepts
  1. Field of play
  2. Use of equipment
  3. Playing courtesies
D. Skills and Strategy—Introduce rules and terminology at most appropriate times.
  1. Skills
    a. How to hold the stick—when running, when near the ball or goal
    b. Dribble
    c. Drive and Fielding
    d. Push-Pass
    e. Flick
    f. Passing
    g. Dodge—right dodge, left dodge
    h. Tackle
    i. Goalkeeping
  2. Tactics and Strategy
    a. The Bully
    b. Penalty Stroke
    c. Corner—long corner, short corner
    d. Free Hit
    e. Defense Hit
    f. Push-In
    g. Offensive playing hints
    h. Defense playing hints

SKILLS AND TECHNIQUES

Too much stress cannot be laid on the importance of doing all practices while moving. The proper relationship between ball and feet is most important and can only be gained by always practicing strokes while one is running or walking. The essence of stickwork is footwork. Make the feet assume the proper relationship to the ball, not the ball to the feet. Keep the eye on the ball at all times.

Holding the Stick

Fundamental Position. With the heel of the stick resting on the ground in front of the left foot, allow the top of the handle to fall into the fingers of the left hand. Grip the stick easily. Lift the stick to a horizontal position in front of the body with the toe of the stick pointing up. Place the right hand immediately below the left in the same relative position. The V formed by the thumb and index finger of each hand will be in line with the toe of the stick. Allow the stick to drop to a perpendicular position so the heel of the stick is in front of and very slightly to the right of the right foot with the flat face pointing directly ahead. The left forearm should be in a straight line with the stick. The grip with both hands should be tight but not tense. This is the *fundamental position* for all stroke production. The left hand will never change its position. For some strokes the right hand will be farther down the handle.

Learning Cues (See Figure 12-3)

1. The stick must be held firmly but comfortably.
2. The left hand is placed on the handle so that the back hand points upward and to the right.

FIGURE 12-3. Assuming the grip for the fundamental position.

FIGURE 12-4. Assuming a grip for the zigzag dribble.

Stick hold for Zigzag Dribble. A slight variation in the grip will be noted when the player executes a zigzag dribble (Figure 12-4). Place the stick flat on the ground, reach down, place the V formed by the grip at the top of the stick. Remember to align the V's on both hands as this encourges free turning of the stick. The zigzag dribble, a series of alternate forehand taps and reverse stick taps, gets its name from the pattern of the stick as it moves in a zigzag fashion over the ball and in front of the player. The left hand turns the stick as the right hand relaxes allowing the stick to move into a reverse stick position.

FIGURE 12-5. Dribbling—note the arms are well away from the body in the running position.

Dribble

This is a series of short strokes used to carry the ball down the field. As running speed is increased, the ball is hit harder but should be close enough at all times to be under complete control. The position for the dribble is the fundamental position except that the right hand is about four inches lower on the stick. The arms are relaxed, the left arm away from the body, the left shoulder leading slightly. The stick moves straight forward and backward, with most of the impetus coming from a left wrist motion. The player should be in a proper position for running, with the ball in front of the right foot but slightly to the right to prevent kicking the ball. The left hand remains on the stick in its usual position and the right hand is slid down only as far as is necessary for stick control, so as to maintain a good running position (Figure 12-5).

Zigzag Dribble. This dribble is used prior to the attempt to move around an opponent. The ball is tapped on alternate sides by the use of a forehand tap and reverse stick tap (Figure 12-6). Better ball control is insured as the stick is close to the ball at all times. The zigzag action of the ball causes the opponent to delay momentarily in attempting to take the ball away, thus giving the player with the ball the time either to set up a teammate for a pass or to break by the defender.

Practice Suggestions

1. Begin by moving in a straight line—tap ball with the emphasis on ball control, concentrate on the ball and staying low. Push the ball out in front of the body; prevent the ball from being to the side of the body.
2. Move in a circle first clockwise, then counter-clockwise. Set up traffic cones and practice dribbling in one direction then in another direction.

FIGURE 12-6. The zigzag dribble.

3. Practice the technique of zigzag dribbling; concentrate on keeping the ball within a path the width of the shoulders and hips.
4. Once good control is acquired, add a defender in front of the dribbler. Use that player only to knock the ball away from the dribbler if the dribbler taps the ball too far in front.
5. With a defender standing 5 to 8 yards away, practice using the zigzag dribble in an attempt to move around the defender. At a later time another player may be used in a 2 on 1 situation to set up a pass. As dribbling proficiency increases, players should be encouraged to execute a dodge.

Drive

The drive is a strong hard stroke used for passing and shooting. The hands are usually close together for this stroke. The stick swings in a perpendicular plane with a pendulum-like motion in the direction the ball is to travel (Figure 12-7). The stick may not be lifted above the shoulder on either the back swing or the follow-through. Body weight, shoulders, arms, and wrists, quick down swing, all combine to give the stroke its force. One must be careful not to flick the wrists on the follow-through or the stick will rise too high and result in a violation. Note, however, that the wrists will be cocked on the back swing. To be assured of an accurate stroke, allow the body weight to follow through with the stick pointed in the direction of the pass.

Drive Straight Ahead. The ball should be ahead of and slightly to the right of the path the right foot is to take. The left shoulder faces the path of the hit and should be practiced that way so it can be executed at any instant.

Drive to the Left. The ball should be in front of the body and so placed that at the moment of impact

FIGURE 12-7. The drive—hands are together throughout the swing.

of stick and ball, the weight will be behind the stroke and the stick will be in a position perpendicular to the ground.

Drive to the Right. The ball is to the right of the body. The farther to the right the ball is to be passed, the more its position will be behind that of the fundamental position. The right foot should be forward as the stroke is made. The body pivots from the hips so the right shoulder drops back and the left shoulder is brought around in the direction of the pass.

Hard Drive for Goal. This is the same as a straight drive, but the emphasis should be on pointing the left shoulder toward the path the ball is to take. The ball should be opposite the heel of the left foot so the weight of the body is behind the stroke. Follow through by reaching toward the path the ball has taken. Avoid pulling back on the stroke, which will occur when the ball is behind the forward foot at the moment of impact of ball and stick.

Fielding the Ball

The ball must be fielded or controlled when it comes to a player and before it is passed or played. A "two touch sequence" is used when thinking about fielding and passing. The first touch stops the ball and the immediate second touch passes or drives the ball. Meet the ball in a set position; then execute the stop and pass.

Learning Cues

1. Keep stick in direction of the ball, eyes watch ball, stick is lowered so ball meets the blade squarely (first touch).
2. With an easy grip, give with the blade; the top handle will be ahead of the blade.
3. With the left wrist and arm over the top of the handle and the ball under control, pass the ball (second touch) or dribble.

Practice Suggestions

1. Fielding and passing should always be practiced while moving, once the initial learning takes place. Emphasize the importance of going to meet the ball.
2. Begin by having player A roll the ball to player B; emphasize two touches, foot position, and left wrist and left arm over the top of the handle.
3. Introduce a passive defensive player and play two on one keep away. Later, as proficiency is gained, add an active defensive player.

4. As the students' drive becomes more powerful, practice long drives and ball reception followed by an immediate return pass as the player cuts to the right or left. Encourage movement and passing to an open area.
5. Partners may receive a pass, then repass the ball to the other partner cutting by for a drive on goal.

Push-Pass

The push-pass is used for short, accurate passing or shooting when there is no time or necessity for a drive. This pass can be executed quickly off of a dribble or after receiving a pass. The body crouches more for the push-pass and the flick (to be discussed later) than for other strokes. The left shoulder is pointed in the direction of the pass with the left foot forward. The right hand is 6 to 8 inches lower than in the fundamental position. *There is no back swing.*

Learning Cues

1. Starting with the left shoulder and left foot facing the direction of the pass and on contact with the ball, the top of the stick is slightly ahead of the ball.
2. Both arms move forward to their limit of reach, the left hand pulls back and the right pushes forward. The pull and push are done quickly.
3. The stick continues through in the direction of the pass, the right leg finishes in an extended position.

The Flick

This is also a wrist stroke *without the backswing.* The ball will rise slightly. It is used for

FIGURE 12-8. Executing the flick.

shooting when deep in the circle, as a technique to move a ball over the top of a defender's stick, and for passes to a marked player. The flick is especially valuable for shooting at close range inasmuch as the direction the ball is to take is concealed. Also, since this stroke is off the ground, it is more difficult to stop. Although the flick may be executed with a moving ball—a difficult move—on free hits that are awarded a player the ball is stationary.

Learning Cues (See Figure 12-8)

1. The hand and foot position are the same as that for the push-pass.
2. The ball is played further forward, the blade of the stick is held slightly upward and the top of the handle inclined toward the player's body.
3. The stroke and follow-through are executed like the push-pass.

Practice Suggestions

1. Using partners or three or four players to a group, begin with a stationary ball, players 5 to 10 yards apart. Practice the push-pass and flick. Emphasize the mechanics and follow-through as well as the accuracy of the pass.
2. Using a similar group, execute a push-pass and direct the partner to execute a flick off the moving ball. One partner may begin by rolling the ball to the other while practicing the flick.
3. With partners or with two lines 5 to 10 yards apart, practice the flick-pass from a stationary position to the right side of another player cutting downfield. Various passing patterns may be executed with the use of the push-pass or flick-pass being practiced to the stick side and reverse stick side.
4. Set up groups of three players, designating a passer, a defensive person, and a receiver in each

group. Continue the practice remembering to keep within the context of the game.

Passing

Passing is the very essence of the game of field hockey. Passing includes the ability to execute an accurate, well-placed and well-paced pass to a teammate moving out of the defensive zone or toward the attacking zone. It also involves the ability to move to an open space while not in possession of the ball in order to set up a pass or moving away from the attacking zone to receive a back pass in order to change the direction of the attack. Teams that employ a hit and chase style of play will have minimal opportunities to establish a cohesive offensive or defensive plan. The team having the ability to make accurate, precise passes and maintain possession of the ball for 4–6 passes will have the most scoring opportunities and will control the tempo of the game.

At any time during a game, a player should have two to three avenues available to execute a pass if the team has good field balance and proper depth, (i.e., the relationship of forwards-midfielders-defense people). A lot of time during practice should be devoted to passing, in combinations of 2, 3, or 4 players. As students become more proficient, drills should be developed that will include 3 on 2, 4 on 3, 2 on 1 situations where the passers and players without the ball must confront a defender, as is the case in a game. A few points to remember about passing are essential:

1. Draw an opponent toward you to create space for a teammate before passing.
2. Keep passes simple and precise.
3. If you are a receiver, move to an open space and

into a position so your teammate can make a good pass.

4. Sometimes a pass backward is as effective as a pass forward into a congested zone.
5. Be aware of the position of your teammates at all times; know what passing routes are available.

Dodge

The dodge is used when a player who is in possession of the ball wishes to evade an opponent who is approaching from the front. The effectiveness of the dodge is derived from deceiving the opponent. Therefore, the player should learn a variety of dodges. It is particularly important to teach beginning players how to dodge. There is a natural tendency to move directly into the opponent, which of course is illegal. Introduction at an early stage in the unit and provision for continued practice are vitally important.

Learning Cues

1. Always approach the opponent in the same position so that the intention will not be revealed by movement of hands or changes in body-ball relationship.
2. Increase pace to change timing. Do not slow down to do a dodge, and be sure to accelerate once past the opponent.
3. Execute the dodge just before the opponent is within reach of the ball. Remember that both players are moving, thus this point will be considerably farther away than might be expected.

Right Dodge.   Sometimes called "dodge to non-stick side." The player in possession of the ball sends the ball ahead and close to the non-stick side of the approaching opponent. The player herself passes on the stick side of the opponent and meets the ball again behind her. In other words the ball goes right and the player goes left (Figure 12-9A). The stroke has only the force of a dribble and the ball goes just enough off line to the right to miss the opponent's left toe. This is not a pass and should have neither the force nor change of direction of a pass. Remember to execute this dodge before the opponent can reach the ball but be close enough to her so that she has no opportunity to move to her left and thus block the ball.

Left Dodge.   In this play, both ball and player go to the left of the approaching opponent (Figure 12-9B). Shortly before the ball is within reach of the opponent, the player steps left, pulls the ball left a short distance (not more than six inches), then continues straight ahead. For success, the timing must be accurate and the ball must be played squarely left, not diagonally. The ball must remain on the player's right throughout the dodge.

Practice Suggestion

1. Partner A dribbles toward a stationary partner B; practice the right dodge and left dodge. Next allow partner B to become first a passive defender, then an active defender. As a variation either the right or left dodge may be executed; once past the opponent execute a flick or drive to a teammate moving downfield. It is important to practice dodging as part of the class as soon and as often as possible.

Tackle

The key to becoming an accomplished tackler is being prepared and forcing the opponent to move in one direction or the other. The tackle is a technique used in an attempt to take the ball away from an opponent who is controlling it. A player should be able to tackle from the left, right, or front. Since a successful tackle is dependent on timing, practice should always be with two players, both moving.

A second key to good tackling is the ability to force the opponent when possible to the left or stick side by overplaying to the left. If the opponent dribbles right, the defender must execute the tackle with a reverse stick. While the front tackle is not always possible, it is important for the tackler to recover from the missed attempt quickly and catch up to the dribbler in order to attempt a right or left tackle. This maneuver is called "tackling in retreat" because the defender is now heading for the goal line (own). When moving left or right after a missed front tackle, the crucial part becomes the half turn or the first step because it brings the player into a position facing the goal line.

Front Tackle.   This is used to tackle an opponent in possession of the ball who is approaching from directly in front. Do not stand still to make the

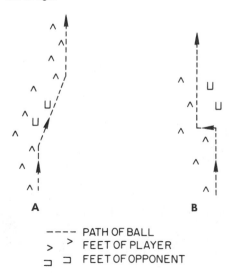

FIGURE 12-9.   (A) Diagram of a right dodge, non-stickside. (B) Diagram of a left dodge.

---- PATH OF BALL
> FEET OF PLAYER
⊐ FEET OF OPPONENT

FIGURE 12-10. In the front tackle, continually pressure the ball by jabbing and retreating.

tackle. The defender assumes a basic athletic stance, weight forward, feet shoulder width apart, knees flexed slightly, head up, eyes watching the opponent. The stick is held low to the ground, across the thighs, the hands further apart than for the normal dribble. As the opponent approaches, lunge quickly to the left, extending the right leg and left arm and the stick; poke the ball away and attempt to gain possession. Remember, physical contact is *not* allowed; meet the opponent stick to stick.

Learning Cues

1. Keep the eye on the opponent's stick and the ball, anticipating any move the opponent may make to deceive.
2. Time the tackle so it is unexpected. Slow or increase the pace to achieve this deception.
3. Control the body stance so as to be alert and ready to move quickly in any direction.
4. Continually jab and retreat, pressuring the ball.

Tackle to the Left. If a tackle must be executed in retreat, force the opponent right or left by overplaying to that particular side. The defender must execute a half turn so as to be facing the goal line.

Learning Cues

1. Step right facing the goal line, swing the left foot around and proceed to run alongside of the opponent; hips should be close to and aligned with opponent's hips.
2. Holding the stick with the left hand, extend the arm and stick attempting to poke the ball away from the opponent or draw the ball in toward the tackle.

Tackle to the Right. Execution of a tackle to the right side is much the same as one to the left, with a few exceptions. To turn, step with the left foot and bring the right foot around. The defender will execute the same lunge but will utilize a reverse stick to make the tackle.

Practice Suggestions

1. Any drill formation using one on one. Begin with the front tackle and move on to tackling to the left and right. Emphasis should be placed on the turn facing the goal line (practice just the turn, then add the rest of the maneuver).
2. Like dodging, tackling may be started early and done in combination with dribbling.

FIGURE 12-11. Tackle to the left.

FIGURE 12-12. Tackle to the right.

Goalkeeping

Goalkeeping requires different skills from other positions. In addition to good stickwork, the goalkeeper must have alertness of mind to be able to anticipate, good agility, courage, and good concentration. The goalkeeper is well protected with mask (may be optional, but for a class it should be mandatory), gloves, pads for the legs, and hard shoes. A canvas kicker may be used over regular shoes as long as the shoe is well padded. The goalie has the privilege of using the feet for stopping and directing the ball. The goalie may also stop the ball with the flat hand; however, the ball may not be batted.

Stance. A basic athletic stance with a few modifications would describe the stance of the goalie. The feet are shoulder width apart, weight evenly distributed on the balls of the feet, legs slightly flexed, a slight lean forward, the arms hanging in front with the forearms parallel to the ground. Grasp the stick with palms facing out; the blade end will be up and slightly ponting away from the right goal post. The head should be up watching the ball.

Goalkeeping Principles. The goalkeeper is the last line of defense. Aside from some individual moves that might be employed for specific opponents, here are three important principles to practice and remember.[1]

1. The goalkeeper should narrow the possible goal mouth area the shooter has to aim by moving with caution toward the shooter. This maneuver takes away or narrows the angle the shooter has

available to shoot toward the goal mouth.
2. The goalkeeper should remain stationary when the opponent is in the scoring area. Charging toward the shooter can have spectacular results but if the goalkeeper miscalculates the shot, it can result in a goal.
3. The goalkeeper should line up with the ball, i.e., the ball should be in a line with the goalkeeper and the goal line.

Technique. The beginning goalkeeper should meet the ball with legs together and "give" on impact, so that the ball drops almost dead. It is then cleared with the inside of the foot hard and accurately, either toward the sideline or to the player who is ready to receive it and relay it up the field. With more experience the goalie may learn to reach out to catch and redirect the ball with the side of one foot, especially a well-directed shot that is impossible to reach with two feet. The stick is used only for emergency clears.

Getting the ball out of reach of the oncoming forwards is as important as stopping the initial shot. Balls not aimed between the posts should be allowed to go over the goal line untouched. When a forward is coming down alone or loses control of the ball, the goalkeeper will learn to come out fast to meet her. Experience will best teach the goalkeeper when this should be attempted.

The goalie should never allow a defense player to block her vision. It is the job of the defense to prevent a shot and of the goalkeeper to stop it. The goalkeeper must avoid fouls such as obstruction or keeping the foot against the ball and must not fall down.

The goalkeeper should follow the game intently

[1]Vonnie Gros, *Inside Field Hockey* (Chicago: Contemporary Books, 1979), pp. 58–59.

all the time. There are long periods when there is little to do, but it is important to maintain concentration.

Practice Suggestions

Students should always wear protective equipment when practicing or in a scrimmage situation.

1. Reaction drills—roll ball to right, straight-on and left. Emphasis is on maintaining balance and concentrating on the ball.
2. Practice should also be devoted to employment of basic goalkeeping principles. This can be done by first rolling the ball, then adding one player 1 on 1.
3. Place a goalie in goal in a 5 on 5 scrimmage situation, and indicate where the ball is to be cleared. Emphasis should be placed on hard clears to the outside of the goal mouth, avoiding clears across the goal mouth.

TACTICS AND STRATEGY

Bully

This is the play used to:

1. Start the game at the beginning, after half time, and after a goal has been scored.
2. Restart the game after simultaneous fouls by two opponents.

Formation. One player from each team takes the bully by standing astride the line and facing the side line squarely, with her goal on her right. The ball is placed between them. All other players shall be nearer their defending goal than the ball and at least 5 yards from the bully.

Execution. The hands are well apart on the stick to give strength to the stroke to be used. Some teachers advocate always rotating the right hand

FIGURE 12-13. The bully.

slightly to the right, thus enabling the player to execute any play to complete the bully without making her intentions obvious. To bully the ball, each player strikes the ground on her own side of the ball with the heel of the stick, then strikes the opponent's stick over the top of the ball with the flat side of the stick. This is done three times, after which the ball must be hit by one of these players before it is in general play.

Play to Complete a Bully. Every player should know at least three plays to be used to complete a bully and be able to execute them interchangeably.

1. *Reverse Stick:* After hitting sticks for the third time, the stick is turned over, without a shift of the hands, so the toe is down and the ball is tapped back with a firm wrist motion. It can be tapped back and immediately passed by the same player to a teammate on the right, or it can be tapped back harder to the defense who is backing up the bully. This last play opens up the game and is difficult for the opponents to stop.
2. *Pass Right:* One of the players will play the ball between the opponent's stick and right foot, thus passing to a teammate on her right if the play is well executed.
3. *Pass Left:* The ball is drawn slightly toward the player, enough to be out of reach of the opponent. At the same time, the player will step back with the left foot and, without obstructing her opponent, pass forward to the left inner or left wing.

Penalty Stroke

The penalty stroke is awarded to the attacking team when a foul—either intentional or unintentional—was committed that prevented a goal inside the shooting circle by the defending team.

Formation. The penalty shot is taken at a point 7 yards from the center of the goal line. Aside from the shooter, the remaining players must remain outside the shooting circle behind the 25-yard line until the ball is played.

The Play. The goalkeeper must keep both heels on the goal line, not leaving the goal line or moving the feet until the ball is played. The player taking the penalty shot must use a push, flick, or scoop. Once the referee whistles for the play to begin, the shooter is allowed one stride to the ball before shooting. Faking or any other deceptive moves are not allowed. The attacker may only touch the ball once. After a successful goal, play is restarted by a center bully. If the try is unsuccessful, the defense is awarded a free hit from the 16-yard line.

Corner

This formation is awarded as an advantage to the attacking team and has two variations: *long corner* and *short* (or *penalty*) *corner* (Figure 12-14).

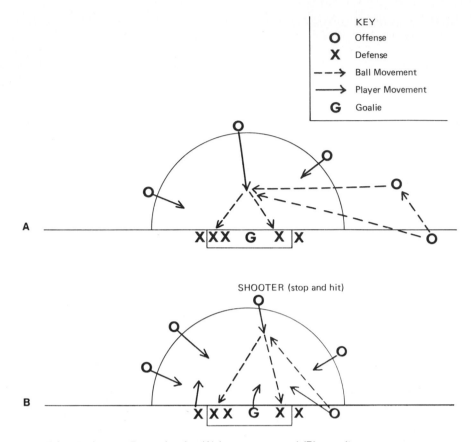

KEY

O — Offense

X — Defense

- - -> — Ball Movement

——> — Player Movement

G — Goalie

FIGURE 12-14. Formation for (A) long corner and (B) penalty corner.

1. *Long Corner.* Sometimes called simply a *corner,* this formation is awarded when the ball is unintentionally sent over the goal line, not between the posts, off the stick of a defender. The ball is placed 5 yards from the corner on either the goal line or side line, preferably on the goal line, on that side of the goal where the ball went out.

2. *Short Corner.* Sometimes called a *penalty corner,* this formation is awarded when:
   a. The ball goes over the goal line off a defender's stick with no attempt being made to keep it in the field of play.
   b. The ball goes over the goal line off the person of the defense.
   c. The defense fouls in the circle.

Formation. The ball is placed on the goal line not less than 10 yards from the nearer goal post on either side of the goal, according to the choice of the attacking team. A member of the attacking team, usually the wing, takes the corner hit. The other forwards arrange themselves around the circle, their sticks and feet outside the line. The halfbacks are in position to back up the forwards. The defending team has six players including the goalie, usually the defense, with their sticks and feet behind the goal line. Each player should be opposite the stick of the person she is marking. No player may be nearer than five yards to the player taking the hit. These

players may move as soon as the ball is hit. The other members of the defending team, usually the forwards, may not be nearer than the 50-yard line and may not cross that line until the ball has been hit then everyone is in play.

The Play. The designated offensive player pushes or hits the ball along the ground to a forward who stops the ball. A shot should follow immediately by the strongest hitter on the team. This player should be quick in addition to being an accurate shooter. The success of a corner lies in a hard hit, a good initial push, and the consequent stop.

Free Hit

A free hit is awarded to the opposite team when a foul is committed anywhere on the field, except inside the circle.

Formation. For a free hit outside the circle, the ball is placed on the spot where the breach occurred and is usually played by the defense player of the team fouled against in whose area it lies. However, a forward could also play the ball. For any free hit, all other players must be 5 yards away. The ball must be motionless.

The Play. The player taking the free hit may use any legitimate stroke, but may not raise the ball above the knee into the circle. After taking the hit, she may not play the ball again until it has been touched by another player. Free hits should be taken quickly so as to take full advantage of the penalty before the opposing team gets placed.

Defense Hit

A defense hit is awarded to the defending team when:

1. An attacking player hits the ball over the end line
   a. not between the goal posts.
   b. between the goal posts but from outside the circle.
2. The ball is unintentionally hit over the goal line by a defense player from beyond the 25-yard line.

Formation. The ball is placed 16 yards from the end line exactly opposite the spot where it left the field of play and always outside the circle. It is taken by the defense player in whose area the ball is placed. The ball must be motionless, and all other players shall be at least 5 yards away.

The Play. The ball is put in play as for a free hit, with the defense player using any legal stroke.

Push-In

When the ball has been completely rolled over the sideline by one team, the opposing team is awarded a push-in. Any member of the team may execute the push-in. However, the ball must remain on the ground; it cannot be hit or lifted. If the experiment push-in rule is used, a flick may be used as long as the ball goes no higher than the knees.

Formation. The ball is placed on the sideline while the defenders form a semicircle no more than 5 yards closer to the ball. The pusher may have the feet in bounds or over the sideline as the push-in is being executed.

The Play. Successful execution will result when the push-in is made quickly since the defenders are 5 yards away. Once the whistle blows indicating the out of bounds, the push may be executed without another whistle to start play. The premium is on getting the ball to the point where it crossed the line and getting it in play. Once the ball is hit by the player executing the push-in, it cannot be played again by that player until it is hit by another player.

Basic Strategy Hints

1. Stick may not be raised above the shoulder. It is better to keep it below the knee.
2. Use only the flat side of the stick.
3. Field the ball before hitting it. Never hit on the fly.
4. When receiving a pass from behind, the player should be looking back over the shoulder, and

be in a running position with the feet going in the direction of the attacking goal.
5. Go to meet a pass coming toward you.
6. A player should move away from a teammate with the ball to make a space into which the ball may be passed.
7. In order to avoid obstruction, you should turn in a clockwise direction around the ball; don't pull the ball around you.
8. Do not touch an opponent with the stick or the body.
9. Do not abruptly cut in front of another player whether the player has the ball or not.
10. Pass when a teammate is free to receive the ball rather than wait to draw an opponent.

Basic Offensive Suggestions

Once the ball is in a team's possession, then the players on that team must think about advancing the ball toward the opponent's goal. Advancement is executed by dribbling and through a series of passes. No matter what formation is being used, the following key principles must be employed if the attack is to be successful.

1. *Movement to an open space.* The key to receiving a pass or setting up a pass is to move to an open

FIGURE 12-15. Player positions. Note team balance (depth), possible passing routes, and opportunities for 2 on 1 or 3 on 2 situations.

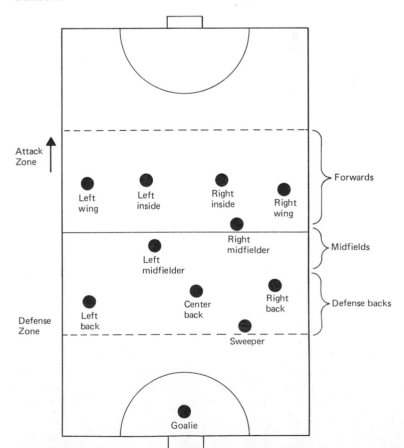

area. Such a maneuver can draw a defensive player away from a key attacking zone or can place the offensive player in a position to receive a pass and maintain possession.

2. *Playing without the ball.* Closely related to the principle stated above is the responsibility of the player to act as a decoy to create space for another teammate or to create space to add to general defensive confusion. It further provides a teammate another avenue of attack or passing choice.

3. *Ball movement.* Keep the ball moving in every way possible—short, long, and wide—through a series of short or long passes. Being able to change rapidly the position of the ball on the field increases the chance of defensive confusion and never allows the defense an opportunity to remain settled. Players should not discount lateral passes or back passes as effective ways to move the ball.

4. *Team balance.* Depth and good field balance are very important. Besides positional relationship of the forward attackers or goalkeeper to other teammates, there should always be a teammate in front of or behind you to pass to or to support a particular position. The use of movement without the ball helps to maintain team balance. Remember that balance also refers to width, and continually emphasize the importance of not becoming too one-sided.

5. *Goal-mindedness.* The team that wins is the team scoring the most goals. A constant offensive pressure employed by *all* members of the team will usually result in more scoring opportunities.

Basic Defensive Suggestions

Once the ball is in the possession of the opposing team, then all players on the team without the ball must become defensive minded. Defense involves total concentration on the game and an awareness of the offensive players in the vicinity. In addition to the principles previously discussed, the good defender must understand several others.

1. *Always being prepared.* Being able to switch from offense to defense without a moment's delay is going to save valuable yards. It may also make the difference in regaining possession of a ball momentarily lost and turning back to your advantage.

2. *Player responsibility.* It is vital to have an awareness of the basic defensive responsibility relative to a specific zone coverage or player. Being able to mark an opponent without the ball in order to prevent that player from receiving a pass or to decoy that player is good defensive strategy. In such a position it is important always to know the position of the ball and the location of your own goal.

3. *Pressure.* The player in possession of the ball must be kept under constant defensive pressure. Maintaining such pressure on the player will result in inaccurate passes or force an opponent away from a set play.

4. *Defensive depth.* If an offensive player gets behind a defender assigned coverage, then another defender must be assigned the area to pick up that responsibility. Once the opponent moves past a defender, it is important for that defender to switch into an unoccupied position or to recover and catch the attacker.

5. *Individual defensive control.* Play the game under control at all times; an unnecessary rush or a rush out of control will allow an attacker to move easily by with a dodge or another decoy. Further burden is then placed on the defense and will create a 2 on 1 or 3 on 2 situation.

TERMINOLOGY

Advancing Foul committed when the ball rebounds from a player's person.

Alley Area of the field between the sideline and the five-yard or alley line.

Bully Play used to start or restart the game. Opposing players alternately strike the ground and each other's sticks three times, then play the ball.

Circle Same as *Striking circle.*

Corner A play following certain infringements of the rules; the formation used in such a play. See *Long corner* and *Short corner.*

Covering Defensive anticipatory position much nearer the defending goal than the play at that given time. As opposed to *marking.*

Defense hit Term used to denote play when the ball goes over the goal line under certain circumstances. The ball is placed 16 yards from the end line opposite the spot where it left the field.

Dodge Play used to evade an opponent while maintaining control of the ball.

Dribble Series of short strokes used to take the ball down the field while maintaining constant control of it.

Drive Hard stroke with a back swing. May be done to right, left, or straight ahead.

Fielding Controlling an approaching ball before it is passed or played.

Flick A wrist stroke having no back swing. Ball rises slightly. Stick is brought around the ball during execution. Good for close shooting or passing to a marked player.

Foul Infringement of rules. Penalty may be a free hit, short corner, or penalty stroke.

Free hit A play following certain infringements of rules. Taken by a player on the team fouled against.

Holding the whistle Term used when the umpire allows play to continue after a foul when, in her opinion, this is more advantageous to the team fouled against than stopping play and awarding a penalty.

Long corner The play awarded to the attack after the ball goes over the end line *unintentionally,* off the stick of a defender. The ball is placed five yards from the corner.

Lunge (or Left-hand lunge) Stroke used in attempting to take the ball from an opponent on the player's left. May be used for a pass or follow-up shot when a long reach is necessary.

Marking Defensive position when the player stays close to her opponent.

Obstruction A foul made by placing the body or any part of it between the opponent and the ball so as to interfere with the opponent's effort to play or reach the ball.

Offside A foul committed by a player receiving the ball while in an illegal position.

Penalty corner See *Short corner.*

Penalty stroke A shot awarded to the attacking team when a defensive player intentionally commits a foul to prevent a sure goal.

Push-in Method of putting the ball into play after it has gone over the sideline.

Push-pass A quick wrist stroke having no back swing. The ball does not rise. When the strike is executed the stick faces the direction of the pass in contact with the ball. Accurate and easy to receive.

Reverse sticks Turning the stick over to play a ball on the left, or to tackle a player on the right.

Scoop Stroke without back swing in which the ball is lifted slightly with the toe of the stick. Can be used as a dodge.

Short corner The play awarded to the attack for a foul by the defense inside the circle or when the defense *intentionally* hits the ball over the end line. The ball is placed 10 yards from the goal post. Also called *penalty corner.*

Stick side The player's right side. So called because the stick meets the ball on that side of the body.

Sticks Raising the stick above the shoulder at either the beginning or end of a stroke. It is a foul.

Striking circle The goal-shooting area; the curved line that encloses it.

SELECTED REFERENCES

American Alliance for Health, Physical Education, Recreation, and Dance. *NAGWS Field Hockey Guide.* Reston, Virginia: AAHPERD, 1980.

ARMBRUSTER, DAVID A., FRANK F. MUSHER, and DALE MOOD. *Sports and Recreational Activities for Men and Women,* 7th ed. St. Louis, Mo.: The C.V. Mosby Company, 1979.

BARNES, MILDRED J. *Field Hockey: The Coach and The Player.* Boston: Allyn & Bacon, Inc., 1979.

DILLAHUNT, et al. *Field Hockey for Teachers.* Iris Hills, Brooklyn, Mich.: Saulk Valley, 1976.

GROS, VONNIE. *Inside Field Hockey.* Chicago: Contemporary Books, 1979.

POWELL, AGNETA. *27 Hockey Stickwork Games and Rotations.* Available from Sophia Dickson, 905 Sterling Street, Plainfield, N.J. 07062.

USFHA MANUAL FOR COACHES. The Official Manual of the United States Field Hockey Association: North Chill, N.Y., 1979.

Periodicals

Eagle. Published 8 times yearly by USFHA, National Office: 4415 Buffalo Rd., North Chill, N.Y. 14514.

Audio-Visual Materials

AAHPERD. Educational Media Services, Dept. B, 1201 16th St., N.W., Washington, D.C. 20036. *Field Hockey.* Super 8 series of color films.

GOLF

THIS CHAPTER WILL ENABLE YOU TO:

+ Identify the parts and features of a golf course.
+ Identify the various clubs and other equipment, know their function and proper care.
+ Describe and after practice execute the following skills: grip, stance, swing (irons and woods), pitch, chip, and sand shots, putting, and various golf exercises.
+ Identify and carry out the courtesies associated with the sport.
+ State and interpret the major official rules of golf.

NATURE AND PURPOSE

One of the greatest advantages of golf lies in the age range of those who are able to participate. Both young boys and girls and old men and women can be found participating at many golf courses. In recent years the United States Golf Association has sponsored Junior Golf Programs (ages 9 to 17); therefore more and more children are becoming interested in playing at a very early age. Many private and public golf courses have extensive instructional programs for the junior golfer and sponsor golf tournaments all summer long. Most public and private clubs have also set aside specific playing times for the juniors in order to encourage their participation.

Golf may be played by strokes or by holes. The objective is to play a ball from a teeing area to a hole, a prescribed distance from the tee, in the fewest strokes possible. An official round is eighteen holes. In stroke play, the winner is the person taking the fewest number of strokes over an entire eighteen holes of play. Each hole is given a rating of par determined by the length of the hole (see Figure 13-1). In match play, or play by holes, the winner is the golfer who wins the greater number of holes despite the final total in strokes. Stroke play is considered more exacting, since each shot is of equal value, whereas in match play, a loss of two or more strokes on a hole may be recouped by a one-stroke victory on a later hole.

Golf is one of the few sports that allows a handicapping system among participants. Handicapping is a means of equalizing competition among golfers of differing abilities. The player with the lower average score is required to give strokes to the higher average golfer. In stroke play the higher average player subtracts these strokes from his total

to get a *net* score. This is compared with the other player's *gross* or total score to determine the winner. In most handicap play the strokes are usually computed in relation to the difference between par and the average score of the player. Thus, many can compete in a tournament on a handicap basis. In match play the strokes are subtracted from the higher average player's score on holes designated as the most difficult. That is, a handicap of five would allow the player to subtract one stroke from his score on the five most difficult holes.

THE COURSE

The course is the whole area within which play is permitted. It is the duty of authorities in charge of the course to define its boundaries accurately. Most courses consist of eighteen holes; however, there are many nine-hole courses. Golf scores are based on eighteen holes of play, with the par usually varying between 70 and 72. Each hole consists of many

FIGURE 13-1. Directions for computing par on a golf course.

FOR MEN	
Par 3	Up to 250 yards, inclusive
Par 4	251 to 470 yards, inclusive
Par 5	471 yards and over

FOR WOMEN	
Par 3	Up to 210 yards, inclusive
Par 4	211 to 400 yards, inclusive
Par 5	401 to 575 yards, inclusive
Par 6	576 yards and over

162

common components and some not so common components (see Figure 13-2). A player tees a ball up on a wooden or plastic tee in the teeing area, in line with or no more than two club lengths behind the tee markers. Generally there are three sets of markers on a tee: the farthest from the hole are for championship play, the middle markers are generally for men, and the markers closest to the hole are where women initiate play. From the tee, the golfer hits to a fairly well-groomed area called the fairway and from there, hits to a closely cut area of the hole called the green. Generally the area to the right and left of the fairway where the grass is long and other obstacles may be found is known as the rough. Most courses include obstacles such as sand traps, bunkers, water hazards, out-of-bounds, and trees placed in strategic positions to penalize a poor shot made by a golfer. There are specific rules governing play that the golfer must understand when confronted by one of these obstacles. These will be discussed later on under the heading Rules of Golf.

SCORING

Figure 13-3 represents a typical score card. The golfer will note the yardage given for each hole dependent on the set of markers from which play is initiated. Also included is information on the course rating, the par designation for a particular hole as well as the hole's difficulty as expressed in men's or women's handicap. Thus the hole having the men's handicap designation of 7 (hole number 6) means that it is the seventh hardest hole on the course. If the golfer had a handicap of 7, he would be given a deduction of 1 stroke from his score in order to equalize the competition. In this example, the golfer would also receive a 1 stroke deduction on holes 7, 11, 2, 13, 1, and 12.

The par designation is the number of strokes that an expert would take to play a hole. It is usually the number of shots from the tee to the green plus two strokes for putting. Thus an expert playing a par four hole would take two shots to reach the green

FIGURE 13-2. A typical hole.

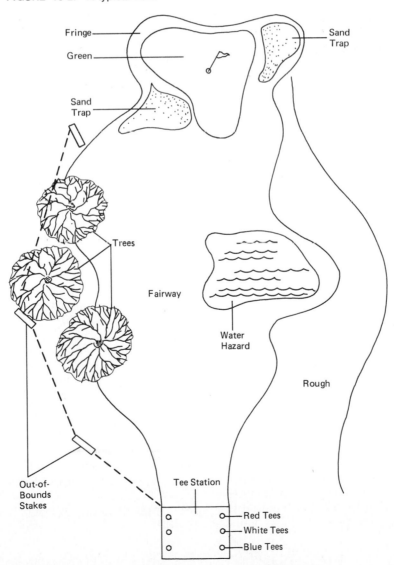

SCORE CARD

HOLE	1	2	3	4	5	6	7	8	9	OUT	10	11	12	13	14	15	16	17	18	IN	Total
Championship BLUE	440	545	250	350	175	385	420	385	480	3430	520	440	525	420	205	350	385	185	405	3435	6865
Men's WHITE	365	515	245	325	160	380	415	350	455	3210	450	420	510	405	150	325	380	180	395	3215	6425
PAR	4	5	3	4	3	4	4	4	5	36	5	4	5	4	3	4	4	3	4	36	72
Men's Handicap	5	3	13	15	17	7	1	11	9		12	2	6	4	18	14	10	16	8		
Won + Lost – Halved O																					
Women's YELLOW	360	490	245	320	160	365	410	350	440	3140	440	405	510	405	150	320	370	175	395	3170	6315
PAR	4	5	4	4	3	4	5	4	5	38	5	5	5	5	3	4	4	3	4	38	76
Women's Handicap	5	1	17	9	15	7	11	13	3		4	10	2	16	18	12	8	14	6		

COURSE RATING 70.5

DATE _____ PLAYER _____ ATTEST _____

FIGURE 13-3. Score card.

and two putts to hit the ball into the hole. Sometimes a golfer will hit a ball from the tee into the hole in less than par. A score of 1 under par is a birdie, two under par is called an eagle, 3 under par on a par five is a double eagle, and 2 under on a par three is a hole in one, the golfer's dream.

EQUIPMENT

Clubs

A set of golf clubs consists of woods, irons, and a putter. The beginner may not wish to invest in a complete set of expensive clubs. Many of the less expensive clubs will suffice in the beginning. A minimum set should contain two woods, four irons, and a putter. The recommended choices would be a driver and a number 3 wood, the 3, 5, 7, and 9 irons, and a putter. While it is possible to obtain a full set by gradually adding the missing clubs, such as the numbers 2 and 4 woods and the 2, 4, 6, and 8 irons, as well as the sand wedge, a better plan is to play with the basic set until a fairly high level of skill is reached. At that time, a golf professional should be consulted to fit the player with a better and completely matched set of 14 clubs of his choice. The most popular 14 clubs are the driver, numbers 3 and 4 woods, numbers 2 through 9 irons, a pitching wedge, a sand wedge, and a putter. A set of clubs may cost anywhere from around $40 to several hundred dollars. Generally the beginning golfer can purchase a starter set for approximately $75 to $100.

The Putter. The putter is a golf club carried by all golfers; it is used primarily on the putting green to hit the ball into the cup. Today there are as many putter designs as there are golfers. The putter comes in various sizes, shapes, and colors. In choosing a putter, the key points to look for, according to the noted golf instructor Dick Aultman, are first, that the putter when soled flat on the ground allows you to look directly over the putting line; secondly, that it should be simple to aim, and third, that it be easy to control.[1]

Choosing Clubs

Golf clubs are precision instruments. They vary in design for men, women, and children. A golfer's shotmaking ability is affected by many factors directly related to the construction of the golf club. Among these factors are swingweight, length of the club, shaft flexibility, clubhead design, and the grip.

Swingweight. Determined by a swingweight scale, swingweight is the relationship among the weights of a club's component parts—grip, shaft, and head. Scales to measure swingweight may be found in most pro shops. Swingweights are usually designated by the symbols C and D followed by a number ranging from 0 to 9. Women usually use a lightweight club that has a swingweight of C4 to C7; stronger women might use a C9 or even move to the D classification. Men's clubs start at D0; an average male golfer would use a swingweight of D0 to D4. Children's clubs are generally lighter.

Length of the Club. An important point to remember is that the higher the *number* of the club, the shorter the club's *length*. The woods have the longest shafts while the 9 iron, pitching wedge, and sand wedge have the shortest shafts.

In addition, the shorter clubs have a more sharply-angled club face (greater degree of loft). The combination of club length and club loft determine in part the distance a golf ball can be hit under normal conditions. If a golfer can execute a good shot each time, there is an approximate ten-yard difference between each club used. Figure 13-5 indicates the degrees of loft of specific clubs.

[1]Dick Aultman, "Golf Primer," *Golf Digest* (May 1979), p. 113.

164

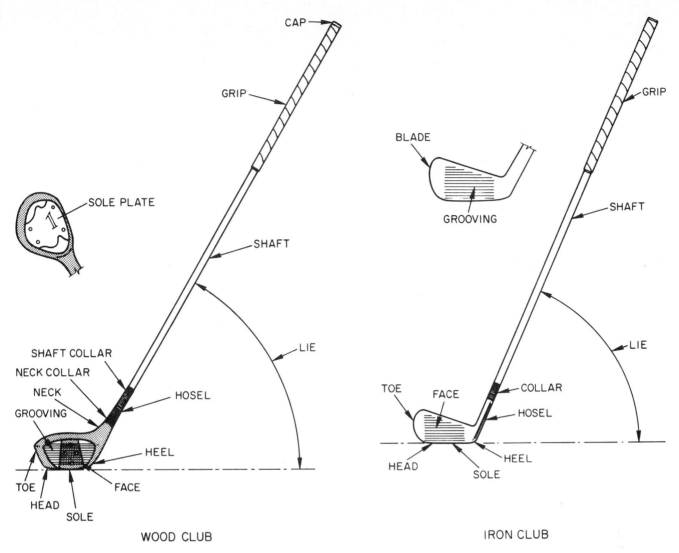

FIGURE 13-4. Parts of a wood club and an iron club.

FIGURE 13-5. Club lofts. The loft of any one club will vary a few degrees. The manufacturers' recommendations are shown here.

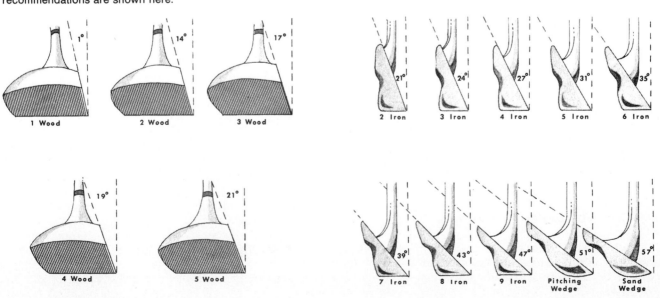

Women's golf clubs are one to two inches shorter than men's clubs. Children's clubs are shorter still. Some companies today are making fully matched sets of junior clubs, but they are quite expensive.

Shaft Flexibility.   The amount of flexibility of the club's shaft plays an important role in golf, because it determines the golfer's "feel" of the clubhead. Companies generally make shafts with five different flexibilities: extra stiff to stiff, used only by very long hitters; regular or medium stiff, used by the average man and the longer hitting women; medium flex and flexible shafts, used by most women.

Clubhead Design.   The design of the clubhead is important in the selection of clubs. Players who drive less than 175 yards are advised to use wood clubs with relatively shallow faces and with a loft of 10 degrees in order to gain additional height. Those who drive between 175 and 225 yards should have a deeper-faced club with a loft of 9 degrees. Players who drive over 225 yards usually use the deepest-faced club with a loft of 8 degrees. The difference in face depth of the irons is not too important, since most irons have practically the same face depth.

Grip.   Grips are generally made of leather or rubber and vary from the thin, for short-fingered players, to the standard size, for big-handed and/or long-fingered players. A good guide is, "If it feels right, it is for you."

Balls and Tees

Golf Balls.   Golf balls come in a variety of types and in a wide price range. It is not necessary for beginners to buy the most expensive ball. Less expensive balls generally have a thicker covering and are more durable.

The distance a ball travels is largely determined by the amount it is compressed by the clubhead at impact. A ball which is tightly wound has a high compression and rebounds further from the clubface than a low compression ball—if both were flattened the same amount on the clubface. Beginning golfers should use the 80 to 90 compression ball while the good golfer should use the 90 to 100 compression golf ball.

Tees.   Tees are made of wood, plastic, or even light metals. Wooden tees are considered best and are usually least expensive. It makes little or no difference what type of tee a golfer uses.

SUGGESTED LEARNING SEQUENCE

Golf can be taught a number of different ways and from various starting points. Many of the skills can be learned and practiced indoors as well as outdoors. The availability of space and equipment (clubs, balls, screens, rugs, or mats) are important factors to consider. For beginning golfers, audio-visual aids can play a significant role in the learning process, for they serve to reinforce many of the concepts explained during the initial stages of instruction. Another point to remember is that psychomotor and cognitive material is much better learned when presented together at the appropriate time. For example, etiquette and the rules governing play on the putting green are more meaningful during a lesson on putting than during a lesson devoted to the rules of golf. Finally, it is important to become proficient in the basic swing techniques before attempting to move on to the more advanced skills and techniques.

A.   Introduction to Golf
    1. Nature and purpose of the game
    2. Choosing the right equipment
    3. Care of equipment
B.   Etiquette and Rules of Golf. These should be introduced as deemed most appropriate for learning during different class intervals.
C.   Skills and Techniques
    1. Grip—overlap, interlocking, ten-finger
    2. Stance—address position
    3. Building a swing
        a. Woods
        b. Irons
    4. Types of shots
        a. Chip—Pitch shot
        b. Sand shot
        c. Putting
D.   Strategy on the Course. This should be introduced as deemed most appropriate for learning.

SKILLS AND TECHNIQUES

Golf is game requiring control, concentration, and coordination. It is characterized by a great deal of upper body movement—the arms, hands, and shoulders—revolving in different planes around a fairly stationary base—the lower half of the body. The following key concepts will be helpful to the beginning golfer as the various skills are being learned.

1.   In order to cause the ball to rise in the air when struck, generally the golfer must hit down on the ball. Scooping or attempting to flick the wrists as the ball is contacted usually results in mishits. Clubs are designed with specific degrees of loft; let the loft take care of the flight.
2.   The club is an extension of the hands and arm. Think of the club as being your arm and the clubhead as your hand. Therefore any change in your body position during the swing results in a

change in other body parts which has a direct relationship to the success or failure of the shot being attempted.

3. The swing is basically the same for all the clubs you use except for the special shots.

The Grip

The correct grip is the most important fundamental skill to be learned by golfers of any skill level. It can determine in great part the path of your swing, and consequently the directional flight of the ball. There are three types of grips used in golf: the overlapping grip (Vardon grip), the interlocking grip, and the ten-finger grip (Figure 13-6). The Vardon or overlapping grip is the one most commonly used. In this grip the little finger of the right hand overlaps the index finger of the left hand. The interlocking grip is used by the golfer who has small hands and short fingers. In this grip, the little finger of the right hand *interlocks* with the index finger of the left hand. Both grips have the advantage of having the hands work as a unit, because the hands are joined together. The ten-finger grip is used by the golfer who has small hands; it is used frequently by beginning junior golfers. The ten-finger grip enables the golfer to take a strong hold, but there is a tendency for the hands to slip apart at times.

When assuming a grip, the fact that it may not feel comfortable is no reason for the golfer to think that it is incorrect. However, the grip should not feel like a vise; rather it should feel firm yet somewhat relaxed. Tenseness in the grip will cause a restricted swing; the golf swing should flow.

Learning Cues—Overlapping Grip (right-handed golfer)

1. Using a 5 iron or 7 iron, place the sole of your club flat on the ground, supporting the end on your left thigh; left arm should be hanging naturally.
2. Place the left hand on the club so the hand lies across the middle front of the index finger and back across the palm.
3. Close the fingers around the club—pressure should be felt in your last three fingers. The index finger will be placed like a trigger finger, the thumb is wrapped alongside of the shaft so that a V appears formed by the forefinger and thumb.
4. Check the V. It should point toward the right shoulder; the back of the left hand should also point to your intended line of flight.
5. Place the right hand on the shaft with the handle across the open palm at the middle of the index finger; the little finger should overlap the index finger of the left hand.
6. Close the right hand; the life line of the right palm should be placed over the left thumb.
7. The palms should face each other; the V formed by the index finger and thumb of the right hand should also point toward the right shoulder; the club face should be square to the line of flight.

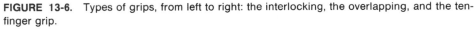

FIGURE 13-6.   Types of grips, from left to right: the interlocking, the overlapping, and the ten-finger grip.

FIGURE 13-7. Assuming the overlapping grip. Note the two V's and their alignment with the right shoulder.

Practice Suggestions

1. Place class in a circle and have them grip and regrip the club.
2. Allow class to pick out a target and work with partners. Have partner A assume a grip and then have partner B check the position of the Vs and the position of the club face to note if it's square to the target. Reverse the procedure.
3. Place class in a circle formation with plenty of space between students. Have them assume the grip, pick up the club so that it is parallel to the ground, and draw a circle or a figure 8 in the air. This helps to develop the feel of the club.

The Stance and Address

The stance and address involve assuming a good grip, position of the feet and shoulders to the line of flight, and position of the club face in relation to the line of flight.

There are three types of stances that may be taken when addressing the ball preparatory to hit-

ting it (Figure 13-8). The open stance is taken with the left foot pulled farther away from the intended line of flight than the right foot. The closed stance has the right foot pulled farther away from the intended line of flight than the left foot. The square stance, with both feet lined up equidistant from the line of flight, is probably the best for almost all shots, especially for the beginner. It is considered better to instruct the beginner with the fundamentals of the swing from one stance and explain to the golfer the various adaptations. As mastery is gained, modifications can be made to fit the situation.

Learning Cues

1. Determine the line of flight to a target, place a club on or draw a line in the direction of the target.
2. Step up to the line with both feet together, toes touching the line. Assume a good grip, stand erect with the club, holding the club in front of you.
3. Place the sole of the club flat on the ground and square to the target by bending at the waist.

FIGURE 13-8. The three types of stances, left to right: open, square, and closed.

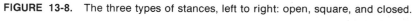

4. Spread the feet shoulder width apart, toes touching the line and turned out slightly; weight should be equally distributed and the knees slightly flexed as they would be prior to sitting.
5. The arms should be hanging from the body naturally; the hands should be slightly forward of the clubhead.

The position of the ball and distance from the golf ball will depend on the club being used. The shorter the club the closer to the ball the golfer stands. Obviously with a wood or a long iron, you will be standing further from the ball. The position of the golf ball will also depend on the club being used. For long irons (2 and 3) and woods, the ball is positioned just off the left heel (Figure 13-9). For a shorter to mid-iron, the ball is played nearer the middle left of the stance.

FIGURE 13-9. Address position for long iron or wood.

The Swing

Developing a rhythmical, coordinated, and smooth swing that produces solid contact at impact is fundamental to the game of golf. Basically, there is no difference in swinging a wood club or an iron club. In swinging a golf club, the attempt is to swing it back and through a long, large elliptical circle. The important point is that the clubhead leaves the ball and returns along the same line to the same point each time it is swung. The player should consider the body as the center of this circle and the arms as the radius. It is necessary for the golfer to pivot the body around a vertical axis and allow the arms to follow firmly in a natural plane.

The thought required to swing the club should be kept as simple as possible. Cluttering the move-ment with excess thought is detrimental to the beginning golfer, rather than helpful. It is helpful for the beginner to think of the swing in four parts: (1) the backswing or takeaway, (2) at the top, (3) the downswing, and (4) the follow-through. In practicing, care should be taken to follow a simple sequence of motion each time the golfer addresses and swings at a ball. Although we frequently think "practice makes perfect," it should be rephrased as "practice makes permanent." Therefore haphazard practice is almost as bad as no practice at all. Much practice and thought should go into learning this most fundamental aspect of the game.

Learning Cues

A. The Backswing or Takeaway (Figure 13-10)
1. Assume the address position along a target line, the left side initiating the move away from the ball inside the line of flight.
2. The arms swing the clubhead back close to the ground.
3. The shoulders turn, the right arm bends at the elbow.
4. The wrists are cocked, the left arm is fairly straight and firm, head is steady looking at the ball.
5. The left arm is parallel to the ground, the left knee is rotated and flexed at the knee, weight on the inside foot of the right side.

FIGURE 13-10. Backswing.

B. At the Top (Figure 13-11)
1. The left arm is parallel to the ground, wrists are cocked, club shaft is nearly parallel to the ground.
2. Right elbow is fairly close to the side, pointing downward.

FIGURE 13-11. Position at the top of the swing.

3. The hips and shoulders should be turned, the left shoulder is under the chin.

C. The Downswing
1. The initial movement is made with the hips along the line of flight (weight transfer to left side).
2. The left arm and shoulder pull toward the ball, the right arm is inside and close to the body during the return to impact point.
3. The wrists are uncocked as late as possible in the downswing, the hands will be slightly ahead of the ball at contact.
4. The head and eyes remain fixed on the contact point.

D. Follow-through (Figure 13-12)
1. The hands and arms continue through during the swing.
2. The clubhead remains low throughout until the arms are extended, then the hands and arms follow-through in a natural line.
3. At the finish, the hips and shoulders have turned so that you are facing the intended target.
4. Weight has transferred to the left side, the right leg is bent at the knee toward the left leg.

Practice Suggestions

Many warm up exercises can be used that approximate the rhythm and pattern of a full swing. In addition, golf is a target game and therefore the beginner should always use a target for a point of reference as an indicator of how the ball is being hit.

A. Without a Ball or Club
1. Assume a stance with arms hanging naturally in front of you. On command, pivot back swinging the arms as you would in a takeaway position and swing through with the arms finishing high. Repeat several times checking head movement and weight transfer.
2. Against a wall. Stand 12 to 18 inches from the wall, assume a stance and place forehead against the wall. On command, go through the swing sequence. This drill helps to note importance of keeping the head steady.
3. With a towel rolled up and grasped at either end, assume a stance and go through swing sequence. A club grasped at either end can serve the same purpose.

B. With a Club and Ball
1. Assume a stance with feet together. Execute a backswing, then step with the left foot toward the target as you begin the downswing. Try it first without a ball, then with a ball. This will give the beginner a sense of weight transfer.
2. Without a ball, practice the swing and note the cut of the grass made by the swing. It should indicate direction.
3. With a ball, begin hitting toward a designated target, first with short irons and moving gradually toward longer irons. Note the pattern formed by the golf balls—are they close together or far apart.

SUITING CLUBS TO SHOTS

The Wood Shots

The woods are used for the longest shots in golf. The driver is primarily used for shots from the teeing ground, where the ball may be mounted on a

FIGURE 13-12. Halfway through the follow-through. Note weight transfer, head remaining almost behind the ball.

tee. The number 3, 4, and 5 woods are all used for extra distance when hitting from the fairway. Each is graded for a slightly shorter distance than the lower numbered club. The higher the number of the club, the greater the height of the shot.

For the drive, the ball should be approximately in line with the instep of the left foot. With the number 3, 4, and 5 woods, the ball can be played slightly on the inside of the left heel.

In playing shots from the fairway where the ball is resting on depressed ground, it is often best to choose an iron. In selecting a wood for a fairway shot, the lie should always be carefully considered. If there is doubt of success, an iron should be chosen. A poorly-played wood shot is never as effective as a well-played shot with one of the irons. In the rough, the lie must be exceptionally good to warrant the use of one of the woods.

The Long Irons

The number 2, 3, and 4 irons are considered the long irons. They are used on the fairway when maximum distance is desired, but when the lie is such that the use of a wood is not deemed advisable. The irons, being shorter, allow the plane of swing to be more upright. Consequently, the player is closer to the ball. Irons give greater accuracy and offer more control of the shot. They also impart backspin to the ball, allowing better placement of the shot.

In choosing the proper club, always select one that does not require straining for distance. Under-clubbing may cause the player to press and sacrifice accuracy for distance. A number 3 iron swung with a three-quarter swing is more easily controlled than a number 5 iron swung as hard as possible. There is no premium for an exceptionally long shot with a particular iron when another, longer iron might be used and more accuracy obtained. The irons are graded to be used at various distances, and there is a proper club for each distance. This may vary with individuals, but each player must determine what club is proper for him. There is no disgrace in using a number 2 iron when a stronger player used a number 5 iron for the same distance. What matters is, who went the closest to the hole with the club he or she used.

With the longer irons the stance involves a somewhat shorter stride, and the ball is played between the left heel and the center of the body. The golfer stands closer to the ball, since the shaft of the club is shorter than the wood. In hitting all iron shots, the club meets the ball just prior to the bottom of the downswing, taking a little turf after the ball is struck.

The Medium Irons

This name applies to the number 5, 6, and 7 irons. They are the middle-distance clubs among the irons. They offer greater accuracy and also allow the player to achieve some distance. The medium irons can often save strokes on the score. Many holes can be negotiated with a good tee shot and a well-placed one with an iron—leaving only an average length putt. These clubs can substitute for an approach shot if played well onto the green. They can also compensate for a slightly missed tee shot in many cases. Out of the rough, they give enough loft to the ball to get out of trouble and still give fair distance. These clubs are often used for chip shots close around the green, where entry is not obstructed by traps or hazards. All in all, they are very useful clubs for a multiplicity of purposes.

The Short Irons

This category includes the number 8 and 9 irons and the sand wedge. They have a high pitch to the face of the club and are used for short shots around the green and in getting out of the rough, hazards, and traps. These clubs are designed so that they impart a great deal of backspin to the ball and therefore little roll at the end of the shot. The ball is hit on the downstroke and some turf is taken. Here, accuracy is the main concern and thus the backswing is shortened. The pivot and body action is reduced and more of the swing is produced in the action of the arms and hands. More advanced golfers play these shots with a slightly open stance.

SPECIAL SHOTS

The short approach shots discussed in this section—the pitch, chip, sand shot, and putt—are frequently called the golfer's scoring strokes. A high percentage of shots taken during a round of golf consist of these four types; therefore the more proficient you become the lower your scores will become. One of the key elements in these shots involves "feel"; consequently the shots must be practiced frequently in order to develop a comfortable feeling. Most of these shots, with the exception of a fairway sand shot, are executed near the green or on the green itself.

The Pitch Shot

The pitch shot is generally executed with a high lofted iron such as the 8, 9, pitching wedge, or sand wedge. The golfer will execute a pitch when within less than 90 yards of the green or when near the green but confronted with a sandtrap, bunker, or water hazard between the ball and the green. A pitch shot is designed to be hit high, with backspin so that when it hits the green it will stop quickly with a minimum of roll. The swing will range from a full swing when 70 to 90 yards from the green to a partial swing (1/4, 1/2, 3/4) when nearer the green.

When executing a full pitch shot, swing mechanics will be the same; when executing a partial swing, some change needs to be made.

Learning Cues

1. Assume a square or open stance; use your normal grip.
2. The feet are moved closer together in an open stance.
3. The hands "choke" down on the handle with most of the weight on the left side throughout the swing.
4. The distance to the hole will determine the length of the backswing—cock wrists.
5. Bring arms and hands down and through as you make contact with the ball; keep your hands moving toward the target. *Do not* flip your wrists at contact; keep the left arm and wrist firm.

The Chip Shot

The chip shot is generally executed with any iron club from a 5 through 9. The club selected usually depends on the distance from the hole and the amount of roll necessary to reach the hole. Many instructors recommend that the beginner select one particular iron and develop the feel necessary for that club. The chip shot is designed to be executed when the ball lies off the green. When done properly, the ball spends a minimum amount of time in the air and a maximum amount of time rolling on the green. The shot is executed with a partial swing.

Many experts recommend that the golfer use a putting stroke to chip when the ball is just off the green, because it gives increased accuracy.

Learning Cues (Figure 13-13)

1. Stance and grip—feet narrow, stance is open, weight on left side, ball is played off the left heel.
2. To gain greater feel, the hands are placed near the bottom end of the handle.
3. The swing is executed with the wrists fairly firm (very little break) and the swing is down and through the ball. The hands should continue to lead the clubhead through the shot. The clubhead should be square to the target.
4. There is very little or no body movement aside from the arms.

Practice Suggestions

1. Experiment with different clubs when chipping. Set a target 20, 30, 40 feet away. Chip to the target noting the flight pattern and the landing point.
2. Place an object (such as a golf bag or a 2 × 8 inch strip) between the hole and your ball. Chip over the object. This will force you to hit down and through the ball.
3. For pitch shots, move various distances away from the target and note the length of your backswing and follow-through.
4. For short pitch shots, use a basket as a target and try to pitch the ball into the basket.
5. Place an object between the ball and the target and pitch over the target.

FIGURE 13-13. Chip shot. The stance is open, weight on the left side; the ball is positioned near the left heel. Note position of the wrists, which remain firm during the follow-through.

FIGURE 13-14. Sand shot. The stance is open, club face is open; club may not be grounded before the shot.

The Sand Shot

The sand shot is usually a difficult shot for the beginner to master because sand does not have the firmness of the fairway nor does the ball set up as it does on grass. A specially designed club called a sand wedge is used to execute the shot. Again "feel" is an important element that determines success. There are various ways to get out of a sand trap. With traps that are flat, near the green, and with no lip, the beginner might try putting the ball out of the trap, provided the ball is not buried. For shots with a low lip near the green, the golfer may try a chip shot. However for shots in a deep trap and with the ball buried in the sand, the golfer must execute an explosion shot. Remember, a golfer may not ground a club in a trap without incurring a penalty.

Learning Cues (Figure 13-14)

1. Address the ball with an open stance, with the feet securely planted in the sand.
2. The ball is played opposite the left foot, the weight is on the left side, and the club face is open.
3. Focus on a point one to two inches behind the ball; use very little body movement during the swing; wrists are cocked, aim to left of the target.
4. Make sure the clubhead accelerates into and through the sand, and complete the swing.

The Putt

Putting is probably the most important phase of the game, and too often one of the most neglected. Concentration and confidence are two of the primary requirements for good putting, and can be gained best through practice of fundamental tech-

niques. Forms of putting differ widely, but basic fundamentals are much the same.

Learning Cues

1. Place hands on the club with the palms facing each other and in line with the face of the putter. When closing the fingers around the putter reverse the overlap of the little finger and index finger. The grip should be made near the bottom end of the handle for better control.
2. Stand with feet in line with the direction of the putt; this may not be directly at the hole. Weight is placed on the left foot.
3. Ball should be placed opposite the left heel.
4. Stand with your eyes looking directly over the path of the ball. This should place you closer to the ball than normal.
5. The backswing, initiated with the arms, and keeping the wrist fairly firm, should be low and along the line of flight.
6. The forward stroke should return along the same line keeping the putter face square to the putting line. The hands should lead the putter through the stroke.

Some important points about putting must be remembered by the beginning golfer. First, the putter head must continue to accelerate through the ball. Secondly, keep the putter head low to the ground and concentrate on making solid contact with the ball. Finally, learn to read the green.

By approaching the ball from the rear, the golfer can "read" the green. Since few greens are absolutely flat, the golfer must determine which way the ball will curve and to what extent. More important, however, is the distance the ball must travel. The player should study each green to determine its speed by considering the way the grass grows, how it is cut, and how hard the turf is. If the distance of the putt is accurately judged, the golfer will seldom leave himself a difficult second putt. On the other hand, if the distance is badly misjudged, even though the direction is accurate, there may be a long, bothersome putt waiting.

HELPFUL HINTS

1. For downhill shots, use a lofted club, a wide stance, and play the ball back so as not to hit the hill on the downswing.
2. For uphill shots, use a straight face club, feet well apart for balance, and play the ball opposite the left foot. Let the club follow the contour of the hill.
3. For sidehill shots (standing below the ball), use a shorter grip, aim to the right and open the stance, and play the ball back to make certain you hit the ball first and not the turf.
4. For sidehill shots (standing above the ball), use a longer grip, close the stance, and flex the knees to get down to the ball—don't lean.
5. If you slice, try closing your stance, closing the left hand, and placing the right hand farther over the shaft. If you hook, do the reverse.
6. Remember there is a maximum body pivot and backswing on woods for distance. As the clubs become shorter and the distances decrease, the body pivot and backswing also decrease.
7. Study each shot carefully, but don't delay other players.
8. Learn to control your shots before trying for distance.
9. Learn the distances you hit with each of your clubs. Play your own game—not your opponent's.
10. Always select the club that will not require straining for distance.
11. Learn to judge distances.
12. Study the roll of the green by approaching your ball from the rear.
13. Concentrate on each shot and take your time.
14. Relax before hitting every shot. Taking a fairly deep breath and then exhaling just before starting the swing is a good method of relaxing.
15. Study the speed and direction of the wind, condition of the course, and the terrain to be covered on each shot.
16. After you have played, attempt to analyze your game and work on those phases that need improvement.
17. Remember that good golfers not only play, but practice as well.
18. Learn the rules of golf and golfing etiquette.
19. Hit drives to the center of the fairway except in unusual circumstances.
20. Play to the safe side of the greens if there is no contour; play to the downhill side if they slope.

SAFETY CONSIDERATIONS

Golf can be a dangerous game if attention is not given to your play and the play of others. Whether golf is being played in a class situation, on a practice range, or while playing a round, basic safety rules must be observed.

General Rules

1. Never hit a shot until you are sure those in front of you are out of your range. If you hit another player, you may be liable for damages.
2. Never swing a club, especially on the tees, unless you are sure no one is standing close to you.
3. If the warning "Fore" is given, it is often dangerous to turn to see where the ball is coming from. It is best to cover the head for protection and turn away from the direction of the warning.
4. In the event of a thunderstorm, it is not wise to remain outdoors. Shelter should be sought in a closed building protected against lightning. Large or small unprotected buildings are alternatives in the order given. If remaining outdoors is unavoidable, keep away from open spaces and hilltops. Also, stay away from isolated trees, wire fences, and small shelters in exposed locations. Shelter may also be sought in caves, depressions or deep valleys and canyons, the foot of a cliff, or in a dense stand of trees. Umbrellas held overhead in exposed places are dangerous.
5. Never practice in an area where others are playing. Most golf courses have special practice areas.
6. Never hit practice shots while playing a round. It not only wastes time but is dangerous.
7. Only one person should hit at a time. The person farthest from the hole should play first.
8. Knowing and applying the rules of golf and golfing etiquette will increase your safety on a golf course.
9. Carry a towel and wipe hands dry, particularly on hot humid days and rainy days.
10. Know the distances of specific clubs and distances you can hit the ball.

In Class—Rules for the Instructor

1. Plan the lesson well in advance, checking such things as formation, target areas, methods of retrieval.
2. Allow no one to swing a club unless instructed to do so.
3. Provide plenty of space between golfers.
4. If stations are used, provide for adequate distance between groups.

In Class—Rules for the Student

1. Do not retrieve a golf ball until asked to do so; never step out of line to pick up a "muffed" shot.

2. Do not walk too close behind other golfers swinging the golf club.
3. If working with a partner, stand in front and to the side of your partner, not behind.
4. Listen to instruction, follow prescribed rules.

ETIQUETTE AND PLAYING COURTESIES

Since golf is a polite game with a well-defined code of ethics, it is important for every golfer to observe common courtesies while on the course.

In General, While Playing the Course

1. Be polite at all times, know the rules of golf so decisions can be made quickly without causing undue delay.
2. Be aware of the local rules and regulations that govern play on a course.
3. Do not hit practice shots between regular shots—it is an infraction of the rules.
4. Abstain from obscene language, loud talk, and club throwing.
5. Plan ahead and be ready to play your next shot without undue delay. The player farthest from the flag stick shoots first.
6. Do not talk, move around, stand too close or directly in line of a shot when another player is preparing to shoot.
7. Never play a shot until the group ahead is completely out of range.
8. While looking for a lost ball, do not unduly delay the play of others. Allow a group playing behind you to go through by signalling them to do so and do not resume play until they are out of range.
9. After each shot, pick up the divot or loose grass and replace it with your hand in the divot mark. Pat it down with your foot.
10. Fill holes made in bunkers and smooth the sand after playing from a trap. Be sure to rake all sand traps upon leaving them.
11. Keep pull carts and motorized carts off the green area.
12. Yell "Fore" if a ball is in danger of striking another person.
13. The person having the honor (lowest score on the preceding hole) tees up first.
14. Notify your partners when you wish to change a golf ball.

On the Putting Green

1. As soon as a hole has been completed, the player should leave the green. Do not total the scores and record them on the green.
2. Allow the person farthest from the hole to putt first.
3. When lifting a ball on the green, mark it with a coin.
4. Never lay a bag of clubs down on the green.

5. Do not throw the flag stick off to the side. Always lay it down gently, away from all play, and replace it when the hole has been completed.
6. Do not damage the hole with the stick or by standing too close to the hole.
7. Repair ball marks on the green.
8. Upon completion of the hole, the group should move off the green to record scores.
9. Do not drag your feet or in any way scuff the green.

RULES OF GOLF

The rules of golf have been developed and are periodically upgraded by two coordinating bodies—the United States Golf Association (USGA) and the Royal and Ancient Golf Club of St. Andrews, Scotland. The rules undergo continual study and are revised by these two bodies every four years. The USGA publishes a rule book each year and offers it for sale at a minimal cost. It is strongly recommended that serious students obtain a copy. A booklet entitled *Easy Way to Learn Golf Rules* is available at a minimal cost from the National Golf Foundation.

Local Rules

In constructing the rules which uniformly govern all golf play in the United States, the United States Golf Association recognizes that certain local conditions such as climate, variable physical conditions, and characteristics of golf courses may necessitate modifications of the rules. These modifications are termed Local Rules and are designed to protect the golf course and make the game more enjoyable. A player is responsible for becoming acquainted with the Local Rules before playing. Sources of information concerning Local Rules include the golf professional, the score card, golf course bulletin board, and players familiar with the golf course.

The United States Golf Association limits the extent to which Local Rules may modify the USGA rules. Players should refer to the United States Golf Association Rules of Golf Appendix to familiarize themselves with the limitations.

Summary of Important Golf Rules

1. A player may have a maximum of 14 clubs in the golf bag at any one time. Penalty for exceeding the maximum: disqualification.
2. A player must tee up his ball between the tee markers or anywhere in the rectangle two club lengths behind them. Violation of the rule: two-stroke penalty.
3. An intentional swing at the ball must be counted as a stroke, even if the player "wiffs" it.

4. A ball is considered lost if not retrieved in five minutes.

5. A ball must be played as it lies except as provided for in the rules. Violation of the rule: two-stroke penalty.

6. Loose impediments such as grass, leaves, a flag stick, vehicle, or bench may be removed in order to hit a golf ball. If it must be re-dropped, it must be done no more than one club length from the original spot and no nearer the hole.

7. If a player hits a ball out of bounds, the player must take a one-stroke penalty and play the ball from the original spot.

8. When a ball is hit into a water hazard, the player may drop a ball behind the hazard, keeping the spot at which the ball crossed the hazard between himself and the hole. Penalty: one stroke.

9. A player is allowed to drop a ball out of casual water, but not nearer the hole.

10. A player, while in the act of putting on the green, whose ball hits another player's ball is assessed a two-stroke penalty in medal play. The opponent must replace his ball at the original spot. A player while putting off the green, whose ball hits another ball on the green is not assessed a penalty.

TERMINOLOGY

Ace A hole in one.

Address The position taken by a player in preparing to start a stroke.

Apron The area immediately surrounding the green.

Banana ball A slice.

Best ball tournament Competition in which the better score of a partnership on each hole is used as the team score.

Birdie The score of one under par on a hole.

Bogey A score of one over par on a hole (United States rules). In countries playing the British rules, a bogey is the score an average golfer should make on a hole; on easier holes, par and bogey might be the same score.

Casual water Temporary accumulation of water which is not recognized as a hazard on the course.

Course rating The comparative difficulty of a specific course. Usually computed by a committee of a local association in order to have uniform handicapping for all courses within a district.

Divot Sod cut with the clubhead when executing or attempting to execute a shot.

Dogleg A hole which has a sharp bend in the fairway.

Driver Number 1 wood.

Eagle A score for a hole played in two strokes under par.

Fairway The course between the teeing ground and the putting green, exclusive of hazards.

Flag Banner on top of the flagstick identifying the cup.

Fore A warning cry to anyone of a stroke about to be played or one that has been played.

Go to school Learning the roll of a green by watching a previous putt over the same area.

Ground under repair Any portion of the course so marked that includes material piled for removal or a hole made by a greenskeeper.

Hazard Any bunker, water hazard, or lateral water hazard.

Hole Small cup sunk into the green, into which the golf ball is hit. The hole is 4¼ inches in diameter and at least 4 inches deep.

Honor The side which is entitled to play first from the teeing ground is said to have the honor. This is usually determined by a coin flip on the first tee. Once play begins, the player having the lowest score on the previous hole is said to have the honor thereafter.

Hook A ball in flight that curves from right to left (for a right-handed golfer).

Lie The position of the ball on the playing ground. Also refers to the angle of the clubhead.

Loose impediments Natural objects not fixed or growing and not adhering to the ball, and including stones not solidly embedded, leaves, twigs, branches, and the like, dung, worms, and insects, and casts or heaps made by them.

Match play Competition in which the winner is decided by the number of holes won.

Mulligan or Shapiro Permitting a second hit of a badly played ball—usually on a tee shot. (Not permitted under the rules but by mutual agreement in friendly matches.)

Obstruction An artificial object erected, placed, or left on a course and not an integral part of the course.

Par The standard score for a hole.

Pull-shot To hit a ball straight, but to the left of the target (for a right-handed golfer).

Push-shot To hit a ball straight, but to the right of the target (for a right-handed golfer).

Rough The unmowed terrain on either side of the fairway.

Scotch foursome A competitive round in which two partners play the same ball, taking alternate shots.

Slice A ball in flight that curves from left to right (for a right-handed person).

Stroke play (medal play) Competition in which the winner is decided by the total number of strokes taken from a specific number of rounds, not by individual holes won, as in match play.

Summer rules Playing the ball as it lies from tee through green.

Teeing ground The starting place for the hole to be played.

Trap A hazard, technically known as a bunker.

Waggle Body or club action prior to starting the swing.

Wedge A heavy iron club that is used to loft the ball high into the air. It is also used for special situations, such as getting out of heavy grass or sand.

Winter rules The privilege of improving the lie of the ball on the fairway of the hole being played.

SELECTED REFERENCES

ALTMAN, DICK. *Square-to-Square Golf Swing.* New York: Simon & Schuster, Inc., 1970.

CHUI, EDWARD F. *Golf.* Goodyear Physical Activities Series, Pacific Palisades, Calif.: Goodyear Publishing Co., 1969.

FOSSUM, BRUCE, and DAGRAEDT, MARY. *Golf.* Boston: Allyn and Bacon Inc., 1969.

HOGAN, BEN. *Five Lessons: The Modern Fundamentals of Golf.* New York: A.S. Barnes and Co., Inc., 1957.

NANA, VIRGINIA L., and ELWOOD CRAIG DAVIS. *Golf,* 3rd ed. Dubuque, Iowa: Wm. C. Brown Company, Publishers, 1975.

NICKLAUS, JACK. *My 55 Ways to Lower Your Golf Score.* New York: Simon & Schuster, Inc., 1964.

THOMPSON, DONNA HAZEL, and JULIA CARVER. *Physical Activities Handbook for Women.* Englewood Cliffs, N.J.: Prentice-Hall, Inc., 1974.

TOSKI, BOB. *The Touch System for Better Golf.* New York: Simon & Schuster, Inc., 1971.

WATSON, TOM, and FRANK HANNIGAN. *The Rules of Golf.* New York: Random House, 1980.

WIREN, GARY. *Golf.* Englewood Cliffs, N.J.: Prentice-Hall, Inc., 1971.

Magazine Articles

AULTMAN, DICK, and Editors of *Golf Digest.* "A Golf Primer." *Golf Digest* (May, 1979) pp. 1–24.

Golf Digest's Professional Teaching Panel and Advisory Staff. "The Art of Putting—The Stroke." *Golf Digest* (December 1975) 68–71.

METZ, ROBERT V. "Teaching Golf to Large Groups." *Journal of Physical Education and Recreation* (November–December 1976) 27–28.

PATE, JERRY. "Good Putters Are Made—Not Born." *Golf Digest* (June 1978) 50–53.

RUNYAN, PAUL. "A Sure Method for Getting Your Chips and Pitches Close." *Golf Digest* (March 1980) 57–72.

WATSON, TOM. "How to Get It Up and Down." *Golf Digest* (August 1978) 43–49.

WATSON, TOM. "My Two Keys to Good Putting." *Golf Digest* (April 1980) 53–57.

WICKHAM, SUZY. "Teaching Youngsters Basic Golf Skills." *Journal of Physical Education and Recreation* (November–December 1976) 25–26.

WIREN, GARY. "The Common Denominator of All Good Sand Methods." *Golf Digest* (September 1975) 94–96.

Audio-Visual Materials

National Golf Foundation Series—16 mm films
For rental:
Film Comm Inc., 108 West Grand Avenue, Chicago, Illinois 60610.
Golf—A Special Kind of Joy (16 min.)
How to Build a Golf Swing (32 min.)

For purchase:
National Golf Foundation, 200 Castlewood Drive, North Palm Beach, Florida 33408.
The Short Approach Shot (9 min.)
The Special Challenge Shots (14 min.)
Putting—Golf's End Game (12 min.)
Courtesy on the Course (18 min.)

Loop Films—8 mm
Athletic Institute, 200 Castlewood Drive, North Palm Beach, Florida 33408.
The Grip
The Full Swing
The Short Approach
The Putt
The Sand Explosion
Uneven Lies—Uphill, Downhill, Sidehill

Association Films Inc., 866 Third Avenue, New York, N.Y. 10022. *Come Golf With Me* (16 mm, 28 min.) Features Laura Baugh.

Modern Talking Pictures, 5000 Park Street, North, St. Petersburg, Florida 33709. *Move Along—Enjoy Golf* (16 mm, 27 min.) Features Arnold Palmer and Amy Alcott. Rules and etiquette.

Shell Film Library, 1433 Sadlier Circle, W. Dr., Indianapolis, Indiana 46239. Shell's Wonderful World of Golf Series (22 films—16 mm, 50 min. each) Features 18-hole matches of golfing greats.

14 GYMNASTICS FOR MEN AND WOMEN

THIS CHAPTER WILL ENABLE YOU TO:

♦ Understand how a competitive gymnastics meet is organized, administered, and scored.
♦ Identify the various events which comprise competition in gymnastics for men and for women.
♦ Comprehend the judging system used in evaluating the gymnast's performance during competition.
♦ Appreciate the importance of acquiring safety habits and attitudes when working out.
♦ Become acquainted with the national and international gymnastics organizations.
♦ Analyze and perform selected skills involved in competitive gymnastics events.

NATURE AND PURPOSE

When we speak of gymnastics today, we generally mean artistic gymnastics. The term *artistic gymnastics* was introduced in 1960 for the purpose of clarifying and differentiating among the various contemporary forms of gymnastic programs. Artistic gymnastics utilizes the heavy apparatus and the floor exercise area. For men, the events contested are: *floor exercise, pommel horse, still rings, long horse vaulting, parallel bars,* and *horizontal bar.* For women, the Olympic order of events is: *side horse vaulting, asymmetric (uneven parallel) bars, balance beam,* and *floor exercise.*

Artistic gymnastics is primarily an individual sport, in the sense that a performer executes a routine on a piece of apparatus and is scored for his/her performance by a panel of judges. The scoring is based on a ten-point scale, with appropriate deductions being taken from a number of categories. Judging will be covered in more detail later in the chapter. Despite the individual nature of the sport, team scores are kept also, with six performers constituting a team and the top five scores from that team constituting the team score for that particular event. In most major competitions, i.e., the Olympic Games and the World Gymnastic Championships, the gymnast performs both compulsory routines and optional routines. The compulsory routines are "set" routines established every four years, from one Olympic year to another. Every athlete in the competition performs the compulsory routines first, and then optional routines at another designated time period. The optionals are routines made up by each athlete, and are characterized by elements of risk, virtuosity, originality, and difficulty of combinations. It is in the optional routines that the gymnast's free spirit, élan, and inimitable style are demonstrated.

Other popular forms of gymnastics include *modern rhythmic gymnastics* and *sport acrobatics.* Trampolining was once a major part of competitive gymnastics in the United States, but this event was dropped from competition in 1964. This resulted in the formation of the United States Trampoline and Tumbling Association, which still sponsors competition in these events. Space does not permit the coverage of these excellent gymnastic activities, but they are gaining widespread recognition as important divergent forms of gymnastics.

GYMNASTIC FEDERATIONS AND ASSOCIATIONS

Governing bodies have been established that serve to develop, organize, and administer programs of gymnastics in the schools, universities, clubs, and for their respective countries. These organizations have powers to sanction, determine the process of selection, establish rules and policies, and to act as supervising agents in ascertaining that appropriate procedures are followed in the best interests of the athletes.

The Fédération Internationale de Gymnastique is an organization comprised of member nations from all over the world. The FIG is responsible for the conduct of major international gymnastic competitions, including the Olympic Games and the World Gymnastic Championships.

The United States Gymnastics Federation is the governing body for all amateur gymnastic competitions in the United States. Founded in 1964, the USGF has performed a remarkable service to the sport of gymnastics by fostering international recognition for the United States role in the sport, by developing a training program of national magnitude, and by serving as a communications and resource center for distributing materials, registering athletes, providing insurance coverage, conducting national championships, and selecting members for international teams.

The United States Association for Independent Gymnastic Clubs was formed in response to the tremendous growth in private gymnastic clubs across the nation. The USAIGC assists its members in the conduct of their programs and businesses, and has proved a boon to the burgeoning private gymnastics industry. This organization hosts its own national championship meet, and has provided the necessary leadership in meeting the needs of its constituents in legal, financial, and program development areas.

The United States Gymnastics Safety Association was founded in order to provide more qualified leadership in the private and public sectors of gymnastics and to promote safety in the sport. The USGSA works closely with federal agencies, such as the Bureau of Product Safety, that are concerned with providing safety standards, educational input, and meaningful programs to promote the safety of participants.

The National Collegiate Athletic Association is the governing body for collegiate sports for men. The NCAA publishes a rule book each year that serves as a guide for the conduct of all collegiate gymnastics competition for men in the country. The NCAA hosts a national championship at the Division I, II, and III levels in gymnastics. Most of the male gymnasts representing the United States in international competitions come from the ranks of NCAA member institutions.

The Association of Intercollegiate Athletics for Women is the governing body for collegiate sports for women. This organization is the counterpart of the NCAA. Begun in 1972, the objective of the AIAW is to provide women athletes greater opportunities for self-realization through an organization specifically attuned to their needs and interests. The AIAW hosts collegiate championships at the Division I, II, and III levels of competition.

The majority of female athletes representing the United States in international gymnastics competition come from the private gymnastics club level. This phenomenon is the result of earlier "peaking" of the female athlete, dealing with such characteristics as weight-strength ratio, aspiration/ability level, incentive/motivation factors, and socio-economic conditions. The AIAW program however has done a magnificent job in developing the competitive program for women at the collegiate level. As a result we find many more "elite level" gymnasts continuing on with their competitive careers in the collegiate ranks.

These national and international organizations govern the sport of gymnastics, controlling the conduct, direction, and development of the competitive programs in their own respective sphere. Each of the United States gymnastics organizations pub-

lishes a rule book, guide, handbook, or similar publication setting forth its organizational format, policies, and regulations for the forthcoming competitive season or, as is the case with the United States Gymnastics Federation, for the next four-year period. The USGF is the overall authority for the sport, providing national and international leadership, and having the sole right to sanction international competitions and to select the gymnasts who will represent the United States.

RECREATIONAL GYMNASTICS

We have been discussing the competitive artistic gymnastics programs. In addition, both in schools and private clubs there are recreational gymnastics programs, but these are more informal and not bound by the same rules and regulations that pertain to the aforementioned programs. Recreational gymnastics serve the needs of those individuals who have an enthusiasm for the sport of gymnastics, but perhaps do not have the time, ability, aspiration, or motivation for competing that marks the more advanced competitive gymnasts. Recreational programs may take the form of intraclub or intramural type activities. The rules are established locally in concert with the purposes and objectives of the program. It has been variously estimated that there are between 520,000 to 600,000 female competitive gymnasts in the United States, and approximately 190,000 to 200,000 males engaged in the competitive sport. Approximately *three times* as many people—a truly impressive number—are involved in recreational gymnastic programs.

Gymnastics lends itself well as a recreational activity for a number of reasons:

1. It does not require any set number of people or groups.
2. Individuals may select whatever event they wish to work out on, and can perform whatever skills their experience and ability permit.
3. Age is not a factor. Many people engage in gymnastics as a lifetime, carryover activity. Ethnic organizations such as the Turnverein (German heritage) and the Sokols (Czech heritage) sponsor age-group competitions that have a classification for people 50 years of age and older.
4. No special equipment is required other than the apparatus itself.
5. The activity is well suited to year-round participation, and may be conducted either indoors or outside.

In order to present relevant, consistent information, the material that follows will pertain specifically to competitive rather than recreational gymnastics.

COMPETITIVE FORMAT AND SCORING SYSTEM

Prior to the start of the competition, a draw is conducted to ascertain:

1. The group to which an individual or team will belong during the competition.
2. The order within the group in which the performers will compete.
3. The event that the group will start with, after which they will rotate in the Olympic order.
4. The number assigned to each gymnast, to be used throughout the competition.

The judging is based on a ten-point scale. As each performer completes his or her routine, the judges evaluate the performance; these scores are taken to the head scoring table where they are checked for accuracy and then tabulated. The performer's score is represented by a raw score, determined by averaging the two middle scores of the four judges. This raw score is added to each of the other scores received in the succeeding events (a total of four for women, and six for men), and this total represents the "all-around" score for the performer during the meet. In the case of individual competition this procedure completes the scoring process for the meet, following a rank ordering of the contestants. However, in the case of team competition, the team's five highest scores, from their total of six in each event, are totaled for all of the events, and this figure represents the team's score for the meet.

NOTE: The procedure just described is the one that is utilized in international competition. There are variations in scoring procedure among the different U.S. governing bodies such as the USGF, NCAA, AIAW, USAIGC, etc. For rules and regulations governing the conduct of meets within the jurisdiction of these organizations, the reader is referred to the booklets published by them.

Judging of Competitive Gymnastics

1. Vaults are each rated in value, with 10.00 being the highest possible value. Women perform two vaults and the score of the best vault is counted, except in finals competition, when the scores of the two vaults are averaged. Men perform one vault only.
2. The routines are scored on a scale of zero to ten, in tenths of a point.
3. For women, the breakdown of points is as follows: difficulty, 3.00; bonus points, 0.50; combinations, 2.50; execution and virtuosity, 4.00 points.
4. For men, the breakdown of the points is as follows: difficulty, 3.40; combination, 1.60; risk, originality, and virtuosity, 0.60; execution, 4.40 points.

5. Four judges shall be used per event, except in international meets, where a fifth judge will be used. (For women, in finals competition in international meets, six judges will officiate.) The head judge will determine if the scores of the judges are within an acceptable range, specified in the rules.
6. The highest and lowest scores are eliminated, and the two middle scores are averaged to determine the performer's score for each event.
7. Requirements for Balance Beam: The time limit for balance beam is between one minute ten seconds and one minute thirty seconds. The gymnast must use the entire length of the beam and must show variations in rhythm and level. A 360-degree turn on one leg, a leap or jump, an acrobatic series, and acrobatic elements in at least two directions are required.
8. Requirements for Floor Exercise (Women): Women's floor exercise is the only event accompanied by music. The routine must be performed between one minute ten seconds and one minute thirty seconds. The gymnast should show changes in levels and in rhythm. She should make use of the entire 12 meter by 12 meter area. The gymnast should combine acrobatic series with gymnastic elements of turns, leaps, jumps, steps, balance elements, and body waves to create a routine in harmony with her music and personality. This event allows the gymnast an opportunity for self-expression.
9. Requirements for Uneven Bars: The uneven bar routine should show several directional and bar changes and must show movement under the low bar and over the high bar. Stops or intermediate swings are to be avoided. The ten required elements should include at least three of the following: upward or circular swings, kips,[1] swing to handstand, turns around the longitudinal axes, turns around the horizontal axes, flight elements, and height elements.
10. Requirements for Floor Exercise (Men): The men's floor exercise must form a harmonious, rhythmical, whole composition, alternating movements of balance, hold parts, strength, leaps, kips, agilities, flexibilities, and tumbling movements. The exercise must cover the entire floor space, with movement in a variety of directions. Movements of a personal and postural expression are deemed valuable.
11. Requirements for Pommel Horse: The exercises must be composed of clean swings, without stops. Circles of one and both legs must be performed as well as forward and reverse scissors, one of which must be done consecutively. Double leg circles must predominate, and all

---

[1]A *kip* is a basic connecting movement going from an underswing to a front support.

three parts of the horse must be used as well as both sides.

12. Requirements for Still Rings: The work on the rings must contain movements alternating swing, strength, and hold parts, all without noticeable movement of the rings. The routine must contain at least two handstands, one of which must be executed with strength and the other attained with swing from a hang, inverted hang, or support. Hold parts must be held between three and five seconds, and must be of a difficulty level commensurate with moves such as the cross, front lever, inverted cross, planche, etc.

13. Requirements for Long Horse Vaulting: The horse is placed lengthwise, with the distance between the board and the horse individually determined by the performer. All vaults must be executed with support of one or both hands, and the hands must be placed within the specified zone areas of the horse. The distance of the run is up to the discretion of the gymnast, but the length cannot exceed 20 meters.

14. Requirements for Parallel Bars: The exercises must consist of swinging, flight, holding moves, and strength. The swinging and flight moves should predominate. The exercises must contain at lest one part strength, a grip change (either above or below the bars), at least one hold movement, and there can be no more than three stops during the duration of the routine.

15. Requirements for Horizontal Bar: The exercises must consist exclusively of swinging movements without stops. Valuable variations of giant swings should predominate, and one vaulting movement over the bar is required. Direction changes, body shape alterations, and hand releases are considered important ingredients by the judging panel.

SAFETY CONSIDERATIONS

It is most important that the gymnastics enthusiast follow a few basic safety procedures when preparing to work out. Gymnastics is a potentially hazardous sport; yet when good judgment is used and reasonable precautions are taken there should be no reason for accidents to occur. Although not a safety guarantee, the following procedures are strongly recommended:

1. Never work out alone. Someone should always be available in the gym who is competent to spot, assist with the adjustment of the apparatus, and to provide general supervision.
2. Be sure to have mats both under and around the apparatus you are working on.
3. Always check the apparatus to see that it is properly secured, stable, and adjusted.

4. Don't attempt skills that you have not been instructed in, or that you suspect you may not be able to perform. Use caution in practicing new skills until you can perform them proficiently.
5. It is important that you warm up before attempting any skills. Gymnastics demands a good deal of strength and flexibility, and a warmup period of ten to twelve minutes that emphasizes moving through moderate ranges of motion is essential to avoid strain and possible injury.
6. Work on skills in progressive stages. Skipping developmental steps in gymnastics is "asking for trouble," so be sure you practice the lead-up skills and build gradually to a successful performance.

SUGGESTED LEARNING SEQUENCE

For every skill in gymnastics there are a variety of lead-ups and progressions that are designed to insure both the safety and success of the performer. The skills described in this chapter provide a basic introduction into selected performance experiences in gymnastics. The suggested sequence is outlined below and each of the competitive events is described in the next section, Skills and Techniques.

A. Introduction to Artistic Gymnastics—include history and development
B. Scoring in Gymnastics
C. Safety Considerations
D. **Men's Competitive Events**
  1. Floor Exercise
    a. The Handstand
    b. Handstand Forward Roll
    c. Back Extension to Handstand
    d. Front Handspring
  2. Pommel Horse
    a. Front Support Position
    b. Single Leg Cuts
    c. Full Leg Circles
    d. Front Scissors
  3. Still Rings
    a. Back Circle to Back Hang
    b. Muscle-Up
    c. Back Lever
    d. Back Uprise
  4. Long Horse Vaulting
    a. Straddle Vault
    b. Squat Vault
    c. Cartwheel Vault
  5. Parallel Bars
    a. Swing from Shoulders
    b. Shoulder Stand
    c. Front Uprise to Straddle Support
  6. Horizontal Bar
    a. Cast to a Swing
    b. Single Leg Uprise
    c. Fron Hip Circle
    d. Back Hip Circle

Women's Competitive Events
1. Side Horse Vaulting
    a. Squat Vault
    b. Straddle Vault
    c. Handspring Vault
2. Uneven Parallel Bars
    a. Beat Swing Straddle Mount
    b. Back Hip Pullover Mount
    c. Stride Circle Forward
    d. Straddle Underswing Dismount
3. Balance Beam
    a. Straddle Aerial Mount from the End
    b. Pirouette on One Foot
    c. Cartwheel with Quarter-Turn Dismount
4. Floor Exercise
    a. Tinsica
    b. Front Walkover
    c. Back Walkover
    d. Roundoff

SKILLS AND TECHNIQUES—MEN'S EVENTS

Men's competitive events comprise: floor exercise, pommel horse, rings, vaulting (long horse), parallel bars, and horizontal bar.

Floor Exercise

The men's floor exercise event requires that the routine be done within a specified time period of 50 to 70 seconds. The gymnast must cover the entire 40 × 40 foot area with a predominance of complex tumbling skills. These tumbling skills must be ac-companied by transitional movements including balance, flexibility, and strength elements that need to be executed with rhythm and harmony. There are no hard and fast requirements as to the type or sequence of movements that a gymnast must execute, but the entire routine must be aesthetically appealing. It is recommended that the gymnast build the entire routine in difficulty, and finish with a strong tumbling pass, leaving a positive impression at the conclusion.

The Handstand.   The handstand is the very symbol of the sport of gymnastics. It is used in some form in every event, and its successful accomplishment is of paramount importance to future successes that a gymnast might enjoy in the sport. A conceptual model for demonstrating the correct technique is presented in Figure 14-1A. Note that the entire body is tightly stretched—very long and very straight. A straight line should be able to be drawn through the body from hands to feet. The idea here is to align each of the body parts one on top of the other so that the performer's weight is positioned directly through the midline of the body and directly over the hands or base of support. Although this straight-line body position appears rather simple and straightforward to understand, success in the actual performance requires a great deal of practice, with particular attention given to the proper alignment of each body part.

The handstand is basically a balancing posture with the weight supported over the hands. It is essential that one first acquire the proper "body shape" which, although generally described as a straight line, is actually slightly curved. In order to

FIGURE 14-1.   (A) Handstand.   (B) Bar hang.   (C) Back-lying handstand.

A   B   C

perform consistently successful handstands, it is essential that the performer be physically able to assume a straight-line body position, to know what this position "feels" like, and to know how to arrive in this position in the most efficient manner.

Learning Cues—Handstand Progression

1. The performer should hang from a horizontal rail and practice assuming a one-segment body shape position (Figure 14-1B). Besides enabling you to concentrate on correct body shape, this bar hang technique requires the use of many of the very same muscles that are required in the execution of the handstand.
2. The performer assumes a back-lying position on the floor. Very slightly, raise the arms, keeping the head and shoulder girdle forward while at the same time lifting the legs from the floor. These body parts are thus elevated until the hollow in the low back area is flat on the floor. The resultant dynamically-curved, single-segment body position should be that of a "horizontal handstand" position (Figure 14-1C).

Note that in the bar hang and the horizontal handstand techniques, the abdominal and gluteal muscles are very tight, while the chest is both concave and somewhat rounded. The head is held neutral between the arms, and the elbows, knees, and toes are all extended.

To get into the balanced handstand position, you first assume the correct body position for a handstand while standing erect. From this position you stride forward with the non-kicking leg, flexing slightly at the knee, and with the kicking leg you thrust the body to the inverted position, supporting yourself over the hands. This skill should be performed with as much of a single-segment body shape as possible, therefore eliminating any unnecessary, compensatory body shape changes.

With the body in the inverted handstand position, the balance is maintained primarily with the wrists and secondarily with the shoulder girdle. A concerted effort should be made to maintain a straight arm-trunk, head-trunk, and hip-trunk angle, while keeping a fully elevated shoulder girdle.

The reason for devoting so much attention to the handstand position is that the controlled handstand is probably the single most important skill to master in the sport of gymnastics. Even the most proficient gymnasts in the world practice handstands daily in their training regimen.

Handstand Forward Roll. This skill is initiated from the standing handstand position above. From the erect standing posture the performer thrusts into the handstand position, momentarily supporting himself in the inverted handstand (Figure 14-2). The performer then allows the entire body unit to fall in a forward direction. As this occurs, the body undergoes a slightly altered position and assumes a some-

FIGURE 14-2. Handstand forward roll.

what concave shape. The elbows remained extended and locked while the chin is gradually brought toward the chest. The body is kept relatively straight (a slight dynamic curve), until the shoulder blades make contact with the floor, at which time the performer may either tuck the legs into the body, straddle the legs, or maintain straight legs while piking at the waist to assume the standing position from a variety of different body shapes.

Back Extension to Handstand. This skill should simulate a mirror image of the handstand forward roll just described. The object of this skill is to lift the body backward, with straight arms, into the handstand position. Since this requires considerable force, the body must pick up a lot of backward momentum as the body weight transfers to the buttocks. As the buttocks contact the floor, a forceful hip extension to the vertical starts the body rotating backward. As the performer rolls onto the upper back, the arms are extended overhead with the hands rotated inward, fingers pointing toward one another. The body maintains its relatively straight but concave shape, with the head tucked forward. The forceful extension of the hips is then abruptly stopped. This abrupt stopping action of the hip extension allows the momentum to be transferred to the total body for use in pressing against the floor with the arms and hands, bringing the body into vertical alignment (Figure 14-3).

A fully extended handstand position completes the skill, with no part of the body transcending the vertical during the course of the execution until all body parts line up with one another at the vertical position at the same time.

FIGURE 14-3. Back extension to handstand.

Front Handspring. This movement, which can be incorporated into a variety of front tumbling sequences, may be executed either from a stand, a skip step, or a run. As the performer steps out from the hurdle, the body is driven vigorously up and forward, through the handstand position. The angle of the total body at the moment when the hands make contact with the floor is at that point in which the straight line of the body transcends the 45-

degree angle from vertical. This "angle of input," which is referred to as "blocking" in gymnastics, is necessary to facilitate the transfer of horizontal momentum to vertical lift. Upon hand contact with the floor, the support leg forcefully extends at the knee joint, creating increased forward rotation of the entire body as the shoulder girdle dynamically extends to full elevation.

When the performer approaches the hand entry onto the floor, the center of gravity is kept comparatively low so that the dynamic extension of the shoulder girdle has a maximum effect on elevating the center of gravity (Figure 14-4A).

In preparing for the landing, the performer maintains complete body extension until just before making contact with the floor. The arms remain directly overhead and in line with the trunk, while the legs are reaching for the mat. Upon contact with the floor, the hips, knees, and ankle joints lightly flex to absorb the impact of the landing. The attainment of a fully extended standing position with the arms overhead represents the final objective in completing the skill.

Practice Suggestions—Handspring Progression

Two methods may be used in practicing this skill to ensure the safety of the performer:

1. Handspring Timer. A spotter should stand approximately two feet in front of the performer who is about to attempt a handspring. As the performer "blocks" with her hands for the repulsion phase of the handspring, the spotter catches her at the hips, taking the bulk of the performer's weight across his shoulders as the performer lifts

FIGURE 14-4. (A) Front handspring. (B) Handspring timer. (C) Handspring with towel.

A

B

C

from the floor (Figure 14-4B). This technique enables the performer to practice the takeoff for the handspring without having to worry about the rotation or the landing.

2. Handspring with Towel. For this method we use a towel that is split down the middle approximately twenty inches, or a towel sufficiently large so that the performer can step into it and bring it up around the waist. With the towel thus wrapped around the waist and two spotters—one on each side—holding an end of the towel, the performer may take any number of trials without fear of either over-rotating or under-rotating the handspring. The spotters simply run along beside the performer supporting her by means of the towel and assisting with any aspect of the skill that needs attention (Figure 14-4C).

FIGURE 14-6.   Single leg cuts.

to pommel horse. The gymnast should strive to attain the following characteristics (see Figure 14-5):

1. The body is stretched and leaning slightly forward so that your center of gravity traverses the middle of the horse.
2. The hands are gripped slightly forward of center on the pommels.
3. The shoulders are firmly depressed and the elbows remain straight.

Single Leg Cuts.   Typically, a performer mounts the horse thereby initiating motion for swing immediately. Therefore, even the beginner should jump into the front support position from slightly off to the side so that motion is created. The performer then lifts the right leg up to the right side in a pendulum manner, bringing the leg over the right outer zone of the horse, and swinging it down in front of the horse. As the leg approaches the right hand, the right hand grip on the pommel is released, and immediately replaced again after the right leg has crossed over the pommel (Figure 14-6). The performer is now in a stride support position on the horse with the right leg forward and the left leg behind, in the original starting position. The right leg is then returned to the original front support position in the exact opposite manner that it was brought forward.

Once the technique is secure, variations of leg cuts may be attempted. These serve to introduce the performer to the intricacies of pommel horse work and to instill an appreciation for the difficulty involved.

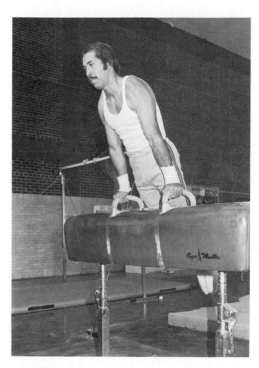

FIGURE 14-5.   Front support on pommel horse.

Pommel Horse

This event, although not the most spectacular nor the most daring, is generally considered to be the most difficult event to master in men's gymnastics. The gymnast must maintain constant swinging movements, in the circular dimension with the legs together, and in the pendulum fashion with the legs apart. Furthermore during the course of his routine the gymnast is required to perform on all three parts of the horse—the neck, the saddle, and the croup—as well as on both sides, thereby necessitating the inclusion of travels, hops, and turns during the performance.

Front Support Position.   This position is basic

Variations of Leg Cuts, From Front or Rear Support:

1. Right leg cut in to the right—return (as described in the text).
2. Left leg cut in to the left—return.
3. Right leg cut in to the right—left leg cut in to the left—right leg cut back out to the right—left leg cut back out to the left.

Full Leg Circles. The full leg circle is similar to the leg cut in the initial stages, but instead of stopping the leg when it is swung to the front of the horse, the leg continues to move around the opposition side of the horse before returning to the starting position (Figure 14-7). The following example will describe a full leg circle right. The right leg swings to the right, crossing over the right outer zone of the horse, coming down in front of the horse. The right hand is released, and then regrasps the pommel as the leg crosses over the pommel. Then the right leg continues toward the left, swinging up and over the left outer zone of the horse, as the left hand releases and then regrasps the left pommel as the right leg returns to the starting, front support position. Thus, the right leg completes a full circle over the horse, moving from the right to the left, over and around the horse.

Variations of Full Leg Circles:

1. Right leg full circle right (as described in the example).
2. Left leg full circle left.
3. Right leg full circle left.
4. Left leg full circle right.
5. Each of these circles may be repeated from the rear support position.

FIGURE 14-7. Full leg circle.

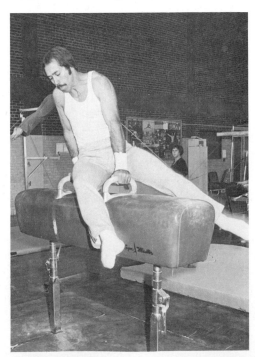

FIGURE 14-8. Front scissors.

Front Scissors. From the stride support position with the right leg forward, the front scissors is merely a question of swinging both legs to the left and higher than the level of the horse. Bring the right (front leg) rearward over the left outer zone while at the same time cutting the left leg forward over the left outer zone (Figure 14-8). The left hand releases its grasp on the pommel during this "scissoring" action and regrasps the pommel after the legs have crossed over it. At the completion the performer should be in a new stride support position, but with the legs on opposite sides of the horse rather than as when the move started.

Still Rings

The ring event requires the greatest amount of strength of any of the six events. The gymnast must perform two different types of handstands: one must be characterized by dynamic swing into the handstand position, the other by slow, controlled, pressing movement that reflects strength. Additionally, the gymnast must show a static strength movement, frequently typified by the "iron cross," which must be held for a total of two seconds at least. Ideally, the routine is composed of 60 percent swinging movements, and 40 percent strength movements.

Back Circle to Back Hang. From the hanging position, the performer tucks the knees into the chest as the arms are pulling the performer upward. As the knees approach the chest, the performer circles backward, slowly extending himself to a fully stretched hang backwards. Although not a competitive movement, this skill is a good introductory one, and it provides the performer with a means of developing excellent range of motion through the shoulder girdle.

Muscle-Up. There are a few easy ways to arrive in an upper support position on the rings. One means is to do a "muscle-up." This move requires getting a "false grip" on the rings; that is, to grasp the ring so that the ring itself is held not only in the palm of the hand but also across the wrist. This will permit the performer to move from a hang position to an upper support position, whereas it is extremely difficult to get above the wrist angle if the ring is held in a straight hang position. The muscle-up is performed by doing a pull-up as high as one can go, then leaning forward and doing a push-up. Done in one motion, and with a bit of momentum, this skill is very easy to master.

Back Lever. Another easily performed strength movement on rings is the back lever. The performer will generally begin this movement from an inverted hang position, lowering himself down backward with stretched body to the horizontal plane, parallel to the floor. As the body nears the horizontal position it becomes increasingly difficult to control, so the performer must strain to maintain the proper position.

Back Uprise. The back uprise is common to the rings, parallel bars, and horizontal bar. During the initial phases of learning, the performer may execute the move from a hang-swinging position. After a bit of momentum has been built up with three or four swings, the legs are driven rearward and upward as vigorously as possible. Once this movement has been initiated, the performer attempts to stop the vigorous leg swing, permitting the momentum to transfer to the total body, while the arms are pulling forward and downward. Through the combination of leg lift, momentum transfer, and arm pull, the body should rise up into the straight-arm-support position on top of the rings. Timing accuracy plays an important part in the success of this skill; therefore trial followed by analysis will permit the performer to recognize where he may be in error if there are repeated failures in execution of this skill.

Long Horse Vaulting

This is the most unusual event in gymnastics competition. In vaulting, the gymnast runs to the horse and vaults over it, using a variety of body positions to do so. The difficulty of the vault is determined by the complexity of the vault during the flight phases, i.e., from the board to the horse, and from the horse to the landing. The vault is judged in terms of height, distance, and execution, as well as the control demonstrated in the landing.

Straddle Vault. The performer approaches the vaulting board with near maximum speed, very

quickly forces the feet forward to the crown of the board, and then repulses as quickly as possible. The hurdle from the floor to the crown of the board should be relatively short, low, and flat, with a vigorous thrust of the legs just prior to contact on the board. As the performer leaves the board, he stretches his body toward the far end (neck) of the horse, preparing to repulse from the horse with his hands immediately on contact (Figure 14-10). As this thrusting action takes place the performer seeks additional height through the oblique upward dimension; the legs are then straddled, and the performer clears the end of the horse, coming to a controlled landing.

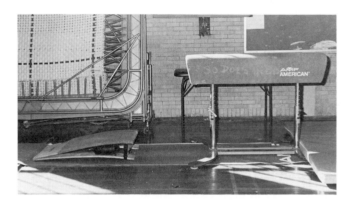

FIGURE 14-9. Long horse vaulting equipment.

FIGURE 14-10. Straddle vault.

Squat Vault. The performance requirements are the same for the squat vault as for the straddle vault, except that in the arm repulsion phase the performer tucks up the legs instead of straddling them (Figure 14-11).

Cartwheel Vault. Again, the approach, hurdle,

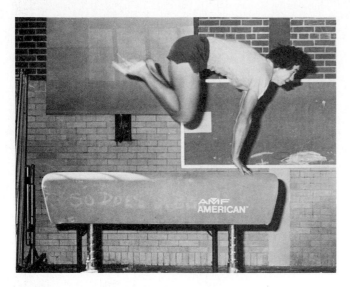

FIGURE 14-11.   Squat vault.

FIGURE 14-12.   Cartwheel vault.

and takeoff are the same as previously described. As the performer leaves the board he attempts to turn the body a quarter turn and then cartwheels across the top of the horse (Figure 14-12). The landing is a sideward body position, so the performer needs to ascertain that he is competent in controlling the entry onto the mat so that there is no great adverse strain at the knee joint in absorbing the impact of the landing.

Parallel Bars

The parallel bar routine must be executed predominately with swinging type movements. The

gymnast must swing through the handstand position with turns and releases of the hands, and also somersault-type moves both above and below the bars. These swinging movements must be done with many changes of level, direction, and (preferably) body shape.

Swing from the Shoulders.   From a straight-arm-support position, the performer initiates swing by extending the feet forward, stretching the body, and pivoting from the shoulder girdle area. The body swings freely forward and backward using the shoulder joint as its axis of rotation. The performer seeks to get as much extension as possible on both ends of the swing, and gradually builds the height of

FIGURE 14-13.   Swing from the shoulders.

FIGURE 14-14.   Shoulder stand.

the movement so that it transcends the horizontal plane at either end of the swing continuum (Figure 14-13).

Shoulder Stand. This skill may be arrived at either by the utilization of strength—pressing into the position—or by swing. The performer inverts the body, making certain to keep the center of gravity as high above the point of support as possible, then lowers himself onto his shoulders on the parallel bars. The elbows are spread as wide as possible, with the hands a comfortable distance behind the shoulders to provide a stable base of support (Figure 14-14).

Front Uprise to Straddle Support. From a short two or three step approach, the performer dives between the bars, placing his arms above and outside of the rails, and grasps the rails with his hands forward of the armpits. As the body swings forward from this extended dive position, the feet thrust to a 45-degree angle, followed immediately and simultaneously by a hip thrust and arm pulling action (Figure 14-15). This procedure brings the hips (cen-

FIGURE 14-15. Front uprise to straddle support.

ter of gravity) toward the hands (base of support), providing stability and control of the movement. As the legs approach the horizontal position they are separated and straddled over the rails, bringing the performer to a straddle sitting position on top of the bars.

Horizontal Bar

This is decidedly the most spectacular, daring, and venturous event in men's gymnastics. The gym-

nast must remain in constant motion as he transcends from one variety of giant swing to another by means of turns, hops, and circles around the bar in a variety of body positions. The routine requires simultaneous hand changes and releases while the body twists, somersaults, and vaults over the bar. Finally, the dismount must be high, with twisting and somersaulting of a multiple nature being performed prior to landing. The horizontal bar event combines the thrill and excitement of the circus performer with the style, grace, élan, and charisma of the competitive gymnast.

Cast to a Swing. Because swing is the prime requisite for work on the horizontal bar, it is advantageous to begin our exercises with an elementary swing type movement. The cast is essentially a pull-up movement with the arms, followed by a piking action at the hips, and then a total extension of the body at an angle somewhat higher than horizontal (Figure 14-16). This motion will produce a rather large amount of swing form which the performer may execute any number of sequential moves. As the performer swings in the "long hang" position following the cast, he should feel exhilarated by a sense of freedom and flight. Characteristic of this flight phase are the sensations of speed, power, and motion. To become a true gymnast the performer must relate to these sensations—to appreciate their vast potential and learn how to control them and be able to create exciting experiences from them.

FIGURE 14-16. Cast to a swing.

Single Leg Uprise. Upon reaching the point of maximum forward swing, the performer flexes one leg at the hip, compresses it to the body, rides the motion to the end of the back swing, and then vigorously thrusts the leg forward and down (Figure 14-17). This action forces the hamstrings (tendons at back of the thigh) against the bar, and brings the upper body to a stride support position on top of the bar. Significant points to keep in mind: (a) maintain straight arms throughout the move; (b) keep as tight

FIGURE 14-17. Single leg uprise.

FIGURE 14-18. Front hip circle.

a compression of the leg to the chest as possible at the point of flexion at the hip joint; and (c) ride the movement all the way to the end of the back swing before attempting to come to a stride support position on top of the bar.

Front Hip Circle. From the straight-arm-support position on the horizontal bar, the performer pushes down on the bar, elevating the center of gravity slightly above the level of the bar, yet maintaining a comparatively straight body (Figure 14-18). From this extended and elevated position, the performer leans out in front of the bar, falling with as straight and extended a body as possible. After the stretched body has transcended the horizontal plane, the performer pikes at the waist, bringing the upper body into as tight a compressed shape as possible. The object is to circle around the bar forward, returning to the starting position as quickly as can be managed. The important learning points are: (a) lift the body at the initial phase to overbalance the center of gravity; (b) lean out as far as possible in order to acquire as much angular momentum as you can; and (c) then dynamically close the body after transcending the horizontal plane so as to shorten the radius and thereby increase the rotatory force around the bar.

Back Hip Circle. From straight-arm-support position on the bar, the performer brings the legs slightly forward under the bar. From this position of slight closure, sufficient force is acquired to cast off the bar backward, taking the gymnast up and backward to a free support on the bar (Figure 14-19). As the legs come back into the bar, the hips are com-

FIGURE 14-19. Back hip circle.

pressed, and the head is thrown backward. The shortened radius of the body causes the performer to circle backward around the bar rather rapidly. As the performer begins to complete the circling action, the body is again extended, lengthening the radius and slowing down the rotation. The objective is to complete the backward circling action of the body, returning to the starting position.

SKILLS AND TECHNIQUES—WOMEN'S EVENTS

Women's competitive events are: vaulting (side-horse), uneven parallel bars, balance beam, and floor exercise.

Side Horse Vaulting

The female gymnast performs two vaults—either the same vault twice or two different vaults—and the best score of the two is the performer's score for that event. The gymnast must possess speed, power, agility, and total body awareness, for in a few seconds she must fly through the air, repulse off of the horse, perform a complicated controlled skill in the post-flight phase, and then land with maximum control.

In general, a very fast, accelerating but controlled approach is of critical importance to maximizing the execution of all vaulting skills. The performer should run upright, but with a slight, total body lean forward. As the performer moves into the hurtle, the arms begin to lift forward and upward, the feet are brought quickly to the crown of the board, and in front of the center of gravity. The hurtle should be comparatively short, very flat (low), and extremely quick.

Squat Vault. Following the approach and hurtle phase, the performer drives off the board with an instantaneous and forceful extension of the legs. She immediately assumes a hollowed body shape and gets to the horse as fast as possible. Upon contacting the horse, the hands push vigorously downward, and at the same instant, the gymnast moves into the "squat" position, or fully tucked body shape (Figure 14-21). In the post-flight phase, the performer attempts to elongate the body again after clearing the horse, flexing lightly at the ankles, knees, and hips upon landing to absorb the force of the entry into the floor. The arms remain over the head and in line with the trunk until the performer has acquired control of the landing.

The gymnast should conceive of vaulting as a stepwise approach that is constantly moving upward: from the floor to the board, up again to the horse, then up a third time for the post-flight phase. It is important to emphasize this upward motion in all types of vaults, for frequently we see gymnasts come in too high on their pre-flight to the horse, hence coming *down* for their entry onto the horse. This of course negates any capability to acquire power for the post-flight phase of the vault.

Straddle Vault. The movements for the straddle vault are the same as those described for the

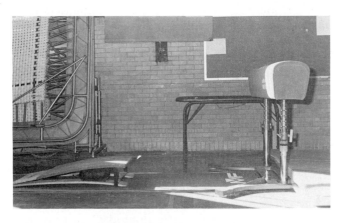

FIGURE 14-20. Side horse vaulting.

FIGURE 14-21. Squat vault.

FIGURE 14-22. Straddle vault.

squat vault until hand contact is made with the horse. At this point, the legs are forcefully extended to the sides until they clear the horse (Figure 14-22), at which time they are brought together again in preparation for the landing.

Handspring Vault. Handspring vaults require a more extended body shape during the pre-flight phase and a greater body angle upon hand contact with the horse (Figure 14-23). For these reasons greater amounts of lift and forward rotation must be generated at takeoff. To meet these requirements, the gymnast needs to: (a) maximize the forward horizontal speed of the run and hurdle phases; (b) stand upright during impact rather than leaning backward; and (c) minimize the amount of time on the board by instantly and forcefully extending the total body unit upon actual contact with the board. A comparatively flatter pre-flight shape is required so that maximum amplitude can be realized. Again, actual hand contact with the horse should be made as the performer is still moving upward. The shoulder girdle is lightly flexed during the pre-flight phase, and then vigorously extended at or just prior to contact. The body undergoes slight modifications in that it assumes a very slight overextension during the post-flight phase, and continues in this manner into the landing.

Uneven Parallel Bars

Moving swiftly and powerfully, using a predominance of swinging moves from the hands, the gymnast demonstrates strength and a tremendous sense of timing and awareness when working the uneven bars. As the gymnast moves around, between, under, and over the bars, going from one bar to the other in a virtuoso display of circles, twists, and somersaults, she gives a performance worthy of Wonder Woman. This dynamic and exciting event is culminated with difficult dismounts of multiple twisting or rotating movements around one or more axes of the body.

Beat Swing Straddle Mount. The performer stands behind the high bar and, following a short run, hurtle, and jump to the high bar, the body is stretched somewhat backward, swinging into the low bar. Emphasis should be placed on the fully elevated shoulder girdle and relatively strong swing into the low bar. As the hips contact the low bar, the legs swing forward and upward, wrapping tightly around the low bar. From the tightly closed position, the legs are then swung down and back, immediately followed by a vigorous stopping of this action as the arms begin a "pull-up" movement on the high bar (Figure 14-24). The legs then straddle as the hips are tightly flexed, causing the body to swing forward over the low bar. The legs are then extended forward and down, coming to a back-hang-support position over the low bar.

Back Hip Pullover Mount. The performer stands close to the low bar, either in front or behind it. The feet are placed directly underneath the low bar, and the hands are placed in an overgrip position on top of the bar. The performer takes a short step forward with one leg and as this leg first flexes and then dynamically extends, the other leg kicks vigorously up and backward over the bar (Figure 14-25). The elbows remain flexed so that the center of gravity can be brought quickly to the bar. The legs are joined as they drop backward over the bar, and at this point the head and shoulder girdle lift up and forward, bringing the body to a straight-arm-support position on top of the bar.

FIGURE 14-23. Handspring vault.

FIGURE 14-24. Beat swing straddle mount.

FIGURE 14-25. Back hip pullover.

FIGURE 14-26. Stride circle forward.

Stride Circle Forward. This skill may be performed on both bars and in both directions, but our example will be done on the low bar, facing outward. The performer has one leg forward over the bar, and the other stretched backward behind the bar (Figure 14-26). The hands are in a reverse grip, palms facing forward (this grip is used for all forward moving skills with the exception of the front hip circle). The gymnast next lifts the body off of the bar by depressing the shoulders and keeping the arms stretched and locked. She then leans forward, placing the bar well down on the front of the thigh of the back leg. The center of gravity is thus overbalanced and the performer continues to lean well forward as the descent phase of the move begins. Due to the extended body and forward lean, the performer circles very swiftly around the bar with her hands being the primary support point during the circling action. As she nears the three-quarter mark of the circle, the front leg is pressed against the bar, further propelling her up and forward, causing the circling action of the body to be completed, and the performer finishes the move in just the same position as she started.

Straddle Underswing Dismount. This skill is initiated from a straight-arm-support position on the low bar, facing outward. The performer casts with as much amplitude as possible, piking at the hips as the apex of the cast is realized, and bringing the feet onto the low bar just barely outside of the hands (Figure 14-27). The tightly compressed body shape is very important at this point so that the gymnast is able to achieve maximum angular momentum. The gymnast begins her downward swing with the head

FIGURE 14-27. Straddle underswing dismount.

in tight between the arms and the legs, consciously exerting a continual compressing action so that the flexion at the hip is maintained. Keeping this position throughout the descent phase, the swing through the bottom, and the ascent phase, the performer "rides" this position until reaching the horizontal position (back parallel to the floor), on the ascent phase. At this point the legs are thrust vigorously forward and upward (at approximately a 45-degree angle). Attention is first given to the extension of the feet, followed by an extension of the hips, and then a final extension of the arms, as the body assumes a slight overextension (as if the back were extending up and over an imaginery rope stretched across and at right angles to the body). As the gymnast releases the bar, the body is extended, the arms are overhead, and she prepares for the absorption of the landing.

Balance Beam

The balance beam is often referred to as the "side horse" of women's gymnastics. The event has earned this dubious distinction as a result of the difficulty in mastering the wide assortment of moves that are executed on the beam, including dance combinations involving leaping, turning, jumping; acrobatic skills such as walkovers, aerials, flexibilities; and tumbling skills. The working surface of the beam is only 3⅞ inches wide and 16 feet 4 inches long, and the beam is positioned approximately 4 feet off the floor. Considering these dimensions, it can be readily understood that the margin for error is quite small. Great concentration and control are demanded during the 70 to 90 seconds that the performer is executing her routine.

Straddle Aerial Mount from the End.   The gymnast faces the end of the beam with the hands placed on top of the beam. From this position she jumps to a support on the hands while lifting the legs forward and upward in a straddled position until the legs are parallel with the top of the beam (Figure 14-28). Keeping the legs high, the gymnast makes a full 180-degree turn while in the straddled position, before lowering the body down to the beam. The mount is completed with the legs still held up in the straddle position and the gymnast facing directly opposite from the direction in which the mount was initiated.

FIGURE 14-28.   Straddle aerial mount.

Pirouette on One Foot.   The term "pirouette" commonly refers to a turn about the longitudinal axis of the body. A pirouette can be done on the hands, the feet, and even on other body parts such as the seat. Typically, the move is done from a standing position on one foot (Figure 14-29). The amount of the pirouette, as well as the variety of body shapes can be altered to conform to the needs of the gymnast and the aesthetic appeal that is desired. The performer pushes off of the ball of the foot on the trail leg, while simultaneously extending the hip, knee, and ankle joints of the front leg. The trunk should be held erect and the center of gravity of the body should bisect the foot of the turning leg. The arms provide added impetus to the turn by swinging through a relatively wide arc initially, then closing to the mid-line of the body. Only the ball of the support foot is in contact with the beam's surface, and the ankle should remain tightly extended throughout the entire movement. The performer should attempt to stop the turning action before arriving in the intended position so that an over-rotation does not occur.

The movement should culminate in an erect standing posture, with one leg placed on the beam behind the other. The abdominal muscles should be tightly contracted and the gluteus muscles squeezed so that the hip joint is more easily controlled. The shoulder girdle as well as the hip girdle should finish at right angles to the beam, with a slight plié movement finishing the final aspect of the pirouette.

Cartwheel with Quarter-Turn Dismount.   The performer must determine the amount of room she

FIGURE 14-29.   Pirouette on one foot.

will need to perform the cartwheel, making sure to allow for a relatively evenly spaced foot, hand, hand placement rather than bringing both of the hand placements too close together—a customary error in this move. As the performer's hands contact the beam in a one-two sequence, the slightly flexed front leg pushes vigorously, taking the performer into the quarter turn as well as into the vertical position. The legs are together at the top of the turn and the previously depressed shoulder girdle returns to a dynamically elevated position just before the body reaches the vertical plane. The strong thrust of the legs combined with the elevation of the shoulders provides the impetus to repulse from the beam. By pushing fore-downward with the front hand, and back-downward with the rear hand, the performer initiates a quarter twist about the longitudinal axis of the body. Once airborne, the performer's body continues to rotate forward while also rotating about its long axis. In order to prevent overrotation, the arms are held relatively wide on the dismount, thereby increasing the radius of rotation, hence slowing down the amount of rotatory force that has been generated (Figure 14-30). The performer should try to land in a rear standing position, with the arms directly over the head, and in line with the trunk.

FIGURE 14-30. Cartwheel with quarter-turn dismount.

Floor Exercise

In 70 to 90 seconds the gymnast must perform a routine covering a 40 × 40 foot area, demonstrating the grace and beauty of a ballet dancer as well as the power and precision of the circus tumbler. At the same time, the gymnast has to reflect her own inimitable personality, projecting a style, flair, and élan that are indigenous to the theatre performer. Music is of prime importance, and must be selected so that it is a cohesive part of the total routine.

Tinsica. The Tinsica is often described as a cartwheel done straight forward (Figure 14-31). Actually, there are a number of variations of the Tinsica, all of them being accepted as legitimate forms of the move. The performer steps forward on the takeoff leg from either a standing or hurtling position, depending upon the amount of flight that she wants to project. The hands are then placed on or close to a line which lies at right angles to the body, in an alternate hand–hand fashion. The first leg over, i.e., the landing leg, is on the same side of the body as the second hand that contacts the floor in the alternate hand placement movement. The body is rotated obliquely as the performer moves through the inverted position, then returns to the straight ahead position on the landing. The move-

FIGURE 14-31. Tinsica

ment is illusory in nature, for it appears that more things are happening than actually are. The movement may be executed as a spring type move, like a handspring, or it may be executed without flight, like a front walkover. The important points to keep in mind are that the hands land in an alternate fashion, spaced well apart, and the first leg down is on the same side of the body as the second hand that touches down.

Front Walkover. The initial movement for the front walkover is identical in nature to the step-up to handstand. As the lead leg continues to move up and forward, rotating around the hip joint axis, the weight of the body shifts onto the hands entirely. The legs are held in a wide splits position following the initial kick to handstand (Figure 14-32) and they remain that way until the performer lands the lead leg for the standing portion of the move. As the center of gravity transcends the vertical, the shoulders maximally extend, drawing as much arch through the upper back as possible and thereby allowing the foot to come closer to the hands on the landing. The head is held neutral between the arms throughout the move, the performer watching her hands at all times until she assumes the erect standing position.

FIGURE 14-33. Back walkover.

FIGURE 14-32. Front walkover.

Back Walkover. The performer begins this movement from a standing position, arms overhead, one leg elevated fore-upward. The gymnast leans the entire straight body backward with no apparent arching or bending whatsoever. After the hips have moved behind the support leg the gymnast then arches backward, keeping the head and arms in as nearly a straight-line relationship as possible, and maintaining a totally elevated support leg. The weight transfers to the hands just as they make contact with the floor, and the support leg is thrust to the vertical, or handstand position. The lead leg continues to precede the movement, so that the body is in an inverted splits position immediately following the supporting leg's departure from the floor (Figure 14-33). By the time the support leg arrives in vertical, the lead leg is just about to touch down on the floor. The gymnast then extends off of

the floor with a strong elevation through the shoulders, keeping the body hollowed all the way to the erect standing position.

Roundoff. Mastery of the roundoff is essential because it is crucial to the development of backward tumbling sequences and is one of the most commonly executed movements in floor exercise and tumbling work. There are a variety of ways used in initiating the hurdling techniqe. We recommend an approach similar to that used for a cartwheel in terms of hand placement, but less separation between the hands (Figure 14-34).

The gymnast steps out with the lead leg, leaning forward at the hip joint and preparing to place the lead hand on the floor. As this hand touches down, the lead leg is thrust straight upward to the vertical position. The body begins to turn toward the side handstand position, arriving there at the same time as the second hand touches down. The body continues its turn through the longitudinal axis another quarter turn as the hands and arms push vigorously off of the mat. The body is dynamically hollowed, head held neutral between the arms, and the hip girdle rounding into the landing. It is wise for the gymnast to practice this movement over and over until she is completely successful in completing the turning movement through the vertical, getting maximum extension from the hands and arms in the repulsion phase, and maintaining a completely hollowed body on the descent phase. The gymnast should then combine this movement with a little "punch jump" on the landing. This will assist her in acquiring the speed and proper body position to follow up the roundoff with any additional backward tumbling movements.

A   B

FIGURE 14-34. Roundoff: (A) start,   (B) inverted position.

SELECTED REFERENCES

BOWERS, CAROLYN et al. *Judging and Coaching Women's Gymnastics.* Palo Alto, Calif.: National Press, 1972.

COOPER, PHYLLIS. *Feminine Gymnastics,* 2nd ed. Minneapolis, Minn.: Burgess Publishing Company, 1973.

GEORGE, GERALD. *The Magic of Gymnastics.* Santa Monica, Calif.: Sundby Publications, 1970.

GEORGE, GERALD. *The Biomechanics of Women's Gymnastics.* Englewood Cliffs, N.J.: Prentice-Hall, 1980.

NORTHRIP, JOHN W. et al. *Biomechanical Analysis of Sport.* Dubuque, Iowa: Wm. C. Brown Co., 1974.

SZYPULA, GEORGE. *Tumbling and Balancing for All,* 2nd ed. Dubuque, Iowa: Wm. C. Brown Co., 1968.

Additional Sources

Sundby Sports, Inc., 410 Broadway, Santa Monica, Calif. 90401. *International Gymnast Magazine.*

National Collegiate Athletic Association, Nall Avenue at 63rd Street, Shawnee Mission, Kansas 66222.

United States Gymnastics Federation, P.O. Box 7686, Fort Worth, Texas 76111.

HANDBALL AND RACQUETBALL

THIS CHAPTER WILL ENABLE YOU TO:

♦ Select equipment necessary to play handball and racquetball.
♦ identify and put into practice the rules governing handball and racquetball.
♦ Identify and develop the basic skills, namely the forehand stroke, the backhand stroke, the serve, and the back wall shot.
♦ Employ the basic strategy necessary to play the game.
♦ Identify and put into practice the safety considerations necessary for a successful game of handball or racquetball.

NATURE AND PURPOSE

Handball and racquetball are related competitive sports in which the hand (or a racquet) is used to serve and return the ball. In their principal variations these games can be played by two opponents (as a singles game), by three opponents (as a cut-throat game), or by two opposing pairs of players (as a doubles game). In this chapter, whatever is said about handball also applies to racquetball, unless otherwise stated.

Although the game can be played on one or three walls, the four-wall enclosed court provides perhaps the greatest challenge to skill and the most competition. The four-wall game is discussed primarily here, but most of its related description is meaningful to the other variations of the game.

The game is won by the first side scoring 21 points. A match is won by the first side winning two games. The third game, or tie-breaker, is usually played to only 11 points. There is no tie score nor requirement to win by two points, as in some games.

A player may use either the right or left hand for hitting the ball (or holding the racquet), but only one hand at a time may be used to play the ball, and the ball must be struck only once in each instance.

PLAYING AREA AND EQUIPMENT

Court. The standard four-wall handball court is 40 feet long × 20 feet wide × 20 feet high (Figure 15-1). An outdoor single-wall court is 34 feet long × 20 feet wide × 16 feet high (Figure 15-2). The four-wall court is divided into a front court and a back court or equal dimensions by a line called the *short line,* running parallel to the front wall. Five feet in front of the short line is another parallel line called the *service line.* Eighteen inches from and parallel

with each side wall a line is drawn to form a box, termed the *service box,* where the partner of the server, in doubles, must stand while the ball is being served.

Ball. The handball is made of black rubber, has a diameter of $1\frac{7}{8}$ inches and weighs 2.3 ounces. In racquetball a seamless rubber ball is used that is $2\frac{1}{4}$ inches in diameter and weighs approximately 1.4 ounces. If one-wall handball is to be played in a physical education class, it would be advisable to use the racquetball ball.

Gloves. The rules of handball require that gloves be worn. This is not only for protection but to keep perspiration off the ball as much as possible. In racquetball, gloves are not required by the rules; however, many players prefer to wear them for a better grip and reduced slippage due to perspiration.

Racquet. The racquetball racquet will have a maximum head length of 11 inches and a width of 9 inches. The handle may not exceed 7 inches in length. The racquet frame may be made of any material, with popular types made of aluminum, steel, or fiberglass. The strings of the racquet must be gut, monofilament, or nylon. The price of racquets ranges from $10 to $100. For physical education classes a less expensive solution is to use wooden paddle racquets that cost much less.

Goggles. Racquetball players are encouraged to wear eye protection of some type. Special racquetball goggles are available in various price ranges and styles.

BASIC RULES

A strong point in favor of handball is the simplicity of the rules governing the game. Any person can become familiar with the basic rules in one or two class sessions. In 1958 the Amateur Athletic Union, the U.S. Handball Association, and the YMCA agreed upon a unified set of handball rules that would be applicable throughout the country, and in 1959 these rules were adopted by the Jewish Welfare Board. A summary of the latest rules is given below.

The Game

In the act of serving, the server drops the ball on the floor (between the short and service lines) and on the first rebound the ball is struck in such a manner that it will first hit the front wall and on the rebound land upon the floor back of the short line, either before or after striking one of the side walls. After the ball is legally served, one of the players of the receiving team returns the ball by striking it either on the fly or on the first bounce so that it will strike the front wall before striking the floor either directly or after having struck one or both of the side walls, back wall, ceiling, or any combination of these surfaces. The receiving side then returns the ball to the front wall, and play continues until one side is unable to return the ball legally, which will then constitute either a point or a handout.

Playing Regulations

The choice for the right to serve shall be decided by the toss of a coin, and the player or side winning the toss starts the first and third games. The server may stand any place in the service zone. When the server or serving side loses the service, he or they shall become the receiver and the receiver the server; they alternate in this fashion in all subsequent services of the game. The serve must be made within the service area; stepping on the line, but not beyond, is permitted. In serving, the ball must be bounced on the floor and struck on its first rebound from the floor. If the server attempts to hit the ball on this rebound, and fails, he is out. The server may not bounce the ball more than three times in the service zone in making a service. Violation of this rule retires the server. A server shall not serve until his opponent has had a fair opportunity to get placed. The server's partner, in doubles, must stand within the service box with his back to the side wall, both feet on the floor, until the ball passes the short line on its return from the front wall.

If a player's partner is hit by a served fly ball while standing in the service box, it counts as a "dead ball" without penalty, but does not eliminate

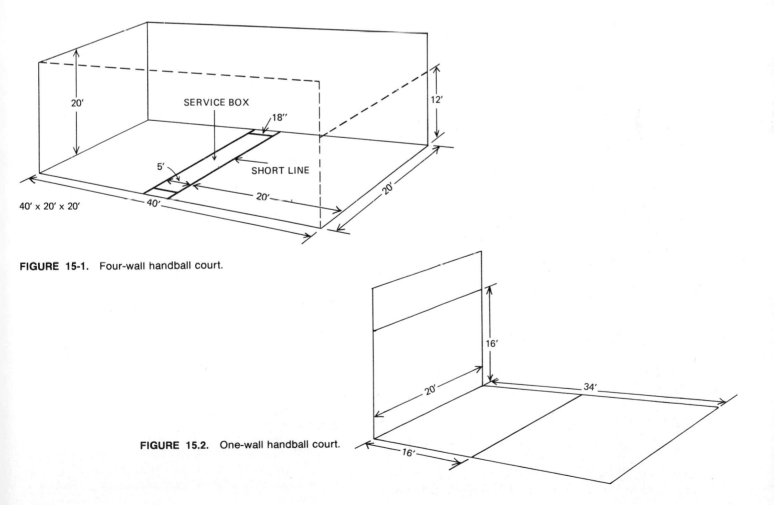

FIGURE 15-1.   Four-wall handball court.

FIGURE 15.2.   One-wall handball court.

any short or long fault preceding this service. If he is hit by a served ball on the bounce, it is a short ball. If the served ball should pass behind the partner and strike the floor back of the short line, it is a dead ball.

In doubles the side starting each game is allowed one handout only. After that both partners are permitted to serve. Players in doubles must follow the same order of service throughout the game. It is not necessary for players to alternate serves to their opponents.

If a ball is swung at and missed, it may be played again, providing it is hit before bouncing twice on the floor. If a player swings at and completely misses the ball and if in his, or his partner's attempt to again play the ball there is an unintentional interference by an opponent, it shall be a hinder. If the completely missed ball should on the fly or first bounce strike an opponent, it is a penalty against the opponent—a point, or handout, as the case may be.

Receiving Service

The receiver or receivers must stand at least five feet back of the short line while the ball is being served. The receiver may play the ball on the first bounce or volley it, provided he does not cross the short line. The receiver may not play an illegally served ball.

Illegal Service

Any two of the following serves in succession retires the server:

1. When the served ball hits the front wall and fails to strike the floor back of the short line on the fly.
2. When a served ball hits the front wall and two side walls before striking the floor.
3. When a served ball hits the front wall, side wall, and back wall before striking the floor.
4. When a served ball hits the front wall, then the ceiling or back wall before striking the floor.
5. When the server steps beyond the short line or service line in the act of serving.
6. Failure of the server to properly return a ball in play.
7. A served ball hitting the ceiling, floor, or side walls before striking a front wall.
8. A served ball which hits the front and side wall, or front wall and floor, or front wall and ceiling at the same time (crotch ball).

SUGGESTED LEARNING SEQUENCE

A. Introduction
   1. Origin and development
   2. Equipment
   3. Safety

B. Rules and Procedures of Play
   1. Playing area
   2. Scoring
   3. Serving
   4. Hinders
C. Skills and Techniques
   1. Forehand shot (sidearm stroke)
   2. Overhead stroke
   3. Back Wall shot
   4. Backhand shot (Racquetball)
   5. Service
      a. Forehand serve   c. Lob serve
      b. Drive serve   d. Z serve
   6. Kill shot
D. Playing Strategy

SKILLS AND TECHNIQUES

Forehand or Sidearm Stroke

The forehand stroke is the primary offensive stroke in handball and its mastery is essential in order for you to achieve a winning game. The most efficient stroke occurs at knee height and is similar to the motion of bending over to skip a flat stone across a body of water or throw a sidearm pitch in baseball (Figure 15-3).

Learning Cues

1. Position your body as if you were a baseball batter, facing the side wall.
2. Raise the striking hand to the height of your ear in a "cocked" position (Figure 15-4).
3. As the ball is struck, step forward with the front foot (shifting weight form back to front foot).
4. Simultaneously with the step, drop your striking shoulder, rotate your body to enable your forearm and hand to move forward in a plane parallel to the floor (Figure 15-5).
5. Contact the ball at the vertical center of your body.
6. The wrist moves past the elbow in a snapping motion.
7. Ball is struck by the hand at the base of the fingers.
8. Follow through ahead of the front knee.

Practice Suggestions

1. Stand facing the side wall in a ready position. Bounce the ball in front of you easily, striking the ball as it rebounds at about knee level. Start a series of practice shots near the short line, then move back 5 feet and hit a series, then back 5 feet more, and so on.
2. Stand facing the side wall (five feet away) in a ready position. Toss the ball easily against the side wall so that the ball will rebound up from the floor into a striking position for a forehand shot.

FIGURE 15-3. Forehand or sidearm stroke.

FIGURE 15-4. "Cocked" position.

FIGURE 15-5. Contact position.

Overhead Stroke

The overhead is the stroke that is used to strike the ball at eye level or higher, and is very similar to a baseball catcher's throw or a quarterback's pass in football.

Learning Cues

1. Position toes toward the side wall and open shoulders to the front wall.
2. Weight is on the rear foot.
3. Bring cupped hand to the ear, cocked (Figure 15-6).
4. Weight shifts to the front foot as the arm moves up and forward.

5. Ball is struck above and in front of the head.
6. Ball is struck by the fingers with a wrist snap.
7. Follow through in the direction you wish the ball to take (Figure 15-7).

Practice Suggestions

1. Stand in a ready position deep in the court. Bounce the ball vigorously on the floor so that it rebounds up into a striking position for the overhead.
2. From a position deep in the court, throw the ball high against the front wall so that it bounces high to you, returning it with an overhead stroke. Move your body as soon as possible to the striking position.

FIGURE 15-6. Overhead "cocked" position.

FIGURE 15-7. Overhead follow-through.

Back Wall Shot

The back wall shot, unique to handball and racquetball, rebounds from the front wall to the floor and then off the back wall before the opponent can get into position to play the ball. If you want to become an above average player you have to learn to play this shot successfully. The stroke most applicable for the back wall shot is the forehand stroke in which the forearm is swung parallel to the floor. This offers a balanced and powerful method of hitting the ball.

Learning Cues

1. Face the back wall or the area of the back wall that the ball is in.
2. Move the ball toward the front wall.
3. As the ball rebounds from the wall and begins to descend, pivot on your right foot (for a right hand shot) and turn your body, stepping toward the front wall.
4. Hand and arm locked above the ear.
5. Strike the ball at the vertical mid-point of your body.
6. Let the ball drop as low as possible.
7. Follow through in the direction you want the ball to follow.

Practice Suggestions

1. Facing the back wall, toss the ball against the back wall, letting it bounce toward the front wall from the floor. You move with the ball, positioning yourself for a back wall shot.
2. Facing the back wall, toss the ball against the floor to the back wall, but before it bounces on the floor, position yourself for a back wall shot.

Backhand Shot

While the handball player needs to develop both hands equally well in playing both sides of the court, the racquetball player must learn to use the backhand shot. The backhand shot is similar to a tennis backhand, but the stroke is much shorter and uses more wrist snap.

Learning Cues

1. Position your body by facing the side wall (opposite side of the forehand stroke).
2. Rotate the racquet in your hand ⅛ of a turn toward the front wall.
3. Cock the racquet back near the ear, pelvis turned (Figure 15-8).
4. As the ball is struck, step forward with the front foot, shifting the weight from the back leg to the front leg.
5. Simultaneously with the step, bring the racquet forward and contact the ball in line with the front foot, but away from the body (Figure 15-9).

FIGURE 15-8. Backhand "cocked" position.

FIGURE 15-9. Backhand position on contact.

6. As the ball is struck, uncock the wrist, snapping the ball towards the front wall.

Practice Suggestions

1. Standing at mid-court, facing the side wall, bounce the ball easily into the backhand hitting area. Hit a series of shots from this area, back up 5 feet, hit another series, back up another 5 feet, and so on.
2. Stand at mid-court, facing the side wall. Toss the ball easily against the side wall so that the ball rebounds up from the floor into the striking area for a backhand shot. Repeat this series from deeper in the court.

Service

The service, the beginning stroke of each point, must be successfully placed in order to continue the point, but the service can also be an offensive weapon if developed to its potential. You may serve from anywhere in the service area, the most advantageous spot being in the center, so that you may direct your serve to either side. You must drop the ball into the serving zone, strike it on the first rebound, causing the ball to strike the front wall and rebound over the short line and land on the floor.

Drive Serve. The drive serve is a low, hard serve placed so that it returns close to the side wall and drops dead in the back corner, or a low, hard serve that strikes the floor and wall just behind the short. If possible, the drive serve should not rebound off the back wall, thereby giving your opponent a back wall shot. The drive serve should be struck with the same techniques described in the forehand stroke.

Lob Serve. The lob serve is a high ball placed on the front wall which permits the ball to return in an arc, hugging the side wall, and striking the floor a few feet past the short line in such a manner that the ball rebounds again and drops gently into the corner. The lob serve may be struck either with an underhand or an overhead stroke, the underhand stroke being generally easier to develop in the beginning.

Z Serve. The Z serve is named from the Z pattern formed by the ball. Standing near the left wall of the service area, serve the ball so that it strikes the extreme right side of the front wall a few feet from the corner, approximately 4 feet above the floor, then strikes the right wall, angles past in front of the server, strikes the floor, and finally strikes the left side wall from which it spins off nearly parallel to the back wall (Figure 15-10). The Z serve should be struck with a low forehand, almost underhand stroke. The Z serve could also be executed from the right side of the service area.

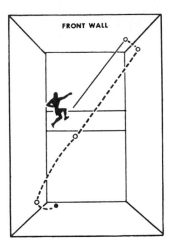

FIGURE 15-10. The Z serve.

Kill Shots

A "kill" shot is actually a placement hit so low that there is little or no possibility of a return. Generally hit with a forehand stroke, you do not hit "down" on the ball but let the ball drop to knee height before contacting it with a powerful stroke. Kills can either be front wall kills or corner kills. The front wall kill is stroked straight ahead, hitting so low on the front wall that the ball bounces twice before your opponent can hit it. The corner kill is hit low, but is aimed toward either corner formed by the front and side walls. The ball should strike either the front or side wall and it immediately will then carom into the side or front wall, producing an angled return that is low and slowed considerably by the ball striking the two wall surfaces.

PLAYING STRATEGY

Handball and racquetball are games in which a premium is placed on analyzing the opponent's strong and weak points. Some players are unable to use their left hand with much effectiveness in handball or they have not developed a strong backhand shot in racquetball. When facing such an opponent, a player should direct a majority of his shots so the opponent is placed at a disadvantage. Players should vary their strategy by employing fast balls alternated with lobs (high, soft shots) in sufficient frequency to get the opponent off balance. The change of pace is particularly effective on the serve, and many good players use it to advantage. In playing doubles, partners should agree on the area that each is to cover and assign the areas so each player may take advantage of any particular strong points he may have.

Players should work for a desirable position on the court. It is usually good strategy to maintain a position in the well—near the middle of the court and close enough to enable one to play low balls and corner shots. By skillful placing of shots, a player can keep an opponent in such a position that he will be at a disadvantage in returning crosscourt angle shots. Think ahead and make the first play a forerunner to a second or third play that will result in an error by the opponent, or afford the opportunity to place a passing or kill shot. If an opponent persists in playing close to the front wall, he can be driven out of position by high lob shots that go over his head but do not strike the back wall with sufficient force to rebound any distance. In the final analysis, a careful scrutiny of your opponent and his style of play is the first step in planning a campaign that will be most effective. Pick out his weak points and take advantage of them.

SAFETY CONSIDERATIONS

1. Dress properly for the game. Always wear rubber-soled shoes to ensure firm footing.
2. Always warm up thoroughly before beginning competition.
3. Do not play a dead ball, because your opponent may turn and get struck in the face.
4. Do not deliberately hit an opponent with the ball in the hope that he will call a hinder on the play. You may both get hurt, and ill feeling will develop.
5. After you play the ball to the back court, do not watch the ball; you may get hit in the face by a returning ball.
6. Allow your opponents room to make the play. Don't crowd or you may be struck.

HELPFUL HINTS

1. Practice "kills" alone. Play the ball around an imaginary opponent and work on the various arm strokes.
2. If your hands swell from playing, soak them in hot water before entering the court, and swelling will be minimized.
3. Gloves are worn by a majority of handball players. Your enjoyment of the game will be increased if you wear a pair of gloves that fit your hands well. Always hang gloves up to dry after using them.
4. Do not rush the ball. Wait for it and you will not only save energy but play a better game.
5. Control is more desirable than speed.
6. Serve each ball so that it is difficult for the opponent to return it. Try to get several ace serves in each game.

7. A ball hit close to the floor has less bounce and is more difficult to return. The forehand stroke is best for this shot; practice regularly on this play.
8. Watch good players and pattern your play after those who have mastered the game.
9. As a playing courtesy, the opponent is entitled to a fair and unobstructed opportunity to play the ball.
10. If there is any doubt about a play, it is advisable to play the point over.

TERMINOLOGY

Ace A service which completely eludes the receiver.
Back wall shot A shot made from a rebound off the back wall.
Box See *Service box.*
Ceiling shot A shot striking the ceiling first, then the front wall.
Crotch The juncture of any two playing surfaces, as between the floor and any wall.
Crotch shot A ball that strikes the front wall and floor simultaneously. Not good.
Cut throat A three-man game in which the server plays against the other two players, with each player keeping an individual score. Not played in official competition.
Drive shot A power shot against the front wall which rebounds fast, low, and in a straight line.
Fault An illegally served ball.
Handout Retiring the server who fails to serve legally or when the serving team fails to return a ball that is in play.
Hinder Accidental interference or obstruction of the flight of the ball during play. Point will be played again.
Kill A ball directed to the front wall in such a way that it rebounds so close to the floor that it is impossible to return.
Passing shot A placement driven out of opponent's reach on either side.
Rally Continuous play of the ball by opponents.
Run-around shot Ball that strikes one side wall, the rear wall, and other side wall.
Screen A hinder due to an obstruction of vision by opponent.
Server Person (or persons, in doubles) in the "hand-in" position and eligible to serve.
Service box Area within the service zone bounded by the side wall and a parallel line 18 inches away; denotes where server's partner must stand in doubles when serve is being made.
Service court The area in which the ball must land when returning from the front wall on the serve.
Service zone The area where the server must stand when serving the ball. Located between the service line and the short line, usually 5 feet wide, and extending across the court.

Short line A line on the floor parallel to front wall and equidistant from front and back wall. Serve must carry over this line on its return from the front wall.

Shoot To attempt kill shots.

Volley To return the ball to the front wall before it bounces on the floor.

SELECTED REFERENCES

Amateur Athletic Union. *Official Handball Rules,* current ed. 231 West 58th Street, New York, N.Y. 10019.

BRUMFIELD, CHARLES, and JEFFREY BAIRSTOW. *Off the Wall.* New York: The Dial Press, 1978.

FAIT, HOLLIS, JOHN SHAW, and KATHERINE LEY. *A Manual of Physical Education Activities,* 3rd ed. Philadelphia: W.B. Saunders Company, 1967.

FITZGIBBON II, HERBERT S., and JEFFREY N. BAIRSTOW. *The Complete Racquet Sports Player.* New York: Simon & Schuster, 1979.

FLEMMING, A. WILLIAM, and JOEL A. BLOOM. *Paddleball and Racquetball* (Goodyear Physical Activity Series, ed. J. Tillman Hall). Pacific Palisades, Calif.: Goodyear Publishing Co., Inc., 1973.

KEELY, STEVE. *The Complete Book of Racquetball.* Northfield, Ill.: DBI Books, Inc., 1976.

MACLEAN, NORMAN. *Platform Tennis, Racquetball and Paddleball.* New York: Drake Publishers, 1977.

MAND, CHARLES L. *Handball Fundamentals.* Columbus, Ohio: Charles E. Merrill Publishing Company, 1968.

O'CONNELL, C.J. *Handball Illustrated.* New York: The Ronald Press Company, 1964.

Official International Racquetball Association. *Racquetball Rules.* 4101 Dempster St., Skokie, Illinois.

SQUIRES, DICK. *The Other Racquet Sports.* New York: McGraw-Hill Book Co., 1978.

WHITE, JESS R. *Sports Rules Encyclopedia.* Palo Alto, Calif.: National Press Books, 1961.

YESSIS, MICHAEL. *Handball,* 2nd ed. Dubuque, Iowa: Wm. C. Brown Company, Publishers, 1972.

YURIC, THOMAS. *Handball.* Philadelphia: W.B. Saunders Company, 1972.

Audio-Visual Materials

The following are available from AAHPERD Educational Media Services, Dept. B, 1201 16th St., N.W., Washington, D.C. 20036, or from The Athletic Institute, 200 N. Castlewood Dr., North Palm Beach, Florida 33408. Racquetball Series (16 mm or Super 8 Cassettes):

Fundamentals of Racquetball
Racquetball Shots
Racquetball Series and Serve Returns
Strategy for Singles, Doubles, Cut Throat.

ORIENTEERING

THIS CHAPTER WILL ENABLE YOU TO:

♦ Identify the parts of a liquid-filled compass and how it works.
♦ Utilize fundamental topographic map reading techniques and skills.
♦ Utilize basic compass techniques and skills.
♦ Navigate an orienteering course using a topographic map and a liquid-filled compass.
♦ Identify the basic terminology necessary to understand the activity and sport of orienteering.

NATURE AND PURPOSE

Orienteering is a cross-country type of activity in which the participant utilizes the skills of topographic map reading and following directions by compass or other means to navigate over unfamiliar terrain. The skills of orienteering can be used to enjoy many outdoor pursuits such as camping, backpacking, hiking, cross-country skiing, fishing, and hunting, or for competing in the sport of orienteering. Called "the thinking sport," competitive orienteering requires great mental acuity, problem solving and decision making, along with cardiorespiratory fitness, as the orienteer can cover distances from two up to ten miles in navigating an orienteering course. With today's back-to-nature interests by people of all ages the skills of orienteering can be valuable in improving environmental awareness and self-reliance in the out of doors.

Participants of all ages and levels of ability can take part in orienteering as a recreational activity or competitive sport. In competitive orienteering, courses with various degrees of difficulty are set up to allow for differences in skill levels; therefore, all participants can achieve success. For many, just completing the course can be a satisfying experience.

Orienteering is an excellent coeducational activity. The techniques and skills can be easily taught to both boys and girls and men and women. The environmental setting makes for social acceptance. Since outstanding physical ability is not necessarily the limiting factor, girls often achieve the same success as boys.

Competitive Orienteering

Point-to-point or cross-country orienteering is the most common type of competition. This event requires the competitors to navigate through a prescribed series of control points shown on a topographic orienteering map (Figure 16-1), with all competitors visiting the controls in the same order. At the start of the event, competitors receive a clue card (Figure 16-2). The clue card identifies the control markers by letter code and describes a prominent feature in which the control marker has been set. The competitors leave the starting line at equal intervals of time, for example, one minute intervals; so that the event becomes for each a contest of route selection and physical skills with the time to complete the course determining the order of finish. To insure that each competitor has visited the control markers, a code or punch is located at each control and must be marked on a competitor's scorecard (Figure 16-3). In competitive orienteering, courses of different levels of difficulty are set up to allow for the differences in navigational and physical skill abilities of the contestants. These courses are designated by colors: white, yellow, orange, green, red, and blue, with white and yellow being for the novice, orange and green for the intermediate, and red and blue for the advanced orienteer. Course difficulty is determined by the number of controls, distance between the controls, and the difficulty of the placement of the controls in the field. For example, compare the distance between controls and the total distance of the red course shown in Figure 16-4 with the distances of the white course shown in Figure 16-1. The red course is obviously much more difficult.

EQUIPMENT

Maps. The most essential item of equipment for successful orienteering is the map. For children just beginning, a map of a schoolyard, local park, or

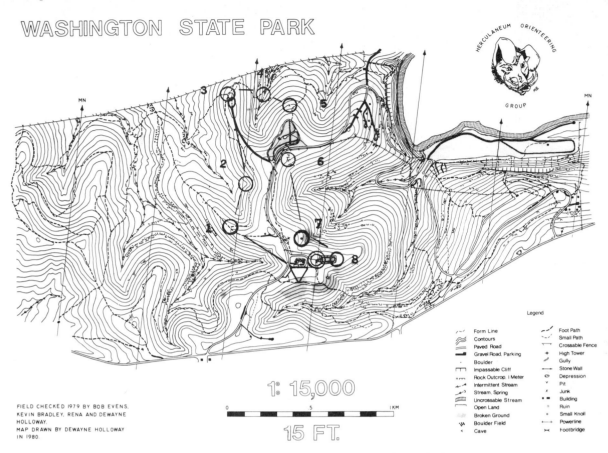

FIGURE 16-1. Topographic orienteering map showing a white course used by beginning orienteers. (Map courtesy of the St. Louis Orienteering Club and Dewayne Holloway.)

Day 1 White Course 2.7 km.

1	(WA)	The trail junction
2	(WB)	The re-entrant (head)
3	(WC)	The trail junction
4	(WD)	The re-entrant
5	(WP)	The junk
6	(WE)	The fence corner
7	(WF)	The depression
8	(HW)	The earth bank

Follow streamers to finish

FIGURE 16-2. Competitors' clue card for the white course shown above. (Courtesy of St. Louis Orienteering Club and Dewayne Holloway.)

ROSE ORIENTEERING CLUB CONTROL CARD

Name

Course   Class

Finish		
Start		⭕⭕
Elapsed		

11	12	13	14	15	16	17	18	19	20
1	2	3	4	5	6	7	8	9	10

FIGURE 16-3. Competitors' score card. (Courtesy Rose Orienteering Club.)

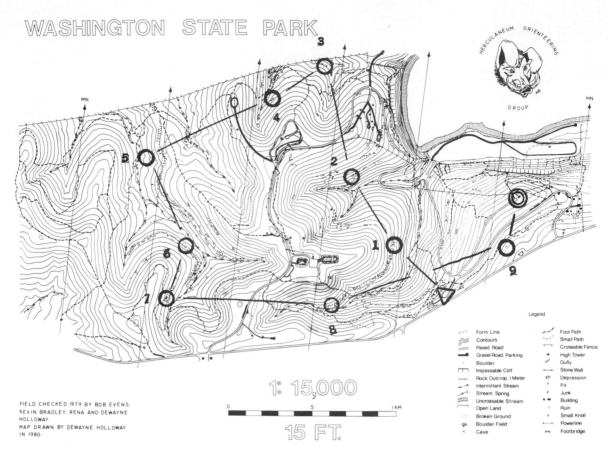

WASHINGTON STATE PARK

HERCULANEUM ORIENTEERING GROUP

FIELD CHECKED 1979 BY BOB EVENS,
KEVIN BRADLEY, RENA AND DEWAYNE
HOLLOWAY.
MAP DRAWN BY DEWAYNE HOLLOWAY
IN 1980.

1: 15,000

15 FT.

0   .5   1 KM

Legend

	Form Line		Foot Path
	Contours		Small Path
	Paved Road		Crossable Fence
	Gravel Road. Parking		High Tower
	Boulder		Gully
	Impassable Cliff		Stone Wall
	Rock Outcrop. I Meter		Depression
	Intermittent Stream		Pit
	Stream. Spring		Junk
	Uncrossable Stream		Building
	Open Land		Ruin
	Broken Ground		Small Knoll
	Boulder Field		Powerline
	Cave		Footbridge

FIGURE 16-4. Topographic orienteering map showing a red course used by advanced orienteers. (Map courtesy of the St. Louis Orienteering Club and Dewayne Holloway.)

forest preserve, drawn to scale, is sufficient; however, for the advanced orienteer, large-scale topographic maps showing selected man-made and natural features are necessary. These topographic maps usually drawn on a scale of 1:24,000 are produced by the United States Geological Survey (USGS) of the Department of the Interior. Recently, more accurate and highly developed orienteering maps have been produced. These maps, usually drawn on a scale of 1:15,000 and developed from current aerial photographs, have been accurately field checked and printed in the standard international orienteering colors: blue (water features), black (man-made features), green (vegetation features), brown (contour features), and yellow (clear areas). Although colored maps are more meaningful and precise, black-and-white maps can be successfully used and are less expensive.

Orienteering maps provide the following important information to the orienteer:

1. *Map Scale.* Each map contains a certain scale which is proportional between a distance on the map and the actual distances in the field. For example, a scale of 1:15,000 on a topographical map means that one unit of distance on the map equals 15,000 units of actual distance in the field. A bar scale representing map distance is located in the margin of the map.

2. *Directions.* The top of an orienteering map represents geographic north; therefore, the other cardinal directions are: south (the bottom), east (the right), and west (the left). Most orienteering maps will have the magnetic-north lines already drawn on the map. These lines, called the declination lines, represent the degree difference between the magnetic north direction and true north direction. The angle of declination on USGS topographic maps can be found in the margin.

3. *Elevation Features.* A topographic map is distinguished from a planemetric map (roadmap) in showing the shape and elevation changes of the terrain by brown contour lines. Each of these lines represents a constant elevation, in feet or meters, above sea level. The space between each line on a topographic map represents a vertical distance called the contour interval. The contour interval is given below the bar scale at the bottom of the map sheet. In areas of the United States with little elevation, the contour interval will be 5 to 10 meters (or feet) to more accurately represent the land features, while contour intervals of 10 to 20 meters (or feet) are found in more mountainous areas.

4. *Other Map Features.* Other important man-made or natural features such as power lines, roads, trails, bridges, buildings, fences, boulders, cliffs, streams, lakes, marshes, or ponds are also shown on the map. These features are either drawn to actual scale or displayed symbolically with the description of each symbol found in the map's legend (see Figure 16-1).

Compass. The second most essential item of equipment for successful orienteering is the compass. The protractor type compass with the liquid-filled housing (Figure 16-5) is the most widely used compass in orienteering today because it permits the orienteer to take a bearing and measure its distance quickly and accurately. The parts of the compass and their basic function are as follows:

1. *Base Plate.* The transparent rectangular plate on which the compass housing is mounted is called the base plate. The front edge and one of the side edges are marked off in inches and millimeters for measuring map scale or distance.

2. *Compass Housing.* The degree markings are found on the outer rim of the rotating compass housing. Each mark represents one degree and they are numbered in intervals of 20. (It should be noted that 0° and 360° coincide and are both north.) Once the compass is set correctly, the degree bearing is

FIGURE 16-5. The protractor compass.

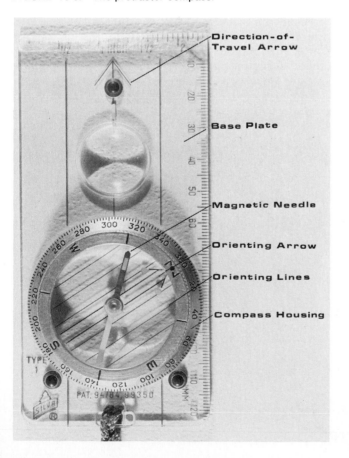

taken at the index pointer on the rim of the housing.

3. *Orienting Arrow.* Located inside the compass housing is the orienting or north-seeking arrow. Its function is to assist in orienting the compass. The compass is oriented by holding the compass in such a way that the orienting arrow is lined up with the magnetic needle both of which will be pointed north.

4. *Magnetic Needle.* The free floating needle located inside the compass housing is called the magnetic needle. The north end is painted red and always points to magnetic north unless affected by a metal object.

5. *Orienting Lines.* Located inside the compass housing and running parallel to the orienting arrow are the orienting lines. These lines assist in determining declination by setting them parallel to the magnetic lines on the map, with north on the compass pointing to north on the map.

6. *Direction-of-Travel Arrow.* At the upper end of the base plate is located the direction-of-travel arrow which is used for determining the direction of travel when the compass is oriented.

SUGGESTED LEARNING SEQUENCE

Whole Method

The direct or whole method is recommended for teaching younger children and novice orienteers when suitable terrain with linear features such as trails, roads, fields, etc., is available. In this method beginners will run or walk through the woods on a real orienteering course as their first introduction to orienteering, the only preliminary teaching being a knowledge of the map symbols, techniques of orienting the map, and map reading by thumb. Controls are set in such a way that the beginner needs only to follow linear features such as trails, roads, or other distinct and easily recognizable features. After these techniques and skills are mastered and confidence gained, a knowledge of contour lines, map scale, handling a compass, and measuring distance may be introduced.

Part-Whole Method

While the "whole" method of teaching is often used with children and novice orienteers, the most widely used and accepted method of teaching is the "part-whole" method. In this method the basic techniques and skills of using the map, the compass, and map and compass together are taught before the orienteer attempts to navigate an orienteering course. In attempting to navigate an orienteering course, an orienteer using this method should start with a novice or white course (such as shown in Figure 16-1), and progress to a more advanced or red course (such as Figure 16-4), once the basic orienteering techniques are mastered.

BASIC TECHNIQUES AND SKILLS

Map Reading. Since the map is the primary tool for navigation in orienteering, it is essential to teach basic map reading techniques and skills first.

1. *Orienting the Map.* Orienting the map simply means keeping the map turned so that north on the map corresponds to north in the field regardless of the direction the orienteer travels. Orienting the map can be done either by inspecting the surroundings and aligning the terrain features with those on the map or by using the compass. The steps in using the compass to orient the map are as follows:

a. Set the compass dial at 360°. Then place the compass on the map with the edge of the base plate parallel to one of the magnetic north lines, making sure the direction-of-travel arrow points north.

b. Rotate the map and compass until the magnetic needle is over the orienting arrow. The map is now oriented with respect to magnetic north.

2. *Map Reading by Thumb.* In using this technique the map should be folded so that it can be easily held and read as only the immediate area in which you are orienteering is showing. The tip of the thumb is then placed on the map corresponding to the place in the field where you are standing and pointing in the direction you will travel. As the orienteer travels along, the thumb is moved to the place on the map corresponding to the location in the field where the orienteer has traveled. This technique assists in keeping the map reader ori-

ented, as the terrain features that lie ahead can be easily analyzed and checked.

Compass Reading. The compass can be used with a map or by itself. For the beginning orienteer, the steps in taking a bearing and traveling with the compass by itself should be taught first. These steps are as follows:

1. The orienteer stands facing in the direction of the destination he plans to go. With the direction-of-travel arrow pointed in this direction, the compass housing is turned until the north end of the orienting arrow is lined up with the north end of the magnetic needle.

2. Once the compass is set, the orienteer picks out a prominent feature such as a tree or hilltop in line with the direction-of-travel arrow. He travels to that feature, takes another bearing, and continues until reaching his destination.

Additional Procedures. Taking a bearing and traveling with a compass and map involve additional procedures and should be done with precision. Three basic steps are used in this process:

1. Put the edge of the base plate from your present place of location to your destination making sure the direction-of-travel arrow is pointing in the direction you plan to travel (see Figure 16-6).

2. Turn the compass housing until the orienting lines are parallel to the magnetic lines and the orienting arrow is pointing north on the map (see Figure 16-7). When magnetic north lines are not present, the orienting lines can be set parallel with the meridian lines—the lines running true north to south. In this case the declination (angle of difference in degrees between true north and magnetic

FIGURE 16-6. The first step in taking a bearing from the start to control #1 on the white course (Figure 16-1).

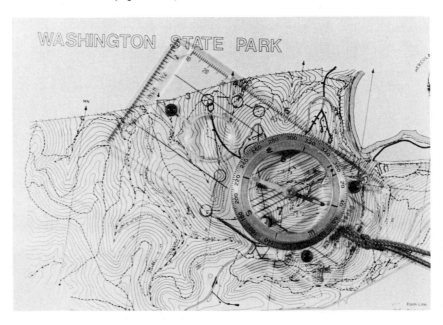

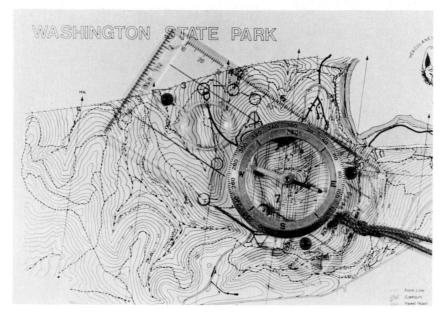

FIGURE 16-7. The second step in taking a bearing from the start to control #1 on the white course (Figure 16-1).

north) must be added or subtracted to the final bearing. This degree difference is given in the margin on topographic maps. To decide whether to add or subtract, think of the rhyme "East is least and West is best." If the angle of declination is *east*, the degree of declination is *subtracted;* if the declination is *west*, it is *added.*

3. The final important step is to turn yourself until the north end of the magnetic needle points to the north end of the orienting arrow (Figure 16-8).

COMPETITIVE ORIENTEERING SKILLS

In competitive orienteering the orienteer must know special orienteering techniques and skills in order to select the fastest and least tiring route between control points.

1. *Pace Counting.* Pace counting involves a two-step approach:

a. In step one, the orienteer measures the distance on the map by using the marked edge of the compass and the map bar scale.
b. Step two involves measuring the distance in the field by pace counting. In pace counting, you count your double step, or each time the same foot hits the ground. This can be practiced by measuring an exact 100 yards or 100 meters over different terrain and counting the number of double steps taken in covering this distance.

2. *Attack Points.* Sometimes called secondary controls, these are large prominent features such as

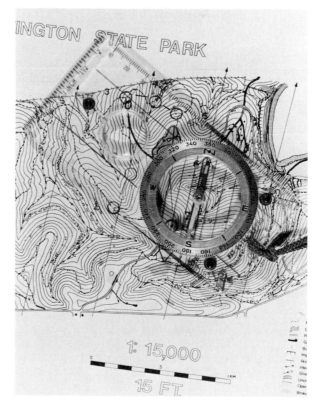

FIGURE 16-8. The third step in taking a bearing from the start to control #1 on the white course (Figure 16-1).

a cliff, building, bridge, trail junction, or other features near the control which can easily be found and identified on the map. Finding an attack point makes the final approach to the control much easier.

FIGURE 16-9. Arriving at a control point, indicated by the prism-shaped cloth control marker, the orienteer checks the code letter on the marker. She then punches her control card with a punch found at the marker to indicate that she has been there.

FIGURE 16-10. Orienteer using her map and compass takes a bearing to the next control point.

3. *Check Points.* After finalizing the route the orienteer should visualize certain prominent features (check points) she will see along the way which will indicate she is on the correct route.

4. *Handrails.* Linear features running parallel to the direction of a control point or an attack point are called handrails. These can take the form of natural features such as a stream, the edge of a field, a ridge or man-made feature such as a road, trail, fence, or power line. Handrails are used by the orienteer as a natural guide to follow toward the control point.

5. *Catching Features.* Long features running crosswise to the orienteer's direction of travel are called catching or collecting features. These features can assist the orienteer in navigation, as upon reaching the catcher the orienteer needs only to turn in the proper direction and follow it until the attack or control point is reached. These "catchers" include the same linear features mentioned as handrails.

6. *Aiming Off.* When control or attack points are located on linear features such as roads, streams, fences, etc., the orienteer aims off, that is, sets the compass toward a point 40 to 60 meters to the right or left of the control point rather than right at it, so that upon arriving at the linear feature he knows exactly which way he must turn, right or left, to find the control point.

SAFETY CONSIDERATIONS

While orienteering is a relatively safe activity, there are some precautions which must be followed.

1. Orienteers should be cautioned to avoid potentially dangerous obstructions and features shown on the map such as cliffs, rock faces, barbed wire fences, or deep rivers and streams.
2. The orienteer should be instructed to wear protective clothing when heavy brambles, briar patches, or thick vegetation exist in the terrain in which orienteering will occur.
3. Before embarking on a course, a safety bearing should be given which will lead the orienteer to a large catching feature such as a road, trail, etc., in the event he becomes lost or totally disoriented.

TERMINOLOGY

Aiming off A technique in which the orienteer purposely aims to one side of a control point so that he will know which way to turn.

Attack point A large prominent visable feature both on the map and in the field, from which the final approach or attack to the control can be made.

Bearing Sometimes called an azimuth, it is a direction measured in degrees from north with a compass.

Cardinal points The four basic directions on a compass: north, south, east, and west.

Catching feature A long, natural or man-made feature running perpendicular to the orienteer's direction of travel.

Contour interval The vertical distance in height between contour lines on a topographic map.

Controls Markers of two colors—usually red and white or orange and white—placed in the field before the orienteering meet starts; used for locating control points on the map.

Control description A word description for the location of a control point.

Declination The degree difference between the magnetic north direction and the true north direction.

Handrail Linear features running parallel to an orienteer's direction of travel which are used to navigate to a control or an attack point.

Magnetic north The direction to the magnetic north pole located north of Hudson Bay.

Map symbols Designs found in the legend on a map; used to indicate landscape features.

Meridians Real lines on the map or imaginary lines in the terrain running true north to true south.

Orienting the compass Turning the compass until north on the compass is the same as north in the field.

Orienting the map Turning the map until north on the map corresponds to north in the field.

Pace counting Method used to measure distance in the field by counting each time the same foot strikes the ground.

Scale A proportion between a distance on the map and the actual distance in the field.

Topographic map A map showing elevation changes by means of contour lines.

SELECTED REFERENCES

Humphrey, Vernon, and Theodore Stroup. *The Orienteering Handbook.* Fort Benning, Ga.: U.S. Army Infantry School, 1971.

Kjellstrom, Bjorn. *Be Expert with Map and Compass.* New York: Charles Scribner and Sons, 1976.

Bengtsson, Hans, and George Atkinson. *Orienteering for Sport and Pleasure.* Brattleboro, Vt.: The Stephen Green Press, 1977.

Boy Scouts of America. *Orienteering.* North Brunswick, N.J.: Boy Scouts of America, 1971.

Disley, John. *Orienteering.* Harrisburg, Pa.: Stackpole Books, 1967.

Audio-Visual Materials

International Film Bureau, Inc., 332 South Michigan Ave., Chicago, IL 60604.
Color Films (rental or purchase):
  1. "Orienteering" (10 minutes).
  2. "The Sport of Orienteering" (24 minutes).
  3. "What Makes Them Run" (20½ minutes).
Filmstrips and Slide Series:
  1. "Adventures with Map and Compass."
  2. "Map and Compass Clinic Kit."

Training Aids and Orienteering Equipment

Orienteering Services USA, P.O. Box 1604, Binghamton, N.Y. 13902.

Topographic Maps

National Cartographic Information Center, 507 National Center, Reston, Va. 22092.

Organizations

United States Orienteering Federation, P.O. Box 1039, Ballwin, Missouri 63011.

Canadian Orienteering Federation, 355 River Rd., Vanier, Ontario, KIL 8B9.

RECREATIONAL SPORTS

Angling
Horseshoes
Shuffleboard
Table Tennis

NATURE AND PURPOSE

Angling is fishing for sport. In particular, it is the employment of the skill of casting to catch fish. Angling has increased steadily in popularity and today countless people of all ages engage in the sport. Over thirty million fishing licenses are issued in the United States each year, and millions of people fish without a license. With this population it is quite possible that more money is spent on angling than on any other sport. Wherever fish and water are to be found, anyone can enjoy this lifetime recreational activity.

The basic skill in learning to become an angler is casting. Despite the fact that this is a relatively simple skill, very few master it because they do not learn under proper guidance.

There are two types of casting: fly and bait. These two types are quite similar but employ different tackle and somewhat different techniques. In *fly casting,* a longer, more flexible rod is used, the line is controlled from the hand, and the light bait is propelled entirely by its own weight and that of the line. The purpose of fly casting is to make it possible to use very small lines and to secure accuracy rather than distance. *Bait casting* requires a shorter, less flexible rod. Distance is gained by the weight of the bait or lure. In bait casting the line is controlled at the reel, rather than by the line as in fly casting.

EQUIPMENT

Fly Casting Tackle

The beginner should first enlist the assistance of an experienced fly fisherman in selecting equip-

ment, as proper equipment in the beginning is very important. The equipment selected should correspond to the type of fishing done.

Rod. The most important piece of equipment is the rod. Fly rods come in different lengths and have different actions and fittings. For the beginner, a rod measuring 8½ feet and weighing 4¼ to 5 ounces is recommended. A rod made of fiberglass would be best suited for general use. The rod should be flexible yet have strength and bend evenly.

Reel. The single action or manual type of fly reel is recommended for the beginner. The reel, which is a storage unit for the line, should have an adjustable drag (a mechanism that increases or decreases the resistance on a line once a fish is hooked), an interchangeable spool, and the capacity to hold enough back-up line in order to play the fish.

Line. The manufacturer's recommendations of line size for the rod should be closely followed. Fly lines today are usually constructed of a core of braided dacron or nylon fibers covered by a plastic coating. They come in various tapers (thicknesses) and weight; the experienced fly fisherman can aid in helping to select the proper line.

Bait-Casting Tackle

There are three types of reels that may be used, one is specifically for bait casting and the other two are used for spin casting (Figure 17-1).

Bait-Casting Reel. The beginner should select a level-wind reel, "level wind" meaning that the line is wrapped evenly on the spool. The reel should fit the rod. Too heavy a reel on a light rod will kill the action of the rod.

Spinning Reel. Spinning reels are divided into two general classes. In the *open type,* the spool upon which the line coils has no cover, leaving the spool and line fully exposed. In the *cone type,* a cone covers the spool and line to protect the line from dirt; to prevent its being touched by lures, twigs, weeds, and other foreign objects; and especially to prevent gusts of wind from blowing it off the spool and causing "gnarling." The line passes through a hole in the center of the cup, directly in front of the axis of the spool shaft.

Most reels are equipped with left-hand action handles, but some of the later types have handles for right-hand use.

The action of the reel spool is the basic difference among the spinning, spin-casting, and standard bait-casting outfit. The spool of a spinning reel does not rotate to release the line on the cast or to respool it during the retrieve. On most reels, it advances and recedes as the line is being coiled on, in order to spool the line uniformly, but it never rotates. On the cast, the line slips off the exposed end of the spool. This action can best be visualized by thinking of a spool of thread. If one end of the spool of thread is held firmly in one hand and the thread end grasped by the other hand and stripped off straight over the opposite end of the spool, the action would be similar to that of the spinning line leaving the reel. The spool also remains stationary on the retrieve. A metal "finger" rotates around the spool, picking up the line and placing it back around the spool. For this reason, there are no backlashes such as frequently happen with the standard reel. This feature especially appeals to the inexperienced caster.

Rod. The beginner should select a good rod that is 5 to 6 feet long and has good action. The same rod can be used for either bait casting or spin casting. Most rods are constructed of some kind of fiber and resin combination.

Line. Generally speaking, a light to medium monofilament line is recommended for the beginner. When pulling on the line for a spinning reel, it is very important to follow the manufacturer's instructions carefully in order to avoid twisting the line. Usually a braided monofilament line is used for the

bait-casting (level-wind) reel, because many fishermen feel it is less likely to backlash.

SKILLS AND TECHNIQUES

The casting of the line onto the water is the most important skill to be developed by the angler. As the various techniques are described in this section you will notice similarities in the use of the fly rod, bait-casting rod, and spinning rod; however, there are differences. Reference will be made to the positioning of the casting arm in relation to the hands on a clock. Most of the movements center on the 10 o'clock to 1 o'clock range of movement. Therefore if you will think of the movement in terms of the hands on the face of the clock, you should have relatively little difficulty in understanding the action of the arms and rod as the learning sequence is described.

Fly Casting

Two important things to remember when learning to fly cast are first, the right hand will grip the handle and become part of the execution of the cast while secondly, the other hand must control the feed of the line as the cast is being made. After sufficient practice, the sequence and action of the two hands will become smooth and rhythmical. Another key point for the beginner to remember is that the cast is primarily a result of the action of the forearm and less of the wrist.

To practice the cast, begin by pulling 15 to 20 feet of line from the tip of the rod and place it on the ground in front of you. The rod is gripped on the handle, the thumb is placed on the top in line with the rod, the fingers are wrapped comfortably around the handle. The wrist is bent until it becomes a parallel extension of the forearm, the elbow is kept in close to the body. The stroke itself, will be best

FIGURE 17-1. Types of reels, clockwise from left: bait casting, automatic fly reel (back), open type, cone type (in foreground).

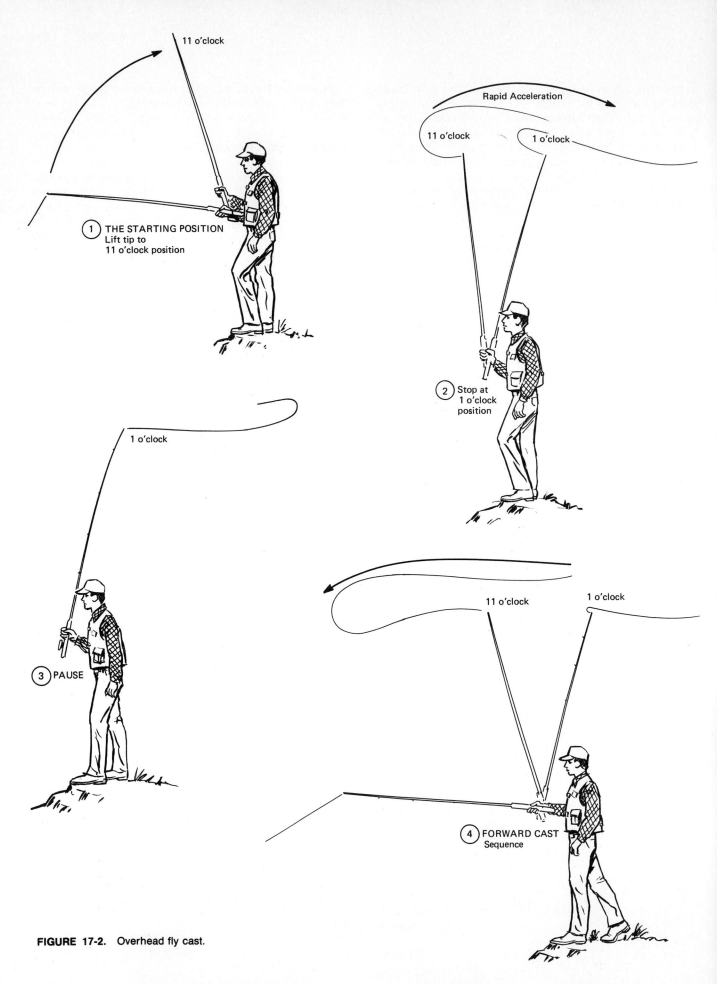

11 o'clock

① THE STARTING POSITION
Lift tip to
11 o'clock position

Rapid Acceleration

11 o'clock   1 o'clock

② Stop at
1 o'clock
position

1 o'clock

③ PAUSE

11 o'clock   1 o'clock

④ FORWARD CAST
Sequence

FIGURE 17-2. Overhead fly cast.

executed between the 11 o'clock and 1 o'clock positions (see Figure 17-2).

Learning Cues

1. Begin by lifting the tip up, rapidly accelerate from the 11 o'clock to 1 o'clock position, the space between the wrist and handle opens slightly.
2. The rod stops at the 1 o'clock position, the line drifts behind the shoulder, wait until it is almost completely unrolled, then begin the forward cast.
3. Accelerate the rod forward to the 11 o'clock position, stop quickly and allow the line to unroll forward, the line should land softly on the surface as the follow-through is completed.

Practice Suggestions

The left hand plays an important role in the cast as it feeds line to the rod on the forward cast or draws line from the reel during a false cast.

1. Slack is taken and the line is grasped between the thumb and forefinger and stripped (drawn) from the reel to an arm's length. Repeat this action two or three times so additional coils are formed.
2. At the end of the forward cast, the line is released from the coil in the left hand, the loop nearest the ends of the finger being released first. It is important to keep the loops separated.
3. As soon as sufficient line is drawn for the length of the cast, complete the cast.

Bait Casting

The action in bait casting is similar to that described for fly casting, with certain important differences. The grip for bait casting is different in that the thumb must be placed on the spool flange for the conventional type, and the reel turned sidewise so that the handle points straight up. The index finger should grip the finger trigger while the other fingers grasp the handle firmly but not rigidly.

In fishing, a good caster learns to cast from any position and with either hand. In target casting, which is the only method of learning accuracy, the caster may stand directly facing the target or slightly sidewise, with the right side (if casting right-handed) toward the target and the right foot slightly advanced. The arms should be held in a relaxed "natural" position with the elbow at or near the side. The target should be aligned by looking at it through the top of the tip.

The overhead casting action has two parts: the backward and the forward motion. Each is equally important.

Learning Cues

1. Stand comfortably; the elbow should be clear of the body, the forearm should become an extension of the rod.
2. The rod is brought up quickly and is stopped at a

one o'clock position; the weight on the lure will bend the rod further back.
3. With no hesitation the rod is brought swiftly to an 11 o'clock position and the thumb eases off the line on the spool.
4. While the lure is in flight, gently apply pressure with the thumb braking the spool and allow the rod to follow through in the direction of the line of flight. The spool is braked to a complete stop as the lure reaches the surface of the water.

The rod must be shifted to the left hand in order to retrieve the plug. The right hand then grasps the handle of the reel and begins to reel in the line. The method of retrieving depends on the type of bait being used. Often the manufacturer supplies printed instructions on proper manipulation so the angler may secure the best results from each type.

Spin Casting

Remembering that there are two types of spinning reels, the open type and the cone type, the cast is made in the same manner as with the bait casting outfit. The only difference is in the control of the line during the cast. With the closed-type reel, the thumb button is pressed then released at the 11 o'clock position and the left hand helps to feather the line and eventually brake it. With the spinning oufit, it is done by pressure upon the line between the forefinger and the rod grip *after* the line has left the spool.

In starting the cast, the line (ahead of the reel) is held firmly against the rod grip with the forefinger of the hand with which the cast is made. While holding the line securely, the pick-up bail or finger is released and moved aside so that it will not interfere with the line during the cast. This is done by turning the handle very slightly in reverse, by pressing a release button, or as required for the particular make of reel.

As with the conventional rod and reel, the direct overhead cast is recommended until proficiency with the new outfit is acquired.

The pressure upon the line is released at the same time and in the same manner as the thumb pressure upon the spool would be released with a bait-casting outfit. During the flight of the lure, control is exercised by decreasing or increasing the index finger pressure on the line against the cork grip.

Practice Suggestions

The beginning angler must learn not only accuracy and form but also develop a "feel" for the casting technique being learned. Distance is secondary in the beginning. Use a dummy lure (no barbs) when practicing.

1. Pick up the rod and practice the forearm and

wrist action without casting. The fly rod enthusiast might want to strip out 30 feet of line and practice the action of lifting, the backcast, the pause, and forward cast.

2. For a class, place a series of plastic hoops at a standard distance and have students hit the target. As proficiency is gained, move the hoops to varying distances, designate high scores for those hoops farthest away and lower scores for those that are nearest to the angler. Individual and team competition can be promoted.

3. Since many people fish from a boat, bring a bench or low backed chairs to class so students can practice the bait cast and spin cast from a sitting position.

NOTE: In all instances, whether dealing with beginners or more advanced anglers, make sure there is adequate space between participants. Single line formations with a two or three arms' length between participants would appear to be safe.

SKILL TESTING—SKISH

Skish is a dry-land game designed to improve one's skill in casting with regular bait-casting and fly-casting tackle. It is an excellent game way to master the skills of accuracy and the control of distance.

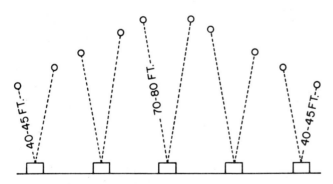

FIGURE 17-3. A skill-testing setup or Skish game using ten targets and five stations.

Bait Casting. Bait-casting rules call for the plug not to exceed five-eighths of an ounce, and the line must be no smaller than nine-pound test. Ten targets, rings not to exceed 30 inches, are randomly scattered distances unknown to the caster. The closest target is not less than 40 nor more than 45 feet from the casting box (4 × 4 feet), while the farthest one should be not more than 80 nor less than 70 feet away. Each target has its own casting box and the contestants move from box to box, taking two casts at each target (Figure 17-3).

Scoring: 6 points are scored for perfect cast on first trial; 4 points for perfect cast on second trial.

The play must fall within the target to score. In the event of a tied score, the one having the greatest number of points on initial casts is declared the winner.

Fly Casting. Fly-casting rules call for regular fly-casting tackle, tied in approved dry fly style and the hook broken off back of the barb. Five targets are placed at distances unknown to the casters, between 20 and 40 feet from the casting boxes.

First round. Caster must start with fly in hand and no slack in line, and is given two and one-half minutes at each target to make three casts.

Scoring: 5 points are scored for perfect cast on first trial; 3 points for perfect cast on second trial; 2 points for perfect cast on third trial. Maximum score is 50 points. (On water, the fly must rest on water until judge calls for score.)

Second round. Time limit is one and one-half minutes (90 seconds) for each target. The caster rolls casts until a "perfect" has been scored on all five targets or until the official calls time. Time begins when the fly drops on the surface. Each perfect score counts 5 points, with a possible score of 25.

Third round—Wet fly. The limit, one to one and one-half minutes. Caster starts with fly in hand and no slack in line. To begin, he extends line to nearest target by false casting and time begins when the fly drops on the surface as a measured cast. Two casts are made, without false casts, at each of the five targets from left to right, stripping the necessary line to reach each target.

Scoring: 3 points are scored for perfect cast on first trial; 2 points for perfect cast on second trial. Maximum possible score is 25 points. In case of a tie, the caster having made the greatest number of initial perfects is declared the winner.

SAFETY CONSIDERATIONS

1. Care and skill must be employed if the angler is to avoid being "hooked" by the fishhook in bait and fly casting.
2. Wading with boots in unknown waters or wearing them in a boat is hazardous and the angler must realize the danger involved. Very few persons are good enough swimmers to survive if wearing boots when a boat capsizes.
3. Lures should not be left in the bottom of a boat or on the shore because they may become imbedded in one's foot or leg.
4. To avoid injury from the bait-casting reel the thumb may be coated with lacquer or covered with adhesive tape.

TERMINOLOGY

Back cast Drawing the rod back; the initial movement in the cast.

Backlash A faulty casting technique that results in a tangling of the line.

Bait Artificial or natural lures that are used to attract fish.

Bait casting The throwing and placing of a lure and line from the rod and reel.

Cork arbor The part of the reel to which the line is attached.

Dry fly fishing Casting a surface fly so that it resembles an insect on the water.

Ferrules The metal connections between sections of the rod.

Fly Artificial bait resembling an insect.

Fly casting Throwing a line with an artificial lure by means of a fly rod.

Forward cast The last movement forward with the rod that throws the bait on the line to the desired spot.

Guides Small loops on the rod through which the line is run.

Leader The strong, transparent material that connects the line to the hook or lure.

Level-wind reel A reel which has a carriage that distributes the line evenly on the spool.

Lure Artificial or natural bait used to attract fish. A hook or hooks are attached to the lure.

Net A device to take the fish safely out of the water.

Reel The mechanism which winds or unwinds the line.

Reel set A part of the rod handle to which the reel is attached.

Rod tip The end of the rod.

Spinner Artificial bait that spins when it is drawn through the water.

Spoon Artificial bait shaped something like a spoon.

Strike When a fish graps the bait.

Tackle Fishing gear; usually refers to the rod and reel only.

Thumbing Controlling the speed of the cast by means of thumb pressure on the reel.

SELECTED REFERENCES

Basic Casting from A to Z. Tulsa, Oklahoma: Zebco.

GERLACH, REX. *The Complete Book of Casting.* New York: Winchester Press, 1975.

KNAP, JEROME J. *Fishing Secrets.* New York: Crown Publishers, Inc., 1977.

National Association of Angling and Casting Clubs. *By-Laws, Rules and Regulations of Casting* (current ed.). University City, Mo.: NAACC.

National Skish Board. *National Skish Guide* (latest ed.). Washington, D.C.: NSB (Bond Building).

SLAYMAKER II, S.L. *Simplified Fly Fishing.* New York: Harper and Row, Publishers, 1969.

HORSESHOES

NATURE AND PURPOSE

Horseshoe pitching has been popular for a long time both as a recreational and competitive sport. The formation of the National Horseshoe Pitchers Association in 1921, has given rise to chapters in nearly every state as well as Canada. The NHPA sanctions local and regional meets for men, women, boys and girls. A World Tournament is held each year for Men and Women while a Junior Boys and Junior Girls World Champion is also decided.

The game is played by pitching horseshoes toward a metal stake some 40 feet (30 for women and juniors) from the pitching point. Points are scored for shoes landing closest to the stake, providing the shoe is not farther than 6 inches from the stake. A ringer (shoe which encircles stake) counts 3 points. The winner is the player who first scores 21 points (informal play) or 50 points (official tournament competition). Players alternate in throwing shoes, with the player who scored one or more points on the previous pitch throwing first. In singles play the players move from stake to stake after each throw, but in doubles one partner is stationed at each stake and makes all throws from there.

PLAYING AREA AND EQUIPMENT

The Court. The official horseshoe court (see Figure 17-4) is 50 × 10 feet with one-inch metal stakes placed 40 feet apart (30 feet for women and juniors). The stakes are centered in a 6 × 6 foot pitcher's box. For informal recreational games, the distance between stakes may be arranged to fit the available space. If courts are to be built on a school ground, it is advisable to build back stops behind each pitcher's box to prevent the horseshoes from rebounding into a student. In schools that lack the space or do not wish to build permanent courts, temporary ones can be built in a place of convenience.

Horseshoes. Horseshoes may be bought at local hardware stores or discount department stores, or may be specially ordered from a number of companies approved by the NHPA. For schools, several physical education and recreation equipment companies sell either official metal shoes or indoor and outdoor rubber horseshoes that are used with wooden stakes. An official shoe should not exceed 7¼ inches in width and 7⅝ inches in length, and should weigh no more than 2 pounds 10 ounces. The opening can be no more than 3½ inches from point to point.

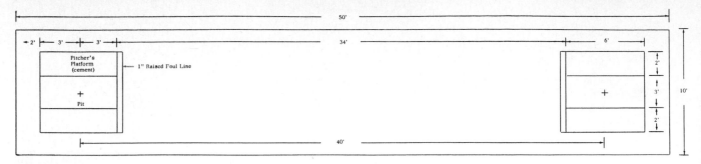

FIGURE 17-4. The official horseshoe court.

BASIC RULES

The National Horseshoe Pitchers Association establishes the official rules of horseshoe pitching.

Simplified Rules

1. A game is divided into innings, and each contestant pitches two shoes in each inning. A game lasts 25 innings (50 shoes pitched by each person).
2. The choice of the first pitch to start the game is decided by the toss of a shoe or a coin.
3. A shoe that has left the pitcher's hand is ruled a pitched shoe.
4. A pitcher's opponent must stand behind the person in action and may not interfere with the pitch in any way.
5. A contestant may not walk to the opposite stake or be informed of the position of the shoes until the inning is completed.
6. Shoes thrown when a foul has been committed are considered shoes pitched; however, they may not receive any point value. Fouls may be assessed for the following:
   a. Illegal delivery of shoe.
   b. Failure of opponent to stay behind the pitcher, or his interfering in any way with the opponent while he is in the act of pitching.
   c. Touching thrown shoes before a measurement has been made.
   d. Thrown shoes which strike part of the pitcher's box or land outside the foul lines and which then rebound into the box.
   e. Stepping on or over the foul line.
7. Ties are broken by pitching an extra inning(s).

Scoring

1. The shoe nearest to the stake scores one point, providing it is within six inches of the stake.
2. Two shoes closer than opponent's shoe score two points.
3. One ringer scores three points and two ringers, six points.
4. A player having two ringers to one by his opponent scores three points.
5. All shoes equally distant from the stake count as ties and no points are scored.
6. A leaning shoe has the same value as that of a shoe lying on the ground and in contact with the stake.

SKILLS AND TECHNIQUES

Players must stand behind the foul line on the pitching platform when pitching. Most players assume a starting stance with the pitching arm closest to the stake and in a position which permits a forward step in the act of delivery of the shoe. The number of turns which the shoe takes in flight usually determines the style of grip to be used. Regardless of the grip used, there are several factors common to all pitches:

1. The shoe should be held parallel to the ground with calks down;
2. The rotation of the shoe should be clockwise; and
3. The open end of the shoe should face the stake when landing.

There are four standard methods of delivery, so the beginner should do some experimenting to determine which method is best for him.

1. In the single turn delivery (see Figure 17-5) the open face of the shoe is directed toward the stake.
2. In the one and one-quarter turn delivery (see Figure 17-6) the open end of the shoe faces the pitcher's left and the thumb is across the top.
3. In the one and one-half turn delivery (see Figure 17-7) the open end of the shoe faces the pitcher.
4. In the one and three-quarters delivery (see Figure 17-8) the open end of the shoe faces the pitcher's right and either of two methods of holding the shoe may be used.

Learning Cues

1. Weight evenly distributed on both feet in the stance, step off on opposite foot, knees bent, eyes on the target, shoulders square to target.
2. While slightly leaning forward, the arm remains straight and falls down and back and retraces the same arc on the forward swing. The pitch must be smooth and rhythmical.
3. At the release the body and arm extend giving proper lift, the forearm rolls in order to turn the shoe.

Practice Suggestions

1. Experiment with various deliveries; usually the one and one-quarter turn delivery is best for a beginner.

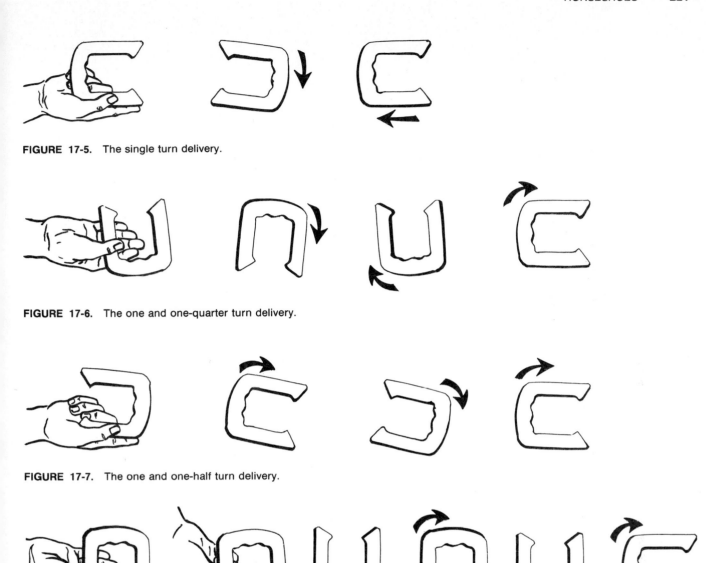

FIGURE 17-5. The single turn delivery.

FIGURE 17-6. The one and one-quarter turn delivery.

FIGURE 17-7. The one and one-half turn delivery.

FIGURE 17-8. The one and three-quarters turn delivery. Two different grips are illustrated.

2. Practice the step and throw without a shoe then add the shoe. Partner should check to see that arc is straight and shoulders square and delivery is rhythmical.
3. Juniors and school age children might start closer to the stake and work their way back to 30 feet.

SAFETY

1. Stand well away from the pitching court when not involved.
2. Be aware of people around you when swinging the horseshoe. Pitch only in the designated area.
3. If setting up courts for a class, make sure there is adequate distance between courts to compensate for erratic throws of beginners.

COURTESIES

1. Observe all the rules.
2. Do not disturb a person who is in the process of pitching.
3. Keep emotions under control.
4. Be aware of the game and the position in the game so you are ready to pitch when your turn comes.

TERMINOLOGY

Calks Raised areas on the heels and toe of one side of the pitching shoe that tend to make the shoe less likely to skid when striking the surface of the pit area.

Double ringer   Two successive shoes which encircle the stake by the same player in the same inning.

Flipped-up shoe   Flipping shoe in air to determine which player takes the first pitch. Instead of calling heads or tails, a player calls smooth or rough.

Heel   The ends of the prongs on each side of the open end of the shoe.

Inning   The pitching of two shoes by each player.

Leaner (also *Hobber*)   Shoe which leans against a stake.

Pit   The area in which the shoe lands.

Pitcher's box   The area which includes the pitching platform and the pit.

Ringer   A shoe that encircles the stake.

SELECTED REFERENCES

National Horseshoe Pitchers Association of America. *Official Rules for Horseshoe Pitching* (current ed.). Federation of 54 State Associations in the U.S. and Canada. (Contact local association for State address.)

RENO, OTTIE W. *Pitching Championship Horseshoes,* 2nd ed. New York: A.S. Barnes and Company, 1975.

The Horseshoe Pitchers' News Digest, published monthly, P.O. Box 1606, Aurora, Illinois 60507.

SHUFFLEBOARD

NATURE AND PURPOSE

The game of shuffleboard may be played by two people (called *singles*) or by four (called *doubles*). The game is played by propelling round wooden discs by means of a cue with a curved end over a hard, smooth surface on which the outlines of a court have been drawn.

The Court.   The court is 52 feet long and 6 feet wide, with a triangular target and scoring diagram at each end (see Figure 17-9). One end of the court is designated as the Head of Court and the other as the Foot of Court.

Equipment.   Each player is provided with a cue stick measuring 6 feet 3 inches maximum; it must have no metal parts touching the playing surface. There are two sets of discs, four in each set, one set painted red and one black. The discs must be 6 inches in diameter, weigh not less than 11½ ounces nor more than 15 ounces, with thickness ranging from three-quarters of an inch to one inch. Shuffleboard is easily adaptable to many types of surfaces; shuffleboard courts can be painted on the floors of classrooms, gymnasiums, hallways, sidewalks, or other concrete surfaces found at schools. Shuffleboard sets can be obtained from most physical education and recreation equipment companies at a very reasonable price. Discs that accompany the cues are usually made of a composition material that can be used both indoors and outdoors and are very durable.

Choice of discs is made by playing one disc to the farthest deadline, with player of the disc closest to it receiving his choice of colors. In starting a game, the owner of red discs shoots first, followed by black, then by red, alternating thus until all discs are shot. In singles play, after all discs are shot from Head of Court, the players walk to Foot of Court and, after tallying the score, continue play toward Head of Court with owner of black discs shooting first.

In doubles, with two players at each end of the court, a game is started with the owners of red discs shooting all discs first from the Head of Court, followed by owners of black discs. Owners of red discs again shoot first from the Foot of Court, followed by black. On the second round, owners of black discs shoot first at each end of the court, followed by owners of red discs. Playing of all discs from one end of the court and back constitutes a round, so in doubles play the lead in starting to shoot changes after each round, while in singles play the lead changes after each half round.

BASIC RULES[1]

Scoring.   The scoring area contains one 10-point area, two 8-point areas, two 7-point areas, and one 10-off area. To count, a disc must lie entirely within one of the scoring areas with no part of the disc touching any side line, except that the separation line in the 10-off area is not considered. A game may end at 50, 75, or 100 points. Play continues until all discs have been shot, even if game point has been reached during the early part of a half round. In doubles, if a tie score results at game point or over, two additional rounds shall be played. If the score is still tied, play continues as outlined. In singles, one additional round shall be played to determine the winner in a tie game. In match play, the winner shall be determined on the basis of the best two out of three games.

Penalties.   From five to ten points shall be deducted from the score of players for certain infractions of playing rules. Five points shall be deducted for the following infractions:

1. All discs not in respective half of 10-off area when ready to shoot.
2. Discs not played from respective half of 10-off area (red played from right side, black from left).
3. Players stepping on or over baseline in making their shot.
4. Players not remaining seated when play is toward their end of the court.

[1]The American Association for Health, Physical Education, and Recreation, *Official NAGWS Recreational Games and Volleyball Guide.* Washington, D.C.: AHHPER.

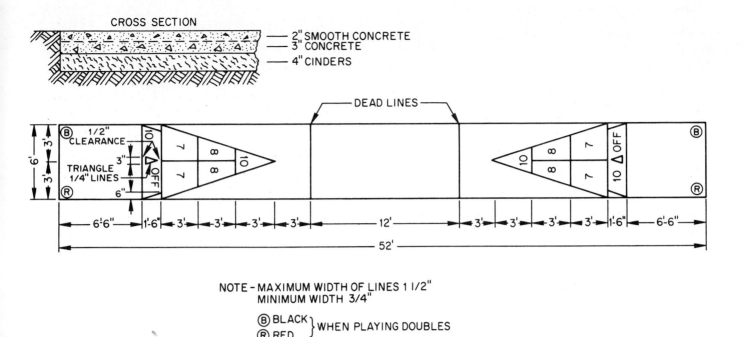

CROSS SECTION

— 2" SMOOTH CONCRETE
— 3" CONCRETE
— 4" CINDERS

NOTE – MAXIMUM WIDTH OF LINES 1 1/2"
MINIMUM WIDTH 3/4"

Ⓑ BLACK
Ⓡ RED } WHEN PLAYING DOUBLES

FIGURE 17-9. Shuffleboard court.

5. Interfering in any way with opponent while he is making a play.
6. Players touching live discs at any time.

Ten points shall be deducted for the following infractions:

1. Player making hesitation or hook shot.
2. Player making remarks to disconcert opponent.
3. Making any remarks which may be construed as coaching a partner while making a play.
4. Player shooting before opponent's disc has come to rest.

Playing Rules. A disc returning or remaining on the court after having struck any object other than a live disc shall be called a *dead disc* and shall be removed from the court before the play is resumed. If a dead disc strikes a live disc, that half round shall be replayed. A disc that stops in the area between farthest deadline and starting point shall be considered dead and be removed from the court. Any disc that stops just beyond the farthest baseline shall be moved a distance at least eight inches from baseline. Any disc stopping more than halfway over sidelines, or which rests or leans on the edge, shall be removed from the court.

SKILLS AND TECHNIQUES

The skills involved in playing shuffleboard are very few; however, it is a game requiring the development of touch, to know just how hard to push the disc. It is extremely important for the shuffleboard player to "read" the surface on which the game is being played, since the disc will react with different speeds on different surfaces. In executing the push or forward thrust of the cue, it is important to place the cue against the disc before the pushing action begins. Do not jab at the disc, because this will result in a loss of power. A few important points must be remembered about the push.

Learning Cues

1. The handle is held at the end, weight forward on the feet, body slightly leaning forward (Figure 17-10).
2. Push by straightening out the elbow, the opposite foot steps forward, the arm straightens and follows through toward the target, knees will be flexed.

Practice Suggestions

1. Have students line up in squads, one behind the other. Place one student at the end of the court to retrieve discs and push them back to students awaiting their turn. Rotate students from pushing position to retrieving position.
2. Place discs in different scoring areas, and allow the students to practice pushing the disc out of the area with their own disc.
3. Practice shooting for position. Develop "feel" for the push by attempting to push the disc to various boxes. Begin with no competition and then add competition.

TERMINOLOGY

Cue Stick used to propel discs toward the target.
Dead disc A disc that returns to or remains on the court after having struck an object other than another "live

FIGURE 17-10. Execution of the push in shuffleboard.

disc." Disc is also dead that stops between farthest deadline and starting line.

Foot of court That end of the court opposite the head.

Head of court That end of the court from which play starts to begin a match.

Hesitation shot This is illegal—the forward motion of the disc must be continuous.

Round The playing of all discs from one end of court and back constitutes a round.

SELECTED REFERENCES

American Association for Health, Physical Education, and Recreation. *Official N.A.G.W.S. Recreational Games and Volleyball Guide* (current ed.). Washington, D.C.: AAHPER.

National Shuffleboard Association. *Official Rules.* Kissimee, Fla.: NSA, Inc., 1965.

TABLE TENNIS

NATURE AND PURPOSE

Table tennis (popularly called Ping-Pong) may be played by two or four people. Equipment consists of a table with a smooth playing surface, a net, balls, and rackets (also called paddles). The game may be played by both old and young and seems destined to remain one of our most popular recreational activities.

EQUIPMENT

The equipment necessary to play table tennis is of simple construction and relatively inexpensive. School physical education programs can have rackets and tables made by the industrial arts department at a very nominal fee. Many physical education and recreation supply companies sell table tennis sets and balls for a very reasonable price. Obviously, as the competitive level and skill increases, more expensive rackets may be wanted.

Table. The table is 9 feet long and 5 feet wide, with a height of 30 inches from floor to top surface (Figure 17-11). Most tables are made of ¾ inch pressed wood or good quality plywood, but other materials can be used. Tables that come in halves and have a collapsible undercarriage are easy to store. Some are constructed so that one half can be folded up into a backdrop and used for a rebound wall in practicing various strokes.

Net. The playing surface is divided by a net secured in the center and parallel to the end lines. The top edge of the net is 6 inches above the playing surface.

Balls. The balls are constructed of celluloid, hollow, 4½ to 4¾ inches in circumference, and weigh between 37 and 41 grains. A good ball should be perfectly round and without wobble when spinning. The United States Table Tennis Association seal of approval on a ball is a good indication of quality.

Racket. A variety of rackets (paddles) can be purchased at most sporting goods stores. Some have grips that will fit your hand size. All have a rubber or sponge covering of some type that covers the playing surface. A covering of inverted sponge is most used and is recommended for all levels of players.

BASIC RULES

Singles Game

Scoring. The winner of a match shall be the player who first scores 21 points, unless both players have 20 points, in which case the winner must gain a two-point lead in order to win. The choice of ends and service at the start of the game shall be decided by toss.

Change of Ends and Service. A game is started with the server making five consecutive services. The receiver follows with five services, each player alternating in this fashion for the duration of the game, unless the score becomes 20-all, in which case the receiver shall make one serve, followed by the original server with one serve, then the receiver, and so on, until a winner is declared. Where the match consists of only one game, or in the deciding game of a match, the players shall change ends at the score of 10. The player who started at one end of the table in one game shall start at the other end in the immediately subsequent game.

The Service. The service shall be delivered by releasing the ball, without imparting any spin upon release, and striking it with the paddle outside the boundary of the court near server's end. Finger spins and rubbing the ball against the racket face are illegal. Any spin imparted to the ball must come from action of the racket upon impact with the ball. The ball shall be struck so that it first drops into server's court and then into receiver's court by passing directly over or around the net.

control, is prevented from making a serve or a return.

Either player shall lose the point:

1. If he fails to make a good service, unless a let is declared.
2. If a good service or a good return is made by his opponent and he fails to make a good return.
3. If racket, or any part of player or clothing, touches the net or its supports while the ball is in play.
4. If the player moves the table in any way while playing the ball.
5. If a player's free hand touches the table while the ball is in play.
6. If, at any time, he volleys the ball. (A volley consists of hitting the ball before it has bounced.)

Doubles Game

The rules for singles games apply to doubles except as indicated below.

Service Line. A one-eighth inch white line drawn down the center of the table parallel to the side lines is called the service line.

A Good Service. The ball must touch first the server's right-half court or the center line on his side

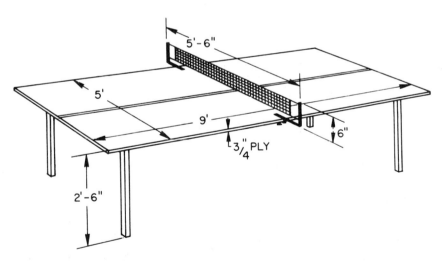

FIGURE 17-11. Table tennis table.

A Good Return. A ball having been served or returned in play shall be struck by the player so that it passes directly over or around the net and lands in opponent's court; provided that if the ball, during play, returns of its own impetus over or around the net, it may be played the same as a returned ball.

Let Ball. The served ball shall be a let if it touches the net or its supports, and later lands in receiver's court. A let shall also be declared when a serve is made before the receiver is ready, unless the receiver makes an effort to strike the ball. It is a let if either player, because of conditions not under his

of the net, and then, passing directly over or around the net, touch the receiver's right-half court or the center line on his side of the net.

Choice of Order of Play. The pair who has the right to serve the first five services in any game shall decide which partner shall do so, and the opposing pair shall then decide similarly which shall first be the receiver.

Order of Service. Each server shall serve for five points. At the end of each term of service, the one who was receiving becomes the server, and the partner of the previous server becomes the receiver.

This sequence of the receiver becoming the server and the partner of the previous server becoming the receiver continues until the end of the game or the score of 20-all. At the score of 20-all, the sequence of serving and receiving shall continue uninterrupted except that each player shall serve only one point in turn, and the serve alternates after each point until the end of the game.

Order of Play. The server shall first make a good service, the receiver shall then make a good return, the partner of the server shall then make a good return, the partner of the receiver shall then make a good return, the server shall then make a good return, and thereafter each player alternately in that sequence shall make a good return.

SKILLS AND TECHNIQUES

Because of the close similarity to tennis, the basic fundamentals regarding stroking the ball may be applied in some instances. Table tennis requires much concentration and excellent reactions. The discussion in this section will deal with some of the beginning skills needed to get the player started.

Grip

The most common grip used by a majority of players is the "shake hands" grip used in tennis (Figure 17-12). The great Chinese players use a grip known as the penholder grip (Figure 17-13). However this style of grip is usually best only for an attacking type of game.

Learning Cues

1. With the racket perpendicular to the floor, grasp the racket as you would shake hands.
2. The last three fingers wrap around the handle

and the forefinger lies close to the lower edge of the racket face.

Strokes

The forehand and backhand push shot should be mastered by the beginner before playing the game. For the right-handed player, the forehand stroke should be used when the ball approaches from the right, and the backhand when the ball approaches from the left. Preparatory to any stroke the player should assume a good athletic stance in a ready position (Figure 17-14). The knees are bent, weight is evenly distributed on the forward half of the foot, arms are in front of the body, elbows bent, racket held parallel to the ground.

When executing both shots, it is important to remember that the ball is directed over the net by a pushing action, not a hitting action. Variations in arm movement and wrist movement will allow spin to be imparted to the ball.

Learning Cues—Backhand Push

1. The ball is played in front of the body at the point of highest contact.
2. As the ball approaches, the right arm is drawn back by pivoting at the elbow, the right shoulder turns and is pointed toward the table.
3. Push the racket forward toward the ball, extend arm in a horizontal plane.
4. Body weight transfers from back foot to forward foot throughout the stroke.

Learning Cues—Forehand Push

1. As the ball approaches, the racket is drawn back; shoulders turn so the left shoulder is pointed toward the table.
2. Push the racket forward toward the ball, arm extended in a horizontal plane; shoulders return.

FIGURE 17-12. The standard "shake hands" grip.

FIGURE 17-13. The penholder grip.

FIGURE 17-14. A good ready position.

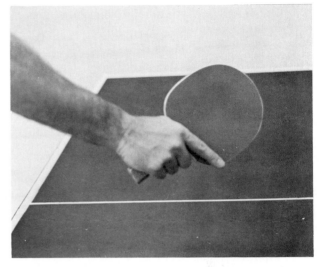

FIGURE 17-15. Position of hand in backhand push.

FIGURE 17-16. Position of body during backhand push shot.

FIGURE 17-17. Position during forehand push shot. Note that left shoulder is pointing toward table.

3. Body weight transfers from the back foot to the forward foot throughout the stroke.

Serves

It is important for the beginner to remember that the ball may not be served from the palm of the hand. In addition the ball must contact the server's side of the table first.

Learning Cues—Topspin Serve (Forehand Side)

1. The body assumes a stance three quarters sideways to the table, the ball rests on the fingers of the left hand, racket assumes position of a forehand push shot.

FIGURE 17-18.   Ready to serve on the forehand side.

FIGURE 17-19.   A folding table can be used as a rebound wall for practice.

2. The ball is tossed upward, the racket face (slightly closed) comes forward and continues forward after the contact.
3. As the racket face follows through it rolls over the top of the ball thus imparting topspin to the ball.

The mechanics for a backhand topspin serve will be essentially the same except the serve is initiated from the left side for the right-handed player.

Practice Suggestions

1. If a folding table is available, fold up one side perpendicularly, so that it can be used as a rebound wall to practice strokes and serves (Figure 17-19).
2. Practice the toss (6 to 8 inches high) needed for the serve, concentrating on a smooth, rhythmical toss.
3. Practice against a wall, either letting the ball bounce once or volleying the ball as long as possible. As a variation, mark a target (circle or square) on the wall and try to hit the ball into the target.
4. To develop a feel for the racket and ball, continuously tap the ball upward off the face of the racket, then downward, while walking. Note the importance of concentration as this drill is executed.

When practicing the strokes and the serve, equal amounts of time must be given to developing skills on the backhand side as well as the forehand side.

TERMINOLOGY

Ace   A service which completely eludes the receiver.
Advantage (ad)   Next point made after a deuce score. It is

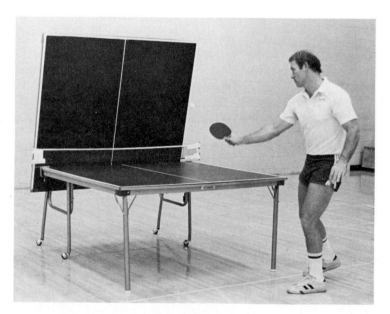

"advantage out" if the receiver wins it and "advantage in" if the server wins. The player wins the match who first wins a point after gaining "advantage."

All Term used to denote an equal score, e.g., 20-all.

Backhand Stroke frequently used by right-handed player when returning a ball hit to his left. The paddle is held so that the back of the hand faces the ball; the ball is usually hit with side of paddle opposite the side used in the forehand.

Backspin A ball hit so that top of ball rotates toward stroker, bottom moving away.

Block shot A half-volley.

Dead ball A ball is dead if a let is called, if the ball bounces twice on the table, and at the conclusion of a point or rally.

Deuce When the score is even at 20-all. To win, a player must score two consecutive points.

Drop shot A shot played so softly that it dies before opponent can reach it, or places him at a disadvantage if he does play it.

Finger spin An illegal procedure whereby spin is imparted to the ball by the fingers in serving.

Forehand A stroke or volley made in such a fashion that the palm is the leading part of the movement. Usually hit with the opposite face of the paddle than that used in backhand. In this stroke the left foot of a right-handed player is toward the table.

Let Means "play the point over" and occurs when the ball strikes the top of net and falls into correct service court, also if a ball breaks or if a player is interfered with by an official or spectator.

Mixed doubles Doubles game in which each team has one man and one woman player.

Push shot A ball struck with a pushing motion of the paddle near the top of the bounce so that no spin is placed on the ball.

Service court In singles, the entire table area on the receiver's side, 5 by 4½ feet. In doubles, the table is divided by a center line so each service court is 4½ by 2½ feet.

Slice A stroke in which the ball is stroked late so that it tends to spin in a direction away from the paddle.

Topspin A ball stroked so that the top spins forward in the direction of flight. Is the opposite of backspin or underspin.

Volley Illegal stroking of ball while it is in the air and before it has touched the table.

SELECTED REFERENCES

American Association for Health, Physical Education, and Recreation. *Official N.A.G.W.S. Individual Sports Guide* (current ed.). Washington, D.C.: AAHPER.

DEWITT, R.T., and KEN DUGAN. *Teaching Individual and Team Sports,* 2nd ed. Englewood Cliffs, N.J.: Prentice-Hall, Inc., 1972.

MILES, DICK. *Sports Illustrated Table Tennis.* Philadelphia: J.B. Lippincott Co., 1974.

SKLORZ, MARTIN. *Table Tennis.* Yorkshire, England: E. P. Publishing Limited, 1973.

VARNER, MARGARET, and J. RUFFORD HARRISON. *Table Tennis.* Dubuque, Iowa: Wm. C. Brown Company, Publishers, 1968.

United States Table Tennis Association. *Table Tennis for You* (current ed.). Philadelphia: USTTA.

SOCCER

THIS CHAPTER WILL ENABLE YOU TO:

‣ Identify and put into practice the rules governing the game.
‣ Practice and then execute the basic skills including kicking, passing, trapping, heading, tackling, the throw-in, and goalkeeping.
‣ Discuss and employ basic offensive and defensive strategy and tactics.
‣ Identify and discuss the nature of the game including player responsibilities, field markings, and player positioning.
‣ Identify and use basic terminology associated with the game.

NATURE AND PURPOSE

Soccer is played by eleven players from each team. The game starts at midfield with a free kick called the kick-off as each team is in its own half of the field. The offensive objectives are to maintain possession of the ball, keep the ball wide until near the goal, and then get the ball in front of the opponent's goal where a player can propel it between the uprights, beneath the cross bar and completely across the goal line for a score. The ball may be propelled with any part of the body except the hands and arms; however, the foot, body, and head are the main parts of the body used.

The defense's main objectives are to contain the opponents and the ball, forcing excessive passes, mark (guard) opponents in scoring position, tackle the opponent, taking the ball away whenever possible, funnel the ball to the middle of the field toward their own goal, and concentrate in front of their goal when the ball is in scoring position. The goalkeeper provides great assistance to the defense by being allowed to use the hands to contact the ball; and he also attempts to clear the ball away from the scoring area by throwing, punting, or drop-kicking it.

Systems of play are comprised of forwards, halfbacks, and fullbacks. The forwards' primary contribution to the system is scoring. The halfbacks support the offense and are the first line of defense. The fullbacks support the offense and are the last line of defense. The fullback's primary objective is defending against the opponents' attack. Systems are numbered from the fullbacks forward (example 4-3-3) depending upon the number of players comprising each of the three lines.

The game is continuous with no timeouts allowed and time is stopped only for an injury, a temporary suspension of play by the official, the end of a period, or a score.

The players use basic skills of kicking, trapping, dribbling, heading, tackling, and throwing (where allowable) to propel or control the ball. The game is low scoring due to the difficulty of executing the skills, plus the nature of some rules.

The game requires constant adjustments by all the players and calls for short sprinting plus slower jogging. Good physical conditioning is necessary. The constant activity, use of the big muscle groups, large numbers competing, and low equipment expense make the game highly suitable for competitors of all ages.

FIELD OF PLAY

A regulation field measures 100 to 120 yards in length and 65 to 75 yards in width (Figure 18-1). The dimensions and areas can easily be modified to suit the number, age, and sex of the participants. The field can be made longer or shorter and various grids can be applied (as discussed later on) to provide practice areas for modified games.

In the list below, the numbers correspond to the numbers in the diagram of Figure 18-1.

1. *End Line.* When the ball goes out of play over this line it is put in play with either (a) goal kick (offense last touched the ball) or (b) corner kick (defense last touched the ball).
2. *Goal Area*—the area where the ball is placed for the defending team to take a goal kick. It is placed on the front line of the area in that half field in which the ball went out of play.
3. *Penalty Area.* Restriction area where (a) the goalie is allowed to play the ball with the hands; (b) the offensive team has to stay out of when the defending team is taking a goal kick; (c) on the goal kick the ball must be kicked out of this

area for the ball to be legally in play; (d) if a foul committed in this area by the defending team results in a *direct free kick*, then a *penalty kick* is awarded to the team fouled.

4. *Side or Touch Line.* A ball going out of bounds over this line is put in play with a throw-in by the opposite team which last touched the ball.

5. *Penalty Kick Mark*—the spot where the ball is placed when a penalty kick results.

6. *Penalty Kick Arc.* This arc is a ten-yard radius from the ball, and players from both teams must stay behind it. On a penalty kick both teams (except one offensive player and the goalie) must be out of the penalty area and at least ten yards from the ball.

7. *Center, Mid, or Halfway Line.* This line (a) insures that both teams are in their own half of the field on the kickoff, and (b) is used to help regulate the offside rule.

8. *Center Circle*—a ten-yard radius circle to restrict players of the defending team on the kickoff. They must stay out of the circle until the ball is contacted.

9. *Corner Arc.* One yard from each corner there is a corner arc. The ball is placed on this arc when the offensive team is taking a corner kick.

10. *Goal Line*—the line between the uprights of the goal. When the whole ball crosses it below the crossbar either on the ground or in the air a goal results.

FIGURE 18-1. Regulation soccer field and markings. (For further explanation of numbers, see text.)

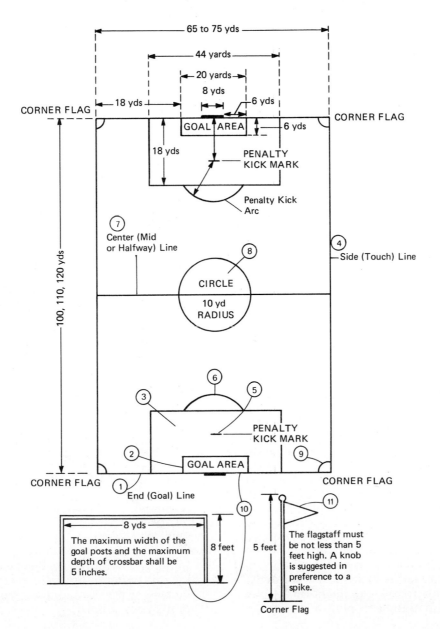

11. *Corner Flag.* The flag is at least 5 feet high and located in each of the four corners to assist in locating the boundary lines.

EQUIPMENT

The only equipment absolutely necessary for playing soccer are a ball and two goals. There are many makes and price ranges of soccer balls manufactured today. The molded ball with a rubber bladder, nylon wound carcass, and compressed waterproof leather or synthetic panels varies in price from $15 to $60. Goals can be purchased for around $200 to $860 a pair, or may be constructed of 2 × 4's or pipe. Soccer shoes ($10 to $63), shin guards ($2.50 to $6.50 a pair) and nets for the goals ($90 to $165 a pair) may be added when progressing from physical education class to intramural to interscholastic competition levels. Gym shoes may be substituted for soccer shoes, thick magazines for shin guards, and chain link fencing for nets. The fact that the game can be played by a large number of players at very little expense makes it particularly appealing. Competition apparel is not a major factor. Colored jersey vests and game jerseys are inexpensive. For pants, gym shorts, sweatsuits, or game trunks may be worn.

BASIC RULES

Kickoff. At the beginning of the game, choice of ends and the kickoff are decided by the toss of a coin. The ball is placed in the center of the field on the half-way line and the team kicking off plays the ball forward from the line. The player usually kicks the stationary ball legally (one circumference of the ball) forward to his teammate attempting to maintain control of the ball. All players from both teams are in their own half of the field with the defending team at least ten yards from the ball. A goal cannot be scored from the kickoff.

Fouls. Fouls and misconduct committed during the course of play result in a free kick to the offended team. The severe infractions, which are most often injurious, result in a direct free kick, meaning a goal can be scored directly from that kick. A direct free kick foul occurring in the penalty area and against the defending team results in a penalty kick, the most severe infraction. Less severe infractions result in an indirect free kick, meaning someone else must contact the ball following the kick before a goal can be scored. When making a free kick, the opponents must be ten yards from the ball, unless standing on their own goal line between the uprights, until the ball is kicked. The ball must be stationary on the free kick, must travel the circumference of the ball to be in play, and may not be re-contacted by the kicker until someone else touches it.

Direct Free Kick Offenses

Offenses for which a direct free kick is awarded are:

1. Handling the ball: intentionally contacting the ball with the hands or arms. This includes the goalie when outside the penalty area.
2. Holding an opponent with the hands or arms.
3. Pushing an opponent; includes the hands or arms.
4. Striking or attempting to strike an opponent; the goalie is also not allowed to use the ball to strike a player.
5. Jumping at an opponent.
6. Kicking or attempting to kick an opponent.
7. Tripping or attempting to trip an opponent.
8. Using the knee on an opponent.
9. Charging an opponent violently or dangerously; includes the goalie in the penalty area or from the rear unless being obstructed.

All direct kicks awarded to the attacking team in the penalty area are penalty kicks.

Indirect Free Kick Offenses

Offenses for which an indirect free kick is awarded are:

1. A player playing the ball a second time before it is played by another player at the kickoff, on a throw-in, on a free kick, on a corner kick, or on a goal kick (if the ball has passed outside the penalty area).
2. A goalkeeper carrying the ball more than four steps or the goalie delays getting rid of the ball.
3. A substitution or re-substitution being made without reporting to the referee, or a substitute replacing the goalie not informing the referee and then handling the ball in the penalty area.
4. Persons other than the players entering the field of play without the referee's permission.
5. Dissenting by word or action with a referee's decision.
6. Ungentlemanly behavior. For persistent infringement of the rules, a warning, or expulsion may follow.
7. Dangerous play by raising the foot too high or head too low while attempting to play the ball, thus endangering a player.
8. Resuming play after a player has been ordered off the field.
9. Offside.
10. Charging illegally (not violent or dangerous).
11. Interfering with the goalkeeper or impeding him in any manner until he releases the ball, or kicking or attempting to kick the ball when it is in his possession.

12. Obstruction other than holding.
13. Player leaving the field of play during the progress of the game without the consent of the referee.

Physical Contact. Body contact is allowed provided it is legal. A legal charge consists of a gentle nudge (not violent or dangerous), shoulder to shoulder, in an upright position, at least one foot contacting the ground, the arms close to the sides of the body, and playing the ball at the exact moment (Figure 18-2). The body may not be used as an obstacle to shield an opponent from getting to the ball unless actually playing the ball at that moment. This is obstruction (Figure 18-3), and allows for an opponent legally to charge the person obstructing, provided the contact is not violent or dangerous.

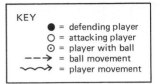

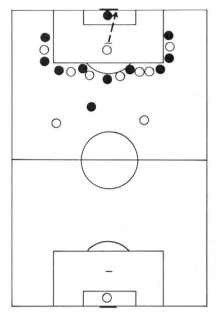

FIGURE 18-4. Penalty kick.

FIGURE 18-2. Legal charge.

FIGURE 18-3. Legal obstruction. Note use of the body to protect the ball while playing it.

Penalty Kick. The penalty kick (Figure 18-4) is taken from any spot on the penalty mark and all players except the kicker and the goalkeeper must be outside the penalty area. The goalkeeper must stand, without moving his feet, on the goal line between the goal posts until the ball is kicked. For any infringement by the defending team the kick is retaken, if a goal does not result. On an infringement by the attacking team, other than the player making the kick, the kick shall be retaken if a goal results. An infringement by the player making the kick results in an indirect free kick by the opposing team at the spot where the violation occurred.

Goal Kick. The ball is in play as long as it is not totally across the boundary lines (goal line or side line), either on the ground or in the air. When it goes out of bounds over the goal line, the ball is put in play either with a goal kick (last touched by the attacking team) or a corner kick (last touched by the defending team). A ball put out of bounds over the side line by a player is put in play with a throw-in by the opponents.

On the goal kick the ball is placed on the front line of the goal area in that half of the field nearest to where it crossed the goal line (Figure 18-5). Any player on the team may take the kick. It is kicked from the ground. The opposing players remain outside the penalty area until the ball is kicked, and the ball must travel beyond the penalty area for it to be in play. The kick is retaken for any infringement.

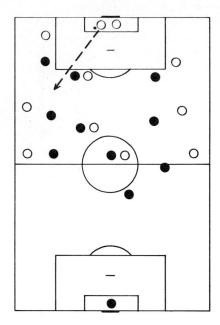

FIGURE 18-5. Goal kick.

Corner Kick. The corner kick is taken by the offense from the arc in that half of the field nearest to where the ball crossed the goal line. A goal may be scored directly from the corner kick (Figure 18-6).

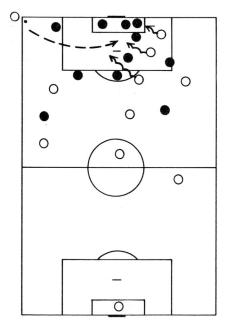

FIGURE 18-6. Corner kick.

Throw-In. The throw-in is taken from where it went out of play. It is thrown equally with both hands on the side of the ball from a point behind the head and delivered directly over the head. Both feet must remain on the ground during the throw and be either on the side line or outside the field of play.

Offside. The players must be concerned with their position in reference to the ball as play progresses. An offside infraction is called if a player is nearer his opponent's goal line than the ball at the moment the ball is played, with limited exceptions. The offside rule is for assisting the defending team so that the offense will not be able to have players continually lurking in front of the goal. This would lead to an unskilled game with team strategy consisting of no more than long, uncontrolled kicks from one end of the field to the other, and back again.

A player nearer his opponent's goal line than the ball at the moment the ball is played is considered *offside* unless: 1) he is in his own half of the field of play (Figure 18-7); 2) there are two opponents nearer

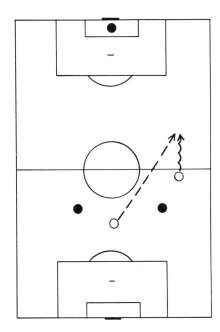

FIGURE 18-7. Player is in own half of field—*Not Offside.*

their own goal line than he (Figure 18-8A); 3) the ball last touched an opponent; 4) he received the ball directly from a dropped ball by the referee, a goal kick, a corner kick, or a throw-in. A player in an offside position does not have to be penalized except if he is gaining an advantage by his position, seeking to gain an advantage, or interfering with an opponent. Once offside, the only way for a player to put himself onside again is if: 1) an opponent next contacts the ball; 2) he is behind the ball when it is next contacted by his teammates; or 3) there are two opponents near their goal when he is in an advanced position of the ball, and the ball is played to him by his teammates. The key factor for offside is always the position of the player in relation to the ball at the moment the ball is contacted.

Dropped Ball. Temporary stopping of play while the ball is still playable results in the game

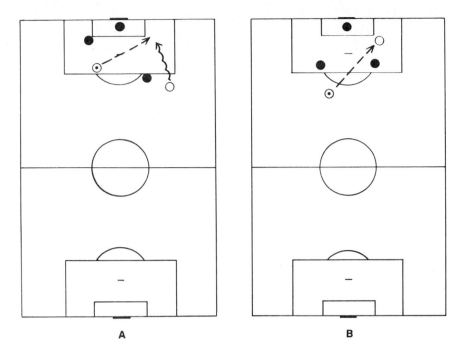

FIGURE 18-8. (A) Two opponents are nearer their own goal line at the moment the ball was played, *plus* the receiver was behind the ball at that moment—*Not Offside.* (B) Two opponents *not* near their goal line—*Offside.*

restarting with a dropped ball. Two opponents face each other and the referee standing between them drops the ball to the ground for either to contact. It is dropped where the ball was when play stopped unless in the penalty area. Then it is brought to the nearest point outside the penalty area and dropped. Common reasons for a dropped ball occurring are: 1) simultaneous contact by opponents causing the ball to go out of bounds, 2) temporary stopping for injury, 3) the ball becoming deflated, or 4) simultaneous fouls by both teams.

Goalkeeper. When the ball nears the scoring area, the goalkeeper enjoys certain privileges not granted to other players while in the penalty area. He may: use his hands and arms to stop a ball from scoring; take four steps with the ball in his possession; punt, throw, or drop-kick the ball; and he is free from interference by opponents while in possession of the ball. He loses these privileges when outside the penalty area.

Scoring. A goal is scored when the whole of the ball passes over the goal line, between the goalposts, and under the crossbar, provided it has not been thrown, propelled by hand or arm, or carried by a player of the attacking side (Figure 18-9). If a member of the defending team, other than the goalie, deliberately deflects the ball with his hand or arm attempting to stop a goal, it should be scored a goal if it crosses the goal line between the uprights. Goals may also be scored on "direct free kicks," penalty kicks, and corner kicks. A goal counts one point for the team scoring the goal. After a goal is

scored, a kickoff is made at the center of the field by the team scored against. Teams change ends after each regular and extra period.

Time and Players. The length of the game, number of substitutes, and when substitutes are allowed to enter the game are rules that vary depending upon the age and ability levels of the players. The organizations governing competition provide rule guides; however, there are only minor differences in them. Men and women are playing by

FIGURE 18-9. Scoring a goal.

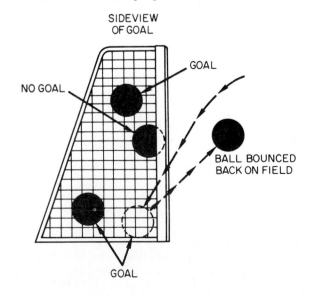

basically the same rules regardless of the organization, and quite often at an early age (6 to 11), the game is played co-ed.

SUGGESTIONS FOR MODIFIED PRACTICE GAMES AND AREAS

Figure 18-10 is a grid model showing various ways of modifying a regulation field to provide areas of different sizes. The larger the area the more competitors possible. Examples are 2 on 1, 3 on 1, 2 on 2, 3 on 2, 3 on 3, 4 on 2, 4 on 3, 4 on 4, 5 on 3, 5 on 4, 5 on 5, etc. A modified goal, objective, or soccer strategy and tactic are used in the games. Cones, flags, or other players are used as two-sided goals. These may be placed opposite each other on the end line of the area, slightly on the field with space behind them or in the middle of the area. One, two, or more goals may be used.

Combining grids allows for actual games with modified field sizes. An example is using grid D, E, and F together, placing a goal on the side line of the actual field and centered in the middle of the area.

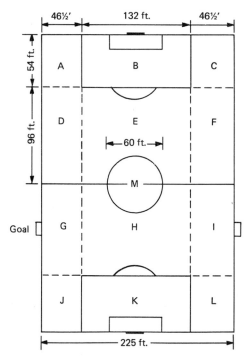

FIGURE 18-10.   Grid for setting up practice areas.

The size of the field is now 96 feet by 225 feet, where an actual game might consist of 6 on 6, 7 on 7, or 8 on 8. Two games may be played at once if grids G, H, and I are used similarly.

Combining areas A through F provides an even wider field, whereby more players can compete in an across field game, as in the foregoing example. The same area (A–F) is used to practice offense

(attackers and midfielders) versus defense (goalie, fullbacks, and midfielders) playing half field as on the regulation field. Scoring objectives are: the offense gets one point for scoring a goal, hitting the goal posts, or causing the goalkeeper to field the ball. Defense scores one point if they get the ball past the halfway line under their control.

Here are some other suggestions for playing games within a restricted area: a given number of consecutive passes without losing the ball receives a point; allow only one contact per player; allow no more than two contacts per player; after receiving the ball the player must out-dribble an opponent; the receiver of a pass must take the ball (pass or dribble) away from his own goal before it next goes forward; every other pass must be in the air; no pass above knee height. The possible modifications are endless.

SUGGESTED LEARNING SEQUENCE

Beginning Level

A. Stretching and Running
B. Basic Rules
C. Fundamental Skills
    1. Kicking
       a. Inside of foot push pass
       b. Instep
    2. Trapping (Receiving)
       a. Sole of the foot
       b. Inside of the foot
       c. Chest
    3. Dribbling
       a. Inside of the foot
       b. Outside of the foot
    4. Heading: Power standing
    5. Tackling: Front
    6. Throw-In: Standing
    7. Goalkeeping
       a. Catch—roll or bounce
       b. Catch—waist or chest
       c. Catch—head or above
       d. Punt
D. Strategies
    1. Tactics
       a. Possession
       b. Space—receiving ball
    2. Group
       a. Superiority around ball
    3. Team
       a. Communication
       b. Functional training combining 2 or more lines
E. Principles
    1. Attacking
       a. Depth/Support
       b. Width
       c. Penetration

2. Defending
   a. Depth/Support
   b. Width
   c. Balance
   d. Delay
F. Systems
   1. W formation (2-3-5)
   2. M-W formation (2-3-5)
   3. Defensive style—zone
   4. Offensive style—static positioning, long pass and short pass
G. Restarts
   1. Corner kick
   2. Goal kick
   3. Throw-in
   4. Kickoff

Intermediate Level

A. Partner Stretching and Interval Training
B. Review Beginning Unit
C. Fundamental Skills
   1. Kicking
      a. Outside of foot
      b. Lofting the ball
   2. Trapping (Receiving)
      a. Outside of foot
   3. Dribbling
      a. Screening
      b. Sole of the foot
   4. Heading: Power jumping
   5. Tackling: Side
   6. Throw-In: Running
   7. Goalkeeping
      a. Catch—fall to side
      b. Tip
      c. Throw—overhand
D. Strategies
   1. Review Beginning Unit
   2. Tactics
      a. Space-creating
   3. Group
      a. Space-restricting
      b. Tempo
   4. Team
      a. Rhythm
      b. Functional training involving tactical passing restrictions
E. Principles
   1. Attacking
      a. Mobility
      b. Improvisation
   2. Defending
      a. Concentration
      b. Control
F. Systems
   1. 3-3-4
   2. 4-3-3
   3. Defensive style—diagonal and man to man
   4. Offensive style—dribbling and fast/slow

G. Restarts
   1. Indirect free kicks
   2. Direct free kicks
   3. Defensive wall

SKILLS AND TECHNIQUES

The fundamentals of soccer are dribbling, heading, trapping, kicking (shoot or pass), tackling, throwing, and goalkeeping. Because the game of soccer is primarily a kicking and trapping game, it is essential that players master the technique of controlling the ball without use of the hands or arms. In observing good soccer players, one sees that they control the ball and keep it reasonably close to their bodies when passing or advancing it down the field. The ball is kept close to the ground and not kicked into the air where it is difficult for the player to keep possession and control.

When learning or teaching each of the skills, the following factors are important for understanding problems—their causes and corrections:

1. Alignment to Ball
   a. Position the body early in preparation to contact the ball.
   b. Position at the best spot in the line of flight for making initial contact.
   c. Prepare the contact surface at the proper angle required for optimum execution.
   d. Be as stable as possible.
2. Base
   a. Position the foot/feet for optimum stability.
   b. Position the foot/feet so that the contact surface can be at the proper angle for execution.
   c. Position the grounded foot/feet in the direction the ball is to be propelled.
3. Whole Body Position
   a. Position of specifically the feet, knees, hips, shoulders, arms, and head before, during, and after ball contact.
4. Power/Absorption
   Power
   a. Ball contact surface—speed of ball.
   b. Joints providing force—range of motion and speed of motion.
   c. Proper line of force (see #5).
   d. Total body parts alignment as they relate to the desired trajectory.
   e. Follow-through (see #7).
   Absorption
   a. Ball contact surface—speed of ball.
   b. Joints involved in receiving force.
   c. Proper line of receiving force (see #5).
   d. Total body parts alignment as they relate to receiving the trajectory and force of the ball.
   e. Direction (away from ball) of body parts used for absorbing the ball.
5. Line of Giving/Receiving Force

a. Correct direction of all body parts related to the desired trajectory, rotation (spin), and final destination of the ball.

6. Ball Contact
   a. Surface and angle of body part used to make contact.
   b. Exact spot on the ball to contact for accomplishing the desired end result.
   c. Alignment to ball (see #1).
   d. Base (see #2).
   e. Whole body (see #3).
   f. Power/absorption (see #4).
   g. Line of giving/receiving force (see #5).

7. Follow-Through
   a. The full range of motion (arc) of the primary power joints used and the exact point at which to stop in order to provide the desired power plus trajectory to the ball.
   b. When receiving the impetus (trapping) of the ball, the primary joints used in recoiling, giving, or absorbing which lead to cushioning the impact—follow-through away from the line of flight of the ball.

Each of these factors will be considered as we discuss the learning cues for performing each specific skill or technique. Either a *B* (Beginning) or *I* (Intermediate) is indicated with each skill or technique to designate the appropriate ability level for presenting that skill. Where suitable, verbal learning cues are given in capital letters.

Kicking (Pass or Shoot)

Kicking is primarily used for passing, shooting, and clearing. The rotation (spin) on the ball denotes proper or improper contact. Different parts of the foot can be used to contact the ball.

Learning Cues—INSIDE OF FOOT PUSH PASS (B)

1. *Alignment to Ball.* Quickly position as near the direct flight (180°) of the ball as possible—ALIGNMENT.
2. *Base.* Place grounded foot toward target, position it to the side of the ball approximately 6″–12″ and either even with or slightly behind the ball depending upon desired flight (on the ground or in the air)—GROUNDED FOOT. Knee slightly flexed.
3. *Whole Body Position.* Contact foot raised with toe pointed out—TOE OUT, feet pointed out—KNEE OUT, and ankle joint locked at 90° angle—ANKLE LOCKED. Draw leg backward from the hip in a straight line. Raise the contact leg to the rear bending the knee until the lower leg is close to parallel with the ground with the inside of the foot facing the ground—COCKED POSITION. Position head directly above ball (to keep ball on ground) or slightly behind the ball (to loft off ground)—HEAD. Hips and shoulders near 90° to approaching ball with slight pivot out as contact leg is drawn

FIGURE 18-11.   Inside of foot push pass. Note legs, ankle, and knee of contact foot.

back. Arms comfortable away from body for balance.
4. *Power.* Power results from the height that the contact foot is raised off the ground, speed that the contact leg is snapped forward to meet the ball, speed of the approaching ball, correct ball/foot contact (hard surface), and the amount of follow-through.
5. *Line of Giving Force.* The foregoing power items applied in the correct line depend upon the approaching flight of the ball and the desired final destination. The correct line involves the body alignment to the ball (as near 180° as possible), direction the grounded foot is pointed, straight linear (180°) cocking of contact leg, and straight linear snap down plus follow-through of that leg—LINE OF FORCE.
6. *Ball Contact.* The correct contact surface is the hard area near the heel of the foot and ankle area with the inside of the foot facing the approaching

ball. The ball is contacted near its midline and either high, middle, or low depending upon the desired speed and trajectory.

7. *Follow-Through.* The height the contact foot and leg are allowed to lift after contact depends upon the desired trajectory and/or force.

Learning Cues—INSTEP KICK (B)

1. *Alignment to Ball.* Same as Inside of Foot Push Pass—ALIGNMENT.
2. *Base.* Same as Inside of Foot Push Pass. The grounded foot is approximately 10 to 18 inches to the side of the ball—GROUNDED FOOT. Knee flexed.
3. *Whole Body Position.* Contact foot lifted with toe pointed down—TOE DOWN, knee rotated in—KNEE IN, and ankle joint locked as near 180° with the lower leg as possible—ANKLE LOCKED. Lift heel

FIGURE 18-12. Instep kick. Note toe, ankle, and knee of contact foot.

upward toward the buttocks—COCKED POSITION. Hip extends and rotates slightly. Position head directly above ball (to keep ball on ground) or slightly behind ball (to loft off ground)—HEAD. Hips and shoulders near 90° to approaching ball with slight pivot out as contact leg is drawn back. Arms comfortably away from body for balance.

4. *Power.* Power results from the height that the contact foot is raised—HEEL RAISED, speed that the contact leg is snapped forward to meet the ball—SPEED, speed of the approaching ball, correct ball/foot contact, and the amount of follow-through.
5. *Line of Giving Force.* The foregoing power items applied in the correct line depend upon the approaching flight of the ball and the desired final destination. The approach angle of the body to the flight of the ball approximates 45°. The grounded foot is pointed toward the intended destination as the remainder of the power joints naturally correct to a direct alignment with the desired line of flight.
6. *Ball Contact.* The correct contact surface is the hard area on the top of the arch. The ball is contacted near the midline and either high, middle, or low depending on the desired speed and trajectory.
7. *Follow-Through.* The height the foot and leg are allowed to lift is dependent upon desired trajectory and/or force.

Learning Cues—LOFTING THE BALL (B)

FIGURE 18-13. Lofting the ball with an instep kick. Note body angle and low contact with ball.

1. *Alignment to Ball.* Same as Inside of Foot Push Pass.
2. *Base.* The grounded foot is approximately 10 to 18 inches to the side of the ball and slightly behind it. Knee flexed.
3. *Whole Body Position.* Same as Instep Kick, except that the head is positioned slightly behind the vertical plane of the ball—HEAD BACK.

4–7. *Power, Line of Giving Force, Ball Contact, Follow-Through:* All same as Instep Kick.

Learning Cues—OUTSIDE OF FOOT KICK (I)

1. *Alignment to Ball.* Same as Inside of Foot Push Pass.
2. *Base.* Same as Instep Kick.
3. *Whole Body Position.* Contact foot lifted with the toe extended down and rotated inward—TOE DOWN AND IN, knee rotated in—KNEE IN, and ankle joint locked—LOCKED ANKLE. Lift heel backward and upward toward the buttocks—COCKED POSITION.
4–5. *Power* and *Line of Giving Force:* Same as Instep Kick.
6. *Ball Contact.* The correct contact area is the hard area on the top outside surface of the foot (Figure 18-14). The ball is contacted near the midline and either high, middle, or low depending upon the desired trajectory and speed.
7. *Follow-Through.* Same as Instep Kick.

FIGURE 18-14. Outside of the foot kick and dribble. Note toe and knee of contact leg.

Trapping

Many surfaces of the body can be used to trap (catch) the ball. Trapping means controlling a ball that is received by a player. There is "immediate" or "deflect" trapping. The first denotes control of the ball right where the player receives it, while the second means redirecting the ball close to the receiver (3 to 4 feet) to avoid an on-rushing opponent. When a body trap is used, a foot trap usually follows in order to "settle" the ball to the ground.

Learning Cues—SOLE OF FOOT TRAP (B)

1. *Alignment to Ball.* Quickly position as near to a direct line (180°) with the path of the ball as possible—ALIGNMENT.
2. *Base.* Body weight is totally supported by the grounded foot as the contact leg is raised with the sole facing the approaching ball.

FIGURE 18-15. Sole of the foot trap.

3. *Whole Body Position.* Ankle of contact foot flexed (90°) with toe higher than heel, toe up, providing a wedge-like surface for ball contact. The contact leg and foot are extended in front of the body, reach out, as the grounded leg provides support with a slight flexion of the knee. Hips and shoulders near 90° to approaching ball. Arms slightly away from body to provide balance and stability.
4. *Absorption.* The ball at contact is cushioned by slightly flexing the knee of the contact leg, slightly flexing the knee of the support leg with a slight pike at the waist which moves the head forward toward the ball—GIVE.
5. *Line of Receiving Force.* The foregoing absorption factors are applied as near a direct line with the path of the ball as possible.
6. *Ball Contact.* The ball is contacted on the top and slightly to the rear by the sole of the foot. The contact foot approximates a 45° angle with the ground providing a wedge between the sole of the foot and the ground.
7. *Follow-Through.* There is negative follow through as the contact leg and foot at impact give in the same direction that the ball is traveling in order to stop the ball.

Learning Cues—INSIDE OF THE FOOT TRAP (B)

1–3. *Alignment to Ball, Base,* and *Whole Body Position:* Same as Inside of Foot Push Pass.
4. *Absorption.* The force of the ball is cushioned by the soft relaxed contact surface, the wedging of the ball against the ground by the contact foot—WEDGE, and the movement of the contact leg away from the path of ball at about the same speed of the approaching ball—GIVE.
5. *Line of Receiving Force.* The foregoing absorption factors applied in the correct line depend upon the path of the ball and the desired final destination for the ball. The correct line involves the body alignment to the ball (as near 180° as possi-

FIGURE 18-16. Inside of the foot trap. Note grounded foot, position of ball, ball/foot contact, and toe and knee position of contact leg.

ble), direction the grounded foot is pointed, angle of the contact foot, and direction the contact leg is moved upon impact.

6. *Ball Contact.* The correct contact surface is the soft area on the inside of the foot near the arch. The ball is contacted on the top and back wedging it to the ground to the rear of the grounded foot for "immediate" control. It is contacted nearer the bottom and back (imparting back spin) in advance of the grounded foot for "deflecting" the ball away from but close to the body.

7. *Follow-Through.* The contact leg lowers the foot on the ball wedging it (immediate control) or the leg and foot make a relaxed, sweeping action "deflecting" the ball away from but close to the body.

Learning Cues—CHEST TRAP (B)

1. *Alignment to Ball.* Quickly position as near to a direct line (180°) with the path of the ball as possible.
2. *Base.* The feet are in a staggered stance with the body weight evenly distributed—STANCE.
3. *Whole Body Position.* The knees are flexed, hips thrust forward bending backwards, shoulders back further than the hips, placing the upper chest near parallel with the ground, the head above the rear foot, and the arms comfortably away from the body for balance—BACKBEND.
4. *Absorption.* Upon ball contact, the knees flex deeper allowing the chest to "give" quickly, absorbing the impact.
5. *Line of Receiving Force.* Same as #4 above. The ball rebounds off the chest in a low upward trajectory, falling to the ground near the feet. Turning the shoulders at impact causes the ball to rebound to the side of the body if desired.

FIGURE 18-17. Chest trap.

6. *Ball Contact.* The contact surface is the high flat part of the chest just below the throat.
7. *Follow-Through.* Following contact and rebound, quickly stand straight and prepare to "settle" the ball to the ground by using one of the foot traps—SETTLE.

Learning Cues—OUTSIDE OF THE FOOT TRAP (I)

1. *Alignment to Ball.* Same as Sole of the Foot Trap. The path of the ball is to the outside of the grounded foot—approximately 6 to 12 inches.

FIGURE 18-18.   Outside of the foot trap.

2. *Base.* Body weight is totally supported by the grounded leg while the contact leg is off the ground.
3. *Whole Body Position.* The contact leg reaches across and in front of the grounded leg—REACH ACROSS, with the ankle rotated inward and down preparing the outside of the foot for contact. The upper body leans—LEAN, at an angle in the direction the ball is to be deflected. The arms are away from the body for balance.
4–5. *Absorption* and *Line of Receiving Force.* The sweeping action of the contact leg from one side of the body to the other—SWEEP, absorbs force and controllably deflects the ball in the desired direction (approximately 90°) away from the approaching flight of the ball. The ankle rotates out with a flicking action—ANKLE FLICK.
6. *Ball Contact.* The contact surface is the outside of the foot and the contact is high on the ball. The

ankle which is rotated inward and downward before contact makes a forceful outward rotation at impact—ANKLE FLICK, flicking the ball to the side of the body as the whole contact leg sweeps across the body.
7. *Follow-Through.* The contact leg sweeps across and in front of the body in the direction that the body is leaning providing controlled re-direction to the ball.

Dribbling

The skill of dribbling involves very controllably propelling the ball with the feet in an effort to move the ball to another area without relinquishing possession to another player. Different surfaces of the foot can be used to dribble.

Learning Cues—INSIDE OF THE FOOT DRIBBLE (B)

1. *Alignment to Ball.* The body is directly behind the ball prior to contact.
2. *Base.* The grounded foot is behind and to the inside of the ball while the other foot is slightly off the ground for contact.
3. *Whole Body Position.* The body is in a continuous running action making repetitive contacts with either foot.
4. *Power/Absorption.* The contact surface (inside of the foot) can provide either force or absorption depending upon how close to the body one wants to keep the ball.
5. *Line of Giving/Receiving Force.* The speed of the running action provides force at contact. Contacting high on the ball takes away force and keeps the ball close while contacting near the middle applies force.
6. *Ball Contact.* The toe of the contact foot is pointed out, knee out, foot slightly off the ground, and sole parallel to ground. The angle of the

FIGURE 18-19.   Inside of the foot dribble.

FIGURE 18-20. Outside of the foot dribble.

FIGURE 18-21. Screening. Note leaning body contact.

contact surface depends upon the path desired for the ball after impact.

7. *Follow-Through.* There is a continuous running action with repetitive contacts by either foot, TAP-TAP, propelling the ball along the ground in a controlled action.

Learning Cues—OUTSIDE OF THE FOOT DRIBBLE (B)

1–3. *Alignment to Ball, Base,* and *Whole Body Position.* All same as Inside of the Foot Dribble.

4. *Power/Absorption.* The contact surface (sole of the foot) is applied to the ball with the degree of force necessary for either stopping it or propelling it in the desired direction.

5. *Line of Giving/Receiving Force.* The degree of pressure by the foot on the ball plus the line of movement by the contact leg determines the force and direction.

6. *Ball Contact.* The contact surface is the sole of the foot, which is applied to the top of the ball. The light rolling of the contact surface over the top of the ball determines force and direction.

7. *Follow-Through.* The contact leg moves in the final desired direction, with light pressure on the ball, in a running action as the ball is propelled in front of the body.

Learning Cues—SCREENING (I)

1–2. *Alignment to Ball* and *Base.* Same as Inside of the Foot Dribble.

3. *Whole Body Position.* The body and ball are under definite control as the body is used to screen the opponent from the ball. Slight leaning contact against the opponent aids in protecting

the ball plus determining the path the opponent desires to take to reach ball.

4. *Power/Absorption.* None.

5. *Line of Giving/Receiving Force.* Light leaning force against the opponent.

6–7. *Ball Contact* and *Follow-Through*—depend upon which dribbling technique (inside, outside, or sole of the foot) the player decides to use to keep away from the opponent. These techniques are often used in combination to feint the opponent prior to breaking away.

Heading

The head is used to play the ball when shooting, passing or clearing the ball. Beginners use the *standing* approach; intermediates use the *jumping* play.

Learning Cues—POWER HEADING, STANDING (B)

1. *Alignment to Ball.* Quickly position as near as possible to a direct line (180°) with the path of the ball.

2–3. *Base* and *Whole Body Position.* Same as Chest Trap (see Figure 18-17).

4–5. *Power* and *Line of Force.* From the foregoing position the whole body snaps forward—SNAP (Figure 18-22). The upper body starts forward as the arms are vigorously thrust backward—ARMS, the weight transfers more to the front foot and the neck snaps—NECK SNAP, thrusting the head toward the ball. All are directed in a straight line toward the approaching ball.

6. *Ball Contact.* The contact surface is near the hair

FIGURE 18-22. Power heading—standing position.

FIGURE 18-23. Power heading—jumping.

line on the forehead. The contact on the ball is dependent upon the desired trajectory and target. Low ball contact propels the ball upward, middle contact propels the ball straight forward parallel with the ground, while high ball contact propels the ball downward to the ground.

7. *Follow-Through.* All power components continue forward following contact providing continued force and direction.

Learning Cues—POWER HEADING, JUMPING (I)

1. *Alignment to Ball.* Same as Power Heading, Standing. Position in the arc of the trajectory

where the ball can be contacted with a maximum height jump.

2. *Base.* A two-foot takeoff provides stability while suspended in air. A running one-foot takeoff provides height in jumping. Use both where desirable.

3. *Whole Body Position.* The arms are close to the side, the back arches, and the neck cocks in preparation for contact.

4. *Power.* The proper contact surface, back, neck, and proper jump timing assist with power as the upper body snaps forward to meet the ball while suspended in mid-air.

5. *Line of Giving Force.* Same as Power Heading, Standing.

6. *Follow-Through.* Same as Power Heading, Standing. A two-foot landing after execution of the skill is necessary for stability.

Tackling

The tackle is a skill used for taking the ball away from an opponent and maintaining control of the ball following that confrontation. Beginners use the frontal approach; for intermediates tackling may be from the side.

Learning Cues—FRONT TACKLE (B)

1. *Alignment to Ball.* Quickly position as near as possible to a direct line (180°) with the path of the approaching player and ball.

2. *Base.* From a running approach the grounded foot is positioned near and to the side of the ball as the full body weight is supported by that foot.

3. *Whole Body Position.* The head is above or slightly in front of the ball, grounded foot and flexed knee. The arms are down and close to the body and the hips are behind the ball. All are in a forward learning position. The contact foot is

FIGURE 18-24. Front tackling.

slightly raised backward with the toe and knee out.

4. *Power.* The knee of the contact leg snaps forward as the contact foot blocks the ball—BLOCK, at the exact same instant that the opponent makes contact.

5. *Line of Giving Force.* At that instant of contact the near shoulder contacts the opponent with a gentle nudge. The straight contact leg is pushed/pulled forward from the groin—DRAG, as the whole body leans into the opponent attempting to knock him off balance.

6. *Ball Contact.* The ball is contacted exactly in the middle with the inside of the foot (see Figure 18-11) at the exact time the opponent makes contact, blocking the ball.

7. *Follow-Through.* The whole body leans into the opponent as the contact foot lightly rolls over the top of the ball causing it to roll over the opponent's foot and propelling it behind the opponent.

Learning Cues—SIDE TACKLE (I)

1. *Alignment to Ball.* The approach angle is from the side at approximately 90° with the path of the player.

2. *Base.* Same as Front Tackle. The grounded foot is firmly planted in a direct line (180°) with the path of the player and ball.

3. *Whole Body Position.* The firm plant of the grounded foot and transfer of total body weight to that foot allows the body to correct itself, facing the oncoming player as in the front tackle. (Refer to Front Tackle.)

4–7. *Power, Line of Giving Force, Ball Contact, Follow-Through.* Same as Front Tackle.

FIGURE 18-25. Side tackling. Note 90° approach angle prior to pivot and contact.

Throw-In

The throw-in is the only time that the players other than goalkeeper can use their hands to propel the ball. This is allowable only when the ball goes out of bounds over the touch line.

Learning Cues—STANDING THROW-IN (B)

1. *Alignment to Field.* Face in the direction that you intend to deliver the ball.

2. *Base.* Either a parallel or staggered stance can be used. The staggered stance (Figure 18-26) provides best stability for a forceful throw.

FIGURE 18-26. Throw-in—standing or running.

3. *Whole Body Position.* From the stance the back arches and arms raise the ball directly over and to a position behind the head.

4. *Power.* The snap forward of the arms, wrists, and upper body provides power.

5. *Line of Giving Force.* All power factors are delivered in a straight line as the body weight transfers to the front foot. The back foot must stay in contact with the ground throughout the throw.

6. *Ball Contact.* The hands must be on the side of the ball and the ball delivered equally with both hands.

7. *Follow-Through*—See #5.

Learning Cues—RUNNING THROW-IN (I)

1. *Alignment to Field.* Same as Standing Throw-in.

2. *Base.* A run prior to delivery with a skip step followed by a stride (staggered) stance is used.

3–7. Same as Standing Throw-in.

FIGURE 18-27. Kneeling catch—roll or bounce ball.

FIGURE 18-28. Standing catch—roll or bounce ball (front and side views).

Goalkeeping

The goalkeeper uses skills for fielding the ball and for clearing it. The hands may be used while in the penalty area. Catches are made in different positions, depending on how the ball arrives.

Learning Cues—KNEELING CATCH—*Roll or Bounce* (B)

1. *Alignment to Ball.* Quickly position in a direct line (180°) with the path of the ball.
2. *Base.* Kneeling (Figure 18-27), the knee of one leg and foot of the other are placed on the ground on opposite sides of the path of the ball for stability and blocking purposes. Standing (Figure 18-28), the feet are placed together in a direct path with the flight of the ball.
3. *Whole Body Position.* Kneeling, the hands and arms are extended downward in front of the body to receive the ball. The lower leg of the kneeling limb is placed at an angle (45° or greater) directly behind path of ball to block it if it gets past the hands. The head is directly above the ball and the shoulders are 90° to the path of the ball. Standing, the upper body bends over at the waist with both legs straight. The hands and arms are extended downward in front of the legs to receive the ball. The head is directly over the ball and the shoulders are 90° to the path of the ball.
4. *Absorption.* The soft contact surface (hands) makes initial contact as the ball is curled to the forearms, biceps, and chest.
5. *Line of Receiving Force.* The movement of the contact surface and absorption factors away from the line of flight at about the same speed as the ball assists in receiving the force.
6. *Ball Contact.* The little fingers of both hands are close together, all fingers are spread and palms are facing the approaching ball. This surface contacts the ball below its center bringing it to the forearms, biceps, and chest in one smooth curling action.
7. *Follow-Through.* Immediately stand up for balance and stability.

Learning Cues—CATCH—*Waist or Chest High Ball* (B)

1. *Alignment to Ball.* Same as catching a rolling or bouncing ball.
2. *Base.* The feet are even in a parallel stance.
3. *Whole Body Position.* The hips and shoulders are

FIGURE 18-29. Catch—waist or chest high ball.

parallel with the goal line. The hands and arms are extended together in front of the body reaching forward for the ball.

4. *Absorption.* The ball traveling at a slower speed is cushioned the same way as when catching a rolling or bouncing ball by first contacting the hands, forearms, biceps, and finally chest. A fast approaching ball is cushioned by taking some of the impact immediately on the body while simultaneously curling the hands and arms around the ball as in catching a rolling ball. A slight jump in the air at contact also aids in absorption.

5-6. *Receiving Force* and *Ball Contact.* Same as catching a rolling or bouncing ball.

6. *Follow-Through.* Bring the knee forward for protection against approaching players, if necessary.

Learning Cues—CATCH—*Ball Head High or Above* (B)

1. *Alignment to Ball.* Same as catching a rolling or bouncing ball.

FIGURE 18-30.   Catch—ball head high or above.

2. *Base.* From a parallel stance raise the knee of one leg forward while the weight is supported on the other (exactly the same if a jump is required).

3. *Whole Body Position.* The hips and shoulders are parallel with the goal line, while the arms extend upward and forward to the desired height for fielding the ball.

4. *Absorption.* The soft contact surface (hands) makes initial contact as the ball is quickly brought to the chest area for protection.

5. *Line of Receiving Force.* Movement by the contact surface and arms is away from the line of flight at the same speed as the approaching ball.

6. *Ball Contact.* The thumbs of both hands are close together, all fingers are spread apart and the palms are facing the approaching ball. This surface contacts the ball near its center and brings the ball to the chest area in one smooth action.

7. *Follow-Through.* Land with two feet in a wide stride stance and lower the hips to a medium standing position for balance and stability.

Learning Cues—CATCH—*Fall to Side* (I)

1. *Alignment to Ball.* With the ball rapidly approaching to the side, drop to the ground on the side of the body attempting to place either the hands or body in alignment with the ball blocking it.

FIGURE 18-31.   Catch—fall to side. Note hands behind ball.

2. *Base.* From a parallel stance the ball-side leg is folded and extended behind the other foot dropping the whole body to the ground on its side.

3. *Whole Body Position.* The body weight is supported on its side and the arms are extended as far as necessary for intercepting the ball.

4-6. Same as catching the ball above the head.

7. *Follow-Through.* As the ball is brought to the chest area both knees are brought forward curling around the ball for protection.

Learning Cues—TIP (I)

1. *Alignment to Ball.* Same as catching a rolling or bouncing ball.

2-3. *Base* and *Whole Body Position.* Same as catching a ball above the head.

4-5. *Power* and *Line of Giving Force.* The contact surface (one or two hands) thrusts upward and backward deflecting the ball over the cross bar.

6. *Ball Contact.* The ball is contacted on its bottom area with the heel of the palm(s) as the wrist(s) is flexed for deflecting the ball upward and backward.

7. *Follow-Through.* The knee is brought forward for

FIGURE 18-32.   Tip—one or two hands.

protection and the landing is on two feet for stability.

Learning Cues—PUNT (B)

1. *Alignment to Ball.* The ball is held with both hands in front of the body.
2. *Base.* From a walking or running motion the body weight is transferred to one foot while the other prepares to kick the ball.
3. *Whole Body Position.* The kicking leg is brought behind the body with a high heel raise as the

FIGURE 18-33.   Punt.

arms are extended in front with the ball in the hands preparing to drop it.

4. *Power.* The proper contact surface, height that the contact foot is raised behind the body, speed that the contact leg is snapped forward to meet the ball as it is dropped, and amount of follow through all provide power.
5. *Line of Giving Force.* The foregoing power factors applied as near as possible to a 180° with the intended flight provide the line and amount of force.
6. *Ball Contact.* The ball is contacted in the back/bottom area. The closer to the ground that the ball falls prior to contact the lower its trajectory. The contact surface is the top hard area of the foot (instep).
7. *Follow-Through.* The contact leg continuing to lift following contact provides both height and force as the body weight is supported by the grounded foot.

Learning Cues—OVERHAND THROW (I)

1. *Alignment to Ball.* The ball is held near the shoulder at the side of the thrower.
2. *Base.* A medium stride stance is used.

FIGURE 18-34.   Overhand throw.

3. *Whole Body Position.* The ball is held in one hand and brought behind the body about head high with the arm flexed (Figure 18-34). The non-throwing arm is extended in front of the body for balance. The knees are slightly flexed. The hips and shoulders are slightly rotated toward the throwing arm.
4. *Power.* The distance that the ball is brought behind the body, speed that the throwing arm is

brought forward and the non-throwing arm is brought back, and follow through of the throwing arm plus upper body all provide power.

5. *Line of Giving Force.* The foregoing power factors applied in a straight line provide maximum force and the desired direction.

6. *Ball Contact.* The ball is held in the palm of the throwing hand and at the back/bottom of the ball.

7. *Follow-Through.* As the ball is released overhand the throwing arm continues forward and the body bends forward providing force and direction.

PLAYING STRATEGY

Skilled execution of the techniques blended with knowledge of principles, tactics, and systems lead to a winning combination in soccer. *Principles* are factors which lead to skillful organized controlled play. *Tactics* denotes the execution of techniques and application of principles in a competitive situation. These fall into categories of individual, group, and team. *Systems* refer to the formational placement of players on the field where they apply techniques, principles, and tactics.

Principles

The basic principles are possession and space. Possession can be by one's own team (attack) or by the opponents (defend). The knowledgeable use of space when attacking or defending is the basis for successful play. The field size (space), understanding of the importance of each third of the field, attack principles and defense principles provide the initial foundation for team play.

Space. The position of players on the large (75 yd. × 120 yd.) field area presents a variety of available spaces. When in possession of the ball, the objectives are to attack the space behind, between, or in front of the opponents or to create new spaces by forcing them to move. The defensive objective is to deny the use of these spaces. The larger the space the more time a player has to maintain possession leading to more controlled play.

Strategic Field Areas. The field is divided into thirds (Figure 18-35). The following factors, when applied in each area, lead to systematic team coordination.

Defend

1. Ball is distributed wide immediately upon possession.
2. Always provide support behind teammate with ball.
3. Do not pass ball across goal mouth.
4. Do not give the ball away.

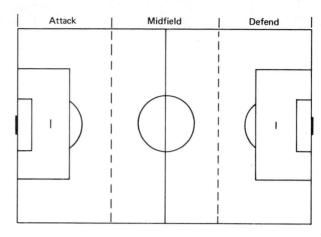

FIGURE 18-35. Strategic field areas.

5. Control pass to midfield area as quickly as possible.
6. When in trouble clear ball: (a) to midfield, (b) out of bounds over sideline, (c) to goalie, (d) over end line (as a last resort).

Midfield

1. Slow down tempo of ball and players.
2. Maintain control.
3. Diagonal cross field flow of ball.
4. Back pass to supporting players—reverse field to opposite side.
5. Penetrate to attack zone.
6. Keep ball wide.
7. Overlap extra players for numerical superiority.

Attack

1. Wide passes for control plus spread defense.
2. Penetrate with ball when possible.
3. Center or cross ball in front of goal mouth, preferably in the air.
4. Short passes, one/two touch contact.
5. Back pass to maintain possession.
6. Shoot whenever possible.
7. Pressure the ball when it is lost.

Offensive Principles. As illustrated in the diagrams (Figure 18-36), the following principles aid the attacking team:

1. *Width*—distributing the ball wide spreads out the defense, opening larger areas for penetrating by either the ball or another player.
2. *Depth/Support*—10 to 15 yard positioning ahead or behind the ball provides additional possible passing angles and enhances possession.
3. *Penetration*—the ball that penetrates past an opponent toward the end line is the most threatening pass to him. The deeper the controlled penetration the better.
4. *Mobility*—the movement by players without the ball to different positions can provide superiority

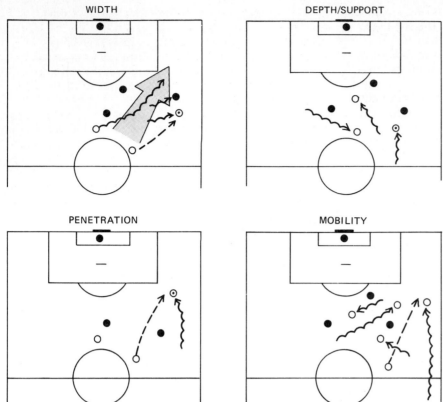

FIGURE 18-36. Offensive principles.

FIGURE 18-37. Defensive principles.

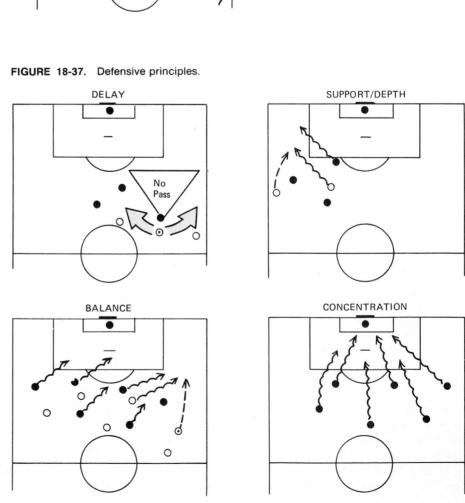

around the ball, create surprise, and create new situations to which the opponents must adjust.

5. *Improvisation*—the ability to adjust to ever-changing situations during the course of play.

Defensive Principles. As illustrated in the diagrams (Figure 18-37), the following principles aid the defending team:

1. *Delay*—positioning in front of the player with the ball so that the ball cannot make immediate penetration, thus buying the important defensive ingredient: time.
2. *Depth/Support*—positioning beside and behind teammates restricting the space and ball/opponent might move.
3. *Balance*—the spread of players across the field protecting all areas.
4. *Concentration*—retreating by all defensive players funneling to the goal scoring area causing congestion.
5. *Pressure*—forcing mistakes through aggressive play.
6. *Control/Restraint*—applying all other principles of defense awaiting the best opportunity for winning the ball. Not committing and being beaten by both the ball and man.

Tactics

The execution of techniques and application of principles in a competitive situation is called tactics. These may be either individual, group, or team.

Individual. A player with the ball has the opportunity to dribble, pass, or shoot, and only has possession of the ball approximately two minutes of a 90-minute game. Developing technique and proficiency in the foregoing skills is important; however, it is more important to learn what to do for the other 88 minutes when one does not have the ball. One must learn how to use the available space for receiving the ball, how to create new space for either the ball or a teammate, and how to apply the principles of attacking or defending.

Group. The basic soccer objective of superiority around the ball initiates group tactics. When superiority is gained the factors of using space, creating space, restricting space, and controlling tempo (time) are applied in small side games. Small side games (2 on 1, 2 on 2, 3 on 1, 3 on 2, 3 on 3, etc.) in restricted areas provide excellent opportunities for learning individual and group tactics.

Team. The grouping of a larger number of players leads to team tactics. Organizing restrictive games often with two lines of players (for example, 4 attackers and 3 midfielders versus 2 midfielders, 4 defenders, and the goalkeeper) requires additional continuity.

Playing within the boundaries of the suggested one-third field areas (see Figure 18-35), the players

can concentrate upon the factors governing systematic team coordination. Communication becomes critical since more players are involved. Short one-word cues aid in communication. Using cuewords such as *square, back, through, lead, leave, touch, carry, turn, settle*, etc., lets teammates know what to do with the ball.

Special rules in such competitions help reinforce specific tactics. Examples for rules are: allow only one touch or two touches per player; a back pass must be used before a penetrating pass; no passes over 15 yards; after receiving a pass the player must dribble past an opponent; all passes must be longer than 15 yards; no passes above knee high; all passes above the head; etc.

The next step in developing playing strategy is the application of principles and tactics within a specific system.

Systems

The formational placement of players on the field is called a system (Figure 18-38). The players

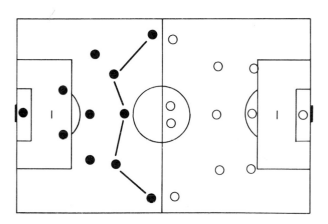

FIGURE 18–38. A systems alignment at kickoff. Numbering: 2-3-5 (W) versus 3-3-4.

are numbered starting with the defenders (fullbacks), midfielders (halfbacks) and then attackers (forwards). The goalkeeper is not included in the numbering. The first attempt to develop new systems occurred when the five forwards of the 2-3-5 system changed their relative positions thus forming either a W or M due to their alignment with each other on the field. Since that first change many new systems have evolved. All systems have strengths and weaknesses. Each evolved due to the specific abilities and knowledge of the players involved. The choice of which system to use should always depend upon those two factors—abilities and knowledge.

Style. Within a system there are varying styles of play. Offensive styles are long pass, short pass, fast, slow, static positioning, improvisational movement, and dribbling. Defensive styles are zone, man to man, switching man to man, rotational, and diagonal.

Many current coaching books discuss principles, tactics, and systems in more detail. The references in this chapter list several books for those requiring additional information.

Dead Ball Situations

When the ball goes out of play or there is an infraction of the rules the game restarts from a dead ball situation. This allows a team the opportunity to initiate set plays. Goal kick, corner kick, kickoff, throw-in, indirect free kicks, and direct free kicks provide such an opportunity. The defending team also has time to prepare. There are many such plays and plans.

References in coaching books can provide a variety of set plays for dead ball restart situations.

Player Positional Responsibilities

Traditionally the player positions were called forwards, halfbacks, fullbacks, and goalkeeper. In recent years the three basic lines are referred to more commonly as attackers, midfielders and defenders. Each line has specific responsibilities related to that particular position. Following are basic responsibilities for each line. It might be pointed out that differing systems of play demand varying responsibilities. The following are very basic; however, additional references in the books recommended can provide extensive information and knowledge.

Attackers

The forward line players which include wings, insides, center forward, or other teammates who overlap into the attacking area.

1. Scoring by shooting (head-foot).
2. Setting up scoring opportunities by dribbling to commit an opponent; centering or crossing the ball in the air into the penalty area; running to create a new space for the ball or a teammate and to receive the ball; distributing the ball strategically and quickly wide, backward, or forward.
3. Performing offensive restarts such as direct, indirect, and corner kicks in scoring area.
4. Pressuring the opponents immediately upon their gaining control.
5. Positioning for counterattacks upon regaining possession of the ball.

Midfielders

1. Supporting the attackers on offense.
2. Redistributing the ball wide, forward, or backward upon gaining possession for sustaining offense.
3. Shooting outside the penalty area.

4. Overlapping into attack area for additional strength or surprise.
5. Retreating, delaying the opponents upon their gaining definite control of the ball.
6. Challenging for a loose ball when there is a 50/50 chance of gaining possession.
7. Receiving goal kicks both offensive and defensive.
8. Taking a majority of the throw-ins.
9. Defending against opponent's corner kicks.
10. Positioning for counter attacks upon regaining control of the ball by one's own fullbacks or goalkeeper.

Defenders

1. Supporting midfielders when attacking.
2. Challenging for ball at midfield when there is a 60/40 chance of gaining possession.
3. Retreating, delaying the opponents upon their gaining definite control of the ball in midfield area.
4. Funneling toward the goal and concentrating in the scoring area.
5. Supporting each other when challenging for the ball.
6. Clearing (kick or head) the ball out of the scoring area and when possible out of the defensive ⅓.
7. Keeping balance across the field; not allowing weakened areas.
8. Positioning wide for counterattacking.
9. Protecting the goal when the goalkeeper leaves the goal mouth.
10. Forming walls for protecting against free kicks.
11. Assisting or taking goal kicks.
12. Overlapping occasionally for added superiority or surprise.
13. Defending against corner kicks.
14. Taking free kicks in defensive ⅓.
15. Sprinting to goal when beaten by both the ball and man.

TERMINOLOGY

Center A pass from the outside of the field near the side line into the center.

Charge The body contact between opponents which may be either illegal or legal.

Chip The lofting of the ball into the air using the instep kick technique: contacting the ball very low causing it to loft quickly with back spin.

Clear Playing (kick or head) the ball a great distance attempting to move it out of a danger area.

Corner kick A direct free kick awarded to the attacking player on the corner arc when the defending team last played the ball over their own end line.

Cross A pass from the outside of the field near the end line to a position in front of the goal.

Dead ball situation The organized restarting of the game following the stopping of play.

Direct free kick   A free kick from which the kicker may immediately score from that initial contact.

Dribble   The technique of the player self-propelling the ball with the foot so that he maintains control while moving from one spot to another.

Drop ball   The method used for restarting the game after temporary suspension of play when the ball is still playable.

Goal area   The rectangular area in front of the goal where the ball is placed for a goal kick.

Half-volley   Contacting the ball just as it hits the ground after being airborne.

Head   The technique of playing the ball with the head.

Indirect free kick   A free kick from which player other than the kicker must contact the ball before a score can result.

Kickoff   The free kick that starts play at the beginning of the game, after each period, or after a score.

Obstruction   The illegal use of the body to shield an opponent from reaching the ball.

Penalty area   The large rectangular area in front of the goal where the goalkeeper is allowed to use the hands to play the ball.

Penalty kick   A free kick awarded for a Direct Free Kick foul in the penalty area against the defending team.

Square pass   A pass that is directed toward the side of a player.

Tackle   A technique for taking the ball away from the opponents.

Through pass   A pass that penetrates between and past the defenders.

Throw-in   The technique used for restarting the game when the ball goes out of play over the side line.

Touchline   The side line of the field.

Trap   The technique used for receiving the ball, bringing it under control.

SELECTED REFERENCES

BEIM, GEORGE. *Principles of Modern Soccer.* Boston: Houghton Mifflin Co., 1977.

CSANADI, ARPAD. *Soccer,* vols. 1 and 2. Budapest: Carving Press, 1965.

CSANADI, ARPAD. *Soccer: Training and Tactics.* New York: International Publication Services, 1965.

INGELS, NEIL B., JR. *Coaching Youth Soccer.* Monterey, Calif.: Page-Ficklin Publications, 1976.

THOMSON, WILLIAM. *Teaching Soccer.* Minneapolis, Minn.: Burgess Publishing Co., 1980.

Audio-Visual Materials

Athletic Institute, 200 Castlewood Drive, North Palm Beach, Fla. 33408. (8mm silent, 16mm sound, and books.)

Champions on Film, Box 1941, 745 State Circle, Ann Arbor, Mich. 48106. (Skill cassettes and sound film.)

"Key Goals to Winning Soccer," National Federation of State High School Associations, P.O Box 20626, Kansas City, Mo. 64195.

Modern Talking Picture Service, 5000 Park Street, North, St. Petersburg, Fla. 33709. Physical Training, The Goalkeeper, Ball Control, The Art of Refereeing, Soccer, The Name of the Game Is Soccer

World's Greatest Sports Movies, 406 E. Tehachapi Blvd., Dept SA, Tehachapi, Calif. 93561.

Governing Bodies—Rules

Association for Intercollegiate Athletics for Women, 1201 16th Street, N.W., Washington, D.C. 20036.

National Association of Girls and Womens Sports, 1900 Association Drive, Reston, Va. 22091.

National Collegiate Athletic Association, P.O. Box 1906, Shawnee Mission, Kan. 66222.

National Federation of State High School Associations, P.O. Box 20626, Kansas City, Mo. 64195.

SOFTBALL

THIS CHAPTER WILL ENABLE YOU TO:

♦ Identify the basic equipment needed in softball and understand the rules pertaining to it.
♦ Understand the rules and the offensive and defensive strategies so that verbalization may be made on the various plays of the game.
♦ Demonstrate the skills of batting, baserunning, sliding, fielding, throwing, pitching, and catching; and of playing the infield and outfield positions.
♦ Identify the terminology necessary to understand the game.
♦ Observe the procedures to make the game safe for participants.

NATURE AND PURPOSE

It is estimated that over thirty million adults and youngsters annually play some form of competitive or recreational softball in the United States. The fact that the game can be played with a minimum of equipment in a reasonably small area contributes greatly to its being played in a variety of places and on a variety of occasions. The keen competition between teams, the advent of lighted parks, the brief time span of a game (approximately one hour), and the variety of age groups participating have brought additional millions to the ballparks to watch their favorite team or person play. The game of softball has truly become one of America's favorite sports for the player and spectator alike.

BASIC RULES

The rules of softball are patterned after those of baseball, making it very similar to the parent game. Pitching and several rules concerning field dimensions and equipment are different. A brief summary of the rules is given below, but players should study a copy of the Official Rules in order to become familiar with all regulations governing the game.

The games of slow pitch softball and fast pitch softball have many similarities: the ball must be pitched underhand, the game is 7 innings long, the purpose is to get on base and score runs. The major difference, as the names imply, is in the speed of the pitched ball. In slow pitch softball, the ball must be thrown underhand with a specific arc (3 to 12 feet) whereas in fast pitch softball the ball is thrown underhand in a straight line with great velocity—much like a baseball. Other differences are noted in the following list.

Slow Pitch	Fast Pitch
No bunting	Bunting
No stealing bases	Stealing bases
Runners may leave the base after the ball crosses home plate	Runners leave base after the pitcher releases the ball
10 players per team	9 players per team
65-foot base paths (Males)	60-foot base paths
60-foot base paths (Females)	
Recommend a mask and chest protector for the catcher	Require a mask and chest protector for the catcher

The Game

The purpose of the game is to score more runs than the opponent. A regulation game consists of seven innings or six and one-half innings if the team second at bat has scored more runs than its opponent. The umpire may call (terminate) a game if five or more complete innings have been played or the team second at bat has scored more runs than the other team has scored in five or more innings. The score of a forfeited game shall be 7–0 in favor of the team not at fault.

Players and Substitutes

A team shall consist of nine players in Fast Pitch, ten players in Fast Pitch with a Designated Hitter, and ten players in Slow Pitch. A team must have the required number of players to start or continue a game. A substitute may take the place of a player whose name is on the team's batting order. Any of the starting players except a Designated Hitter (DH) may be withdrawn and re-enter once provided such player occupies the same batting position whenever he or she is in the line-up. A player, other than the starting line-up, removed from the game shall not participate in the game again except as a coach. The DH may be used for any player provided it is made known prior to the start of the game and his or her name is indicated on the line-up sheet. The DH must remain in the same position in the batting order, may not enter the game on defense, may be substituted for at any time by a player who has not yet been in the game, and may not return to the game when replaced.

Equipment

The official softball bat must be round and made of one piece of hardwood or from bonded wood. Plastic, bamboo, or metal are also acceptable materials. The bat must be no more than 34 inches long, 2¼ inches in diameter at its largest part, and not exceed 38 ounces in weight. It must have a safety grip of cork, tape (not smooth plastic tape), or composition material, and be marked "Official Softball" by the manufacturer.

The official ball must be a regular, smooth-seam concealed-stitch or flat-surfaced ball not less than 11⅞ inches or more than 12⅛ inches in circumference, and weigh not less than 6¼ ounces or more than 7 ounces.

Gloves may be worn by any player, but mitts may be used only by the catcher and first baseman. The pitcher's glove must be of one solid color other than white or grey. Multicolor gloves are acceptable for all other players, but gloves with white or grey circles on the outside giving the appearance of a ball are illegal.

Shoes may be made with either canvas or leather uppers or similar materials. The soles may be either smooth or with soft or hard rubber cleats. Ordinary metal sole and heel cleats may be used if the spikes on the plates do not extend more than ¾ inch from the sole or heel of the shoe. Shoes with rounded metal spikes are illegal.

Masks must be worn by catchers in Fast Pitch and are recommended in Slow Pitch. Female catchers must wear a body protector in Fast Pitch, and it is recommended in Slow Pitch.

All players on a team shall wear uniforms identical in color, trim, and style. Ball caps are considered part of the uniform and are required for all players under U.S. Slo-Pitch Softball Association (USSSA) rules and in Amateur Softball Association (ASA) rules for male players including the catcher. Helmets are permissible for catchers, batters, and baserunners.

Pitching Regulations

In Fast Pitch, the pitcher must take a position with both feet firmly on the ground and in contact with, but not off the side of, the pitcher's plate. Before pitching, the pitcher must come to a full and complete stop for at least one second and not more than ten seconds, facing the batter with both shoulders in line with first and third base and with the ball held in both hands in front of the body (see Figure 19-1). The pitcher may not take the pitching position without the ball. The pitcher may use any wind-up in the delivery provided there is no stop in the forward motion or reverse in the direction of the arm swing. The release of the ball and the follow-

FIGURE 19-1. Pitching position, presenting the ball to the batter.

FIGURE 19-2. Pitching delivery, Fast Pitch.

through of the hand and wrist must be forward past the straight line of the body, and, when the arm passes the body in the forward swing, the hand shall be below the hip and the wrist not farther from the body than the elbow (see Figure 19-2). The pitcher shall not take more than one step which must be forward toward the batter (within the length of the pitcher's plate), simultaneous with the delivery of the ball, and the pivot foot must remain in contact with the pitcher's plate until the stepping foot has touched the ground.

In Slow Pitch, the pitcher can take the pitching position with one or both feet touching the pitcher's plate, but both the pivot and non-pivot foot must be within the length of the pitcher's plate. A full stop must be made for one second and not more than ten seconds with one or both hands holding the ball in front of the body and the shoulders in line with first and third base preliminary to pitching. The pivot foot must remain in contact with the pitcher's plate until the pitched ball leaves the hand. It is not necessary to step, but if a step is taken, it must be forward toward the batter within the length of the pitcher's plate. The pitch shall be released at a moderate speed (umpire's decision—if warned about excessive speed and the act is repeated, the pitcher shall be removed from the pitcher's position for the remainder of the game), and at a perceptable arc of at least six feet and no higher than twelve feet from the ground.

Batting

The batter shall take a position within the lines of the batter's box and may be called out for stepping on home plate or having the entire foot touching the ground completely outside the lines of the batter's box when the ball is hit. A batter is removed from further participation in the game if an illegal bat is used. Players must bat in regular order as indicated in the starting line-up. Batting out of order is an appeal play and if the error is discovered while the incorrect batter is at the plate, the correct batter must replace the incorrect batter and assume the ball and strike count. If the error is discovered after the incorrect batter has completed the turn at bat and before there has been a pitch to another batter, the player who should have batted is out, and the next batter is the player whose name follows that of the player declared out. Any runs scored are cancelled and base runners must return to bases held when the incorrect batter came to the plate. If the error is not discovered until after a pitch is made to the next batter, no one is declared out and all play is legal.

A strike (Fast Pitch) occurs when the ball passes over any part of home plate and is between the batter's armpits and the top of the knees when in a natural batting stance. In Slow Pitch the strike zone is over any part of home plate between the batter's

higher shoulder and the knees when in a natural batting stance.

A foul tip is a foul ball which goes directly from the bat, not higher than the batter's head, to the catcher's hands and is legally caught. In Fast Pitch the ball is in play and baserunners may advance at their own risk. In Slow Pitch the ball is dead.

The batter shall be declared out when an infield fly is hit with baserunners on first and second or on first, second, and third with less than two out (infield fly rule). The batter is also called out in Slow Pitch when the ball is bunted, is hit with a downward chopping motion, or is hit foul after the second strike.

Baserunning

Baserunners must touch the bases in regular order and if forced to return while the ball is in play, the bases must be touched in reverse order. Two baserunners may not occupy the same base simultaneously. The runner who first legally occupied the base shall be entitled to it and the other baserunner must return or be put out. A baserunner is out when he or she: (a) runs more than three feet from a direct line between bases in regular or reverse order to avoid being touched by the ball in the hand of a fielder; (b) passes a preceding baserunner before that runner has been put out; (c) leaves a base to advance before a caught fly ball has been touched provided the ball is returned to a fielder who touches that base while holding the ball, or a fielder with the ball touches the baserunner before returning to the base; (d) fails to keep contact with the base until a legally pitched ball has been released by the pitcher in Fast Pitch (whether on a steal or batted ball); (e) fails to keep contact with the base until a legally pitched ball has reached home plate in Slow Pitch (batted ball only).

A pitcher in Slow Pitch who desires to walk a batter intentionally may do so by notifying the Plate Umpire who shall then award the batter first base.

Dead Ball

The ball is dead and not in play under the following circumstances: (a) on an illegally batted ball; (b) when the batter steps from one box to another as pitcher is ready to pitch; (c) on an illegal pitch; (d) when a pitched ball touches any part of the batter's person or clothing; (e) when a foul ball is not caught; (f) when a baserunner is called out for leaving a base too soon; (g) when any part of the batter's person is hit with a batted ball while in the batter's box; (h) when the batter is hit by a pitched ball; (i) when a blocked ball is declared; (j) when a wild pitch or passed ball in Fast Pitch goes under, over, or through the backstop; and (k) in Slow Pitch after each strike or ball.

Scoring

A base hit results when a batted ball permits the hitter to reach first base safely when no fielding error is involved. A base hit shall not be recorded when a baserunner is forced out by a batted ball, or would have been forced out, except for a fielding error.

Sacrifices are scored when with less than two out the batter advances one or more baserunners with a bunt and is retired at first base, or when a run is scored by advancing runners after a fly ball is caught.

Assists are scored to each player who handles the ball in any play or series of plays which results in a put-out, but only one assist is credited to a player in any one put-out.

Errors are recorded for the player who commits a misplay that prolongs the turn at bat of the batter or the life of the baserunner.

Put-outs are credited to players who catch a batted fly ball, catch a thrown ball that retires a baserunner, or touch a baserunner with the ball while the runner is off the base.

A run batted in (RBI) is a run scored because of: (a) a safe hit; (b) a sacrifice bunt or fly; (c) an infield put-out or fielder's choice; (d) a baserunner forced home because of interference, or in Fast Pitch the batter being hit with a pitched ball, or the batter being given a base on balls; (e) a home run and all runs scored as a result.

Winning and Losing Pitcher

A pitcher shall be credited with a win if he or she starts and pitches at least four innings and the team is not only in the lead when the replacement occurs but remains in the lead the remainder of the game. When a game is ended after five innings of play and the starting pitcher has pitched at least three innings and the team scores more runs than the other team when the game is terminated, he or she shall be declared the winner. A pitcher shall be charged with a loss regardless of the number of innings pitched if replaced when the team is behind in the score and the team thereafter fails to tie the score or gain the lead.

Playing Field

The regulation playing field is 60 × 60 feet square (Figure 19-3); note the accompanying indications of the required distances for Fast Pitch and Slow Pitch. Ground or special rules establishing the

FIGURE 19-3. Softball field, official dimensions.

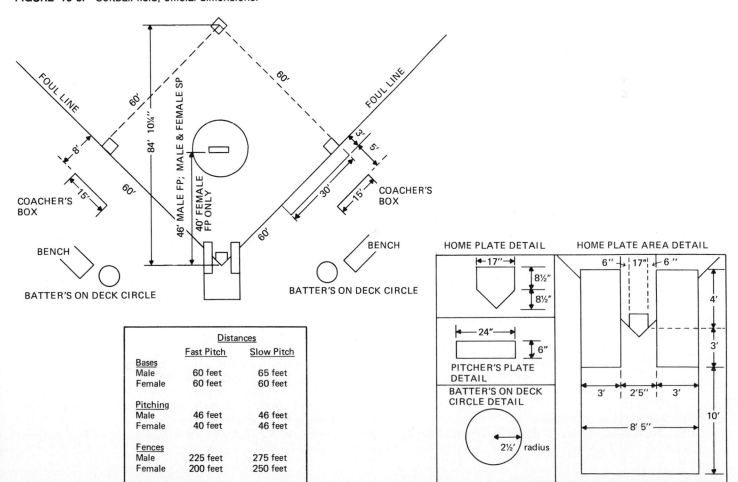

Distances	Fast Pitch	Slow Pitch
Bases		
Male	60 feet	65 feet
Female	60 feet	60 feet
Pitching		
Male	46 feet	46 feet
Female	40 feet	46 feet
Fences		
Male	225 feet	275 feet
Female	200 feet	250 feet

limits of the playing field may be agreed upon by leagues or opposing teams whenever backstops, fences, stands, vehicles, or other obstructions are within the prescribed area.

The home plate is made of rubber or other suitable material and is a five-sided figure 17 inches wide across the side facing the pitcher, 8½ inches long on the sides parallel to the inside lines of the batter's box, and 12 inches long on the sides of the point facing the catcher.

The pitcher's plate is made of wood or rubber, and measures 24 inches long and 6 inches wide. The top of the plate must be level with the ground; the front line of the plate measures the following distances from the outside corner of home plate: male Fast Pitch and Slow Pitch and female Slow Pitch— 46 feet; female Fast Pitch—40 feet.

The bases other than home plate must be 15 inches square and made of canvas or other suitable material and not be more than 5 inches thick. The bases should be securely fastened in position.

Umpires

The umpires are the representatives of the league or organization by which they have been assigned and as such are authorized and required to enforce each section of the rules. The umpire judging balls and strikes is the "Plate Umpire," and the umpire judging base decisions is the "Base Umpire." The plate umpire shall have the authority to make decisions on situations not specifically covered in the rules. The umpires shall not be members of either team. Neither umpire has the authority to set aside or question decisions made by the other within the limits of their respective duties. Each may consult his associate at any time; however, the final decision rests with the umpire whose exclusive authority it was to make the decision and who requested the opinion of the other. The umpire's judgment cannot be appealed on decisions of whether a batted ball was fair or foul, whether a baserunner was safe or out, whether a pitched ball was a strike or ball, or on any other play involving accuracy of judgment.

SUGGESTED LEARNING SEQUENCE

A. Nature and Purpose of Softball
B. Conditioning—Exercises and Drills for developing muscular strength, speed, agility, coordination, and balance.
C. Basic Game Concepts
  1. Field of play and player positions
  2. Equipment
  3. Safety
  4. Playing courtesies
D. Rules—start with those essential to play the

game and expand in depth and comprehensiveness as playing ability increases.
  1. Terminology
  2. Playing field
  3. Equipment
  4. Players and substitutes
  5. The game
  6. Pitching regulations—fast or slow pitch, for whichever game is being taught
  7. Batting
  8. Baserunning
  9. Dead ball—ball in play
  10. Umpires
  11. Protests
  12. Scoring
E. Skills and Techniques. The sequence for teaching skills may vary, but it is difficult to teach softball until throwing, catching, and batting are somewhat accomplished.
  1. Throwing
    a. Grip on ball
    b. Arm motion
    c. Body movement
  2. Fielding the ball
    a. Catching
    b. Ground balls
    c. Fly balls
  3. Batting
    a. Grip on bat
    b. Stance
    c. Stride
    d. Rotation of body and arms
    e. Follow-through
  4. Bunting
    a. Grip on bat
    b. Stance
    c. Direction of bunt
  5. Baserunning
  6. Sliding
  7. Pitching
  8. Catching
F. Playing Strategy. The Fast Pitch game utilizes many strategies of baseball, whereas the Slow Pitch game is the adaptation of field positions to batting strengths and/or weaknesses.
G. Safety Suggestions. Moving people and moving objects can create hazards; therefore, from the first day, safety precautions must be adhered to without fail.

SKILLS AND TECHNIQUES

Softball, while adaptable for general recreational use, is a game that demands a good performance of certain fundamental skills and techniques if one hopes to play on a first-class team. Enjoyment from participation in the game intensifies as skills improve. A careful study of the suggestions outlined here should help give a better picture of correct techniques necessary for performance of the fundamental skills. Observance of these suggestions on the playing field and with the guidance of an instructor should improve the quality of one's play.

Throwing

This is a natural activity ordinarily engaged in by most children, but not all people throw correctly. Throws should be made quickly, accurately, and to the correct base or fielder. Players should be able to throw using an overhand, sidearm, or underhand motion, but more time should be spent on the overhand throw because with it one can attain the greatest accuracy. The sidearm throw imparts a side spin on the ball that causes it to curve.

Learning Cues

1. Grip ball across a seam with index finger and second finger (all fingers if hand is small), thumb underneath, and third and fourth fingers to the side (see Figures 19-4 and 19-5).
2. Point elbow away from body as arm moves backward (see Figure 19-6).

FIGURE 19-4. Two-finger grip for adults.

FIGURE 19-5. Four-finger grip for children.

FIGURE 19-6. Overhand throw—as arm moves backward, point elbow away from the body.

3. Move body weight to foot on same side (rear foot) and rotate trunk in that direction.
4. Keep wrist extended until just before release.
5. Push off with the rear foot and step with the other foot in the direction of the intended throw.
6. Rotate hips, trunk, and shoulders as arm comes forward.
7. Lead with the elbow and snap the wrist as the ball is released opposite the peak of the cap.
8. Practice throwing for accuracy by throwing to a designated spot in warm-up or in competition.
9. Use a natural rhythmical movement.

Practice Suggestions

1. Throw to a partner. Start with a short distance and then increase that distance. Throw to a specified target on the partner such as the chest. Vary the target and the speed of the throw. Stay at a distance until accurate for four out of five throws (preferably all five). Remember that a small angle of error as the ball leaves the hand becomes greater and greater the farther the ball travels.
2. Throw at a target from various distances.
3. Throw to different bases from different field positions.
4. Retrieve bad throws. The player making a bad throw that is out of the reach of a partner should

chase the ball. If it is a good throw but bad catching, the one trying to catch retrieves.

Fielding the Ball

Catching the ball is another fundamental that players must master if they expect to be successful in softball. When catching balls that are to be caught below the waist, the hands are cupped with the little fingers together, palms forward, and the fingers pointing downward or sideward. In catching balls that are above the waist, the hands are cupped with the thumbs together, palms forward, and the fingers pointing upward or slightly sideward (see Figure 19-7).

FIGURE 19-7. Fly ball catching position.

Learning Cues

1. Catch the ball, when possible, close to the throwing side so that the throwing arm can move into position for the throw as soon as possible.
2. Relax the fingers slightly and have the hands and arms give with the ball as it is caught to reduce the force of impact.
3. Catch a ground ball just as it leaves the ground on a bounce or after it has reached the peak of its bounce.
4. Keep the body and glove low on ground balls and move upward to make the catch. One can move more quickly upward and since the body is already low, more bad bounces may be blocked by the body or glove.
5. Stay in front or get in front of ground balls. This

enables you to handle them if they take bad bounces to the left or right.
6. Field ground balls with the feet in a stride position, with the knees slightly bent, and the body crouched (see Figure 19-8). On hard-hit balls it may be advisable to close the feet or drop to one knee to block the ball.

FIGURE 19-8. Fielding ground ball position.

7. Glance at a fly ball that is over your head, approximate its position of flight, then turn and run to the spot where it will fall.
8. Know where to throw the ball before it is caught and then move quickly to accomplish the throw *after the catch.*

Practice Suggestions

1. Catch balls from a partner as indicated under Throwing.
2. Field ground balls with a partner tossing balls at varying speeds and in different directions.
3. Field ground balls hit by a partner at varying speeds and directions. Throws can be made to a catcher next to the hitter or to a base.
4. Catch fly balls thrown by a partner. Gradually increase the distance.
5. Catch fly balls hit by a partner. Throw to a relay person, or directly to a catcher next to the hitter, or to a player at a base.

Batting

The key to offensive softball lies in the effective use of the bat, coupled with base running. To become effective in hitting, which is a complex motor task, one must master several basic fundamentals involving desire, self-concept, knowledge of mechanical principles, and development of strength, endurance, and flexibility. Occasionally good hitters will deviate from the following procedure, but the basic position has the batter taking a position in the

FIGURE 19-9. Batting grip.

batter's box with feet slightly more than hip width apart, knees relaxed and flexed slightly, and with the body bent slightly forward at the hips. The bat is gripped by the handle in such a manner that the second joints of each finger on each hand are in alignment (see Figure 19-9). The bat may be gripped with both hands side by side at the very end, at a short distance from the end, or at a point four to eight inches from the end (called "choking"); or it may be gripped with the hands separated several inches along the handle. The shorter the grip the more of a "chopping" or "punching" motion one should use, but the more accurate the placing of the ball will be into the field desired. The grip at the end of the handle is a free-swinging grip used by long ball hitters. Before hitting, the bat is held in a position over the rear shoulder with the forearm (closer to pitcher) fairly straight and raised so that the elbow is as high as the handle. The back arm is bent slightly with the elbow away from the body (see Figure 19-10). In executing the swing, the body, arms and bat first rotate slightly away from the pitcher. This gives the bat more distance over which to gain momentum and enables the body to exert more torque in hitting. As the bat comes forward, the arms should straighten, the wrists should straighten forcefully just before the ball is hit, and should continue to straighten very forcefully as the ball is hit. The trunk and hips rotate until the batter almost faces the pitcher, and the ball is struck about half an arm's length in front of the shoulder that is closer to the plate. Just before the swing, the forward leg should step forward toward the pitcher—somewhat toward the plate for an outside pitch (closed stance), slightly away from the late for an inside pitch (open stance)—and during the swing the weight should shift over to the front leg which should be straight (see Figure 19-11). The rear foot initiates a push forward but should maintain contact with the ground as the ball is hit. The eyes must be on the ball from the time the pitcher has it until just before one hits the ball.

Learning Cues

1. Select a bat that can be gripped comfortably and can be swung without difficulty. A bat that is too heavy prevents getting around in time to hit the ball, whereas a bat that is too light will make it difficult to hit a long ball.
2. Refrain from taking a long stride; if a step is taken make it a short one and more of a glide.
3. Swing only at good pitches.

FIGURE 19-10. Batting stance.

FIGURE 19-11. Batting position as follow-through starts.

4. Swing the bat parallel to the ground and follow through with the swing.
5. Plant the rear foot and keep it steady. Don't dance around in the batter's box.
6. Lean slightly forward on the balls of the feet.

Practice Suggestions

1. Strike the ball from a stationary tee or from a rope suspended overhead.
2. Hit balls with a fungo bat—fly balls, line drives, ground balls.
3. Have partner toss ball from a distance of two to three yards to the side (about a 45-degree angle) and hit ball into a fence.
4. Get in groups of four or five with batter, pitcher, and two or three fielders. Hit ten or fifteen pitches and rotate. Position groups for safety.

Bunting

This is an effective offensive weapon in Fast Pitch softball but is illegal in Slow Pitch. Although the fielders are closer to the batter in softball than in baseball, it takes just as much time to field and throw a softball as a baseball. Therefore, the batter in softball should have a slight advantage over the baseball player in using the bunt as a means to reach first base safely. The initial stance is the same as for hitting because it is most effective as a surprise maneuver and its declaration must be withheld as long as possible. Just before the pitcher releases the ball, the batter should pivot on the rear foot and bring the forward foot back parallel with the rear foot so that the batter is facing the pitcher.

FIGURE 19-12. Bunting position.

This move is advocated to keep the catcher as far away from the play as possible, especially on squeeze bunts. The knees should be bent and the body should crouch low, especially on low balls. The arms bring the bat downward to a position parallel with the ground over homeplate and perpendicular to the line of flight of the ball. As the bat comes down, one should slide the top hand up the bat to a position beyond the center of the bat where the thumb and index finger grasp the bat on the rear side to avoid having the fingers hit. The arms should be about half flexed (see Figure 19-12). By flexing one arm a little more while extending the other arm, the ball may be guided down either the first or third base lines. The ball should hit the bat near the top hand and the placing of the bat in front of the ball is similar to the movement one would use to place his hand in position to catch the ball. The arms should give slightly as the ball hits the bat to keep the ball from rebounding too far into the playing field.

Learning Cues

1. Refrain from swinging or pushing bat into the ball.
2. Catch the ball on the bat near the top hand.
3. Turn bat slightly to get ball near either foul line. Remember the angle of reflection (rebound) from the bat equals the angle of incidence (hitting) on the bat.
4. Move body up and down and maintain bunting stance rather than moving the arms for high and low pitches.
5. Keep the bat above the ball so that the ball is more likely to be hit downward.

Practice Suggestions

1. Practice turning from batting stance to bunting stance in front of a mirror.
2. Have partner toss ball slowly and bunt.
3. Bunt to a glove placed on the ground at various positions.

Baserunning

One should follow the base lines in running the bases and avoid making large turns in rounding a base. The proper method of running bases is to pull out about three feet from the base line two or three strides before reaching the base and then by timing one's steps, hit the inside corner of the base with left foot. As the left foot hits the base, the body twists slightly to the left so that the right foot will land just beyond the next base line (see Figure 19-13). The runner comes back to the base line and continues. Since the runner must hold his base until the ball leaves the pitcher's hand (Fast Pitch) or reaches home plate (Slow Pitch), a sprinter's stance should be taken with one foot on the base in readiness for a quick departure (whether on a steal or a batted ball). When advancing from first to second, watch the

FIGURE 19-13. Running form—as foot hits base, twist the body.

third base coach for directions. The coach is usually in a better position to see the entire field of play and tell the runner whether to stop at second or continue on to third base.

Learning Cues

1. Follow the most direct path to the next base.
2. Step toward first base with the rear foot after hitting the ball.
3. Look to the coach for directions rather than try to follow the ball because this tends to slow one down.

4. Run across first base, do not jump or leap for the base because this slows one down.
5. Run hard on all plays because routine balls may be misplayed by the defense.

Practice Suggestions

1. Run the bases after hitting in batting practice.
2. Practice hitting the ball and starting for first base.
3. Practice starting from a base with the sprinter's stance.

Sliding

Sliding should never be used by anyone without first having instruction in the technique and then practicing the technique. Runners should learn to slide correctly in order to keep from overrunning a base, and to prevent injury. The hook slide is the most popular technique and is performed by sliding on a thigh and hip with the body leaning away from the base. When sliding on the right hip and thigh, the base is hooked with the left toe, and the right leg should either be bent under the left leg with the right toe pointing backward to keep from getting caught in the ground or extended forward in the air to prevent the spikes from catching in the ground and injuring ankles and knees. The left leg is raised slightly off the ground and as the body, which is slightly to the right of the base line, approaches the base the toe hooks onto the base (see Figure 19-14). One must be certain to start the slide soon enough so that by the time the toe hooks the base the body's momentum is slow enough to avoid pulling the toe off the base. The bent-leg slide is used by players

FIGURE 19-15. Bent-leg slide.

FIGURE 19-14. Hook slide.

who wish to get to their feet quickly in order to advance to another base on an overthrow or misplay. In this slide the player slides on the bent underneath leg with the upper leg making contact with the base (see Figure 19-15). The forward momentum of the slide is utilized to raise the body to an upright position after making contact with the base. The head-first slide is often used when it becomes necessary to return to a base.

Learning Cues

1. Understand the fundamentals of the sliding position, assume it on grass in a stationary position, and then with a short easy run execute the slide. As the slide is learned, increase running speed.
2. Start slide early so that base is not contacted with a great force.
3. Land on as large an area of the thigh and hip as possible. This reduces the landing impact per square inch of body surface.
4. Watch defensive player and slide away from point of catch by throwing body off to that side.

Practice Suggestions

1. Practice on wet grass or in a sliding pit with long pants and socks, no shoes.
2. Judge one another on technique.
3. Slide for a square marked on the grass.
4. Slide into a base opposite catch made by a partner who receives toss from another player. Rotate.

Pitching

The success of a winning team is greatly dependent on the consistency of the pitching. A good pitcher must have control and a variety of pitches that can be used whether it is Fast Pitch or Slow Pitch. The movements of pitching are outlined by the rules. The following types of pitches can be used in Fast Pitch: (1) *Straight Pitch*—fast ball. Grip the ball with palm up, hold the ball in a tripod grip (same as in the overhand throw described previously). Release the ball from the finger tips and thumb with palm up and slightly to the left; (2) *Curve Ball.* Grip is the same but deeper in the tripod. Release occurs between the thumb and forefinger after the wrist is rotated vigorously just before the release to give side spin. When the wrist is rotated clockwise it produces a curve to the right (incurve) and when it is rotated counterclockwise it produces a curve to the left (outcurve); (3) *Drop Ball.* Grip is palm up, thumb to the right, three fingers underneath and little finger to the side. Release occurs by a snap of the wrist upward allowing the ball to roll off the fingers giving it top spin; and (4) *Rise Ball.* Grip is with palm down, thumb underneath, and all fingers on top. Release occurs by a snap of the wrist upward while the thumb pushes against the ball to put backspin on it.

FIGURE 19-16. Pitching delivery, Slow Pitch.

In Slow Pitch the ball should be released about shoulder high, which helps to attain the twelve-foot arc and to drop the ball over the plate (see Figure 19-16). Lower releases tend to flatten the pitch and give it more velocity. Varied spins as well as different speeds on the ball should be developed to keep the batter mixed up in the timing of his swing.

Learning Cues

1. Understand the rules thoroughly.
2. Rotate the wrist prior to release of the pitch. This necessitates knowing where the ball is released and starting the rotation before that point.
3. Make use of the seams to enhance curving movements by grasping ball properly.
4. Pitch to spots in the strike zone and not to the batter.
5. Maintain balance after the pitch so that fielding responsibilities can be carried out.
6. Develop leg and arm endurance and strength.
7. Develop confidence in the ability to pitch the ball to a desired point with different spins and speeds.

Practice Suggestions

1. Throw to a partner who moves the target around the strike zone.
2. Throw to a target—use of an old mat on a wall, fence, or backstop is good. In Slow Pitch use some type of container or a circle on the ground behind the plate.

Catching

The catcher is frequently called the "defensive center of the infield" because the catcher handles all

FIGURE 19-17. Catching position.

Playing First Base

The first-base player in Fast Pitch must always be alert for fielding a bunt as it is used frequently. The field position for this is in toward home plate ten to twenty feet; a greater distance is used with no one on base and a shorter distance with a runner on first and a double-play possibility. In Slow Pitch the playing position is approximately ten feet behind the base but varies in depth and distance from the foul line according to the strength or weakness of the batter. To be in position to receive a throw from another fielder, run quickly to the base when the ball is hit and assume a position facing the fielder with the heels touching the inside edge of the bag (see Figure 19-18). The first-base player should shift the body according to the direction of the throw. When the throw is to the left (toward home plate), bring the toe of the right foot to the edge of the bag by the left heel and then step toward the ball with the left foot (see Figure 19-19). Reverse the procedure (see Figure 19-20) for a throw to the right (toward the outfield).

the pitched balls and is in a position to see all the infield proceedings. The catcher should call the player's name on infield flies, tell the fielder of a bunt where to throw, and keep all players informed of the number of outs. He or she gives the pitcher the signal for the type of pitch to be thrown, gives a target to throw to, makes every effort to block wild pitches with runners on base, and makes plays at home plate. The catcher assumes a squat position as close to the batter as possible without interfering with the swing and with the weight forward on the balls of the feet so that quick movements in any direction can be made (see Figure 19-17). In making a throw, bring the ball up to a position behind the ear, step forward with the left foot, and throw by bringing the arm forward quickly and with a strong wrist snap just prior to release.

FIGURE 19-18. First-base player position waiting for the throw.

FIGURE 19-19. First-base player position reaching for ball to the left.

FIGURE 19-20. First-base player position reaching for ball to the right.

Practice Suggestions

1. Do the footwork without catching until it is an automatic response.
2. Have partner toss balls to both sides of the base.
3. Have fielders throw balls to base.
4. Have coach hit ground balls to fielders and let them throw to first base.
5. Field bunts and ground balls hit to various spots in the first base area.
6. Practice catching fly balls in the vicinity of first base.

Playing Second Base

The fielding position for the second-base player is approximately fifteen feet from second base toward first base and about twelve feet behind the baseline. The position varies with the strength and weakness of the batter. One should attempt to field all batted balls to the first-base side of second base. On a double-play situation from the third-base side, one should move quickly toward the base in a path that puts second base between the person fielding the ball, and the second-base player. Time the move so that the ball is caught as the right foot hits the bag, step forward with the left foot toward the infield and first base to avoid the baserunner, and with a pivot throw to first base (see Figure 19-21).

The shortstop takes a fielding position similar to the second-base player's position but closer to third base; the position varies with the strength and weakness of the batter. One should attempt to field all batted balls to the third base side of second base. On a double-play situation, move quickly to the base in a direct line with second base and the player fielding the ball. Time the move to catch the ball just

before reaching the bag, step to the outfield side with the left foot, drag the right foot across the bag, and pivot and throw to first base. Both the shortstop and second-base player can stop just before they reach second base, catch the ball and touch second base with the left foot, push back with that foot, landing on the right foot, and then pivot and throw to first base.

Practice Suggestions

1. Field ground balls hit to various positions and with varying speeds.
2. Move across the bag and throw to first base.
3. Make the step-back-and-throw maneuver.
4. Complete the double-play situation after fielding ground balls.
5. Make the double-play with a runner moving with the hit ball.
6. Tag runners stealing second base.
7. Catch infield fly balls.

Playing Third Base

The position of the third-base player in Fast Pitch is similar to that of the first-base player—be in a position to field bunted balls by playing in toward home plate ten to twenty feet, depending on the game situation. Attempt to field all batted balls hit down the third-base line and as many as can be reached hit to the second-base side, as the momentum developed by moving in that direction should aid the throw to first base.

Practice Suggestions

1. Field bunted balls and throw to first base and second base.

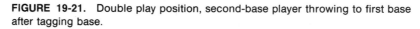

FIGURE 19-21. Double play position, second-base player throwing to first base after tagging base.

2. Field batted balls hit to various positions and with varying speeds. Throw to first base and to second base.
3. Field batted balls and practice the double-play situation.
4. Catch pop-ups in the vicinity of third base.
5. Tag runners stealing third base.

Playing the Outfield

The position of the outfielders should enable them to cover their area from the infield to the fence and it should vary according to the strength and weakness of the batter. The overhand throw is used when throwing to the infield because it is usually more accurate due to the fact that side spin is not put on the ball, which causes it to curve. Use the techniques for fielding ground balls and fly balls.

Practice Suggestions

1. Catch fly balls hit to various positions, including over one's head.
2. Field ground balls hit to various positions.
3. Make throws to second base, third base, home plate, and to a relay player. Do the same with players running the bases.
4. Throw to targets at the various bases.

PLAYING STRATEGY

Fast Pitch softball permits most of the team strategies used in baseball. It is varied according to any given game situation and the philosophical beliefs of the coach. The winning team will be the one that not only masters individual fundamentals but that functions as a unit in the execution of team plays. In Slow Pitch softball there are no offensive plays, since a baserunner cannot leave the base until the pitched ball reaches home plate and cannot advance until the ball is hit or the batter is walked.

SAFETY PROCEDURES

The following safety procedures should be observed in order to minimize the possibility of injuries.

1. Do pre-game throwing on the field in two lines facing one another. If waiting to play on an occupied field, move away from the spectators.
2. Have batting practice organized so that one group does not hit toward another group.
3. Grip the bat tightly so it will not slip from the hands. Keep the hands dry and only use bats with the proper safety grip. Do not swing a bat near other players. Drop the bat, do not throw it, after batting.

4. Stretch the leg muscles before running especially on cool days. Condition the legs by doing extra running.
5. Anchor bases firmly to the ground.
6. Perfect sliding techniques before using them. Always avoid unnecessary slides.
7. Wear proper equipment at all times.
8. Wear a mask when catching.
9. Throw easily early in the season until the arm becomes conditioned. Warm up thoroughly before each game.
10. Keep equipment organized and in the dugout. Do not leave it scattered around or in the playing area.
11. Keep playing field clear of rocks, depressions, obstructions, or any other foreign substance.
12. Learn the correct procedure for calling for fly balls and for covering bases to avoid collisions.
13. Play hard but do not use tactics that would injure an opponent or cause a fight.
14. Learn to accept decisions of the umpires and to avoid anger. A person who is always angry not only increases the probability of making more errors but also of getting injured. Always concentrate on playing the game the best way possible.

TERMINOLOGY

Appeal play A play upon which an umpire cannot make a decision until requested by a player or a coach.

Assist Fielding credit for a player who throws or deflects a batted or thrown ball in which a put-out results, or would have resulted except for a subsequent error.

Battery The pitcher and the catcher.

Batting average The number of hits divided by the times at bat.

Blooper A batted fly ball that goes just over the head of the infielders and just in front of the outfielders.

Cleanup hitter The number four batter in the batting order, a position usually occupied by the team's heaviest hitter.

Control The ability of a pitcher to throw the ball to a desired area when pitching.

Count The number of balls and strikes on the batter.

Cut-off A throw from the outfield that is intercepted by an infielder for the purpose of throwing out a runner other than the intended runner.

Double play Two consecutive put-outs occurring between the time the ball leaves the pitcher's hand and its return to the pitcher.

Error A misplay or mistake by the defensive team that results in prolonging the turn at bat of the batter or the time on base of the baserunner.

Fielder's choice The batter is safe because the defensive player elected to retire a preceding baserunner.

Force out An out as a result of a defensive player with the ball tagging a runner or the base to which the baserunner must go because the batter became a baserunner.

Fungo bat A lightweight bat used in hitting balls to fielders during practice.

Grand slam The batter hits a home run with the bases loaded.

Hit A ball hit in such a way that the batter or preceding baserunners are not retired by good defensive play.

Hot corner The third base area.

Infield fly A fair fly ball that can be caught by an infielder with runners on first and second, or first, second, and third before two are out. The batter is declared out by the umpire.

Keystone sack The second base area.

On deck The player in line to follow batter at the plate. The place for waiting is the "On-deck Circle."

Overthrow A thrown ball that goes into foul territory beyond the boundary lines of the playing field on an attempt to retire a runner who has not reached or is off a base.

Passed ball A legally delivered pitch that should have been held or controlled by the catcher, which allows a baserunner to advance. A dropped third strike that permits the batter to reach first base in Fast Pitch is an error, not a passed ball.

Put-out An out credited to the fielder who last handles the ball on a play that retires the batter or a baserunner.

Running squeeze A play where the runner on third base starts for home with the pitch because he knows the batter is going to bunt the ball.

Sacrifice bunt A play where the batter bunts the ball to advance a baserunner and is thrown out at first base, or would have been if the ball was played properly.

Sacrifice fly A fly ball that is caught and after which a baserunner crosses home plate to score a run.

Safety squeeze A play where the baserunner on third base starts for home after the batter bunts the ball.

Switch hitter A batter who bats both right- and left-handed.

Texas leaguer Same as a *Blooper.*

Wild pitch A legally delivered pitch so wide or low or high that the catcher cannot stop or control the ball, which allows a baserunner to advance.

SELECTED REFERENCES

BLAKE, O. WILLIAMS, and ANNE VOLP. *Lead-up Games to Team Sports.* Englewood Cliffs, N.J.: Prentice-Hall, 1964.

CASADY, DONALD R. *Sports Activities for Men.* New York: Macmillan Publishing Co., Inc., 1974.

DOBSON, MARGARET, and BECKY SISLEY. *Softball for Girls.* New York: Ronald Press, 1971.

Encyclopaedia Brittanica, vol. 20. Chicago: Encyclopaedia Brittanica, Inc., 1972.

GENSEMER, ROBERT, and MARY BEHLING. *Beginning Softball.* Belmont, Calif.: Wadsworth Publishing Company, Inc., 1970.

JONES, BILLIE J., and MARY JO MURRAY. *Softball Concepts for Coaches and Teachers.* Dubuque, Iowa: Wm. C. Brown Company, Publishers, 1978.

KNEER, MARION E., and CHARLES L. McCORD. *Softball.* Dubuque, Iowa: Wm. C. Brown Company, Publishers, 1966.

LITTLEWOOD, MARY. *Women's Softball.* Chicago: The Athletic Institute, 1971.

Merit Students Encyclopedia, vol. 17. New York: Macmillan Educational Corporation, 1976.

NOREN, ARTHUR T. *Softball with Official Rules,* 3rd ed. New York: The Ronald Press Company, 1966.

Official Softball Guide and Rulebook. Oklahoma City: Amateur Softball Association.

Official Softball Rules (current ed.). The International Joint Rules Committee on Softball. P.O. Box 11437, Oklahoma City, Okla.

PORTER, DON E. "Softball: Past, Present and Future." *Journal of Health, Physical Education, Recreation,* 42 (May 1971): 36–37.

WALSH, LOREN. *Contemporary Softball.* Chicago: Contemporary Books, Inc., 1978.

World Book Encyclopedia, vol. 18. Chicago: World Book-Childcraft International, Inc., 1979.

Audio-Visual Aids

Amateur Softball Association, 2801 N. E. 50th, Oklahoma City, Oklahoma, 73111
Softball Rules in Pictures
Flip Chart—covers rules, questions and umpire mechanics
35mm Rule Illustration Slide Set—appeal plays, strike zone, infield fly, interference, fair and foul territory, foul tip, obstruction, overthrow, run does not count, batter is out, etc.

Athletic Institute, 805 Merchandise Mart, Chicago, Ill. 60654
Softball—Eight filmstrip units:
Unit I—The History of Softball
Unit II—Throwing
Unit III—Fielding
Unit IV—Hitting
Unit V—Baserunning
Unit VI—Pitching
Unit VII—Base Play
Unit VIII—Defensive Team Play
Softball—Super 8 mm films demonstrated by members of Orange City, California Lionettes Women's Softball Team.
SB-1 (3:45 min.)—Overhand Throw; Sidearm Throw
SB-2 (3:45 min.)—Catching Above Waist; Catching Below Waist
SB-3 (3:48 min.)—Fielding Long-hit Fly Ball; Fielding Ground Balls
SB-4 (3:42 min.)—Batting
SB-5 (3:42 min.)—Sacrifice Bunt; Bunt for Base Hit
SB-6 (3:42 min.)—Running to First Base; Running Extra Bases; Runner's Lead-off
SB-7 (3:30 min.)—Defensive Run Down
SB-8 (3:42 min.)—Hook Slide; Straight-in Slide

SB–9 (3:42 min.)—Pitching; Windmill Style; Slingshot Style

SB–10 (3:50 min.)—Tag Outs; Force Outs

SB–11 (3:48 min.)—Double Play by Shortstop; Double Play by Second Basewomen

SB–12 (3:15 min.)—The Catcher

Major League Baseball Film Division, Room 402, 1650 Broadway, New York, N.Y. 10019. Films for rental.

Batting Fundamentals (11 min., sound, b & w)—Covers the stance, grip, stride, swing, follow-through and bunting.

Hitting (26 min., sound, color)—Baseball's toughest hitters discuss techniques that make a slugger and demonstrate how it is done.

School Film Service, 549 W. 123rd St., New York, N.Y. 10027

Softball Rules for Boys—Set of six filmstrips. Also set for girls.

Part I—The Game

Part II—Pitching Rules

Part III—Batting Rules

Part IV—Baserunning Rules

Part V—Baserunning Rules (cont.)

Part VI—Officiating

TEAM HANDBALL

THIS CHAPTER WILL ENABLE YOU TO:

♦ Identify and demonstrate the basic skills associated with team handball.
♦ Develop at least one practice formation for each of the basic skills: pass, catch, throw, and dribble.
♦ Understand and demonstrate simple rules and regulations.
♦ Understand and demonstrate free throw, penalty throw, corner throw, throw-in, and throw-off.
♦ Identify and name the positions of players.

NATURE AND PURPOSE

Team handball may be played indoors or outdoors by children or adults of both sexes. Team handball employs fundamental motor skills such as running, throwing, catching, jumping, and defensive and offensive strategies similar to the motor skills used in basketball, soccer, and hockey.

The object of the game is to pass and/or dribble the ball toward the opponent's goal and then shoot the ball into the goal. The ball is played primarily with the hands. However, any portion of the body above the knee can be used to play the ball.

COURT, EQUIPMENT, PLAYERS

The Playing Area

1. The playing area (indoors or outdoors) should be a rectangular surface with dimensions of 126 to 147 feet in length, and 60 to 73 feet in width (Figure 20-1). For a physical education class, a basketball court can easily be adapted to an indoor playing court by taping the goal-area line and the free-throw line.
2. The goal area is a semicircular space marked off by the goal-area line which is drawn in front of the goal at a distance of 20 feet, with a radius of 20 feet from the back inside edges of the goal posts.
3. The free-throw line is drawn as a broken line parallel to and 10 feet beyond the goal-area line.
4. The penalty-throw line is 3 feet 3 inches long and is drawn at a distance of 23 feet from the goal.
5. The goal is in the middle of each goal line and measures 6 feet 7 inches in height and 10 feet in width. If possible, a loose net, measuring 2 feet 8 inches at the top and 3 feet 3 inches at the bottom, should be attached behind the goal post. For a

physical education class, two poles, such as volleyball or badminton poles, with a rope tied across them will serve as a goal.

The Ball

A round ball is used that will vary in weight and circumference according to the age and sex of the players. For males over age 15, the ball should weigh from 15 to 19 ounces and be 23 to 24 inches in circumference; for females and boys under age 15, the ball should weigh 11½ to 14 ounces and measure 21 to 22 inches around. For physical education classes, a playground ball or volleyball will serve the purpose of the game. However, basketballs and soccer balls should not be used.

Players

Each team consists of 7 players (6 court players and 1 goalkeeper) with 5 additional players for substitution. The positions of players are designated as goalkeeper, center half, right and left backs, center forward, and right and left wingers (see Figure 20-1).

BASIC RULES

Duration of the Game

1. Playing times for a regulation game will vary depending upon the age and sex of the players: for men—two periods of 30 minutes with an interval of 10 minutes; for women and junior males—two periods of 25 minutes with an interval of 10 minutes; and for all other players—two periods of 20 minutes with a 10-minute interval.
2. The winning team from referee's coin toss has the choice of either the end, defense, or offense.

3. By referee's whistle, the game must start at the center of the court only by passing the ball to another teammate. All players must be within their own half of the court at the beginning.
4. After each goal is scored, the other team will always start the game at the center of the court.
5. A goal cannot be scored directly from the throw-on.

Playing the Ball

1. The ball can be played in any manner with any part of the body except below the knee. (For violation of this rule a free throw is awarded to the opposition.)
2. The ball cannot be held for more than three seconds if the player is not moving. (Otherwise, a free throw is awarded to the opposition.)
3. The ball can be bounced once or repeatedly with either hand while moving or standing—like a dribble in basketball.
4. Once the ball has been seized with one or both hands, it must be played off within three seconds or after three steps have been taken. (Otherwise, free throw is awarded to the opposition.)
5. Any ball that touches a referee and/or goal post is still playable.
6. Players cannot dive for rolling balls that are on the ground.
7. The ball may be continuously rolled on the ground with one hand.
8. When the ball has passed the touch line, the ball can be put into play by the other team as in basketball, and the throw-in should take place from the point where the ball crossed the touch line.
9. If the ball is touched by a defensive player except the goalkeeper, and travels across the goal line outside the goal, a corner throw is awarded to the attacking team.

Approach to Opponent

Players are not permitted to:

1. Block an opponent with arms, hands, or legs. (Free throw is awarded to opposition.)
2. Hold, hit, push, run into, or jump at the opponent, throw oneself down in front of or endanger an opponent in any other way. (Free throw is awarded to opposition.)
3. Throw the ball intentionally at an opponent or execute a dangerous feint by moving the ball towards the opponent. (Free throw is awarded to opposition.)

The Goal Area

1. No player except the goalkeeper may enter the goal area.

2. A player of the defending team, providing the entry is intentional and for the clear purpose of defense, shall have a penalty throw (23 feet) awarded to the attacking team.
3. There shall be no penalty if a player enters the goal area after playing the ball.
4. Inside the goal-area line the ball belongs to the goalkeeper. No other player shall touch a ball that is lying, rolling, or being held by the goalkeeper inside this area.
5. The ball shall be thrown neither into one's own goal area nor to the goalkeeper. (Penalty throw is awarded to the opposition team.)
6. A ball in the air is not considered to be in the goal area.

The Goalkeeper

1. So long as the goalkeeper remains inside the goal area, the goalkeeper shall be allowed to defend the goal in every possible way including kicking the ball with the feet while the ball is moving toward the goal or is inside the goal area.

FIGURE 20-1. Team handball court and players' positions.

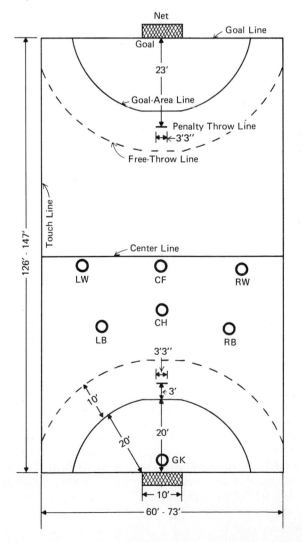

2. The goalkeeper is allowed to leave the goal area without the ball. When he/she does, the same rules apply to the goalie as to the rest of the team.
3. The goalie shall not touch a ball that is lying or rolling outside the goal area.

Scoring

1. A goal is made when the ball has passed the goal line inside the goal with its *entire* circumference.
2. A goal made by the defending team is also scored as a goal.
3. After every goal is made, the other team should start the game from the center of the court.

Penalty Throw

1. When the offensive player has lost a clear chance of scoring by the defensive player's foul, the offensive player shall be awarded a penalty throw from the 23 foot line.
2. During a penalty throw no other player except the goalkeeper shall be allowed between the goal-area line and the free-throw line.
3. The penalty throw shall be aimed directly at the goal.

Free Throw

1. All violations of the rules, except the penalty throw shall have a free throw awarded to the opposing team.
2. All free throws are taken from the point where the violation occurred except a violation between the free-throw line and the goal-area line, in which case the free throw shall be taken at the free-throw line.
3. During a free throw, players of the defending team shall stand 10 feet away from the player having the free throw.
4. A goal may be scored directly from a free throw.

SUGGESTED LEARNING SEQUENCE

Team handball is an activity that can be learned very quickly. It may be played at all levels by both sexes and on a coeducational basis. A basic game can be played at an early stage of the physical education class; offensive and defensive formations and styles of play may be added as the level of skill increases. It is important to discuss terminology, rules, skills, and strategies at a time when most appropriate and meaningful to the discussion of a particular concept.

A. Purpose of the Game
B. Skills and Techniques. The skills of passing, shooting, and dribble are best taught in combination with each other.

1. Passes for short distances
   a. Bounce
   b. Close Hand-Off
   c. Hook
   d. Chest
   e. Shovel
   f. Overhead
2. Passes for medium distances
   a. Ground
   b. Jump
   c. Shoulder (baseball)
   d. Side Arm
3. Catching
4. Dribble
5. Shooting
   a. Jump Shot
   b. Dive Shot
   c. Underhand Shot
   d. Reverse Shot
   e. Side Throw
   f. Lob Shot
   g. Penalty Throw
6. Goalkeeping. Goalkeeping should be started early in the sequence. A few minutes practice each day will add to the quality of the game.
C. Playing Strategies
   1. Offensive
   2. Defensive
D. Rules. Discuss the rule when most applicable to a given situation or skill.
E. Terminology. Terms should be discussed as they arise in the normal progression.

It is recommended that scrimmage time be included in early lessons. The length of scrimmage time will increase as the unit progresses.

SKILLS AND TECHNIQUES

The basic skills to be discussed in this section are passing, catching, dribbling, and shooting.

Passing

Passing is the most important element of team handball. It allows a player to move the ball quickly and accurately so as to advance the ball and set up scoring opportunities. Team handball passing fundamentals are quite similar to those utilized in basketball.

Learning Cues

1. The speed of the receiver as well as the distance between the receiver and the passer will determine how hard the ball should be thrown and the type of pass to be used.
2. For practice purposes the non-throwing arm should be pointed in the direction of the throw. (In actual game situations, more deception must

be used so that the individual does not "tele-graph" his pass.)

3. Use finger-tip control to ensure a more consistantly accurate pass.
4. Maintain proper balance and distribution of body weight to ensure a more accurate pass. Shift your weight from the back to front foot maintaining momentum behind the ball for a crisp pass. (Don't throw a pass when you are off balance except in improvised or emergency situations.)
5. Step forward with the leg opposite to throwing arm.
6. Snap your wrist upon release.
7. Select a pass which is appropriate for a specific situation.
8. After you pass always be ready to penetrate the defense and await a return pass.
9. A properly thrown pass will usually enable your teammates to catch the ball more easily.
10. A generalized rule to keep in mind when passing the ball is always to make a threatening motion (feint) to score before passing to a teammate.

Passes can be divided into three categories characterizing the distance, trajectory, and type (arm form) of the throw.

Short Distance Passes. Passes which are normally used in short distances include:

1. *Bounce*—The ball should be thrown so that it bounces approximately three feet in front of the receiver. The receiver should move toward the ball and try to catch it on the short hop (as in baseball) in such a manner that he is immediately prepared to throw the ball.
2. *Close Hand-Off* (*front and back*)—In this pass (which usually occurs in close quarters around the goal area) the player merely hands the ball to a teammate in a manner similar to an "end-around" (reverse) play in football. Deception is of utmost importance in this pass. It should only be used after considerable practice and by players who are very familiar with each other since the chance for error is much greater than most other passes.
3. *Hook*—This pass is very useful when a player is closely guarded by two or more players. It can also be used when a player is in the air for a jump shot. He simply releases the ball at the top of his jump to one of his teammates who might be penetrating toward the goal. This pass is the same as the "hook shot" in basketball.
4. *Chest* (*push*)—This pass should be one of the most frequently used in short distances. It is one of the most accurate passes and relatively simple to learn. The same fundamentals can be applied as the two-hand chest pass.
5. *Shovel* (*scoop*)—This pass is less frequently used than those passes described thus far. The player

picks a low ball upon the short hop and remains in a crouched position while quickly tossing the ball (underhand) to a teammate.
6. *Overhead* (*two hands*)—One of the methods of putting the ball back into play after it has crossed one of the side lines. The throw is taken by a player of the team which did not cause the ball to go out. The player making the throw must have both feet touching the surface outside the sideline and throw in to the playing area with one or two hands in any manner.

Medium Distance Passes. Passes which are normally used in medium distances include:

1. *Ground* (*"roller"*)—When all other passing lanes are blocked it may, on occasion, be appropriate to roll the ball between a defender's legs. Also, when there is a "scramble" for a loose ball on the court and a player can't control the ball completely, he can roll it to a nearby teammate.
2. *Jump*—When normal passing lanes are impeded, a player can use this pass by jumping into the air and releasing the ball in a manner similar to the shoulder throw.
3. *Shoulder* (*baseball*)—When throwing, the player should not attempt to grip the ball as if it were a baseball. Rather, he should allow the ball to rest in his hand with a flexed wrist and fingers spread wide enough to cover as much of the ball surface as is comfortably possible.
4. *Side Arm*—This pass is the same as the shoulder pass except the positioning and action of the throwing arm may be likened to a ¾ and/or "submarine" pitching motion as in baseball. The length of stride for the lead leg should correspond (approximately) to the length of the pass. For a right-handed throw the right foot can remain in place (with weight back) and the left foot can stride forward simultaneously with the arm-throwing motion.

Catching

An accurate throw will result in an accurate catch.

Learning Cues

1. Whenever possible, players are to catch the ball with two hands to ensure best control.
2. The player should always attempt to catch the ball with his finger tips spread. Whenever possible he should not allow the ball to make contact with the palms.
3. The elbows should be flexed and the body relaxed to absorb the impact of a hand-thrown ball.
4. Whenever possible the player should move forward to meet the ball, maintaining eye contact with the ball as it comes into his hands.
5. Upon receiving a pass, a player should be immediately prepared to shoot, dribble, or pass the ball again.

Dribble

In team handball the dribble is used to advance the ball up the court when a player is not closely guarded and to gain "rhythm" when attempting to move the ball for purposes of attacking the goal or setting up a possible scoring play. Because of their strong basketball orientation, most Americans have a tendency to dribble too much in team handball.

The dribble is similar to that used in basketball except that the player may take three steps when the ball is seized by either one or both hands. When the ball is seized, it must be played off within three steps or three seconds.

Shooting

The primary objective of attacking the goal in team handball is to score. Shooting will not occur in team handball as frequently as in basketball. Players must learn to be patient and work for a good opportunity to score a goal. This does not mean that players should be overcautious, as team handball is an aggressive game in which the offense must continuously attack the goal and generate its own scoring opportunities.

Learning Cues—Basic Shooting Principles

1. The shooter must have a definite throwing direction in mind prior to releasing the ball. Shots blocked and easily caught by the goalie often result in fast-break 2-on-1 situations for the opposing team. The most vulnerable shooting lanes are the high and low corners of the goal mouth. It is generally agreed that shots directed to the lower corners of the goal have greater scoring percentages.
2. The momentum of the shooter should always be toward or perpendicular to the goal.
3. The use of deception is of utmost importance. The shooter should attempt to draw the goalkeeper towards one corner of the goal and depending upon the commitment of the goalkeeper, the player should aim his shot for the opposite corner.
4. The shoulder pass is the most frequently used in team handball shooting.
   a. The ball is held behind the head with the arm cocked to hide the ball from the goalie and make it more difficult for defensive players to take the ball away.
   b. The non-shooting arm remains forward to ward off defenders and assist in maintaining balance.
   c. The shot should be released with a snap of the wrist and follow-through (as in throwing a football or baseball).
5. Many foot movement patterns can be utilized in team handball shots, including hop steps, crossover steps, and running steps. New players are

FIGURE 20-2. The jump shot.

encouraged to experiment with different step and dribble combinations which fit their individual abilities.

Types of Specific Shots

Jump Shot. This shot simply involves the use of the shoulder throw (pass) in which the ball is released at the height of the jump with the momentum of the body directed toward the goal rather than falling away. By jumping high in the air the player is able to see the goal more clearly and determine the direction of his shots.

Dive Shot. This shot also utilizes the shoulder throw. The shooter stretches his body out and directs his momentum toward the goal. He should release the ball at the last possible moment as close to the goal mouth as he can.

Learning Cues

1. The weight is evenly distributed on both feet as the shot is initiated.
2. The body is leaning, moving in a position parallel with the floor.
3. The upper body is thrust upward in a diving action toward the goal.
4. Snap the wrist and release the ball quickly.
5. Break the fall with your chest and both hands positioned at your side about chest level.

Underhand Shot. The side arm or ¾ pitching motion is used in this shot. The right-handed thrower turns (twists) his left side toward the goal. To generate increased power, a crossover step is used with the push-off coming from the rear foot. This shot is used when upper scoring lanes are cut off by the defense. The shot is on a low trajectory with a continuous follow-through.

Reverse Shot (circle). This shot is used around the goal area when the defender is playing behind and/or overplaying to the shooting side. When you are unable to execute a normal shot, lower your center of gravity (bend knees), fake to the strong (normal shooting) side, turn and quickly pivot away from the strong side on your right foot (if you are right-handed) releasing the ball in a side-arm motion. (This is similar to the initial backward motion in the discus throw.) As the ball is released, body momentum should be directed toward the goal.

Side Throw (twister). This is a relatively weak shot but with the proper element of surprise it can be successful. It is most frequently used in close to the goal area when an attempted shot with a regular shoulder throw is stopped by a defender. If you are right-handed, drop your left shoulder, step across your body with your right foot, then execute the same arm motion described for the reverse shot with body momentum directed toward the goal.

Lob Shot. This shot is often used in a 1-on-1 fast break situation and also in certain 2-on-1 situations. When the goalie comes out to challenge, the offensive player lobs the ball over his head into the goal, or to his teammate if this is a 2-on-1 situation. Timing is of utmost importance in the execution of this shot.

Penalty Throw. This throw is taken at the 23 foot penalty-throw line. It is a 1-on-1 situation with the goalie as the only defender. The goalie may move about and come within 10 feet of the penalty line. The player who is awarded the penalty throw cannot move his foot or touch the penalty line until the ball is released. The offensive player has three seconds in which to shoot from the time the referee blows the whistle to begin the throw. The type of shot normally utilized in this situation is the shoulder or side throw. The other players must remain outside the free throw line area until the shot is taken. They should strategically position themselves around the goal to be ready for a blocked shot which might possibly rebound out into the area of play.

PRACTICE SUGGESTIONS—BASIC SKILLS

Drills for team handball basic skills—passing, catching, and dribbling the ball—are similar to those in basketball. Therefore basketball drills should be utilized to practice the basic skills, particularly passing, catching, and dribbling the ball with the following points in mind:

1. The ball is much smaller than the ball used in basketball. Therefore the ball can be easily handled by either one or both hands.
2. It is permissible to take a maximum of three steps or three seconds with the ball in either one or both hands. For example, after catching the ball from another player, you may take three steps and start dribbling. When you stop dribbling, you must either pass or shoot after taking no more than three steps or three seconds.

Goalkeeping

The goalkeeper is the most important defensive player in team handball. The goalie should have quick hands and quick feet, must be fearless of the ball, and be ble to throw the ball well in initiating fast break plays. The goalie can use any part of the

FIGURE 20-3. Setting up for the reverse shot: fake to one side.

FIGURE 20-4. Reverse shot, release with side-arm motion.

body to deflect shots. Within the goal area there is no restriction on how many steps the goalie can take or the time the ball can be held (without the ball, the goalie may become a court player at any time). All rules applying to court players then apply to the goalie.

Learning Cues—Goalkeeping Fundamentals

1. The goalie should know the position of the ball on the court at all times.
2. He should maintain a low center of gravity with weight evenly distributed on the balls of his feet.
3. In blocking shots the goalkeeper's palms should always face out toward the field of play. His hands should be relaxed enough to "give" with a shot to keep it under control in the goal area and not allow the ball to rebound back out onto the field of play.
4. Low shots in close to the goalie's legs should be fielded (blocked) in a manner similar to that which an infielder employs when fielding a ground ball.
5. On shots that are low and to the side, the goalie must stride to the side with his hands and outside foot stretching simultaneously to block the ball.
6. Similar to the goalkeeping used in hockey or soccer, the goalie should move out away from the goal mouth in an attempt to cut down the best shooting angles.
7. Probably the most important and fundamental rule to remember in goalkeeping is to stop the ball by any manner possible.
8. On high hand shots the goalie should not attempt to catch the ball, rather he should deflect the ball over the top of the goal.
9. In defending against the penalty shot, the goalie should move out toward the 23-foot penalty line to cut down the shooter's angle.
10. The goalie should always play one foot out from the goal line to avoid a self-scored goal.
11. When the goalie recovers a blocked or missed shot, he returns the ball to play by means of a "throw-out." In this instance, the ball is free and the defense can try and intercept the pass out and score directly.
12. It is recommended that the goalie wear a protective supporter, long pants, and a long-sleeved shirt to cut down on the "sting" of blocked shots.

BASIC STRATEGY

Defensive Strategies

When the ball is lost, all players of the team become defensive players with certain defensive responsibilities according to the defensive strategies employed.

Generally, defensive strategies are divided into (1) man-to-man defense, (2) zone defense, and (3) a combination of the two. In defensive play, a player should always attempt to keep the opponent in front of him or else the opponent should be slightly overplayed to the shooting arm side. ("Stay between your man and the goal" is a general rule to follow.)

Man-to-Man Defense

Each defensive player must cover one designated player of the attacking team regardless of whether he has the ball or not. The offensive player is continually blocked off and hindered in attacking actions.

Zone Defense

Each defensive player is responsible to protect a particular area against the athlete. Zone defense may require less running, but more teamwork is needed for an effective zone defense.

Combinations

6-0 Defense (Figure 20-5). Six court players stand alongside and in front of the goal-area line, each having the specific responsibility to protect a certain area. The players must coordinate with each other to cover any space uncovered which may be created by one of the defensive players who attempts to attack an opponent with the ball. Taller players should be placed in the center of the defensive zone and smaller players on the outside.

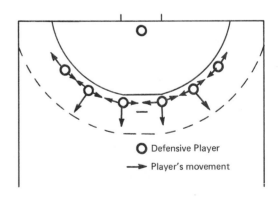

FIGURE 20-5. The 6-0 defensive formation.

5-1 Defense (Figure 20-6). The basic concept of a 5-1 is similar to that of a box and 1 defense used in basketball. Five players stand in front of the goal-area line. One player, pulled out to the free-throw line, has the two assignments of covering the man with the ball and/or covering a good shooter. This player must be an all-round athlete. The fast break is frequently originated by this player.

4-2 Defense (Figure 20-7). Four defensive players encompass the goal-area line and shift as a unit. Two defensive players move out to the free-throw line in order to concentrate on intercepting passes

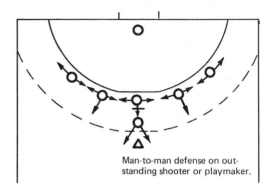

Man-to-man defense on outstanding shooter or playmaker.

FIGURE 20-6.   The 5-1 defensive formation.

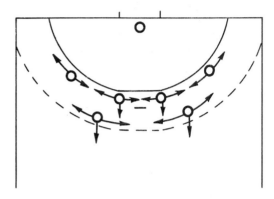

FIGURE 20-7.   The 4-2 defensive formation.

and harrassing the ball handlers to prevent their taking the most advantageous routes toward the goal area. These two players not only have to protect the central axis, but also are responsible for filling in gaps between defensive players behind them.

3-3 Defense (Figure 20-8).   Three defensive players stand on the middle of the goal-area line and the other three players stand in front of the free-throw line. These three players as a unit have to shift toward the attacking point of the offensive team to protect against long-distance shootings. This formation is vulnerable against the team having shots from angles, and requires that the team have a well-versed goalkeeper.

FIGURE 20-8.   The 3-3 defensive formation.

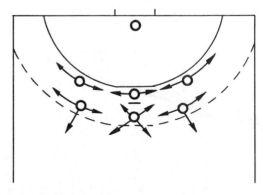

Offensive Strategies

In the deployment of any offensive alignment, every effort should be made to utilize the entire offensive floor area. It is of utmost importance that continuous movement be maintained. Upon receiving a pass, every player should make a motion of threatening to score each time in scoring range. In order to spread the defense out as much as possible, it is important that players maintain good spacing and that most plays be initiated from approximately 40 feet. Team handball is a game of fast continuous movement. Whenever possible, dribbling must be avoided and the ball should be passed quickly between players. Effective screening (similar to that used in basketball) is a key to the success of most offensive patterns in team handball. Screens and double screens can be improvised from any of the offensive formations presented. The following represent some common offensive formations.

2-4 Offense.   This is the most frequently utilized offensive formation in team handball. In this formation the two backcourt players are situated at around 40 feet. The wing players are spread out wide for the best possible shooting angles. The circle runners are strategically positioned between the two wing players at 20 feet. A variety of offensive maneuvers can be initiated from this basic offensive pattern. This offense will spread out most zone defenses and allow opportunities for scoring between the defensive players.

3-3 Offense.   This offense is also effective in spreading out the coverage of a zone defense. If a team possesses three strong shooters, this is an excellent offensive formation to employ. Constant movement of the ball is essential and each player must threaten to score each time he receives a pass.

1-5 Offense.   This offensive formation can best be employed by a team which has some strong inside players who are very physical. Effective inside screening is the key to a successful 1-5 offense. It is of utmost importance that one player always stays back to guard against a possible fast break.

1-3-2 Offense.   One back court player is situated around 40 feet as a playmaker; three players are placed around the middle of the free-throw line; and two players become outside and circle runners between the free-throw line and the goal-area line.

The back court player passes the ball to make a play. The three middle players attempt to block defensive players by whatever means to create an opportunity for the two circle runners to make effective shooting chances. The two circle runners must constantly move and feint to confuse defensive players, and at the same time make a good shot into the goal.

It is recommended that various offensive and defensive strategies should be developed by utilizing knowledge and skills from similar team sports such as soccer, basketball, field hockey, and even football.

TERMINOLOGY

Corner throw When the ball is played over his own goal line by a defending player (except the goalkeeper), on either side of the goal, the game is restarted by means of a throw from the corner of the court by one of the attacking players. The player must place one foot on the corner and throw the ball in, using either hand.

Court player Member of the handball team actually playing on the court, except the goalie.

Dive shot A means of trying to score a goal by launching the entire body into the air toward the goal in an attempt to gain more distance.

Free throw A throw awarded to the opposing team when the other team is in violation of certain rules of the game.

Free-throw line The broken line parallel to the goal-area line at an extra distance of 10 feet; from this line free throws awarded near the goal area are taken.

Goal A goal is considered scored when the ball has passed wholly over the goal line between the uprights and underneath the crossbar of the goal.

Goal area The area of the playing court inside and including the goal-area line.

Goal-area line The semicircular line which is drawn in front of and on either side of the goal.

Goalkeeper (goalie) The player who is allowed to play freely inside the goal area to defend the goal.

Goal line The line forming the end of the court which runs between the uprights of the goal and meets the sidelines at the corners of the court.

Penalty throw A shot attempted by any offensive player when an offensive player is prevented from making a clear goal-scoring chance by foul means. The player attempting the penalty throw is required to make a direct attempt to score a goal from the penalty-throw line.

Referee's throw A ball bounced by the referee to restart the game after an interruption of play caused by players of both teams committing simultaneous infractions of the rules or if the game has been interrupted for some other reason.

Throw-in The method of putting the ball back into play after it has crossed one of the sidelines. The throw is taken by a player of the team which did not cause the ball to go out. The player making the throw must have both feet touching the surface outside the sideline and throw the ball into the playing area with one or two hands in any manner.

Throw-on The method of putting the ball in play at the start of the game and after a goal is scored. The throw is made from the center of the court.

Throw-out The means the goalkeeper takes of throwing the ball onto the court after he has obtained possession of the ball in his goal area. Defensive players may place themselves at the goal-area line.

Throw-off The means the goalkeeper takes of throwing the ball onto the court after he has obtained possession of the ball in his goal area.

SELECTED REFERENCES

Korsgaard, Robert, and S. Jae Park. "Codified Rules of Team Handball." Ball State University, Muncie, Indiana, 1970.

Neil, Graham I. *Modern Team Handball: Beginner to Expert.* Montreal, Canada: McGill University, 1976.

Handbook of the International Handball Federation. Basie, Switzerland, I.H.F., 1960, p. 88.

I.H.F. Information Bulletin. Basel, Switzerland: International Handball Federation, Nos. 95 and 16, 1972.

Official U. S. Team Handball Rules. Jayfro Corp., P.O. Box 400, Waterford, Conn. 06385.

TENNIS

THIS CHAPTER WILL ENABLE YOU TO:

♦ Select tennis equipment that will be appropriate for you.
♦ Demonstrate the proper grips and techniques for the following strokes: serve, return of serve, approach shot, forehand, backhand, volley, lob, overhead.
♦ Understand the scoring procedures and the basic rules of play.
♦ Identify the playing courtesies, safety considerations, and basic terminology associated with tennis.

NATURE AND PURPOSE

Tennis is a game that has always appealed to both sexes and to both young and old. It is considered by many to be one of the best forms of corecreational sports. The pace of the game can be set to the individual's ability, for it may be played merely as a mild form of exercise, or so strenuously that it taxes one's endurance and strength to their limits. Speed, agility, coordination, and endurance can be developed, and indeed are needed to play a sound game of tennis.

The game of tennis can be played either as singles or doubles. The singles game has two participants, one individual opposing the other. The doubles game has four participants, two individuals teaming up to compete against another team of two. The doubles court is 9 feet wider than the singles court, having a 4½ foot alley on each side of the singles court.

The basic rules are the same for men's and women's tennis. To start the game, the server stands just behind his baseline to the *right* of his center service line, and puts the ball into play by striking it in the air in such a manner that it lands in his opponent's right service court. The server has two chances to put the ball into play. The ball that does not land in the proper service court is called a "fault" and is not played. A served ball that touches the net during the flight and lands in the proper service court is called a "let"; it is not counted as a fault nor is it played, but is served again.

The receiver must return the serve on its first bounce to the server's court. The rally continues until one of the players fails to return the ball, either on the fly or after the first bounce within the boundaries of his court.

When the point has been completed, the server stands just behind his baseline and to the *left* of the center service line and serves to his opponent's left service court, continuing to alternate left and right after each point until the game is completed. Upon completion of the game, the server becomes the receiver. Players change sides at the completion of each odd-numbered game.

In doubles, each player serves a game in turn—first a member of one team, then a member of the other team, and so on. The same order of serving is kept throughout the set.

Scoring

Points in tennis are called Love, 15, 30, 40, Deuce, Advantage, and Game.

0, or nothing, is called Love.

First point won by a player is called 15.

Second point won by a player is called 30.

Third point won by a player is called 40.

Fourth point won by a player gives him Game, provided his opponent does not have more than 30 (2 points).

If each player has won three points (40-all), the score is deuce. The next point won by a player gives him advantage. However, if he loses the next point, the score is again deuce. When either player wins two *consecutive* points following the score of deuce, the game is won by that player. The server's score is always given first. The score should be called loudly and clearly after every point.

In scoring, the player who first wins six games wins a *set,* unless both players have won five games; then it takes an advantage of two games to win, so the score could be 7-5, or 8-6, or 9-7, and so on.

In scoring the *match,* the player first winning

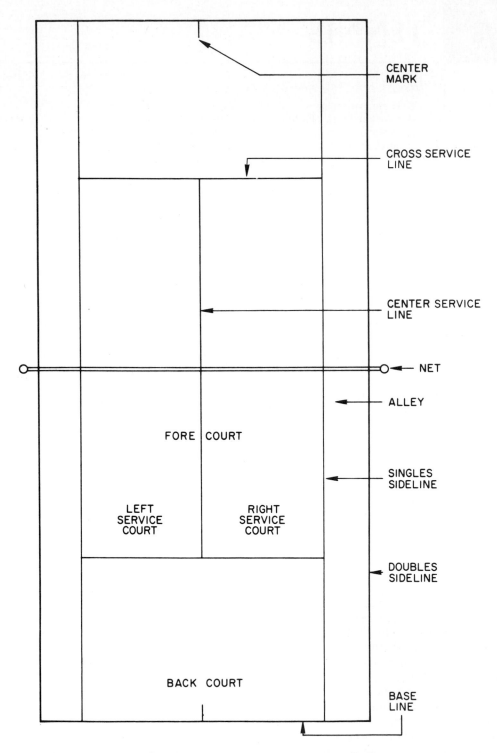

FIGURE 21-1. Lawn tennis court. For dimensions, refer to Appendix C.

two sets is generally declared the winner. In professional tennis matches, the winner of three sets is declared the winner of the men's match, while in the women's game the winner of two sets is declared the winner of the match. For example, match scores could be 6-0, 6-3, 6-2; 9-7, 4-6, 10-8; 2-6, 6-4, 6-4; 6-1, 6-1, 6-3; 4-6, 6-4, 6-4, 6-4; 6-0, 5-7, 7-5, 2-6, 8-6.

The VASSS scoring system (Van Alen Simplified Scoring System) is used today in most tournaments. There are two major aspects to this system. The first, and most popular, is the "nine-point sudden death tie-breaker," which takes effect when the game score is tied at 6 games all. At such times, the best 5 of 9 points are played to determine the winner of the set. The serving order continues, but now each player serves two points at a time until one player wins five points. Players change sides of the court after the fourth point. If the score becomes tied at four points all, the receiver dictates into which service court the ninth point is served. The second aspect of VASSS is termed the "no-add" rule: when the game score is tied at deuce (3-3) the next point wins the game. Again, the receiver dictates into which service court the no-add point should be played.

SELECTION OF EQUIPMENT

The selection of proper equipment is of utmost importance to the beginning tennis player as well as to the professional player. With good equipment the beginning player can eliminate many handicaps, and thereby get more enjoyment from mastering the fundamental skills.

Tennis Rackets

In selecting the racket, the player must give consideration to the weight, balance, grip size, stringing, and quality of the frame.

Rackets are manufactured in three different weights: light, medium, and heavy; they range from about 11 to 15 ounces. Women tend to prefer light rackets while men usually select medium or heavy racket frames. The "feel" of the racket as it is swung should be the most important factor. The person choosing a new racket should test each potential racket. In doing this and understanding the difference in racket composition, rackets can be compared and a selection made.

Most rackets are 27 inches long and measure 9 inches across the racket face. Recently, tennis rackets have been manufactured in different lengths, with oversized racket heads, and using various combinations of materials including wood, aluminum alloy, steel, magnesium, fiberglass, and graphite.

The quality of the racket is very important. The racket frame should be sturdy enough to withstand at least four or five restringings. The less expensive rackets soon lose their shape and are usually not a good long-term investment.

Basically, two types of string are manufactured for a tennis racket: gut and nylon. Gut strings are more expensive but also more resilient and pliable. This type is preferred by most tournament players. Gut requires more care than nylon and is vulnerable to humidity and wetness. Nylon strings do not have the elasticity of gut, but still are very comparable in play, are more durable, are impervious to dampness, and are less expensive. Nylon is very adequate for the beginning player.

When purchasing a racket, the retailer will usually request the player's preference for string tension. The higher the tension, the less control one tends to have because of the string tightness. Also, the racket frame can't withstand as many restringings when it is strung tightly. The recommended tension is between 55 and 57 pounds for beginning and intermediate players.

Rackets are manufactured to be evenly-balanced, head-heavy, or handle-heavy. Head-heavy rackets are preferred by players inclined to be ground strokers or base line players. Handle-heavy rackets are used by individuals who are predominantly net players. It is suggested that beginners select an evenly-balanced racket to start with.

The most important aspect of choosing an appropriate racket is the size of the grip. The grip size of the racket depends upon the hand size of the person. Grips usually range in circumference from four to five inches. Selection of proper grip size may require professional assistance. If the individual grips the racket in an Eastern forehand grip, the

FIGURE 21-2. Parts of a tennis racket.

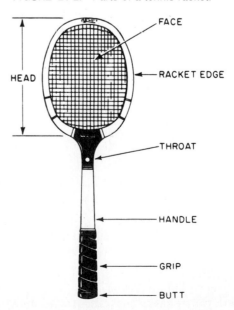

thumb should come just past the first knuckle of the middle finger. Correctly fitting a grip is of the utmost importance.

Tennis Balls

Most tennis balls are pressure-packed with compressed air and marked with numbers for identification. They are manufactured according to United States Tennis Association (USTA) specifications; that is, a ball must weigh two ounces, be two and one-half inches in diameter, and have a wool-felt covering.

Tennis balls are also produced to be court specific. Some are made especially for hard courts (asphalt or cement) by having more felt on the ball's cover. Others are made for soft court play on such surfaces as clay or grass.

SKILLS AND TECHNIQUES

The Grip

The importance of a proper grip cannot be stressed enough. There may be adjustments made in a player's swing, but a proper grip will last a player for a lifetime.

Special names have been given to the forehand grips, based upon the position of the palm against the racket handle.

When the palm sits upon the top right side, the grip is called the *Continental* (Figure 21-3). It requires a strong wrist and is used by some professionals for both forehand and backhand strokes.

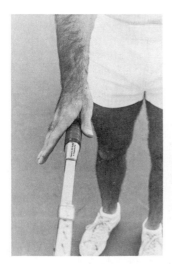

FIGURE 21-3.   Continental grip (front and back views)

When the palm sits on the back side of the handle, it is called an *Eastern* grip (Figure 21-4). The palm and the racket face are on the same plane, which gives the sensation of hitting the ball with the

FIGURE 21-4.   Eastern grip (front and back views)

palm of your hand. This is the most common grip and the one that will be strongly recommended in this chapter.

When the palm rests on the bottom of the handle, so that the palm points at the sky, it is called a *Western* grip (Figure 21-5). This is the least common grip, although some players use it to great advantage.

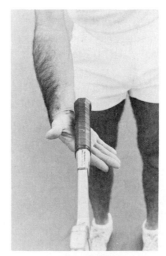
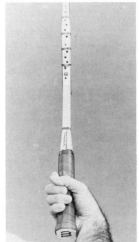

FIGURE 21-5.   Western grip (front and back views)

Eastern Grip.   Since this is the grip that is recommended for the forehand it will be the only grip covered in detail. A teacher that does not have an extensive tennis background can't go wrong by suggesting this grip. It is by far the most fundamentally sound.

If you are right-handed, start by holding the throat of your racket with your left hand so that the racket face is vertical to the ground. Then hold the racket at waist level with the right palm vertical and your fingers pointing slightly downward at approximately a 45-degree angle. The thumb should overlap and lie next to the middle finger, with the index finger spread. Now hold the racket out away from you and look at the top edge of your racket and the top edge of your right palm to see if they are both absolutely vertical. If you play this game correctly you'll rarely hit a shot that requires the racket to vary more than 10 degrees from the vertical position.

You can check your grip between points to see if the palm and the racket head are indeed vertical, but "feel" is all you can rely on as you play, especially if you switch grips between the forehand and the backhand; therefore, begin to think kinesthetically. Close your eyes and try to achieve the perfect grip, then open your eyes and see if you are right.

Eastern Backhand Grip. The backhand grip advocated in this chapter is the Eastern backhand grip. This is attained by putting the palm on the top of the racket, the knuckle of the index finger rides the top right ridge, and the thumb can be placed either behind the racket or underneath. This grip position provides the most stability and requires the least amount of wrist adjustment in order to provide a vertical racket head at impact.

Strokes

All the strokes are described in terms of a right-handed player's actions. There are some general principles that the player must be aware of:

1. Spin of the Ball. The direction in which the ball spins is determined by the trajectory taken by the racket before and after contact with the ball. If the racket comes from below the ball, is vertical at impact, and finishes above the ball, topspin (low to high) will be attained. If the racket starts above the ball and sweeps down to the ball, underspin (high to low) will be attained.
2. Nearly every successful hit is accomplished with a vertical racket head. A player *does not* come over the ball for topspin or under the ball for underspin!
3. With the exception of the serve and overhead all strokes in this chapter will be hit with a locked wrist. The swing will come from the shoulder and not the wrist.

The Serve

The serve is the first ball hit in every point. The motion is very similar to that of a baseball pitcher's throwing motion. A good way to start teaching the serve is just to watch the student throw the ball over the net. Have the student pretend the ball is the racket and don't be satisfied until the perfect motion is attained.

Many beginners prefer to use the regular forehand grip to hit a basic "flat" serve. But intermediate and advanced players should use the Continental grip, halfway between the Eastern forehand and Eastern backhand, in order to facilitate greater ball rotation with less stress on the wrist.

To attain a good service motion it is necessary to coordinate two movements simultaneously—the ball toss and the action of the racket. The toss is made by holding the ball near the finger tips, with the palm up, and then releasing the ball upwards with all fingers letting go at the same time.

Achieving spin on the ball is an important aspect of serving. There are three kinds of serves recommended:

1. Flat. A totally flat serve is a myth because every ball has some amount of spin. This serve has the least amount of spin and is attained by snapping the wrist up and forward through the middle of the ball.
2. Slice. Very much like a curveball in baseball. The racket face must move across the backside of the ball on an almost horizontal plane thus producing sidespin. Using the face of a clock as a reference the righthander would hit from 9 o'clock to 3 o'clock.
3. Topspin. The principle of applying topspin on a serve is basically the same as on a forehand or backhand. Swing from low to high and brush the back side of the ball at about a 45-degree angle. On the imaginary clock hit from 8 o'clock to 2 o'clock.

The Serve Motion

Figure 21-6 shows the sequence of motions involved in the service.

A. Ready Position. It is important to be totally relaxed before attempting to serve. The feet are shoulder width apart and the front shoulder is pointing in the direction the ball will be served. Weight is evenly distributed at this point.
B. To start the motion the players arms go down together and then start up together. Also begin to lean slightly forward.
C. Position C is crucial. At this point the ball is released and shoulder rotation must begin. The racket is slightly above the shoulder and the tossing arm is pointing toward the right net post so the toss will be 10 to 12 inches to the player's right. Height of the toss is 18 inches out of outstretched tossing arm. The object of the shoulder rotation is to let the right shoulder replace the position of the left shoulder. Weight at this point is mainly over the front foot with both feet still in contact with the ground.
D. The racket is forming a loop behind the player's back. The racket *does not* scratch the back but forms a loop. This loop is accomplished by maintaining a loose arm and rotating the shoul-

ders at the proper time. If the racket is hitting or touching the student's back at any time, the motion is out of sync.

E. Point of Contact. At impact the arm should be extended but not necessarily at the peak of one's reach (depending on spin desired). The chin is held upward, and for optimal power both feet should be in contact with the ground though weight should have transferred forward. Notice that contact is made to the right of the player's head and in line with the hitting shoulder.

F. Follow-Through. The right shoulder has replaced the position of the left shoulder and the player's momentum following impact has brought the back foot a step into the court. If the

player wishes to serve and volley, this will naturally become the first step toward the net. If not, the participant may step back and rally off of the baseline.

Serve and Volley

The footwork recommended for serve and volley are to step with the right foot, left foot, right foot, and then bring both feet into alignment (Figure 21-7). The closer you can get to the service line the better.

Learning Cues

1. No fancy movements. Just relax and take your time.

FIGURE 21-6. The service sequence.

A

B

C

D

E

F

| A | B | C | D |

FIGURE 21-7. Footwork for serve and volley.

2. To toss the ball, hold the ball with the finger tips and not the palm.
3. The toss must fit into the motion.
4. Chin up and hit up and out. This is true for all serves.
5. Think positive. Picture in your mind a successful serve before starting the motion.
6. Shoulder rotation and *not* the strength of the arm is the main source of power.
7. Hit the second serve with the same motion as the first; just with more topspin.

Practice Suggestions

1. Hit buckets of balls at specific targets to each service court.
2. Before serving, determine the spin to be desired (flat, slice, topspin) and then evaluate your success accordingly.

Loop Backhand

Figure 21-8 illustrates the sequence of motions involved in executing the loop backhand.

A. Ready Position. In a good ready position the player's feet are shoulder length apart and knees slightly bent. Elbows are winged out and the racket position is at a 45-degree angle to the ground. Note that the player is now holding the racket with an Eastern forehand grip.
B. Backswing. The first move, once determining the ball is coming to the backhand side, is to turn the shoulder and change the grip simultaneously. The grip recommended is the Eastern backhand. The body should be turned enough so that the back of the shoulder is pointing at the oncoming ball.

FIGURE 21-8. Loop backhand sequence.

| A | B | C |

D   E   F   G

FIGURE 21-8. (continued)

C. The backswing viewed from behind. The key points to note here are the position of the player's left elbow and the height of the racket face. The left arm is held high to keep the racket on the front side of the body and prevent it from getting wrapped behind you. This is very important if one is to limit the length of the stroke. The height of the racket face should be at eye level if you are going to loop.

D. Three movements happen simultaneously in this photo. The right foot steps into the ball, the racket drops to the bottom of the loop, and the knees bend to a crouch position. The racket must be below the level of the oncoming ball if topspin is to be achieved.

E. Position D viewed from behind. Notice how low the racket is and also that the racket face is slightly tilted downward. The arm is a radius and if the racket is to be vertical at impact and the wrist remain locked throughout the swing the racket face must be tilted downward at this point. The left hand may be used to help push the racket downward, but this is optional.

F. Impact with the Ball. The racket face is vertical and the arm is extended well in front of the body (8 to 10 inches in front of the right foot). Eyes are focused right on the point of contact. Knees have lifted upward so as to help lift the ball up (topspin) and the hips have rotated toward the net. Body weight has transferred forward slightly before impact.

G. Follow-Through. Following impact let the racket face and knuckles follow the flight of the ball until the arm is fully extended. Freeze at this point and check to make sure that your weight is forward and over your front foot, and also the racket should form an archway. If one was to drop the shoulder straight down, the racket should still form a perfect hitting position.

Learning Cues

1. Change grip and pivot body as early as possible.
2. Cradle the throat of the racket with the left hand—don't let the hitting arm take a solo.
3. Concentrate on bending the knees and getting low. The legs are a tremendous source of power.
4. Work hard to swing easy.
5. Reach forward and out away from the body for contact.
6. Keep the wrist locked.
7. Let the knuckles of the hitting hand be the guide for direction. As the knuckles go, so goes the racket head.
8. Reach out and upwards for the follow-through.
9. Always check the follow-through at the completion of a swing.
10. While the body is lifting, the head must remain stationary. Leave head and eyes glued on point of impact.

Practice Suggestions

1. Hit backhands toward a specific target area either from a ball machine or from someone feeding from across the net.
2. Hit off of a backboard.

Loop Forehand

Figure 21-9 shows the loop forehand sequence.

A. Ready Position. The feet are shoulder length apart and knees slightly bent. Elbows are winged out and the racket is at a 45-degree angle to the ground. The player is holding the racket with an Eastern forehand grip.

B. Backswing. Turn the shoulders so that the back of the left shoulder is pointing toward the oncoming ball. It is important that this movement happens well before the ball crosses the net. Note that racket head is at eye level. The left hand is held in front of the body for balance and may also be an aid on the follow-through.

C. The backswing as seen from behind. The racket should never go back any further than what is shown.

D. Bottom of the Loop. Three movements happen simultaneously in this photo. The left foot steps forward, the racket and knees drop down together. Notice that the racket face is turned slightly downward. The arm is a radius and if the wrist is to remain locked and the racket be vertical at impact then the racket face must be tilted slightly downward at this point.

E. Impact with the Ball. The racket face is vertical and the player's eyes are focused on the point of contact. Legs are lifting upward and hips are turning forward. Body weight has been transferred forward to the left foot.

F. Follow-Through. There are two important

points on the follow-through. One, the palm of the hitting hand should be pointing toward the intended target. Two, the hitting arm should be extended until the shoulder and chin touch, as shown in the photo. Also, the legs are totally extended and all weight is on the left foot.

Learning Cues

1. Rotate both shoulders together when turning the body.
2. Keep the wrist firm and let the palm be the guide for direction.
3. Synchronize the movement of the racket and body.
4. Keep the swing short. Don't let the racket get lost behind the body.
5. Power is generated from the leg lift and hip rotation not just the arm.
6. On completion of the follow-through the palm should face the intended target and the player's chin and hitting shoulder should touch.

FIGURE 21-9. Loop forehand sequence.

A

B

C

D

E

F

7. Always check the follow-through at the completion of the swing.
8. While the body is lifting, the head must remain stationary. Leave head and eyes glued on point of impact.

Practice Suggestions

1. Hit forehands toward a specific target area either from a ball machine or from someone feeding from across the net.
2. Hit off of a backboard.

Lobs

With some practice the lob stroke should resemble the forehand and backhand ground strokes as much as possible. To conceal the lob, remember to turn the front shoulder and have a loop swing identical with the forehand and backhand ground strokes. This also means running to the ball with the racket head up and already back. But instead of turning the racket face down as the racket drops, work on a bevel (slight backward tilt) and lifting the ball high into the air using the opponent's baseline as a target.

Figure 21-10 shows the ready position for the overhead smash. The motion from this point is exactly like that of a flat serve. When teaching, stress keeping the chin up through contact and also reaching up for the ball.

FIGURE 21-10. Ready position for overhead smash.

Backhand Volley

The sequence of motions recommended for backhand volley are illustrated in Figure 21-11.

A. Ready Position. The player is waiting to determine the direction of the ball; he is holding the racket with an Eastern forehand grip.
B. Backswing. The player pivots the body and changes his grip. Actually, there is little or no backswing. The racket should always remain out in front of the body. Notice how the left elbow is held high to keep the racket face on line with the ball.
C. Contact. The key points here are:
    1. The racket head must remain above the wrist.
    2. The ball is contacted well in front of the body—8 to 10 inches.
    3. The arm and racket form a V.
    4. The player's head, racket head, and ball should all be on the same plane.
D. Follow-Through. To gain depth on the volley the racket head should remain above the wrist and ideally the racket face should follow the flight of the ball. The follow-through is very short. From an instructional standpoint, it is good technique to try to have the student freeze the racket right at the point of impact to assure that the wrist isn't breaking.

Forehand Volley

The sequence of motions recommended for forehand volley are shown in Figure 21-12.

A. Ready Position. The player assumes a ready

FIGURE 21-11. Motion recommended for backhand volley.

A   B

A	B	C	D

FIGURE 21-12. Motion recommended for forehand volley.

position; she is holding the racket with an Eastern forehand grip.

B. Backswing. The player pivots the body striving to get the shoulders sideways to the net. The racket should go back as far as the body turn takes it yet never be out of the player's peripheral vision. The less backswing the better.

C. Contact. Reaching forward to the ball, impact should take place slightly in front of the left shoulder. The nature of the swing will give the ball natural underspin. Do not break the wrist or chop at the ball. The arm and the racket form a V and the player's head, racket head, and the tennis ball should be at the same height at contact.

D. Follow-Through. Keeping the wrist firm, try to keep the racket face in line with the ball. Do not let the racket head drop if at all possible.

Learning Cues for Volleys

1. Always step forward and attack the volley. Also, change the grip when necessary.

C	D

A   B   C   D

FIGURE 21-13. Suggested technique for backhand return of serve.

2. Use little or no backswing.
3. Contact well out in front of the body especially on backhands.
4. Keep the wrist locked.
5. Finish with racket head above the wrist.
6. Use the knuckles for direction guidance on the backhand and the palm on the forehand.

Practice Suggestions

1. Hit off of a ball machine or a feeder with a specific target in mind.
2. Alternate hitting a forehand and then a backhand to get used to changing the grip.
3. Hit off of a backboard.

Backhand Return of Serve

The suggested technique for backhand return of serve is analyzed in Figure 21-13.

A. Ready Position. Player should be up on his toes, slightly leaning forward, and holding an Eastern forehand grip.
B. Player pivots the body sideways while changing the grip to an Eastern backhand. The backswing is very short, the emphasis being on a blocking motion similar to the volley.
C. Contact. At this point it is crucial that the returner has stepped forward and is reaching out to contact the ball 8 to 10 inches in front of the body. This shot is hit with underspin. Concentration should be on putting the ball back in play rather than on hitting a winner.
D. Follow-Through. The follow-through is the same archway as described in the backhand ground stroke.

Forehand Return of Serve

The suggested technique for forehand return of serve is illustrated in Figure 21-14.

A. Ready Position. Remember to keep the elbows raised and be ready to move forward.
B. Rotate both shoulders sideways while limiting the length of the backswing. Hold the racket face on the level of the ball and remember that a blocking motion similar to a volley is desired.
C. Contact. The ball is met just in front of the player's left shoulder. A step forward as well as body weight transfer is important. The shot is hit with slight underspin with emphasis on putting the ball back in play.
D. Follow-Through. This position is the same as described on the forehand ground stroke.

Learning Cues

1. Start with a forehand grip rather than in between the two grips.
2. Short backswing, long follow-through.
3. Wrist locked.
4. Always try to have feet moving forward never backward.
5. Contact ball in front of body, especially on the backhand.
6. Follow-throughs are the same as ground strokes.

Practice Suggestions

1. Have a fellow participant practice serves while you hit returns to a specific target area. Alternate between both service courts.

STRATEGY FOR THE BEGINNER

To be effective, strategy must be an automatic response to a given set of conditions. The problem with beginners is that there are no "givens." Therefore it is suggested that beginners not worry about strategy and concentrate on getting the ball back over the net one more time than their opponent. This sounds terribly feeble but that's how Bjorn Borg and Chris Evert's coaches explained it to them at an early age. A player needs to "own" or "control" certain shots before he can become worried about strategy. Of course, if at all possible you should hit to your opponent's weakness whenever the chance arises. The best advice for beginning players is to be able to laugh at the mistakes they make and have fun learning. Things we learn with pleasure we don't forget!

RULES FOR TENNIS[1]

1. *Server and Receiver:* The players shall stand on opposite sides of the net; the player who first delivers the ball shall be called the server, and the other the receiver.

2. *Delivery of Service:* The service shall be delivered in the following manner. Immediately before commencing to serve, the server shall stand with both feet at rest behind the baseline, and within the imaginary continuations of the center-mark and sideline. The server shall then toss the ball by hand into the air and before it hits the ground strike it with his racket. The server is not permitted to touch the court inside the baseline until after the racket has made contact with the ball.

3. *From Alternate Courts:* In delivering the service, the server shall stand alternately behind the right and left courts, beginning from the right in every game. The ball served shall pass over the net and hit the ground within the service court, which is diagonally opposite.

4. *Faults:* The service is a fault if the server commits any breach of rules 2 or 3; if he misses the ball in attempting to strike it; or if the ball served touches a permanent fixture (other than the net) before it hits the ground. However, if he

[1]United States Lawn Tennis Association, *Official Tennis Guide and Yearbook* (current issue).

tosses the ball without making an effort to hit it, there is no fault.

5. *Ball in Play Till Point Decided:* A ball is in play from the moment at which it is delivered in service. Unless a fault or a let is called, it remains in play until the point is decided.

6. *Player Hinders Opponent:* If a player commits any act, either deliberately or involuntarily which, in the opinion of the umpire, hinders his opponent in making a stroke, the umpire shall in the first case award the point to the opponent, and in the second case order the point to be replayed.

7. *Ball Falling on Line:* A ball falling on a line is regarded as falling in the court bounded by that line. Good ball.

8. *Good Return:* It is a good return:
   a. If the ball touches the net, posts, cord or metal cable, strap, or band, provided that it passes over any of them and hits the ground within the court;
   b. If a player's racket passes over the net after he has returned the ball, provided the ball passes the net before being played and is properly returned;
   c. If a player succeeds in returning the ball, served or in play, which strikes a ball lying in the court.

9. *When Players Change Sides:* The players shall change sides at the end of the first, third, and every subsequent alternate game of each set, and at the end of each set unless the total number of games in such set be even, in which case the change is not made until the end of the first game of the next set.

10. *Doubles, Order of Service:* Decided at the beginning of each set. The pair who have to serve in the first game of each set shall decide which partner shall do so and the opposing pair shall decide similarly for the second game. The part-

FIGURE 21-14. Suggested technique for forehand return of serve.

A   B   C   D

ner of the player who served in the first game shall serve in the third; the partner of the player who served in the second game shall serve in the fourth. The order of serving may be changed following the completion of any set.

11. *Doubles, Order of Receiving:* Decided at the beginning of each set. The pair who have to receive the first game shall decide which partner shall continue to receive the first service in every odd game throughout that set. The opposing pair shall likewise decide which partner shall receive the first service in the second game and that partner shall continue to receive the first service in every even game throughout that set. The order of receiving may be changed following the completion of any set.

A complete staff of officials for a tennis match includes a referee, an umpire, a net-cord judge, and at least seven linesmen. However, most dual matches are played with only a referee or, at most, a referee and an umpire.

HELPFUL HINTS

1. Keep your eye on the ball at all times.
2. Strive for accurate placement rather than speed.
3. Always play the game to win, but if you go down in defeat, give your opponent due credit.
4. Play to your opponent's weaknesses.
5. When calling the score, always call the server's score first.
6. Keep your weight on the balls of both feet so you can move in any direction with ease and speed.
7. Acquire an understanding of the fundamentals of stroking, and practice faithfully to master these.
8. Notice how your opponent strokes the ball so when he uses the chop or slice stroke you can play the bounce accordingly.
9. Turn the body sideways to the net on all ground strokes.
10. When stroking the ball, avoid stiff leg action by keeping the knees loose and relaxed.
11. On the ground strokes, return the ball deep into the opponent's back court near the baseline.
12. On the ground strokes, attempt to hit the ball at waist level and on the rise.
13. Hit the ball squarely on the strings of the racket face by hitting "through" the ball instead of chopping under it.
14. The follow-through of the racket is in the direction of the intended flight of the ball.
15. After completing each stroke, return to a ready position, facing the net and loosely grasping the throat of the racket with the left hand to facilitate change of grip if necessary.
16. Well-placed lobs, which are out of reach of the

net rusher, will help keep him away from the net.
17. When serving, attempt to get the first serve in the proper court as often as possible. Stress control and accuracy if a second serve is necessary and concentrate on getting the ball into the proper service area.
18. The server should always have two balls in his possession before starting his service.
19. The receiver should not retrieve or return the ball if the opponent's first serve is a fault. He should remain in his receiving position so the server can immediately follow with his second attempt.
20. Devote periodic practice sessions to correcting specific weaknesses.

PLAYING COURTESIES

To make the game more enjoyable for yourself and for others, you should follow certain court courtesies or rules of etiquette. If one of your tennis balls rolls into another court, wait until the players on the court have finished their rally before asking for your ball. When you return someone's ball that has rolled into your court, roll the ball back to the player asking for it instead of trying to gain some stroking practice. If they are engaged in playing a point, roll the ball back against the screen out of their field of play. If your opponent is interfered with in any way during the play for a point, stop the play, call a "let," and then play the point over. You call lines on your side of the net and let your opponent call lines on his side. When leaving or entering the courts, do not walk behind a player playing a point. Wait until the rally is over, then quickly cross the rear of the court close to the back screen.

SAFETY

1. Warm up sufficiently before starting strenuous play.
2. Stop when injured and report injury to the instructor.
3. Remove rings, bracelets, watches, etc., as they may cause bruises and cuts.
4. Check the playing surface for glass, nails, stones, slippery spots, etc.
5. Stay in line, on mark, or in own area when swinging or hitting.
6. Control emotions; do not throw the racket or hit a ball in anger.
7. Shout a warning when there is danger of a ball hitting someone.
8. Avoid showing off and "horseplay."
9. Be aware of the distances between the baselines and walls, fences, screens, etc.

10. When playing in excessive heat, make sure you have a plentiful intake of fluids.

TERMINOLOGY

Ace A ball served and untouched by the opponent's racket.

Ad An abbreviated form of the word "Advantage."

Alley The 4½-ft. strip on either side of the singles court, used to enlarge the court for doubles.

Approach shot A shot hit inside the baseline while approaching the net.

Backcourt The area between the service line and the baseline.

Backhand Strokes hit on the left side of a right-handed player.

Backspin Spin acquired on a ball dropping from a vertical position, which forces the ball to bounce back toward the hitter.

Backswing The beginning of all ground strokes and service motion requiring a backswing to gather energy for the forward swing.

Baseline The end line of a tennis court, located 39 ft. from the net.

Break Relates to the act of winning a game in which the opponent serves.

Center mark Short mark that bisects the baseline.

Center service line The line perpendicular to the net which divides the two service courts.

Center strap A strap placed at the center of the net and anchored to the court to facilitate a constant three foot height for the net at the center.

Center stripe Same as the center service line which divides the two service courts into halves.

Chip Refers to the short chopping motion of the racket against the back and bottom side of the ball.

Chop Used in the same manner as "chip" by many. Refers to the placement of backspin on the ball with a short high to low forward swing.

Cross-court A shot hit diagonally from one corner of the court over the net into the opposite corner of the court.

Cut off the angle To move forward quickly against an opponent's cross-court shot, allowing the player to hit the ball near the center of the court rather than near the sidelines.

Deep (depth) A shot that bounces near the baseline on ground strokes and near the service line on serves.

Default A player who fails to play his scheduled match in a tournament and thus forfeits his position.

Deuce Scoring term used when the game score is 40-40.

Dink A ball normally hit very softly and relatively high to ensure its safe landing.

Double fault When the server has served two serves out of bounds on the same point.

Doubles line The outside sideline on a court—used in doubles only.

Down-the-line A shot hit near a sideline which travels close to, and parallel to, the same line from which the shot was initially hit.

Drive An offensive shot hit with extra force.

Drop shot A ground stroke hit in such a manner as to drop just over the net with little or no forward bounce.

Drop volley A volley hit in such a manner as to drop just over the net with little or no forward bounce.

Error A mistake made by a player during competition.

Face of racket The hitting surface of the racket.

Fault A serve which lands out of bounds or is not hit properly.

Flat shot A ball hit in such a manner as not to rotate when traveling through the air.

Foot fault Illegal foot movement before service that is penalized by the loss of that particular serve. Common foot faults are: stepping on or ahead of the baseline before the ball has been contacted; and running along the baseline before serving.

Forecourt The area between the net and the service line.

Forehand The stroke hit on the right side of a right-handed player.

Frame The rim of the racket head plus the handle of the racket.

Game A player has won a game by winning four points before his opponent and holding a minimum two-point lead.

Grip of racket That portion of the racket which is grasped in the player's hand.

Ground stroke Any ball hit after it has bounced.

Half-volley A ball hit only inches away from the court's surface after the ball has bounced.

Hold serve To win your own serve. If you lose your own serve, your serve has been "broken."

Let ball Any point which is played over because of some kind of interference.

Let serve A serve which touches the net tape and falls into the proper square and is played over.

Linesman A match official who calls balls "in" or "out."

Lob A ball hit sufficiently high to pass over the outstretched arm position of the net player.

Lob volley A shot hit high into the air from a volleying position.

Love A player with zero points or games to his credit.

Match To win a match is to win the contest between two or four opponents.

Match point If the player holding match point wins the next point, he is the winner.

Midcourt The area in front or in back of the service line of the playing court.

Net ball A ball which hits the net and falls back on the same side as the hitter.

Net man The player who has gained position at the net and is prepared to volley.

No man's land A general area within the baseline and proper net position area where, when the player is caught, he must volley or hit ground strokes near his feet.

Offensive lob A ball hit just above the racket reach of an opposing net player.

Open face racket   A racket whose face is moving under the ball. A wide open racket face is parallel to the court surface.

Overhead   A shot hit from a position higher than the player's head.

Overhead smash   A shot hit from a position higher than the player's head and hit extremely hard.

Overhitting   A player who tends to put too much force into each shot.

Pace   The speed of the ball.

Passing shot   The shot which passes beyond the reach of the net player and lands inbounds.

Placement   A shot hit inbounds and untouched by the opponent.

Poach   To cross over into your partner's territory.

Racket face   The hitting surface of the racket.

Racket head   Top portion of the racket frame which houses the strings.

Rally   The act of hitting balls back and forth across the net. A rally includes all shots other than the serve.

Receiver   The player about to return the opponent's serve.

Retrieve   Normally refers to a fine defensive shot in response to an opponent's well-placed offensive shot.

Server   The player initiating play.

Service line   The end line of the service courts running parallel to the net.

Set   The first player to win six games with a minimum two game lead has won a set.

Set point   The point which, if won, will give the player the set.

Sidespin   A ball hit and rotating on a horizontal plane.

Signals in doubles   Signaling your partner that you are going to poach at the net.

Singles line   The first sideline closer to the center mark and running the entire length of the court.

Slice   Motion of the racket head going around the side of the ball and producing a horizontal spin on the ball; also called a slice.

Tape   The band of cloth or plastic running across the top of the net.

Telegraphing the play   To indicate the direction of one's intended target before actually hitting the ball.

Topspin   The clockwise rotation of the ball at a 90° angle.

Touch   The ability to make delicate soft shots from several positions on the court.

Twist   A special rotation imparted to the ball during the serve causing the ball to jump to the left (of right-handed server).

Umpire   The official used in tournament play to call lines.

Underspin   A counterclockwise spin placed on the ball by catching the backside and bottomside of the ball with the racket head.

Volley   To hit the ball in the air before it has bounced on the court.

SELECTED REFERENCES

BRADEN, VIC, and BILL BRUNS. *Tennis for the Future.* Boston and Toronto: Little, Brown and Company, 1977.

GRAEBNER, CLARK, and CAROLE GRAEBNER. *Mixed Doubles Tennis.* New York: McGraw-Hill Book Company, 1973.

GREENE, ROBERT. *Tennis Drills.* New York: Hawthorn Books, Inc., 1976.

GROPPEL, JACK. *Principles of Tennis Techniques, Drills, and Strategies.* Champaign, Illinois: Stipes Publishing Co., 1980.

KRAMER, JACK. *The Game.* New York: G.P. Putnam's Sons, 1979.

LAVER, ROD. *How to Play Championship Tennis.* New York: The Macmillan Company, 1965.

LOTT, GEORGE. *How to Play Winning Doubles.* Norwalk, Conn.: New York Times Company, 1979.

PLAGENHOEF, STANLEY. *Fundamentals of Tennis.* Englewood Cliffs, N.J.: Prentice-Hall, Inc., 1970.

SEGURA, PANCHO. *Championship Strategy.* New York: McGraw-Hill Book Company, 1976.

TILDEN, BILL. *How to Play Better Tennis.* New York: Simon & Schuster, Inc., 1957.

United States Tennis Association. *USTA Official Encyclopedia of Tennis.* New York: U.S.T.A.

Audio-Visual Materials

AMF Head, 4801 North 63rd Street, Boulder, Colorado 80301. *Go For a Winner* (Mixed Doubles), 16 mm color film; 37 min.

Johnson-Nyquist Productions, Inc., 23854 Via Fabricante, D-1, Mission Viejo, California 92691. *Play It Straight* (Etiquette) 16 mm color film; 27 min.

Converse Rubber Company, Sporting Goods Division, 1454 Ormandy Drive, Baton Rouge, Louisiana 70808 *or* Converse, 333 Serramonte Plaza, Daly City, Calif. 94015. *Practice with the Pros.*

Vic Braden Tennis College, 22000 Plano Rd., Trabuco Canyon, Calif. 92670. *Vic Braden Tennis Training Films:* Forehand Drive (5¼ min.); Backhand Drive (4¼ min.); Half Volley (4¼ min.); Approach (4¼ min.); Forehand Volley (5 min.); Backhand Volley (4¾ min.); Basic Serve (5¼ min.); Overhead (4 min.); Advanced Serve (5¼ min.); The Lob (4 min.); Ball Rotation (4¾ min.); Footwork (4 min.); Singles Strategy (3¼ min.); Doubles Strategy (3¼ min.).

TOUCH FOOTBALL AND FLAG FOOTBALL

THIS CHAPTER WILL ENABLE YOU TO:

♦ Discuss the key points of the games of touch football and flag football.
♦ Identify the differences in equipment, rules, and strategy between flag football and touch football.
♦ Describe the rules governing play.
♦ Analyze and demonstrate the various skills and techniques including the stance, passing, catching, blocking, tackling, and kicking.
♦ Describe the offensive and defensive strategies utilized.
♦ Take proper safety precautions.
♦ Understand and use the basic terminology associated with the game.

NATURE AND PURPOSE

Touch Football

The object of the game of touch football (and its variation, flag football) is to advance the ball over the opponent's goal line without being "tackled." Points are awarded for a touchdown (6 points), a point after touchdown (1 point by kicking, 2 points by running), a field goal (3 points), a safety (2 points), a forfeit (1 point) and by penetration in event of a tie (1 point).

Informal games of touch football are often played in areas any size large enough to give the players running and passing room. In schools and recreation leagues, where the game is played on an organized basis, a regulation football field equipped with goal posts and yard lines is used. A regulation football is used, but players are not required to wear the heavy official football equipment because tackling is not permitted. Runners are stopped by a touch with one or both hands instead of a tackle. The fact that expensive equipment is not needed makes this game appropriate for use in recreational programs and in schools where funds are not available to outfit a regular football team.

The game retains most of the fundamentals of regular football, which gives it a popular appeal in the Fall, when sport pages are filled with news about forward passes, touchdowns, and long runs. An official touch football team is usually composed of seven players, but variations (from five to eleven players) may be used with very little rules adaptation. The game provides an opportunity for the individual interested in football to duplicate in a relatively safe situation many of the skills utilized by widely publicized members of the gridiron game. Most present-day versions of the game resemble regulation football to the extent that names of positions of players, running and passing plays, punting, place-kicking, first downs, and scoring are used in touch football. The tackling element is eliminated in favor of the touch, and in most versions of touch football certain limitations are placed on blocking. In many cases no limitations are placed on eligibility of pass receivers, making it possible for any player to receive a forward pass. This factor makes the game more interesting to players on the line of scrimmage, who seldom have an opportunity to score or handle the ball in regulation football.

Flag Football

Flag football is a variation of touch football in which cloth or plastic flags are worn on both hips by all players. The flag is detached or stripped from a belt (worn by all players) by the defensive player in lieu of a touch. Flags are generally 12 to 15 inches long and 2 inches wide and are attached to the belt by an adhesive substance such as Velcro or by plastic snaps (Figure 22-1). A different colored flag is used by each team.

The basic rules governing flag football are similar to those used in touch football. Holding an opponent or holding onto the flag to prevent detachment are common infractions found in flag football and must be closely regulated. Some contend that utilization of the detachable flag in lieu of the one- or two-handed touch tends to minimize roughness in team play. Officiating is easier in flag than in touch football, since detachment of the flag is readily discernible while there may be arguments regarding the touch.

From a strategic standpoint, flag football would appear to better orient itself to all around offensive and defensive strategy because of the increased difficulty in detaching a flag. Teams will be more prone to include a more balanced running and passing attack; defenses will have to be designed to prevent both strategies.

FIGURE 22-1.   Typical flag and belt worn in Flag Football. Note Velcro attachment.

In order to minimize hazardous play in flag football, the following precautionary measures are suggested:

1. Eliminate the blocking, tackling, or holding the ball carrier by a defensive player attempting to secure the flag.
2. Defensive players must maintain contact with the ground when attempting to secure the flag—no jumping or diving.
3. The ball carrier may not employ a straight-arm or utilize body contact against a defensive player in order to prevent him from securing the flag.

BASIC RULES

The rules for touch football and flag football are generally the same. However, when playing flag football, the rules for blocking, fumbling, and tackling must be strictly enforced. In flag football, any ball carrier without two flags is considered tackled.

Playing Field and Equipment

Playing Field.   An official touch football and flag football field is 40 yards wide by 100 yards long (Figure 22-2). The field is divided into four 20-yard zones and two end zones, each 10 yards in depth.

Goals.   Goalposts are not a necessity; however, lack of goalposts eliminates points after touchdown by kicking and field goals. In these cases, points after touchdown are gained by running or passing.

Uniform.   No special uniform is required. The use of football helmets and football pads is prohibited. Tennis shoes or soccer shoes with molded rubber cleats may be used.

Ball.   A regulation leather or rubber-coated football can be used. It is recommended that a junior sized football be used by younger children.

Flags.   Flags should measure 12 to 15 inches in length and 2 inches in width. They can be made of

cloth and tucked in the elastic top of the gym trunks if belts are not available.

Length of Game

Periods.   Four ten-minute periods constitute a game with a one-minute rest between periods and a five-minute rest between halves. Games may also be divided into two twenty-minute halves with a five-minute rest period.

Overtime.   Tie games may be decided by one of the following methods.

1. Award the game to the team with the greatest number of penetrations inside the opponent's 20-yard line.
2. Award game to team with greatest number of first downs.
3. Give each team four downs from the 20-yard line and award the game to the team advancing the ball the farthest.

Forfeits.   If a team is not ready to play within ten minutes after scheduled starting time, the opponents are awarded the win on a forfeit. Teams refusing to resume play after an order to do so by the referee forfeit to opponents.

Timeout.   Each team is allowed two timeouts

FIGURE 22-2.   The 100-yard Touch and Flag Football field.

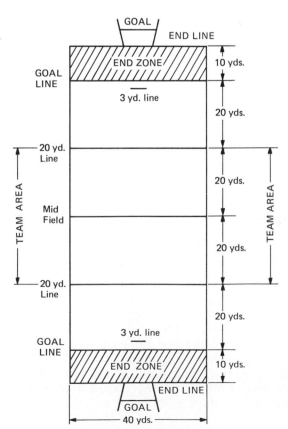

per half. Timeouts are also taken under the following conditions:

1. When ball goes out of bounds.
2. After a score is made.
3. While a penalty is being enforced.
4. At the discretion of the referee.
5. At the end of each period.

Scoring

Scoring is the same as in regulation football:

touchdown:	6 points
field goal:	3 points
safety:	2 points
point after touchdown:	1 point

Players and Officials

Players. A team consists of seven players, although fewer or more players may be used by mutual consent. The offensive team must have at least three men on the line of scrimmage when the ball is put in play.

Substitutes. Any number of substitutions may be made at any time during the game. Substitutes must report to the referee.

Officials. Officials consist of a referee, an umpire, and linesmen.

Playing Regulations

Starting the Game. A toss of a coin by the referee determines which team has the choice of kicking off, receiving, or goals. The loser of the toss has choice of remaining options. Privileges of choice are reversed at the beginning of the third period.

Putting the Ball in Play. The ball is put in play at the start of the game, after a score, and at the beginning of the third period by a place kick from the kicker's 40-yard line. Defensive team members must be 10 yards away when the ball is kicked, and members of the kicking team must be behind the ball. If the ball does not go 10 yards, it must be kicked again. If the ball goes out of bounds after 10 yards, the opponent has a choice of beginning play where it went out of bounds on their own 20-yard line. If the ball is kicked into the end zone and the opponents elect not to run it out, play begins on their 20-yard line.

Fumbled Ball. A fumbled ball at any time is dead and belongs to the team that fumbled the ball at the point of the fumble, the down and point to be gained remaining the same. A fumbled forward pass is ruled as an incomplete pass.

Downed Ball. The ball is dead and the player downed when an opponent touches him with one hand somewhere between his shoulders and his knees. In flag football, the ball is downed or player

tackled when one flag is detached from the belt or the ball carrier loses a flag.

First Downs. A team has four chances to move the ball from one 20-yard zone to the next. If a team does not advance the ball from one zone to the next in four downs, the ball goes to the opponents at that spot.

Passing. The following regulations govern passing:

1. All players on both teams are eligible to catch passes.
2. Forward passes may be thrown from any point back of the line of scrimmage, and lateral passes may be thrown anywhere on playing field.
3. Any number of passes may be thrown in a series of downs.

Penalties

5-Yard Penalty Infractions (from line of scrimmage):
   Offside
   Delay of game
   Less than three players on line of scrimmage
   Illegal motion or shift
   Illegal forward pass
15-Yard Penalty Infractions (from spot of foul):
   Illegal use of hands
   Illegal block
   Unnecessary roughness (push, tackle, shove, trip, holding)
   Unsportsmanlike conduct
   Clipping
   Pass interference

Flagrant violations of rules should be met with automatic disqualification.

RULES FOR COEDUCATIONAL FLAG FOOTBALL

Coeducational flag football is becoming an increasingly popular game. Many variations and modifications can be used. Modifications can be found in *Rules for Coeducational Activities and Sports,* published by the American Alliance of Health, Physical Education, Recreation, and Dance, 1977 and 1980.

SUGGESTED LEARNING SEQUENCE

A. Nature and Purpose of Touch Football/Flag Football
B. Conditioning Aspects—plan drills and exercises that might be related to movements of touch football and flag football.
C. Basic Game Concepts
   1. Field of play

2. Equipment
3. Safety
4. Playing courtesies
D. Rules/Coeducational Rules—rules should be introduced when appropriate and at a time that relates to a specific skill or strategy. This does not mean that all rules must be discussed at one time.
E. Skills and Techniques—skills should be taught in combinations whenever possible; the sequence that skills are taught is up to the individual preference of the instructor.
   1. Stances
      a. three-point stance
      b. upright stance
   2. Ball Carrying
   3. Passing and Receiving
      a. pass patterns
   4. Kicking
      a. punting
      b. place kick
      c. kickoff
   5. Blocking
   6. Tackling
      a. touch
      b. flag detachment
   7. Centering
      a. direct snap
      b. long snap
F. Strategies—offensive game concepts as well as defensive game concepts should be introduced as early as possible so that skills can be practiced within the context of a game.
   1. Offense
      a. T-formation
      b. Shotgun formation
      c. Single wing

2. Defense
   a. pass defense—pass rush
   b. running defense
G. Game Play

SKILLS AND TECHNIQUES

The techniques and fundamental skills associated with touch football and flag football are identical in most instances to regular football. There are two areas, however, where touch football and flag football differ from the parent game; these are in tackling and blocking. The tackle in touch football refers to a touch between the shoulders and knees, while the tackle in flag football refers to the detachment or stripping of a flag by an opponent from a belt that circles the waist. In both touch football and flag football, players cannot leave their feet when blocking. There are other skills that all players must work on since the skills will be used regardless of the position played.

Stances

The stance will vary according to the position played and the function of either the offense or defense. Generally speaking, the three-point stance is used by the players on the line on offense and defense and sometimes by the offensive backs. The upright stance may be used by linebackers, defensive backs, and sometimes, the offensive backs. (See Figure 22-3.)

Learning Cues—Three-Point Stance

1. Feet are shoulder width apart, one foot slightly ahead of the other in a heel-toe relationship.

FIGURE 22-3. Stances: the people on the line are in a 3-point stance; the backs are in an upright stance.

FIGURE 22-4. Proper way to carry a ball.

2. The supporting arm hangs vertically, the back is nearly horizontal, head is up looking ahead, weight is on support hand.
3. The free arm rests on the knee of the forward leg.

Learning Cues—Upright Stance

1. Foot position is much the same as in the three-point stance.
2. Hands are placed just above the knees, back is slightly bent on the waist, head is up, focused downfield.
3. Weight is on balls of the feet.

Ball Carrying

Because of the rules governing play, most players have an opportunity at one time or another to carry the football. The effective ball carrier is one who can start quickly, change direction, dodge, sidestep, and execute fakes that will throw the defensive player off stride. It is important for the ball carrier to follow the blockers in order to elude the defensive players.

Learning Cues (see Figure 22-4)

1. Carry ball in outside arm furthest from the defensive player.
2. One end of the football is placed in the armpit and the other end is held in the palm of the hand with fingers spread comfortably around the end to provide a firm grip.

Practice Suggestions

1. Align a ball carrier facing a defensive player standing 10 yards away. On the signal, have the ball carrier run toward the defensive player, changing the ball as the player changes direction.
2. Same type of formation, have the ball carrier run toward the defensive player using a series of fakes to try to avoid being tackled.
3. Using a blocker, have a ball carrier try to set up

the block on the defensive player by following the interference and setting up a series of fakes.

Passing

The forward pass assumes an important role in touch football and flag football since rules permit everyone to be an eligible receiver. A good passing attack will loosen up the defense and allow the running game to become more effective. There are two types of passes commonly used, the forward pass and the lateral pass. The lateral pass may be thrown in an overhand motion or it may be "pitched" to a player in an underhand motion. The lateral, which cannot be thrown forward, adds much interest and excitement to the game since it can be used anywhere on the field.

Learning Cues—Forward Pass

1. Ball is gripped by the hand on the top; the thumb is opposite the middle finger, the other fingers are spread on the laces (Figure 22-5).

FIGURE 22-5. Gripping the ball for the forward pass. Note that the middle finger and thumb are opposite.

2. As ball is brought up behind the ear, plant the rear foot, step with the opposite foot in the direction of throw as the arm is brought forward.
3. The wrist is snapped downward and palm of throwing hand is rotated outward as the ball is released, thus giving the ball a spiral motion.

Practice Suggestions

1. Place players opposite each other and throw ball back and forth. Begin at a distance of 10 yards and move further away.

2. After you have reviewed certain pass receiver patterns, form two lines, have a player center the ball back to the quarterback, receivers go out for a pass. First begin with short passes and then progress to longer passes.
3. Same formation as #2 but add two defensive linesmen, force quarterback to throw on the run. Another variation is to add two defensive backs and attempt to complete a pass.

Receiving

Pass receivers should become adept at eluding their opponents by dodging, faking, and using a change of pace that will enable them to move past the defensive player. It is important for the pass receiver to focus in on the ball as soon as it leaves the passer's hand, watching all the way to his own hands. Some basic fundamentals must be remembered.

Learning Cues

1. Palms face out, thumbs toward the incoming pass. Catch with the hands and pull into the body.
2. On passes above the chest, thumbs are turned in; below the waist, thumbs are turned out (see Figures 22-6 and 22-7).
3. As the receiver moves away from the passer, fingers are extended, thumbs are turned out; give with ball on contact.
4. On passes caught over either shoulder, the thumbs are turned out, the arm on the ballside

FIGURE 22-8. Catching a football over the shoulder.

(nearest the body) is held below the shoulder, the forearm is held at eye level (Figure 22-8).

Practice Suggestions

1. Form two parallel lines and have passes thrown above chest and below chest to pass receivers.
2. Two lines, passer drops back and throws pass over the receiver's head for over-the-shoulder catch.
3. Two lines, receivers practice pass patterns and catches. Add defensive backs as a variation.

Kicking

The kicking game consists of kickoffs to begin play, punting, and place kicks.

Learning Cues—Punting

1. The punter stands 13 yards behind the line of scrimmage awaiting the center snap; the kicking foot is slightly ahead of the non-kicking foot, arms are relaxed, palms open and up, trunk is slightly flexed.
2. Follow the ball into the hands; the ball is held in the hand of the kicking foot toward the end and underneath. The other hand is placed on the ball with laces up to the front and side. The ball should be slightly tipped, nose downward just below the chest.
3. The kick and step is a step with the right foot, a hop with the left, and a follow-through with the right leg. The kicking foot may finish above the head.
4. The ball is released with the non-kicking hand and guided to the correct position of the foot by the kicking hand prior to release.

Place Kicking and Extra Point. There are two types of place kicks, the traditional head on ap-

FIGURE 22-6 (left).   Catching the ball above the chest, the thumbs are turned in. The arms give with the ball as it is caught.
FIGURE 22-7 (right).   Catching the ball below the waist, the thumbs are turned out.

proach and the soccer style instep kick, which is described in the chapter on Soccer. Some key points to remember for the traditional kick are:

1. Assume a stance two steps behind the spot of the kick; the right foot takes a longer step and the left foot a short step.
2. The non-kicking foot is placed approximately two feet behind and a foot to the side of the ball.
3. With the head down and eyes on the contact point, the body leaning forward, the right leg follows through with a definite leg snap coming at the contact point.
4. The ball is contacted just below the center of the football; the leg should be extended at impact.

The Kickoff. The kickoff follows the same mechanics except the kicker is stationed 8 to 10 yards behind the ball prior to kickoff. Practice and timing are essential in executing the correct form for the place kick during a kickoff.

Blocking

Since the player is not permitted to leave the feet in executing a block, the player must become adept at maintaining balance while retaining a position between the defensive person and the ball carrier. It is important to try to maintain contact with the defensive player and draw him away from the ball carrier. The blocker is not allowed to hold the defensive person, so the hands must be held in close to the body at all times.

Learning Cues (see Figure 22-9)

1. Assume a three-point stance opposite your opponent; the initial steps are short choppy steps to the opponent.
2. Body is in a semi-crouch position, the shoulder and forearms make contact with the opponent's midsection, the head is placed between your opponent and the ball carrier.
3. Drive your opponent away from the ball carrier; use short, choppy steps.

Practice Suggestions

1. Form two parallel lines 2 yards apart. On the signal, block right or block left; the blocker attempts to maintain contact on a blocking position for 3 to 4 seconds.
2. With a center, a ball carrier, defensive player, and offensive player, on signal the ball carrier runs behind the blocker and cuts right or left, depending on the direction of the block.

Tackling

Tackling is the term used to denote the touching of a ball carrier to stop play or, in flag football, the detachment or stripping of the flag to stop play. An important point to remember is that, for the tackle to be valid, both feet of the tackler must be on the ground. A legal touch is between the shoulder and knee of the opponent. The game may be played using a one-hand touch or it may be increased in difficulty by making it a two-hand touch game (Figure 22-10). In flag football, one flag must be

FIGURE 22-9. Blocking—note that the ball carrier cuts away from the block.

FIGURE 22-10. Tackling—a two-hand touch above the waist.

FIGURE 22-11. Tackling, Flag Football style. The ball carrier's hand may not protect the flag.

detached from the belt (Figure 22-11). Body balance and control of body movement and speed are important factors to practice.

Centering

The center plays an important part in touch football and flag football. The center snap is executed at close range (direct snap) if a team uses a T-formation, at longer range if a team uses a shotgun or single wing, and at still longer range on punts and extra point tries. Note that in touch or flag football if the center snaps the ball on the ground before getting to the receiver, it is a dead ball.

FIGURE 22-12. The snap—note the quarter turn of the ball as it is given to the quarterback.

FIGURE 22-13. The direct snap.

Learning Cues—Direct Snap

1. Feet are shoulder width apart, bend at the waist, knees flexed, arms hanging comfortably in front, head up.
2. Quarterback places hands under the crotch of the center, fingers spread, heels of palms together.
3. The center places one hand on top of the ball (laces up) and the other hand alongside and toward the end of the ball. On the signal the arms are rolled toward the quarterback, the ball is snapped back to the quarterback, with the right hand turning the ball ¼ right turn so the ball is placed in the quarterback's hands on its side.

Learning Cues—Long Snap

1. Same starting position although weight may be forward and head lower than the buttocks.
2. Arms are swept toward the receiver, wrist snap to impart spiral on the ball.

STRATEGY FOR TOUCH OR FLAG FOOTBALL

Offensive Strategy

Touch football permits the use of a wide range of offensive plays because of the emphasis on passing and the fact that everyone is eligible to receive a pass. In arranging the offensive strategy, a team should plan a signal system that will denote the kind of play to be used (pass, run, punt), who is to carry the ball and where the ball is to go. Plays should be kept as simple as possible. Numbers may be employed to represent the type of play, the player executing the play or carrying the ball, and the side of the line where the play is to go. The line may be numbered with odd numbers on the left side and even numbers on the right (Figure 22-14). The backs may be numbered: 1—quarterback, 2—right halfback, 3—fullback and 4—left halfback. Thus, after the ball has been centered, the signal "Run 14" indicates a running play through the number 4 hole, with the number 1 back carrying the ball.

FIGURE 22-14. Numbers for offensive holes.

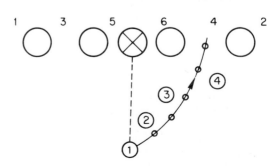

FIGURE 22-15. Types of offensive formations.

Offensive strategy should combine running and passing plays in order to create confusion to the defense. It is not good strategy to constantly employ all passing plays or all running plays. Try to keep the defense guessing; attempt running plays on second down with a lot of yards to go for first down.

Offensive Formations. There are a number of formations that can be created by the offense as long as three people line up on the line of scrimmage before the ball is snapped. Three common formations used in touch football and flag football include (1) the T-formation, (2) the shotgun formation, and (3) the single wing formation (Figure 22-15).

Defensive Strategy

Teams should agree on a plan for the pass and the run defense. For a passing defense, certain players on the line of scrimmage should be assigned to rush the passer, and other players are designated to drop back to help the defensive backs to cover possible receivers. Generally a person-to-person assignment is made for the deep pass receiver while a zone defense is employed by the remaining defensive players to watch for the short pass receivers.

Defensive Hints

1. Assign rushers to contain the passer or runner inside, not allowing the ball carrier the opportunity to break outside the defensive containment.
2. Learn to recognize the opponent's formations and most effective players; set up your defenses accordingly.
3. Listen to see if an opponent is continually using the same cadence; time your rush to the cadence occasionally.
4. Defensive backs: do not turn your back on the pass receiver; learn to run backwards or laterally so that you can always see the ball and the pass receiver.

FIGURE 22-16. Types of pass patterns.

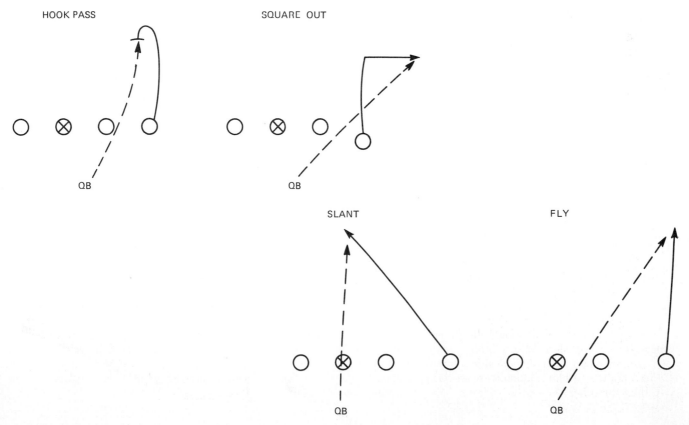

5. Use different pass rushers to confuse the offense; send in linebackers at times as an element of surprise.

Offensive Hints

1. Keep defense guessing by varying running and passing plays.
2. If the defensive secondary plays deep, use many of your players in short passing patterns. When the defense draws in, use the deep pass.
3. If you receive a long penalty, do not try to make it up on one play; use a run and perhaps some short passes.
4. Change your cadence occasionally to pull the defensive team offside.
5. Utilize a quick kick on third down to get your team out of a defensive hole.
6. Let your field position help dictate the type of plays you will use—long passes are dangerous near your own goal line, plays involving deception are best in the vicinity of midfield; use quick hitting or pass plays near your opponent's goal line.

SAFETY

Observance of the following safety precautions will minimize the incidence of injuries.

1. Do not wear any equipment possessing sharp or projecting surfaces that may injure teammates or opponents. This includes rings, belt buckles, and watches.
2. Use rules that prevent leaving the feet in executing the block.
3. Declare the ball dead on all fumbles.
4. See that the playing area is smooth and free from holes and projecting objects that may prove a hazard.
5. Use competent officials who enforce the rules and eliminate rough play.
6. See that adequate treatment is available to players who receive injuries while competing.
7. Players who wear glasses should wear a headband or eyeglass guard.

TERMINOLOGY

Backs Players on the team who ordinarily carry or pass the ball on offense. Stationed behind the linemen.

Backward pass Play in which the ball is thrown or passed in any direction except toward the opponent's goal. Any player may make a backward pass.

Balanced line An offensive formation which has an equal number of linemen on each side of the center. Line is unbalanced if more linemen are on one side of center than the other.

Block Action of offensive linemen and backs in which they use their bodies to ward off defensive players from the ball carrier.

Bootleg play An offensive play in which a back fakes handing the ball to a teammate, conceals it on his hip, and runs in the opposite direction.

Brush blocking Momentary blocking by an offensive player.

Button hook A forward pass play in which the receiver runs toward the defender, turns, and runs back toward passer to receive the pass.

Clipping Action by player in which he throws his body across the back of the leg or legs of a player not carrying the ball. This is likely to cause injury and is a personal foul.

Cross-buck An offensive play in which two backs cross paths in moving toward the line of scrimmage, one faking to receive the ball and the other actually taking the ball.

Cut-back An offensive maneuver in which the back starts wide and then cuts back toward center of the line.

End around An offensive maneuver in which one end wheels around, takes the ball from a teammate, and attempts to run for a gain.

Fair catch A player may make a fair catch on a kickoff, return kick, or kick from scrimmage by raising his hand clearly above his head before making the catch. He may not be tackled, and must not take more than two steps after receiving the ball. The ball is put in play from the spot of the catch by a free kick or scrimmage.

Flanker An offensive maneuver in which a player lines up nearer the sideline than a designated opponent.

Flat pass A forward pass that travels chiefly in a lateral direction and is usually thrown with a flat trajectory.

Handoff An offensive play in which one back hands the ball off to another back who attempts to advance the ball.

Lateral pass An offensive play in which the ball is passed backward or lateral to the line of scrimmage. If ball is thrown toward the line of scrimmage it is a forward pass.

Line of scrimmage An imaginary line, or vertical plane, passing through the end of the ball nearest a team's goal line and parallel to the goal lines. Thus there is a line of scrimmage for each team, and the area between the two lines is called the neutral zone. Any player of either team is offside if he encroaches upon the neutral zone before the ball is snapped.

Naked reverse An offensive play in which the ball carrier takes the ball from another back and attempts to advance without benefit of backfield blockers.

Offside When an offensive player is ahead of the ball before it is snapped. Penalty, 5 yards.

Safety A score made when a free ball, or one in possession of a player defending his own goal, becomes dead behind the goal, provided the impetus which caused it to cross the goal was supplied by the defending team.

Screen pass An offensive maneuver in which a wave of eligible receivers converge in area where pass is to be thrown.

Shotgun offense A formation in which the quarterback lines up 5 to 6 yards behind the center. Usually one or both halfbacks may line up 1 to 2 yards on either side of the quarterback and 1 yard in front of the quarterback.

Shovel pass An offensive maneuver in which a pass is thrown, underhand, usually forward to a back behind the line of scrimmage.

Touchback When the ball becomes dead behind the opponent's goal line legally in possession of a player guarding his own goal, provided the impetus which caused it to cross the goal line was supplied by an opponent. No points are scored on the play, and the ball is put in play by a scrimmage at the 20-yard line.

SELECTED REFERENCES

American Association for Health, Physical Education, and Recreation. *Rules for Coeducational Activities and Sports,* revised ed. Washington, D.C.: AAHPER Publications, 1980.

American Association for Health, Physical Education, and Recreation, Division for Girls' and Women's Sports. *Soccer-Speedball-Flag Football Guide,* current ed. Washington, D.C.: AAHPER.

ARMBRUSTER, DAVIS A., LESLIE ERWIN, and FRANK F. MUSKER. *Basic Skills in Sports for Men and Women,* 5th ed. St. Louis, Mo.: C.V. Mosby Company, 1971.

DINTIMAN, GEORGE B., and LLOYD M. BARROW. *A Comprehensive Manual of Physical Education Activities for Men.* Englewood Cliffs, N.J.: Prentice-Hall, Inc. 1970.

FROMMER, HARVEY. *Sports Lingo: A Dictionary of the Language of Sports.* New York: Atheneum, 1979.

DOWELL, LINUS J. *Handbook of Teaching and Coaching Points for Basic Physical Education Skills.* Springfield, Ill.: Charles C. Thomas Publisher, 1974.

National College Physical Education Association. *Touch Football—Official National Touch Football Rules,* current ed. Chicago: The Athletic Institute.

STANBURY, DEAN, and FRANK DeSANTIS. *Touch Football.* New York: Sterling Publishing Co., Inc., 1961.

Skills Testing

BRACE, DAVID K. *Skills Test Manual: Football.* Washington, D.C.: American Association for Health, Physical Education, and Recreation, 1965.

HEWATE, CAROLYN, and JUNE REYNOLDS. "Flag Football." *Soccer-Speedball-Flag Football Guide.* Washington, D.C.: American Association for Health, Physical Education, and Recreation, 1972.

Audio-Visual Materials

Clearvue Inc., Educational and Audio Training Products, 6666 North Oliphant Ave., Chicago, Illinois 60631. *Touch/Flag Football II: Rules of the Game* (Filmstrip/Guide).

TRACK AND FIELD

THIS CHAPTER WILL ENABLE YOU TO:

♦ Identify the basic rules of the sport.
♦ Demonstrate and perform basic skills and techniques of various running, hurdling, jumping, and throwing events.
♦ Identify the basic terminology used in the sport of track and field.
♦ Set up a training program for a participant in various running and hurdling events.

NATURE AND PURPOSE

The more than thirty track and field events in the Olympics involve walking, running, jumping, and throwing, and require a combination of speed, endurance, and skill. However, the great variety of abilities required for these events enables practically every type of individual, no matter what body type, to participate successfully. Often young men and women do not realize that they have the native ability to become successful in track and field until they give it a try. Many track and field stars "discovered themselves" in physical education classes or intramural sports, and all young athletes are urged to try the various events, as they can usually find one in which they can succeed or often excel. In fact, a coach in properly assessing talent on a team for the first time should conduct a pentathlon competition consisting of five events: sprinting, hurdling, jumping, throwing, and distance running.

Recently in the United States, high schools and colleges have moved to the metric system in the running events so that these outdoor events now include for men the 100, 200, 400, 800, 1500, 3000 meter steeplechase; 5000 and 10,000 meter runs; the 110, 300, and 400 meter hurdles; and the 400 and 1600 meter relays. For women, the outdoor running events include the 100, 200, 400, 800, and 1500 meter runs; the 80, 100, and 400 meter hurdles; and the 400 and 1600 meter relays. The outdoor field events for men include the long jump, triple jump, high jump, pole vault, discus, and shot put with a few states conducting the javelin and hammer events; while the outdoor field events for women include the long jump, high jump, shot put, discus, and javelin.

SUGGESTED LEARNING SEQUENCE

There is no particular order to teach the various running or field events described in this chapter.

Much of what may be taught should depend on the particular need, the length of time available, the characteristics of the learners, and the types of facilities available. It is important to follow prescribed progressions leading up to the completion of a given skill. A pattern whereby certain skills might prove valuable in carrying over learning from one event to another is recommended. For example, principles relating to sprinting could also be applied to the long jump or triple jump, or perhaps to hurdling.

The technique of station teaching would encourage maximization participation. Stations might be set up so students have a break between events, that is, a field event followed by a running event at the next station.

In all instances, rules, strategies, hints, and terminology should be introduced only when most significant to the learning progression and when dealing with that particular event. Safety considerations would be of prime importance during the initial stages of learning because of the types of equipment that might be used.

A. Orientation
　1. Safety considerations
　2. Nature and purpose
　3. Discussion of equipment
　4. Importance of warm up and cool down
B. Rules, Strategy, Skill Development, Terminology, Specific Safety Considerations—Interpretations are given from event to event as it applies to that event.
　1. Running Events
　　a. Sprinting
　　b. Middle and Long Distance
　　c. Hurdles
　2. Field Events
　　a. Shot Put
　　b. High Jump (Flop Style)
　　c. High Jump (Straddle Style)

d. Long Jump
e. Triple Jump
C. Concluding Track Meet

SKILLS AND TECHNIQUES

Sprinting

While speed or sprinting ability is largely determined by inherited traits—the white muscle fiber composition of the body—a sprinter's innate speed can be greatly improved through technique work and training.

Technique Work. Technique work involves improving a sprinter's start, ability to lift or change gears and ability to relax, thereby sustaining speed.

Starting. The starting commands are "Runners to your marks," "Set," and then the firing of the gun. In the "on the mark" position the sprinter may use one of three types of start: the bunch, medium, or elongated (Figure 23-3). These terms refer to the spacing between the blocks as well as the distance of the blocks from the starting line; the choice is determined by the sprinter's body structure, height, and length of limbs.

In the "on the mark" position, the hands are parallel to the starting line, the arms are shoulder width apart, the dominant leg is forward in the blocks with the opposite knee resting on the track, and the head is relaxed. After assuming this position, the sprinter will then slide or roll forward until the shoulders are over or in front of the starting line with the pressure being on the knee and finger tips.

On "set" the sprinter raises the hips until slightly higher than the shoulders. The knees are parallel or at a slight angle to the track in this position. The sprinter feels good power in both legs in this position if the blocks are spaced properly. The head is relaxed with no tension on the neck.

FIGURE 23-2. Excellent "on the mark" position. Sprinter's weight is on hands and right knee, head down and relaxed, weight is out over the hands.

FIGURE 23-1. Jim Ryun, former world record holder for the mile run.

FIGURE 23-3. Sprinter in the "set" position. (A) Bunch spacing. (B) Medium spacing. (C) Elongated spacing.

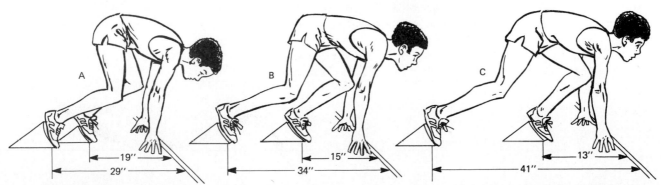

At the gun, the sprinter concentrates on good sprint action driving the arms, lifting the knees, and keeping the driving angle low and forward (Figure 23-4). It is important that the sprinter's movement be forward, not upward, which is the result of the proper "set" position.

Lifting. After coming out of the blocks the sprinter concentrates on lifting or shifting gears by driving the knees high which will continue acceleration. This action continues until the sprinter has reached maximum speed, somewhere between 30 to 40 meters, at which time an upright running position and full running stride length will have been achieved.

FIGURE 23-4. The first step leaving the blocks. (Courtesy of The Athletic Institute.)

Free-wheeling. In this phase, the sprinter works to sustain speed through total body relaxation. Total relaxation is achieved by keeping the hands, arms, and jaws loose, and the shoulders down to reduce tension in the antagonistic muscle groups of the neck.

Finish. The sprinter drives or runs through the tape at the finish in regular sprint form and does not attempt to jump or lunge.

Training Workout Suggestions

In training for the sprinting events, quality work is important over quantity work. Basic work concepts in sprint training should include: long sprints consisting of 200 to 250 meters for the 100 meters, 250 to 300 meters for the 200 meters, and 500 to 600 meters for the 400 meters; medium sprints, consisting of 50 to 75 meters for the 100 meters, 100 to 150 meters (around turn) for 200 meters, and 300 to 350 meters for the 400 meters; and short sprints with the gun consisting of 20 to 30 meters for the 100 meters, 50 to 75 meters for the 200 meters, and 100 to 150 meters for the 400 meters. A weekly competitive season training program is given in Table 23-1. Each of the workouts should be preceded by a good warm-up which includes stretching and flexibility exercises, easy running, sprint drills, and should be followed by a good cool-down of easy running and stretching.

Practice Suggestions—Sprinting Drills

1. *High Knee Drill.* Running 20 to 30 meters, knees are lifted so that thighs are at least parallel to the ground. In performing the drill, it is imperative to emphasize quality lifting and the drill should not be hurried.
2. *Relaxation Drill.* Sprinters in a semi-circle begin on command, run in place concentrating on good arm action, fingers and wrist loose and knees high. On the command "accelerate" sprinters increase arm and leg action while concentrating on maintaining relaxation in the face, shoulders, and hands.
3. *Block Drill.* Sprinter A gets into the blocks in the "on the mark" position. Sprinter B stands facing him with hands on shoulders of sprinter A. Upon continued hand pressure, sprinter A comes to

TABLE 23-1. Weekly Training Program for Sprinting Events

	100 Meters	200 Meters	400 Meters
Monday	4 × 250m at 95% effort/ walk 8 min.	3 × 300m at 95% effort/ walk 10 min.	2 × 600m at 90% effort/ walk 15 min.
Tuesday	baton work; 8–10 × 30–40m gun starts	baton work; 8–10 × 75m gun starts (around turn)	8–10 × 150m gun starts (around turn)
Wednesday	5–6 × 75m at allout/ walk back for recovery	6 × 150m at allout/ walk back for recovery	2–3 × 300m at race pace
Thursday	baton work; 5–6 × 20–30m gun starts	baton work; 6–8 × 50m gun starts	5–6 × 100m at 95% effort
Friday	Meet	Meet	Meet
Saturday	1–2 miles easy distance golf course	1–2 miles easy distance golf course	2–4 miles easy distance golf course
Sunday	Rest	Rest	Rest

"set" position. On the command "go" from sprinter B, sprinter A drives out of the blocks concentrating on driving the arms and lifting the knees while sprinter B continues to offer resistance.

4. *Acceleration Drill.* The sprinter runs 150 meters, increasing speed every 50 meters until at full speed the last 50 meters. The sprinter concentrates on good sprint form and relaxation when accelerating to avoid a breakdown in running form.

Middle Distance and Distance Running

Middle distance races include the 800, 1500 meters, and mile and distance races the 3000-meter steeplechase, 5000, 10,000 meters, and marathon.

Running form in these events is not significantly different from the sprint events except that as the speed of a runner is reduced, the stride length becomes shorter, the body is more erect, and the foot strikes more on the heel in landing.

In training for these events it is important to train both energy systems of the body, the aerobic and anaerobic.

Aerobic Training. This type of training, which improves a runner's endurance or stamina by increasing the ability to take in and utilize oxygen, is accomplished through runs of 3 to 10 miles or longer at different tempos (speeds). An easy tempo involves relaxed recovery running; a brisk tempo involves running at steady state or oxygen balance; and hard tempo involves running beyond steady state but not all out. Using all three tempos in a run produces a type of training called Fartlek (Swedish for "speed play") or playing with speed. Early training should include only easy and brisk tempo runs for several weeks; later hard tempo and hard Fartlek runs with hills may be alternated with easier runs. An example of this pattern of training is given in Table 23-2.

TABLE 23-2. An Aerobic Training Program

Sunday	Long and easy (10 miles, easy tempo)
Monday	Intense (6 miles, hard tempo)
Tuesday	Active rest (5 miles, brisk tempo)
Wednesday	Intense (7 miles, hard Fartlek)
Thursday	Active rest (4 miles, brisk tempo)
Friday	Intense (5 miles, hard tempo)
Saturday	Active rest (8 miles, brisk tempo)

Anaerobic Training. This type of training, which improves the body's ability to run while under oxygen debt, is best developed through intermittent or interval type training. Interval training consists of running a number of short distances at a given pace, interspersed by 1 to 5 minutes of rest or jogging fixed distances. For example: 8 × 200 meters at 30 sec/jog 200 meters. Interval training is used basically to develop race rhythm and for sharpening speed.

Training Workout Suggestions

A weekly competitive season anaerobic training program is outlined in Table 23-3.

Relays

There are two types of relays: the *sprint relays* (400, 800, 1600 meters) and sprint medley (200, 400, 800 meters) and the *distance relays* (3200, 6000) and distance medley (400, 800, 1200, 1600 meters). Four

TABLE 23-3. A Competitive Season Anaerobic Training Program

	800 Meters	1500 Meters	5000 Meters
Sunday	6 miles (easy tempo)	8 miles (easy tempo)	10 miles (easy tempo)
Monday	1 mile (easy tempo) 2 × 600m at race pace/ walk 5 min.; 15 min. (easy tempo)	2 miles (easy tempo) 5 × 800m at slower than race pace/jog 400m; 20 min. (easy tempo)	3 miles (easy tempo) 4 × 1200m at race pace/ jog 600m; 25 min. (easy tempo)
Tuesday	40 min. (brisk tempo)	50 min. (brisk tempo)	60 min. (brisk tempo)
Wednesday	2 miles (brisk tempo) 4 × 400m at faster than race pace/walk 4 min.; 15 min. (easy tempo)	3 miles (brisk tempo) 8 × 400m at race pace/ jog 200m; 25 min. (easy tempo)	4 miles (brisk tempo) 12 × 400m at faster than race pace/jog 200m; 35 min. (easy tempo)
Thursday	20 min. (brisk tempo) 4 × 200m at 90% effort/ jog 200m	30 min. (brisk tempo) 6 × 200m at 90% effort/ jog 200m	50 min. (brisk tempo) 8 × 200m at 90% effort
Friday	20 min. (easy tempo)	30 min. (easy tempo)	40 min. (easy tempo)
Saturday	Meet	Meet	Meet

runners compete for a team, each running an equal distance (except in medley relays), and pass a baton to the next runner. The baton must be exchanged within a 20-meter exchange zone. There are two general methods of exchanging the baton, the visual pass and the blind pass.

Blind Pass. The blind pass is used in the sprint relays. In this exchange the outgoing runner stands in a good sprint position at the back of the 10-meter fly zone located beyond the 20-meter zone (see Figure 23-5). The runner stands on the low side of the lane if the baton is to be received in the right hand and the high side of the lane when the baton is to be received in the left hand. When the incoming runner hits a predetermined mark on the track called the "go mark" the outgoing runner leaves, concentrating on good sprinting action. This "go mark" may vary by 5 to 8 meters and is established by a trial and error method. The baton is exchanged at a given point in the zone, preferably in the last 10 meters of the 20-meter passing zone, without the receiver looking back. The exchange is made by the incoming runner extending the baton forward as far as possible to the opposite hand which has been extended backward, palm back and thumb extended (see Figure 23-6). It can also be received with the palm up, the incoming runner placing the baton downward into the receiver's hand.

Visual Pass. The visual pass is used for all distance relays so that the outgoing runner can judge effectively the fatigue and speed of the incoming runner. The outgoing runner, who is turned toward the inside of the track facing the pole lane, stands on the high side of the lane and receives the baton in the left hand palm up. After receiving the baton in the left hand, it is immediately transferred to the right hand.

Practice Suggestions—Sprint Relay Drills

1. *Four Runner Standing Drill.* Four relay runners standing staggered to the right or left, according to the receiving hand, pass the baton forward from each relay runner. The distance between

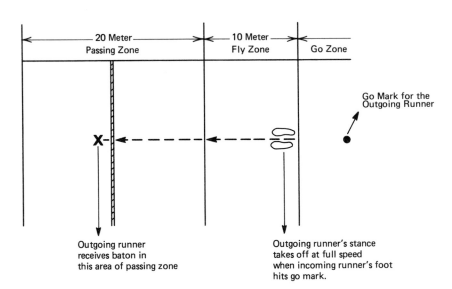

FIGURE 23-5. The blind pass, used for all sprint relays.

FIGURE 23-6. Blind pass. Passer keeps her eyes on the receiver's hand until the pass is completed and she is sure the receiver has a firm grip on the baton.

must allow good extension of the passing and receiving arm.

2. *Four Runner Jogging Drill.* After the standing pass drill is mastered, the runners, using the same techniques, jog around the track passing the baton. Care must be taken to keep the proper spacing between runners to make the drill effective.

3. *One-on-One Drill.* Two relay runners, 2 to 4 feet apart, from a standing start move at full speed on the command "go" from the back runner. The pass is made at full speed on the command "reach" or "hand" by the back runner.

4. *Five Runner Drill.* Four 20-meter exchange zones are marked off around the track. The first relay runner starts out at half speed increasing to full speed 50 to 60 meters from the passing zone. The baton continues around the track for several laps practicing the relay exchanges.

Hurdling

The physical attributes of height or good leg split, speed, flexibility, and coordination with the mental qualities of courage, patience, and concentration are important for success in hurdling.

Hurdling is sprinting and hurdle races must be considered as sprint races. The hurdling action is a step-over or sprinting action and not a jumping, flying, floating, or sailing movement; all teaching is done with this objective in mind (Figure 23-7).

Learning Cues

1. The first step in teaching hurdling is to introduce the wall drill. The hurdler standing a few feet from a wall starts by lifting the lead knee and leg toward the wall, letting the weight fall forward. The leg is planted on the wall at hurdle height. The chest drops down toward the knee and the opposite arm is driven toward the opposite leg. The drill is continued gradually increasing the distance from the wall. Correct hurdling action in this drill is important. The leg is not just swung up from the ground, the thigh and knee are lifted and the foot picked up and planted against the wall, just as if aiming to plant it over a hurdle.

2. The next step is to walk or step over barriers set at 20 to 26 inches high. After the correct lead leg action is mastered in this walk-over drill, the proper action of the trail leg is introduced. The trail action is introduced by having the hurdler stop after the lead leg has landed over the hurdle. The trail knee is then brought up under the arm pit and the foot reaches out for a long step forward.

3. The last step is to run over the hurdles with a high knee stepping action, gradually increasing the speed of the running into full effort as correct hurdling form is executed. The height of the hurdles is raised when correct hurdling technique is achieved.

Hurdle Start. The hurdle start differs from the regular sprint start in that the hurdler must come up to the running position sooner. A high hurdler will take 7 or 8 steps to the first hurdle, an intermediate hurdler 21, 22, 23 or 24 steps. The hurdler who takes an odd number of steps to the first hurdle will have the same leg forward in the blocks as leads over the hurdle. With an even number of steps, the lead leg

FIGURE 23-7. Recommended form in the high hurdles. (From J. Kenneth Doherty, *Modern Track and Field.* Englewood Cliffs, N.J.: Prentice-Hall, Inc., 1953.)

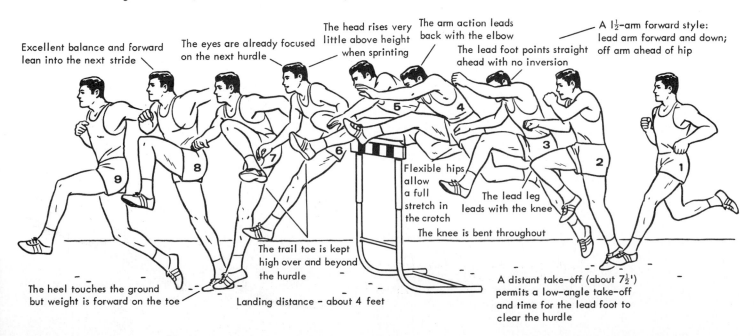

Excellent balance and forward lean into the next stride

The eyes are already focused on the next hurdle

The head rises very little above height when sprinting

The arm action leads back with the elbow

The lead foot points straight ahead with no inversion

A 1½-arm forward style: lead arm forward and down; off arm ahead of hip

Flexible hips allow a full stretch in the crotch

The lead leg leads with the knee

The knee is bent throughout

The trail toe is kept high over and beyond the hurdle

The heel touches the ground but weight is forward on the toe

Landing distance - about 4 feet

A distant take-off (about 7½') permits a low-angle take-off and time for the lead foot to clear the hurdle

TABLE 23-4. Hurdling—A Competitive Season Training Program

	110m Hurdles	400m Hurdles
Sunday	2 miles (easy tempo)	3–4 miles (easy tempo)
Monday	Go over flights of 7, 6, 5, 4, and 3 hurdles 3 times each 1 × 400m at full effort	Go over flights of 8, 6, 4, and 2 hurdles, from blocks, working on stride pattern at race pace
Tuesday	"Five-step" 5 hurdles, 2–3 times 3–4 × 150m at 90% effort/ walk back for recovery	2 × 300m at full effort
Wednesday	Go over 5 flights of hurdles (70 meters) 5 times at full effort 1 × 300m at full effort	Go over flights of 5, 4, 3, 2, and 1 hurdles at race pace
Thursday	5–6 gun starts over 2 hurdles 3–4 × 100m at 90% effort/walk back for recovery	4 × 200m at 90% effort
Friday	Easy stretching and jogging "Five-step" 3 hurdles, 2–3 times	3–4 gun starts over 1st hurdle working on stride pattern
Saturday	Meet	Meet

over the hurdle is the back leg in the blocks. The hurdler determines the lead leg by attempting to hurdle with each leg. The one most comfortable should be the lead leg.

Running between the Hurdles. In the highs a hurdler must take 3 steps and in the intermediates 13, 15, or 17 steps. The intermediate hurdler can use a 14-stride pattern if the lead leg is alternated. The hurdler must concentrate on good sprint action between the hurdles, running up on the balls of the feet, knees high, and arms driving hard with relaxation. Good sprint rhythm between the hurdles is important. The hurdler should never gallop or overstride, which often is caused by not getting a good step off the hurdle with the trail leg.

Practice Suggestions—Hurdling Drills

1. *Wall Drill.* Used to teach basic hurdle techniques of lean, lead leg, and trail leg action.
2. *Ground Hurdling.* Sit on ground in the same position as hurdle clearance. This drill is used for stretching and flexibility as well as teaching hurdling technique.
3. *Five-Step the Side.* The lead leg clears the hurdle to the side without passing over the hurdle, the trail leg comes over the hurdle. Take five quick, short steps to the next hurdle, until clearing several hurdles.

4. *Five-Step the Top.* This drill follows side drill, emphasizing correct hurdle technique over top.

Training Workout Suggestions

Table 23-4 presents a weekly competitive season training program for hurdling. Each of these workouts is preceded by a good warm-up consisting of specific hurdling flexibility and stretching exercises, easy running, and sprint work, and is followed by a good cool-down of easy running and stretching.

Shot Putting

In the past seventy years the world record for the shot put has improved by 21 feet. Improvement in technique and the addition of weight training are the two factors which have brought about this increase in distance.

The technique of shot putting has changed from the side style, hopping across the circle, to the O'Brien style, gliding across the circle, to the latest rotational style performed by spinning across the circle as in the discus throw. The O'Brien style is the most widely used technique today.

O'Brien Style. With the putter facing opposite the direction of the throw, the thrower glides (shifts) across the circle, lifts the shot with the back, hips, and legs, and then explodes with the arm. The emphasis in teaching this technique is to stress the importance of keeping the legs and hips ahead of the upper body and throwing arm, thus utilizing the stronger, larger muscle groups of the lower body.

In teaching the shot technique it is helpful to think of the circle as the face of a clock with the 12 o'clock position at the back of the circle. The circle should also be divided with two lines; one a line of direction, the other a cross line. These lines divide the circle in four equal parts.

Learning Cues

1. *Grip.* The weight of the shot is placed where the fingers meet the palm of the hand. The thumb and little finger support and guide the shot. The three middle fingers are used for power.
2. *Shot Placement.* The shot is placed on the neck under the jaw bone underneath the ear.
3. *Starting Position.* The putter stands at the back of the circle with the right foot in the 11 o'clock position on the line of direction. The putter keeps the eyes focused on a focal point in the back of the circle with the non-throwing arm and shoulder kept square and held back.
4. *Glide.* From the starting position, the body weight drops down over the right leg raising the left leg. The left leg makes an easy swinging motion toward the throwing direction. At the same time the right leg begins its pushing action across the circle. This is a ball to heel motion that causes a stretching action, not a hopping or jumping movement. As the body weight moves toward the

front of the circle the right leg snaps underneath the thrower to the middle of the circle in the 9 o'clock position. The left leg lands at the same instance in the 5 o'clock position just to the left of the line of direction.

5. *Throwing (Power) Position.* This position at the front of the circle is called the power position; it is the key to a successful throw. Hitting this position correctly for a right-handed thrower means the feet and hips are turned to the left side of the circle, the head facing the back of the circle, body weight over the right leg and the right and left legs bent.

Practice Suggestions—Shot Put Techniques

Standing Throws

1. Punch drill—thrower in a throwing position at front of circle without a shot punches hard with throwing arm as if throwing a punch; then with the shot repeats the same action.
2. Hip drill—thrower in a throwing position at front of circle without shot, hands on hips, makes a hard throwing action initiating power from legs and punches right hip hard; then repeats with shot.

Starting Position

1. T-drill—from a standing position the thrower drops down in a T-position as if starting the throw.
2. A-drill—from the standing T-position the thrower drops down and kicks the left leg until the thrower's body is in the A-position.

Middle of Ring

1. Cross bar drill (right leg)—with arms draped over a cross bar the putter snaps the right leg under; the cross bar prevents the shoulders from turning.
2. Cross bar drill (left leg)—with arms draped over a cross bar the putter concentrates on driving the left leg low and to the toe board without turning the upper body.

Finish

1. Side block drill—the putter from a standing position blocks with the left side of the body getting the feel that this part of body acts as a fulcrum.
2. High jump cross bar—with a high jump cross bar set up high on standards the putter throws over the bar learning to lead with the hip and to throw off the back leg.

High Jump (Flop Style)

The flop or back layout style of jumping originated by Dick Fosbury, the 1968 Olympic champion, is currently used by the majority of high jumpers.

Technique. The technique for the flop style of jumping can be broken down into three phases: approach, plant/take-off, and bar clearance.

Learning Cues

1. Approach. The "J" approach is used by most jumpers. This is a run of 3, 4, or 5 strides straight ahead, then 3, 4, or 5 strides on a curve (see Figure 23-8). Speed is important in the approach so the jumper must lean to the inside of the arc in order to maintain velocity into the bar. The stride next to the last stride is longer to enable the jumper to lower the center of gravity for the jump. The last stride (take-off) is from the outside foot, the foot farthest from the bar, and is shorter so that the body is in a lean back position.
2. Plant/Take-off. The lead knee, the knee closest to the bar, is driven up hard and *across* the body toward the opposite shoulder. This action along with the direction of the run helps with the rotation of the back to the bar after lift off. The arms assist the lift at take-off and should be kept tight and close to the body. They come up with the lead knee until shoulder high, then are stopped abruptly in a blocking action. As the take-off is being executed the jumper should look over the inside shoulder.
3. Bar Clearance (layout position). During bar clearance the lead knee remains up with the plant leg

FIGURE 23-8. The "J" approach used in the back layout (flop style) high jump.

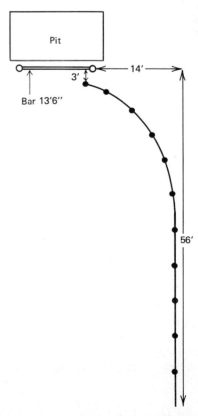

catching up to it. The legs are spread with the knees out in a "frog" position and the feet together. The hands are placed alongside the body. There is a laying back of the head and an arching of the back until the bar passes along the back and hips. At this point the chin is tucked down to the chest so that the body folds up in an L-position.

Teaching Sequence

1. Learn to land on the back or shoulders
   a. Standing at the edge of pit with back to it, jump backwards off both feet.
   b. Jump backwards off a box from both feet.
   c. Continue jumping backwards working on the techniques of placement of hands, legs, and hips.
2. Determine take-off foot
   a. Demonstrate scissors jump standing first and then from three steps.
   b. Experiment with scissors jump from each side landing on the feet in the pit.
   c. Jog five steps and jump into pit.
   d. Continue jumping putting together the knee drive, arm drive, and leg plant.
3. Bar Clearance
   a. Lying on edge of pit, legs hanging down, tuck chin to chest, lifting upper body to raise lower legs.

Practice Suggestions—Drills for the Flop

1. *Approach Drill.* Run a circle with a 17 feet radius. Learn to relax while running the arc, dropping the inside shoulder.
2. *Plant/Take-off Drill.* In the open field, away from the pit, take 3 to 4 running strides with the last two utilizing the long-short rhythm. Plant the take-off foot driving the lead knee across. Repeat the drill popping up into the air with good vertical lift.
3. *Clearance Drill.* Bouncing in pit, jump up as high as possible then lay back as if clearing the bar working on the proper techniques of bar clearance.

High Jump (Straddle Style)

Technique. Like the flop style, the straddle technique can be broken down into three phases: approach, plant/take-off, and bar clearance.

Learning Cues

1. Approach. The jumper uses a straight line approach in contrast to the arc approach used in the flop. For an experienced jumper, a 7 to 9 stride approach is recommended. The beginner will take fewer strides. A checkmark for the start of the approach should be established. The jumper must use speed into the plant/take-off, but for a fast run-up exceptional strength is needed in the hips and legs. The angle of approach should be between 20 and 45 degrees.
2. Plant/Take-off. The jumper takes off on the inside foot, the foot closest to the bar in this style of jumping. There is a longer pendulum stride prior to the last stride which lowers the hips preparing the jumper for vertical lift. In the last stride the take-off foot lands heel first and out in front of the body so that the jumper is in a lay back position (see Figure 23-9). Both arms are back to assist in

FIGURE 23-9. Proper straddle jump form.

FIGURE 23-10. Recommended form in the long jump, using a modified hitch kick.

the lift. As the take-off foot is planted, the lead leg is brought through fast. The jumper may lead with either a straight lead leg or a bent lead leg.
3. Bar Clearance. The head, lead leg, and outside arm reach across the bar first. The trail leg, bent at the knee, is pulled upward. Following these actions the chest and hips pass over the bar with the crotch directly over the bar (Figure 23-8). While on top of the bar the jumper tucks the chin to the chest. The lead arm as it passes over the bar should be pulled back and up, which rotates the hips and trail leg away from the bar.

Practice Suggestions—Drills for Straddle

1. *Plant/Take-off.* The jumper moves down the field in a straight line making a series of two-stride jumps. The jumper uses the long-short stride pattern, simulating the last two strides of the jump.
2. *Vertical Lift.* With a four-step approach from the pit the plant is made with the outside leg and both arms are driven upward. The rotation is made, and the jumper lands in the pit on the foot of the lead leg. When the jumper can perform this drill successfully, a crossbar is added and the jumper continues to repeat the drill as the bar is raised.

Long Jump

The long jumper must possess good sprint speed, a rhythmic consistent stride pattern, and great spring.

Learning Cues

The basic technique of the long jump can be broken down into the following phases:

1. The Run-up or Approach. During the approach the jumper must get to the take-off board with maximum controlled speed and be in a position to lift. Therefore, relaxation and consistency of stride length is important during the approach. To ensure that the jumper hits the take-off board with consistency, checkmarks are established in the following manner:

a. The jumper, one stride from the take-off board, runs in the opposite direction of the jumping pit 12 to 16 strides until the same foot that is to hit the take-off board lands on the track.
b. The jumper continues with 4 to 5 run throughs in this direction until the take-off foot hits consistently at the same point.
c. The jumper then places a checkmark at that point and standing one stride away hits the mark with the same foot as the take-off foot.
d. Now running toward the jumping pit the jumper makes 4 to 5 run throughs until hitting the board consistently.
e. The checkmark may be moved forward or backward depending on whether the jumper is over or under the take-off board.
2. Plant/Take-off. Much like in the high jump, the next-to-last stride is a longer or settling stride preparing for the gather or lift. The last stride is shorter and the take-off foot hits in a heel-toe action. The free leg comes through as in a normal running stride.
3. The Flight. After leaving the board the jumper can use one of three types of techniques in the air: the hitch kick, hang, or sail. The *hitch kick* is done with a run-in-the-air action (see Figure 23-10). The *hang* is performed by letting the legs hang down, the hips are forward and the upper body back. In the *sail* the legs are tucked up under the body. The purpose of these flight positions is to prevent forward rotation and to get good leg extension in landing.
4. The Landing. The important technique in landing is to get good leg extension. This can only be achieved when the flight position is done correctly. Upon impact in landing the jumper must work through the jump in order not to sit back. This is done by dropping the chin to the chest and driving the arms back forcefully behind the body.

Practice Suggestions for Long Jumping

1. *Pop-ups.* Performed by doing repeat short runs of 5 to 7 strides; the jumper settles in the next-to-last stride, shortens the stride, pops off the board with

TABLE 23-5. Basic Rules, Safety Instructions, and Helpful Hints for Track and Field Events

EVENT	BASIC RULES	SAFETY INSTRUCTIONS	HELPFUL HINTS
Sprinting	1. One false start disqualifies a runner. 2. A starter may not touch on or over the line before the firing of the gun. 3. Some part of each foot must be in contact with the track in the blocks.	1. Warm up thoroughly before starting. 2. Don't jump or lunge at the finish tape. 3. Don't take starts after a hard training session.	1. Think action at the gun and concentrate on good sprinting action out of blocks, not jumping or lunging. 2. Come up gradually into the running position after leaving the starting blocks.
Hurdling	1. Entire body must pass over the hurdle. 2. A hurdler may not interfere with a hurdler in another lane.	1. Warm up and stretch well before hurdling. 2. Never attempt to go over a hurdle from the wrong direction.	1. Get a good lean or attack at the hurdle. Don't bend from the waist. 2. Lead with a bent knee. 3. Stay up on balls of the feet in sprinting between hurdles.
High Jump	1. The jumper must make a jump from one foot. 2. Three trials are allowed at each height. 3. Displacing a bar, passing under it, crossing the line of the bar extended, or leaving the ground shall count as a foul and trial.	1. Make certain the pit is positioned correctly. 2. Don't jump without spiked shoes to prevent slipping. 3. Use a heel cup or heel pad to prevent bruises.	1. Don't decelerate into the last few strides. 2. Don't try to rotate off the ground—it destroys vertical lift. 3. Use the arms at take-off to help vertical lift.
Long Jump	1. Touching in front of scratch line or passing the line extended shall count as a foul and trial. 2. The jump shall be measured at right angles to the board and at the point of landing closest to the take-off.	1. Keep the landing pit area soft and smooth. 2. Wear jumping shoes with heel cups or rubber pads in take-off heel.	1. Keep the chest and head up at take-off. 2. Run up off the take-off board. 3. Throw the stomach out after take-off.
Triple Jump	1. During the hop and step phase the free leg must not touch the ground. 2. The legal measurement of a jump is the same as described in the long jump. 3. A scratch jump is the same as described in the long jump.	1. Wear heel cups or rubber pads in both jumping shoes. 2. Keep the landing pit area soft and smooth.	1. Lead with the knees during the hop and step. 2. Keep the thighs parallel with the ground during the hop and step. 3. Keep the cadence of the hop and step even.
Shot Put	1. Touching on top or outside with circle or toe-board with any part of the body constitutes a foul. 2. The thrower must enter and leave by the back of the circle.	1. Roll the shot back to the circle—don't throw it back. 2. Practice in a protected area.	1. Get the right leg up under the body quickly during the glide. 2. The left and right leg should hit at the same time at the front of the circle. 3. Keep the legs ahead of the upper body.
Relay Races	1. The baton must be passed inside the 20-meter passing zone. 2. The baton must be carried in the hand throughout the race. 3. After passing the baton, the runner may not interfere with an opponent.	1. After passing the baton, remain in your lane until all others have passed. 2. Pass the baton to opposite hands, right to left or left to right, to avoid a collision.	1. The incoming runner "attacks" the passing zone until the baton is exchanged. 2. The incoming runner "looks" the baton into the receiver's hand. 3. The pass is made directly ahead, never across the body.

high body carriage, continuing a normal leg action, and lands with the legs under the body.
2. *Flight Pop-ups.* The jumper performs the same type of pop-ups as described above but this time working on the in-the-air action—hitch kick, hang, or sail.
3. *Landing and Extension Pop-ups.* A similar drill only trying to perform correct landing procedures as to leg extension, collapsing of the knees, and driving the arms back forcefully.

Triple Jump

The triple jump, formerly called the "hop, step, and jump," is an event requiring good speed, great leg strength, and excellent coordination.

Learning Cues

The technique in the triple jump can be broken down into the approach, plant/take-off, flight, and landing.

1. Approach. To ensure hitting the take-off board with consistency, checkmarks are established using the same method as in the long jump. However, the approach is slower and more controlled than in the long jump.
2. Plant/Take-off. Since the movement at take-off is more forward than upward as compared to the long jump, the jumper does not need to settle or gather at take-off. The take-off foot is planted flat with the center of gravity directly over the foot.
3. Flight. The first phase of the flight is the hop. The hop, or first jump, is performed by bringing the take-off leg forward after it has fully extended from the take-off board. The thigh of the hopping leg is held parallel to the ground. The hopping foot lands flat in preparation for the next phase. The step, or second jump, is performed by bringing the free leg forward and parallel to the ground, riding it forward until there is a good thigh split. The third phase, or jump, utilizes the same technique as described in the long jump. However, the hang or sail should be used rather than the hitch kick as there is less time to perform the action.
4. Landing. The landing techniques are the same as those used in the long jump with the exception that most jumpers sit out in landing rather than falling forward as in the long jump.

Proper knee action, with thighs parallel to the ground, and equal rhythm are the whole key to good performance in the triple jump.

Practice Suggestions—Drills for the Triple Jump

1. *Standing Triple Jumps.* Begin teaching the triple jump by using the standing triple jump. Start by emphasizing an even rhythm. In this drill a marker should be placed at equal distances to aid in establishing this even cadence.
2. *Short-Run Triple Jumps.* Once the standing jumps are mastered, progression is made by doing short run (5 to 6 stride) triple jumps. Again, it is important to stress even cadence. The key to the even rhythm is keeping the step phase approximately the same distance as the hop and jump phase.
3. *Hopping Drills.* Single leg hopping of 20 to 40 meters is excellent for learning technique and developing leg strength. In this drill, stress the knee coming up parallel to the ground.
4. *Bounding Drills.* Alternate bounding from one leg to the other for 30 to 60 meters is also good for learning technique and for conditioning. In this drill it is important to keep the thighs parallel to the ground, lead with the knees, and get a good leg split by delaying the bounding action.

TERMINOLOGY

Aerobic running Running done at speeds of low intensity so that oxygen intake and oxygen output are the same; therefore, this type of running can be sustained for a long period of time.

Anaerobic running Running done at speeds of great intensity so that oxygen intake is less than oxygen output; therefore, this type of running can only be sustained for a short period of time.

Anchor leg The last leg for a runner on a relay team.

Baton A stick passed from one relay runner to another.

Blind pass A nonvisual baton exchange used in sprint relays.

Crossbar The bar which a high jumper or pole vaulter must clear.

False start Moving or jumping before the gun is fired.

Fartlek A Swedish term for "speed play" describing a type of training in which a runner uses various running speeds over a long distance. This type of training is usually done in a forest, golf course, or other area away from the track.

Flight One lane of hurdles. A round of trials for a given number of field event contestants.

Flop style The style of high jumping in which the jumper's back passes over the bar.

Fly zone The 10-meter zone outside the passing zone used by the outgoing runner to get a flying start.

Gather In jumping events, the settling or lowering of the hips during the last few strides prior to take-off.

Heat Preliminary race whose winners qualify for the semi-finals or finals.

Hitch kick A running-in-the-air action during flight in the long jump used to prevent forward rotation.

Interval training A type of running training containing four variables: the number of repetitions, distance, tempo of run, and rest interval.

Passing zone The 20-meter zone in which the baton in a relay must be exchanged (passed).

Relay leg The distance each runner travels in a relay.

Straddle style Style of high jumping in which the jumper's stomach passes over the bar.

Take-off board A board from which the long jumper takes off.

Throwing sector The specified arc in which a thrown implement must land.

Toe-board A board, in the form of an arc, on which or over which the shot-putter must not step.

Trial An attempt in a field event.

TAC The Athletics Congress, the new governing body of track and field in the United States.

SELECTED REFERENCES

BOWERMAN, J. WILLIAM. *Coaching Track and Field.* Boston: The Houghton Mifflin Company, 1972.

BUSH, JIM. *Dynamic Track and Field.* Boston: Allyn and Bacon, Inc., 1978.

COSTILL. *A Scientific Approach to Distance Running.* Los Altos, Calif.: Track and Field News, 1979.

DOHERTY, J. KENNETH. *Track and Field Omnibook,* 3rd ed. Los Altos, Calif.: Track and Field News Press, 1976.

FOREMAN, K., and V. HUSTED. *Track and Field Techniques for Girls and Women,* 2nd ed. Dubuque, Iowa: Wm. C. Brown Company, Publishers, 1971.

National Collegiate Athletic Association. *Official Track and Field Guide* (current ed.). New York: National Collegiate Athletic Bureau.

National Federation of State High School Athletic Associations. *Track and Field Rules* (current ed.). Washington, D.C.

POWELL, JOHN T. *Track and Field Fundamentals for Teacher and Coach,* 3rd ed. Champaign, Ill.: Stipes Publishing Company, 1971.

STEBEN, RALPH E., and SAM BELL. *An Administrative Approach to the Science of Coaching.* New York: John Wiley & Sons, 1978.

Periodicals

Track and Field News. Box 296, Los Altos, Calif. 94022.

VOLLEYBALL

THIS CHAPTER WILL ENABLE YOU TO:

 ◆ Describe and execute in game play the skills of overhand pass, forearm pass, serve, spike, and blocking.
 ◆ Describe, discuss, and put into practice the rules of power volleyball during a game or match.
 ◆ Apply basic offensive and defensive principles during a game or match.
 ◆ Describe and play in a game or match the 6-6 offense and 4-2 offense.
 ◆ Describe and play in a game or match the man-back defense and the man-up defense.
 ◆ Describe play in power volleyball using the correct terminology associated with the sport.

NATURE AND PURPOSE

Volleyball is played by two teams of six players each on a court 60 by 30 feet, divided into two halves, with a net 8 feet high (7 feet 4¼ inches high in women's volleyball). The players are designated as left, center, and right forwards and left, center, and right backs. When it is a team's turn to serve, every player rotates one position clockwise and the right back serves (see Figure 24-1).

The object of the game is to keep the ball from striking the floor on your side of the net and to return it so that it strikes the floor on your opponents' side before they can return it. The ball is put in play from behind the rear boundary line by the right back, who serves it across the net into the opponents' court. The ball is then volleyed back and forth until one team or the other fails to return the ball. If the serving team makes the error, it loses the serve. An error by the receiving team gives one point to the servers. A team can score only when it serves and it continues to serve as long as it scores.

Teams are permitted three hits to return the ball across the net. One player may execute two of the three hits, but not two in succession. Exception: A block of a spike is not considered as one of the three hits, and the blocker may immediately play the ball again.

The serve must go directly from the server to the opponents' court without touching a teammate or the net, which would result in a side-out.

A match consists of the best two of three games at the high school level, the best of five at the collegiate level. Ends of the court are changed after each game, and at the middle (8 points) of the final game (third or fifth).

Volleyball games are played to 15 points, but teams must win by at least 2 points.

SUGGESTED LEARNING SEQUENCE

A. Introduction—Nature and Purpose
B. Overhand Pass
C. Forearm Pass
D. Spike
E. Rules and Procedures of Play
F. Service
G. Blocking
H. Offense
I. Defense

As is the case with many activities, drills and skills should be put in a competitive and game-like situation as soon as possible. Games using only the overhand pass or forearm pass are good practice.

SKILLS AND TECHNIQUE

Overhand Pass

Balls received above the waist are best played with the two-hand overhand pass. This provides the most accuracy and control because more control points result from the positioning of the fingers on the ball, and it gives an extended absorption and acceleration period.

Learning Cues

1. Body position includes feet shoulder width in a staggered stance with either foot forward, knees slightly flexed. Hands are ready, held high above the forehead. (See Figure 24-2.)
2. Finger position is described as forming an equilateral triangle on the ball with the thumbs and forefingers serving as the sides of the triangle, but the forefingers being approximately 4 inches

NET

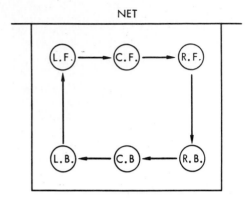

FIGURE 24-1.   Team position and rotation.

FIGURE 24-2.   Body position, ready for overhand pass.

FIGURE 24-3.   Hand position on the overhand pass.

apart, the thumbs 2 inches apart, and the remaining fingers resting on the ball. The palms do not touch the ball. (See Figure 24-3.)
3. Ball is contacted in front of the forehead, approximately 6 inches above the head.
4. Ball is viewed through the forefingers and thumbs.
5. Fingers, wrists, and elbows flex as the ball makes contact, creating an "absorption," and allowing the ball to come within approximately 2 inches of the forehead. (See Figure 24-4.)

FIGURE 24-4.   Hand and arm position during absorption.

6. Fingers, wrists, and elbows then extend upward, following through to a "surrender" position.

Practice Suggestions

1. Practice overhand passing by placing volleyball in your hands in the correct position for initial contact. Absorb and pass ball upward, then recatch ball in same position. Repeat. Gradually reduce the amount of time that the volleyball is held between passes.
2. Pass the ball from a sitting position to develop the power from the upper extremities.
3. Overhand pass to a partner or against a wall, let the ball bounce on the floor, then pass off the bounce. Position body early.
4. Have partner toss volleyball into position for an overhand pass, you return ball to partner with a pass. Have partner toss ball slightly right and left, forcing you to change body position.
5. Execute an overhand pass to yourself, turn 90° and pass, 180° and pass, 360° and pass.

Forearm Pass

The forearm pass is excellent for playing balls that cannot be returned with the overhand pass. It is sometimes called a "bump" or "dig," and is almost always used to return serve. This technique is unusual and will require a longer time to master than the overhand pass. Combining the forearm pass with a dive or a roll greatly increases the area covered by a volleyball player.

Learning Cues

1. Body position includes the feet spread shoulder width, weight on the balls of the feet, with one foot slightly ahead of the other in a heel-toe relationship. The players body is in a semi-squat position with the knees flexed approximately 90° and the back fairly erect or vertical. (See Figure 24-5.)
2. Hands are connected by placing the back of one hand into the palm of the other and folding the thumbs down evenly. (See Figure 24-6.) The fingers are pointed toward the floor by cocking the wrists downward.

the pass, with the arms remaining extended and parallel to the floor. The momentum for the pass comes primarily from the extension of the legs into a standing position. Many times the speed of the ball is enough to provide a return with the forearm pass. A common mistake is for players to swing the arms upward during the forearm pass, but this is not good technique and should be used only when returning a deeply hit ball or from out-of-bounds.
5. Absorption when returning hard-hit spikes or serves can be accomplished by playing the ball on the fleshy part of the forearm and relaxing the arms slightly upon contact.

Practice Suggestions

1. Without ball, assume correct starting position for forearm pass, then through an extension of the legs and hips, rise through the striking motion without swinging the arms.
2. Have player execute as in (1) but strike a ball held out by a partner, with both hands, approximately 4 feet from the floor.

FIGURE 24-5. Body and hand position for forearm pass.

FIGURE 24-6. Body position after contact of forearm pass.

3. Arms are extended in front of the body with elbows locked and rotated toward each other, which exposes the fleshy part of the forearm to the ball. The angle between the extended arms and the trunk is approximately 90 degrees.
4. Ball contact is made on the fleshy part of the forearm (approximately 2 to 6 inches above the wrist). Eyes should remain on the ball throughout

3. Have partner toss volleyball high enough so that it will rebound from the floor, and have the player execute a forearm pass of the rebound. Emphasize good form and upward direction of the ball.
4. Return a tossed volleyball. Emphasize good form and upward direction of the ball.
5. Return a tossed ball that is thrown to the right or

left of the player. Emphasize body position.

6. Forearm pass into a basketball basket or to a prescribed area of the court from a tossed ball.
7. Return served balls from opposite court. Try to pass balls to a given area, approximately 15 feet high.

The Dig Pass. The one-hand dig pass is used to return low balls that would be out of reach of the two-hand pass. The fist is closed, and the ball is struck with the heel of the hand and the *second* joint of the fingers; or the fingers are curled, and the ball is struck with the heel of the hand and the *first* joint of the fingers. The ball need not be hit with much force because it rebounds forcefully from the hard fist. The back of the hand is another effective method of "digging" the ball, particularly if you are diving forward to play the ball.

Spike

The spike is the primary offensive weapon in power volleyball that provides the excitement of a home run, a knockout punch, or a touchdown. The spike is the process of driving a volleyball with force from your side of the net down into your opponents' court so that it strikes the floor before they can return the ball.

FIGURE 24-8. Body position just prior to contact of the ball while spiking.

FIGURE 24-7. "Gathered" position, preparing to spike.

Learning Cues

1. The approach to the spike is made to align the body with the ball. The spiker begins 8 to 10 feet from the net. As the spiker sees the set ball, he quickly takes a directional step toward the ball (left foot for right-handers). On the second step the spiker begins to swing both arms backward, steps toward the ball, bringing the shoulders parallel to the net. The third step is small bring-ing the rear foot parallel to the front foot, with the arms swung backward as far as possible, and the body in a "crouched" or "gathered" position (see Figure 24-7).
2. In jumping, the heels are planted hard, both arms swung forward and upward (as in a basketball rebound), primary motion is upward. The jump should be made from both feet.
3. As the arms reach the top of their arc the spiking arm is cocked—elbow higher than the shoulder, back slightly arched, wrist cocked (see Figure 24-8).
4. The player completes the spike by dropping the non-hitting arm and striking the ball with an up and over movement of the spiking arm. Contact should be made as high as possible and in front of the hitting shoulder.
5. The ball should be struck with the open hand (fist is legal, but lacks control and power), with initial contact made with the heel of the hand and then the wrist snapping forward bringing the palm and fingers over the ball.
6. Follow through to the waist, being careful not to touch the net.
7. Land on the toes of both feet that are shoulder width apart, absorbing the impact by flexing the knees to a crouched position, which also helps to regain balance.

Practice Suggestions

1. Have players stand facing a wall some 12 to 15 feet away. Player will cock spiking arm to a ready

position, toss the volleyball to the correct spiking position in front of the shoulders, and strike the ball as in spiking. Player should attempt to hit the ball to the floor some 3 feet from the wall causing it to rebound against the wall and up into the air toward the spiker. Initially, have the spikers catch the ball each time and re-set to themselves, and as they progress have the spikers continuously return the ball by spiking.

2. Place a chair adjacent to the net and 2 feet away. Have a partner stand on the chair, laying a volleyball in one hand while holding the ball away from the chair and above the net. Player should then make the approach and spike the stationary ball. Emphasize form on approach as well as the striking motion.
3. Start in ready position for a spike, have partner toss the volleyball 5 to 8 feet above the net and 2 feet from the net ("set" the ball). Player approaches and spikes the ball. Repeat.
4. Spiker stands with the ball adjacent to the net at one end. Partner (setter) stands adjacent to the net near the center of the net. Spiker passes the ball to the setter (who will set the ball in the proper area) then quickly back up to the correct starting position in preparation to spike. As the set is made the spiker then approaches and spikes the ball. This drill helps the spiker understand what his position should be when a "set" is imminent.

Serve

The serve is the technique used to begin the play of each point. Emphasis should be placed on the serve, for a team may score only when serving, and an unsuccessful serve removes any chance to then score. In power volleyball the serve has been developed to the extent that it is a scoring tool. The overhand serve is primarily used and in its variations can be very difficult to return. For beginning players who do not handle the ball well, the underhand serve is recommended.

Underhand Serve. The underhand serve is used by beginning players or by players who desire a great deal of control on their serve. The underhand serve is similar to the slow pitch in softball, a horseshoe pitch, or a delivery in bowling.

Learning Cues

1. Body position includes a staggered stance, with the left foot slightly forward (if right-handed), approximately 2 to 8 feet behind the back line, and the body facing the direction you want ball to go.
2. Ball is held in the left hand, about 12 inches in front of the body to the right of the right hip. This puts the ball in front of the right shoulder.
3. The striking arm is brought back in a pendulum motion, then swings forward toward the ball.

4. The ball is struck from the holding hand, not tossed into the air, which increases error.
5. The striking hand may be open, closed (fist), or semi-closed (ball strikes the heel and first digits of the hand).
6. Follow through in the direction you wish the ball to go.

Practice Suggestions

1. Serve to a partner only 10 feet away until proper contact is consistent, then increase the distance to 20 feet until consistent, then 30 feet.
2. Practice serving from the backline into specific areas of the opposite court. Have a partner stand on those areas to return the balls to you.

Overhand Serve. The overhand serve is used primarily by power volleyball teams because with practice it can be most effective as an offensive weapon, either to immediately score a point on an ace serve, or force a poor return, which will not allow the opponents to set and spike the volleyball.

Learning Cues

1. Body position is 2 to 10 feet from the baseline in a staggered stance (left foot forward for right-handed players).
2. Ball is held in both hands in front of the right shoulder. Left hand is under the ball, right hand on top.
3. Softly toss the ball about 2 feet high and 18 inches in front of the right shoulder. A high toss is not required nor desired.
4. The arm is then cocked as a catcher's throw or quarterback's pass, with the weight on the rear foot.
5. Weight is then shifted to the front foot while bringing the striking arm forward (as throwing a baseball).
6. Hand–ball contact occurs slightly above head level in front of the shoulder. Actual contact occurs between the heel and lower palm of the hand on the center of the ball. Contact is sharp and solid.
7. There is no follow-through. After contact, the arm is stopped in a jabbing motion. This action will result in the ball reacting like a knuckleball in baseball, veering as it approaches the opponent.
8. The overhand serve should travel in a path parallel to the floor, not rising more than 2 to 3 feet above the net. An overhand serve that loops over the net is no more effective than an underhand serve, and is more difficult to control.

Blocking

Blocking is the technique employed by one, two, or three defensive players to counteract the advantage gained by a good spike on the part of the offensive team. Essentially, it is the act of jumping with arms extended directly in front of the ball at the time it is hit, and either returning the ball immediately down into the opponents' court, or deflecting the flight of the ball up and back, permitting the blocking team to establish a set and spike offensive situation.

Learning Cues

1. Body position includes hands held at or slightly above shoulder height in an area adjacent to the ball and net.
2. Watching the ball and the spiker, the blocker anticipates where and how hard the ball will be hit. Timing is critical in blocking.
3. The blocker prepares to jump by flexing the legs 90° and by bringing the arms down and slightly out from the sides for added lift as he jumps.
4. As the blocker jumps, the arms are brought upward and over the net to contact the ball. The hands and arms are quickly withdrawn, preventing contact with the net. The hands should be rather close together, preventing a gap through which the spike might penetrate. Concentrate on "putting your hands on the ball."
5. Eyes should remain open and follow the ball, ready to play it a second time, or preparing to spike, or ready to block again.
6. Generally a two-man block is used, including the middle front player and his teammate to either side. The center blocker is a key man because he must move quickly right or left and pair up with the outside blocker to form the two-man block.

Practice Suggestions

1. Practice blocking technique alone, without a spiked ball.
2. Practice blocking technique with a partner (2-man block) without a spiked ball.
3. Practice blocking technique while having a teammate jump and throw the ball as if spiking into your court.

4. Two lines of players at one end and opposite sides of the net. Both players face each other, slide two steps toward the center of the net, jump, simulate a block by touching palms and return to the floor without touching the net, immediately slide two more steps and repeat. Repeat again until you get to the end of the net.
5. Practice blocking techniques while teammates are practicing spiking by blocking their spikes.

Offensive Play

Offenses in power volleyball have developed widely in the last ten years. While the techniques of passing and spiking have changed relatively little, the methods by which the spike is obtained vary greatly.

In most beginning programs or physical education classes, the 6-6 offense would be the simplest to administer. The 6-6 refers to the fact that all six players spike when rotating to the spiking positions and that any of them will also be setters when rotating into a setting position. The 4-2 offense is very similar, except that four members of the team are basically spikers and two members are used essentially as setters. For the alignment of the 4-2 offense, see Figure 24-9.

The 4-2 offense is certainly possible for use in physical education classes. It does allow for the smaller players to develop their skills as a setter and therefore become an integral part of the volleyball team. The 4-2 offense is relatively simple, but still includes some of the concepts used in the more complex 5-1 or 6-0 offense.

In preparing to receive a serve, players should face the server in a semi-crouched position, prepared to return the ball with a forearm pass. Every attempt should be made to direct the first pass to the center front position (setter, either with or without switching) with an arc of 12 to 16 feet. This high pass gives the setter ample time to get to the ball. The

FIGURE 24-9. The 4-2 offense.

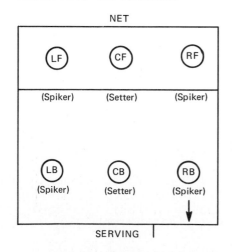

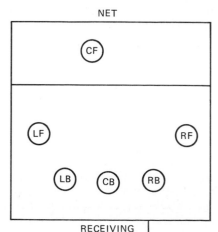

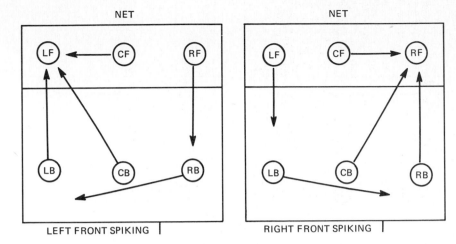

NET   NET

LEFT FRONT SPIKING   RIGHT FRONT SPIKING

FIGURE 24-10. Spike coverage, 4-2 offense.

setter positions himself under the ball and faces the direction he plans to set the ball for the spiker.

The setter will attempt to pass or "set" the ball 6 to 10 feet above the net, 2 to 3 feet from the net, and near the sideline. This sideline set gives the spiker three advantages: (1) The center blocker has a greater distance to travel. (2) The spiked ball may rebound back out-of-bounds. (3) A ball spiked diagonally across court has a greater area in which to land for a point.

Team coverage on the spike is shown in Figure 24-10.

It is necessary for the spiking team to form a cup around the spiker to defend against a blocked spike that returns immediately back into their court. The players not in the cup follow the ball, looking for a ball that is blocked high and deep.

When the offensive team is serving, the front line players are close to the net in preparation for the blocking of a spike.

Defensive Play

Defenses in power volleyball may vary as widely as the offenses, but the primary job of the defense is to offset the spiking action of the opponents. This can be done by blocking and rejecting the ball back into the opponents' court, or blocking and controlling the ball on your own side of the court, which should result in a passing-setting-spiking combination.

The initial defensive play by a team is the return of the serve. Without complete court coverage and a well-placed first pass to the center man in the front row, the desired spike will not materialize. Court position for serve reception is shown in Figures 24-11 and 24-12.

Note that receiving players do not have a teammate in front of them, so there is no confusion as to who should play the serve, each player being responsible for the area in front of him. The setter in the front row should not play the serve so that he may be prepared to set the pass directed to him.

Most teams will have good spikers that sometimes cannot be blocked. Court coverage, or defensive coverage of a blocking situation is then necessary to be sure that all areas of the court are defended.

Two of the most common coverages include the man-back defense and the man-up defense.

FIGURE 24-11. Serving with 4-2 switching offense.

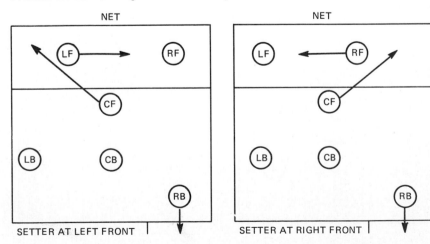

NET   NET

SETTER AT LEFT FRONT   SETTER AT RIGHT FRONT

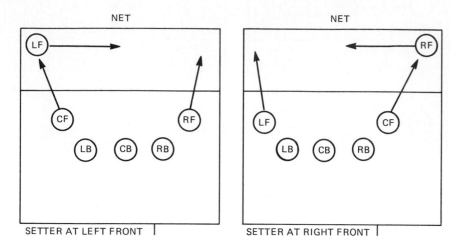

NET   NET

SETTER AT LEFT FRONT   SETTER AT RIGHT FRONT

FIGURE 24-12. Serve reception with a 4-2 switching offense.

Man-Back Defense. The man-back defense or 2-4 defense provides good deep coverage with four players stationed near the court's perimeter and two men blocking. The starting positions and areas covered by each player are shown in Figure 24-13. The blockers should attempt to protect more against the sideline spike by the positioning of the block. This defense would be used by a team whose players are not particularly tall but very quick and agile.

Man-Up Defense. The man-up defense, or 2-1-3 defense is shown in Figure 24-14. The man that is "up" is the center-back player who moves to a position behind the block and covers all dinks, or deflections that fall short. The blockers should attempt to protect against a cross-court spike by establishing their block to the inside of the spiker. It is hoped that the spiker will attempt to hit down the line where the right-back defensive player is waiting. This defense would be used by a team that is tall and blocks well.

SIMPLIFIED RULES

Volleyball rules are simple and can be learned quickly by beginners. The simplified rules follow. The penalty for practically every foul is the loss of the ball for the side serving or loss of the point if the receiving side fouls.

1. The ball must be served by the right back from *behind* the rear line, right of the 10-foot mark, and may be hit in any manner with the hand.
2. Only one serve is allowed per side per point and it must land within the opponents' court. If it touches the net it is side-out.
3. It is a foul for players to touch the net, or to step completely over the center line.
4. Lifting or throwing the ball while it is in play is a foul. The play must be a distinct hit of the ball.
5. A ball landing on a boundary line is "in."
6. A point may be scored only by the side serving.

FIGURE 24-13. Responsibilities in the man-back (CB) defense. Blockers protect sideline.

FIGURE 24-14. Responsibilities in the man-up (CB) defense. Blockers protect against cross court.

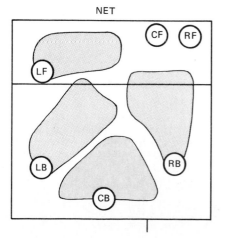

NET

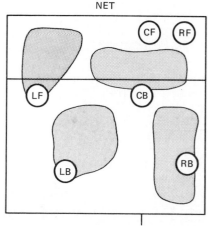

NET

7. If a ball touches a player or a player touches a ball, he is considered as having played the ball. If the ball hits two or more blockers after being spiked, it is considered as having been played just once. A block is not considered as one of the three allowable hits.
8. The ball may be played only three times by one team in a volley, and a player may not play it twice in succession but may play it twice if it is played by a teammate in between.
9. Players of the serving team must rotate clockwise when receiving the ball to serve.
10. When two opponents simultaneously hit the ball out of bounds or touch the net at the same time, the point is played over.
11. Players may shift position after the ball is served, but back row players are not permitted to block or spike.
12. Balls may be played only with body parts above the waist. Ball may not be kicked.
13. First serve or choice of court side is decided by a coin toss. Teams alternate opening serves with each game.
14. Net height is 8 feet for men, 7 feet 4¼ inches for women. Physical education classes may adjust net height to age and ability of their students.
15. Players substituted for may return only for their replacement.
16. Ball may be blocked over the net, but may not be touched before the spike. You may not block a set.
17. Ball being spiked must be on your side of the net, but you may follow through over the net.
18. Back row players may spike from behind the 10-foot spiking line.

TERMINOLOGY

Block Defensive play by players (or a player) in the forward positions who place their hands and arms above the net so that a spiked ball rebounds into the opponents' court or back to their own.

Bump pass The forearm pass made on low balls.

Carrying the ball The ball must be clearly batted. If it rests momentarily in the player's hands, it is considered illegal.

Dig pass A pass made with the hand slightly cupped or with the fist of one hand, usually on a difficult play.

Dink A soft shot off the fingertips used when faking a spike.

Double foul Infraction of rules by both teams during the same play.

Forearm pass A pass made off the forearms. Used to play served balls, hard-driven spikes, or any low ball.

Free ball A return of a ball by the opponent that may easily be handled.

Kill A spike that cannot be returned.

Overhand pass A pass made by contacting the ball above the head with the finger pads.

Point A point is scored when the receiving team fails to return the ball legally to the opponents' court.

Rotation Shifting of the players, clockwise, when gaining the ball from the opponents.

Serve The method of putting the ball in play over the net by striking it with the hand.

Set The placement of the ball near the net to facilitate spiking.

Setter Person assigned to set the ball.

Side out Side is out when the serving team fails to win a point or plays the ball illegally.

Spike A ball hit with a strong downward force into the opponents' court.

Spiker Person assigned to spike the ball.

SELECTED REFERENCES

ANGLE, JERRY. *Modern Volleyball Drills.* Huntington Beach, Calif.: USVBA Publications, 1978.

BARTUCCI, BOB. *Championship Volleyball.* West Point, N.Y.: Leisure Press, 1979.

COLEMAN, JAMES, and TARAS LISKEVYCH. *Pictoral Analysis of Power Volleyball.* Huntington Beach, Calif.: USVBA Publications, 1972.

McMANAMA, JERRE I., and DONALD SHONDELL. *Volleyball.* Englewood Cliffs, N.J.: Prentice-Hall, Inc., 1971.

SANDEFUR, RANDY. *Volleyball.* Pacific Palisades, Calif.: Goodyear Publishing Co., 1970.

SLAYMAKER, THOMAS, and VIRGINIA BROWN. *Power Volleyball.* Philadelphia: W.B. Saunders Company, 1970.

United States Volleyball Association. *Rule Book* (latest ed.). Colorado Springs, Colo.: *USVBA.*

Periodicals

USA Volleyball Review, 1750 E. Boulder, Colorado Springs, Colo. 80909. *Volleyball Review.*

Volleyball Magazine, 17272 Newhope Street, Fountain Valley, Calif. 92708. *Volleyball Magazine.*

Audio-Visual Materials

USVBA Publications, P.O. Box 286, Huntington Beach, Calif. 92648. *This Is Volleyball* (Film) 16mm, 30 min.

Athletic Institute, 705 Merchandise Mart, Chicago, Ill. 60654. *Power Volleyball* (Loop Film Series).

Association Instructional Materials, 600 Madison Avenue, New York, N.Y. 10022. *Volleyball U. S. A.* (16mm, 17 min. BW).

NCAA Film Series, P.O. Box 2726, Witchita, Kan. 67201. *Volleyball* (Loop Film Series). Super 6, 3½ min. each; series of 6.

USVBA Films, 1750 E. Boulder, Colordo Springs, Colo. 80909. *Volleyball For Women.* Features U.S. Womens Team.

WEIGHT TRAINING

THIS CHAPTER WILL ENABLE YOU TO:

♦ Identify and compare the key points associated with Olympic lifting, powerlifting, athletic weight training, and body building.
♦ Identify the differences and similarities among weight lifting equipment.
♦ After practice, demonstrate the various skills and techniques necessary to execute the various weight training lifts.
♦ Identify and discuss facts and myths as related to female weight lifting.
♦ Identify the necessary safety concerns of weight training.
♦ Become familiar with basic terminology required to carry out a successful weight training program.

NATURE AND PURPOSE

During the past two decades, the effectiveness of carefully planned weight training as a method of improving body development and sports performance has been accepted on the basis of well-controlled studies. Although being musclebound, having reduced localized muscle endurance, and loss of speed and agility were once thought to result from weight training, such claims have no physiological basis.

Much may be gained from the systematic and intelligent application of modern weight training principles. Using the principle of overload (taxing the muscles beyond their normal daily activities), coupled with progressive resistance through a full range of motion appears to be the most effective means of acquiring dynamic strength. The closer the weight lifting movement simulates the actions in sports, the greater the transfer of strength to motor performance. Weight lifting is also an excellent way to develop flexibility, provided the exercise is executed through the entire range of motion. Muscle enlargement does not reduce muscle endurance, because an increase in capillarization usually accompanies the cross-sectional increase of muscle fibers, which helps to delay the onset of fatigue. Weight training does not necessarily affect cardiorespiratory endurance unless movements are executed for this specific purpose. Increasing the cardiorespiratory endurance requires specific training. To achieve this, heart and respiratory rates must be intensely increased and maintained at higher than normal resting values for a duration of time. Systematic weight training that applies the principles of resistance, overload, and specificity will have positive effects on motor performance parameters and contribute to successful participation in sports.

Many individuals become involved in weight training as a means of gaining or losing weight. The use of weight training is of greater benefit to gaining body weight than to losing it. This is due to the activities' physiological effect upon the body. The overload principle causes proteins to be readily incorporated into the muscle thus increasing muscular mass (hypertrophy), while on the other hand the energy expenditure of weight lifting is too low to be of much benefit in body weight reduction. However, the overweight person may want to include weight training as part of a reduction program to increase body tone while reducing with diet and an aerobic program.

Many centers of rehabilitation find the use of weights valuable in developing weak or injured muscles, strengthening underdeveloped muscles, or rebuilding muscles affected by atrophy following casting or hospitalization.

EQUIPMENT

Variable Resistance Machines

This type of machine is manufactured by many companies under a variety of names. The most widely used is the Universal Gym (Figure 25-1). While this type of machine is available in separate units, it is most commonly found as a jungle gym arrangement on which several athletes can work out at one time. The units consist of weight stacks connected by pulleys to levers or lifting bars. The levers and pulleys allow variable resistance through a fixed and oftentimes limited range of motion.

Nautilus

An improvement upon the variable resistance machine is the Nautilus equipment (Figure 25-2). Through unique and innovative engineering the machines offer a near true weight through the entire range of motion. The range of motion along with the specificity of the movements have also been improved. The Nautilus concept claims increased cardiovascular benefits while improving muscular strength; however, many claims made by Nautilus are supported by the manufacturer's own research. Nautilus has been found by many coaches to be an excellent way to maintain strength in-season.

Isokinetic Equipment

Probably the most talked about and misunderstood equipment available today are isokinetic devices. The term isokinetic means "moving at a constant speed." These machines require no weights as the resistance felt from this equipment is self-generated. The machines are capable of being set at a variety of training velocities. If the athlete is capable of moving through a range of motion which approaches this velocity, then resistance is felt through that range. If the velocity is not reached, resistance is not felt. For this reason to train on these devices requires a highly motivated athlete with constant supervision. The significance of training at a variety of velocities is found in the physiology of the muscle fibers. Since muscle fibers are of a

FIGURE 25-1. The Universal Gym, a widely used variable resistance machine.

FIGURE 25-2. The Nautilus pullover torso machine.

FIGURE 25-3. The Orthotron isokinetic machine.

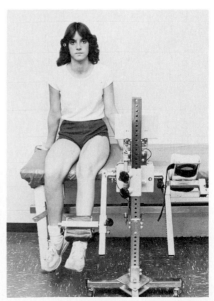

fast and slow nature, it is felt that training at fast and slow speeds will increase recruitment of these fibers.

The value of isokinetic devices in rehabilitation is well founded. The Orthotron and Cybex II (Lumex Inc.) are most commonly used for rehabilitation while the Mini Gym is used for sports training. One problem with isokinetic devices is that they do not relate well with other forms of strength training. There is also doubt as to their effectiveness in building muscular bulk.

Free Weights

The oldest forms of weight training have been done with free weights. There are two types: the Olympic form and the standard one-inch barbell. A well-equipped training room will have both types of bars. The Olympic bar offers more balance, is more durable, and is a must for power and Olympic lifts. If properly used with supervision from an experienced lifter, free weights offer the most substantial strength program available. The cost of equipment is low but the risk may be high with improper accessory equipment or lack of supervision.

Other Equipment

The following items may become necessary to the lifter as the training becomes more intense.

Lifting Belt. The lifting belt is made of thick leather and is used to give physical support to the lower back and moral support to the mind. There are two types of belts, training and competition. The training belt is 5 inches wide and gives a wide support to the lower back. The competition belt is 4 inches wide and may not exceed this in Olympic and power lifting. The belt is generally worn with free weight squats and cleans.

Lifting Straps. Lifting straps are loops of leather or canvas belting about one inch wide. The straps are placed around the hands and then under and around the bar. With an overhand grip the lifter secures the strap and the bar is held tightly to the hand. Straps are used with dead lifts and cleans for training only. Lifting straps may not be used in competition.

Knee Wraps (Super Wraps). Wraps are long, 3-inch wide strips of tough elastic material. They are worn extremely tight around the knee to add spring to the rebound phase of the squat and clean. They are needed only with heavy weights and may be worn in competition.

Super Suits. Super suits are made of tough elastic material and look like wrestling gear. The suit gives support and spring to the body during heavy squats and cleans. They are generally not worn in training but are normally always worn in competition.

THE FEMALE WEIGHTLIFTER

The fundamentals, techniques, and training programs described in this chapter are directed at both sexes. The female athletes need strength training every bit as much as their male counterparts, if not more. Competitive power lifting and body building are also becoming very popular among women across the country. Coeducational weight training classes offer no problems in terms of training programs, in fact they are very effective ways of destroying weight lifting myths concerning females.

myth: Women are not as strong as men.

fact: Through elementary school, middle school, and well into high school, females are as strong if not stronger than their male counterparts, although with age and training men will surpass women pound for pound.

myth: Women should execute lifts differently because they are built differently.

fact: Anatomical differences in bone and muscle are so slight that they have no bearing on lifting technique.

myth: Women will become extremely muscular if they lift heavy weights.

fact: Women can increase strength up to 70 percent with little change in physical appearance. It is the male hormone (testosterone) which causes the noticable hypertrophy in men. Most women have such small amounts of this hormone that bulk muscularity is next to impossible. Women body builders who do show extreme hypertrophy have (1) very low body fat, (2) unusually high levels of testosterone, or (3) may take anabolic steroids (a testosterone-like drug).

myth: Women (as well as men) are concerned that their muscles will turn into fat if they stop working out.

fact: Just as lead cannot turn into gold, muscle cannot turn into fat. Muscle generally atrophies (becomes smaller) when training ceases. People who appear to have become fat after they stopped training may not have changed their eating habits and consequently may be gaining weight.

myth: Women should not train during various stages of the menstrual cycle.

fact: The overwhelming majority of female athletes report no adverse effects on performance due to this physiological process.

Most women who have begun training with weights find they have gained the following benefits:

1. Increased physical strength improves their performance in sporting events.
2. There is a decrease in overall body fat while developing muscular tone.
3. There is an improvement in self-image and a feeling of well-being.

SUGGESTED LEARNING SEQUENCE

Weight training as part of a physical education program should be approached as a skill-oriented class and not merely as an activity. Weight training requires an overall philosophy, the development of techniques, and the ability to execute the skills of each lift.

A four day a week lifting program is recommended which splits the various lifts into two groups. Monday and Thursday lifts emphasize legs and back while Tuesday and Friday lifts emphasize upper body. If time restricts the number of lifts which may be accomplished, then some leg and back lifts may be done on Monday and some may be done on Thursday. The same arrangement can be used with the upper body lifts. A practical approach for utilization of equipment would be to split the class into two groups containing subgroups of three students (matched for strength if possible). By doing this, one group can do Monday/Thursday lifts on Tuesday and Friday, thus allowing the proper amount of time needed to execute a proper program. The subgroups of three students lift as a team and are responsible for spotting each other when this is required. Each member of the subgroup should complete a set before any member repeats a set.

The following instructional approach is recommended:

1. Students should be informed of the various forms of strength training and how they differ.
2. Each lift should be demonstrated to the student with emphasis placed on key points as well as safety factors. Students should also understand the purpose of each lift. (Olympic lifts may be omitted from the demonstration as they are not part of the training program.)
3. If the course meets five times a week, the non-lifting day should be devoted to instruction about related areas (stretching techniques, aerobic exercises, guest speakers or lifters).
4. Begin the lifting schedule as soon as techniques have been demonstrated and safety tips have been emphasized.

Outlined below is a basic plan which may be adopted as is or with modifications. If this plan does not meet the needs of your program, many different lifting schedules may be found in the books listed in the reference section. This program may be done almost entirely on variable resistance machines (Universal Gym), totally with free weights, or in combination. Students should begin with an amount of weight which can be handled through the recommended number of repetitions. The first set should be lighter than the second or third set. The student may increase the weight in a set when there is no longer difficulty in completing the last few reps of the second or third set.

FW = Free Weights; VRM = Variable Resistance Machines

MONDAY AND THURSDAY LIFTS:

EXERCISE	SETS	REPS
Back		
Dead lifts (FW)	2	5
Bent over rows (FW)	2	10
Lat pull overs (FW)	2	10
Lat pull downs (VRM)	2	10
Biceps and Forearms		
Barbell curl (FW or VRM)	2	8
Reverse curl (FW or VRM)	2	8
Legs		
Squats (FW)	1	10
	1	5
Leg lunge (FW)	2	10
Leg press (VRM)	2	10
Leg extentions (VRM)	2	10
Leg curls (VRM)	2	10
Calf		
Donkey calf raise	2	15
Dorsal flexion	2	15
Abdominals		
Sit-ups	2	15 (may vary)

TUESDAY AND FRIDAY LIFTS:

EXERCISE	SETS	REPS
Power cleans (FW)	3	5
Shoulders		
Military press front (FW or VRM)	2	10
Military press back (FW or VRM)	2	10
Dumbbell shrugs (FW)	2	10
Chest		
Bench Press (FW or VRM)	3	5
Incline Bench Press (FW)	3	5
Triceps		
Lying triceps extensions (FW)	2	10
Calf		
same as Mon/Thur		
Abdominals		
same as Mon/Thur		

SKILLS AND TECHNIQUES

Correct lifting form is essential not only for obtaining quick results but also for safety.

The Grip

The overhand, palms down, grip is used in practically all exercises. The thumbs may be hooked underneath the bar or in some instances, as in the bench press, may remain on the same side of the bar as the other fingers. This requires more balance and is not recommended to the novice lifter.

FIGURE 25-4.   The overhand grip.

The underhand grip is the exact opposite of the overhand grip, with palms placed upward under the bar. This grip is used in executing the curl maneuver.

FIGURE 25-5.   The underhand grip.

The alternating grip, with one hand palm down and the other hand palm up, is favored for dead lifts. Regardless of style, the hands must be spaced evenly

FIGURE 25-6.   The alternating grip.

on the bar in order to execute the lift properly as well as provide safety.

When involved in Olympic or power lifting, the use of chalk on the hands is recommended. The chalk will increase the bar/hand friction, thus facilitating a better grip.

The Feet

When the bar is being lifted from the floor, as in cleans or dead lifts, place the toes approximately under the bar with the feet spread about one foot apart. The feet should always be in the same line although the distance between them may vary. Many beginners have the fault of not starting close enough to the bar; consequently, when they start the lift the bar swings toward the feet instead of going straight up. Many experienced lifters find that a slight angling outward, not more than 15 degrees, of the feet is a more comfortable and efficient lifting style. This is a technique which should be developed as the lifter improves.

Breathing

Breathing should come naturally during the course of the exercise, letting the body regulate the demand. Forced gasping and hyperventilating (rapid puffs of breath) only interfere with proper breathing and may even lead to lightheadedness. The best pattern of breathing is to inhale during the lifting phase and to exhale with the return movement. As the weight increases, many lifters find it more effective to take one deep breath and hold it through the repetition of the lift. The lifter should never hold a breath for more than one repetition. This puts undue pressure on the body cavities as well as the blood vessels of the head. Getting a purple face in the weight room will not improve your lifting ability.

The Bar and Body Placement

A technique which is of utmost importance in a weight room is lifting a bar from a power rack or squat stands. Injuries which occur during this phase of lifting with free weights can most always be traced back to carelessness on the part of the lifter. To properly place your body under the bar to execute a lift check the following items:

1. The bar should be no higher than the shoulder nor more than 3 to 4 inches below the shoulder.
2. Grip the bar evenly and space your hands wider than your shoulders.
3. Move under the bar in such a way that the midpoint of the bar is on line with your backbone.
4. The bar should rest on the base of the neck and the shoulders.

5. If the muscles of the neck and shoulders lack the mass to cushion the bar, foam pads or towels should be wrapped around the bar so as to protect the bony parts of the back. This is extremely important for young lifters and as a rule is a good policy for women to follow.
6. By bending at the knees, align your body as vertically as possible under the bar.
7. With the head up, lift straight up with hip and leg power to a vertical position.
8. Step backwards out of the rack no more than 2½ feet.
9. With spotters on both ends of the bar, execute the lift.
10. Rerack the weights by stepping back into the rack, with alignment by spotters, and set the weight down.

TRAINING PROGRAMS

As weight training has come of age and specificity has become a recognized factor in a successful program it has become difficult to recommend training programs without knowing what equipment is available and what purpose the program will serve. There are recent publications which speak to many specific programs in weight training. For this reason specific programs will not be proposed but rather comments concerning programs will be presented. For training manuals, refer to the references at the end of the chapter.

Light Conditioning Programs

These types of programs cover the broadest range of weight trainers from in-season athletic programs to the programs typically offered to the general public at spas. The programs generally consist of a three day a week lifting routine. All of the basic lifts would be done at this time with a brief stretching and warm-up followed by one set of 10 to 15 reps of the various lifts. This is the "circuit or circus" training approach, also known as the "get them in—get them out" routine. This approach is a lifelong battle which gives non-dramatic results.

Heavy Conditioning Programs

Programs in this area are practiced by a smaller group of lifters containing pre-season athletes, power lifters, Olympic lifters, and body builders. The programs run from a 4 to 7 day week with muscle groups worked rather than the entire body. The average workout would be around two hours; however body builders, prior to a contest, may actually train on a split day routine, thus doubling the workout time. This is a very effective program if you can afford the time. The general rule followed in heavy training is to thoroughly overload and exhaust the muscle each time it is trained with at least one day between training of that muscle group again. Overtraining in heavy programs is a real problem and it affects different people at different times. Constant muscular pain with a loss in strength are the warning signs. The large muscle groups are the first to be affected, especially the lower back.

A heavy training program, although there is much variation, may consist of a 5×5 approach of 5 sets with 5 reps, not including a warm-up or stretch. A current variation of the 5×5 approach is to include one day of extremely high rep work at around 50 to 60 percent of maximum.

An important point concerning heavy training for sport specificity is that the movements of the sport should also be done before or after the lifting. This will allow new motor skills to develop with the new strength gains.

DESCRIPTION OF TRAINING GROUPS

Olympic Lifting

Olympic lifting requires strength, power, and quickness. In competition there are two lifts: the two-hand snatch and the two-hand clean and jerk. Training for competition requires explosive lifts such as power cleans as well as bench press, military press, and parallel squats for strength development. Olympic lifters are also concerned with muscular endurance and often include running in a training regime. Although Olympic lifting is an Olympic sport, its popularity in this country has dropped off dramatically in past years. This drop-off is due to several reasons:

1. The reluctancy of lifters to adopt modern training techniques.
2. The lack of experienced strength coaches.
3. A new emphasis on power lifting.
4. The acceptance of body-builders in society.

In competition the competitor attempts to lift the heaviest weight he can in each lift, and the individual with the highest total is declared the winner in his body weight class as established by the Amateur Athletic Union.

Two-Hand Snatch

1. Place the bar on the floor horizontally in front of the lifter.
2. Grip the bar with both hands, palms down, at least shoulder width apart.
3. With the legs bent, drive with the legs and pull with the arms until the bar is supported vertically above the head with straight arms.

4. The lifter may split the legs or squat with the weight in order to achieve the vertical arm position. The lifter must stand erect upon completion of the lift.
5. The lifter must stand motionless with feet in the same line to be judged a good lift.

Two-Hand Clean and Jerk

1. Place the bar horizontally on the floor in front of the lifter.
2. Grip the bar with both hands, palms down, at least shoulder width apart.
3. The bar is brought to the shoulder from the floor in one continuous motion with bent or split legs.
4. The bar may rest on the chest while the feet must return to the same line with straight legs before continuing with the jerk.
5. By bending the legs and then extending them and the arms vertically, bring the bar to a vertical extension above the head.
6. The lift is complete when the lifter is motionless with the weight vertical above the head and feet on the same line.

Power Lifting

While flexibility and explosive power are of utmost importance in Olympic lifting, power lifting relies mainly on sheer strength. Although technique is important, the power lifts are easier to master than the Olympic lifts, because power lifts are not explosive and require less muscular endurance. The power lifts are the bench press, the parallel squat, and the dead lift. As in Olympic lifting, the competitor attempts to lift the greatest amount of weight in each lift. The largest total lifted wins the individual weight class. The competition begins with the parallel squat, and the lifter must have one of three attempts judged good to continue into the other lifts. While power lifting is not an Olympic sport, it is very popular in the United States with women as well as men.

Bench Press (see Figures 25-7 and 25-8)

1. The lifter lies horizontally with head, trunk, and buttocks on the bench.
2. The palms are placed up against the bar with the thumb placed on the same side as the other fingers or hooked on the opposite side. Placement of the hands may not exceed 32 inches between forefingers.
3. The bar is pressed vertically to straight arm length and held for two seconds.
4. The bar is lowered to the region of the chest but may not sink into the chest.
5. The bar is then raised evenly to a vertical position without moving the trunk, buttocks, or feet. Movement is grounds for disqualification.

Parallel Squat (see Figures 25-9 and 25-10)

1. Begin in an upright position with the bar resting across the shoulders.
2. The head should be held up.
3. The back should be flat with the small of the back kept arched.
4. The feet are 12 to 16 inches apart and in the same line.
5. Keeping the back straight, squat slowly with the weight until the tops of the thighs are parallel with the floor.
6. From the squat position, drive with the legs and hips to an upright position. The small of the back should remain arched slightly so as to prevent leaning, which may lead to injury.

FIGURE 25-7. Starting position for proper execution of the bench press.

FIGURE 25-8. The bar is lowered to the chest region with the back flat on the bench.

FIGURE 25-9 (left).   Starting position for the parallel squat.
FIGURE 25-10 (right).   With the back flat, the weight is lowered to a position where the thighs are parallel to the floor.

Dead Lift (see Figures 25-11 and 25-12)

1. Place the bar on the floor horizontally in front of the lifter.
2. Begin in the squat position, thighs parallel to the floor, head up, feet 12 to 14 inches apart, and back flat.
3. The palms are placed on the bar approximately shoulder width apart, using a palms down grip or an alternating palms up, palms down grip.
4. The lift may also be done with the increasingly popular "sumo" style. The only difference is that the feet are spread widely apart, 36 to 40 inches, with the hands placed about 14 inches apart.
5. With the arms straight and the back flat, drive upward with leg and hip strength.
6. Pull with the back once the bar is past the knees.
7. The lift is complete when an upright body position is attained.

Training includes a few other lifts besides those which would strengthen secondary muscle groups involved in the power lifts. These lifts will be discussed in the next section. For information concerning training schedules for Olympic and power lifting, consult the references listed at the end of the chapter.

Body Building

Body building for men and women is an activity which is growing rapidly in this country. Reasons for this are many, although media coverage and the popularity of self-improvement are the main contributors. Body building is as much an art form as it is a sport and may well be called a form of kinetic sculpture. Body builders are not concerned with muscular strength, although all maintain a strength which matches their muscular size. They do not

FIGURE 25-11.   Begin the dead lift close to the bar, back flat and head up.

FIGURE 25-12.   End the dead lift standing erect.

train with the specificity needed for a particular sport activity, yet all are athletic. Body builders train with weights to achieve muscularity with symmetry. This requires a multitude of lifts which are variations of the lifts described in the weight conditioning section. Rather than attempt to describe each of these lifts in detail, the reader is referred to the literature suggested at the end of the chapter.

Weight Training for Conditioning

Weight training in the pre-season and during the season is important for every athletic team or conditioning class. The key to a successful weight training program is specificity and supervision. Specificity means that the program should be designed to fit the needs and movements of the athlete. Supervision by a strength coach or a member of the teaching/coaching staff is important from a safety standpoint as well as a means of building morale. This section will describe a number of the lifts commonly used in building a strength program. It will not, however, attempt to put together any programs for different sports. For this type of information, the Selected References will be helpful.

Behind the Neck Press. This is an excellent exercise for the development of the shoulders, especially the deltoid group. The exercise may be done with a barbell or with a machine.

1. With the barbell resting behind the head on the shoulders, inhale and press the weight to a vertical position above the head.
2. Lower the weight until it nearly touches the shoulders behind the head and exhale.
3. The exercise may be done standing or seated.

The Military Press. Again this is an excellent

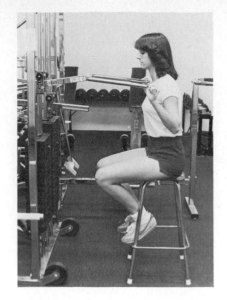

FIGURE 25-15. Starting position for the military press.

FIGURE 25-16. Raise the bar to a vertical position above the head.

FIGURE 25-13. Begin the behind the neck press with the barbell resting in this position.

FIGURE 25-14. Raise the bar to a vertical position above the head.

lift for shoulder development and may be done with free weights or on a machine.

1. With the barbell resting on the chest, inhale and press the bar to a vertical position above the head.
2. Lower the weight until it nearly touches the chest and exhale.
3. The exercise may be done standing or seated.

Bent Over Rowing. Rowing has long been used as an overall back developer. It will add thickness and width to the lats while developing strength very quickly. This exercise must be done with a barbell.

1. Place the barbell horizontally on the floor in front of the lifter.
2. Bend at the hips and grip the bar palms down, shoulder width apart. Bend the knees slightly to remove hamstring tension.
3. With the back stationary and flat, pull the bar to the chest.
4. Slowly lower the bar to near the starting position (bar need not touch the floor).

the weight off of the chest or arching the back and pushing with the legs to achieve the lift are toying with injury. Many coaches, especially football coaches, boost their athletes' bench press achievements by actually teaching the bounce and arch as part of the lift. The athlete will gain more physiologically and mentally if taught the proper technique in this exercise. The lift should be done with free weights and spotters, but may also be done on a machine.

Upright Rowing. This lift is often done to supplement training for Olympic lifting. The front deltoids and the trapezius musculature are thoroughly exercised. The lift must be executed with a barball and may be done explosively or at a slower speed.

1. Grip the bar palms down, about shoulder width apart.
2. Begin by standing with the bar held at the level of the thighs.
3. Pull the bar straight up the front of the body to the area of the chin (speed may vary).
4. Slowly return the bar to the front of the thighs.

FIGURE 25-17. Starting position for bent over rowing.

FIGURE 25-18. Raise the bar to this height to complete the lift.

The Bench Press. Much controversy continues as to which muscle gains the principal benefit from this exercise. Most biomechanic experts would agree it primarily exercises the anterior deltoid and triceps with the pectoralis major a secondary mover. To put more emphasis on the pecs, the incline bench press may be incorporated in advanced training programs.

The correct procedure for the bench press has been outlined earlier under power lifting. It should be emphasized at this point that athletes, trainers, and coaches who recommend benching by bouncing

Dumbbell Lat Pullover. This is a lift for all sports from tennis to the shotput. The exercise is designed to work the musculature of the back and rib cage. For this reason it should be included in all training regimes for track events. The pullover should be done with a dumbbell but may be done with a light barbell. Traditional lat work is done on some form of lat pull down machine and will not be described in this text.

1. Lie crossways on a flat bench with only the upper shoulder region supported by the bench.

FIGURE 25-19. Start the dumbbell lat pullover with hips low and shoulders flat on bench.

FIGURE 25-20. Keeping the hips low, raise the arms to a vertical position above the head.

2. The knees should be bent with the feet flat on the floor.
3. The buttocks should dip slightly to keep an arch in the small of the back.
4. Grip the weight by cupping the hands in such manner that the palms are against the weight plates. This will cause the weighted ends to be in an up-and-down position.
5. Extend the arms vertically so that the weight is over the face.
6. Lower the weight slowly in an arch so as to miss the head until the weight is nearly touching the floor behind the bench.
7. Return the weight to the vertical position slowly by contraction of the lats, keeping the arms nearly locked out.

The Barbell Curl. The curl is well known to anyone who has ever touched a weight. The exercise builds the biceps, and is tremendously overused, especially by teenage boys. It is most often used to increase the size of the arms for visual rather than functional reasons, and therefore should be considered a body building exercise. Coaches will generally have little trouble getting males to do an arm workout. The lift may be done with a straight barbell, a bent (E-Z curl) barbell, dumbbells, or machines. All provide slightly different results in terms of appearance.

1. Grip the bar palms up, about shoulder width apart.
2. Begin with the bar in front of the thighs and the elbows kept at the sides.
3. Contract the biceps so that the bar moves in an arch toward the shoulders.
4. Slowly lower the bar against gravity to ensure a good stretch to the starting position and repeat.

FIGURE 25-21. Begin the barbell curl with the bar in front of the thighs and the elbows at the sides.

FIGURE 25-22. Contract the biceps and raise the bar in an arch toward the shoulders.

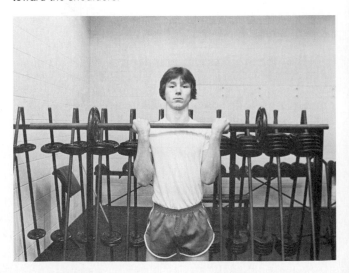

The Reverse Curl. The reverse curl is done to strengthen the forearm and biceps. The lift is most effective when done with a barbell.

1. Grip the bar with palms down, about shoulder width apart.
2. Start with the elbows at the sides and the bar in front of the thighs.
3. Move the bar in an arch toward the chin.
4. Lower the bar to starting position and repeat.

Donkey Calf Raise. When traditional calf machines are not available, the donkey calf raise will give the best all round calf development. This exercise is done with a partner and does not involve

weights. The partners should be approximately the same weight.

1. Place the feet on a calf board (2 × 4 on 2 × 4 blocks) with the balls of the feet on the board and the heels off the board.
2. Bend at the waist until the back is flat while supporting the body weight on a chair or bench.
3. The partner should sit on the exerciser's back, on the hips if possible.
4. The lifter should then lift up as far as possible onto the toes.
5. Once the toes are locked out, lower the heels until they pass beyond the calf board, and then repeat.

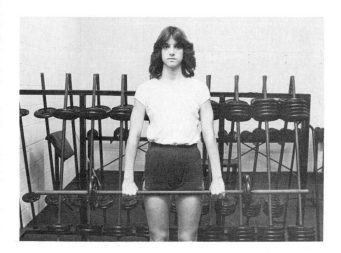

FIGURE 25-23. Begin the reverse curl with palms down.

FIGURE 25-24. Contract the biceps and raise the bar in an arch toward the shoulders.

FIGURE 25-25. Begin the donkey calf raise with heels lower than toes.

FIGURE 25-26. Complete the lift by raising up on toes.

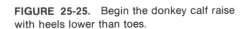

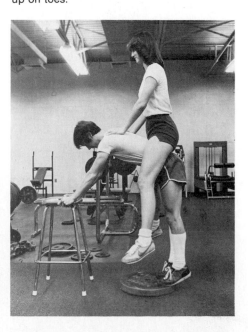

The Parallel Squat.   The parallel squat, described in the power lifting section, is the ultimate exercise for leg development. It has long been used to develop strength and size in the leg. Done properly the parallel squat will give very quick results. The current belief held by many coaches that the parallel squat will damage the knees is both biomechanically and medically unfounded. The use of a bench for the athletes to squat to is very popular but not necessary. In fact, bouncing up and down on the bench may lead to more serious injuries due to aggravation of the spine. If safety is the reason for bench use, the problem can be eliminated by using spotters at both ends of the bar or by the use of safety squat racks.

Leg Lunge.   The lunge is done to strengthen the thigh and is an exercise that might be used as a means of stretching prior to doing squats. The motion of the lunge should be mastered without weights before actual weighted lifts.

1. Begin the lift with the bar resting across the back.
2. Take a lunging step forward, about three to four feet, so that the rear knee dips and touches the floor.
3. Return then to an upright, starting position.
4. Balance is of utmost importance with this lift and any amount of weight should be worked up to gradually.

Dumbbell Shrugs.   The shrug is probably the best exercise for development of the trapezius and neck muscles. It is a must for additional training in the power lifts. The lift may also be done with a straight bar; however, the best results are obtained with the dumbbell.

1. Begin the exercise with dumbbells in both hands and arms at the sides.
2. Raise the shoulders as far as they will go towards the ears.
3. Hold that position for a three count and relax.

FIGURE 25-29 (left).   Begin the shrugs with dumbbells at the sides.
FIGURE 25-30 (right).   Keeping the arms straight, shrug the shoulders upward.

FIGURE 25-27.   Begin the leg lunge in this position.

FIGURE 25-28.   Lunge forward with a straight back until opposite knee touches the floor.

FIGURE 25-31. Triceps extensions begin with bar held vertically over the face, arms locked out.

FIGURE 25-32. Bar is lowered to position behind the head and then raised to vertical position.

4. The lifter may also roll the shoulders while executing the lift.

Lying Triceps Extensions. The tricep extensions work to strengthen the posterior portion of the arm. This exercise should be done as a secondary lift with the bench press. The exercise may be done with a bar or a machine.

1. Lie on your back on a flat bench.
2. Grip the bar, which should be behind your head on the floor, with a palms up position about 12 inches apart.
3. Raise the bar such that it is positioned vertically over the face with the arms locked out.
4. Lower the bar from the elbows while keeping the upper arm in a near vertical position. The bar should be lowered to the forehead or just beyond the head.
5. Extend the forearm back to the vertical position.

Leg Extensions. The leg extension works directly on the quadriceps muscle group. The exercise can be done with a weight boot but most workout areas are now equipped with extension machines. The leg extension is generally part of a rehabilitation program for people who have weak knees or who have recently undergone surgery.

1. Sit on the bench of the extension machine and put your feet behind the lower pad so that your toes point out. You should sit so that you are leaning slightly back. This will put the quadriceps at the optimal angle for maximum extension.
2. Hold on to the sides of the bench and raise the lower weighted bar so that your legs are parallel to the floor.
3. If the lifter cannot achieve full extension, there is too much weight on the machine.
4. Slowly lower the weight to the starting position.

FIGURE 25-33. Begin the leg extension in this position.

FIGURE 25-34. Extend legs so they are parallel with the floor.

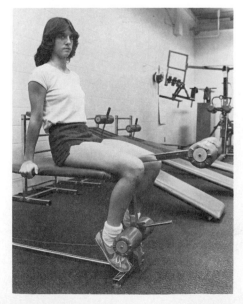

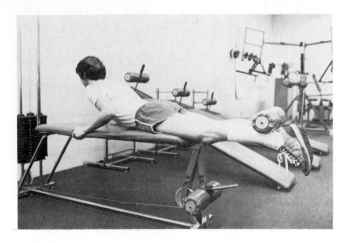

FIGURE 25-35. Begin the leg curl in this position.

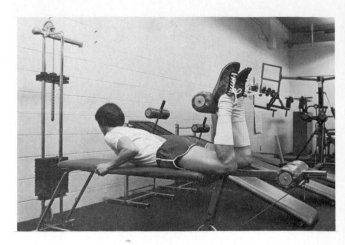

FIGURE 25-36. Flex the legs so they are vertical to the floor.

The Leg Curl. The leg curl is a most effective way of strengthening the hamstrings of the leg. Unless the athlete is on a good parallel squat program, there is a tendency for the quads to become too strong in relationship to total quad/hamstring strength. While the exercise may be done with weighted boots, most leg extension machines are built to allow performance of the leg curl.

1. Begin by lying stomach down on the machine and position the heels behind the heel pad.
2. Prop yourself up slightly with your elbow so as to keep the hamstrings as prime movers of the lift.
3. Contract the hamstrings and attempt to touch the heels on the buttocks.
4. Slowly return to the starting position and repeat.

Dorsal Flexion of the Foot. A group of muscles on the front of the lower leg are generally forgotten about in training except by body builders. Yet it is this musculature which causes many athletes a great deal of trouble in the form of shin splints. While the exact cause of all shin splints is not known, it is generally a result of an overdeveloped calf muscle and an underdeveloped anterior tibial muscle (front of the lower leg). This condition is found in many runners and may also result from prolonged wearing of high heels. The exercise is simple and really requires no equipment other than what may already be found around the home.

1. Begin in a seated position with the feet hanging freely above the floor.
2. A weighted device is hung from the toes so that resistance is felt. The weight may be as simple as a bucket with water or sand in it. This allows the amount of resistance to be altered without much trouble.
3. Contract the foot so as to bring the toes up and point to the knee (active dorsal flexion).
4. Relax the foot and repeat. Repetition is the key to this exercise.

The Power Clean. The power clean is probably the most total body lift that can be successfully executed short of the clean and jerk. More than any

FIGURE 25-37 (left). Contract the foot and point the toes upward.
FIGURE 25-38 (right). Relax the foot and let the toes point downward.

other single lift, the power clean will significantly improve the vertical jump with greater total body strength. All training programs should include the clean to some intensity. The lift must be done with free weights, preferably Olympic weights.

1. Begin with the bar horizontally at the feet of the lifter.
2. Grip the bar, palms down about shoulder width apart.
3. The feet should be placed inside the hands so as to provide a firm base of support.
4. Squat low as in the beginning dead lift position.
5. The head should be up with gaze fixed toward the ceiling.
6. Drive with the hips and legs to lift the bar from the floor.
7. Continue to drive with the legs as the bar gains acceleration and as the bar passes the knees, pull with the back and shoulders.
8. As the bar reaches the chest region it will begin to lose momentum.
9. At this point there is a need for the body to move slightly under the bar as the elbows drive

FIGURE 25-39. The power clean starting position.

FIGURE 25-40. Initial pull phase should not be rapid.

FIGURE 25-41. Rapid acceleration phase—note extension onto the toes.

FIGURE 25-42. The bar has lost momentum—time to move under it.

FIGURE 25-43. The catch phase—knees are bent.

forward under the bar to catch the weights on the chest. This movement of the arms should be somewhat passive as this is not a reverse curl. If the lifter must reverse curl the weight, the weight is too heavy or there was insufficient momentum in the drive phase.

10. The lifter will find it necessary to bend at the knees in order to achieve the correct catch position. When bending occurs, stand erect with the weights before lowering them to repeat.

Points to ensure a successful training lift in the clean are:

1. The bar should move almost vertically up the front of the body.
2. This is an explosive lift, therefore rapid acceleration of the bar is important.
3. Do not jerk the weight from the floor with the arms, rather drive it up with the legs.
4. Extend up on the toes when possible to increase leg drive force.
5. Do not actively reverse curl the bar back to the chest.

SAFETY IN THE WEIGHT ROOM

1. Stretching exercises and a warm-up should precede the training program.
2. Until you are familiar with the movements involved with the lift, do not attempt a great amount of weight on the bar.
3. Collars should always be used on the bars and they should be secure.
4. Keep adequate distance between the lifters and the equipment in the training room.
5. Always use spotters on the squats and the bench press.
6. Dropping of weights other than on a lifting platform is uncalled for. Likewise weight stacks on machines should not be banged up and down.
7. It is always best to partially unload both sides of a weight bar before removing the final weights.
8. When weight pate racks are available, replace all weights after use.

TERMINOLOGY

Barbell A steel bar 5 to 7 feet long on which circular iron plates of known weight may be placed.

Cheating A lift which is executed with the addition of muscle groups other than the prime movers involved in the lift.

Clean The power clean or beginning phase of the clean and jerk.

Dumbbell A short barbell, 12 to 16 inches, with fixed or removable weight plates.

"Lats" The latissimus dorsi muscles of the back.

Overload principle Progressively increasing the intensity of the workouts over the course of the training program.

Quadriceps The four muscles of the front of the thigh.

"Pecs" The pectoralis major muscles of the chest.

Rep Repetition or the continuation of identical motions.

Set The completion of a predetermined number of repetitions.

Specificity The development of a training program aimed at increasing one's ability to succeed in a particular skill.

Spotter Individual responsible for the safety of the lifter. Generally two spotters are used, one at each end of the bar, in lifts such as the squat and the bench press. They are not used in Olympic lifts.

SELECTED REFERENCES

BRIGGS, G.M., and D.H. CALLOWAY. *Bogert's Nutrition and Physical Fitness.* Philadelphia: W.B. Saunders Co., 1979.

Dairy Council Digest. *Nutrition and Athletic Performance.* 46(2) 1975.

O'SHEA, J.P. *Scientific Principles and Methods of Strength Fitness.* Reading, Mass.: Addison-Wesley Publishing Co., 1969.

SCHWARZENEGGER, A., and D.K. HALL. *Arnold: The Education of a Body Builder.* New York: Simon and Schuster, 1977.

STONE, W.J., and W.A. KROLL. *Sports Conditioning and Weight Training.* Boston, Mass.: Allyn and Bacon, Inc., 1980.

STRAUSS, R.H. *Sports Medicine and Physiology.* Philadelphia: W.B. Saunders Co., 1979.

ZANE, F., and C. ZANE. *The Zane Way to a Beautiful Body: Through Weight Training for Men and Women.* New York: Simon and Schuster, 1979.

WRESTLING

THIS CHAPTER WILL ENABLE YOU TO:

♦ Identify and discuss the key points associated with a wrestling match.
♦ Identify the differences in equipment, weight classes, and strategy between high school and collegiate wrestling.
♦ Identify rule differences between high school and collegiate wrestling.
♦ After practice, analyze and demonstrate the various skills and techniques necessary to participate in a wrestling match.
♦ Describe the offensive and defensive strategies utilized in wrestling.
♦ Identify the basic terminology associated with the sport of wrestling.

NATURE AND PURPOSE

There are two worldwide styles of wrestling— the "Greco-Roman" and the "free-style"—both of which are represented in the Olympic games. In America we use a variation of the free-style, in which the wrestlers start in an upright position and one attempts to pin the shoulders of the other to the mat for one second (two seconds in high school). This style of wrestling, as practiced in the schools and colleges of this country, is commonly called "catch-as-catch-can."

All matches occur on a protective mat within a circle 32 feet in diameter. A smaller circle of 10 feet in diameter is located at the center of the mat, and this is where the opposing wrestlers begin to wrestle.

Matches last for 6 minutes in high school and 8 minutes in college. High school matches are divided into three 2-minute periods; college matches are divided into a 2- 3- 3-minute system. There are no rest periods between periods.

The first period always begins with both opponents in a standing position and facing each other on either side of the small circle at the center of the mat.

The second and third periods are begun with both wrestlers in a "referee's position," in which one wrestler is in a down-man position and the other in a top-man position. Both wrestlers change positions at the end of the second period.

If during the course of the match neither wrestler is able to successfully pin his opponent's shoulders to the mat for the required one second (two seconds in high school), the winner may be determined by a point system.

There are five ways to score points against an opponent:

1. *Takedown*	2 points
2. *Escape*	1 point
3. *Reversal*	2 points
4. *Near fall*	2 or 3 points
5. *Time advantage* (college)	1 point

Weight Classification. In order for two wrestling opponents to be evenly matched in size, weight classifications have been developed to allow opponents to wrestle at the same approximate weight.

HIGH SCHOOL	COLLEGE
98 lb.	118 lb.
105	126
112	134
119	142
126	150
132	158
138	167
145	177
155	190
167	Unlimited
185	
Unlimited	

Wrestling contains numerous holds involving throws, lifts, and twists. A great amount of strength is an important asset but not a prerequisite. A wrestler must have quickness, physical conditioning, and a knowledge of leverage points.

BASIC RULES

To win a fall, the shoulder blades of one's opponent must be held in contact with the mat continuously for one full second (two seconds in high school).

RECOMMENDED MAT SIZE
WRESTLING MAT

CIRCULAR MAT
38' OVER-ALL DIA. 28'
DIA. CIRCLE; 10' DIA
INNER CIRCLE

Any hold may be used except certain holds considered dangerous to the safety of one's opponent. These are as follows:

ILLEGAL HOLDS

Hammerlock above a 90° angle

Twisting hammerlock

Full nelson

Front bendlock without the arm

Headlock without the arm

Straight head scissors

Overhead double arm bar

Over-scissors

Strangle holds

Body slams

Twisting knee lock

Key lock

Bending, twisting, or forcing the head or any limb beyond its normal limits of movement

Locking the hands behind the back in a double arm bar from the neutral position

Full back suplay from a rear standing position

Any holds used for punishment alone

If no fall (pin) is secured, the decision goes to the contestant who has scored the most points during a match.

STARTING THE MATCH

Contestants begin the match from a standing position, facing one another. When a contestant takes his opponent to the mat within the first two minutes, both continue to wrestle until a fall is declared or until the 2-minute time limit is reached.

If neither secures a position of advantage before the two minutes have elapsed, the remaining time is divided into two periods of mat wrestling. The referee flips a coin, and the winner of the "call" chooses the top or bottom position for the start of the second period. A fall in the second period terminates that period and the bout. The loser of the coin flip in the second period alternates positions starting in the third period. A fall by one wrestler takes precedence over a greater number of points earned by the other prior to the fall.

Certain rules differ between high school and collegiate wrestling. They are outlined in Table 26-1.

Team Point System for Dual Competition
(High School & College)

1. *A loss* either by decision or by fall—0 points
2. *Draw* (tie)—2 points each team
3. *Decision*
   a. Less than 8 points—3 points
   b. 8 points or more—4 points
   c. More than 12 points—5 points
4. *Fall* (pin)—6 points
5. *Forfeit*—6 points
6. *Default*—6 points
7. *Disqualification*—6 points

Individual Scoring System

1. *Takedown* (2 points)—For each takedown of opponent to mat and securing a position of advantage.
2. *Escape* (1 point)—Escape from a position of disadvantage to a neutral position.
3. *Reversal* (2 points)—Reversal from a position of disadvantage to a position of advantage.
4. *Near Fall* (2 points)—Both shoulders of the defensive wrestler held momentarily (stopped) within 4 inches of the mat or less, or when one shoulder of the defensive wrestler is touching the mat and the other shoulder is held at an angle of 45° or less, for less than 5 seconds.
5. *Near Fall* (3 points)—Same situation as above, but wrestler is held in this position for more than 5 seconds.
6. *Time Advantage—College* (1 point)—One minute or more of net accumulated time in the advantage position.
7. Points may also be scored if an opponent is stalling, commits certain technical violations, or applies an illegal hold.
8. A fall terminates the match and all points scored up to that point are disregarded.

SUGGESTED LEARNING SEQUENCE

A. Nature and Purpose of Wrestling
B. Conditioning Aspects. Plan drills and exercises that might be related to movements of wrestling.

TABLE 26-1. Rules of High School and Collegiate Wrestling

	HIGH SCHOOL	COLLEGE
Uniforms	One or two piece uniform is optional.	One or two piece uniform is optional.
Starting Position	Knee on near side must be down on mat.	One knee must be on the mat but not necessarily the "near" knee.
Riding Time	No riding time.	One point for one minute or more accumulated time advantage.
Fall	Two seconds (pin)	One second.
Length of Match	Three 2-minute periods.	First period: two minutes; 2nd and 3rd periods: 3 minutes.
Weigh-in	Shoulder-to-shoulder weigh-in within a maximum of one hour and a minimum of one-half hour before the time a dual meet is scheduled to begin.	Five-hour maximum, one-half hour minimum.
Competition	A wrestler weighing in for one weight class may be shifted to a higher weight, provided it is not more than one weight class above that for which his actual stripped weight qualifies him.	A contestant may wrestle any weight class above the one for which he weighed in.
Overtime	In a completely new match warnings and penalties are not accumulative from match to overtime period.	Same—time advantage is listed sixth in order.
Number of Matches	May not compete in more than four full-length matches in a day.	No similar rule.
Unlimited Weight Class	Must weigh a minimum of 175 lbs.	Must weigh a minimum of 177 lbs.

C. Basic Wrestling Concepts
    1. Wrestling area
    2. Equipment
    3. Safety
    4. Sportsmanship and courtesy
D. Rules
E. Skills and Techniques. Skills should be taught in combination whenever possible. The sequence that the skills are taught is up to the individual preference of the instructor.
    1. Escapes and Reversals
       a. Referee's position
       b. Sit out and turn in
       c. Outside switch
       d. Side roll
       e. Stand-up with inside leg
    2. Breakdowns and Rides
       a. Near arm, tight waist, into double waist ride
       b. Head lever and tight waist
       c. Near ankle and cross face
       d. Far ankle and near waist
    3. Pinning combinations
       a. Half nelson
       b. Arm bar and half nelson
       c. Cross face cradle
       d. Near cradle
    4. Stance and Drop-step
       a. Square stance
       b. Lead foot

    5. Takedowns
       a. Double-leg
       b. Single-leg
       c. Fireman's roll
F. Strategies. Offensive as well as defensive wrestling concepts should be introduced as early as possible so that skills can be practiced within the wrestling match.
G. Wrestling matches

SKILLS AND TECHNIQUES

Mat Wrestling

To begin the second and third periods, or at any time during the first period one contestant has a position of advantage over his opponent when they go off the mat, the wrestlers begin wrestling from the "referee's position" (Figure 26-1).

The "bottom" man (wrestler in a position of disadvantage, or defensive man) assumes a stationary position on his hands and knees facing the official. He must keep both knees on the mat at the rear starting line. The heels of both hands must be on the mat in front of the forward starting line.

The "top" man (wrestler in position of advantage, or offensive wrestler) assumes a position on one or both knees to the side of his opponent. The near arm is placed loosely around the defensive

FIGURE 26-1. The referee's position, right and left views.

wrestler's waist, and the palm of the other hand is placed on the back of the near elbow. The head must be placed on the midline of his opponent's back.

On signal from the referee both wrestlers begin to wrestle. The objective of the bottom man is to execute a reversal in order to gain a position of advantage. The top man's objective is to turn the opponent over and hold his shoulders to the mat for the time required to secure a fall. The systematic procedure for attaining this objective is to break his opponent down and then work for a fall.

ESCAPES AND REVERSALS

The wrestler in the bottom man position has numerous opportunities open to him which facilitate execution of offensive moves enabling him to escape from or reverse his opponent. In order to facilitate these movements the wrestler must pos-

sess an astute sense of balance, timing, explosiveness, and deception. It is important that the wrestler prevent having his arms or legs from being "tied up" and that he maintain a good base of support. The wrestler who possesses these skills will have a distinct advantage over his opponents.

Sit Out and Turn In

Learning Cues

1. Bottom man assumes referee's position.
2. Wrestler steps up with outside leg and grasps wrist of opponent's far arm.
3. Sit through with inside leg and maintain grasp of arm.
4. Pivot on inside shoulder and hip to face opponent.
5. Bring free arm upwards to prevent opponent from following.

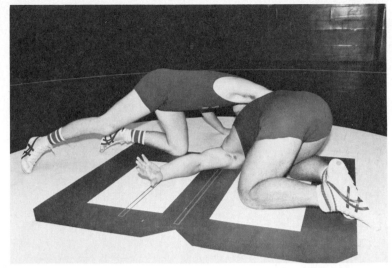

FIGURE 26-2. Sit out and turn in.

Outside Switch

Learning Cues

1. Assume bottom man referee's position.
2. Bring inside arm across body to release grip of opponent.
3. Shift weight to inside hand and outside foot, while lifting knee of outside foot off mat.

4. Pivot on outside foot and sit through bringing inside leg towards side of outside foot.
5. Throw outside arm over outside arm of opponent and place into crotch of opponent, swinging wide to apply pressure against opponent's shoulder.
6. Pull opponent forward while pivoting on hip that is closer to opponent, thereby coming to a top man position.

FIGURE 26-3. Outside switch.

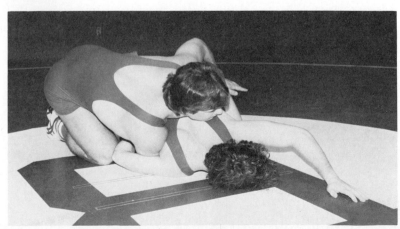

Side Roll

Learning Cues

1. Assume referee's position with partner in slightly overbalanced high position.
2. Lift off knees to tripod while grasping with outside hand and arm the outside arm of opponent and locking tightly behind opponent's elbow.

3. Move outside knee close to inside knee, collapse onto outside hip and shoulder, thereby executing roll. Maintain tight lock on opponent's arm during roll.
4. With opponent on back, pivot towards opponent's legs until coming to a chest-to-chest, perpendicular position.

FIGURE 26-4. Side roll.

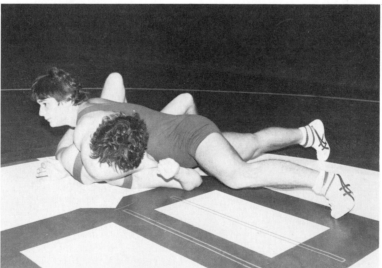

Stand-up with Inside Leg

Learning Cues

1. Assume bottom man referee's position with partner on top.
2. On signal, thrust weight upward and backward into opponent while stepping up with inside leg.
3. Grasp outside arm of opponent at wrist with your outside hand, and come to a standing position and push opponent's hand to side.
4. Pivot away until facing opponent.

Practice Suggestions

1. Without partner, assume bottom man referee's position. Execute step-by-step progression of the sit out and turn in, outside switch, the side roll reversal, and the stand-up at reduced speed.
2. Same as above, on signal execute the escape, a reversal, or stand-up at normal speed.
3. Assume referee's position, with partner assuming passive role. Execute the escape, a reversal, or stand-up at reduced speed.

FIGURE 26-5. Stand-up with inside leg.

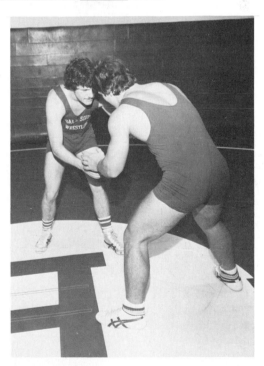

4. Same as #3, except partner offers resistance. Execute on signal the escape, a reversal, or stand-up at normal speed.

BREAKDOWNS AND RIDES

In order to secure a fall the wrestler must be able to break down his opponent and maintain control in order to prevent a reversal. Realizing that the opponent has four bases of support, the wrestler must take away one of these bases in order to initiate a breakdown. By breaking the opponent down to a prone position the opponent's base of support is destroyed. From this position the likelihood of escape by the opponent is eliminated and he is put into a position whereby a fall is possible.

The ride is the act of maintaining the opponent in a prone position under control by utilizing various holds and leverage points.

FIGURE 26-6.   Near arm, tight waist breakdown into double waist ride.

Near Arm, Tight Waist Breakdown and Double Waist Ride

Learning Cues

1. Assume a top man referee's position.
2. At the whistle, tighten waist control and break down near arm at elbow, pulling in towards waist.
3. Shift weight forward and against opponent's hips to facilitate breakdown to prone position.
4. Maintain weight on top of opponent and grasp wrist of opponent's near arm with both hands (double wrist ride) to maintain control.

Head Lever and Tight Waist Breakdown

Learning Cues

1. Assume referee's position with partner.

2. On signal, slide hand on elbow to wrist, and tighten waist control.
3. Place head in near armpit of opponent and drive forward, pulling arm backward and to side.
4. Shift weight forward and drive opponent towards removed base of support to prone position.

Near Ankle and Cross Face Breakdown

Learning Cues

1. Assume referee's position.
2. On signal, remove hand from waist and grasp near ankle. With near arm execute cross face, by reaching across face of opponent and grasping far arm above the elbow.
3. Lift ankle and break down far arm, driving weight forward and towards removed base of support, to prone position.

FIGURE 26-7.   Head lever and tight waist breakdown.

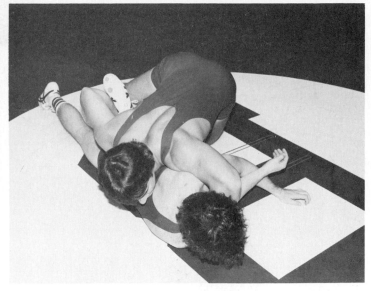

FIGURE 26-8. Near ankle and cross face breakdown.

Far Ankle and Near Waist Breakdown

Learning Cues

1. Assume referee's position.
2. On signal, reach with far arm to far ankle of opponent and grasp.
3. Place near arm around waist of opponent, lift far ankle.
4. Drive weight perpendicular to opponent towards removed base of support to prone position.

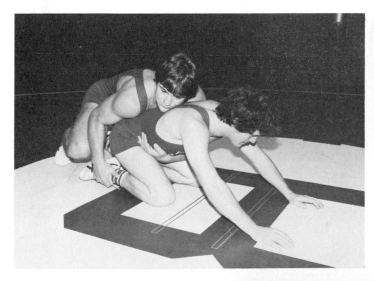

FIGURE 26-9. Far ankle and near waist breakdown.

Practice Suggestions

1. With partner, assume referee's position, partner in passive role. Execute breakdown in step-by-step progression at reduced speed.
2. Same as above, execute breakdown at normal speed.
3. Same as above, except partner offers resistance; execute breakdown at normal speed.

Counters to Breakdowns

Near Arm, Tight Waist. Defensive wrestler on whistle moves near arm towards far arm and posts. Far hand grasps opponent's hand around waist and wrestler sits out.

Head Lever, Tight Waist. Defensive wrestler turns near arm inward with palm up. Drop elbow to mat while pivoting inward to free arm.

FIGURE 26-10. Half nelson.

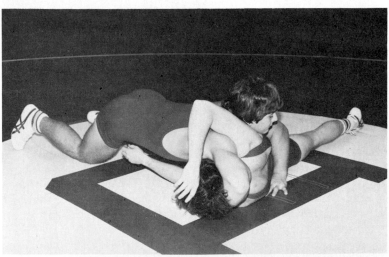

Near Ankle, Cross Face. Defensive wrestler straightens leg to free from grasp. With free hand reach up and grasp arm of opponent at waist and pull arm off, releasing grip.

Far Ankle, Near Waist. Defensive wrestler straightens leg or reaches back with far hand to grasp opponent's hand. Then post the foot he controls and push hips into him until grasp is released.

PINNING COMBINATIONS

Once the opponent has been broken down to a prone position the wrestler's objective is to secure a fall in order to win the match outright. Various pinning combinations are utilized to position the opponent on his back to facilitate the fall.

Half Nelson

Learning Cues

1. Assume a prone position with double wrist ride.
2. Wrestler crosses over to other side of opponent, but maintaining double wrist ride.
3. Slide near hand under near arm of opponent and

place wrist on opponent's head and move perpendicular to opponent.
4. Pry up opponent's arm, sliding arm around head and turning under.
5. Drive forward, turning opponent to his back and lifting his head. Maintain wrist lock and prone position.

Practice Suggestions

1. Assume prone position with partner in double wrist lock. Execute step-by-step progression of pinning combination at reduced speed with partner maintaining passive role.
2. Same as above, execute pinning combination at normal speed.
3. Same as above, except partner offers resistance; execute pinning combination at normal speed.

Arm Bar and Half Nelson

Learning Cues

1. Assume prone position in head lever ride, or double wrist ride.
2. With near arm, slide under near arm of opponent

FIGURE 26-11.   Arm bar and half nelson.

until hand is on shoulder in perpendicular position.

3. Cross over to other side of opponent, while maintaining arm bar, to perpendicular position from opponent.
4. Slide free hand under near arm of opponent to a half nelson.
5. Drive weight forward, prying arm upwards and turning opponent onto his back.

Cross Face Cradle

Learning Cues

1. Assume prone position with a cross face on opponent.
2. Grasp far leg of opponent behind knee.
3. Drive head of opponent towards his knee by walking around the head towards far knee and lock hands.

4. Wrestler turns opponent towards him onto opponent's back.
5. With far leg, lock free leg of opponent. Slide near leg under hips of opponent.

Near Cradle

Learning Cues

1. Assume referee position.
2. Wrestler moves near arm on elbow to a position over the opponent's head, with the elbow joint resting on the back of the neck.
3. Other hand moves from waist to around near leg of opponent at knee joint.
4. Lock the hands in front of the opponent's chest, and force head downwards and leg upwards.
5. Wrestler brings right leg up and sits through onto hip, thereby turning opponent onto his back.
6. Once opponent is on back, wrestler continues

FIGURE 26-12. Cross face cradle.

pivoting until on top of opponent, and then returns to a prone position perpendicular to opponent.

Practice Suggestions

1. With partner maintaining a passive role, assume a referee's position. Execute the pinning combinations in step-by-step progression at reduced speed.
2. Same as above, execute pinning combination at normal speed.
3. Same as above, except partner offers resistance; execute pinning combination at normal speed.

Counters to Pinning Combinations

Half Nelson. Defensive wrestler locks arm of offensive wrestler above elbow. Drive elbow to the mat and throw near leg high and across top wrestler's body into a pinning situation.

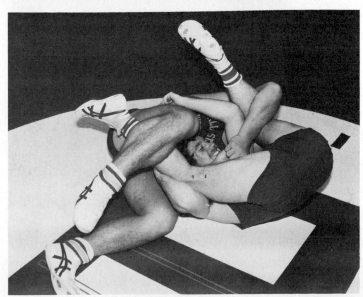

FIGURE 26-13. Near cradle.

Half Nelson and Arm Bar. Defensive wrestler turns body away from opponent and keeps head high. Straighten far arm to counter arm bar. Pull hand off neck to counter half nelson.

Cross Face Cradle. Defensive wrestler locks his legs and then straightens legs while turning to a prone position to break grip of opponent.

Near Cradle. Defensive wrestler brings free leg forward and plants near arm firmly on mat. Sit through hand while throwing head back into opponent's armpit to break grip.

THE STANCE AND THE DROP-STEP

The stance may vary according to the individual preference of the wrestler. Two basic stances are utilized: the square stance and the lead-foot stance. It is important in the stance to use a sliding step rather than a crossover step in execution of movement from side to side.

Square Stance

Learning Cues

1. Feet are shoulder width apart and parallel.
2. Knees and hips are flexed.
3. Head held in an upright position; the back straight at a slight angle from the waist.
4. Elbows close to the sides, hands in front, with palms facing the mat.
5. Weight on the balls of the feet, and equally distributed.

Lead-foot Stance

Learning Cues

1. One foot slightly forward of the other foot, shoulder width apart.
2. Knees and hips flexed.
3. Head and back in same position as in square stance.
4. Hands in front with elbows close to body, palms facing downward.
5. Weight on the balls of the feet, and equally distributed.

Practice Suggestions—Stances

1. Place class in evenly spaced lines. Assume a square or lead-foot stance. On the signal, move them to the right, left, forward, or backward.

Drop-step

In order for a wrestler to be effective on his feet and to gain control over an opponent he must be

FIGURE 26-14. (A) Square stance. (B) Lead-foot stance.

A   B

FIGURE 26-15. Drop-step.

able to penetrate the defense of the opposing wrestler. Penetration allows the wrestler to lift an opponent off of his base of support, thereby neutralizing his balance and power. The drop-step is an effective maneuver used to penetrate the opponent's defense.

Learning Cues

1. Using a lead foot, step and stretch as deep and as far as possible.
2. Lower chest down near knee of front leg.
3. Move back foot up behind front foot.
4. Head in upright position, back straight over front knee.
5. Weight over front foot.
6. Elbows next to body, hands in front, palms pointing downward.

Practice Suggestions

1. Align wrestlers in line, facing opposite side of mat. On signal, wrestler leads with one foot and steps into drop-step pattern. Trail leg follows and stomps mat, then proceeds to step through with that leg. Continue drill across entire length of the mat. Do 8 to 10 repetitions.
2. Facing a partner standing 6 feet away, begin drop-step pattern and penetrate into partner, chest against partner's thighs. Straighten back and lift partner off mat; still on your knees, carry him four or five steps.

TAKEDOWNS

The takedown is a maneuver used by a wrestler in a neutral position to take his opponent to the mat and gain control. Much of the offense found in wrestling occurs with the takedown, and good wrestlers are very proficient at this skill. The takedown consists of three components: the set-up, penetration, and the follow-through.

Double-Leg Takedown

Learning Cues

1. Drop-step towards opponent, penetrating as deep as possible.
2. Place chest against opponent's thighs, head to outside of legs against the hip.
3. Wrap arms around thighs and lock hands.
4. Lift opponent and turn towards side opposite of head, return opponent to mat on his side.
5. Move to a position of control.

Single-Leg Takedown

Learning Cues

1. From wrestling stance, perform drop-step, stepping to side of opponent.
2. Place head to inside of hip, shoulder against leg, arms locked around leg.

FIGURE 26-16. Double-leg takedown.

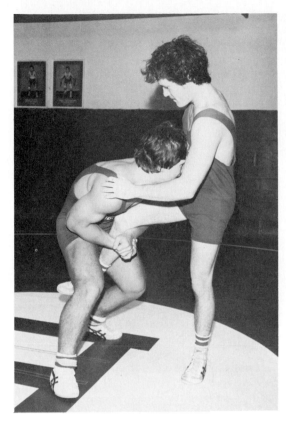

FIGURE 26-17. Single-leg takedown.

3. Lift leg of opponent and come to a standing position, head against inside of opponent's thigh.
4. Exert force downward and away from opponent's one base of support, causing opponent to fall to mat.
5. Move to a position of control.

Practice Suggestions

1. With partner in passive wrestler role, execute double-leg and single-leg takedown maneuver in step-by-step progression at reduced speed.

2. Same set-up, execute double-leg or single-leg takedown at normal speed.
3. Same set-up, execute series of feints prior to performing the double-leg or single-leg takedown. Partner offers resistance.

Fireman's Roll Takedown

Learning Cues

1. Assume collar-bicep tie-up position with partner.

FIGURE 26-18. Fireman's roll.

2. Execute drop-step into partner, lead leg between partner's legs, knee of trail leg on mat.
3. Duck head under arm of partner, cradling neck into armpit.
4. Maintain grasp of bicep, place other hand around near leg, and lift off mat.
5. Pivot onto outside hip and side, carrying partner over your shoulders.
6. Turn partner to his back and maintain a chest-to-chest, perpendicular position.

Practice Suggestions

1. With partner, place hand on collar of partner, with other hand grasping bicep on opposite side. Maintain basic stance and move about using hands to maneuver partner from side to side and

forward and backward as set-up prior to take-down.
2. From bicep-collar tie-up, execute fireman's roll to point of lift, at reduced speed, then at normal speed.
3. Same set-up, execute entire fireman's roll at reduced speed, then at normal speed. Partner offers resistance.

Counters to Takedowns

One effective defense against another wrestler is by utilization of the hands to ward off attempts at control. As another maneuver, once the opponent penetrates the hands the wrestler must sprawl on top of the opponent whereby the hips are dropped and the legs are thrown back. This reduces the effectiveness of the opponent's penetration. A third line of defense calls for the wrestler to maintain a square position to the opponent, and execution of a cross face or quarter nelson will enhance this maneuver.

STRATEGY

1. Learn to set up your maneuvers. Your chances of making them work are many times better when you surprise your opponent.
2. The best time to gain an advantage is just as your opponent relaxes or is slightly off-balance from countering another move.
3. In general, get parallel to escape and perpendicular to pin.
4. Move in the direction in which your opponent has the least support.
5. Learn to wrestle in series; that is, if one move does not work, try another immediately, or if it does work, follow through to the pin.
6. Sound knowledge of fundamentals, top physical condition, and a strong desire to win are the ingredients necessary for success in wrestling.
7. Explosive moves are more effective than slower ones. Learn not to rely on strength when it can be avoided, or else you will tire yourself unnecessarily.
8. While waiting for your match, watch other wrestlers to learn different methods of attack and strategy.
9. Warm up thoroughly prior to the beginning of your match.
10. Be aggressive and make the opponent wrestle your style of wrestling.

SAFETY

1. Remember the basic rule: Anything that endangers life or limb is illegal in amateur wrestling.
2. Be sure you are properly conditioned before beginning to compete.
3. Be sure there is adequate room for the workout; more injuries occur as a result of rolling onto or falling over other pairs than from wrestling with opponents.
4. Warm up properly. The neck, especially, should be exercised prior to wrestling, as the muscles in it are ordinarily little used.
5. Roll when you fall, learn which maneuvers are likely to be most hazardous, and, insofar as possible, know when to resist the opponent's pressure and when not to.
6. Do not compete in an obvious mismatch. This applies both to size and ability.
7. Insist on only qualified officials.

8. See that mats of the surrounding area are properly padded and that no physical hazards exist in the facilities or equipment.
9. Use protective equipment as needed, such as headgear and kneepads.
10. Keep mat and clothing as clean as possible.
11. Be sure all injuries are promptly and properly treated.
12. A physical examination before the season gets under way is imperative.
13. Keep nails short and the hair clean and at appropriate length. Do not wear jewelry of any kind or other objects that might injure you or your opponent.
14. Do not participate when you have infections or injuries—wait until they are cleared by a competent physician.
15. Do not reduce weight drastically in a short period of time.

PLAYING COURTESIES

1. Refrain from engaging in excessively rough play as it may cause injuries and ill feelings.
2. Refrain from questioning decisions of officials.
3. Refrain from swearing or throwing of equipment.
4. Always shake the opponent's hand at the conclusion of the match regardless of the outcome.
5. Encourage other team members to do as well as they can during their matches.

TERMINOLOGY

Bottom position A four point stance assumed at the start of a period or when the referee signals a restart. A position of disadvantage.

Breakdown A maneuver in which the wrestler in the position of advantage forces the opponent flat to the mat.

Bridge Supporting one's weight on the feet and head, with the back arched, thus keeping the shoulders away from the mat.

Control One wrestler is positioned in such a way that his opponent is immobilized or restrained.

Counter A block or a movement which prevents the execution of a maneuver by the opponent.

Cradle A pin hold executed by pulling the opponent's head and leg together and holding his shoulders to the mat.

Cross body A means of breaking the opponent down and controlling him until a pin can be applied; it is executed by grapevining one of his legs, stretching across his back, and holding his opposite arm just above the elbow.

Cross face A maneuver used either as a counter or as an offensive breakdown by reaching across the side of the opponent's face and grasping his opposite arm just above the elbow.

Double-leg takedown A takedown performed by gaining control of both of the opponent's legs.

Escape Coming from a position of disadvantage to a neutral position.

Fall Holding both of the opponent's shoulders to the mat simultaneously for one or two seconds. Same as a pin. This terminates a match.

Half nelson A means of turning the opponent to his back by prying an arm upward, using his head as a fulcrum.

Head lever A means of breaking the opponent to the mat by exerting pressure with the head on his arm at the armpit, at the same time pulling backward on the corresponding wrist.

Near fall A position in which the offensive wrestler maintains his opponent in a controlled pinning situation.

Neutral position Both wrestlers face each other on their feet or knees with neither maintaining control.

Referee's position Starting position for the opening of the second or third periods and for all restarts not from a neutral position. Wrestlers assume a top man and bottom man position as directed by the referee.

Reversal A means of scoring by moving from a position of disadvantage to a position of advantage.

Set-up Maneuver by which a wrestler tries to gain an advantage by feinting, pushing, pulling, or making noises to distract an opponent.

Single-leg takedown Maneuver used by an attacking wrestler to gain control of one of an opponent's legs.

Sit-out Maneuver from a position of disadvantage (bottom man) for the purpose of either escaping or reversing. The wrestler sits, throwing his legs in front of him, and turns quickly.

Stand-up An escape executed by standing up from a bottom man position.

Suplay Illegal takedown whereby the wrestler picks up his opponent around the waist and falls backward in an attempt to put the opponent's shoulders to the mat.

Switch A reversal executed by bottom man by applying leverage near the opponent's shoulder and sitting out to side.

Takedown Taking the opponent down to the mat and attaining control over him.

Top position Wrestler is above and behind the bottom wrestler, with one arm encircling the waist and another placed on the elbow of the near arm. A position of advantage.

SELECTED REFERENCES

BORING, W.J. *Science and Skill of Wrestling.* St. Louis, Mo.: C.V. Mosby Company, 1975.

CARSON, R.F. *Championship Wrestling: Coaching to Win.* Cranbury, N.J.: A.S. Barnes and Co., Inc., 1974.

CARSON, R.F. *Complete Book of Single and Double Leg Takedowns.* West Nyack, N.Y.: Parker Publishing Co., Inc., 1979.

CARSON, R.F., and B.R. PATTERSON. *Principles of Championship Wrestling.* Cranbury, N.J.: A.S. Barnes and Co., Inc., 1972.

DOUGLAS, B. *Wrestling—the Making of a Champion: The Takedown.* Ithaca, N.Y.: Cornell University Press, 1972.

Editors of the Coaching Clinic. *Best of Wrestling from the Coaching Clinic.* West Nyack, N.Y.: Parker Publishing Co., Inc., 1978.

HOPKE, S.L., and W. KIDDER. *Elementary and Junior High School Wrestling.* Cranbury, N.J.: A.S. Barnes and Co., Inc., 1977.

JOHNSTON, J.K., C. DALGEWICZ, and D. WHITE. *Wrestling: Skills and Strategies for the Athlete and Coach.* New York: Hawthorn Books, Inc., 1979.

National Collegiate Athletic Association. *Official Wrestling Guide.* Shawnee Mission, Kan., 1979.

SCIACCHETANO, L., and J. MCCALLUM. *Sports Illustrated—Wrestling.* New York: J.B. Lippincott Co., 1979.

UMBACK, A.W., and W.R. JOHNSON. *Successful Wrestling: Its Bases and Problems,* 2nd ed. Dubuque, Iowa: Wm. C. Brown Company, 1972.

APPENDIX A
Sources of Rules

The following national organizations, athletic associations, and companies publish rules and guides on various sport activities. Some of the national organizations have regional and state affiliates where rules can be obtained. You should check the telephone directory for the nearest office in your area for further information.

NATIONAL ORGANIZATIONS

Amateur Athletic Union of the United States (AAU)
231 West 58th Street
New York, New York 10019

Rulebooks and guides governing amateur athletics

Basketball	Swimming and Diving
Boxing	Water Polo
Gymnastics	Track and Field
Handball	Weight Lifting
Judo	Wrestling

National Collegiate Athletic Association (NCAA)
Box 757, Grand Central Station
New York, New York 10017

Rulebooks and guides

Baseball	Skiing
Basketball	Soccer
Football	Swimming
Gymnastics	Track and Field
Ice Hockey	Wrestling

National Association for Girls and Women in Sport
    (NAGWS)
American Alliance for Health, Physical Education,
    Recreation and Dance
1900 Association Drive
Reston, Virginia 22091

Rulebooks and guides

Archery	Racquetball
Badminton	Skiing
Basketball	Soccer
Bowling	Softball
Fencing	Speedball
Field Hockey	Squash
Flag Football	Swimming and Diving
Golf	Synchronized Swimming
Gymnastics	Team Handball
Lacrosse	Tennis
Orienteering	Volleyball

National Federation of State and High School Athletic
    Associations (NFS)
7 South Dearborn Street
Chicago, Illinois 60603

Rulebooks and guides for high school activities (Check state athletic associations for rules governing specific sports in your state.)

Baseball	Soccer
Basketball	Swimming
Football	Track and Field
Touch Football	Wrestling
Six-man Football	

COMPANY SOURCE FOR MULTIPLE ACTIVITIES

General Sportcraft Company, Ltd.
140 Woodbine Street
Bergenfield, New Jersey 07621

Rules

Banball	Quoits
Bocce	Shuffleboard (Deck)
Croquet	Spiral Tennis
Darts	Table Tennis
Deck Tennis	Takraw Game
Field Hockey	Tether Ball
Horseshoes	Tether Tennis
Paddle Tennis	

OTHER ORGANIZATIONS, ASSOCIATIONS, AND COMPANIES

Aerial Tennis

Sells Aerial Tennis Co.
Box 42, Kansas City, Kan. 66103

Angling

American Casting Education Foundation
P.O. Box 51, Nashville, Tenn. 37202

Federation of Fly Fishers
P.O. Box 1088, West Yellowstone, Mont. 59758

Trout Unlimited
4260 East Evans, Denver, Colo. 80222

Archery

National Field Archery Association
Rt. 2, Box 514, Redlands, Calif. 92373

American Archery Council
23 E. Jackson Blvd., Chicago, Ill. 60604
(Indoor Target)

Badminton

American Badminton Association
20 Wamesit Rd., Waban, Mass. 02168

Dayton Racquet Co.
302 S. Albright St.,
Arcanum, Ohio 43504

Baseball

American Amateur Baseball Congress
P.O. Box 44, Battle Creek, Mich. 49016

(Umpire's Handbook. Scorer's Handbook—Rules not
   included. Rules in Pictures. Tournament Manual.
   League organization.)
National Baseball Congress
Box 1420, Wichita, Kansas 67201
(Copyrighted rules. Nonprofessional Guide)
American Legion
Box 1055, Indianapolis, Ind. 46206
Babe Ruth League, Inc.
524½ Hamilton Ave., Trenton, N.J. 08625
Little League Baseball, Inc.
P.O. Box 925, Williamsport, Pa. 17704
(Umpire's Handbook)
Boys Baseball, Inc.
P.O. Box 225, Washington, Pa. 15301
(Bronco; Pony; Colt)
The Sporting News
2018 Washington Ave., St. Louis, Mo. 63166
"Knotty Problems of Baseball" (professional rules)

Basketball   *See* AAU, NCAA, NAGWS, NFS

Bicycling
Amateur Bicycle League of America
Box 669, Wall Street Station, New York, N.Y. 10005
Bicycle Federation
1101 Fifteenth St. N.W., Washington, D.C. 20005
International Bicycle Touring Society
2115 Pasco Dorado, La Jolla, Calif. 92037
National Bicycling Foundation
P.O. Box 1368, Homestead, Florida 33030

Billiards
Billiard Congress of America
20 N. Wacker Dr., Chicago, Ill. 60605

Bocce
Lignum-Vitae Products Corp.
96 Boyd Ave., Jersey City, N.J. 07303

Bowling (Duck Pin)
National Duck Pin Bowling Congress
1420 New York Ave., N.W., Washington, D.C. 20005

Bowling (Ten Pin)
American Bowling Congress
5301 South 76th St., Greendale, Wisc. 53129
Women's International Bowling Congress
5301 South 76th St., Greendale, Wisc. 53129

Boxing   *See* AAU

Corkball
Rawlings Sporting Goods Co.
2300 Delmar Blvd., St. Louis, Mo. 63166

Cross-country Skiing   *See* Skiing

Dartball
Wisconsin State Dartball Commission
9333 W. Lincoln Ave., West Allis, Wisc. 53214

Fencing   *See also* NAGWS
Amateur Fencer's League of America
601 Curtis St., Albany, Calif. 94706

Field Hockey   *See also* NAGWS
U.S. Field Hockey Association
4415 Buffalo Rd., North Chili, N.Y. 14514
(Official manual)

Fishing   *See* Angling

Floor Tennis
U.S. Floor Tennis Association
1580 Sherman Ave., Evanston, Ill. 60204

Football (Junior League)
Pop Warner Football
3664 Richmond St., Philadelphia, Pa. 19134

Football   *See* NFS, NCAA

Golf
U.S. Golf Association
Liberty Congress Road, Far Hills, N.J. 07931

Gymnastics   *See* AAU, NCAA, NAGWS
U.S. Gymnastics Federation
P.O. Box 7686, Fort Worth, Texas 76111

Handball *See* AAU
U.S. Handball Association
4101 Dempster St., Skokie, Ill. 60076

Horseshoes (Professional)
National Horseshoe Pitchers Assn. of America
9725 Palm St., Bellflower, Calif. 90706

Ice Hockey *See* NCAA

Ice Skating
Amateur Skating Union
4135 N. Troy St., Chicago, Ill. 60618

Indoor Hockey
Cosom Corporation
6030 Wayzata Blvd., Minneapolis, Minn. 55416

Lacrosse *See* NAGWS

Lawn Bowling
American Lawn Bowling Association
1525 Ridge Court, Wauwatosa, Wisc. 53213

Marble Shooting
National Marbles Tournament
Cleveland Press Bldg., Cleveland, Ohio 44101

Orienteering
United States Orienteering Federation
P.O. Box 1039, Ballwin, Missouri 63011
Canadian Orienteering Federation
355 River Rd., Vanier, Ontario, KIL 8B9

Paddleball
Rodney J. Grambeau
Sports Bldg., University of Michigan,
   Ann Arbor, Mich. 48109

Racquetball
Official International Racquetball Association
4101 Dempster St., Skokie, Ill. 60076

Roller Hockey

    National Roller Hockey Association
    97 Erie St., Dumont, N.J. 07628

Roque

    American Roque League, Inc.
    4205 Briar Creek Lane, Dallas, Texas 75214

Scoopball

    Cosom Corporation
    6030 Wayzata Blvd., Minneapolis, Minn. 55416
    (Rules for 26 different games)

Shuffleboard (Table)

    American Shuffleboard Leagues, Inc.
    533 Third St., Union City, N.J. 07087

Skating (Figure)

    U.S. Figure Skating Association
    575 Boylston St., Boston, Mass. 02116

Skating (Roller)

    U.S. Amateur Roller Skating Association
    120 West 42nd St., New York, N.Y. 10036

Skating (Speed)

    Amateur Skating Union of the U.S.
    4135 N. Troy St., Chicago, Ill. 60618

Skeet Shooting

    National Skeet Shooting Association
    3409 Oak Lawn Ave., Suite 219, Dallas, Texas 75219

Skiing *See also* NCAA

    U.S. Ski Association
    1726 Champa St., Denver, Colo. 80202
    (Downhill, Slalom, Giant Slalom, Jumping, Cross-country,
        FIS and USSA rules)
    Citizen and Club Cross-Country Racing Committee
    USSA, Denver, Colorado

Skin Diving (Competitive) *See* AAU

Smash

    Smash
    1024 North Blvd., Oak Park, Ill. 60303

Soccer *See* NCAA, NAGWS

Softball *See also* NAGWS

    Amateur Softball Association
    2801 N.E. 50th, Oklahoma City, Okla. 73111
    (12″ fast and slow pitch)
    Umpires Protective Assn. of Chicago
    Apt. 710, 3550 Lake Shore Dr., Chicago, Ill. 60657
    (16″ Softball)

Speed-A-Way

    Marjorie S. Larsen
    1754 Middlefield, Stockton, Calif. 95204

Speedball *See* NAGWS

Squash Racquets

    U.S. Squash Racquets Association
    200 E. 66th St., New York, N.Y. 10021

Swimming *See* AAU, NCAA

Swimming (Synchronized) *See* AAU, NAGWS

Table Tennis

    U.S. Table Tennis Association
    210 Saturn Dr., North Star, Newark, Del. 19711
    Nissen-Sico
    930 27th Ave., S.W., Cedar Rapids, Iowa 52402

Team Handball

    Jayfro Corp.
    P.O. Box 400, Waterford, Conn. 06385

Tennis *See also* NAGWS

    U.S. Tennis Association
    51 E. 42nd St., New York, N.Y. 10017
    (Guide; Rules; Umpire's Handbook)
    Dayton Racquet Company
    302 S. Albright Street, Arcanum, Ohio 45304

Tether Ball (Inflated Ball)

    W. J. Voit Rubber Corp.
    3801 S. Harbor Blvd., Santa Ana, Calif. 92704

Touch Football

    The Athletic Institute
    805 Merchandise Mart, Chicago, Ill. 60654

Track and Field *See* AAU, NFS, NCAA

Turf Bowling *See* Bocce

Volleyball *See also* NFS

    U.S. Volleyball Association
    1730 East Boulder St., Colorado Springs, Colorado 80909

Water Polo *See* AAU

Weight Lifting *See* AAU

Wrestling *See* NCAA

APPENDIX B
How to Conduct Tournaments

TYPES OF TOURNAMENT DRAWINGS

Various kinds of bracket arrangements may be used in conducting tournament competition. The type of elimination is usually determined by several factors: (1) type of activity, (2) number of entries, (3) amount of playing time, (4) playing space and equipment, (5) age of participants, (6) officials available.

With a large number of entries it is sometimes desirable to run a combination tournament, for example, a double elimination–single elimination tournament. The winners of the double elimination brackets compete in a single elimination tournament to determine the ultimate champion.

Number of Byes. The first step before making a drawing for the bracket arrangement is to determine the number of entries.

When the number of competitors is 4, 8, 16, 32, 64, 128, or any higher power of 2, they shall meet in pairs. When the number of competitors is not a power of 2, there shall be byes in the first round. For example: if there are 13 entries, a bracket of 16 with three byes is required. The purpose of having byes is to bring into the second round a number of competitors that is a power of 2. To determine the number of byes, subtract the number of competitors from the next higher power of 2; to determine the number of competitors in the first round, subtract the number of byes from the total number of competitors. If the byes are an even number, half of them shall be placed at the top of the draw and half at the bottom of the draw; if they are an uneven number, there should be one more bye at the bottom than the top. The byes at the top half shall be the names drawn first. The next names drawn shall be placed in the first round. The byes in the bottom half are drawn last.

Seeding the Draw. It is a common practice to select the best teams or individuals and place them in the bracket so that they will not meet in the early rounds of the play. Two or more entries may be seeded—usually the four best are selected in a sixteen-name bracket and eight in a thirty-two name bracket. The seeded entrants are usually placed in the 1st, 5th, 9th, 13th, etc., bracket positions. The No. 1 and 4 seeded teams are generally placed in the first and fifth positions of the top bracket and the No. 2 and 3 seeded teams in the ninth and thirteenth positions of the lower bracket, or No. 1 and 3 in the upper with No. 2 and 4 seeded teams in the lower half.

Single Elimination Tournament

If the contestants are of equal strength or their strength is not known, have a drawing for positions in the bracket. If the strength is known, seed the best teams so they will not meet in the early rounds. Place the seeded entries in the 1st, 5th, 9th, 13th, etc., positions.

All byes must occur in the first round of play. The total number of games played is always one less than the number of entries. To determine the number of games that the winner would have to play, count the powers of two in the number of entries; e.g., with 32 entries the winner plays 5 games.

Double Elimination Tournament

Two defeats eliminate an entry in this tournament. The losers in the first rounds move into the losers' bracket. The teams which advance farthest in either bracket meet each other in the final game. Should the winner of the losers' bracket defeat the winner of the first-round bracket, the teams are rematched for the championship when one team will have lost two games.

Byes are distributed in the first round of the original elimination brackets as in a single elimination tournament, but in the first round of the losers' brackets byes must be arranged to avoid giving a second bye to an entry that has already had a bye. Also, at all stages of the losers' bracket, avoid

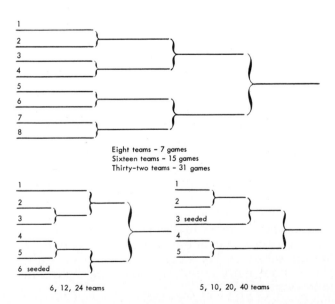

Eight teams – 7 games
Sixteen teams – 15 games
Thirty-two teams – 31 games

6, 12, 24 teams   5, 10, 20, 40 teams

FIRST ROUND

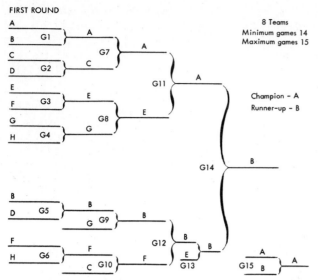

8 Teams
Minimum games 14
Maximum games 15

Champion – A
Runner–up – B

Formula for total number of games, with N representing Number of entries: $2(N-1)$ = Minimum Games to Play; $2(N-1) + 1$ = Maximum Games to Play.

7	6	5	4	3	2	1
6-1	5-7	4-6	3-5	2-4	1-3	7-2
5-2	4-1	3-7	2-6	1-5	7-4	6-3
4-3	3-2	2-1	1-7	7-6	6-5	5-4

Note that the figures go down on the right side and up on the left. No. 7 draws a bye in the first round and the others play as indicated. With an odd number of teams, all numbers revolve and the last number each time draws a bye.

For Even Number of Teams. With an even number of teams the plan is the same except the position of No. 1 remains stationary and the other numbers revolve about it until the original combination is reached. For example, with 8 teams:

1-2	1-8	1-7	1-6	1-5	1-4	1-3
8-3	7-2	6-8	5-7	4-6	3-5	2-4
7-4	6-3	5-2	4-8	3-7	2-6	8-5
6-5	5-4	4-3	3-2	2-8	8-7	7-6

In essence there are two things to remember: (1) With an even number of teams, No. 1 remains stationary and the other numbers revolve. (2) With an odd number of teams, all numbers revolve and the last number each time draws a bye.

pairing entries that have met in earlier rounds, if possible.

This type tournament is seldom used unless the entries are eight or less in number. If more than eight entries, double the process and the two winners meet for the title.

Consolation Tournament

There are two types of general use: The consolation type tournament is generally used only when the number of entries is 8 or 16. In No. I bracket arrangement only the losers in the first round of play compete for consolation title. In No. II, the losers in all the rounds except the final of the upper bracket compete for 3rd and 4th place.

In both tournaments every team plays at least two games before being eliminated.

Round Robin Tournament

In this simple but efficient method, each team plays every other team once with the final standing determined on a percentage basis.

The following formula will apply to any number of teams, whether the total is odd or even. With an odd number of teams there is the same number of rounds; with an even number of teams there is one less number of games than teams.

For Odd Number of Teams. Assign a number to each team and then use only the figures in drawing the schedule. For example, in a league with 7 teams start with 1, putting down figures in the following order:

Ladder Tournament

In a ladder tournament the competition is arranged by challenge and the tournament requires a minimum of supervision. A player may challenge either of the two players above him in the ladder. If the challenger wins, he exchanges places with the

FIRST ROUND BRACKET - 16 ENTRIES

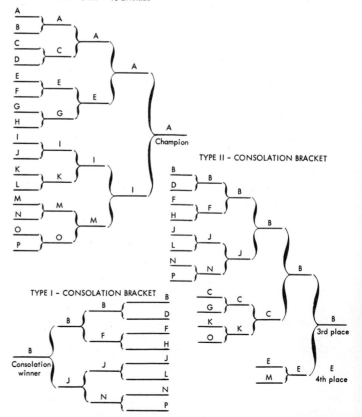

loser in the ladder. All challenges must be accepted and played at an agreed time. Players draw for positions in the ladder; a starting and closing date for the tournament must be announced. Each player carries his handicap against all players, in case handicaps are used.

Pyramid Tournament

The pyramid tournament is similar to the ladder tournament except the design allows for more participating and challenging. After the original drawings are made any player may challenge any other player in the same horizontal row. If he wins he may then challenge anyone in the row above—the two change places in the pyramid.

```
         TABLE TENNIS
    1  _____
    2  _____
    3  _____
    4  _____
    5  _____
    6  _____
    7  _____
    8  _____
    9  _____
   10  _____
```

COMPUTING GOLF HANDICAPS

A popular approved system of handicapping is based upon the five best-to-par scores. When the difference between the total of the five best scores and the total of the five pars is 0 through 3, either above or below, the handicap is SCRATCH.

For other differences use the following table.

	HDCP		HDCP		HDCP
4–9	1	35–40	6	66–71	11
10–15	2	41–46	7	72–78	12
16–21	3	47–53	8	79–84	13
22–28	4	54–59	9	85–90	14
29–34	5	60–65	10	91–96	15
				etc.	

The handicaps listed above were figured by the Short Formula: taking $4/5$ of $1/5$ of the difference between the total of par for the five rounds played and the total of the five best-to-par scores, one-half or over to count as a stroke.

Adjusting Strokes in Handicap Matches

Although the U.S. Golf Association recommends $7/8$ of the difference between handicaps in match play (play by holes), as in the table below, some clubs allow the full difference between handicaps

and others; the player with the lesser strokeplay handicap allows the player with the greater handicap $3/4$ of the difference, a fraction of one-half or over counting as one stroke. The strokes allowed are used on certain holes as designated on the club score card.

When the difference between handicaps is:

1 give 1 stroke	11 give 10 strokes	21 give 18 strokes
2 " 2 "	12 " 11 "	22 " 19 "
3 " 3 "	13 " 11 "	23 " 20 "
4 " 4 "	14 " 12 "	24 " 21 "
5 " 4 "	15 " 13 "	25 " 22 "
6 " 5 "	16 " 14 "	26 " 23 "
7 " 6 "	17 " 15 "	27 " 24 "
8 " 7 "	18 " 16 "	28 " 25 "
9 " 8 "	19 " 17 "	29 " 25 "
10 " 9 "	20 " 18 "	30 " 26 "

TABLE A-1. Tournament Schedule Calculator

Teams Entered	Byes Top	Byes Bottom	SINGLE ELIM. No. Games	DOUBLE ELIM. No. Games	ROUND ROBIN No. Games
4	0	0	3	6 or 7	6
5	1	2	4	8 or 9	10
6	1	1	5	10 or 11	15
7	0	1	6	12 or 13	21
8	0	0	7	14 or 15	28
9	3	4	8	16 or 17	36
10	3	3	9	18 or 19	45
11	2	3	10	20 or 21	55
12	2	2	11	22 or 23	66
13	1	2	12	24 or 25	73
14	1	1	13	26 or 27	91
15	0	1	14	28 or 29	105
16	0	0	15	30 or 31	
17	7	8	16	32 or 33	
18	7	7	17	34 or 35	
19	6	7	18	36 or 37	
20	6	6	19	38 or 39	
21	5	6	20	40 or 41	
22	5	5	21	42 or 43	
23	4	5	22	44 or 45	
24	4	4	23	46 or 47	
25	3	4	24	48 or 49	
26	3	3	25	50 or 51	
27	2	3	26	52 or 53	
28	2	2	27	54 or 55	
29	1	2	28	56 or 57	
30	1	1	29	58 or 59	
31	0	1	30	60 or 61	
32	0	0	31	62 or 63	

APPENDIX C
Athletic Field and Court Diagrams

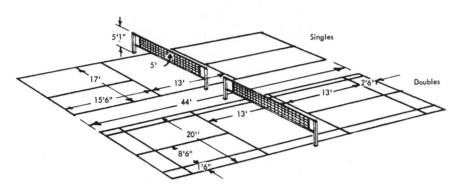

BADMINTON COURT

Measure to outside edge of boundary lines.

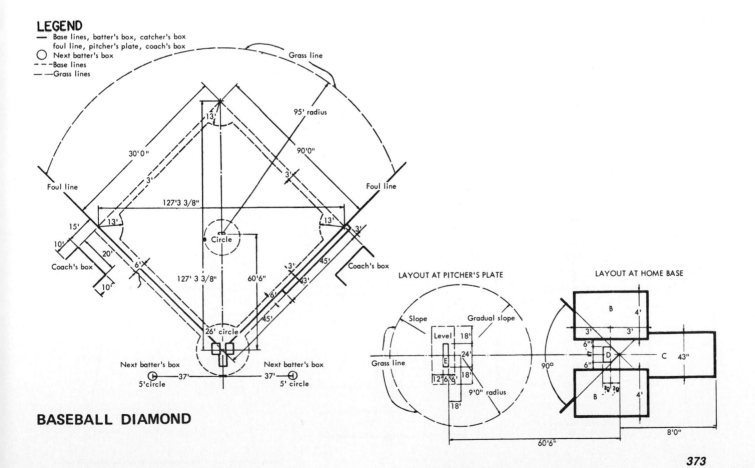

LEGEND
— Base lines, batter's box, catcher's box foul line, pitcher's plate, coach's box
◯ Next batter's box
– – – Base lines
— Grass lines

BASEBALL DIAMOND

LAYOUT AT PITCHER'S PLATE

LAYOUT AT HOME BASE

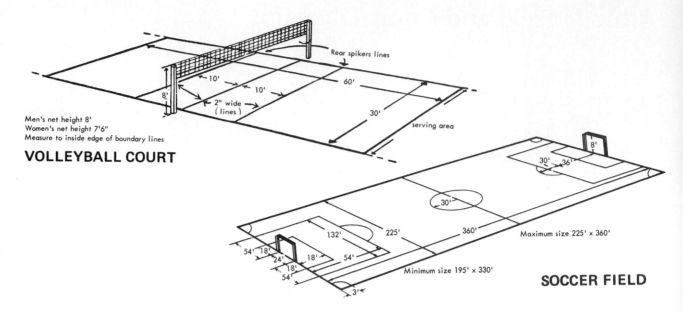

Men's net height 8'
Women's net height 7'6"
Measure to inside edge of boundary lines

VOLLEYBALL COURT

Rear spikers lines

10'

10'

2" wide
(lines)

60'

30'

8'

serving area

SOCCER FIELD

30'   36'

8'

30'

132'   225'   360'   Maximum size 225' x 360'

54' 18'
24'
18'   18'   54'
54'

Minimum size 195' x 330'

3'

BASKETBALL COURT

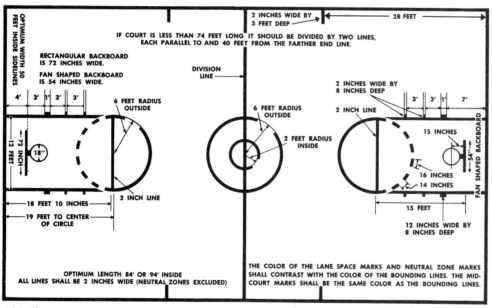

2 INCHES WIDE BY
3 FEET DEEP

28 FEET

IF COURT IS LESS THAN 74 FEET LONG IT SHOULD BE DIVIDED BY TWO LINES,
EACH PARALLEL TO AND 40 FEET FROM THE FARTHER END LINE.

OPTIMUM WIDTH 50 FEET INSIDE SIDELINES

RECTANGULAR BACKBOARD
IS 72 INCHES WIDE.

FAN SHAPED BACKBOARD
IS 54 INCHES WIDE.

DIVISION
LINE

6 FEET RADIUS
OUTSIDE

6 FEET RADIUS
OUTSIDE

2 FEET RADIUS
INSIDE

2 INCHES WIDE BY
8 INCHES DEEP

2 INCH LINE

4'   3' 3' 3'

72 INCH
12 FEET

18"

15 INCHES

3' 3' 1'   7'

FAN SHAPED BACKBOARD

54"

16 INCHES
14 INCHES

18 FEET 10 INCHES
19 FEET TO CENTER
OF CIRCLE

2 INCH LINE

15 FEET

12 INCHES WIDE BY
8 INCHES DEEP

OPTIMUM LENGTH 84' OR 94' INSIDE
ALL LINES SHALL BE 2 INCHES WIDE (NEUTRAL ZONES EXCLUDED)

THE COLOR OF THE LANE SPACE MARKS AND NEUTRAL ZONE MARKS
SHALL CONTRAST WITH THE COLOR OF THE BOUNDING LINES. THE MID-
COURT MARKS SHALL BE THE SAME COLOR AS THE BOUNDING LINES.

**Left End Shows
Large Backboard
for College Games.**

MINIMUM of 3 FEET
Preferably 10 feet of unobstructed space outside.
If impossible to provide 3 feet, a narrow broken
1" line should be marked inside the court parallel
with and 3 feet inside the boundary.

SEMICIRCLE BROKEN LINES
For the broken line semicircle in the free
throw lane, it is recommended there be
8 marks 16 inches long and 7 spaces
14 inches long.

**Right End Shows Small
Backboard for High School
and Y.M.C.A. Games.**

BASKETBALL BACKBOARDS

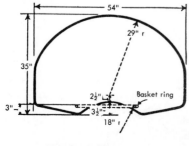

54"

29" r

35"

2½"
Basket ring

3"
3½"

18" r

18"

Modified backboard

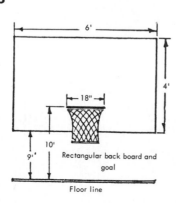

6'

4'

18"

10'

9'

Rectangular back board and
goal

Floor line

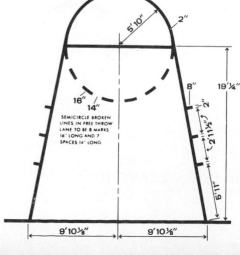

5'10"   2"

8"   2"

16"   14"

19'¼"

SEMICIRCLE BROKEN
LINES IN FREE THROW
LANE TO BE 8 MARKS
16" LONG AND 7
SPACES 14" LONG

2'11½"   2"

6'11"

9'10⅛"   9'10⅛"

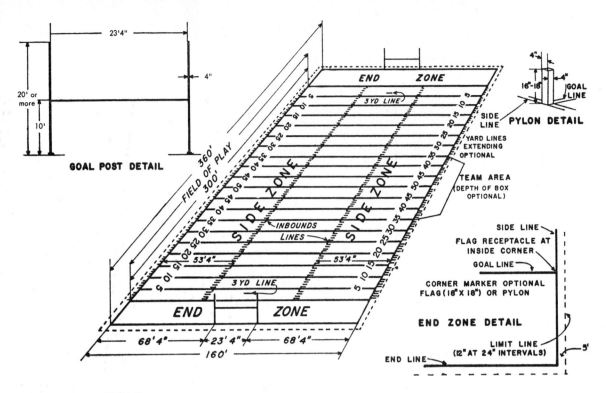

GOAL POST DETAIL

PYLON DETAIL

END ZONE DETAIL

FOOTBALL FIELD

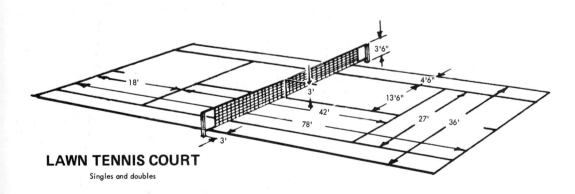

LAWN TENNIS COURT
Singles and doubles

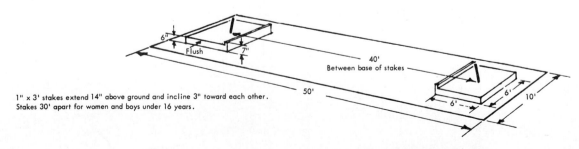

1" x 3' stakes extend 14" above ground and incline 3" toward each other.
Stakes 30' apart for women and boys under 16 years.

HORSESHOES

FIELD HOCKEY

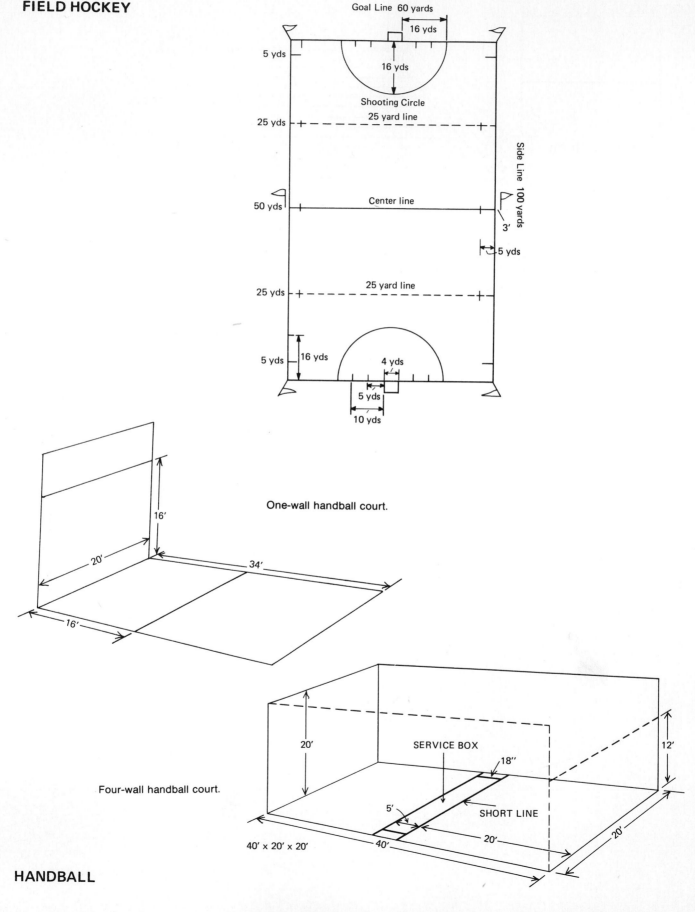

Goal Line 60 yards

16 yds

5 yds

16 yds

Shooting Circle

25 yard line

25 yds

Side Line 100 yards

Center line

50 yds

3'

5 yds

25 yard line

25 yds

16 yds

4 yds

5 yds

5 yds

10 yds

One-wall handball court.

16'

20'

34'

16'

Four-wall handball court.

20'

SERVICE BOX

18''

12'

5'

SHORT LINE

40' x 20' x 20'

40'

20'

20'

HANDBALL

SOFTBALL FIELD

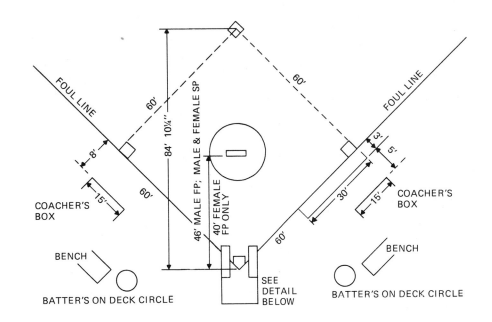

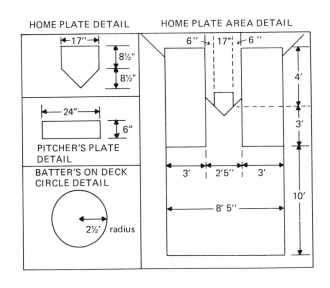

	Distances	
	Fast Pitch	Slow Pitch
Bases		
Male	60 feet	65 feet
Female	60 feet	60 feet
Pitching		
Male	46 feet	46 feet
Female	40 feet	46 feet
Fences		
Male	225 feet	275 feet
Female	200 feet	250 feet

HOME PLATE DETAIL

HOME PLATE AREA DETAIL

PITCHER'S PLATE DETAIL

BATTER'S ON DECK CIRCLE DETAIL

APPENDIX D
Sources of Audio-Visual Materials

Audio-visual materials should be considered as an integral part of the instructional program, and not as entertainment or something to be used on rainy days. Audio-visual materials are supplementary aids to enhance the teaching process. They should not be used as substitutes for the teacher, nor can they take the place of good teaching methods.

The following procedures should prove helpful to the instructor when using A-V materials.

1. Always preview the film or aid before class use in order to become familiar with the material and to make sure it is appropriate for the lesson being taught.
2. Prepare the class in advance by pointing out the features that students should watch for and indicating how the aid will help them in the lesson.
3. After showing the aid, provide an opportunity for class discussion in order to clarify points and to emphasize important parts.
4. It is often advisable to view the film a second time. Some instructors find it helpful to show a film as an introduction to an activity and to rescreen it after students have had an opportunity to practice the activity or particular techniques. There is usually more interest in the second screening because the activity is now more meaningful to the students.
5. Be sure to provide a satisfactory room for viewing projected aids. The effectiveness of a motion picture, for example, may be lost if the students cannot see the picture easily or hear the commentary.
6. Provide students with the means of evaluating the contribution of the visual aid.
7. Be sure you know how to operate the projection equipment, and always have things in readiness when the class arrives.

Catalogues describing available printed, film, and other materials may be obtained upon request from the sources listed below. Sources marked with an asterisk (*) have printed materials only.

AAHPERD Educational Media Services
Department B
1201 16th Street, N.W.
Washington, D.C. 20036

AIMS Instructional Media Services
626 Justin Avenue
Glendale, California 91201

Albion Films
1710 N. LeBrea Avenue
Hollywood, California 90028

Amateur Softball Association
2801 N.E. 50th
Oklahoma City, Oklahoma 73111

American Film Registry
831 South Wabash Avenue
Chicago, Illinois 60605

*American Foundation for the Blind
15 West 16th Street
New York, N.Y. 10011

*American Junior Bowling Congress
5301 South 76th Street
Greendale, Wisconsin 53129

American Physical Fitness Research Institute
824 Moraja Drive
Los Angeles, California 90049

*American Shuffleboard Co., Inc.
210 Paterson Plank Road
Union City, New Jersey 07087

Anargyros Film Library
1813 Fairborn Avenue
Los Angeles, California 90025

Association Films, Inc.
866 Third Avenue
New York, N.Y. 10022

The Athletic Institute
805 Merchandise Mart
Chicago, Illinois 60654

The Athletic Institute
200 Castlewood Drive
North Palm Beach, Florida 33408
(Golf films)

Audio Film Center
2138 E. 7th Street
Mt. Vernon, N.Y. 10550

Avis Films
2408 W. Olive Avenue
Burbank, California 91506

*Babe Ruth Baseball
P.O. Box 5000
1770 Brunswick Avenue
Trenton, New Jersey 08625

*Bear Archery, Advertising Dept.
4600 S.W. 41st Blvd.
Gainesville, Florida 32601

*Ben Pearson/Himalayan Industries
P.O. Box 7465
Pine Bluff, Arkansas

Brandon Films Inc.
200 West 57th Street
New York, N.Y. 10019

Bureau of Audio-Visual Instruction
University of Wisconsin
P.O. Box 2093
Madison, Wisconsin 53701

Carousel Films, Inc.
1501 Broadway
New York, N.Y. 10036

Castle Films Division
1145 Park Avenue
New York, N.Y. 10036

Chicago Tribune Motion Picture Bureau
435 N. Michigan Avenue
Chicago, Illinois 60611

* Cisco Kid Tackle, Inc.
2630 N. W. First Avenue
Boca Raton, Florida 33432

Coronet Instructional Films
65 E. South Water Street
Chicago, Illinois 60601

* Duckpin Bowling Council
1420 New York Ave., N.W.
Washington, D.C. 20005

Educational Activities, Inc.
P.O. Box 392
Freeport, N.Y. 11520

Educational Screen and A-V Guide
434 S. Wabash Avenue
Chicago, Illinois 60605

Educators Guide to Free HPER Materials
Educators Progress Service
Randolph, Wisconsin 53956

Film Associates
11559 Santa Monica Blvd.
Los Angeles, California 90025

Film Trends
8060 Melrose Avenue
Los Angeles, California 90046

* Floor Tennis Co.
2030 West Morse
Chicago, Illinois 60645

General Mills Inc. Film Center
P.O. Box 1113
Minneapolis, Minn. 55440

General Motors Corporation
Public Relations Staff—Film Library
General Motors Building
Detroit, Michigan 48202

General Sportcraft Co., Ltd.
140 Woodbine Street
Bergenfield, N.J. 07621

Journal Films
909 W. Diversey Parkway
Chicago, Illinois 60614

Library of Congress Catalog
Motion Pictures and Filmstrips
Building 159, Navy Yard Annex
Washington, D.C. 20541

Major League Baseball Film Division
Room 402
1650 Broadway
New York, N.Y. 10019

McGraw-Hill Film
1221 Avenue of Americas
New York, N.Y. 10036

Modern Talking Picture Service
5000 Park Street, North
St. Petersburg, Florida 33709

* National Bowling Council
1919 Pennsylvania Ave., N.W.
Suite 504
Washington, D.C. 20006

National Collegiate Athletic Association
NCAA Film Division
1221 Baltimore Street
Kansas City, Missouri 64105

National Federation of State and High School Athletic
    Associations
7 S. Dearborn Street
Chicago, Illinois 60603

* National Horseshoe Pitchers Association of America
803 East 12th Street
Falls City, Nebraska 68355

* National Wheelchair Athletic Association, Inc.
40-24 62nd Street
Woodside, N.Y. 11377

NET Film Service
Audio-Visual Center
Indiana University
Bloomington, Indiana 47401

Rarig Film Service, Inc.
834 Industry Drive
Seattle, Washington 98188

School Film Service
549 West 123rd St.
New York, N.Y. 10027

Schwinn Bicycle Co.
1856 N. Kastner Avenue
Chicago, Illinois 60639

Shell Film Library
1433 Sadlier Circle W. Drive
Indianapolis, Indiana 46239

Society for Visual Education, Inc.
1345 Diversey Parkway
Chicago, Illinois 60614

Teaching Film Custodians, Inc.
25 West 43rd Street
New York, N.Y. 10036

The Travelers Film Library
One Tower Square
Hartford, Connecticut 06115

United States Golf Association
Liberty Corners Road
Far Hills, New Jersey 07931

United States Tennis Association
51 East 42nd Street
New York, N.Y. 10017

APPENDIX E
Metric and English Equivalents

LENGTH

1 millimeter (mm)	= 0.04 inch
1 centimeter (cm)	= 10 millimeters = 0.4 inch
1 meter (m)	= 39.4 inches = 3.3 feet = 1.1 yards
1 yard (yd)	= 0.9 meter
1 foot (ft)	= 30 centimeters
1 inch (in)	= 2.5 centimeters

DISTANCE

1 meter (m)	= 39.4 inches = 3.3 feet = 1.1 yards
1 kilometer (km)	= 1,000 meters = 0.62 mile
1 mile (mi)	= 1.6 kilometers

WEIGHT

1 gram (g)	= 0.035 ounces
1 kilogram (kg)	= 2.2 pounds
1 ounce (oz)	= 28 grams
1 pound (lb)	= 0.45 kilogram